The proper emotion is wonder.

—Ralph Waldo Emerson

To my parents,
Lillian Sklaire Stephens and
Bernard Stephens

Contents

". . . a lively and original historical introduction. . . . There is a particularly useful account of the development of reporting . . . and at every stage Mr. Stephens' wide knowledge of his subject furnishes him with striking facts and analogies."

—JOHN GROSS, *New York Times*

". . . delightful . . . a straightforward, well-written account, mostly chronological, of how people have communicated over centuries."

—STEVE WEINBERG, *St. Louis Post Dispatch*

"The use of interesting anecdotes, examples, and specifics makes *A History of News* a pleasure to read. History is presented as drama, as struggle, and as comedy, not as a chronological collection of names and dates."

—RICHARD STRECKFUSS, Associate Professor of Journalism, *University of Nebraska, Lincoln*

"Mitchell Stephens' *A History of News* combines impressive scholarship and first-rate writing. [It] is a provocative work that should be read by journalism students and practicing journalists."

—ELIOT FRANKEL, *The Tennessean*

"The book's breadth is staggering. . . ."

—ILENE BARTH, *Newsday*

". . . thorough, scrupulous and witty . . . [Stephens] has written not an inside-baseball book but one for the general reader; he has given the news and those who disseminate it a degree of legitimacy previously unsuspected by or of them, and he makes a powerful case for treating 'the news' as seriously as any other aspect of common human interest and endeavor. *A History of News* is in all respects first-rate, and original, work."

—JONATHAN YARDLEY, *Washington Post*

"A unique history of a unique business—the gathering and dissemination of news, without which the modern world could not be imagined, much less function."

—CLIFTON DANIEL, former managing editor of the *New York Times*

"Enlightening and provocative, as well as wonderfully readable, [Stephens'] analogies between past and present are deft and convincing."

—JOSEPH FRANK, author of *Beginnings of the English Newspaper*

THIRD
EDITION

A
HISTORY
OF
NEWS

MITCHELL STEPHENS
New York University

New York   Oxford
Oxford University Press
2007

Oxford University Press, Inc., publishes works that further Oxford University's
objective of excellence in research, scholarship, and education.

Oxford   New York
Auckland   Cape Town   Dar es Salaam   Hong Kong   Karachi
Kuala Lumpur   Madrid   Melbourne   Mexico City   Nairobi
New Delhi   Shanghai   Taipei   Toronto

With offices in
Argentina   Austria   Brazil   Chile   Czech Republic   France   Greece
Guatemala   Hungary   Italy   Japan   Poland   Portugal   Singapore
South Korea   Switzerland   Thailand   Turkey   Ukraine   Vietnam

Published by Oxford University Press, Inc.
198 Madison Avenue, New York, New York 10016
http://www.oup.com

Oxford is a registered trademark of Oxford University Press

Library of Congress Cataloging-in-Publication Data

Stephens, Mitchell.
   A history of news / by Mitchell Stephens. — 3rd ed.
      p. cm.
   Includes bibliographical references and index.
   ISBN-13: 978-0-19-518991-9 (alk. paper)

      1. Journalism—History. 2. Reporters and reporting—History.   I. Title.

PN4731.S686 2006
070.9—dc22

                                                        2006043893

Printed in the United States of America
on acid-free paper

Preface

Although this book spends most of its time in the past, its purpose has always been to shed light on the present—on the nature, the effects and the limitations of the news we receive today. The original edition, published by Viking and then Penguin, was the first book to view contemporary American journalism from an extended historical perspective.

In deference to the many students who began using the book, a number of additions were made to the previous edition, published by Harcourt Brace: Boxes were added, many of which highlighted connections between older news systems and issues in contemporary journalism. A new chapter on mass circulation was added, which made it possible to give a fuller account of American journalism history and to expand the book's discussion of the role of women and minorities. A detailed timeline was also prepared, along with a handful of questions, intended to provoke thought, at the end of each chapter.

This time around, along with mulling over blogs, pondering control of the press in the early 21st century and updating discussions of recent developments in news, my goal was to beef up some of the international references.

This has been one of the only journalism histories published in any country that encompasses the cross-cultural human striving after news—in Africa and Latin America, among Native Americans, in Greece and Rome, in China, in Venice and Amsterdam, in Germany, France and England, as well as in the American colonies and then the United States. In an effort to have a little better go at that tough task, short references have been added in this edition to journalism in, for example, India, Japan, Russia, Italy, Germany, Australia, Afghanistan and Africa.

All these additions have not, however, changed the book's basic approach: going far back in time to gain perspective on what is, or might soon be, happening today.

Acknowledgments

I spent much of my time, as this book was researched and written, delighting in the work of two or three millennia of newsmongers. My first debt is to them. I hope I have made a small start toward repaying it by examining their work—appreciatively, if not always uncritically—in an expanded historical context.

I am also in the debt of those friends and colleagues, journalists and scholars, who took the time to comment—not always uncritically—on early drafts of these chapters. Arthur Engoron, Jim Hauser, Neil Offen, Bruce Weaver and Daniel Lazare read all or much of the manuscript and repeatedly forced me to clarify my thoughts and wordings. Gerald Lanson, Michael Hoyt, Joseph Frank and Joshua Mills offered valuable suggestions on parts of the manuscript. And Michael Peachin, Lawrence Weiss, Walter Guzzardi, Anna Tsing, Carl Prince, Cyrus Gordon, Mel Edelstein, Robert Darnton, Eugene

Borza, Herbert Gans, David Kronick and Blanche Schleier helped improve individual chapters or sections.

I am grateful to the staff at the British Library, the Bibliothèque Nationale, the New York Public Library, Bobst Library at New York University, the Public Record Office, Lehman Library at Columbia University and the New-York Historical Society, and to those librarians here and in Europe who helped track down information or photographs. Thanks to Joseph Spieler for guidance and support, and to Bruce Shostak for his editing. François Moureau shared information on *nouvelles à la main*. Raymond Firth was kind enough to share his photos of the chief in Uta. My students pursued many of these questions with me and tested my answers to them. I also appreciate the assistance of Stan Schwartz, Sandra Hathaway, Meiyu Song, Paula Basirico, Donna J. Klick, Joost Heinsius, Gabriel Gluck, Avital Fryman and Roy Attanasio.

David Mindich contributed many valuable suggestions to the previous edition—some based upon his own important research, some based upon his wide reading.

In recent years I have had the opportunity to serve as a history consultant to the Newseum that the Freedom Forum has been building in Arlington, Va. Some of the material in this book has been found, in three dimensions, in that museum. And the previous edition of the book (particularly its boxes, chronology and illustrations) was improved by what I learned from working with Eric Newton, Loren Ghiglione, Peter Prichard, Jerry Friedheim, Maurice Fliess, Ralph Appelbaum, Deborah Wolff, Chris Miceli, Ann Farrington, Joel Bloom, Kathryn Scott, David Doyle, Chris Wells, Mary Ann Watson, Michael Emery, Brenda Reed, Jeffrey Schloshberg, Evelyn Reilly, Leslee Kukie, Eugenia Ryner, Nancy Stewart, Beverly Kees, Cara Sutherland, Marion Rodgers, Ev Dennis and Charles Overby.

Thanks to my long-time editor at Harcourt Brace, the dedicated and talented Cathlynn Richard. The previous edition was improved by the advice and useful suggestions offered by David Abrahamson, Northwestern University; William Coté, Michigan State University; Anthony R. Fellow, California State University, Fullerton; Robert V. Hudson, Michigan State University; Owen V. Johnson, Indiana University; Samuel Kennedy III, Syracuse University; Marvin Olasky, University of Texas at Austin; Nancy Roberts, University of Minnesota, Minneapolis; Donald Shaw, University of North Carolina at Chapel Hill; Richard Streckfuss, University of Nebraska–Lincoln; and Bernell Tripp, University of Florida.

Thanks to Vitaly Vinichenko for his close reading of and insightful comments and suggestions for the current edition. I had help from three excellent researchers on this edition: Erin Marie Coe, Maria Kolesnikova and, in translating some German, Svetlana Shelest.

Lillian Sklaire Stephens read through a draft of the previous edition and forwarded a supply of articles while I was in France. Bernard Stephens pitched in on the research and was the second person to read and edit these chapters—thoroughly, as always. My wife, Esther Davidowitz, was the first; many of my ideas were shaped in conversations with her.

Chronology

ca. 100,000 B.C. to ca. 3500 B.C.

ca. 100,000 B.C.
Language arrives with *homo sapiens*.

ca. 40,000 B.C.
Settling of Americas. News spreads by word of mouth.

ca. 8000 B.C.
Agriculture and more stable societies. Meeting places, travel, messengers, criers, smoke signals and drums aid the flow of news.

ca. 3500 B.C.
Chinese domestication of the horse increases speed of news.

ca. 3100 B.C. to 1400 B.C.

ca. 3100 B.C.
The oldest known writing systems—tablets in Uruk in Mesopotamia and Egyptian hieroglyphics. Symbols represent words.

ca. 2500 B.C.
Tablets written in cuneiform in Mesopotamia and what is now Syria contain lists of possessions, agricultural records, school texts, literary works, state treaties.

ca. 1500 B.C.
The first alphabet developed by the Canaanites.

ca. 1400 B.C.
Charges against the mayor of Nuzu in Mesopotamia recorded in cuneiform script on clay tablets.

ca. 1200 B.C. to 443 B.C.

ca. 1200 B.C.
An account of Greek battle with Troy survives in the Homeric epics, *The Iliad* and *The Odyssey*.

ca. 750 B.C.
Greeks add vowels to the alphabet created by Canaanites. Versions of this Greek alphabet will be used throughout Europe.

490 B.C.
Athenians turn back first Persian invasion of Greece. Legend says that an Athenian messenger named Pheidippides runs from Marathon to Athens with first word of the victory—then dies of exhaustion.

443 B.C.
Greek writer Herodotus works on his history of the wars between Greece and Persia—generally considered the first Western history.

430 B.C. to 334 B.C.

430 B.C.
When the Greek philosopher Socrates, according to Plato's *Charmides*, returns from the battle to take Potidaea (one of the initial battles of the Peloponnesian War), he goes to a gymnasium in Athens where he tells the news and obtains some news of his own.

404 B.C.
Athens defeated in Peloponnesian War. Thucydides, the great historian of this war, dies without completing his history.

351 B.C.
In the *First Philippic*, the Greek orator Demosthenes notes the extent to which Athenians are preoccupied with the exchange of news by word of mouth: "Thus we all go about framing our several tales."

334 B.C.
After defeating the Persians at the Grankos River, Alexander the Great allows newly married Macedonian soldiers to return home for the winter and sends 300 captured Persian shields to Athens. Both gestures may have been intended to spread news of his victory.

323 B.C.

Alexander the Great dies. Within 13 years Alexander's empire will be in pieces. The absence of a news system capable of spanning this empire may have contributed to its demise.

ca. 145 B.C.

Civic life in the Roman Republic centers around the Forum, with its open-air meeting space, speakers' platform and government buildings. Each day Romans go to the Forum to hear the latest news.

59 B.C.

Julius Caesar orders public posting of the *acta*, daily records of goings-on in the Senate and elsewhere in the Roman Republic.

51 B.C.

The efforts of Cicero—the Roman orator, philosopher and politician—provide our best look at forms of written news available to upper-class Romans, including personal letters, copies of the *acta* and professionally produced news packets.

44 B.C.

Julius Caesar assassinated in Rome. Cicero's letters record dramatic political struggles following this event, also well reported in the *acta*.

47

Roman *acta* include human-interest stories and sensationalism. The writer Pliny the Elder says the *acta* for the year A.D. 47 report that a phoenix is being displayed in Rome.

105

Paper invented in China, according to legend, by Ts'ai Lun. Takes more than 1,000 years to reach Europe.

221

The Han dynasty creates the Chinese Empire, which lasts until 221 and employs a robust system of written news.

222

Last year for a contemporary reference to the roman *acta*.

455

The Vandals, a Germanic tribe, sack Rome. Demise of the Roman Empire leads to trade and literacy decline in Europe. Flow of news from afar dries up.

618

The Chinese Empire rebuilt under the T'ang dynasty, which lasts until 906. The *tipao*—official newsletters—are important sources of news for elite groups within the Empire. Block printing, invented in China during this period, is used to reproduce copies of the *tipao*.

960

The Sung dynasty in China begins—featuring a wide variety of news organs, now read by the literati as well as by government officials. However, before the demise of their dynasty in 1279, Sung emperors begin to censor and suppress nongovernmental newssheets.

986

The Vikings, under the command of Leif Eriksson, sight Greenland, which they will briefly settle 15 years later. News of their discovery of "Vinland" is recorded in handwritten "sagas."

1041

Between 1041 and 1048, a Chinese artisan, Pi Sheng, uses moveable type to print. Invention is not a big success. Chinese has too many different characters to make such a system practicable.

1160

Rabbi Benjamin of Tudela begins his travels, which will take him from Spain through Italy, Greece, Constantinople, Syria, Jerusalem, Damascus, Bagdad, Egypt, Assyria, Persia and to the frontiers of China. Benjamin writes an account of his trip in Hebrew, perhaps an early form of travel news.

1241

Printing arrived in Korea from China by 950. In 1241, the Koreans make the first successful moveable type from metal—bronze. Soon the country faces a shortage of bronze.

ca. 1250

Spoken news remains the dominant form of news in medieval Europe. According to a 13th-century French poem, news of deaths, royal decrees and the arrival of new wine are all being "cried" through Paris.

1275

Marco Polo, of Venice, reaches court of Kublia Khan, ruler of China. Polo finds himself in jail with a writer, to whom he dictates the story of his travels.

1352

Laurence Minot, a court poet, accompanies the English armies as they capture the French town of Guines during the Hundred Years War and produces an eyewitness account of the battle—handwritten, in verse.

1431

Joan of Arc, who inspired and led a French resurgence in the Hundred Years War, is captured and burned at the stake. News before the printing press is so unreliable that it is difficult to be sure anyone is really dead. At least one false Joan of Arc wanders about after the real one is executed.

1432	ca. 1450	1455	1467
Detailed account of young Henry VI's entry into London composed and written down by the poet John Lydgate.	The letter press is first used by Johann Gutenberg.	The War of the Roses begins (lasts until 1485). Word of mouth is so important as a news medium during this war that the English guard the roads out of Calais in an attempt to keep news of their troubles from spreading.	Privileges—official permission to engage in printing—are first distributed in Berne. Bestowing and denying printers privileges becomes a major form of government control of the press, practiced with particular skill by England's Queen Elizabeth.

1470	1471	1471	1481
The oldest known news publication printed on a letter press, an Italian report on a tournament, appears—an early form of sports news.	One Londoner, John Paston, writes of the news or "flying tales" that can be obtained simply by walking in London. Those "tales," like most spoken news, are limited, however—for almost 6 days after one crucial battle in the War of the Roses, Paston writes, London had "non certynges" as to its outcome.	A handwritten newsletter with detailed account of King Edward IV's victory in the battle of Tewkesbury, during the War of the Roses, is prepared, in both English and French, by one of the king's servants.	Sultan Mohammed II, who plays a major role in founding the Ottoman, or Turkish, Empire, dies. Two years later, Edward, the Prince of Wales, obtains a copy of a handwritten letter, originally produced by an Italian in Constantinople, containing news of the sultan's death.

1493	1494	1502	1509
Columbus returns from his journey, and news of his discoveries circulates in many printed editions of his own letter.	French king Charles VIII's invasion of Italy. Forty-one different printed newsbooks reporting on it have been found.	Ferdinand and Isabella of Spain require all printed works to be licensed, which means approved in advance, by government or church authorities. Another form of press control was practiced in Spain even before Columbus departed on his first voyage: burning offensive books by the Inquisition.	A printed newsbook reports on the proxy wedding of 12-year-old Mary, daughter of the English King Henry VII, and 8-year-old Prince Charles of Austria, heir to the the throne of the Holy Roman Empire. An example of published gossip or celebrity news.

1517	1521	1529	1536
Martin Luther, leader of the Protestant Reformation, posts his controversial *95 Theses*. Word of these *Theses* spreads through Europe in a month, thanks largely to the printing press.	In Germany, the Edict of Worms, which formally declares Martin Luther an outlaw, also includes a requirement that printers submit to prior censorship.	The Ottoman Empire, under Sultan Suleiman, lays seige to Vienna. Thirty-three printed works reporting on this seige have been located.	Continued development of European postal systems, with handwritten letters used with more frequency for news. A German lawyer Christoph Scheurl is paid by the court of Mainz for his handwritten newsletters.

1538	1538	1541	1561
A French-printed newsbook includes an eyewitness report on an eruption of Mount Vesuvius.	All printed works in England must be licensed after this date. The Stationers Company—an organization of printers—helps enforce this system.	Oldest surviving example of printed news in the Americas, an eight-page newsbook, printed in Mexico City and written by a notary public named Juan Rodriguez, reports on a storm in Guatemala.	In France, flogging becomes the first-time penalty for those who circulate defamatory or seditious broadsides or pamphlets. Repeat offenders are subject to the death penalty. Press remains tightly controlled in France until the French Revolution in 1789.

1566
Handwritten newssheets—known as *gazzette* or *avisi*—appear weekly in Venice. Probably the oldest known direct ancestors of the modern newspaper.

1568
The House of Fugger, the top group of financiers in Europe, has agents around the world sending it handwritten letters filled with news. These are not, however, available to the public.

1571
Pamphlet printed in England, justifying Queen Elizabeth's arrest of the Duke of Norfolk. Now believed to have been secretly written by Elizabeth's chief minister, Lord Burghley.

1577
Sighting of a comet discussed in at least 111 European books or printed pamphlets.

1588
Michael von Aitzing in Cologne begins printing a biannual summary of political and military events—an ancestor of the printed newspaper.

1588
English confrontation with and defeat of the Spanish armada is the subject of at least 23 printed news ballads in England, including three by Thomas Deloney.

1605
The Bloudy booke, or the Tragicall and desperate end of Sir John Fites (alias) Fitz printed in England. Newsbook with a mix of sensationalism and moralizing that is typical of this period.

1609
Oldest surviving European printed newspapers first published weekly in German in 1609. One, probably printed in Strasbourg as early as 1605, is by Johann Carolus and titled *Relation: Aller Furnemmen*. The other in Woffenbüttel is published by Lucas Schulte and called *Aviso Relation ober Zeitung*.

1609
A newsbook mentioning, in Galileo's words, "a glass by means of which distant objects could be seen" inspires him to work on his telescope.

1613
Sir Thomas Overbury poisoned to death in his cell in the Tower of London. Fifteen different news ballads and newsbooks have survived about his murder or the trials and punishments that followed.

1614
A report on "a strange and monstrous Serpent (or Dragon)" found living in a forest in Sussex is printed in England. Typifies attention given to the supernatural in newsbooks and news ballads, as well as their credibility problems.

1615
Newssheets printed from engraved inked tiles—called "kawaraban," which means "title sheets"—begin to appear in Japan, filled with gossip, scandal and sensationalism.

1616
William Shakespeare dies. No mention of Shakespeare's death in any surviving newsbook or news ballad. Printed news in England in 1616 reports, instead, on such topics as the confession and execution of a witch and the drowning of four drunks in the Thames.

1618
Amsterdam, a center for business and trade, gets its first newspaper, the *Courante uyt Italien, Duytslandt, &c.*

1618
Thirty Years War begins in Europe. News of these battles between Catholics and Protestants fills early printed newspapers.

1620
First newspaper in English printed in Amsterdam by Pieter van de Keere, dated Dec. 2, 1620, begins with the words, "The new tydings out of Italie are not yet com." The first newspaper printed in French *Courant d'Italie & d'almaigne, & c.*, was printed in Amsterdam earlier that year.

1621
Oldest surviving issue of the first English newspaper actually printed in England, *Corante, or weekly newes from Italy, Germany, Hungary, Poland, Bohemia, France and the Low countreys*, dated Sept. 24, 1621. Publisher listed as "N.B."

1622
An editor—perhaps the first in the history of newspapers—begins organizing the material in England's only newspaper into a coherent narrative Editor is probably Thomas Gainsford.

1622
In a printed pamphlet justifying his decision to dissolve Parliament, English King James I complains that this effort to obtain public support requires him to "descend many degrees beneath Our Selfe."

1624
A particularly sensational newsbook, *The crying Murther: Contayning the cruell and most horrible Butcher of Mr. Trat*, printed in England. Newsbooks and news ballads reporting on violent crimes are common in Europe in the 16th and early 17th centuries.

1624

Count Ernst Mansfeld, a German mercenary fighting for the Protestants in the Thirty Years War, is made into a "media star" by the early English newspapers. When he visits London in 1624, cheering crowds follow him in the streets.

1624

One of the series of early English newspapers, *The continuation of the weekly newes,* contains an advertisement for a map its two publishers, Nathaniel Butter and Nicholas Bourne, have printed. May be the first English newspaper ad. Followed a month later by a similar ad for a book in two Dutch corantos.

1626

The Continuation of Our weekly newes . . . in England prints a correction—a significant step toward increasing the credibility of printed news.

1630

Nave of St. Paul's Cathedral in London becomes the place to go for people who want the latest news. One early newspaper, published in 1630, describes "the Pauls walkers" as "the greatest talkers of Newes."

1631

Nouvelles Ordinaires de Divers Endroits, the first newspaper published in France, appears. Followed a few months later by Théophraste Renaudot's *Gazette de France,* which lasts until the French Revolution.

1634

The *Gazette de France* publishes an account of the trial of Galileo for holding that "the sun is the center of the universe." However, the writer's sympathies are with the Inquisition, not with Galileo's "absurd and false" ideas.

1641

As the authority of the king deteriorates, newspapers begin appearing in England that report on national news. First is *The Heads of Severall Proceedings In This Present Parliament.* Five such weeklies are soon being printed in London.

1644

John Milton publishes *Areopagitica*—a pamphlet defending press freedom during the English Civil War.

1644

Manchus conquer China. This news does not find its way into a Dutch newspaper until 1650.

1645

Oldest surviving example of news printed in Britain's American colonies titled: *A declaration of former passages and proceedings betwixt the english and the narrowgansets*—a government-sponsored account of wars with Native Americans.

1645

Friar Marin Mersenne, from a convent in Paris, circulates news of science through handwritten letters.

1645

At least eight different weekly or biweekly newspapers—"corantos"—on sale in Amsterdam.

1649

King Charles I beheaded in England, and newly freed English newspapers report the story.

1650

The first coffeehouse in England opened in Oxford. By the 18th century, in London, there are hundreds, perhaps thousands of these centers for exchange of news. French cafés begin at about the same time, serve the same purpose, and last much longer.

1650

World's oldest surviving printed daily newspaper—*Einkommende Zeitung (Incoming News)* published by Timotheus Ritzsch in Leipzig.

1655

Oliver Cromwell restores press controls in England. Only two newspapers are now being printed in English, both by Marchamont Nedham, who had switched sides twice during and after the Civil War.

1663

Charles II is restored to the throne of England and has cleared the field for newspapers written by his partisans: Roger L'Estrange's *Intelligencer* and, in 1665, Henry Muddiman's long-lived *Oxford,* then *London Gazette.* L'Estrange also serves as censor.

1663

Roger L'Estrange arranges for correspondents to forward news for use in his *Intelligencer* in London.

1665

First scientific periodical, *Journal des savants,* published weekly in France. Followed later that year by the Royal Society's *Philosophical Transactions,* published monthly in England.

1670

The term "newes paper" is used for the first time (we know of) in a letter in England.

1679	1687	1688	1688
The Licensing Act restricting the press lapses in England, and a flurry of new newspapers arrives to take advantage of newfound freedom with expanded local news. Among them is Benjamin Harris's sensationalistic *Domestick Intelligence Or News both from CITY and Country*.	Isaac Newton's *Principia mathematica* published. Becomes the subject of a number of reviews in Europe's new scientific periodicals, one of which is said to inspire the German philosopher and mathematician Leibniz to write three papers and cause Newton himself to revise his text.	William of Orange lands in England to lead the "Glorious Revolution," bringing his own printing press with him.	Despite the spread of printing and development of newspapers, literacy remains the exception rather than the rule in Europe. According to one estimate only 40 percent of adult males in England can read. Literacy levels, of course, are much lower for women, who are denied access to education.

ca. 1688	1690	1695	1700
Nouvellistes, specialists in telling the news, stand at their regular spots on the corners and in the gardens of Paris. Crowds gather around them. *Nouvellistes* will be found in Paris through the 18th century.	Benjamin Harris publishes America's first newspaper, *Publick Occurrences Both FORREIGN and DOMESTICK*, in Boston on Sept. 25, 1690. The governor and council of the colony of Massachusetts close the paper down after its first issue.	The Licensing Act, which lapsed in England in 1679, ends permanently in 1695, after the "Glorious Revolution." Without the requirement that newspapers be licensed, it becomes more difficult for authorities to control their content.	Greater London now has a population of 670,000, too large for spoken news to easily traverse.

1702	1702	1704	1704
First successful daily newspaper printed in English, the *Daily Courant*.	King William III, who took the throne of England with Mary in the "Glorious Revolution," dies on March 8, 1702. This news is proclaimed in London within eight hours. Word of the king's death doesn't reach his American subjects until May 17.	Daniel Defoe enters political fray in London with his distinguished *Review*, a journal of opinion which he publishes until 1713.	America's second newspaper—its first successful newspaper—the *Boston News-Letter*, published by town's postmaster, John Campbell.

1711	1712	1719	1721
The *Spectator*, published and written by Joseph Addison and Richard Steele, first appears in London on March 1, filled with observations and wit of remarkably high quality. Published daily until Dec. 6, 1712.	A stamp tax imposed on newspapers in England. Raises the cost of every copy of a newspaper. Clearly designed to keep news out of the hands of the lower classes.	William Brooker's *Boston Gazette*, America's third newspaper, publishes on Dec. 21. Andrew Bradford's *American Weekly Mercury* in Philadelphia, first newspaper published outside of Boston, debuts the next day.	James Franklin's *New England Courant* becomes the third newspaper available in Boston and features America's first newspaper crusade: an attack on smallpox inoculation.

1725	1729	1729	1732
New York's first newspaper, the *New-York Gazette*, published by printer William Bradford.	Benjamin Franklin, after escaping apprenticeship to his brother James, takes over the *Pennsylvania Gazette* and transforms it into the best-looking, best-written, liveliest and most profitable newspaper in the colonies.	Pamphlet printed by the proprietors of coffeehouses in London accuses newspaper publishers of hiring people to snoop, eavesdrop and loiter in search of an interview—it accuses them, in other words, of hiring reporters.	The first foreign-language paper in the British colonies is the German-language *Philadelphia Zeitung*, started by Benjamin Franklin. Lasts only a few issues.

1735

A jury finds John Peter Zenger, publisher of the *New-York Weekly Journal,* innocent of seditious libel—a triumph for press freedom.

ca. 1735

In France, salons serve to facilitate exchange of news. Madame Doublet's salon probably attracts the richest supply of news.

1738

Elizabeth Timothy becomes the first woman to publish a newspaper in America—the *South Carolina Gazette* in Charleston—when her husband, Lewis, dies on Feb. 4.

1739

First successful foreign-language newspaper in Britain's colonies, the *Germantown Zeitung,* begins publication near Philadelphia.

1739

The coffeehouse vogue at its peak in England with 559 coffeehouses in London.

1756

More than 800 authors, printers and booksellers in France are imprisoned in the Bastille between 1600 and 1756.

ca. 1760

Early newspapers in America, like the early European newspapers, include little local news, because they cannot compete with word of mouth.

1765

American press rises in protest against the Stamp Act, which would place a tax on each sheet of paper used to print a newspaper. The British Parliament eventually backs down and repeals the Act.

1767

British Parliament institutes a series of taxes—the Townshend Acts—on goods imported into America, including, significantly, paper. With John Dickinson's "Letters from a Farmer in Pennsylvania to the Inhabitants of the British Colonies" providing the rationale, the newspapers mount a full attack on import duties.

1768

Illegal pamphlets—*libelles*—filled with wild attacks upon the monarchy and other elements of established society, appear frequently in France under the Old Regime. According to one contemporary, more than 100 persons are imprisoned for circulating such pamphlets in 1768.

1770

Newspapers in London begin testing the prohibition against reporting on Parliament. In 1771, an effort by the House of Commons to crack down on these violations of its privacy fails. By 1774, at least seven London newspapers are covering Parliament—though no note taking is allowed.

1770

"Nonimportation agreements," policed in large part through the press, force Parliament to remove all the Townshend Act taxes except that on tea.

1773

The Boston Tea Party planned in the house of an editor of the *Boston Gazette.*

1774

Britain responds to the destruction of tea in Boston Harbor with the Intolerable Acts. First Continental Congress meets in Philadelphia from Sept. 5 to Oct. 26, and approves a boycott of British goods and, in the event of violations, directs "the truth of the case to be published in the gazette."

1775

Revolutionary War begins with the "shot heard round the world" and the battles of Lexington and Concord in Massachusetts on April 19. News of these two battles does not reach New York for four days. It does not appear in the pages of the *Georgia Gazette* in Savannah until May 31.

1776

One of the great "opinion pieces" of all time, Thomas Paine's *Common Sense,* is published as a pamphlet on Jan. 9, helping turn America toward independence.

1776

The Second Continental Congress in Philadelphia adopts the Declaration of Independence on July 4. Text is first printed in Philadelphia on July 6, but does not appear in South Carolina until Aug. 2.

1777

First daily newspaper in France appears on January 1: the *Journal de Paris.*

1783

Reporters finally permitted to take notes in British Parliament. Shorthand replaces a formidable memory as a job qualification.

1783

America's first daily newspaper (81 years after the first successful English daily, 133 years after the first printed daily newspaper appears in Germany, 1,842 years after the Roman *acta* were first posted daily in the Forum) is Benjamin Towne's *Pennsylvania Evening Post.* Towne is indicted for treason a few months later.

1786	1788	1789	1789
First newspaper in America printed west of the mountains: the *Pittsburgh Gazette.* John Scull and Joseph Hall lug their small printing press across the Alleghenies by wagon. Securing supplies is a constant struggle: At one point they have to print their newspaper on cartridge paper borrowed from a military post.	Because of strict press controls, Paris has only four newspapers.	French Revolution begins with storming of Bastille on July 14—inspired in part by a false report. July 17 issue of the *Gazette de France* in Paris ignores event. The people of France turn to unreliable word of mouth. Rumors help fan the "Great Fear" that sweeps through the countryside in the summer of 1789.	*Declaration of the Rights of Man* in France labels "the freedom to communicate thoughts and opinions . . . one of the most precious" of those rights.

1786 to 1789

1789	1790	1790	1791
The first United States Congress approves the Bill of Rights. The first of these 10 amendments to the new U.S. Constitution states that "Congress shall make no law . . . abridging the freedom of speech, or of the press."	Toppling of the Old Regime in France leads to an explosion of journalistic activity. Readers can choose among 335 different newspapers in Paris.	Benjamin Russell of the *Massachusetts Centinel and Republican Journal* goes out to the docks of Boston to obtain early copies of newspapers and gather news from travelers—a step toward reporting.	James Perry, perhaps the most innovative editor in London in the late 18th century, dispatches himself to Paris to observe firsthand the French Revolution. His reports help his paper, the *Morning Chronicle,* achieve an "amazing circulation."

1789 to 1791

1792	1793	1794	1797
French revolutionaries begin cracking down on the country's newly free and wildly partisan press. The Paris Commune orders the editors of Royalist journals arrested.	Jean Paul Marat, publisher of one of the angriest of the newspapers that appear during the French Revolution, is assassinated.	John Bell, proprietor of the *Oracle and Public Advertiser,* becomes one of the first war correspondents by sending himself to Flanders, where British soldiers are battling French troops.	George Washington leaves office after two terms. Benjamin Franklin Bache's *Aurora,* one of the loudest of the partisan newspapers dominating American journalism, greets the occasion with a bitter attack upon Washington.

1792 to 1797

1798	1799	1800	1800
President John Adams signs Alien and Sedition Acts. The latter makes it a crime to "write, print, utter or publish" attacks against the U.S. government. Federalists use it, or common-law prohibition against seditious libel, to indict leading Republican (anti-Federalist) editors in New York, New England and Philadelphia.	No *Declaration of Rights* in Napoleon's new constitution in France. Soon Paris will once again have only four, strictly monitored, newspapers.	Thomas Jefferson becomes president, in part in protest against the Sedition Act. The Republicans allow the Alien and Sedition Acts to lapse.	Thomas Jefferson persuades a Philadelphia publisher, Samuel Harrison Smith, to move to Washington, where Smith starts the *National Intelligencer*—first significant Washington newspaper, a triweekly established Oct. 31.

1798 to 1800

1806	1807	1808	1808
Meriwether Lewis and William Clark return from explorations as far as the Pacific Ocean on Sept. 23, but the news does not find its way into newspapers in Boston until Nov. 6.	The *Times* of London assigns Henry Crabb Robinson to cover the ongoing Napoleonic Wars. Robinson goes first to Altona, Germany, then to Corunna, Spain, and stays with story until 1809.	The *Times* of London now has, in addition to Henry Crabb Robinson, at least five full-time, though sometimes seasonal, reporters. Reporting is developing much more slowly in the United States.	The first Spanish-language newspaper in what became the United States, *El Misisipi,* printed in New Orleans.

1806 to 1808

1814	1814	1815	1815
France's armies, under Napoleon, near defeat in Europe, but news to America is typically late, incomplete, and sometimes inaccurate.	Steam engine first used to print a newspaper, the *Times* of London. Before its use, the *Times* prints 250 sheets an hour, with the steam press, 1,100.	The Treaty of Ghent, ending the War of 1812, is signed in Ghent, Belgium, on Dec. 24, 1814. The Battle of New Orleans fought between British and American troops on Jan. 8, 1815, killing about 2,000.	Aaron Smith Willington of the *Courier* in Charleston, S.C. rowed out to the harbor on a "news boat" to get early word of the Treaty of Ghent.

1818	1819	1820	1822
The first "packet" ships make regularly scheduled trips across the Atlantic. Set departures and set destinations significantly quicken and smooth flow of news to the United States from Europe.	A reporter for the *Times* of London produces a controversial eyewitness report on the massacre of protesters in Manchester known as "Peterloo."	Expensive "mercantile papers" printed on large "blanket sheets" come to dominate journalism in the United States, and emphasize news of interest to merchants.	Nathaniel Carter is sent to Washington by the New York *Statesman and Evening Advertiser*, becoming probably the first full-time Washington reporter. His first report includes, fittingly, an unidentified source.

1825	1827	1827	1828
The United States is said to have more newspapers circulating to more people than any nation on earth.	First urban mass-transit system in the United states arrives, in the form of a 12-passenger coach on Broadway in New York—a sign that American cities are beginning to grow too large for spoken news to easily traverse.	First African-American newspaper in the United States, *Freedom's Journal*, appears on March 16, edited by John B. Russwurm and Samuel Cornish.	Elias Boudinot publishes the first issue of the *Cherokee Phoenix*—partly in English, partly in Cherokee—in New Echota, Ga. First Native American newspaper. The *Phoenix* is suspended after presses are seized by the Georgia Guard in 1835.

1828	1830	1830	1830
In one of the first examples of cooperative news gathering, most of the major New York newspapers have been sharing the expense of sending "news boats" into the harbor to gain early word of news from Europe. However, the cooperation ends in 1828, and the papers begin to compete.	Thurlow Weed, a major force in Whig politics in New York State and the nation, founds the *Evening Journal* in Albany.	James Gordon Bennett sent to cover murder trial in Salem, Mass., for New York's *Courier and Enquirer*. The states are passing laws limiting the power of judges to hold reporters in contempt of court. The federal government passes such a law in 1831.	*Godey's Lady's Book*, the most important of the early women's magazines, debuts in Philadelphia.

1830	1831	1831	1832
Circulations of legal newspapers in England continue to be held down by the stamp tax on each copy. The *Times* of London is selling 10,000 copies a day in a city of 2 million.	French writer and politician Alexis de Tocqueville visits the United States—writes of the importance of newspapers in its political system.	William Lloyd Garrison publishes the first issue of the *Liberator*, the impassioned abolitionist weekly, in Boston. Garrison is denounced, threatened and assaulted. The Mississippi Legislature will offer a $5,000 reward for information on anyone trying to circulate the *Liberator*.	Agence Havas, the first significant private news agency, opens in Paris. Charles Havas sells translations of foreign news to the city's newspapers.

1833

Benjamin Day launches the first successful "penny paper" in the United States, the *New York Sun.* Cheap price immediately begins to attract a large, working-class audience.

1834

New British government negotiates with Thomas Barnes, the reform-minded editor of the *Times,* until it can win his approval of its policies.

1835

James Gordon Bennett founds the remarkably innovative but often reviled *New York Herald.*

1835

Benjamin Day's *New York Sun* reports the discovery of life—in the form of talking man-bats—on the moon.

1836

Penny papers in England, unstamped and therefore illegal, are amassing large circulations—and crusading for Britain's disenfranchised poor. However, in 1836 Parliament finally listens to the liberals and reduces the stamp tax to only one penny. The unstamped papers disappear.

1836

Two successful American penny papers, the *Philadelphia Public Ledger* in 1836 and the *Baltimore Sun* the next year, started by William M. Swain, Arunah S. Abell, and Azariah H. Simmons.

1836

When the body of a prostitute, Ellen Jewett, is found in her bed in New York, James Gordon Bennett launches one of the first journalistic investigations. He conducts one of the first newspaper interviews—with the madame of the house of prostitution where Ellen Jewett worked. Circulation skyrockets.

1836

Among the collection of new penny papers in New York are two intended particularly for women: *Women,* which had a very short life in 1834, and the *Ladies Morning Star,* which lasts just a little longer in 1836.

1836

France's first "cheap" newspaper is Émile de Giradin's *La Presse.*

1837

Elijah Lovejoy, an abolitionist editor, killed by a mob in Alton, Ill., on Nov. 7.

1838

First steamships—the Sirius, on April 22, and then, a few days later, the Great Western—cross Atlantic Ocean, making the trip in as little as 13 days.

1840

A "moral war" is launched against James Gordon Bennett's *New York Herald* by newspapers in New York and as far away as England. All "respectable people" are called upon to boycott the *Herald.* Circulation falls by one-third. But by 1850 Bennett's *Herald* is selling 30,000 copies a day—more than any other newspaper in the United States.

1841

On April 10, Horace Greeley begins publication of another new penny paper, the *New York Tribune.* The *Tribune*—a Whig and then Republican paper, with solid news coverage and strong, abolitionist political views—becomes perhaps the most respected newspaper in the United States.

1842

Showman Phineas T. Barnum manages to coax or trick newspapers into providing extensive coverage of acts like Tom Thumb—the young midget whom Barnum first exhibits in 1842.

1844

Margaret Fuller, perhaps the most distinguished of the few women who are able to establish careers in journalism in the first half of the 19th century, takes a job as a staff writer for Horace Greeley's *New York Tribune.*

1844

On May 1, Samuel Morse demonstrates the power of his new telegraph by announcing to a crowd gathered at a railroad station in Washington the ticket nominated by the Whig party.

1846

Battles of the Mexican War covered primarily by reporters for New Orleans newspapers—nine dailies there in 1847. The *New Orleans Picayune,* trying to beat the competition, sends fast boats carrying composing rooms to meet steamers from Mexico carrying news. The news was set in type on board, ready to be printed as soon the boat docks.

1846

The first newspaper on the Pacific Coast is the *Oregon Spectator.* California's first newspaper, the *Californian,* in Monterey, appears later that year.

1846

The London *Daily News* begins publication, with Charles Dickens as founding editor.

1847

The *Ram's Horn,* an African-American newspaper, started in New York by Willis A. Hodges, with Frederick Douglass as the nominal editor. Later that year, Douglass, a former slave, publishes the first issue of the *North Star,* his own widely read and respected weekly newspaper in Rochester, N.Y.

1848

The *New York Herald* boasts printing "ten columns of highly important news received by electric telegraph" in one issue.

1848

Most of New York's major newspapers, at times using the name "Associated Press," join to share the expense of chartering a steamer from Boston to meet ships from Europe at Halifax, Nova Scotia, and of telegraphing the news from Boston. Soon "New York Associated Press" correspondents begin selling news to out-of-town newspapers.

1848

Women's rights convention meets in Seneca Falls, N.Y., from July 19 to 20—the beginning of the struggle for equal rights for women. Amelia Bloomer's eight-page monthly, the *Lily,* edited with the help of Elizabeth Cady Stanton, appears the next year.

1848

Revolutionary newspapers spring up on the Continent including one published by Karl Marx, called the *Neue Rheinische Zeitung.* Its last issue will be printed in red.

1850

On April 17, reporter Jane Grey Swisshelm sits in the Senate gallery—becoming the first woman to cover Congress. Swisshelm made an arrangement with Horace Greeley of the *New York Tribune* to send him reports from Washington for $5 a week.

1851

Henry J. Raymond, with two partners, founds the *New York Times* as a penny paper. It quickly establishes itself as one of the most thorough, responsible and respectable newspapers in the country.

1854

William Howard Russell establishes role of the dashing war correspondent while covering the Crimean War for *Times* of London. His inspirational accounts inspire the poet Tennyson to write "The Charge of the Light Brigade." His critiques of British military policy eventually lead to the government's resignation.

1854

The days of the one-person newspaper are passing; the *New York Tribune* now employs 14 reporters and 10 editors.

1854

Henry David Thoreau's critique of contemporary American society, *Walden,* is published. Thoreau is scornful of the obsession with "news."

1855

The British stamp tax on newspapers eliminated. London newspapers enjoy continued circulation growth. The *Times* sells 60,000 copies a day by 1855.

1857

Jane Grey Swisshelm begins publishing the *St. Cloud Democrat* in Minnesota, fighting against slavery and for women's rights. A mob wrecks her press and throws her type into the river, but Swisshelm carries on.

1858

First transatlantic cable, built by Cyrus W. Field, completed in the summer of 1858, setting off huge celebrations. Although the cable breaks, a new one is completed by 1866.

1858

In London, Paul Julius Reuter starts the wire service that will bear his name by distributing telegraphic news to London newspapers. In Berlin in 1855, Bernard Wolff began a similar service. Both men had worked for Agence Havas.

1859

John Stuart Mill publishes *On Liberty,* which includes a powerful argument for the freedom to express unpopular views.

1860

Pony Express begins to carry mail from Missouri to California in 1860. In 1841, news of President Harrison's death took 3 months and 20 days to reach Los Angeles. Overland transport could make the trip from St. Louis in 22 days by 1860. The Pony Express cuts this time in half.

1860

Civil War does more for the development of American journalism than any other event. Details of a big battle could enable a Northern newspaper to sell five times its normal circulation. Bennett's *Herald* sends 63 reporters to cover the war.

1861

First telegraph line completed to San Francisco on Oct. 24, 1861, making the much-heralded Pony Express instantly obsolete.

1864

Union government briefly suspends or denies postal privileges to a number of pro-Southern newspapers in the North, including the *Chicago Times,* the *New Orleans Picayune,* the *Journal of Commerce,* the New York *Daily News* and the *Day-Book.*

1865

Reporters, rushing to transmit newsworthy information over often unreliable telegraph lines, get in the habit of compressing most crucial facts into paragraph-long dispatches, such as the report in the *New York Tribune* on the assassination of President Abraham Lincoln. This is a step toward the "inverted pyramid" writing style.

1867

Paper made from wood pulp instead of rags first begins to be used. It is cheaper and makes possible future price cuts.

1868 — Elizabeth Cady Stanton founds the women's rights newspaper the *Revolution* with Susan B. Anthony.

1868 — The invention of the typewriter begins to relieve those who edit copy and set type on newspapers from the burden of deciphering handwriting.

1869 — Transcontinental railroad is completed.

1870 — Thanks to the telegraph and transatlantic cable, news that a republic has been proclaimed in Paris on Sept. 4, following the defeat of Napoleon III, appears in the *New York Tribune* on Sept. 6.

1868 to 1870

1870 — *New York Times* begins an investigation that will lead to the arrest and conviction of "Boss" William Marcy Tweed, leader of the Tammany Hall organization that controls city government in New York.

1870 — World's most powerful wire services—Reuters, Havas and Wolff—agree to divide up global news gathering and transmission. The "Ring Combination" lasts until 1934, with the Associated Press in the United States, which forms an agreement with these three other wire services in the 1890s, playing an increasingly large role.

1872 — *New York Tribune* Editor Horace Greeley, one of the founders of the Republican Party, runs for president of the United States as a Democrat. Dies shortly after losing the election.

1872 — James Gordon Bennett Jr. assigns intrepid reporter Henry Morton Stanley to locate Dr. David Livingstone's whereabouts in Africa for the *New York Herald*. The famous line "Dr. Livingstone, I presume?" is from Stanley's story.

1870 to 1872

1873 — Scottish physicist James Clerk Maxwell publishes his theory of electricity and magnetism, concluding that they both travel in electromagnetic waves. Radio will be transmitted on those waves by the end of the century.

1875 — Yee Lenn publishes what is probably the first Chinese-language newspaper in the United States, *Wah Kee* in San Francisco.

1876 — The telephone, a crucial tool for reporters, is invented by Alexander Graham Bell.

1878 — Joseph Pulitzer buys two St. Louis dailies and combines them into the *St. Louis Post-Dispatch*.

1873 to 1878

1883 — Joseph Pulitzer purchases the *New York World* on May 11, and brings his "new journalism" to New York. Circulation immediately begins to climb.

1884 — The German inventor Paul Nipkow uses a rotating disk with spiral perforations to produce electronic signals—a very primitive ancestor of television.

1885 — Pultizer's *World* mounts a classic attention-getting campaign to raise money to build a pedestal so the Statue of Liberty can be erected.

1886 — Linotype, invented by Ottmar Mergenthaler, casts the first line of newspaper type at the *New York Tribune*.

1883 to 1886

1886 — President Grover Cleveland is perhaps the first president to make use of an expert in public relations. George F. Parker, a former newsman, is hired by Cleveland and the Democratic National Committee as a "press agent."

xxii

1886 — Heinrich Rudolf Hertz, the German physicist, begins a series of experiments that confirm James Clerk Maxwell's theory of electromagnetic waves and succeed in producing radio waves.

1887 — Intrepid reporter Nellie Bly (Elizabeth Cochrane) feigns insanity to expose conditions in the Blackwell's Island Asylum—her first assignment for the *New York World*.

1887 — William Randolph Hearst takes over his father's failing *San Francisco Examiner* and transforms it into a sensationalistic, crusading, self-promoting and progressive newspaper. By 1890 it is also a successful newspaper—making a $350,000–$500,000 profit each year.

1886 to 1887

1889

In a classic example of "stunt journalism," the *New York World* sends Nellie Bly around the world, with the goal of completing the journey in less than 80 days. Riding ships, trains, horses and sampons, Nellie Bly makes her way, triumphantly, back to New York after only 72 days.

1889

Westinghouse Electric Company becomes one of the first private companies to hire a full-time press agent, trying to defend its new alternating current system against charges that it is dangerous.

1890

Journalist Jacob Riis, a reporter for the *New York Sun*, publishes his explorations of New York's slums in a book, *How the Other Half Lives*, which is designed to awaken the better-off to the abominable conditions under which people are living elsewhere in their cities.

1892

A mob wrecks the press Ida B. Wells uses to publish her newspaper, the *Memphis Free Speech*, after she investigates the lynching of three African-American businessmen.

1892

The use of the "who, what, how, when and where" lead paragraph for news stories becomes more widespread in newspapers. Theodore Dreiser is introduced to it with his first job in journalism, at the *Chicago Globe*.

1893

Lincoln Steffens covers the panic of 1893 for the *New York Evening Post*, then a very serious and sober newspaper—and is forced to leave out the fact that he had seen a financier weep. Later, while working as a police reporter for the *Evening Post*, Steffens maintains he "made a crime wave," by reporting previously ignored burglaries.

1895

William Randolph Hearst buys the *New York Journal*, setting the stage for an intensely competitive period in the popular press marked by frequent recourse to sensationalism—known as "yellow journalism."

1895

Guglielmo Marconi, experimenting in the fields of Italy, develops "wireless telegraphy"—radio. He patents his system in England in 1896.

1896

Alfred C. Harmsworth borrows the techniques of American "new journalism" in his new *Daily Mail* in London, with instant success. "We've struck a gold mine," Harmsworth confides. Soon Harmsworth, now Lord Northcliffe, also owns the *Times* and three other London newspapers.

1896

Adolph S. Ochs purchases the *New York Times*, whose circulation had sunk to 9,000 copies a day, and sets it on course to become the most respected and influential newspaper in the United States.

1898

William Randolph Hearst and Joseph Pulitzer, in the midst of a circulation war in New York, compete with each other to sensationalize reported Spanish atrocities in Cuba and the sinking of the United States battleship *Maine* in Havana harbor—helping lead the country into the Spanish-American War.

1900

The number of daily newspapers in the United States has quadrupled between 1870 and 1900—to 1,967 English-language, general-circulation dailies.

1901

On January 1, Alfred Harmsworth transforms Joseph Pulitzer's *New York World* for one day into a small, breezy, well-illustrated paper—the prototype of the "tabloid."

1902

McClure's Magazine begins printing Lincoln Steffens' investigations of political corruption, "the Shame of the Cities," and Ida M. Tarbell's investigation of John D. Rockefeller's Standard Oil trust, two classic examples of "muckraking."

1903

Alfred Harmsworth introduces the *Daily Mirror* in London, the first widely circulated modern "tabloid"—or small-sized—newspaper.

1905

George F. Parker, together with Ivy L. Lee, form one of the nation's first independent public relations firms, with clients including the Pennsylvania Railroad and John D. Rockefeller Jr.

1906

On Christmas Eve, instead of dots and dashes, ship wireless operators hear Reginald A. Fessenden reading St. Luke's Gospel. Fessenden has invented a way to carry full sound on the wireless. This achievement is followed closely by Lee De Forest's upgrade of the vacuum tube, significantly improving radio reception.

1908

The University of Missouri establishes the first separate school of journalism.

1910

Number of U.S. daily newspapers peaks at 2,600. W.E.B. Du Bois begins the *Crisis*—a magazine for African-Americans filled with news, opinion and literature.

1913

There are now 323 socialist newspapers in the United States with a total circulation of 2 million copies.

1914	1914	1915	1916

The number of daily foreign-language newspapers in the United States peaks at 160.

Edward Wylis Scripps, who organized the first modern newspaper group in the United States in 1895, owns a "chain" of 33 newspapers.

More than 2,200 English-language daily newspapers in the United States.

Frank A. Munsey, who owns the *New York Press*, buys the storied *New York Sun* and merges the two newspapers. The first of Munsey's series of "consolidations," establishes a disturbing trend in the newspaper business, one that will continue until the present day—a steady decline in the number of newspapers.

1917	1917	1919	1920

One week after President Woodrow Wilson leads the United States into World War I, he hires a press agent to organize support for the effort—George Creel, whose title is chairman of the Committee on Public Information. Creel also serves on the censorship board.

After the United States enters World War I, Congress passes the Espionage Act. Under the Espionage Act, the U.S. government revokes the mailing privileges of many nonmainstream—particularly socialist—newspapers.

The first successful "tabloid" newspaper in the United States, the *New York Illustrated Daily News*, debuts on June 26, 1919, soon shortening its name to the *Daily News*.

KDKA in Pittsburgh, the first commercial radio station, begins operations under Westinghouse executive Harry P. Davis, broadcasting results of the 1920 Harding-Cox presidential election on Nov. 2, 1920.

1922	1923	1923	1923

Number of U.S. radio stations skyrockets to 576, as does the number of radios—about 100,000 sold in 1922. The American Telephone and Telegraph Company begins to set up a primitive network of stations. A "toll" is charged for use of airtime on these stations—a method of financing that leads to true commercial radio.

Henry R. Luce and a partner launch *Time*, the weekly news magazine. *Newsweek* follows in 1933. Luce also introduces *Life*, *Sports Illustrated* and *Fortune*.

American Society of Newspaper Editors is formed. Drafts the "Canons of Journalism"—a code of ethics, which is adopted by 107 newspapers.

Yiddish-language newspaper known in English as the *Jewish Daily Forward* is being published in 11 different American cities. It has a total circulation of 250,000.

1923	1925	1926	1926

Baltimore newspaperman H. L. Mencken founds the *American Mercury Magazine*, to which he will bring his broad vocabulary, sharp humor and often cynical observations.

Harold Ross starts the *New Yorker*, in which he intends to present a light, satirical perspective on the news. It does more than that, becoming—thanks to the quality and depth of its reporting, analysis, criticism and fiction—one of the most respected magazines in American history.

Half of all the radio sets in use in the world are in the United States—$5\frac{1}{2}$ million of them. Young inventor Philo T. Farnsworth conducts first successful experiments with electronic television.

AT&T agrees to sell its network of commercial radio stations to RCA—the Radio Corporation of America. This becomes the "red network" of the National Broadcasting Company, a newly formed RCA subsidiary. RCA's own smaller network is dubbed the "blue network."

1927	1927	1927	1928

The radio network that will soon be known as the Columbia Broadcasting System is founded. William S. Paley and his family buy CBS a year later.

There are now 733 radio stations in the United States, and their signals are beginning to interfere with each other. Congress enacts the Radio Act, establishing a Federal Radio Commission to assign radio frequencies and grant licenses. It will be replaced by the Federal Communications Commission in 1934.

The *New York Times*, in its coverage of the controversial execution of Nicola Sacco and Bartolomeo Vanzetti, uses the classic inverted pyramid form for a news story.

Most of what we know about the exchange of news in preliterate societies comes from anthropological reports—produced in the 19th or 20th centuries. L. H. Samuelson's observations of the Zulu's "human wireless telegraphy," for example, date back to the 1870s and were published in 1928.

1930	**1931**	**1933**	**1937**
William S. Paley hires Ed Klauber, who was night city editor of the *New York Times,* to organize a news team for CBS. Klauber brings in Paul White, who worked for United Press. Meanwhile, KMPC, a radio station in Beverly Hills, sends 10 reporters out into the streets of Los Angeles—the largest news gathering effort yet for radio.	The U.S. Supreme Court establishes the bedrock doctrine of freedom of the press in *Near v. Minnesota,* ruling that prior restraint of the press is allowed under only the most unusual of circumstances.	President Franklin Roosevelt takes office. He is the first president to make use of the new electronic media to communicate regularly with a large portion of the citizenry. His radio talks are known as "fireside chats."	The Hindenburg—the largest rigid airship, or dirigible, ever built—crashes and explodes while trying to land in Lakehurst, New Jersey. Herb Morrison of WLS, Chicago, is making a sound recording of the Hindenburg's landing. His dramatic account is broadcast on NBC hours later.

1940	**1941**	**1941**	**1943**
Edward R. Murrow's vivid radio reports from London for CBS, during the Battle of Britain, which begin "This is London . . ." make the torments that city and country are experiencing particularly real to American listeners.	Television broadcasting begins in U.S. Federal Communications Commission permits 18 T.V. stations to begin transmiting on July 1. Two of them are ready to go that day—the New York stations of NBC and CBS. That year CBS broadcasts two 15-minute television newscasts a day to tiny audience in New York.	The Mutual network is broadcasting a football game at 2:22 p.m. EST, when wire services flash: "White House says Japs attack Pearl Harbor." An announcer interrupts game. At 2:31, John Daly of CBS goes on air with news of the attack. Dec. 7, 1941, is a Sunday, and there are no Sunday afternoon newspapers. Pearl Harbor is a radio story.	The Federal Communications Commission forces NBC to sell one of its two networks. NBC's "blue network" is renamed the American Broadcasting Company in 1945.

1945	**1946**	**1947**	**1949**
A newspaper strike in New York provides an opportunity for sociologist Bernard Bereleson to study the effects of their absence: "It's like being in jail not to have a paper," one New Yorker tells him.	A. J. Liebling begins writing his pointed, informed and witty column, "The Wayward Press," in the *New Yorker.* The era of the professional press critic begins.	A commission chaired by University of Chicago President Robert M. Hutchins, and supported financially by Henry Luce, issues a report on "A Free and Responsible Press." The Hutchins Commission, composed of a group of distinguished thinkers, suggests that the press must be more than just free; it must be responsible.	After the war, television grows rapidly, with more than 100 stations in the U.S. Two regular newscasts are broadcast: *CBS TV News,* with Douglas Edwards, and NBC's *Camel News Caravan,* with John Cameron Swayze. In France a newscast, *Le Journal Televise,* begins broadcasting three times a week; and by the end of the year twice a day.

1951	**1954**	**1952**	**1956**
Edward R. Murrow and his producer, Fred Friendly, debut their *See It Now* documentary series on CBS television by showing, simultaneously, a live scene from New York Harbor and a live scene from San Francisco.	Senator Joseph McCarthy's "red" scare costs many their jobs and cows others into silence. Edward R. Murrow and producer Fred Friendly are among the only figures in broadcasting secure enough and courageous enough to take McCarthy on—on *See It Now,* March 9.	The word "anchor" is used, probably for the first time, to describe the role of Walter Cronkite during CBS television coverage of 1952 presidential conventions.	The Italian liner *Andrea Doria* sinks off the coast of Nantucket, and Don Hewitt, the aggressive director of CBS evening newscast, takes anchorman Douglas Edwards and gets film of the sinking ship.

1960	**1961**	**1963**	**1963**
For the first time, two major candidates for president— Richard M. Nixon and John F. Kennedy—debate each other on national television.	Gordon McLendon starts the first successful all-news radio station, XETRA. It broadcasts to Los Angeles—from Tijuana, Mexico.	The early television newscasts are only 15 minutes long. On Labor Day, CBS begins the first half-hour network newscast. Walter Cronkite, who took over the *CBS Evening News* in 1962, is the anchor.	Nov. 22, 1963, assassination of President John F. Kennedy in Dallas. According to one estimate, 68 percent of the American people, learn the news within half an hour. Nonstop television coverage includes the shooting of the man accused of the assassination, Lee Harvey Oswald.

1964

In *Sullivan v. New York Times,* a landmark decision, the U.S. Supreme Court rules unanimously that a public official may win a libel lawsuit only by proving that the story is false and published with "actual malice"—which is defined as "reckless disregard for the truth."

1965

CBS, with considerable reluctance, airs correspondent Morley Safer's report on the "wasting" of a Vietnamese village, Cam Ne, by U.S. Marines. President Lyndon Johnson calls CBS President Frank Stanton to protest.

1968

The Kerner Commission, appointed by President Lyndon Johnson to study the causes of the riots that have broken out in many American cities, criticizes the media for failing to communicate the problems of blacks in American society.

1971

A copy of a secret Defense Department history of the Vietnam War is given to the *New York Times.* When *Times* is prevented, for a time, from printing the "Pentagon Papers," *Washington Post* steps in, then *Boston Globe.* Supreme Court finally rules that government's argument for prior restraint of the press is not sufficiently strong in this case.

1973

Washington Post reporters Bob Woodward and Carl Bernstein investigate a break-in at the headquarters of the Democratic National Committee in the Watergate apartment complex in Washington.

1974

Barbara Walters, one of the first women to achieve stardom in television news, is hired by ABC to co-host its evening newscast—for a then unheard of salary of $1 million.

1980

R. E. (Ted) Turner launches his 24-hour-a-day *Cable News Network*—the first all-news television network.

1981

President Ronald Reagan is shot and seriously wounded. Videotapes of the attempted assasination are shown on ABC, CBS and NBC within half an hour of the shooting. Both Dan Rather on CBS and Frank Reynolds on ABC deliver obituaries for White House Press Secretary James Brady, who is seriously wounded but alive.

1982

USA Today, a national newspaper featuring short, breezy stories and lots of color, begins publication. Satellite transmission enables the paper to be printed simultaneously at 32 different printing locations around the United States.

1983

Reporters are blocked from covering the initial stages of the U.S. invasion of the Caribbean island of Grenada. The military does not bring along representatives of the media, and a group of journalists that manage to land on the island is prevented by U.S. military officials from reporting what is happening for two days.

1986

When the world's worst nuclear-power accident occurs at Chernobyl in what was then the Soviet Union, people in the area are told by officials that there is nothing to fear, while news audiences in the rest of the world must make do with rumors and speculation.

1991

The worldwide news system continues to strengthen. People in countries around the world, for example, are able to watch the bombs drop down upon Iraq—live—during the Persian Gulf War in 1991.

1993	1994	1995	1995
Cable television lines can carry telephone calls. Telephone lines can carry television signals. Computers seem capable of involving themselves in all these forms of communication over all these different lines including the new, multimedia World Wide Web. "Convergence" the media moguls call it, and they race to form business alliances to exploit the potential.	News audiences in the U.S. became obsessed with yet another sensational news story: the accusation that former football star O. J. Simpson has murdered his wife and her friend. Many Americans now have dozens of cable television channels to choose from. A few of those channels lose themselves in coverage of Simpson's year-long trial.	News organizations and technology companies race to place news on the Internet, which seems to hold the promise of making vast quantities of information almost instantly available to plugged-in computer users around the world. Time Warner's Pathfinder "home page" on the World Wide Web proves particularly popular.	Disney purchases ABC. Time Warner purchases CNN. Westinghouse purchases CBS. Huge global media corporations seem to grow larger and larger—with worldwide television networks, their own movie studios and their own news operations.

1996	1998	1999	2001
Coverage of U.S. presidential campaign appears on numerous television networks and spills over to talk shows, the World Wide Web, and even MTV.	Matt Drudge's *Drudge Report* breaks the news that President Bill Clinton was having an affair with an intern named Monica Lewinsky. The term is not yet in use, but his political, conservative, gossipy, hyper-news-alert website may qualify as the first notable "blog"—or personal news site.	Al-Jazeera, an Arab-language satellite news channel, begins broadcasting 24 hours a day and is soon attracting large numbers of viewers in the Arab world. It provides them with a perspective on events in the Middle East and elsewhere that is often different from that of Western news organizations like CNN and the BBC.	As terrorists steered planes into the WTC towers in N.Y. and the Pentagon, people in the U.S., and much of the world, yearn for news. That yearning is satisfied, initially, by television—with reports from the ash-covered streets of N.Y., horrifying video of the planes slicing into the towers and the calming explanations of familiar anchors. Newspapers follow with fuller discussions of who and why.

2003	2004	2006
In the buildup toward the Iraq War, the national borders that had long obstructed the flow of news seem to disappear—on the Internet. Americans interested in looking beyond the American perspective, for example, can easily read what, for example, England's *Guardian* has to say on its website.	For the first time, fully keeping up with news of a highly charged and competitive American presidential election campaign (John Kerry challenging President George W. Bush) seems to require reading blogs online. They prove a source of gossip and attacks, but also a source of quick and often telling analysis not often found in the "mainstream media."	Audiences for traditional print and broadcast news media grow older and smaller, as new news outlets continue to appear on cable and satellite channels, on the Internet and even on cell phones. Once again humans are devising new ways to obtain news, though the nature of the news they obtain remains familiar.

(left margin labels: 1993 to 1995; 1996 to 2001; 2003 to 2006)

Introduction

Our society certainly pays enough attention to news. We watch news, read news, debate news, marvel at, puzzle over, curse and sometimes seem to be drowning in news. The news stream runs fast enough for all of us to feel its rush. But our understanding of the substance in which we are immersed is incomplete. The news itself is too pervasive; it seems too transparent. Those who speculate on its flavor, its nature, too often are wrong.

Critics and scholars squint; they sight against their thumbs. But how is it possible to gain perspective on a substance that is all around us? History should provide the answer, but journalism history in the United States has too long been limited only to the experiences of our own journalists, which means to only the past few centuries. American journalism historians, therefore, too often seem like theater historians who have never studied Shakespeare or Sophocles. European historians, to be fair, can be similarly shortsighted.

This book is unique in attempting to view the development of American journalism in an extended, international historical context. It discusses spoken news, handwritten news and early forms of printed news, before getting to newspapers, reporting and electronic forms of news. And it considers news in Africa, Athens, Rome, China, Venice, Amsterdam, Paris and London before arriving in Boston, New York, Los Angeles and Emporia, Kansas.

The means humankind has employed to spread news are considered in this book in the order in which they arrived (with some doubling back to trace the origins of newspaper reporting); however, that does not always translate into a smooth chronological presentation. Methods of gathering and disseminating information have developed at different speeds in different societies; so in examining written news, for example, it will be necessary to jump from discussions of Rome in the first century B.C. to China in the seventh century A.D., then to England in the late 15th century.

Enlighten me now, O Muses tenants of Olympian homes, For you are goddesses, inside on everything, know everything. But we mortals hear only the news, and know nothing at all.

—The Iliad[1]

1

The chronology is also upset by the fact that, as C.S. Lewis has observed, "humanity does not pass through phases as a train passes through stations."[2] A particularly lively forum for the exchange of news by word of mouth—the coffeehouse—flourished in England well after the development of the newspaper, and in some countries the coffeehouse has survived even the introduction of television. Some news media are also more likely than others to leave behind records of their existence, further confusing the chronology. Evidence of the workings of the oldest news medium—word of mouth—is the least likely to be preserved. That is why so many of the examples in the opening section of this book bear 19th- or 20th-century dates. (The timeline included in this edition arranges many of the events mentioned in these chapters—and additional others—in a strict chronological order.)

Unlike words such as *information* and *communication,* which seem to have gained their current meanings only in the second half of the 19th century,[3] the English word *news* has been used in roughly the same way for at least 500 years. And its synonym *tidings* can be traced back to Old English. In fact, most languages appear to have a term for this category of information. Nevertheless, the definition of news this book relies on might have seemed rather narrow to some of the news-mongers and journalists it discusses. Many considered news inseparable from the kind of moral instruction tagged onto this stanza from an English news ballad printed in 1586 and reporting the destruction of the market town of "Beckles Suffolke" (the once "faire" town itself is speaking):

> But now beholde my great decay,
>   Which on a sodaine came;
> My sumptuous buildings burned be
>   By force of fires flame:
> A careless wretch, most rude in life,
>   His chymney set on fire,
> The instrument, I must confess,
>   of God's most heavie ire.[4]

Others would have had difficulty imagining news without overt political content. This small news item appeared in the *Boston Evening-Post* during the battle over the Stamp Act in 1765. Its ostensible subject was the execution of a man for an unrelated crime:

> Saturday last was executed, Henry Halbert, pursuant to his sentence, for the murder of the son of Jacob Woolman.—*He will never pay any of the taxes unjustly laid on these once happy lands.*[5]

In refining news as a commodity, the elaborate mechanisms for its collection and distribution created in the past two centuries have made it easier to see news as a substance independent of moralizing and polemic. "Newspapers," the *Times Literary Supplement* suggested in a 1955 editorial, "should outgrow the phase of knight-errantry and concentrate . . . on performing a function as useful to society as the daily delivery of milk."[6] Most journalists today demonstrate some ability to separate this news-delivery function from the goals of uplifting or persuading, which seemed so important to so many of their predecessors. (Of course, shared values and selective perceptions continue to taint the supply of news, despite the great show made of eradicating subjectivity.)

O. J. Simpson and Historical Perspective

It has been happening with some regularity. The mass tragedies and world-altering political events seem to recede for a few months, and the cable networks, along with news websites and some blogs, occupy themselves by obsessing—hour upon hour, day after day—over some insignificant crime. Perhaps a husband is suspected of murdering his wife; perhaps, under suspicious circumstances, a young woman has disappeared or a young girl has been killed. The evidence is pored over. Expert after expert is consulted. The trial, if there is a trial, is covered as if the fate of the world, not just that of some troubled individual, is at stake.

And we—lots of us—watch, until we get bored. Then we—some of us—complain: "Trivial." "Shameless." "Don't they have anything else to talk about?"

The granddaddy of such modern-day news obsessions was the case, in 1994 and 1995, against former football star O. J. Simpson, who was accused of murdering his wife and her friend. Simpson, in a controversial verdict, was acquitted. But for the better part of a year it seemed as if all the political, social and economic issues in the country and the world had been forgotten, and the news media could talk of little else.

According to an *ABC News* poll, 9 out of 10 viewers believed that journalists were spending too much time on this case. Yet millions of people continued to watch, listen to, click on and read the stories.

One of the main purposes of this book is to provide the perspective needed to understand such journalistic phenomena. One of its points is that news organs—even before there were newscasts and newspapers, let alone cable networks and blogs—have always indulged themselves in such sensational stories (see Chapter 7). The book also suggests that there have always been individuals, going back to Cicero in Rome, who have complained about them.

O. J. Simpson drives the freeways of Los Angeles in 1994 with television cameras, and much of America, watching. They will continue watching until his trial ends in a verdict of innocent in 1995.

From this perhaps idealistic perspective, and for the purposes of this book, news can be defined as *new information about a subject of some public interest that is shared with some portion of the public.* Historical data usually lack the requisite freshness to qualify as news; art, for the most part, does not offer that layer of compelling information; government intelligence is reserved for private use; chitchat often is of only personal interest—though in smaller communities, with smaller publics, reports on family or friends often are newsworthy.[7]

The more serious-minded among us today might pronounce the definition of news presented here not too narrow in attempting to separate news from moral and political instruction but too broad in accommodating gossip, sports news and similar frivolities. However, a thread worth untangling and examining runs through accounts of fires, executions, political struggles and Brad Pitt's latest romance—whether communicated by drum, printed balled, CNN, the *New York Post* or a blog.

News is, in effect, what is on a society's mind. Has a bill been passed? Has anyone been hurt? Is a star in love? Through the news, groups of people glance at aspects of the world around them. Which of the infinite number of possible new occurrences these groups are able to see, and which they choose to look at, will help determine their politics and their philosophies.

Through our newspapers, magazines, newscasts and websites we see a world of wiggling economic curves, incessant crime, natural disasters, dancing superstars and spectacular catches. Is that view inevitable or arbitrary? What are the strengths and limitations of that particular selection of reality? What else might we be seeing? These questions are best answered by examining what societies in other eras have seen through their news.

Questions

1. This book focuses on continuities in the exchange of news, not cultural differences. To what extent does the exchange of news today reflect such differences? Does the news exchanged by people in cities differ from that exchanged in more rural areas? Does the news vary from country to country? Are young people interested in different kinds of news than their parents?

2. What forms of communication are excluded by the definition of news presented here? Is there news in television talk shows? Do films or recordings contain news? Is there news in advertising?

PART ONE

SPOKEN NEWS

1 Why News?—
The Thursty Desyer That All
Our Kynde Hath to Know

With our morning, evening and late evening television newscasts, our newspapers and magazines, our 24-hour news channels, our satellites and our websites, late 20th-century Americans appear to receive and desire more news than any previous people. "We have become a country of news junkies," concludes Helen Thomas, a long-time White House correspondent.[2] Indeed, our era would seem to be characterized by an obsession with the news.

So it might be surprising to learn that more than 275 years ago the English—though they had no radio, television, satellites or computers, and though men obtained much of their news at the coffeehouse—thought *their* era was characterized by an obsession with news. The condition was described in a 1712 newspaper as "the furious itch of novelty," and it was said to have "proved fatal to many families; the meanest of shopkeepers and handicrafts spending whole days in coffeehouses, to hear news and talk politicks, whilst their wives and children wanted bread at home."[3] Similar behavior had been noted in the mid-17th century in Cambridge. "Scholars are so Greedy after news . . . that they neglect all for it," one concerned observer complained.[4] Just as we are hardly the first people to believe we live in both the most exciting and the most frightening of times, we are hardly the first to believe ourselves unique in the attention we pay to the current events that are exciting or frightening us so.

A comparable appetite for news could also be found in 16th-century England. A newsbook reporting on a military expedition in 1548 announced it was out to satisfy "the thursty desyer that all our kynde hath to know."[5]* Nor were the En-

There is no Humour in my Countrymen, which I am more enclined to wonder at, than their general Thirst after News.

—Joseph Addison, 1712[1]

---

* Original punctuations and spellings (with the exception of the *f* for *s* or the *v* for *u*) are preserved wherever possible in this book. (They are not always preserved in citations, however, and modern spelling is, of course, employed in translations.)

Meeting Digitally

A hunger for news can be found in both the least and the most technological of societies. We can share news today by sending short text messages or gossipy instant messages, by joining online news groups or chat rooms specializing in everything from news of particular neighborhoods to news of particular hip-hop performers.

The Internet and the cell phone, like paths in Outer Mongolia, have become places where people "meet" and, therefore, places where they find new ways of asking and answering a very old question: "What's new?"

glish the only people before us who thirsted after news. In the middle of the fourth century B.C., for example, Demosthenes portrayed his fellow Athenians as preoccupied with the exchange of news: "Thus we all go about framing our several tales."[6]

The desire to pass on tales of current events could be found even in cultures that did not have writing—let alone printing presses or computers—to whet or satisfy their thirst for news. Observers have often remarked on the fierce concern with news that they find in preliterate or semiliterate peoples. A missionary writing in 1857 about a Zulu tribe in southern Africa observed behavior similar to that Demosthenes remarked upon in Athens: "The men, especially, having no serious occupation, spend much of their time telling and hearing some new thing."[7]

Further evidence of the extent to which news has occupied thoughts can be found in the extent to which it has dominated conversations—from Manhattan dinner parties to the paths of Outer Mongolia. "The first question Mongols put to each other when they meet," a researcher reported in 1921, "is invariably the same: What's new? And [then] each of the interlocutors begins to pour out his whole supply of news."[8]

It is difficult, if not impossible, to find a society that does not exchange news and that does not build into its rituals and customs means for facilitating that exchange. Indeed, there are many societies in which that exchange seems to consume much of their members' time and attention. Take the inhabitants of Tikopia, a Polynesian island in the western Pacific, for a final example. According to the anthropologist Raymond Firth, when the Tikopia met within a village, they cross-examined one another about events they had witnessed. When they met on the beach, they automatically swapped the stories they had collected. When they met on inland paths, they began to brief one another on their respective villages. Upon arrival from another side of the island, a visitor could expect to undergo an interrogation on the latest news before any other business would be transacted.[9]

During Firth's two stays on the island—in the 1920s and the 1950s—speech was virtually the only form of communication available to the Tikopia. Yet, according to Firth, the inhabitants of the island were able to exchange a "vast" amount of news each day by word of mouth. In fact, the Tikopia used the same word for news, *taranga,* that they used for speech.

What is the cause of this obsession with news that we share with the people of 16th-, 17th-, and 18th-century England, with the people of Athens, Outer Mongolia, Tikopia, and, undoubtedly, with most of humankind? Firth suggested that the Tikopia's "avid interest" in news could be explained by the small size and the isolation of their community, which forced them to focus on "the minutiae of social existence in their tiny area." Yet many Americans believe our current obsession with news is a function of just the opposite condition: of the power and involvement of our community, of life in the "global village."

Both these theories must be wrong. We do not follow news because of anything unique or idiosyncratic about our society; the Tikopia did not follow it because of anything unusual about theirs. This obsession can only be explained by qualities we and the Tikopia and the rest of humankind share.

The Need for News—A Social Sense

For a period of time while he was living on Tikopia, Raymond Firth would walk every day from his house in the village of Faea to the temple of the chief in Uta. And every day the chief in Uta would greet him with the same question: "Any news from Faea?"[10]

Why do we ask such questions? What motivates us to search for news?

One approach to understanding the news' attraction is to examine how people respond to its absence. Some references to the torments of life without news can be found in anthropological accounts and historical records: Firth mentions the "anxiety" the Tikopia displayed when deprived of news of some kinsmen; a letter written in 1461 described London before news of a battle had been received as a "sory cite"; in 1814 a New York newspaper complained that lengthy interruptions in the flow of news from Europe on Napoleon's fate had the effect of "leaving us for a while in a state of breathless anxiety."[11]

There are, in addition, reports of a Frenchman in 1871, who had been confined to his house for many days during a period of turmoil, having "begged for a newspaper"; of ranchers exiled to the open spaces of central Wyoming early in this century having experienced "a starvation of print"—a deep hunger for newspapers.[12] And this is how the English poet George Crabbe described in 1785 the situation of those "far from town" when the post failed to arrive with their supply of newspapers:

> We meet, but ah! without our wonted smile,
> To talk of headachs, and complain of bile;
> Sullen we ponder o'er a dull repast,
> Nor feast the body while the mind must fast.[13]

The gloom occasioned by the absence of news has become even more noticeable in the 20th century—both because of the brightness of the light normally emitted by modern news media and because upon occasion that light has abruptly been turned off. For 17 days, beginning on June 30, 1945, a newspaper strike almost completely shut down the medium most New Yorkers had relied on for most of their news. The sociologist Bernard Berelson studied the reaction to the strike of a sample group of New Yorkers.[14]

*A participant in the news system on the island
of Tikopia.*

"Is it very important that people read the newspaper?" Almost everyone Berelson
interviewed answered with a "strong 'yes.'" The newspaper's importance, most agreed,
lay in its coverage of what Berelson labels the "'serious' world of public affairs." New
Yorkers in the summer of 1945 were being deprived of updates on the last months of
World War II and on the first months of the Truman administration. However, despite
their avowals of the importance of such news, Berelson found that only about one-third
of those he interviewed during the strike could say they missed the chance to keep up
with particular "serious" stories.

Readers, Berelson learned, have other, less noble-sounding uses for their newspapers: They use them as a source of pragmatic information—on movies, stocks or the
weather; they use them to keep up with the lives of people they have come to "know"
through the papers—from the characters in the news stories to the authors of the
columns; they use them for diversion—as a "time-filler"; and they use them to prepare
themselves to hold their own in conversations.

This list might serve as an outline of the basic functions news performs in any society. When he asked Firth for news each morning, the Tikopian chief, like approximately one-third of New York newspaper readers in 1945, exhibited some concern with
public affairs; Firth reports that the chief was eager to learn of the activities of his coun-
terpart in Faea. In addition, the chief was looking for information of potential pragmatic
value—on the fishing in Faea, for example—and he was interested in following the lives
of the villagers in Faea: Had there been any illnesses or deaths there?

A desire for diversion must also have spurred the chief's request for news. Firth em-
phasizes the "delight" the Tikopia took in news. They looked to news for much more
than a terse listing of information; they wanted elaboration, drama, emotions. Among
the great attractions of the news is its seemingly inexhaustible supply of tales with which
we can delight and divert each other. The exchange of news ensured that the chief's daily
encounter with that anthropologist would pass pleasantly, and it gave the chief a supply

The Thirst

News is never as important as when we are afraid.

Americans were afraid on Sept. 11, 2001, as hijacked airplanes were steered into the two World Trade Center towers, causing them to collapse, and into the Pentagon. No one knew what might happen next.

Most of the citizens of this country—so unused to being attacked—settled themselves in front of their televisions. (Newspapers were too slow; fledgling Internet news sites crashed with the increased traffic.) They watched reporters and producers like Christian Martin, Rehema Ellis, Don Dahler, Anne Thompson and Byron Pitts, often covered with the dust of the fallen towers, attempt to gather and transmit information on and images of what was happening. They watched anchors like Tom Brokaw, Peter Jennings, Dan Rather and Aaron Brown attempt to separate rumor and fact.

And many, many Americans felt, as they sat and watched, an ancient thirst: for facts, for knowledge, for a sense of what was happening now, for a sense of what might happen next, for an idea of why—for news.

of news from Faea that he could share during the course of his day. The news Firth brought to the chief, like the news in a newspaper, had what Berelson terms "conversational value."

These various uses of news seem universal; still, Berelson's list appears incomplete. The specific personal and social tasks the news accomplishes for New York newspaper readers or for a chief on Tikopia are there, but Berelson himself sensed in the comments of the news-deprived people he interviewed a longing for something more "diffuse and amorphous." The basic need for news appears to be not only more amorphous but more powerful than this list of functions indicates.

There was an insistency to the chief's daily question—"Any news from Faea?"—that is not entirely explained by the need to learn about fishing conditions or to be entertained by well-told tales. ("A master-passion is the love of news,/Not music so commands, nor so the Muse," Crabbe wrote in 1785.)[15] And some of the victims of the newspaper strike of 1945 quoted by Berelson clearly were expressing more than mere inconvenience or boredom. They were in pain:

> I am like a fish out of water. . . . I am lost and nervous. I'm ashamed to admit it.

> I feel awfully lost. I like the feeling of being in touch with the world at large.

> If I don't know what's going on next door, it hurts me. It's like being in jail not to have a paper.

> You feel put out and isolated from the rest of the world.

> I am suffering! Seriously! I could not sleep, I missed it so.[16]

These comments recall the much more awful plaints of those who have been deprived of sight or hearing. And perhaps the news is best seen as one of our senses—as a

Pulling the Plug on the Press

The steady flow of news is easy to take for granted in modern democracies. Often it takes an interruption of that flow for us to realize its importance.

On June 25, 1975, Indian Prime Minister Indira Gandhi proclaimed a state of emergency and severely restricted political freedom in the country. That night police cut off power on the street where many of the country's major newspapers were published, and strict censorship was soon imposed on newspapers and magazines.

The people of India knew what they had lost. After democratic freedoms had been restored, and Gandhi had been defeated at the polls, the circulation of daily newspapers in India shot up by 40 percent (Jeffrey).

sense that leaps over the synapses between people, a social sense. The news, viewed from this perspective, is our eye on occurrences beyond the reach of our sight, our ear on conversations beyond the range of our hearing. It is our way of monitoring what is going on in other huts, in Faea, and in other villages.

Is this not why a regular supply of information on current events *feels* so indispensable? As is the case with our biological senses, the importance of the news transcends the importance of the items upon which it focuses. More than specific information on specific events, the great gift a system of news bestows on us is the confidence that we will learn about *any* particularly important or interesting events. The news is more than a category of information or a form of entertainment; it is an awareness; it provides a kind of security.

It does not matter whether we are used to following news across an island or around the world; when the news flow is obstructed—depriving us of our customary view—a darkness falls. We grow anxious. Our hut, apartment, village or city becomes a "sorry" place. However large our horizons were, they grow smaller. "Without news," writes the historian Pierre Sardella, "man would find himself incommensurably diminished."[17] This, perhaps, is the most terrible of the consequences of the limitations governments have so often placed on the free flow of news.

The sociologists Harvey Molotch and Marilyn Lester credit our interest in news to an "invariant need for accounts of the unobserved."[18] The humanoids in whom our genes developed must have survived in part because they were curious about the "unobserved," with its potential threats and potential rewards. Our compulsive interest in events in the next village may have been born of that instrumental curiosity, but it has grown into a generalized need to remain aware. And it is that need, whatever its origin, that is behind the chief's daily request for news from Faea, behind our newspaper reading, and behind our newscast viewing.

We may savor the insights, the stimulation that the choicest news items bring, but we are driven to ingest this mix of current information each day by a hunger for awareness. That is the source of our obsession.

Catching Up

"Hardly a man takes his half hour's nap after dinner but when he wakes he holds up his head and asks 'What's the news?'"

Henry David Thoreau wrote this in the middle of the 19th century—a time when after-dinner naps were more common and methods of learning "What's the news?" more limited (McKibben). It was not then possible to turn on CNN or peruse that hour's headlines on some online computer service.

Thoreau reported on all those news-hungry nappers with considerable disdain. He argued that we should have deeper, more significant concerns than learning, for example of "one man robbed, or murdered, or killed by accident" (see Chapter 15).

Nonetheless, this need to catch up with news we have missed—while napping or away, because it took place out of sight or beyond hearing—exists today; it existed among preliterate people; it seems basic to being human.

The Urge to Tell

In Palestine early in the 20th century, an Arab woman went up to the sister of a man who had been away for years and exclaimed, "Happy news [for] thee, Halime!"

"Tell!" demanded the man's sister. But it was not to be that easy.

The first woman asked, "What wilt thou give me for my news?"

"One shilling."

"Is it a chicken that I announce?" the news-bearer said, with some annoyance.

The two women haggled back and forth, until finally the man's sister agreed to pay four shillings. "Thy brother returned from America!" she was then told.[19]

This exchange sounds wrong. In fact, these Palestinians are the exception that proves a rule: Most of the world's peoples have given away the news they have stumbled upon without charge. Although news is sometimes manipulated for political, social or economic profit, most individuals when asked "What's new?" have not haggled; they have responded. Even where news dissemination becomes a profession, those professionals, while they may charge for their products, have found that they can obtain most of their raw material—fresh information—from their sources without financial charge.[20]

Unlike food, shelter or clothing, most news has value only in the telling; it is worthless when wrapped in silence. And news spoils too quickly to allow it to be squirreled away for future use. Had there not been an established tradition of rewarding the bearer of good news in Palestine, that man's sister could simply have refused to pay anything. She would have learned soon enough that her brother had arrived, and the other woman would have been denied the joy of informing her.

There are occasions when hoarding news might bring economic advantages: Being the only inhabitant of a village who knows the fish are feeding near the north end of the fjord might lead to some large catches. But lips are loosened in most societies by a value

Blogs

The "blog"—a "Web log" often reported, written, edited and produced by one person—took journalism by surprise and by storm in the years after the turn of the millennium. Matt Drudge's *Drudge Report,* which broke the news that President Bill Clinton was having an affair with an intern named Monica Lewinsky in January 1998, may have been the first notable blog, though the term was not used to describe his site. By the 2004 presidential campaign in the United States, the influence of bloggers—free with opinion, free with rumors and speculation, often early with important analysis and facts—had itself become a major news story.

Soon there were millions of blogs. High school students, porn stars and even journalism professors had their own. And something returned that had seemed to be missing in the world of news produced by large organizations and read or viewed by masses: the ability of individuals, lots of them, to be news-tellers.

system that encourages the free flow of information. Among the Lapps at Revsbotn Fjord in northern Norway in the 1950s, anyone who failed to share findings on where the fish were running would be "regarded with disdain."[21]

Not that we bother to calculate the perishability or economic utility of some choice bit of news before we share it or wait for a nudge from social pressure to spread the news we have collected. We give news as we receive it—eagerly. We are, most of us, free and enthusiastic news-tellers.

When bearer and hearer get together, their exchange usually commences either with a general request for information by the news-hearer ("Any news from Faea?") or with a teasing introduction from the news-bearer ("Happy news [for] thee, Halime!"), followed by an expression of interest by the news-hearer ("Tell!"). Then the news itself is related—a story is told—and the person who has heard it is expected to respond with some gesture of appreciation or, better, surprise. The privilege of summing up after the news has been presented is usually reserved for the newsmonger. (The CBS newscaster Walter Cronkite would close his televised news exchanges with the archetypal summation "And that's the way it is.")

From such exchanges, listeners can expect to receive potentially useful information, entertainment and the blessing of invigorated awareness. But while contributing all this to their audiences, newsmongers are hardly shortchanging themselves. The act of telling news brings with it a series of ego gratifications: the opportunity to appear well informed, knowledgeable, current (to indulge in "the vanity of the 'first to know' ");[22] the chance to capture attention, to perform and win appreciation; and the privilege of branding events with one's own conclusions.

There is also a more subtle reward: News-tellers gain the right to have their own perceptions and experiences enhanced by externalizing them, by sharing them. The Bella Coola Indians of British Columbia, for example, were anxious to proclaim marriages or divorces in front of as large a crowd as possible because the "validity" of these transactions would depend "on the presence of witnesses"; their "importance . . . on the number of witnesses."[23] Newsmongers have that power to invest validity and importance, to transform the happenings they have experienced or witnessed into events with the stature of news.

This power, these pleasures—worth many shillings to most to us—have inspired numerous excursions to the battlefield, the scene of the crime or the next village. When a bishop arrived in a Tucano Indian settlement in Brazil in 1956 on his way to pay a surprise visit to some missionaries, one of the Indians hopped in his canoe and traveled 30 kilometers at night just for the honor of informing the missionaries of the impending visit.[24] The search for the joy that Indian expected to receive in telling his news is what makes newsmongers. It moves news.

News, then, is both pulled and pushed through our society, through Tikopia society, through all societies: the uninformed anxious to obtain news, the informed eager to give it away. Even without the benefit of sophisticated information technologies, the news, driven by these complementary desires, can attain impressive speeds.

Questions

1. Does the intensity of the obsession with news today vary among different age groups, economic classes, social groups or cultural groups?

2. What examples are available in contemporary societies of the strength of the human need for news?

3. A few newscasts and news publications recently have outraged many journalists by paying sources for stories. Consider this practice in light of the discussion of "The Urge to Tell" section in this chapter.

News in Preliterate Societies—
In the Ordinary Way

2

A European living among the Zulus in Africa in the 19th century once made the mistake of using his servants' cooking pot to boil the fat off a piece of a crocodile. That was a serious defilement of the pot according to the natives, for whom even touching a crocodile was taboo. His servants quit in consternation. In search of a replacement, the European hurried to neighboring villages, but the news had preceded him: The crocodile was mentioned wherever he went. No one would take the job.

In some desperation, the European ventured farther out, hoping to "outstrip" the news, and in a distant village he did indeed find a man who promised to send a servant. But the man added one request: Please do not feed that servant crocodile![2]

The Zulus, who live in the northeastern section of South Africa, take their name from the clan of the king Shaka, who unified them by force early in the 19th century.[3] They had not developed a form of written communication on their own when they began encountering European settlers in Shaka's time[4] yet the Zulus possessed and maintained the ability to spread news rapidly and over great distances without writing—an ability that often amazed those Europeans who had an opportunity to observe it. L. H. Samuelson, a missionary's daughter who lived among the Zulus, remembered learning in 1872 of the death of the Zulu king 300 miles away by word of mouth, days before the settlers' newspapers had the story. Such journalistic feats, she wrote in 1928, were not atypical of the Zulus:

> Whatever takes place is known for miles round, in an incredibly short time,—what happens in the morning is known everywhere, long before sunset. During the recent wars we often heard from natives of attacks which had taken place, even before the special editions of the papers had been distributed.[5]

This rapid circulation of news is evidence of more than just the desire of individuals to know and tell; it is evidence of a societal commitment. News could not have traveled this far, this fast, among a people without access to printing press or electricity unless its dissemination was encouraged by edict, custom and ritual. And the Zulus were not unique in their ability to circulate news or in the effort, conscious or not, their society put into encouraging its circulation.

Oral news systems must have arrived early in the development of language, some tens or even hundreds of thousands of years ago. At its most basic, the exchange of news requires only the simplest of indicative or declarative statements. And the dissemination of news accomplishes some of the basic purposes of language: informing others, entertaining others, protecting the tribe. For example, Hopi Indian children who spotted a Caucasian entering their village, in the days when that was still a portentous occurrence, were trained to yell out just one word: "Bahana!" ("white person"). That warning cry would then be "echoed throughout the pueblo," until all were aware of the alien presence.[6]

Yet most of our information about spoken news systems, despite their age, comes from relatively recent anthropological literature, such as that on the Zulus, the Hopi or the Tikopia. Attempts to look back further are hindered by the fact that speech does not "fossilize."[7] Instead, to understand the news systems used by the innumerable exclusively oral societies that have appeared and disappeared since humans first began to talk, we must turn to literate observers of such systems. Some scattered historical references to communication in the gymnasiums of Athens or on the street corners of Paris have survived, but for the most part a study of spoken news is beholden to the reports of the missionaries, colonial administrators and anthropologists who have examined life in preliterate societies.

Most of the examples of oral news systems discussed here were selected from observations made in the 19th or 20th century—in that brief interregnum between attempts by the "civilized" to enslave or annihilate the "uncivilized" and the spread of that most seductive of "civilizing" forces, television. (Because many of these news systems have already begun to succumb to the invasion of 20th and 21st century media, they are referred to here in the past tense.) Most of these examples, therefore, were recorded by observers who had grown accustomed to relying on newspapers, radio or television for much (but not all) of their own news.[8] Perhaps that explains why so many of these observers, like the missionary's daughter who watched information spread among the Zulus, were surprised, even shocked, to witness how word that a taboo had been broken or a king had died sped across the plains or through the forests without the benefit of a printing press, electricity or even writing.

We would expect preliterate peoples to be mystified by modern journalism, but Europeans or Americans who have lived with these people seem just as mystified by their news systems. They return from the field using words like "extraordinary," "unbelievable," "incredible" or "almost incomprehensible."[9]

The oral news systems employed by the Zulus and by most of humankind throughout most of human history are neither incredible nor incomprehensible; they feature a series of logical and effective methods for gathering and disseminating information, methods that testify to the importance these societies placed on the circulation of news. The roots of our own journalism lie in such methods.

"Human Wireless Telegraphy"

The neighbors did not have to be notified when a member of the Zulu tribe died. The sound of lamenting emanating from the household of the deceased brought them the news.[10] Such vocal displays of grief obviously had other purposes. In most societies they fulfilled a religious duty: sending off, perhaps, the newly liberated spirit or announcing its impending arrival to the gods.[11] Psychologically attuned observers might suggest that the production of these mournful sounds also accomplished a more down-to-earth purpose: releasing the emotions occasioned by the death of a loved one and, thereby, beginning the process of purging those emotions.

L. H. Samuelson labels the Zulus' news system, of which she was in some awe, "human wireless telegraphy." If their ability to circulate news seems mysterious, almost telepathic, it may be because the behaviors the Zulus and similar peoples relied on to circulate news did perform other, often more visible functions. The religious and the psychological explanations for the Zulus' loud laments can seem sufficiently compelling to mask their role in spreading news or to make that role appear incidental. It was not.

Most of the various rituals with which preliterate societies respond to death have one quality in common: loudness. The Ibo of Nigeria, for example, would bang on a large wooden drum after a death; the Toradja on the Celebes Islands would fire a gun.[12] These may be somewhat less cathartic behaviors than screaming and moaning, but they are audible at even greater distances. The Siwans, who live by an oasis in north Africa, greeted death with a clamorous show of grief like that of the Zulus: the female relatives would commence a loud wail—"Yaiiii-yai-yai-yai-yai-yai-yaiiiiiiiii!—with other women hastening to join the chorus until, according to one observer, "the house of the deceased is packed to the doors with women raising this dismal cry." But at some point, tradition called for mourning Siwan women to climb to the roof of the loftiest house to continue their wail.[13] The need to purge emotions does not explain this ascension to the roof; the need to spread the news as far as possible does.

Many of the institutions and customs of preliterate societies conceal a similar journalistic purpose. In the 1920s at Siwa Town, the Siwan "graybeards" assembled in the evening under the *dululas*—sun shelters made of rushes and mud. These shelters provided some relief from the heat and an opportunity to socialize, but the shelters also were a significant component in the Siwans' news system. Visitors to the town stopped at the shelters to gossip; the men of the camel corps came by "to hear the latest news." "It is incredible how soon the most secret facts are known there," an observer remarked.[14]

Any place where people met or gathered in these societies would fill with "the latest news." When Zulus met along a path, they exchanged greetings, shared a pinch of snuff, and then one would say, "Tell me the news of the country."[15] Elsewhere it was a campfire or the village well or the town square.[16] In such open-air news marts—and there must have been one in every village in the world—the breezes of conviviality carried information from person to person, transforming news-hearers into news-bearers until an entire society was informed.

Few locales drew such large, relatively diverse crowds as a marketplace. News may not have been the most important commodity exchanged there, but the market's importance in the local news system was well understood by the people who frequented it.

Moving People Moves News

The first great improvement in the speed of news was not the telegraph or the radio but the domestication of the horse, which was first accomplished in China in about 3500 B.C. Humans bearing news could be carried by horses much faster than by their own legs. The wheel, which goes back to the fifth millennium B.C., helped too. Wheels together with horses produced chariots.

Before electricity was "domesticated"—used to carry human messages—similar improvements in the speed with which news moved were produced by all improvements in transportation: better roads, better chariots, relays of horses, better boats and then, in the 19th century, steam ships and steam-powered railroads.

When the Ibo of Nigeria wanted to spread some news, they said, "I will speak of it in the market."[17] Indeed, a crucial relationship is established at the marketplace: the symbiotic relationship between news and trade. News—word that a hunt has been successful, for example—helps the merchants at the market plan their strategies, and the goods that are being traded there attract people and therefore attract news.[18]

There seems almost a physical law operating here: When people gather in a pleasant spot, news sparks between them, stirring them, causing them to swirl and buzz, to argue and laugh. A society's political meetings, sporting events, and festivals aid the flow of news by convening such critical masses of people. They too are among the hidden mechanisms behind this "human wireless telegraphy." A Zulu chief, for example, would avail himself of the troupe of warriors gathered for the "Dance of the First Fruits" to announce laws, regulations and orders. The warriors were then expected to pass on the announcements—along with word that the season's fruits could now be eaten—to the rest of the tribe.[19]

Something—shoppers strolling to a market, warriors returning from a ceremonial dance, mail, delivery trucks, electrons in a wire—must move if news is to flow. Preliterate peoples might dispatch their news on puffs of smoke; they might transmit it on sound waves—the Toradja made sure their villages were never too far apart to be able to hear one another's drums.[20] However, in an oral society news moved for the most part as people moved. Traveling was as important as congregating for the circulation of news. Does this not help explain the warm reception guests—travelers—so often received?

Among the Nootka of Vancouver Island in Canada, chiefs invariably invited visitors to their villages, or tribe members who had just returned from a trip, to a feast where they were "expected to recount to their host all the latest novelties." The other guests at such feasts were given the leftover food so that when they returned to their homes they could hold their own feasts for friends and relatives and, significantly, pass on "the latest novelties."[21]

Trade was perhaps the primary motivator of travel—further evidence of its importance to the spread of news.[22] On the island of Jamaica in the 1950s, part of the responsibility of the "higglers," who purchased food from farmers to sell at the market in Kingston, was to keep those farmers informed of occurrences in the city.[23]

Preliterate peoples, like most peoples, were enthusiastic gossipers. It was an activity at which some among them inevitably excelled. At the turn of the 20th century such an individual—one of the Havasupai Indians, who live near the Grand Canyon in Arizona—"breezed through the door and eased her plump body into a chair" in the room where an outsider was settling a dispute.

> She was Vesnor's wife, a giggling woman . . . whose ears were attuned to gossip. She had come to gather news, first hand, so that she might gleefully dispense it later to an eager audience.[24]

Some of what such busybodies "gleefully dispensed" was mere chitchat—of little interest to a public of any size; some presumably represented mere carping or cattiness—opinion, not information. However, the gossip indulged in by men and by women like Vesnor's wife might also have included information on such substantive matters as deaths, births, marriages, hunts, scandals and disputes. There is, in other words, a significant area of overlap between gossip and news.* Through their wanderings, their curiosity, and their chattiness, busybodies helped news items large and small leap the divides between the different courtyards, the different kinship groups, that constitute a community.[25] The fact that so many busybodies have been female may help explain why they have often been disparaged. It is difficult to imagine news finding its way through these communities without them.

To Western eyes, the members of such oral societies may not often have seemed to have been engaged in the process of news gathering and dissemination. Instead they were gossiping, trading, traveling, feasting, attending ceremonies, meeting on paths, collecting at gathering places, lamenting deaths; yet unobtrusively, almost invisibly, word of the pot defiled by a crocodile spread.

The Amplification of News— Messengers, Criers and Minstrels

There is a randomness to the news that drifts through a marketplace or falls from the tongue of a traveler. The spread of a particular item is often dependent on whim and circumstance; word of an event may lurch forward or stall with variations in mood, weather or season.

Leaders of larger societies require more precision and reliability from a news system. When the Zulu king was heavy with news—a threat against the nation, perhaps, or

---

* The word *gossip* is used to describe both a form of communication and a subject about which people communicate—personal, even intimate, information. The role of gossip in the news, in this latter sense, is discussed in Chapter 7.

The Zulu king with his advisors and bodyguards in 1930.

some important new laws—he could not wait for the "Dance of the First Fruits" to deliver it; he could not trust the normal flow of travelers in and out of the capital to spread the word to his many, widely scattered subjects.

The problem was solved with the use of trained news specialists. The Zulus employed runners to transmit the king's news. These messengers would be dispatched to the various chiefs spread about the kingdom. The chiefs, in turn, made sure word was passed to the heads of families and homesteads, who informed the rest of the populace.[26] Through the work of such runners, leaders such as the Zulu king achieved what all authorities at some point desires: a degree of control over the flow of news to their subjects.

Journalism's progress along the road from busybody to newscaster has depended on an increasing ability to amplify the news—to endow it with the power to travel farther, faster, and to arrive with less distortion. The use of messengers was among the first of these amplifications.

The news exchanged in marketplaces or by travelers had been a democracy of anecdote and information—all subject to the same obstacles, all with approximately the same likelihood of being heard. The use of messengers, however, granted significant advantages to an elite selection of news items. This news gained speed as dawdling and detours along the route from source to receiver were reduced; it gained power as discipline and devotion were applied to its circulation. These news items were now more likely to remain coherent over distances, more likely to reach specified destinations. And in amplifying news, messengers—like the more powerful methods for transmitting news that would follow—ensured that additional attention would be paid to its content. Before being placed in the hands of a messenger an item of news might be mulled over, even edited.

Whoever controlled the messengers could select which anecdotes and information would be favored by this treatment. Therefore, whoever controlled the messengers gained not only a conduit to the members of a society—the ability to inform them of new

The First Marathon

Probably the best known instance of news being carried by a messenger is said to have taken place in Greece in 490 B.C. At the time, Greek soldiers, mostly from Athens, were fighting a much larger army of Persian soldiers on the plain of Marathon.

According to one version of the legend, an Athenian messenger, Pheidippides, ran all the way from Marathon to Athens, a distance of more than 25 miles, with word of a huge Greek victory. After reporting this glorious news, the story goes, Pheidippides died of exhaustion. The marathon running races of today commemorate his feat.

regulations—but gained a measure of power over the selection of news the members of a society received—the power, for example, to ensure that they received news of triumphs but not necessarily of debacles. Messengers were controlled, for the most part, by kings, chiefs, headmen. They were rarely channels of dissent.

Such messengers (the Greek god Hermes may be the archetype) delivered more than news. Much of their time would be spent carrying instructions or personal communications between officials or distributing wedding invitations. But messengers often deposited information of public interest at locations where it might be distributed to the public.

Among the Fox Indians in the Midwest, "ceremonial runners" circulated word of deaths, tribal councils, treaties and other occurrences. These messengers made the rounds of the huts each spring and fall to collect news. A clue to their significance can be found in a comment by an elder of the Fox Indians early in this century—about 60 years after the death of the last of the tribe's messengers: "It is hard not to have a ceremonial runner," he told an anthropologist. "That is why [this generation] has a hard time in hearing when anything has happened." (The lack of new ceremonial runners cannot be blamed exclusively on the onslaught of modern communication technology, however; this was a position with great religious significance, and the job description had apparently included celibacy as well as speed.)[27]

A European in Vietnam in 1821 had an opportunity to observe how news was amplified by a member of a different class of news specialist:

> He threw himself backwards, projecting his abdomen, and putting his hand to his sides, and in this absurd attitude uttered several loud and long yells.

Thus began the performance of a news crier. Our narrow-minded observer's review: "truly barbarous."[28] Nonetheless, such exuberant news crying was perhaps the most regular and trustworthy form in which news was presented to preliterate societies. Criers usually followed prescribed routes, often appeared at prescribed times of day and frequently brought news obtained directly from its source—the local potentate.[29] They further strengthened the communication between leader and led.

The crier for the liberal faction of the Hopi tribe at the turn of the 20th century.

Indeed, news criers, like messengers, resided for the most part in the leader's pocket. The crier for the Winnebago Indians in the Midwest, for instance, was required to meet with the chief each morning for instructions.[30] Authorities used them to perform a necessary governmental function—the publication of gatherings, orders and ordinances. (Among the Siwans of North Africa, after an announcement had been proclaimed by a crier on three consecutive days, ignorance of the announcement was no longer accepted as an excuse.)[31] Leaders also used criers in their efforts to control the news received by their followers. This ability to influence perceptions was so well respected by a group of Hopi Indians at the turn of the 20th century that when they found themselves divided politically, two criers were selected: one beholden to the liberal faction, the other to the conservatives.[32]

How did the news accommodate itself to this form of delivery? As do most methods for amplifying news, criers added a degree of formality. If the Khasi, who live in a highland area of northeastern India, had to gather to settle a dispute, their criers, waiting until evening when all the inhabitants of a village had returned, would call out the information. One such cry has been translated. It begins with an attention-grabbing yell:

> *Kaw!* thou, a fellow-villager; thou a fellow-creature; thou an old man; thou, who are grown up; thou who are young; thou a boy; thou a child; thou an infant . . . *Hei!* because there is a contest. *Hei!* for . . . cause to sit together. *Hei!* for . . . cause to deliberate . . .[33]

Such cries were ornate because those who were listening expected a bit of entertainment along with their news; they were strictly structured so they could be easily remembered; and they addressed their audience in direct, personal terms because people in such societies knew no other way of addressing each other. In other words, these cries were typical of formal public speech in preliterate societies.

The communication of news does not require such showy wordings, but they can be useful. Rhythm, rhyme and melody are also optional, but because they are entertaining and because they are aids to memory, these techniques too can be put to the task of disseminating newsworthy information. The problem is that songs or poems take time to compose. They are well suited for recording history or legend—the *Iliad* is an example—but less adept at keeping up with the news. News of the Greeks' hard-won success at Troy must have spread long before a poet, blind or otherwise, fashioned it into verse.

Nevertheless, with a repertoire of stock tunes and a gift for rhyme, some minstrels did succeed in transforming events into song with sufficient dispatch for their compositions to qualify as news. A man who served as a minister in the Serbian government in 1873 recalled walking into coffeehouses and inns and hearing an account of a speech he had made that very day recited by such minstrels—*goosslari*—to the tune of a national song.[34]

So along with messengers and criers, there is a third, much smaller group of news specialists: those who sing or recite news in verse. This branch of the profession includes the *barrāh,* Gypsy musicians who would wander through the marketplaces among the Rif in Morocco "announcing to the listening throng . . . the noteworthy news items of the day";[35] the bards of India, who would "carry news of local and dynastic interest from one village to another" and whose specialty was "to versify the events in which they participate";[36] and the *griots* of west Africa, who would sing songs of praise or ridicule and who were "the channel by which all gossip and rumor passes."[37]

Some of these early news specialists, like the Fox's celibate ceremonial runners, were revered; others, however, were disparaged, even ridiculed. In certain areas of west Africa the *griots* were considered so lowly a caste that they were denied the right to burial—it was believed that their corpses might pollute any land under which they were interred.[38] And the heralds who filled this role for the Bella Coola Indians of British Columbia often were the butt of jokes: It was not uncommon for the host of a ceremony to throw the herald his bag of food at such an angle that it would splatter over him.[39] (Are there not reminders here of the enmity that has been directed at some newspaper and broadcast journalists?)

Nonetheless, societies placed enough importance on these individuals, whatever their status, to honor them with a secure place in custom and ritual. Where tested ways cannot be preserved for future generations by writing them down, religion must function as a sort of societal DNA—passing along the cultural code by fostering the replication of certain crucial behaviors. In many societies religious tradition emphasized the importance of selecting messengers or criers. The Bella Coola's heralds, for example, were said to have been established by the wish of a god "as expressed to the first people in the beginning of time."[40]

Newsworthiness

A group of Zulus was in hostile territory for a wedding in 1918 when suddenly they were attacked. An immediate priority for the members of that seriously outnumbered wedding party was to spread news of their plight, to get help. The women in the group handled

News in Song

News spreads so fast by other means today that it rarely tarries long enough to find its way into song—particularly songs that take many months to record and distribute. However, in the United States in the 1950s and 1960s folk singers often discussed and commented on topical issues such as civil rights or the Vietnam War—as Gypsy musicians, Indian bards, and west African *griots* might have. And this tradition has occasionally been revived in more contemporary forms of popular music.

When four students were shot by National Guard troops at Kent State University in 1970, the group Crosby, Stills, Nash and Young had some success with an angry rock and roll song about the incident. And more recently the Rolling Stones recorded a song, "Sweet Neo-Con," criticizing the Bush Administration.

Rap music, with its sometimes extemporaneous rhymes, has had some success in recent years in fitting in mention of current events, particularly in live performances.

that task by dashing up to the hills and shouting. Soon the alarm spread, and their tribesmen swarmed in to defend them.[41]

Perhaps the most valuable news we can receive is warning of a clear and present danger—the British are coming, Pearl Harbor has been bombed, a hurricane is on the way, a wedding party has been attacked. Sometimes, as it was with those Zulu women, news is simultaneously a call for help.[42] But news of danger does not always arrive with a request for action; an alarm may be sounded simply as a warning. In a Zapotec village in Mexico, the church bells would ring to warn the village of threats ranging from bandits to an earthquake or a rainstorm.[43] Any news system must make some provision for spreading alarms.[44] (Thomas Jefferson once called newspapers "the only tocsin of a nation.")[45]

Death ranks as another inescapable news story—whether proclaimed by wailing or obituary. All societies must also find means for disseminating news of war, which unlooses both death and danger. After members of the Abipon tribe in Paraguay in the 18th century fought a battle some distance from town, a horseman was sent back to spread the news. The scene that followed was observed by a missionary:

> As soon as this messenger is espied from a distance, a crowd comes out to meet him; striking their lips with their right hands, and accompanies him to his house. Having preserved the profoundest silence he leaps down from his horse on to a bed; whence, as from a rostrum, he announces the event of the battle, with a grave voice, to the surrounding multitude. If a few of the enemy are killed and wounded, he begins his story with *Nalamichiriñi;* they are all slaughtered, which . . . receives the applause of the bystanders . . . The number of captives, wagons, and horses, that have been taken, are then detailed with infinite exaggeration, for of each he asserts that they are innumerable. . . .

Eventually, however, all war reporters have to impart some bad news. The Abipon horseman put that task off until the end of his story, for good reason:

The mention of the death of one of their countrymen entirely destroys all the pleasure which the news of the victory had excited; so that the announcer immediately finds himself deserted by his late attentive listeners. . . . All the women unloose their hair, snatch up gourds and drums and lament.[46]

Danger, death, and war all have great impact, but news does not have to be so dramatic, so directly concerned with the physical safety or freedom of the community to have practical value. For the Tikopia the movement of ships was always newsworthy, because ships brought food to the island; for the Rwala Bedouins it was important to know that a new grazing ground was fertile, so a scout would carry back an armful of grass and let the grass tell the story.[47]

Nor does the thirst for news abate when practical concerns end. As noted in the previous chapter, we also turn to the news for pleasure, for entertainment. If news of a pasture upon which their animals might graze was important to the Bedouins, even news of an inaccessible pasture would have been of interest. And word of the ambush of that Zulu wedding party continued to spread even after the practical matter of coming to their aid had been addressed.

We examine our surroundings initially for threats or for the information we need to survive, but inevitably our focus widens. From the spectator's perspective, sporting events—such as the races announced by a crier to Tewa Indians in New Mexico[48]—are classic examples of subjects that are newsworthy without being directly connected to the well-being of the news audience. Human interests demand that news carry us beyond thoughts of safety and succor to the diverting, even the trivial. And those who lived in oral societies demonstrated as much of a fascination with such stories as we do.

The Nootka of Vancouver Island exchanged the usual complement of practical news: on "the abundance of salmon in this or that river," on a chief's plans to hold a ceremony, on the killing of a sea otter, on talk that the chiefs were planning war. However, the Nootka also pricked up their ears at word that someone was having an affair with someone else's wife. And the tale of a suitor who tumbled into a barrel of rainwater while sneaking out the window of his lover's house "spread like wildfire up and down the coast."[49]

The qualities that modern journalists look for in news, as outlined in journalism textbooks, include impact, emotional appeal, conflict, timeliness, proximity, prominence and the unusual. Were standards for measuring news value in oral culture much different?

A rainstorm or the presence of bandits in a Mexican village was news primarily because of its potential *impact* on people's lives. Death too had impact, perhaps magnified by the widespread belief that it provided a clue to the mood of the gods. The suitor's tumble into the barrel had *emotional appeal*—it was at once sexually titillating, embarrassing and funny. *Conflict* was one of the qualities that made news out of war, a footrace, or a man's affair with someone else's wife. Had those Bedouin scouts brought back clumps of brown grass to show that a pasture had been fertile a month ago, it would not have been nearly as newsworthy—*timeliness* was all important. The *proximity* of the grazing ground, the footrace, or the lovers—their accessibility or familiarity—also helped determine the degree of interest they elicited. And evidence of the extent to which the *prominence* of individuals determined their newsworthiness can be found in

How Practical Is News Today?

Some years ago a *New York Post* editor argued that crime news serves a practical purpose: "You make people more aware. You make them more careful. You make them more responsive." But it is not that easy to make the case for the practical value of crime reporting, which too often seems instead to make readers or viewers more paranoid (see Chapter 8). Once you have purchased an extra door lock and mastered some basic street smarts, how useful is it to learn of another particularly gruesome or particularly odd homicide? (See Stephens, "Crime Doesn't Pay. . . .")

A terrible crime is news primarily because it is unusual, because it features conflict and has a kind of emotional appeal, because, in other words, it is interesting not because it has that much impact on our lives (see Chapter 7).

The service pieces that newspapers and newscasts run—how to test for breast cancer, where to find the best child care—certainly are practical. And some breaking news—a tax cut, discovery of a new cancer treatment—certainly can have impact upon many lives. But most breaking news is too unusual to be representative, too far removed from our daily experience to be useful.

As citizens, we want to be informed of outbreaks of fighting overseas and political scandals back home; a chain of events they touch off might someday affect our lives. However, it is a stretch to contend that we follow these events primarily for practical reasons.

the ritual with which the Toradja on the Celebes Islands responded to death: Ordinarily they would fire a gun, but if it was a chief who had breathed his last, 10 cannon shots would be fired.[50]

At the heart of modern journalism is the search for the last item on this list—*the unusual.* Our news is very much about those events that manage to distinguish themselves from the clip-clop of ordinary experience. Oral societies had no less a taste for the unusual. In the hamlet of Kakapalayam in southern India, whenever someone broke a law and was arrested, whenever someone's life was shattered by an accident, a crowd would gather to find out what happened. "On all such occasions, when anything out of the way takes place," two observers report, "the tea shops . . . have some brisk business. The people neglect their looms with a view to find out the local news."[51]

If the basic standards of news judgment in oral societies appear similar to those used in our society, so do the basic types of stories. We have in common reports of accidents, earthquakes, military expeditions, sports, weather, death and violations of the law. We too spread alarms—though the dangers, if life expectancies are any guide, may be growing more distant. Our economic news at present may not include facts on the fertility of individual pastures, and ship movements may have been relegated to the agate type, but the reports we receive on the money supply or the commodities markets perform essentially the same function as the armful of grass brought back by a Bedouin scout.

The splash an occurrence must make to be considered news varies, of course, with the size of the audience reached by a news medium. If some of the news that circulated through preliterate societies still seems unfamiliar, perhaps it is because their measures of news value were calibrated for even smaller audiences than those attracted by our small-town newspapers or radio stations. As a result, the newsmakers in these societies did not have to be quite so prominent; the out-of-the-ordinary occurrences did not have to be quite so bizarre.

The presence of a larger audience—the result of a higher degree of amplification—also tends to add formality, even a hint of propriety to the news. We share with the Nootka a weakness for stories like that of the suitor who fell in the barrel, but his flop would have to be more dramatic, or the suitor more prominent, not only to whet the interest of news organizations today but to overcome their reluctance to publicize so personal a matter. (Were the suitor a candidate for president or were he murdered, that reluctance would quickly be overcome.)

Admittedly, the composite picture of news in oral societies presented here has its limitations. To make the more precise comparison between news in a *particular* oral society and our news we would need a more complete accounting of news in one such society than is now available in the anthropological literature. (It would also be useful if that literature included more comments from the members of those societies about their news.)

It is, of course, possible to exaggerate the extent of the congruity between the news disseminated by busybody, messenger or crier and that disseminated in the late 20th century by newspaper or newscast. Attitudes toward the news undoubtedly have shifted somewhat as ceremonial runners have given way to secular news announcers. News, though now more trustworthy, is less prized, its revelations rarely perceived as divine. And variations certainly have appeared, and continue to appear, in the range, complexity, comprehensiveness, accuracy, emotionalism, credulity and objectivity of news accounts—variations considered in detail in this book. Nevertheless, the basic topics with which those news accounts have been concerned, and the basic standards by which they evaluate newsworthiness, seem to have varied very little.[52] Indeed, the evidence that is available from this wide sample of preliterate cultures all points to one conclusion: that humans have exchanged a similar mix of news with a consistency throughout history and across cultures that makes interest in this news seem inevitable, if not innate.

Is it surprising that the concerns of the news appear to have changed so little? To what other topics could the news devote itself? Can we imagine a news system that disdained the unusual in favor of the typical, that ignored the prominent, that devoted as much attention to the dated as the current, to the legal as the illegal, to peace as to war, to well-being as to calamity and death? The particular amalgam of anecdote and information that humans call news undoubtedly reflects some of the most basic categories and standards by which the human mind evaluates phenomena in the social world.

There is an additional explanation for the success of this mix of news: It seems to satisfy not only individual cravings for information, for entertainment, for awareness, but societal needs for safety and solidarity. The importance to the group of warnings of danger and reports on fertile fields is clear, and news of the leader's laws and regulations help that leader to coordinate behavior—presumably for the good of the group. But the exchange of news also has more subtle contributions to make to the strength of the group. Societies depend on news of violations of the law to reinforce understanding of their laws and fear of their punishments; they depend on accounts of the out of the ordinary to strengthen the consensus on what qualifies as ordinary. Indeed, the members of a society can be said to be renewing their membership each time they exchange news on the situation and fortunes of that society—its battles, its ceremonies, its sporting events. From this perspective, each report or item of gossip recognizing the prominence of a leader is a reacknowledgment of the centrality of that leader; each shared perception—of danger, of humor—each shared reaction—fear, grief, outrage—reawakens a sense of shared destiny and shared purpose.

Oral news systems had significant inadequacies in fulfilling individual and societal needs for news. Future news media would be able to extend human awareness, and societal bonds, over much larger areas. But the set of common interests out of which they would create that awareness, and form those bonds, would remain basically unchanged.

The Edge of the World

One observer of the news system employed by the Zulus was impressed by the "certainty and celerity" with which news traveled.[53] Celerity, yes. News of the pot defiled with crocodile did spread with impressive speed; and with the use of runners the Zulus could accelerate their news still further. But certainty? Elementary school teachers have a game that demonstrates how unreliable oral communication can sometimes be. They have students whisper a message from person to person around the room. The message soon becomes unintelligible.

Oral societies were not quite as vulnerable to misunderstandings as that classroom game might suggest. Because they knew the world through word of mouth, members of these societies had to train themselves to achieve a certain precision in their whispering. The use of news specialists further improved the accuracy of their communication. Employing a messenger to carry the news over a distance, or a crier to distribute it to an entire village, at the very least reduced the number of individuals—each capable of adding distortion—through which a news item had to pass. The use of objects to supplement oral reports also could increase their reliability. A Bedouin scout's report on the fertility of a pasture could hardly be doubted if he was carrying an armful of grass.

Nevertheless, any news system that is based primarily on multiple exchanges among individuals is going to be subject to distortion and inaccuracies. Tongues—no matter how well trained—will occasionally slip; there will be lapses in comprehension. And how many stories can be backed up by an armful of grass? Messages may not have consistently grown unintelligible in these societies, but they could not be consistently relied upon either.

Consider the experience of Ukokko's brother, a member of the Yahgan tribe at the southern tip of South America. After receiving word that Ukokko and his family had been shipwrecked and murdered on an island, this devoted brother quickly gathered some friends and set out in search of revenge. However, the gang of angry avengers soon found themselves "in a very awkward situation": After presumably charging with weapons raised onto the island where Ukokko had landed, they learned that the news—as was often the case—had been incorrect. Ukokko was safe; he had not been mistreated. The anthropologist who passes along this story notes that among the Yahgan "most news . . . is communicated from mouth to mouth." "The facts," he says, "are inevitably altered in various ways."[54]

Oral societies were particularly vulnerable to the storyteller's natural temptation to exaggerate. The feared bush cows inevitably created a sensation for the Tiv in Nigeria when a few of them wandered down from the hills every five or six years. One week in 1950 a Tiv town received a visit from three bush cows. They may have injured one man. The news quickly spread, but just as quickly the number of casualties grew. Soon it was being reported that three men had been injured, another killed. Then in the hands of a "song maker" it became 10 wounded, two dead, and six bush cows.[55] Each person who played a role in spreading the story had an opportunity to improve upon it, and, of course, there was nothing on paper to give the lie to these embellishments.

Freedom from paper, with its ability to harden facts, made it easier for the news to bend in the direction not only of drama but of hope. Raymond Firth recorded a score of inaccurate rumors of ships said to be about to dock at Tikopia, rumors* that were generated, he surmised, by simple wish-fulfillment.[56] Spoken news is also flexible enough to accommodate most stereotypes: Bush cows are vicious; therefore, they must have wounded more than one man.

Journalists working in any medium will surrender at some point to the comfort and convenience of stereotypes. But stereotypes settle particularly easily into spoken news, and they have special value for those who attempt to spread news in a preliterate society. Formulas, clichés, and stereotypes—from the stock phrases of Homeric epics ("clever Odysseus") to the vicious bush cows of the Tiv—are easy to store and then recall from our memories—always an important consideration in an exclusively oral society where the forgettable will be quickly forgotten.[57] The more minds and memories an item of news is filtered through, the more the imprint of the stereotypes lurking in those minds and memories will be felt on that news item. In other words, the heroes grow braver, the bush cows more murderous, as the news is relayed from person to person through a society.

The limitations inherent in spoken news go beyond such inaccuracies and distortions. Despite their remarkable speed, oral news systems have limited breadth. As distances grow, the number of people required to move the news grows—with the attendant risk of additional distortions. Runners and travelers may have enabled news of a king's death to travel 300 miles, but that must have tested the limits of the system. The great expanses of jungles or deserts were opaque to news of less radiant personages, less charged events or more complex circumstances.

News cannot do its work for a society unless it can penetrate that society. Oral culture, the historian Brian Stock writes, "suits small, isolated communities."[58] Empires, even nation-states, could not be kept informed by the mechanisms available to such a culture. In 1954 the residents of a remote village in India, without access to any modern news media, were queried on their knowledge of current events. News that India had gained its independence had reached them all, but no one in the village had heard of the

---

* The difference between rumor and news, in these societies at least, was mostly a matter of degree. Few news stories were seen as entirely trustworthy; few rumors were presented or received as entirely discreditable. Rumor was news that was less likely to prove true.

Cold War, no one knew of the partition of India and Pakistan, and only one person in the village, the headman, had heard of the country's prime minister, Jawaharlal Nehru.[59] The village's news system simply did not reach all the way to New Delhi, let alone Moscow or Washington.

From the perspective of a society dependent for its news upon individuals meeting, chatting, running or proclaiming, the political world, and even the known world, ends at some point. Its edge may be a three-day run away or a three-week caravan trip away, but most of the other cultures in the world are lost in the void beyond.

Such limitations in spoken news are more than mere anthropological curiosities. Gathering places, travel, busybodies, messengers, criers and minstrels were the sources humankind relied on for news for tens of thousands of years. The limitations of spoken news enforced limitations on the cultural perspectives and political possibilities available to most of the world's population.

Questions

1. What other uses of language are as important as the exchange of news?

2. What places contribute to the exchange of news in modern societies?

3. Discuss some of the ways in which the role played by messengers and criers in oral societies differs from that played by professional journalists today.

4. Find contemporary examples to illustrate each of the seven qualities mentioned here as making occurrences newsworthy.

5. Does our world today have an "edge"? In other words, are there places or cultures today into which our contemporary news system fails to penetrate?

The Survival of Spoken News— Publishing the Whisper of the Day

3

Outside of the bush, when we think of news, we tend to think of information that arrives with the aid of a machine. Consequently, when European or American writers are looking for an analogy that might help their readers understand news systems in preliterate societies, they call upon an electronic or mechanical news organ. Not only did the Zulus employ "human wireless telegraphy," but the horsemen in Outer Mongolia who would "gallop away into the green spaces in a hurry to share . . . news" were the "Mongolian telegraph." Topical songs in the Mexican village of Tepoztlán were "a sort of newspaper of the folk," and the Mongour peddlers who moved news as they traveled were "the 'radio' of the country."[2] Although such analogies have value, their repeated use can obscure more direct similarities between cultures, similarities that can make the rapidity with which "secret deeds got whispered abroad" by the Zulus "without telegraph wires, postal correspondence, news agencies, or newspaper"[3] seem somewhat less amazing.

Spoken news not only has helped keep many Asian, African and Native American societies informed, entertained and aware, it has played a significant role throughout the history of Western civilization. In Athens, talk of current events filled the agora and the gymnasium. In Rome, the news center was the Forum, where a man of politics or business could spend the morning "hearing the latest news from the provinces."[4]

In medieval Europe, spoken news was the dominant form of news. A 13th century French poem, "Les Crieries de Paris," explains how deaths, royal decrees and the arrival of new wine were all cried through the *quartiers* of Paris.[5] Travel played such a significant role in circulating news in the 15th century that during some of the worst periods of the War of the Roses, the English guarded the roads out of Calais in an attempt to keep news of their country's troubles from reaching other nations.[6] Richard III considered word of mouth so powerful and dangerous a news medium that he felt it necessary to admonish towns against the "telling of tales and tidings whereby the people might be stird to commocions."[7]

In 17th century London, the nave of St. Paul's Cathedral—"Paul's walk"—served as an informal news exchange, reminiscent of the Siwan sun shelters or the agora: ". . . the news of the continent, the ocean, and the town was brought fresh to Paul's and canvassed with a din of voices."[8] (From the perspective of the countryside, the entire city had always appeared a large news exchange. In 1471 John Paston wrote of the news, or "flying tales," that could be acquired by walking in London as we might speak of the news available in a newspaper.)[9] And as late as the 18th century, watchmen or bellmen—who cried the hour, gave fire warnings, discussed the weather, and announced deaths—would walk the streets of England at night, wearing heavy greatcoats and carrying poles, rattles and lanterns.[10]

The commercial possibilities of spoken news (as will be discussed later in this chapter) were exploited in England and France in the 17th and 18th centuries by the proprietors of coffeehouses and by professional *nouvellistes*.* And, of course, less organized methods for moving news by word of mouth—simple back-fence, park-bench, barbershop, general-store newsmongering—have survived through the 19th and 20th centuries and into the 21st century in Europe and America.

However, this ability of our ancestors to exchange news without the aid of a printing press or electricity is routinely overlooked. Spoken news, difficult enough to see in the bush, becomes practically invisible in the shadow of more advanced news media. *We* invented the telegraph; *they* conjured up "human wireless telegraphy." That most of the world shared a reliance on gathering places, travelers, busybodies, messengers and criers is rarely acknowledged.

When a tradesman on the Isle of Skye in Scotland returned from a trip to the far end of the island in the 1950s, he was greeted by the standard opening question: "What's fresh?" He then proceeded to pass on all the news he had picked up that day. Yet that tradesman himself was guilty of overlooking spoken news. "You'd wonder where these people get all the news," he commented to an outsider, after himself having provided a significant supply.[11]

This attitude, as common among journalism historians as among Scottish tradesmen, adds additional blind spots to our already incomplete view of the history of spoken news—and therefore to the history of journalism in Europe and America. It obscures understanding of the news forms that our ancestors long relied upon and that we are now losing.

Coffeehouses and *Nouvellistes*

One method for moving news that has reached a high level of development in the West employs nothing more technologically sophisticated than an accommodating place and a stimulating beverage. The beverage pulls people in and loosens their tongues; the place fills with news. In rural Ireland in the 1930s, to select one of countless possible examples, an anthropologist found that the pubs were among the places where "the important news of the countryside disseminates itself."[12]

---

* *Nouvelles* is the French word for "news."

The drink of choice in England in the 17th and 18th centuries (uncharacteristic of the English as this may sound) was coffee. "One Jacob, a Jew," opened the country's first coffeehouse in Oxford in about 1650. (Coffee was probably introduced to England from the East by the Jews, whom Oliver Cromwell had allowed to immigrate in the middle years of the 17th century.)[13] The stimulation of the brew proved conducive to conversation, and coffeehouses were soon filled with loquacious men (women were not permitted inside) and all the news they brought with them.

By 1661 in Oxford, the high-minded were complaining that, with the popularity of the coffeehouses, scholarly work had ceased and that "nothing but news and the affaires of Christendome is discussed."[14] And Cambridge would be no better off. This couplet, from a satire called *The Student,* was written about Cambridge in 1751:

> Dinner over, to *Tom's* or to *Clapham's* I go,
> The news of the Town so impatient to know.[15]

In London, by the 18th century, there were hundreds, perhaps thousands, of houses similar to Tom's or Clapham's, where patrons could sit around a large table and obtain coffee (at a penny a cup), warmth, camaraderie and news. Contemporary writers viewed the pull of coffee and coffeehouses with a mixture of awe and derision that critics of television news might find familiar. The ballad *News from the Coffe-House* was printed in 1667:

> . . . There's nothing done in all the World,
>   From Monarch to the Mouse
> But every Day or Night 'tis hurld
>   Into the Coffee-house . . .
> Here Men do talk of every Thing,
>   With large and liberal Lungs,
> Like Women at a Gossiping,
>   With double type of Tongues . . .
> You shall know there, what Fashons are;
>   How Perrywiggs are Curl'd;
> And for a penny you shall heare,
>   All Novells in the World. . . .[16]

In 1712 Joseph Addison described in the *Spectator* how unfounded reports of the death of the king of France, Louis XIV, inspired the patrons of St. James's Coffee-House in London:

> I found the whole outward Room in a Buzz of Politics. The Speculations were but very indifferent toward the Door, but grew finer as you advanced to the upper end of the Room, and were so very much improved by a Knot of Theorists, who sat in the inner Room, within the steams of the Coffee Pot, that I there heard the whole *Spanish* Monarchy disposed of, and all the Line of *Bourbon* provided for in less than a Quarter of an Hour.[17]

Louis XIV lived another three years, but discussions at coffeehouses often were less speculative and more reliable. In 1740 Sir Robert Walpole ordered a "handsome pres-

In 17th- and 18th-century England, coffeehouses were centers for the exchange of news. This unsympathetic engraving from Edward Ward's Vulgus Britannicus, *printed in 1710, shows that the discussions there occasionally grew heated.*

ent" for the master of Lloyd's coffeehouse, who had given him the first account of Admiral Vernon's taking of Porto Bello.[18]

Each London coffeehouse developed its own character. Lloyd's attracted ships' officers, traders, merchants and bankers, and specialized in shipping news. (Ship insurance contracts were auctioned off at a latter incarnation of the house; eventually it was taken over by its patrons—who would form the powerful corporation of insurance agents that still uses the name Lloyd's.)[19] Will's coffeehouse was known for its collection of "wits," including John Dryden and Addison. In Mile's coffeehouse the topic was politics: ". . . the arguments in the Parliament House were flat, to the discourses here," noted one observer. There were even mock ballots taken on public issues in Mile's.[20]

London was so thoroughly saturated with coffeehouses that, like our modern magazines, they were forced to seek out narrow audiences. One was known as the Stock Exchange, another the Tennis-Court. The New York coffeehouse was frequented by men interested in discussing trade with the colonies. The Grecian attracted scholars.

"Narrowcasting"

A basic rule of communication: The more outlets available of any particular medium in any one area the more narrow the audiences they will seek out.

Americans now have the choice of hundreds of magazines, so there are magazines on everything from sea kayaking to community theater. With the arrival of dozens and now hundreds of cable channels, television is moving in the same direction. We already have a food channel and a history channel. Can a community-theater channel be far behind? An it is becoming increasingly difficult to come up with an interest to which the million-channel Internet does not cater.

"Narrowcasting," J. C. R. Licklider labeled this in the mid-1960s (Negroponte). London coffeehouses in the early 18th century provided some of the earliest examples of narrowcasting.

There was also a Theatre coffeehouse, a Literary coffeehouse and even a Tilt-Yard coffeehouse, which attracted "mock-military . . . fellows . . . who manfully pulled the noses of such quiet citizens as wore not swords."[21]

Londoners would often visit more than one coffeehouse each day to sit, drink and exchange news. A letter in the *Spectator* (probably written by Alexander Pope) described a fellow who might be seen "publishing the Whisper of the Day by eight a Clock in the Morning at *Garraway's,* by twelve at *Will's,* and before two at the *Smyrna.* . . ."[22]

The English began losing their taste for coffee later in the 18th century. With the encouragement of a government anxious to spur trade with India, a gentler stimulant, tea, would soon fill their cups. Pressure from women, who were denied access to coffeehouses, undoubtedly also contributed to their decline. Gentlemen began taking their conversations to the private confines of the club; others turned to pubs to rediscover the contribution alcohol could make to sociability and the dissemination of news.[23]

The French had begun their longer-lived affair with coffee at about the same time, and in Paris in the 17th and 18th centuries the news-hungry were beginning to collect in the cafés.[24] But as news centers those cafés faced stiff competition from the city's many parks and gardens, where groups would gather regularly to regale each other with the doings of the great and the world's great doings.[25]

Some of these groups of *nouvellistes á la bouche* (by the mouth) were well organized, with their own officers and their own carefully maintained pipelines of information. One member would have a friend in an embassy, another an acquaintance at the court, another knew someone in the office of a minister, or in the kitchen of a prelate or the stable of a prince. Other groups of *nouvellistes* collected around a single well-informed individual, such as the *bonhomme* who held forth on the terrace of the Feuillants each day for 30 years and was considered so influential that Louis XVI was reputed to have been curious about his opinion.[26]

Spreading news, while avocation for some *nouvellistes,* was vocation for others—they expected a few coins after a performance. These professional news-tellers might develop a special area of expertise, and the interested knew which corner to visit for the most informed update on politics or war or culture.[27] The wares of such Parisian news merchants were obtained through a combination of enterprise and extrapolation that outraged as many as it intrigued. "They have bridges on all the rivers, secret routes in all the mountains," wrote Montesquieu. "They lack only good sense."[28]

As the 18th century progressed, some news began to wander from the gardens and the cafés of Paris indoors to the elegant reception rooms of the city's finest hostesses. A group of politicians, magistrates, physicians, academicians, ecclesiastics and poets, for instance, would gather each day in the apartment of Madame Doublet, on the second floor of a Paris convent, and, under the supervision of the dedicated *nouvelliste* Louis Petit de Bachaumont, exchange whatever news of politics, literature, the arts and society the participants had come upon in the course of their day.[29]

Looking back from the perspective of an era in which news is never farther away than the nearest radio, television or computer, it is easy to dismiss these *salons* as mere settings for the idle to act out their literary and social pretensions, just as it is easy to allow the coffeepot to dominate our view of the coffeehouse or the whiskey bottle to confuse our perspective on the tavern. It is easy to overlook the ache that helped drive our ancestors to these rooms—the same ache that motivated so much of the behavior of the Zulus or the Tikopia: a hunger for news.[30]

The Decline of Spoken News

The coffeehouse and the *nouvelliste* were already facing competition in 18th century Europe from the written and printed forms of news that were sprouting in some profusion from pens and presses (although the growth of printed news was still circumscribed in most countries, France in particular, by government regulation). The long process of erosion of oral culture—begun, according to the classicist Eric Havelock, with the transcription of Homer[31]—was accelerating.

Writing and print began to be used even by the purveyors of spoken news themselves, who were, despite the disparaging comments of critics such as Montesquieu, literate as well as resourceful individuals. The coffeehouses subscribed to all the available newspapers, and some *nouvellistes* reworked their collections of news into handwritten newsletters, which were sent to the provinces for a fee. Bachaumont even began retailing the news brought to Madame Doublet's salon in a periodic newsletter, later preserved in a series of books.

In the 19th century, newspapers, fortified by the arrival of the telegraph and the steam press, were able to obtain news in minutes and reach circulations of tens and, in some cases, hundreds of thousands. While they did not instantly eradicate spoken news, these powerful dailies did begin eradicating understanding of the importance of spoken news. Early publishers had acknowledged their debt to their forebears in the titles they selected for their newspapers—*Herald, Mercury, Messenger.* (*Post* or *Newsletter* honor a different branch of the family.) But increasingly, journalism and the press, specifically the newspaper press, began to be thought of as synonymous, as they are thought of as synonymous in much journalism history today.

People were still speaking news—for although more and more subjects fell within the purview of the press, even newspapers had difficulty keeping up with the word of mouth that continued to race from busybody to barber to street corner to tavern across most of the world's villages and towns. But this was news of mere local interest, spread by uninfluential people, with unamplified voices. Spoken news settled into the background—invisible even to some of those who spread it—leaving a hole in the history of journalism and leaving a mystery at the heart of the history of journalism.

"The subject of deepest interest to an average human being is himself," the 19th century New York editor Horace Greeley once noted. "Next to that he is most concerned with his neighbors. Asia and the Tongo Islands stand a long way after these in his regard."[32] The editors of most early 21st-century newspapers and local newscasts in the United States seem to agree with Greeley's reading of the audience—they fill their pages or screens with significant amounts of local news or news of their metropolitan areas. The mystery is this: Why do so many of the examples of journalism that have survived from the decades and centuries before Greeley made his statement seem to have neglected local news?[33]

The answer is not that our ancestors had more interest in the residents of the Tongo Islands than in their neighbors; rather, it is that they entrusted the information they most prized—local news, community news—to the news medium they relied on most, to a medium archaeologists and historians will never discover under a sandy tell or in a dusty attic: the human voice.

Spoken news is finally beginning to earn its anonymity today. In the more developed urban and suburban communities of the most developed countries, the busybody appears to be going the way of the ceremonial runner. *Nouvellistes* in these communities are more likely to be found propped up in front of television sets than discoursing in cafés. Most of the residents of such communities shop not at marketplaces but at supermarkets, where the talking is done by synthesized voices. Their town squares gather mostly pigeons and the homeless; their travelers are interrogated only by the desk clerk at the Holiday Inn.

Spoken news continues to play a significant role in more rural areas, in the less developed regions of the world and in those countries where the flow of printed or broadcast information is tightly controlled. It still handles some news of the smaller communities to which most of us belong—the workplace, the block. But in the West, at least, these pockets of resistance are shrinking.

The new news media are triumphing. They are triumphing as cities and suburbs grow too broad for spoken news to traverse, and as smaller communities—thanks to easier travel and the substitute "communities" of radio, television and the Internet—begin to lose the cohesion that had enabled them to move their own news. The new news media are triumphing by weaning us from neighborhood characters and events, and seducing us with news of the larger, more glamorous world of metropolitan area and nation— news of neighborhood burglaries displaced by reports of robberies and murders downtown; the escapades of the neighborhood beauty displaced by gossip about film, television or music stars.[34] And the new news media are triumphing because their speed and power in the end put even the Zulus' "human wireless telegraphy" to shame.

Oral news systems are dependent on talk. Today we spend large portions of our time reading, watching and listening—silently.

Before his death in the middle 19th century, the last of the ceremonial runners who had spread news among the Fox Indians in the Midwest was said to have warned his tribe about life without him. That warning was issued to a people settled in areas already filling with newspapers, a people whose grandchildren would be able to keep current on events anywhere in the world at any hour of the day with radio and television. Nonetheless, there are reasons why the descendants of the Fox, whether living on a reservation or living in a condominium, might miss their ceremonial runners.

The news that whizzes by on radio waves in the air above us, or arrives in computer-processed columns in our newspapers, is a distant, impersonal news. We cannot ask questions of our newsmongers; their reports are tailored to us en masse, never to us individually. And in cities and suburbs, the scale by which our news organs measure newsworthiness is too large for most of the events that actually touch our lives to register. It is now possible to know what was served for dinner last night at the White House, but it is becoming more difficult to find out why an ambulance pulled up to a house down the road last night. It is possible to learn exactly why a space shuttle exploded, but it is becoming more difficult to find out what is being built on a lot around the corner.

The new news media have assumed the franchise, but they have not picked up all the services. We are losing news of our neighborhoods. And to the extent that the exchange of news helps bind neighborhoods, we risk losing those neighborhoods and our identity as participants in them.

Moreover, as the news we receive has begun to abandon our streets and communities in favor of momentarily more exciting locales across town or even overseas, our ability to participate in this news has diminished. Busybodies, ceremonial runners and crowds in the marketplace reported on us, taking note of when *we*—not Hillary Rodham Clinton, not Tom Cruise—celebrated, when *we* mourned and when *we* fell into rain barrels. Without them the bulk of humanity appears to have been pulled from the stage and seated in the balcony, our opportunities to make news on our own reduced to the occasional chance to wave should a television camera deign to pan our crowd.

That ceremonial runner's specific warning to his people was said to have been: "You will have no one who will go about telling anything that happened to you."[35] Is that the curse of life without a system of spoken news?

Questions

1. This chapter argues that spoken news has been "practically invisible" in Europe and America. What is it about spoken news that has made it so easy to overlook?

2. The more there are of a particular medium, the more specialized each becomes. This chapter offers modern magazines, cable television, the Internet and London coffeehouses as examples of this principle. Give another example.

3. Why are spoken news systems stronger in rural areas than in cities or suburbs? Are they likely to remain strong there?

PART TWO

WRITTEN NEWS

4 News and Literacy—
The First Story That Comes to Hand

Early in this century, a divorce among members of the Khasi tribe in India would be announced by a crier walking through the village:

> *Kaw*—hear, O villagers, that U___ and K___ have become separated in the presence of elders. *Hei!* thou, O young man, canst go and make love to K___ for she is now unmarried, and thou, oh spinster, canst make love to U___. *Hei!* there is no let or hindrance from henceforth.[2]

Cicero, the Roman philosopher and politician, was informed of similar news in the year 50 B.C. through a letter written by a friend and a fellow politician, Caelius:

> Paulla Valeria, the sister of Triarius, has divorced her husband without assigning any reason, on the very day that he was to arrive from his province. She is going to marry D. Brutus. She had sent back her whole wardrobe.[3]

A gulf separates these two reports. One, relying on easily memorizable formulas, relates the information in the most personal, the most concrete terms: ". . . thou, O young man, canst go and make love to K___. . . ." The other—although it is addressed to one individual, not a whole village—is impersonal, dispassionate (even ironic), and halfheartedly analytical. (Caelius notes that no explanation was provided but presents the wardrobe as a possible clue to the woman's thinking.) Among the many factors that might explain the palpable difference in mentality between this village crier and this Roman politician, one stands out: literacy.

Writing, because of its implications for the development of human thought, deserves a share of the byline on our civilization. With the ability to note, to record, the mind is freed from the burden of memorizing past wisdom. Formulas lose some of their hold on language and thought. And with the store of wisdom no longer limited to the capacity of a generation's memory, knowledge begins to ac-

So little pains do the vulgar take in the investigation of truth, accepting readily the first story that comes to hand.

—Thucydides[1]

43

How Will Television, Like Writing, Change Us?

Writing changed the way human beings thought. The arrival of the printing press in Europe in the 15th century did, too (see Chapter 7). Can we expect television and related modern technologies to work similar changes upon us?

Scholars, media critics and most of the rest of us have been looking for evidence of television's effects almost since it was first invented. Has it made us more violent? Less social? More like preliterate people? Less serious? More materialistic?

A lesson from the history of communication: It takes time for a new information technology to develop the forms that will unleash its power. Their alphabet was more than two centuries old before the Greeks jotted down the first histories and philosophies. More than a century passed after Gutenberg invented the printing press be-

fore the first novels and newspapers appeared. Yes, things seem to move faster now. Nevertheless, it is likely that we haven't yet seen all that television can do; it is likely that the forms— the programming—that will make best use of this medium have not yet appeared.

Television is a revolutionary technology, as writing and the printing press were, but the television revolution is still very young. The consequences of television viewing (most of them negative) pounced on by its critics so far may prove to have been products only of its immature years.

It would have been unwise to judge the consequences of writing before Herodotus and Plato. We may be making a similar mistake with television.

cumulate over the generations—Cicero could read, and presumably build upon, the work, for example, of Thucydides. Furthermore, once words and ideas are impressed on clay tablets or jotted down on paper, they gain weight; they can be studied independently of the objects to which they refer; they can be compared, juggled, rearranged. Thoughts, once written down, can more easily be rethought.

Researchers such as anthropologist Jack Goody and Walter Ong, a professor of humanities, have concluded that the literate see the world differently from the way the preliterate do. In an oral society, the question of whether, for example, the dew is a thing of the sky or of the earth would seem pointless, nonsensical. What in their world might occasion such a distinction? But the literate compile lists, and because dew cannot be placed in both columns, the various attributes of dew, sky and earth must all be considered.[4] Among the outgrowths of such exercises in abstract reasoning is a flowering of cognitive skills, including the ability to categorize and analyze. The literate can separate themselves from words and therefore from situations; they can stand back and mull them over. We owe science, and the myriad technological wonders it has spawned, to writing—this most revolutionary of technologies.[5]

News could not escape the effects of this transformation in thought processes. Although formulas are too convenient for even the most literate of journalists to surrender entirely, the literate mind was able to recast them, settling on formulas with attributes other than ease of memorization. News could, for example, be topped with headings giving the place and date of its origin or a summary of its contents, and it could be arranged or presented chronologically, by location or according to a quality as abstract as its "newsworthiness." Preliterate societies seem to employ the same basic standards of newsworthiness used by modern news organizations; nevertheless, the process of *explicitly* rating and organizing occurrences according to some imposed hierarchy of newsworthiness—deaths before injuries; six-column headline for earthquake, one column for fire—appears to be a construct of the literate mind.

And broader changes in the nature of news can also be attributed to writing. Caelius and other literate newsmongers owed their predilection for dispassion and analysis in part to their literacy, to the objectification of language and, consequently, of thought that writing provides. Indeed, the gradual switch over the centuries from reliance on spoken news to the use of the written word to transmit news may have contributed to the modern journalist's proclaimed allegiance to objectivity.[6]

Reading and writing, of course, did not immediately work their magic on all segments of the population. Cicero and Caelius are hardly representative of Roman society; Rome appears to have had its criers.[7] The transformations took centuries, millennia, to take hold. Literacy spread, among the upper classes at least, with the efficient alphabet and primary schools of Greece and Rome, but it declined again during the Middle Ages.[8]

And news was particularly slow to feel the full force of the literate mind, because writing, unaided by the printing press, is a poor news medium.

The Demands of News

The ability to speak is part of our genetic inheritance; the ability to write is not. Writing, perfected relatively late in the development of the species, is a craft that must be taught to each new generation.[9]

The oldest surviving evidences of a writing system are the pictorial symbols for words impressed on a collection of clay tablets from about the year 3100 B.C. There is no reason to believe that these tablets, produced in Uruk in Mesopotamia, were put to any journalistic uses. Indeed they do not seem to have been put to any literary uses—the tablets are covered with lists of commodities and records of transactions.[10] (Commerce, not art, appears to have spurred the development of this preeminent intellectual tool.)

Greater efficiency in writing was achieved with greater separation between symbol and object. In the cuneiform script developed by the Sumerians in Mesopotamia, the symbols became easier to draw—more abstract—and pronunciations, not just objects, began to be represented. Cuneiform tablets dating from the middle of the third millennium B.C. in Mesopotamia and what is now Syria are still concerned primarily with matters of commerce—lists of possessions and agricultural records. But some of those tablets feature school texts, some fragments appear to have been used for literary works and some record the texts of state treaties.[11]

Newspapers today will occasionally reprint the exact wording of treaties. Might these treaties, written in cuneiform characters on clay tablets 2,500 years before the birth of Christ, have functioned as a form of written news? Probably not. Words are entrusted to hard surfaces to give them permanence. When a state treaty was recorded in clay, its terms were protected against the distortions, convenient or otherwise, of individual memories. But writing's permanence, although it can be crucial for governance and law, is of much less value for news.

The written word, through its ability to last, can preserve the past and regulate the future. Journalism, however, is concerned with the present, and writing had a great deal of difficulty keeping up with the present. Perhaps a clay tablet might have contained the first public mention of a treaty that had otherwise been kept secret. But in normal circumstances, why would leaders wait for the clay tablet to spread news of a treaty? Why would they not simply announce it and talk about it? Why would their subjects not simply ask? News moves fast, and writing is slow. It takes time to form words on soft clay. In a village or small city, most occurrences will be discussed well before they are recorded.

A group of tablets written in a cuneiform script in the 15th or 14th century B.C., about a thousand years after those treaties, discusses a topic even more familiar to modern newspaper readers: official corruption. The tablets display a series of charges against the mayor, named Kushiharbe, of the town of Nuzu in Mesopotamia. He is accused primarily of thefts and extortion: "So declares Ninuari: 'Kushiharbe robbed me from my own storehouse. Two shekels of gold, one ox, and two rams I paid to Kushiharbe; then he restored to me (what he had stolen).'" But an additional charge was also leveled against this mayor: that he had had illicit intercourse with a married woman named Humerelli. Apparently mindful of the need for impartiality, the writer of the tablets includes not only the damaging testimony of Palteya, who says he procured the woman for the mayor, but Kushiharbe's response to the charges: "I swear that Palteya did not bring Humerelli to the trysting house of Tilunnaya, nor did I have intercourse with her!"[12]

Although this record of charges against a mayor from the second millennium B.C. resembles a modern report on a trial or even a work of investigative journalism, again it is hard to imagine that the tablets played much more than an ancillary role in spreading word of Kushiharbe's alleged crimes through Nuzu. Perhaps a traveler who had missed all the local scuttlebutt on Mayor Kushiharbe might have learned the news by reading the tablets, but to conclude that the tablets were responsible for informing the city's residents of the news, we would have to assume that the abundant evidence of their mayor's rapaciousness had not been discussed well before the scribe had been instructed, the cuneiform had been drawn, the clay had dried and the tablet had been displayed. (Certainly, this news would have been widely discussed at the time of Kushiharbe's trial; trials were conducted in public.)

The great strength of writings such as these is the stable and secure home they provide for words, but an item of news is transient. It passes through a community for a few days, then it is gone. A medium that enables a report to settle in for an extended visit threatens to change its nature, to encumber that report with added legal or historical responsibilities.

The extra weight the written word carries does have some value for news. The charges against Kushiharbe must have commanded more respect on clay tablets than they did as chatter in the marketplace. Even if the townspeople found the information on these tablets redundant, the tablets may have played a role, for those able to read them, in confirming reports of the mayor's crimes. If redundant information can be news, perhaps these tablets qualify. But their primary function seems more likely to have been legal or historical than journalistic.

The final step in the development of writing was the adoption of an alphabet. An alphabet without vowels was used by the Canaanites in Syria and Palestine by 1500 B.C.[13] The Greeks contributed vowels about 750 years later—creating the alphabet still used, with modifications, in Europe and many of its former colonies today.[14]

A slower medium can play a more significant role in disseminating news if it can reach a larger audience. (This is the explanation for the great success of the printing press.) But here, too, writing, even with the assistance of the Greek alphabet, fell short. As early as the seventh century B.C., Greeks published laws and decrees by inscribing them on the walls of public buildings or on *stelae*—slabs of stone or wood that were displayed in public places.[15] Certainly, Greek leaders could better maintain their rule by having their decrees writ in stone or wood, but it seems unlikely that these inscriptions actually spread news to as large an audience as could be reached by simply announcing the treaties or decrees and allowing the normal flow of conversations in public places to carry word to the rest of the populace.

The audience that could be reached by an inscription on stone or wood was restricted, in any case, by the severe limitations in literacy that persisted until the fifth century B.C. in Greece and much longer in the rest of the world.[16] Virtually all healthy humans are able to hear news; the potential audience for written news has never been quite that large.

News and History

It is axiomatic in journalism that the fastest medium with the largest potential audience will disseminate the bulk of a community's breaking news. Today that race is being won by broadcasting and the Internet. Consequently, daily newspapers are beginning to underplay breaking news about yesterday's events (already old news to much of their audience) in favor of more analytical perspectives on those events.[17] In other words, dailies are now moving in the direction toward which weeklies retreated when dailies were introduced. As the use of writing advanced over the centuries, writers began taking a similar route. Condemned to being scooped on so much current information by word of mouth, they adopted more analytical approaches to the world, contenting themselves with recording, if not inventing, literature, philosophy, science and, of course, history.

When Herodotus put pen to papyrus (in the last half of the fifth century B.C.), it was to write not news about the present but history about the past (the wars between Greece and Persia in the first half of that century) for the use of the future: "that time may not draw the color from what man has brought into being. . . ."[18]

Another great Greek writer of nonfiction prose, Thucydides, did in fact write about the events of his lifetime (the Peloponnesian War of the second half of the fifth century);

however, his writing was slow, painstaking, deeply analytical. There is no evidence that it was circulated to or even intended for contemporaries. "I have written my work, not as an essay to win the applause of the moment," Thucydides explains, "but as a possession for all time."[19] News lives for the moment and its applause.

In Thucydides' writing we can glimpse what a mind invigorated by literacy can accomplish, but Thucydides was not writing, and probably could not have written, news. Aside from the difficulties the handwritten word had in capturing the news, the expectations Thucydides had for his words would have made it impossible even to attempt such a chase. When Thucydides died, probably shortly after Athens' final defeat in the Peloponnesian War (404 B.C.), he had yet to write about the last six and a half years of the war.

The difference between news and history, or other attempts at a deeper analysis, can be found in those six and a half years and in the attitude of a writer like Thucydides. History exists, in part, as a rebuke to the shortsightedness, the superficiality, the frenzy of news—as a critique of "the first story that comes to hand."

Writing was for tortoises such as Thucydides; news is spread by hares. News of the Peloponnesian War—undoubtedly lacking the certainty for which Thucydides strove, undoubtedly lacking his broad perspective, but six and a half years more current—circulated not in writings on stone or papyrus, but in speeches and conversations.

Socrates, a contemporary of Thucydides, was capable of playing the hare. According to Plato's *Charmides,* after Socrates returned from service as a foot soldier in the Athenian struggle to take Potidaea—one of the initial battles of the Peloponnesian War—he stopped by a gymnasium to talk and, inevitably, exchange news. Socrates wanted to be brought up to date on the current state of philosophy (a form of specialized news) and on young men of remarkable wisdom or beauty. His own contribution to this discussion was "news" from the army—Socrates' acquaintances at the gymnasium requested "a complete account."[20]

The minds of those who participated in such discussions in Greece in the fifth century B.C. undoubtedly were affected by the rapid growth of literacy. Certainly, there is large distance between the war report that must have been contributed by Socrates and that produced by an Abipon messenger with his "infinite exaggeration" of his comrades' conquests. Socrates spoke without the benefit of the time for research, reflection, and analysis possessed by Thucydides when he wrote; yet unlike the Abipon messenger he was predisposed toward detachment and truth. In a society literate enough to produce a Thucydides and a Socrates, spoken news must often have been exchanged less agonistically, with less of a weakness for the fabulous. Under the influence of literacy, news may have taken a hesitant first step on the long, perhaps endless, road toward objectivity.

Still, this indirect effect was virtually the only effect writing had on the exchange of news at this time, even in Athens. Writing would not be able to compete directly with word of mouth as a news medium until a new element was added to the competition: a pressing need to move news regularly over vast distances. And that would require societies spread over vast distances.

Questions

1. This chapter draws a distinction between the dispassionate, analytical, literate style of news (represented by a quote from a letter from Caelius in Rome to Cicero) and the preliterate style (represented by a quote from a Khasi crier). What, if any, advantages are there to the preliterate style?

2. Summarize the disadvantages writing—without the help of a printing press or a computer—has as a news medium.

3. As a rule, writing was good for recording history, bad for exchanging news. What forms of communication have been good for exchanging news but bad for recording history? Why?

News and Empire—The Thought Stream of the Group Mind

5

Alexander the Great died at the age of 32 in 323 B.C. Within 13 years of his death, Alexander's potential male heirs, two of his wives, and his mother had been murdered; his armies had gone to battle against each other; his officers—Ptolemy in Egypt, for instance—were establishing their own kingdoms; and Alexander's empire, which had stretched from Greece to India, was in pieces.

Governments obtain much of their authority by instilling fear or commanding deference.[2] In some Greek city-states, centuries before Alexander's death, an original method of achieving legitimacy and thereby commanding deference had been devised: anointing leaders with the expressed will of the citizenry. Alexander had employed more traditional techniques: relying on the strength of his army and on respect for his person—as king and son of a king; as an unflinching, effective, arguably just ruler; and even, toward the end of his short life, as a divinity. Word of Alexander's approach was enough to cause most of the cities of the known world to tremble and bow. None of his potential successors—an as-yet unborn son, a half-brother rumored to be half-witted, and various feuding officers—would be able to manage that trick.

Deference and fear help establish a government's authority, but subtler forces maintain it. The members of a large society—autocratic or democratic—cannot be expected to shake and swoon constantly. To prevent authority from lapsing between shows of force, coronations or elections, societies rely on an image impressed into the heads of their members, an image of unity and shared purpose. Authority also rests, in other words, on a feeling of allegiance.

If citizens can maintain a sense of participation in a society, they will, in most circumstances, be implicitly acknowledging the established authority as the embodiment of their unity and agent of their shared purpose. If those who survived Alexander had possessed a stronger image of themselves as participants in a single empire, might they have better preserved the coherence of that empire?

A White Ford Bronco Brought Them Together

The couple had been seated in the furthest corner of this restaurant because the man had neglected to wear a jacket. The other guests might be offended, the maitre d' had explained. The occupants of nearby tables were all fancily dressed; many seemed from out of town.

However, before the evening was finished all those in this section of the restaurant were chatting amiably. This was the evening when the former football star O. J. Simpson had been located driving in his white Ford Bronco, after apparently trying to escape arraignment in the murder of his wife and her friend.

News—"Hey, did you hear O. J. escaped?" "Do you think he really did it?"—had once again demonstrated its power to unify, to bring people together.

Societies depend for their unity and coherence on a sense of group identity. A group identity can be forged by geography, ethnicity or shared experiences. That identity is then preserved in history, art and religion, just as personal identities are preserved in memories, aspirations and values. But an individual's sense of self is sustained day to day, even minute to minute, by more mundane thoughts—the succession of perceptions and sentiments that incessantly crackle across a consciousness, continually reminding a mind of its own existence. And a society too depends on the flow of a stream of perceptions and sentiments from a shared perspective—in this case a societal perspective—to provide its members with day-to-day, minute-to-minute reminders of the existence and the significance of the group. To think a society's thoughts is to belong to that society. News provides the requisite set of shared thoughts.*

The more complex a society's structures, the more work history, art, religion *and* news will have in maintaining that society's self-identity. The intricate systems of authority in place atop Athens in the fifth century B.C. were supported not only by a rich culture but by a lively system of spoken news—centering on the daily hubbub in the agora.[3]

Athenians shared news of the *polis* and the theater. Zulus shared news of the king and the "Dance of the First Fruits." Americans today share news of presidential elections, the World Series, the Academy Awards. Which party, team or film we happen to support is unimportant. Citizens strengthen these processes, their participants and the society they represent simply by bestowing their attention upon them.[4]

Society, explains the sociologist Edward Sapir, is not "a static structure"; it is constantly being "reanimated or creatively reaffirmed" as its members communicate with

---

* The point here is not *for* whom those who spread news speak (authorities, dominant groups, themselves), but *to* whom the news they spread speaks (a close approximation of the group as a whole) and *about* what that news speaks (group values, group regulations, group structures, group leaders).

one another.[5] The exchange of news is responsible for much of that reanimation or creative affirmation.

Alexander appears to have depended primarily on written messages and a system of messengers to maintain contact with his various conquests; he had some success in staying in touch with the West while he was conquering the East.[6] However, inevitable limitations in the messages that could be exchanged on primitive roads and sea routes over the vast empire Alexander was establishing had definite consequences for the stability of that empire.

The historian Eugene N. Borza acknowledges that difficulties in communication over these unprecedented distances contributed "to the gradual increase of particularist sentiment in Greece and elsewhere" and "undoubtedly encouraged the activities of the more independent-minded of the king's staff who ruled in the West."[7] Borza's analysis is limited to the transmission of information of obvious pragmatic value: Was there a significant delay before Alexander learned of Sparta's rebellion? Could Alexander communicate administrative directives to the various corners of his empire? But the impediments that less immediately practical information must have faced in traversing this overgrown empire may also have been critical.

Alexander's accomplishments and personality made him the most newsworthy personage of his time. Yet, unless his satraps and subjects were able to receive regular reports on the progress of his army, regular gossip about their king and his entourage, a regular supply of anecdotes about the empire, the hold even Alexander maintained on that most valuable of territories—the attention of his subjects—could easily have begun to weaken, encouraging "particularist sentiment" and "independent-minded" activities.

No meeting place could attract all the officials Alexander had implanted around his empire, let alone all his subjects. After his victory over the Persians at the Granikos River in 334 B.C., Alexander allowed newly married Macedonian soldiers to return home for the winter, and he sent 300 captured Persian shields to the Athenians. Both gestures may have been intended in part to spread news of Alexander's great victory,[8] but how frequently can the newly betrothed be sent home? How much can be inferred from a shield? There is evidence that whatever contact Alexander was able to maintain with the West diminished during his later years in the East.[9]

Government is a performance, and news is the medium in which it is performed.* Without news systems capable of reaching the large majority of their subjects, leaders are in danger of losing their audiences.

Alexander's less-newsworthy heirs, hindered in any case by their tenuous claims on the throne, may have inherited an empire that was not only too big to police and administer successfully but too big to know itself—too big, given the slowness of communication and the lack of sophistication of the available news media, to cohere.

---

* It is tempting to view a concern with image in politics as a recent phenomenon for which we are indebted to television or perhaps press agentry. However, the attention that was paid thousands of years ago to the disposition of trophies (like those Persian shields), to the construction of monuments and to the commissioning of panegyrics demonstrates that leaders were minding their images long before they could polish them on television or even in the press.

The free flow of news obviously holds dangers for authorities. Had a more effective news system traversed his empire, Alexander might have become more vulnerable to interference in his affairs by newsmongers and their audiences. Yet the absence of a vigorous, societywide news system poses a more basic threat to a government: It deprives authorities of an important, if not crucial, means of sustaining the allegiance of the governed; it weakens their ability to create what Marshall McLuhan has called a "social consciousness" (something quite different from a social conscience).[10]

Of course, many other factors help determine the viability of governments, and many other factors contributed to the dissolution of Alexander's enormous empire. This is not an attempt to replace the standard list. Nor is it a proposal for a monovariable theory of political history—with the effectiveness of a system of news as the sole variable. Nevertheless, the role of this one generally overlooked factor ought to be considered

The sharing of news is no guarantor of political stability; it is a subtle, generally invisible political force. While not necessarily powerful enough on its own to encourage the members of a society to *march* in the same direction, a successful system of news can help keep a society *oriented* in the same direction—toward Rome, for example.

News of Rome

In the year 51 B.C. Cicero was sent to Cilicia as proconsul. Cilicia is in Asia Minor, located in what is now southern Turkey, and, like most of those who must spend time far from home, Cicero felt cut off. "I am here in a district where news penetrates very slowly," he complains in one of his letters.[11]

Spoken news could not have traveled from Rome to Cilicia without subjecting itself to the misunderstandings, partiality and forgetfulness of each person asked to transport it. The greater the distance, the greater the potential distortion. The content of a written message, however, will not vary, no matter how far it is carried. And the speed advantage the whisper and the shout normally have over the process of writing something out becomes negligible when information travels out of town. A traveler carrying a written message can move as quickly as a traveler who has committed that message to memory, especially if the message is written on a surface more portable than clay tablets. (Rome controlled Egypt—the source of the world's supply of papyrus.)

Writing became the medium of choice for relating news over distances. Rome's dominions stretched over great distances, and unlike Alexander's empire, Rome was able to develop a system of written news equal to the task of traversing them.

Despite Cicero's complaints, a remarkable variety of written news did make its way to Cilicia. In fact, at one point while he was out of Rome, Cicero protests to Caelius, a politician whom Cicero had asked to keep him informed, that he is being bothered by too much unimportant news from Rome:

> . . . reports of "the gladiatorial pairs," "the adjournment of trials," [a] "burglary [*compilationem*] by Chrestus," and such tittle-tattle as nobody would have the impertinence to repeat to me when I am at Rome?[12]

Cicero, the Roman statesman, philosopher and consumer of written news.

Cicero's correspondence during his stay in Cilicia—a period of little more than a year—is consumed by the exchange of news and by discussions of the exchange of news. It provides what is probably the most substantial evidence we have of the written news available to Romans 2,000 years ago.

The letters Cicero received from friends in Rome were themselves a significant news medium, as personal letters can still be today. "Indeed letter writing was invented," Cicero observed, "just in order that we might inform those at a distance if there were anything which it was important for them or for ourselves that they should know. . . ."[13] However, Caelius sent written news to Cilicia in forms other than personal letters:

> As you were leaving me, I promised to write you a very careful and full account of all that happened in the city; well, I have been at some pains to get hold of a man who would report every detail—so minutely, indeed, that I fear you will regard his efforts in that line as a mere excess of loquacity. . . . Decrees of the Senate, edicts, gossips, rumors—they are all there.[14]

Cicero and Tabloid TV

When Cicero complains, more than 2,000 years ago, that he is being sent too much "tittle-tattle," he sounds something like those who protest that there is too much "junk" on television.

Cicero's specific dislikes? "Reports of the 'gladiatorial pairs'"—or a type of sports news—"the adjournment of trials" and a "burglary"—the kinds of stories that tabloid TV programs might cover.

People have been following such stories, and high-minded people like Cicero have been complaining about them, for many millennia.

In his next letter Caelius calls the "packets" he is forwarding a "collection of notes on city affairs [*commentarium rerum urbanarum*]."[15] Almost a year later he refers to them again after a discussion of the struggle between the Senate and Caesar:

> How each has voted, you will find in my memoranda of affairs in the city [*commentario est rerum urbanarum*]; and you must pick out of them what is noteworthy. There is much which you must skip, especially the detailed accounts of the games and funerals, and all the rest of the tittle-tattle. But the great part is useful.[16]

Who produced the "collections of notes" or "memoranda of affairs" (depending on the translation) that Caelius sent to Cicero? Caelius implies that he was paying for the service; he jokes that these reports threaten to "exhaust" his "purse."[17] Apparently they were the work of one or more scribes, functioning, it would seem, as professional newswriters. (Indeed, if an alternative translation of the word *compilationem,* as "compilation," is accepted, then the Chrestus mentioned in the letter from Cicero cited above is no longer a burglar, but the first professional journalist whose name has survived.)[18]

For whom were these packets of news intended? Clearly, not solely for Cicero in Cilicia; if they had been written specifically for Cicero, Caelius could have asked the scribe to emphasize the political news his friend craved and forget the "impertinences." Copies probably were circulating to a wide-enough audience to make catering to Cicero's specific interests impractical. And this must have been an audience with an interest not only in votes of the Senate, but in games, gladiators, gossip and other "tittle-tattle," an audience with what would today be labeled "popular" tastes.

Where did the news in these collections originate? C. A. Giffard, who has studied Roman journalism, suggests that one source was gossip "picked up in the marketplace," but that much of the news in the packets sent to Cicero must have been copied from what were perhaps the most notable elements in the Roman news system—the *acta senatus* (the transactions of the Senate) and the *acta diurna populi Romani* (the daily transactions of the Roman people—also referred to by various other names, including the *acta urbana* or simply the *acta.*)[19]

The Senate in Rome may have kept a record of its activities—the *acta senatus*—as early as 449 B.C.[20] But according to the Roman historian Suetonius, these records were first made public—along with a more general account of political and social life in

Rome, the *acta diurna*—in 59 B.C., during the first consulship of that leader of the popular party, Julius Caesar:

> Caesar's very first enactment after becoming consul was, that the proceedings [*acta*] both of the Senate and of the people should day by day be compiled and published.[21]

These handwritten newssheets were published by displaying them daily in a public place. Scribes would then copy the *acta*—by hand, of course—and sell them to those who were disinclined or, like Cicero in Cilicia, unable to seek out the original.[22]

Based on Caelius' description, the news packets he secured for Cicero probably contained selections or complete copies of both the *acta senatus* and the *acta diurna.* There is no doubt that someone was sending Cicero copies while he was living in Cilicia. "I have the city gazette [*acta* is frequently translated as "gazette"] up to the seventh of March," Cicero wrote his friend Atticus in 51 B.C.[23]

The original copies of the *acta,* written on papyrus, were placed in archives in Rome and transformed by time into historical records. However, the diligent medieval monks to whom we owe the survival of copies of so many classical compositions—Cicero's letters among them—apparently did not devote their energies to these works of mere journalism.[24] No copies of the *acta* have survived; instead, we must reconstruct their content from allusions to them in more favored writings.[25]

In 44 B.C. Cicero's role was reversed. He was now home in Rome helping to keep his confederates in the provinces informed. This was the year Caesar was assassinated, and in a letter to Cornificius, an ally who was serving as a governor in Africa, Cicero makes clear that the dramatic political struggles that followed the assassination were being covered in the *acta:*

> I am well aware that the record of transactions in the City [*rerum urbanarum acta*] is being sent to you. Did I not think so, I should myself write you a full account of them, and especially of the attempt made by Caesar Octavian [to murder Antony].[26]

Eight months later Cicero is writing to the man who organized Caesar's assassination, Cassius, now with his army in the East:

> The scandalous conduct of your relative Lepidus [who had allied himself with their enemy Antony] and his amazing fickleness and inconstancy I imagine you have already learnt from the daily gazette [*ex actis*] which I am assured is being sent to you.[27]

There is evidence that the *acta* were subject to censorship and manipulation; they were, after all, government publications.[28] However, Rome's major political and military occurrences appear to have been well covered. These newssheets also focused, according to those who had a chance to read them, on less momentous news: government announcements, news of the law courts, births, deaths, marriages,[29] official ceremonies and building projects. "It suits the dignity of the Roman people to reserve history for great achievements, and to leave such details to the city's daily register [*diurnis urbis actis*]," scoffed Tacitus early in the second century A.D.[30]

Other writers, however, delighted in the details captured in these newssheets. The *acta* appear to have contained a rich supply of human interest stories. In his *Natural His-*

tory, written in the first century, Pliny the Elder attributes to the *acta diurna populi Romani* the story of the execution of a man whose dog simply would not leave his dead master's side, even going so far as to follow his master's corpse into the Tiber River in an effort to keep it afloat. With more skepticism, Pliny notes that the *acta* for the year A.D. 47 reported that a phoenix was displayed in Rome.[31]

Nor was sensationalism slighted. It was the "custom" of the Emperor Commodus (A.D. 180–192) "to order the insertion in the city gazette [*actis urbis*] of everything he did that was base or foul or cruel, or typical of a gladiator or procurer," the *Historia Augusta,* not the most reliable of sources, notes.[32]

How long did the Romans continue producing their newssheets? The *Historia Augusta* mentions an item that appeared in the *acta* as late as A.D. 222,[33] which would mean they were posted for at least 280 years—approximately as long as newspapers have been published regularly in America. Undoubtedly the content of these newssheets varied over that long span of time. We do not know what mix of news could be found in each copy of the *acta* or how that mix might have changed. However, we do know that a vigorous news organ was pumping a rich source of current information through Rome and the provinces during the last decades of the Roman Republic and for much of the history of the Roman Empire.

The evidence indicates that news from the *acta* circulated widely. Copies had to be made by hand, of course, but the rich or the enterprising could put slaves to the task. (Industrious teams of Roman copyists had shown themselves capable of producing, in short order, a thousand copies of a single document.)[34] And plebians in Rome could stand where the original was posted and read the news themselves, or listen as others read it. Furthermore, each copy that was made of the *acta* must have passed through numerous hands, with the information it contained then spread further by word of mouth.

News originating in the *acta* flowed out of Rome along sea routes and along the paved arteries constructed by Roman troops and captives throughout Europe and the Middle East. (The Roman Empire is estimated to have completed a network of 49,000 miles of roads.[35] For the sake of comparison, the United States interstate highway system covered less than 47,000 miles in 2006.) The Empire's swift imperial post seems not to have been employed in disseminating these newssheets—the government's responsibility ended when the *acta* were posted[36]—but patricians could hire horses and make use of traveling friends and servants to move copies of the *acta* and other correspondence. Caelius writes of handing one of his letters to Cicero's freedman for delivery.[37]

As a result, Roman politicians such as Cicero, Cornificius and Cassius were able to remain current on Roman politics while in Asia Minor, Africa or the Middle East. The statesman Pliny the Younger, more than 100 years after Cicero's death, sought respite from the pressures of Rome in Tuscany, but he asks a friend not to "drop your habit of sending me the city gazette [*urbana acta*] while I am rusticating in this way."[38] And soldiers too were able to keep up with the *acta.* "The daily records of the Roman people [*diurna populi Romani*] are read attentively in the provinces and the armies," Tacitus, discussing A.D. 66, writes in his *Annals.*[39]

The Roman Empire survived for half a millennium—from 27 B.C. to A.D. 476—at its peak stretching from southern Scotland to southern Egypt. And news flowed through this empire with remarkable efficiency. It would be 1,000 years before information would again spread so rapidly, with such integrity, in the West. Clearly, the unprecedented power and stability achieved by the Roman Empire helped facilitate the development of such a sophisticated news system. But the power and stability of the empire also owed something to its news system.

Rome's leaders struggled for control of the news. Various news items or even news media were employed as weapons in their political battles. Julius Caesar's decision to publish the *acta senatus* in 59 B.C. was probably intended to weaken the power of his opponents in the Senate. And Caesar seems to have made use of the *acta* to spread news of his dramatic, perhaps even staged, refusal of Antony's offer of a crown.[40] News, as Caesar well knew, can help or hurt political factions. Indeed, it is the performance of the news in this role that politicians have found most persuasive. The argument here, however, is that the circulation of news, regardless of whom it happens to embarrass or flatter at any given moment, in the long run strengthens a society and that it strengthened the Roman Empire.

Communication is generally credited with two state-building functions: coordination of society and socialization of its members.[41] Rome's system of written news certainly performed both these functions. Governors in the provinces, to cite the most obvious example, could use the news they received to bring their rule into conformity with the latest Senate decrees. And Roman officials and soldiers in the provinces swallowed regular doses of Roman values while enjoying news of politics, crime, ceremonies and faithful dogs. But an additional, equally powerful though generally overlooked, political force must also have been unleashed by these traveling newssheets, letters and news packets.

Whether the news was of Caesars or gladiators, the periodic perspectives on life in Rome that were transmitted on the empire's neural system of seaways and all-weather roads made it easier to continue to feel like a Roman while living outside of Rome. Although we do not know how much of this news the conquered peoples of the provinces were exposed to and whether it facilitated their assimilation into the Roman world, the supply of written news does appear to have helped ensure that *Romans* stationed in the provinces retained their identity as Romans.

Cicero was desperately homesick for Rome when he first arrived in Cilicia, but that homesickness might have begun to fade without the frequent reminders of home those letters and packets of Roman news provided. Had his eyes not been able to return so frequently to affairs in the Senate, would Cicero have grown more interested in affairs in Cilicia, where his power and prerogatives were so much greater? Would he have terminated his stay there so quickly? Had Cornificius not been in such close touch with disputes in Rome would he have become more interested in protecting his position in Africa than in lining up behind Cicero and the Republicans on the issues that were dividing Rome? Would Cassius, rather than cross the Hellespont and begin marching west toward confrontation with Antony and Octavius, have contented himself with carving out a barony in Asia Minor?

The Roman Empire had a strength, a tradition and an economic base that Alexander's short-lived empire a few hundred years earlier had not been able to achieve. But Rome also had a precocious system of written news that kept the image of Roman society in front of its officials and soldiers wherever they were stationed, making it much more difficult for Rome's satraps to turn away and contemplate life as a Ptolemy in the provinces.

It took Cleopatra to divert Mark Antony's attention from Rome. More frequently the leaders of Rome's armies, unlike Alexander's officers after his death, passed up whatever opportunities they might have had to establish their own fiefdoms; instead, their legions eventually began marching back to—or on—Rome.

News Through China

In size, power and longevity the Roman Empire had one rival: the Chinese Empire formed during the Han dynasty, from 202 B.C. to A.D. 221, and then reconstituted beginning with the T'ang dynasty in 618. Not surprisingly, the Chinese, like the Romans, employed an advanced system of written news.[42]

Government officials stationed in the provinces throughout the mammoth Han empire, which included at its height Manchuria, Mongolia and Korea, faced a constant struggle to keep abreast of events at court. They began setting up residences in the capital staffed by their agents, who functioned as correspondents. The practice became institutionalized under the name *ti*—defined in the statutes of the early Han dynasty as "the residence of provincial prefects for the purpose of communicating official reports."[43]

The distances were too great for these agents to rely on word of mouth to communicate with their employers. At some point they began collecting the information into handwritten newsletters—*tipao* (*pao* is "report")—which were then forwarded to the officials in the provinces. These newsletters were filled with official edicts, news of promotions and dismissals, memoranda by ministers or other authorities, and reports on the activities of the court.[44] Lin Yutang, who has written one of the few books in English discussing early journalism in China, refers to the *tipao* as "Metropolitan Gazettes."

A superior writing surface had arrived toward the end of the Han dynasty. Paper was invented in China by, according to legend, a eunuch named Ts'ai Lun in A.D. 105. (It would take more than 1,000 years for paper to reach Europe.) The system of roads and relays necessary to move written news with dispatch was also in place during the centuries of the Han dynasty, centuries shared in large part by that equally well-paved empire to the west.[45] Indeed, the Chinese journalism historian Ko Kung-chên suggests that the *tipao* were quite similar to Rome's *acta*.[46]

From the third through the sixth centuries the Chinese were divided and subject to invasion by non-Chinese peoples to the north and west. The empire was rebuilt under the T'ang dynasty (618–906), during which references to the *tipao* as important sources of news began to appear. In the eighth century, for example, a friend reported to a surprised official that he had read "in the *tipao* that the post of Secretary of Edicts was vacant, and the Grand Secretariat twice recommended your name. . . ." At some point the central government created a "Bureau of Official Reports," a sort of official news agency, to handle the flow of information into and out of the capital, and under its control the various *tipao* appear to have been combined into a single newsletter sent to all the provinces.[47]

Ko notes that information circulating in the *tipao* helped make management of such a large empire feasible. But if a community was being united here, it was a community of government officials—the *tipao* were not intended for the masses.[48] These newslet-

News from Home Today

Rome and China were unmatched in their time for their ability to keep their citizens—at least their well-connected citizens—informed of news back in the capital while they were away. But the flow of information from afar was, of course, nothing like it is today.

It is now possible for an American to live, say, in southern Russia and not only watch movies and listen to music from back home but to watch ABC's *World News Tonight* every morning. Then there's CNN, which can be seen in a large percentage of the countries in the world and, of course, the endless Internet.

Information flows in the other direction also: Programs in Spanish, French, Korean and Hebrew for example, are now available on American cable systems. And relatives can be reached by telephone or e-mail.

The result is that modern travelers and immigrants can stay more connected to their homes than ever before. Might this slow the assimilation of immigrants into their new cultures?

---

ters circulated widely enough among officials that the newly developed Chinese technique of block printing was used to reproduce copies of some issues during the T'ang dynasty.[49] And news from the capital undoubtedly seeped out into the populace by word of mouth from the officials who saw copies of the *tipao*. But, in general, it appears that those who ruled China in these years were content to follow one of Confucius's less demanding suggestions: that they keep their subjects uninformed.[50] Literacy was confined to an elite group, and there is no evidence that copies of the *tipao*—unlike copies of the *acta*—were ever posted in a public place.

When, after another period of internal warfare, China was reunited in a somewhat smaller incarnation under the Sung dynasty (960–1279), news organs began to flourish and their audiences to expand somewhat. The *tipao* were now being read by the literati as well as by officials, and additional government-sponsored and even private newsletters began appearing. This outburst of journalistic activity so enraged one 12th-century official, Chou Linchih, that he petitioned the emperor to control such "sensational news," circulated by "agents of the residences," which he said was "misleading the public":

> In recent years, whenever there is news in the air and the public is held in suspense, these agents would snatch the chance and write the news down on little scripts and circulate them abroad. This is the so-called *hsiaopao* [a term that now means "small newspapers"]. For instance, they often say "So-and-so was summoned to an imperial audience today" or "So-and-so was dismissed," or "So-and-so got an appointment."

If news that "So-and-so was summoned to an imperial audience today," "So-and-so was dismissed" or "So-and-so got an appointment" strengthened belief in the importance of such audiences, dismissals and appointments, as well as in the system of authority behind them, then Chou Linchih, like most officials, was too annoyed to sense it.

He saw instead the threat to the confidentiality and, potentially, the exclusivity of decision making posed by the spread of unauthorized information about a government:

> I rather think that trivial as the subject seems to be, the spreading of news through such channels is injurious to the administration and demands our attention. I humbly petition that Your Majesty should issue an edict prohibiting their circulation with definite forms of punishment attached to it.[51]

The Sung emperors were persuaded; they began to censor and suppress these non-governmental newssheets. China's news organs would remain under government control and, to a large extent, under government management until the European encroachments of the 19th century.

Authorities make poor journalists. Their sensitivity to the injuries news items might cause their administrations leaves them insufficiently sensitive to public interest in their audiences, dismissals and appointments, as well as in their edicts and scandals. Consequently, the populace has no choice but to rely for much of its news on seepage, on rumor, on unreliable word of mouth.

China entered the history of journalism early. The paper and presses on which the world's newsbooks and newspapers would be printed owed their origins in part to developments in China. An argument can be made that the first printed newspapers appeared in China—if not the *tipao* (which remained in existence for hundreds of years) or the *hsiaopao* then possibly one of the other government-sponsored periodicals that circulated with some regularity over the centuries.[52] Yet the lead in the exploitation of written and especially printed news would be taken by the journalists of more liberal states.

News Across Europe

After the dissolution of the Roman Empire in the fourth and fifth centuries, literacy in Europe declined. Books were reproduced in ornate, difficult to decipher handwritings and in a language—Latin—that the majority of the population did not speak. Transportation and trade also declined during these centuries. Written news was among the many casualties.

Handwritten manuscripts did occasionally play some role in disseminating information on contemporary events in medieval Europe. The manuscript produced by the 12th-century traveler Benjamin of Tudela certainly contained news, as did the account dictated a century later by that most famous of all travelers, Marco Polo. Some news undoubtedly spread, too, in the accounts of celebrations and wars produced by medieval heralds. "It was their duty to attend their masters in battle," one historian reports. "They were enabled to record the most important transactions of the field with fidelity." And there must have been news in some of the verses produced by such court poets as Laurence Minot in the 14th century and John Lydgate in the first half of the 15th century.[53] Nevertheless, there is no indication that written news in medieval Europe moved with a volume or efficiency anywhere near that achieved in Rome and China.

Europe would not again develop an advanced system of written news until the alphabet, in Eric Havelock's words, "was returned to the service of the vernaculars"—

languages that people actually spoke;[54] until a standardized, efficient script was developed; until the monasteries lost their monopoly on writing; until trade revived; and until ideas began to circulate with more vigor. These advances did not all wait for the Renaissance,[55] but they coalesced in the Renaissance. And the climate for the development of written news was further improved in Renaissance Europe by the commitment of some of its rulers—including Frederick III of the Holy Roman Empire, Louis XI in France and Edward IV in England—to more efficient postal services.[56]

In the 15th century, handwritten "newsletters" began trickling across some of the same paths copies of the *acta* had followed more than a dozen centuries earlier. News of the death of the Sultan Mohammed II in 1481, for instance, was reported in a newsletter sent by an Italian in Constantinople to his brother in Western Europe. The French chronicler Philippe de Commynes appears to have seen a copy of this newsletter while in Venice; the newsletter was translated into French, and a copy, which still survives, was made in Flanders no later than 1483 for Edward, the prince of Wales.[57]

For news from afar, writing's strength as a news medium remained its advantage over word of mouth. The chances of the English obtaining reliable news by word of mouth from Constantinople were slim indeed; these were years in which the English had difficulty learning whether their own kings or former kings were still alive. In the 15th century, there were, for example, false reports that Richard II still lived, that Edward IV was dead and that Henry VII had been defeated. In an age when facts often seemed vaporous, the written word was prized for its relative weight. The distinction between an oral and a written report was sometimes expressed in 15th-century England as a distinction between "flying rumours" and "certain knowledge."[58]

In the 15th century, Europe's leaders were beginning to use written news to spread "certain knowledge" of their triumphs. A newsletter describing Edward IV's successful efforts to reclaim his crown in 1471 was issued in both English and French.[59] The newsletter says it was "compiled and put in this forme . . . by a servaunt of the Kyngs, that presently saw in effect a great parte of his exploytes, and the resydewe knewe by true relation of them that were present at every time." This admittedly partial but undeniably industrious writer includes impressive details on battles, including Edward's success in routing his enemies at Tewkesbury:

> The Kynge, full manly, set forthe even upon them, enteryd and wann the dyke, and hedge, upon them, into the cloose, and with great vyolence, put them upe towards the hyll . . . many of them were slayne, and . . . many drownyd; many rann towards the towne; many to the churche; to the abbey; and els where; as they best myght.[60]

The rulers of Europe used writing not only to publicize themselves but to keep themselves informed, to gather intelligence. By 1497 an observer in London would comment on how "thoroughly acquainted with the affairs of Italy" King Henry VII was.[61] Like most European rulers at the time, Henry relied on a network of diplomats and agents who reported back to London in handwritten letters. (Sending back information has always been among the diplomat's primary responsibilities.) City officials too gathered written reports on the events that were swirling around them, often arranging reciprocal exchanges of information with other cities. In the municipal archives of

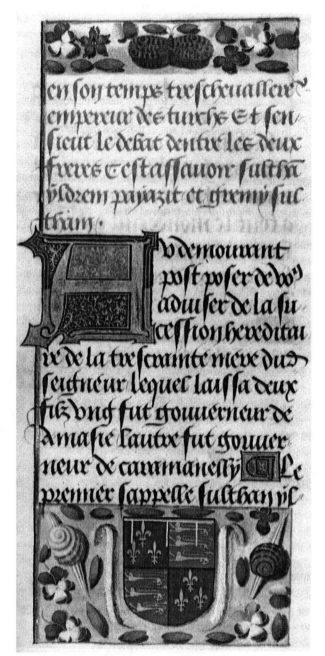

When Sultan Mohammed II died in 1481, an Italian in Constantinople passed on the news in a handwritten letter sent to his brother. Copies of this letter traveled across Europe. This is an illuminated page from a copy in French made in Flanders for the British royal family, under the title "Testament de Amyra Sultan Nichemedy. . . ."

Frankfurt-on-Main are three different accounts, supplied by officials in three different cities, of one battle in the 1540s.[62]

Handwritten letters also served certain private individuals in their struggle to keep informed. In England in the 1450s, John Fastolf concluded a letter to John Paston, a landholder, with this plea: "This is the tydinges that I have. I pray you send me some of yours."[63] There was a certain desperation to this struggle in 15th-century Europe. The "tydinges" available to the writer rarely seem as abundant as the curiosity of the reader. "As for ony othir tydyngges, I can noone," an apologetic correspondent is forced to admit to John Paston in 1462.[64]

Sketchy though it often was, news of the emerging nations of Europe was, nevertheless, being spread through these letters to an influential group of their citizens. A letter from an acquaintance in London in 1485 informed Sir Robert Plumpton "that the Kings [Henry VII's] gud grace shall weede my lady Elizabeth (and so she is taken as quene). . . ."[65] Elizabeth was the daughter of the former king, Edward IV; this was news that Henry Tudor, straining to establish his legitimacy after the bloody dynastic struggles of the War of the Roses, very much wanted circulated. And although only a small, privileged group had access to such letters, the news they contained presumably trickled down to those without correspondents in London, even to some of the illiterate, by word of mouth.

Centralized nation-states—like that the Tudors would develop in England—require a news medium capable of focusing the attention of citizens around the nation on the government. Written news—in the form of newsletters and private correspondence—was beginning to demonstrate in Renaissance Europe, as it had demonstrated in Rome and China, that it could orient a limited but important audience toward the monarch.

By 1508 the attention of the English people would be directed to the proxy wedding of Henry VII's and Elizabeth's daughter by a news medium capable of reaching a larger audience—the printed pamphlet. Even with the help of word of mouth, letters from acquaintances in London could not command such crowds.

Nevertheless, as the 16th century progressed, handwritten letters and newsletters continued to supply news to a uniquely influential audience—composed not only of princes, statesman, and nobles, but of Europe's growing contingent of news-hungry traders and financiers.

"Cosmopolitan Commerce"

In 1815 the banker Nathan Rothschild received advance word on the outcome of the Battle of Waterloo from one of his agents, who had rushed the news across the Channel. Rothschild is said to have then used the information to his advantage on the London Stock Exchange.[66] Such an alertness to current events has proved itself of value in many different eras in all such speculative forms of business.

Grain traders, for example, must learn of any drop in supplies of wheat that could lead to an increase in its price. They must learn of any interference with harvests or trade routes that might lead to a drop in supplies. They must know when armies, with the potential to ravage fields and interrupt trade, go on the march. News accounts prepare

Business and Journalism

From marketplaces to the "Fugger News-Letters" to the first daily newspapers (see Chapter 10) to the online, subscription edition of the *Wall Street Journal,* the particular need business people have to keep up-to-date on developments around the world has always spurred the exchange of news.

News—early news—can mean money in business, so supplying business people with news has been a lucrative strategy for journalists. In the 1980s and 1990s, to choose a recent example, Michael Bloomberg, who would go on to become mayor of New York City, constructed a new and successful enterprise by providing computer terminals with which businesses could access the latest financial news. Bloomberg's business-news-driven empire has now expanded to include radio and television services.

---

traders to anticipate events, and the better prepared they are, the more money they can make.

Venetian merchants early in the 16th century craved information on the ships that carried spice from India to Portugal. Reports that some ships had been lost or captured might send prices soaring in Venice; reports of a safe arrival in Lisbon could cause them to plummet. And Venetian merchants also were attuned to military news. In 1532 Venice received word that the Turkish fleet—always a threat to the city and its trading partners—had returned to port, and the promise of an uninterrupted supply dropped the price of wheat at Venetian markets. But then reports arrived that the Holy Roman Emperor Charles V had passed Venetian territory on his way to Spain, and the resulting anxiety caused the price of wheat to rise.[67] In later decades, traders at the money market in Antwerp would strain for information on Spain's fortunes in the Americas—a source of much of Europe's silver—while financiers in Antwerp would search out news on the prospects of the various governments who were floating loans there.[68]

As news of the forces that shape events allows more and more traders to begin anticipating events, prices in a market will begin to respond to those anticipations as much as to the events themselves. In 1506, for example, the pope and the Holy Roman Emperor formed an alliance that seemed to threaten Venice. No armies were on the march, no trade routes had been threatened but according to a diarist in Venice at the time, the flour market responded "as if enemies were already at the gates of Venice."[69] So traders must even be prepared to anticipate the anticipations. The secret of success at this game of "as if" is obtaining still more news—news that allows traders to see even further into the future.

No other enterprise, save diplomacy, is as dependent on news from afar as is commerce, and in 16th-century Europe—where print was still too crude and too scattershot, and spoken news too unreliable—that meant a dependence primarily on written news.[70] Some members of the mercantile community invested in their own couriers or postal systems, asking their agents around the world to double as correspondents. They created, in essence, their own systems of written news. No one appears to have been more successful at this than the 16th-century German financier Count Philip Eduard Fugger, who gathered what may be the most extensive surviving collection of written news.

The House of Fugger—which had lent money to most of Europe's Catholic royal families—was already in decline when the news accounts in this collection were received, from 1568 to 1605. (Most of those royal families had declared bankruptcy between 1557 and 1559.) Nevertheless, the house still had contacts and agents stationed around the world. Philip Eduard Fugger—a few generations removed from the man who had established the preeminence of the house, Jakob Fugger II—saved the letters, full of news, those contacts and agents sent, added some news from other sources and at some point had his collection copied. The copies are now in the Vienna National Library.[71]

Included among the 36,000 manuscript pages in Fugger's collection are only three listings of exchange rates,[72] and financial news—insolvencies at the exchange at Antwerp, the arrival of gold from "New Spain"—is scarce. Instead, in his effort to remain aware, the count collected a rather representative sample of general interest news, distinguished only by a broad, international perspective.

Fugger apparently was not immune to the appeal of sensationalism, as these details from a report on some executions in 1592 in Saragossa, Spain, indicate:

> Don Juan de Luna had his head cut off from the front and Don Diego from the back, Ayerbe and Dionysio Perez merely had their throats cut, then they were laid down and left to die by inches. Pedro de Fuerdes they strangled with a rope. When he was dead he was quartered and the four quarters hung out in the streets of Saragossa. . . .[73]

Nor were the metaphysical and the bizzare neglected in the news Fugger collected. This is from an account in 1601 of "a weird happening" involving an Italian soldier:

> . . . one night he complained to his wife, to whom he had been married by the Church seven years ago, that he had great pains in his belly and felt something stirring therein. An hour thereafter he gave birth to a child, a girl. . . .

(The soldier, according to this letter, later told authorities that he was half man, half woman.)[74]

The majority of the reports in what have come to be called *The Fugger News-Letters,* however, concern the procession of battles, disasters, plots, miracles, royal births, deaths and marriages that people normally have seen as marking their eras. These are also, by and large, the events about which international traders and financiers would want to have remained current.

The industriousness of the best news system money could buy in the 16th-century can be seen in the number of reports Fugger collected on the Spanish armada and its confrontation with the English navy. At least 30 reports on the subject, sent between January and November 1588, can be found in this collection.[75] Money could not necessarily ensure accuracy, however; many of Fugger's correspondents passed on rumors about the armada that proved false (see Chapter 13).

The news Fugger secured appears to have been intended for him, his family and his business associates. There is no evidence that the count pursued a sideline in the news business and arranged to have this news sold.[76] We are dealing here with a form of *private news* and, given the definition of news proposed in the Introduction, that is something of an oxymoron.

However, written news of a similar sort was being retailed in parts of Europe, including Germany, by the middle of the 16th century. Consider, for example, the career of Christoph Scheurl, a widely traveled, well-connected German lawyer. Scheurl routinely divided his letters into two parts: one for personal comments, the other for the news he had collected. Martin Luther called Scheurl "the eye and the ear of Germany."[77] He appears to have lost his amateur status in about 1536, when he began forwarding newsletters to the court of Mainz in return for game and wine. Scheurl had other clients—though it is not clear what they paid or even if they paid.[78] He also had competition.

The flow of news in Renaissance Europe was intimately connected to the postal service. In fact, a distinction was commonly made between "ordinary" newsletters—which had been sent by the regular, usually weekly, post—and "extraordinary" newsletters—something akin to newspaper extras, sent by special messenger. There is reason to believe that postmasters themselves dabbled in the news business and produced their own newsletters for special clients, based on the news that passed through their offices.[79]

Perhaps the most professional written-news service in Germany in Fugger's day was that of an Augsburg copyist, Jeremias Crasser, and his successor, Jeremias Schiffle.* Crasser and Schiffle called themselves *nouvellanten*. They appear, however, to have devoted themselves more to copying and circulating news than to compiling it. We know that their list of clients included two Nuremberg merchants and, not surprisingly, Count Philip Eduard Fugger. Indeed, a significant proportion of the news in Fugger's collection may have been forwarded to him by Crasser and then Schiffle.[80]

In the 16th century, men like Philip Eduard Fugger and the other customers of Crasser and Schiffle were functioning in a society whose breadth exceeded that of the Roman Empire. They were engaged, as one historian has put it, in "cosmopolitan commerce."[81] Capital, having traversed city walls and the borders between nations, now regularly crisscrossed the Continent. Commodities were regularly shipped across the oceans. To encompass these transactions, an international community was being created.[82] And like any community, it was sustained in part by its news. Indeed, this community, lacking a shared land, was probably even more dependent on its news to unite it.

The written news—resolutely cosmopolitan in perspective—that flowed into and out of Europe's trading centers enabled businesspeople such as Fugger to share a perspective, to share a view of a large and coherent, if not predictable, world—a world in which it was possible to imagine cargoes arriving, interest being paid, profits being made. The 16th century, historian Pierre Sardella reports, saw the arrival of an international, global "sensibility."[83] Through the news they shared, the wheat traders of Venice, the silver traders of Antwerp, the merchants of Nuremberg, the financiers of Augsburg and their trading partners around the world were being drawn together into a society based on this new sensibility: on common interests—the fate of some ships sailing from India to Lisbon—and on common values—a belief in the rights of capital.

The work of the letter writers, agents, and *nouvellanten* of 16th-century Europe helped sustain an image of an international society that transcended national boundaries. It gave legitimacy to the great empire without an emperor in which international trade and finance functioned.

---

* The most significant advances in handwritten journalism in the second half of the 16th century arrived in Venice, but these belong to the history of periodicity and the newspaper.

Systems of news can help support many different kinds of societies—centralized political groupings such as England under the Tudors, subsocieties of interest groups or even dissidents, or supersocieties like those the Romans and Chinese imposed upon their provinces. The international community of trade and finance in the 16th century was in effect another supersociety—an imperial order in which only a small percentage of the inhabitants of any local area had citizenship.

The bulk of the population not only lacked the capital to participate in this community, it could not afford news of this community. For written news is among the most expensive of news forms: Agents or correspondents abroad are required to gather the information, and couriers are often required to transport it. Each copy is handmade. Sardella makes clear that these news systems were beyond the means of most Venetians in the early 16th century.[84]

Of course, another news medium had arrived in Europe by the 16th century. Early forms of printed news tended, if anything, to be less thoughtful, less comprehensive, more "popular" in their choice of subject matter than written news. But each copy could be produced much more cheaply; more segments of society could be reached. (Fugger was not oblivious of printed reports; some were copied—by hand—and included in his collection.)[85] As printed news developed, additional international communities would also be created—the "Republic of Letters," sustained by late 17th- and early 18th-century *journals,* prominent among them. And in subsequent centuries new varieties of printed news—The *Times* of London in the 19th century, for example, or, some would argue, the West's powerful wire services today—would help support the imposition of new empires upon the globe.

Questions

1. Most government leaders today tend to be suspicious of, if not antagonistic toward, journalists and the reports they produce. According to this chapter, what basic point about the political effect of news are these leaders missing?

2. What disadvantages did the Roman news system have compared to our own? What, if any, advantages?

3. What qualities made written news successful in Rome and China, and yet so unsuccessful in most of the rest of the world?

4. Why were written accounts more likely to dispel false reports in Renaissance Europe than spoken accounts?

5. What evidence exists that those who are engaged in commerce continue to have a special need for news today? Do any have private news systems like that used by the Fuggers?

PART THREE

PRINTED NEWS

6 Controlling the News—
The Undeceiving of the People

In school most of us are introduced to two events from the fifteenth century: The first is Columbus's discovery, or rediscovery, of America in 1492; the second is Johann Gutenberg's invention, or reinvention (the Chinese and Koreans deserve some credit), of the letter press, employing movable type. The impact of Columbus' voyage is obvious. Perhaps the impact of Gutenberg's machine becomes clearer when we consider what the printing press, fewer than 40 years after it cut its teeth on the Bible, was able to do for news of Columbus' voyage.

When Vikings sailing from Greenland 500 years earlier had discovered and temporarily settled an attractive land still farther west, the news had to rely on word of mouth and the written word for its passage back across the North Atlantic. This new land had probably been first sighted (by Europeans) in 986; Vikings, under the command of Leif Eriksson, first landed in "Vinland" 15 years later. In about 1070 the German cleric Adam of Bremen interviewed the King of Denmark and was told "of yet another island. . . . It is called Wineland."[2] So the news had reached Denmark, and those few in Germany who saw Adam's handwritten history also learned of the discovery, though by then the story was about 70 years old. In the end, however, conversation and writing proved unable to propel news of the Viking discovery deeply enough into European consciousness for Vinland to secure a place in the worldview Columbus would encounter.

When Columbus returned to Europe with his two remaining ships in March 1493, news of his remarkable accomplishment also began to spread by word of mouth. The explorer apparently handled much of the early public relations himself, disseminating the news as he made the rounds of banquets and celebrations, as he was received by various notables, and as he talked with the people who hailed him on the street and along the road to Barcelona and the Spanish court. To reinforce his own account of his new route to "the Indies," Columbus had brought back with him parrots, gold and even "Indians."[3]

. . . if any read now-a-days, it is a play-book, or a pamphlet of news.

—Robert Burton, 1621[1]

71

A letter from Columbus describing his discoveries in "the Indies" was first printed, in Spanish, in Barcelona in 1493, probably before Columbus arrived in that city to be received by the Spanish court. This is the first page of that early newsbook.

The news also began to travel in a few handwritten letters. There is evidence that a letter arrived in Florence by the end of March with information on the discovery of an island inhabited by people "wearing certain leaves about their genitals but nothing more."[4] And Columbus himself produced the most thorough written account of his adventure, forwarding to the court one or perhaps two letters completed on board the *Nina* by March 14.

Medieval Europe had methods for circulating news of this weight. Even without seeing the parrots or reading Columbus' own letters, conversations with travelers, formal proclamations or letters from acquaintances would eventually have informed many Spaniards that ships had sailed west and reached land. In time, travelers and correspondence would also have acquainted some of the more cosmopolitan inhabitants of cities such as Florence or Augsburg with Columbus' accomplishment. However, those oral reports would inevitably have been delayed and distorted as they spread and those hand-

News of the Real Discoverers of America

The first humans to set foot in America came from Asia, not Europe; probably by foot, not by ship; perhaps 40,000 years before Columbus or the Vikings. The "ice-bridge peoples," they are sometimes called, because they may have walked across an ice bridge between Siberia and Alaska. Their descendants, who populated two continents, are the Native Americans or the people Columbus mistakenly stuck with the label "Indians."

These original discoverers of America had no writing, let alone a printing press, to spread word of what they found. Instead they must have relied upon spoken news, with its inability to remain accurate over distance. It is doubtful that much reliable news of America spread back to Asia. No record of these discoveries survives in any culture.

written letters would have been available only to a limited audience and would have been vulnerable to the errors or the editing of each hand that recopied them. One letter written in Italy about Columbus' voyage, for example, reported that it took 16 days to reach land (it took 33); a letter from a Barcelona merchant stated that Columbus was "in a province where men are born with a tail" (Columbus had reported that some natives told him such men existed in another province).[5]

Leif Eriksson had returned from his voyage to an isolated outpost on Greenland; Columbus returned to one of the more sophisticated corners of Europe. Even if there had been no printing press, news of Columbus' voyage would have penetrated farther. Yet it still would have suffered from lapses in speed, reach, accuracy and credibility similar to those that must have obscured the Vikings' accomplishment.

However, the printing press had arrived in Spain 23 years before Columbus returned,[6] and it was put to work spreading news of his voyage. The letter Columbus wrote to the Spanish court was set in type, printed and distributed in Barcelona probably as early as April 1. So by the time Columbus himself made his entrance into Barcelona in the middle of April, *hundreds* of copies of a pamphlet describing his discoveries *in his own words* must have already been circulating. One copy has survived:

> I found a great many islands peopled with inhabitants beyond number. . . . The people . . . all go naked, men and women, just as their mothers bring them forth; although some women cover a single place with the leaf of a plant, or a cotton something which they make for that purpose. They have no iron or steel, nor any weapons; nor are they fit thereunto; not because they be not a well-formed people and of fair stature, but that they are most wondrously timorous. . . .[7]

This or a second, similar letter Columbus forwarded to the Spanish court was translated into Latin on April 29, 1493, and printed in Rome early in May, where it became, according to one Columbus biographer, Samuel Eliot Morison, a "bestseller."[8] Three separate Latin editions of Columbus' letter were printed in Rome that year. The letter was reprinted in Paris, probably shortly thereafter, where, as in Rome, it reappeared in two additional editions during the year. And before the year was out, editions of Columbus' letter would also be printed in Antwerp, Basel and Florence.[9]

Thus the letter press Gutenberg had developed—the invention of the century—was able to circulate a firsthand account of Columbus' voyage—the story of the century—to a significant portion of literate Europe within months of his return. Columbus' voyage helped demonstrate the power of Gutenberg's press as a method for moving news. And the letter press arrived in a Europe whose geographical, philosophical and economic frontiers were about to race outward, a Europe ready for a news medium equipped to give chase.

News was published before it was printed, but print would transport news to a larger public, at faster speeds than it had ever before known. (Printing is so effective a means of publication that the words would become synonymous.) As writing had, the printing press would go on to rearrange human thinking—changing, wrote Francis Bacon, "the appearance and state of the whole world."[10] Like writing, it would lead to a procession of scientific discoveries and a reordering of the arts. But, unlike writing, the printing press would also lead to a procession of journalistic advances, advances that would be accelerated by the newspaper but would not wait for the newspaper.

A more primitive form of printing had been available in Europe perhaps half a century before Gutenberg developed his letter press. A page could be printed by rubbing a sheet of paper against an inked block of wood carved to produce an impression of pictures or words. Both the paper and the technique were Chinese inventions that had apparently completed the long journey to Europe.[11] There is some evidence that block printing was used to publish newssheets in the 15th century, particularly in Germany.[12] (In Japan as early as 1615, newssheets—called *kawaraban*—were printed from engraved clay or wood plates.)[13] However, Gutenberg's letter press, in which each letter could be removed and reused after a page was printed, offered huge advantages of speed, convenience and quality of impression. (The Chinese—and later the Koreans—had been experimenting with moveable type in earlier centuries, though not on a press. Their ability to exploit this technique was also limited by the multiplicity of written characters with which they had to work.)[14]

News followed Bibles, Latin grammars, and almanacs in the rush to make use of the early letter presses. One of the first printed works that might qualify as news was an Italian report on a tournament printed in about 1470 (the press had arrived in Italy in 1464). From these first decades of the letter press, some scattered pamphlets also survive on the wars with the Ottoman Empire: A report on the Turkish wars was printed in Augsburg in 1474; a letter reporting on the Turk's success in taking the Genoan colony of Caffa was printed shortly thereafter (most likely in Italy in 1475); and additional German publications on the Turks appeared in 1480 and 1482.[15]

Print presented the nascent journalist with a gift well beyond the means of mere handwriting: a large audience. The letter press, it has been argued, introduced the world to mass production.[16] The world would soon be using it to produce masses of news and news for the masses. In 1483 the owner of one press charged three florins for each 20 pages to print a book that a scribe might have copied for one florin for 20 pages. But that press could produce 1,025 copies for the money, the scribe one copy[17]—three times the

A reproduction of Johann Gutenberg's printing press.

expense, a thousand times the audience. An item of new information of public interest, once set in the movable type Gutenberg had devised, was able to reach a much larger public. And each printed copy that marched off a press had a crucial advantage: It was an exact replica. Those thousands of readers would each receive the same story, with no *added* errors, distortions or embellishments.

In a society that depends on word of mouth or handwritten letters for its news, reliability is always at issue. "No one ever hears twice alike about English affairs," a Milanese diplomat stationed in London complained to his government in 1471. The diplomat's problem was well illustrated on April 6, 1483, when the mayor of York learned "on what appeared to be excellent authority" that Edward IV had died. A requiem mass was sung in York on April 7. Edward IV, however, though fatally ill, was still alive. Information twisted and turned like this all across Europe. In October 1525 criers in Paris announced that King Francis I of France had died in captivity, though he too was alive and would live for another 21 years. Deaths were so difficult to confirm that, according to the historian C. A. J. Armstrong, "the end of the Middle Ages teemed with imposters who impersonated the dead." There was a false Richard II, a false Joan of Arc, a false Charles the Bold.[18]

The printing press did not protect the news from the falsehoods of either deceptive or deceived printers—some of their products were wildly incredible. But with the ability to produce a thousand exact copies of documents, statements or news reports, the

The Beginnings of the Information Age?

Those of us today who are well off enough to lead well-equipped lives are constantly bombarded with information: on politics, on business, on science, on entertainment, on sports, on weather, on crime. The "information age," our era has been labeled.

This book presents a few possible candidates for the technology that might be credited with giving birth to this information age, the tele-graph, with its ability to move information almost instantly across great distances, is one (see Chapter 15). Radio, specifically the first all-news radio station, is another (see Chapter 16).

But no invention changed the amount of information available to humankind as radically as that nonelectric, hand-operated machine that arrived in Europe in the 15th century: the printing press.

printing press did at least guarantee that the original news item had not been distorted between the press and the reader. Readers could accept or dismiss the work of the printer without fear that additional falsehoods had been added in transmission or transcription. The vulnerability of a message along the road from the battlefields where the fate of kings was being determined to the towns where news of their fate was so eagerly awaited was considerably reduced. And that was a crucial step toward a world where the dead assuredly were and would stay dead.

It would take some time before the full power of the printing press was felt throughout European society. Lack of literacy would limit readership of printed news. As late as the Reformation, the bulk of the population of Europe "remained relatively indifferent to writing"; by 1688 according to one estimate, only 40 percent of all adult males in England could read.[19] Transportation difficulties would limit the spread of printed news. The *Nuremberg Chronicle* was printed on July 12, 1493, without any mention of Columbus' journey, and the first hard evidence that news of his voyage had crossed the English Channel is a letter written in 1496![20] And finally, authorities, fearful of the geysers of information beginning to erupt within their domains, would severely restrict the subjects upon which printed newssheets could report.

Johann Gutenberg had presented Europe's leaders with a new tool. Many Renaissance rulers would take advantage of the opportunity to publish their news more widely; many were eager to exploit the printed word's potential for what the 17th-century English censor and journalist Roger L'Estrange termed "the *Undeceiving of the People.*" However, authorities also grew concerned that the flow of news might "deceive" citizens into underestimating the wisdom, right and indispensability of their leaders. They succumbed to the fear that their subjects might be, as L'Estrange put it, "Juggled out of their Senses with so many Frightful *Stories* and *Impostures.*"[21]

Even with limitations in literacy and transportation, even before the arrival of the newspaper, print proved itself a remarkably powerful news medium. But printed news would not soon escape the domination of Europe's anxious leaders.

News Management and Manipulation—The Newsbook

Those with arguments to make to a society did not need the printing press to convince them that news items could strengthen or weaken their cases. Leaders may not have perceived the subtle role the circulation of news played in drawing together their societies, but they certainly had seen how word of the birth of a son or the fall of an enemy could bolster their authority, while word of a blunder or defeat could threaten it. Efforts had been made to commandeer the news and turn it to political advantage since the earliest days of messengers and criers.

There was enough of an appreciation of the power of news in late medieval Europe to motivate efforts to hide deaths, close roads by which bad news might spread, commission panegyrics to the sovereign's valor and launch and disseminate false rumors. News manipulation, even the production of "disinformation," was well enough recognized as a political skill that a British diplomatic letter, written in 1578, could observe that "the Turks have learnt excellently to imitate Christians in putting out false news."[22]

In his oral reports and his two letters written to the court, Columbus probably was engaging in a form of news management or public relations: extolling the territories he had discovered in an effort to enhance his reputation and stimulate interest in future expeditions. In one of the letters, for example, Columbus descants on the prodigality of an island he had visited:

> . . . the mountains and hills, and plains and fields, and land, so beautiful and rich for planting and sowing, for breeding cattle of all sorts for building of towns and villages. There could be no believing, without seeing, such harbours as are here, as well as the many and great rivers, and excellent waters, most of which contain gold. . . .[23]

News was managed and manipulated before Gutenberg, but those concerned with the power of individual news reports must quickly have realized the potential power of the machine that was so effective in amplifying Columbus' promotional effort on behalf of "the Indies," the machine that helped Martin Luther's 95 theses, posted in 1517, become "known throughout Germany in a fortnight and throughout Europe in a month."[24] The printing press would intensify the battle for the control of news.[25]

Europe's rulers were among the first to exploit the power of the press. In England in 1486, Henry VII had printed and distributed the papal bull confirming his shaky claim to the throne.[26] (The first printing press had arrived in England in 1476.) And in France, the press became an important tool in Charles VIII's campaign to persuade a skeptical public of the merits of his invasion of Italy.

Charles VIII marched into Italy one year after Columbus returned from his first voyage to America, 126 years before the first newspaper would be printed in French, and 360 years before "the first war correspondent" is supposed to have galloped to within sight of a battlefield.[27] Yet the preparations of Charles' army, its successes, its discovery of the riches and pleasures of southern Italy and its painful retreat received extensive

Masters of News Manipulation

The manipulation of news, which took on new urgency for government leaders after the printing press, developed in the 20th century into an art and a profession: public relations (see Chapter 14).

Among the masters in United States:

- James Haggerty, press secretary to President Dwight Eisenhower in the 1950s, who used to squirrel away stories that he might then release to make it seem the president was working on days when he was in fact playing golf.
- President John Kennedy, who showered his abundant charm on certain select journalists and was rewarded with kinder, gentler coverage.

- President Richard Nixon, who noted that attacks get placed on the front page, while responses to those attacks are buried near "the deodorant ads" and who, therefore, often attacked.
- President Ronald Reagan's White House and campaign staff, Michael Deaver, David Gergen, and others, who not only knew the proper moment to release the red, white and blue balloons at Reagan appearances, but who managed to keep their many colleagues focused on a single, carefully crafted message each day, which ensured that that message made the network evening newscasts.

coverage in printed pamphlets. The French bibliographer J. P. Seguin has located 41 different pamphlets on the campaign, which lasted ten and a half months—from September 1494 to July 1495; others presumably were printed and lost.[28]

Such pamphlets were often called "relations," and later, "newsbooks." Unlike a newspaper, each usually focused on a single event. These newsbooks were small—perhaps 14 by 22 centimeters. They ranged from 4 to 28 pages in length, and were illustrated by large initial letters and woodcuts.[29]

No new news medium immediately establishes its own self-sufficient news system; it attaches itself to the systems that are already in place. As early television newscasts relied on newsreel film, newspaper reporting and radio correspondents, the first printed newsbooks were frequently read aloud in public to enable them to reach even the illiterate, and their content generally consisted of the text of a letter. (This accords with McLuhan's theory that the content of any new medium will be the medium that preceded it.)

The bulk of the newsbooks on Charles' march through Italy reproduced the text of letters from named or unnamed participants in or observers of the invasion, including Charles VIII himself. The king's letter to Parlement reporting on the battle of Rapallo, for example, was printed in a newsbook in September 1494. Handwritten letters on matters of state were already flowing steadily between Italy and Paris at the end of the 15th century.[30] With the help of the printing press, which had first arrived in Paris in 1470, hundreds or even thousands of additional copies of these written letters could be produced.

Charles's scheme to press his claim on the crown of Naples had seemed foolhardy to many of his subjects. The newsbooks on the invasion appear to have been designed, in part, to counteract that impression. One reprints a letter reporting on the position and strength of the formidable army the king had assembled, including the number of "bombards" it possessed and their size—some so "enormous" it took 60 horses to move them. This information, the author of the letter explains, was "dictated" to him by an eyewitness. In other words, this report is based on an interview. In one of the later newsbooks Charles goes out of his way to contradict the pessimistic rumors that had been spreading about his health. Other newsbooks contort themselves in an attempt to associate this invasion of Italy with a crusade against the Muslim peril.[31]

These early printed war reports also emphasize the ease with which the French armies conquered and dwell upon the marvels the soldiers discovered in the cities they captured—marvels that included "Greek wines, sour wines and rosé wines, sweet wines, muscadel wines . . . and [wines] that were so strong that they warmed one's stomach as if one had eaten strong spices." (Only when we read a Frenchman describing the wines found in Italy as "the best in the world" do these publications seem truly dated.) By July the military and oenological adventure had soured, however, and one newsbook reports with some candor that Charles' retreating army was straggling home—hungry, thirsty and overrun by "sutlers and thieves."[32]

Authorities found additional uses for the printing press in succeeding centuries. During the reign of Francis I in France (1515–1547), the government routinely printed the text of treaties—with preambles placing them in the most favorable light.[33] In England in the 16th century, Henry VIII would use the press to spread news of his complex marital arrangements, along with his rationalizations for them and for the split with Rome they would precipitate.[34]

Monarchs, who fancied their power absolute, often found it humbling to have to appeal to the masses gathered by a printing press. In a pamphlet printed in 1622, James I of England complained that justifying in print his decision to dissolve Parliament required him to "descend many degrees beneath Our Selfe." Nevertheless, James and other monarchs would make that descent again and again in the battle for public support.[35]

The oldest surviving publication printed in Britain's American colonies that might be said to contain news represented an attempt by the government to use the press to influence public opinion. Its title: *A declaration of former passages and proceedings betwixt the English and the Narrowgansets, with their confederates, Wherein the grounds and justice of the ensuing warre are opened and cleared. Published, by order of the Commissioners for the united Colonies: At Boston the 11 of the sixth month 1645.*[36] The oldest surviving example of printed news in all the Americas is a report printed in Mexico City on a storm in Guatemala in 1541.[37]

The government's use of the press was occasionally more duplicitous. In 1571 a pamphlet had appeared in England justifying Queen Elizabeth's arrest of the Duke of Norfolk for participating in an alleged Spanish plot to put Mary, Queen of Scots, on the English throne. The pamphlet announced that it consisted of a letter written by one "R. G." to his brother-in-law. Instead, it is believed to have been composed by Lord Burghley,[38] Elizabeth's chief minister and the engine of Norfolk's demise.

With or without such subterfuges, the views held by governments were being aired in these early newsbooks—in official publications, in subsidized publications and in the publications of other loyal or toadying printers. Usually, however, theirs was the only side of the argument that was set in print. That pamphlet on the arrest of the Duke of Norfolk, for example, advertised itself as an attempt to "stop the lying and open slaunderous mouthes of the evill and seditious" by explaining "the cause that the Duke of Norffolke is newely commytted to the Towre."[39] But although the claims, or potential claims, of the "evill and seditious" that Norfolk might be innocent (and he was proclaiming his innocence up to the moment he was hanged) must have been on the mind of Lord Burghley as he wrote this newsbook; there is no evidence that this view of events ever received the attention of a printing press. No newsbook survives entitled, for example, *The discoverie and confutation of the tragicall fiction devysed by the Queenes Majestie against a loyall Subject* or *A defence of the honour of the Duke of Norffolke*.

In print, at least, the public was "undeceived" without ever having had the opportunity of being deceived—for authorities combined their use of the early presses with forceful measures designed to ensure that potential enemies could not use them.

Press Controls

Controlling "lying and open slanderous mouthes" or even handwritten letters seems beyond the power of earthly authorities. Printed reports, however, can be controlled. The printing press may have been the first means of circulating information that would in fact prove mightier than the sword, but it had one great drawback as a weapon: its bulkiness made it difficult to conceal[40] and, consequently, easy for authorities to regulate.

In one particularly energetic effort to evade government controls, a secret Puritan printing press in England from 1588 to 1589 was smuggled from Kingston to Northamptonshire, then to Coventry, then to Wolston Priory. This press had been dismantled again and was on its way to Lancashire when a curious crowd figured out what was in the boxes and called the authorities.[41] Mounting an attack with a printing press would require a secluded, secure location (a colony in America would do nicely). In 16th-century Europe such locations were not readily available to Puritans or to supporters of the Duke of Norfolk, at least not within the boundaries of the countries they were trying to influence.

When they were not exploiting the printing presses themselves, monarchs and their ministers busied themselves monitoring the presses—which were ostensibly in private hands—and making sure the news others printed on them was not, as a British jurist was to put it some years later, "possessing the people with an ill opinion of the government."[42] One of the gentler methods of control they employed was the awarding of exclusive "privileges" to print certain information or even certain types of information. Privileges were distributed as early as 1467 in Berne. In England, Queen Elizabeth excelled in the manipulation of these privileges—shuffling them about among printers, "rewarding here and penalizing there."[43]

Governments also controlled the output of the presses through more straightforward transactions: paying for kind and helpful words. Francis Bacon may have helped earn himself a payment from the queen of 1,200 pounds by writing a pamphlet, in 1601, reporting on the alleged conspiracy against the crown led by his former patron, the popular earl of Essex.[44]

Earthquake or Storm?

It is the oldest surviving news report printed in the Americas—in Mexico City in 1542. And atop the front page of this eight-page newsbook are Spanish words saying "Relation"—a widely used name for early news reports—"of the earthquake." However, the report on this terrible event in Guatemala, written by a notary public named Juan Rodriguez, speaks not of an earthquake but of a "storm . . . so great that floods rushed boulders and trees and those of us that witnessed it were astonished" (Gutiérrez).

Did an earthquake help release those flood waters in the form of a tsunami? Or is this an early example of a misleading "headline"?

European authorities were not adverse to taking sterner measures either. Just before Columbus departed on his first voyage, the Inquisition had begun burning books in Spain. And in 1502 Ferdinand and Isabella required that all printed works be licensed by government or church authorities.[45]

In England, the number of printers was strictly limited. As the simplest route to securing one of the few dozen available positions as a master printer in 16th- and early 17th-century England, printers' widows were in great demand as wives. All works printed in England had to be licensed after the year 1538; printers themselves—through their organization, the Stationers Company—not only registered licensed works but were empowered to inspect each other's shops and warehouses for unlicensed works.[46] In Germany, the Edict of Worms in 1521 required printers to submit to prior censorship and obtain permission to publish from church or government authorities.[47] (The divisions produced in Germany by the Reformation, however, contributed to what one historian calls "a great glut of pamphlet-type printed matter.")[48] In France, the regulations were as stiff or stiffer. After 1561 flogging became the penalty for disseminators of defamatory or seditious broadsides or pamphlets the first time they were caught, and death the penalty for recidivism.[49]

Under Tudor rule in England, one printer was put to death—William Carter, a Roman Catholic convicted of having printed an allegorical attack on the queen's religious policies. In fact, the targets of most of these controls on the press were tracts inspired by dissident religious beliefs.[50] Religion was a subject that caused many a printer to risk a fine, a jail sentence, a flogging or even death in 16th-century Europe. Political issues independent of religious beliefs, to the extent that political opinion was able to organize itself unaided by religious feelings, do not often seem to have inspired such passion.[51] And the mere commercial advantage presented by some bit of news, say, an exclusive on the real explanation for the Duke of Norfolk's arrest, was rarely of sufficient worth to risk the wrath of authorities.

The bonds restricting printers would bend and break in succeeding centuries as printers swelled with belief in such political causes as the rights of Parliament, the rights of the people and even the liberty of the presses. In the 17th century, England would move from rigid press controls to a period of press freedom during the civil war in the

1640s, then back again. In France, between the years 1600 and 1756 more than 800 authors, printers and booksellers would cause sufficient discomfort to the government to be thrown into the Bastille.[52]

Even in the 16th century there were some cracks in the censorship on the Continent, with its easily penetrable borders. And English eyes, despite the island's greater isolation, could not be completely protected from provocative print. During the brief reign of Queen Mary (1553–1558), for example, the Protestant forces, suddenly the object of persecution themselves, were able to smuggle into England a number of pamphlets favorable to their cause.[53]

Nevertheless, most 16th-century printers and newswriters—unburdened by a cause worthy of smuggling or martyrdom, intimidated, if not actually imprisoned, by testy authorities—were content to take the hand of the monarch and respectfully, if occasionally rambunctiously, follow along.

A Fear of Controversy

The presence of the licenser, hovering over the early newsbooks, seems most palpable when the topics these publications underplayed or ignored are considered.

Perhaps the major continuing news story in Europe in the 16th century was the war with the Turks, who were battling for territory in southern and eastern Europe. The hysteria with which news of their advances was greeted can be seen in the title of one of the many German newsbooks published in 1529 on the Turkish attack on Vienna: *The siege of Vienna in Austria by the most terrible tyrant and destroyer of Christianity, the Turkish Emperor known as Sultan Suleiman. . . .*[54]

The Turks entered a Europe that was poorly prepared to resist their progress but increasingly well prepared to report on it. One bibliographer, Carl Göllner, has located 33 publications discussing Suleiman's siege of Vienna, printed across Europe in French, German, Italian and Latin. Altogether Göllner lists 2,463 surviving publications printed in Europe from 1501 to 1600 on the wars with the Ottoman Empire. Some are just essays, arguing, for example, that the "cruell power of the Turkes, bothe may, and ought for to be repelled [by] the Christen people," as one English pamphlet in 1542 put it.[55] But most of these publications did present their readers with fresh information on the battles or treaties; most contained news.

The battle in 1571 at Famagusta, a heavily fortified Venetian outpost on Cyprus, proved one of the more significant in this long struggle, not so much because of its results—the Turkish siege of the town succeeded—but because allegations of Turkish atrocities after Famagusta's fall helped spur Venice, Spain, and the pope to merge their fleets to fight the "cruell power of the Turkes." The newsbook that appeared in England in 1572 recounting details of this battle and some of the atrocities that followed, *The true Report of all the successe of Famagosta . . . ,* provides a good indication of how international news made its way onto the early printing presses. It contains a letter from "Earle Nestor Martinengo," who had survived the siege, to the "Duke of Venice." The letter, originally printed in an Italian newsbook,[56] was "Englished out of Italian" for this pamphlet.

Martinengo's report was filled with remarkable detail. The newsbook includes sections on each of the six Turkish assaults on Famagusta. "They battered and holde with so great rage," he explains in his account of the third assault, "that on the 8 of July, with the same night also, was numbered 5000 cannon shot." When the outpost surrendered, Martinengo reports that he managed to hide where he could observe the treatment of the prisoners at the hands of the Turkish general: ". . . they being unarmed . . . and bound, were lead one by one into the market place, before hys pavilion, being presently cutte and hewen in sunder in his presence." Martinengo himself was, according to his letter, able "to geve . . . the slippe, and to flye"—escaping in a small boat with a "saile made of two shirtes."[57]

This English newsbook on the siege of Famagusta, however, is the exception that proves an important rule. Göllner found a total of eight English publications that appear to contain news of battles against the Ottoman Empire (they appeared from 1532 to 1593). Of those, seven report on "most Noble victorie[s] of the Chrestiens over the armie of the great Turke." Famagusta is the *only* Turkish victory reported on in any of these surviving pamphlets.[58] The European armies hardly achieved a victory rate of seven to one in their efforts to check the Turkish advance; the reverse would be closer to the truth. Bad news for "the Chrestiens" was clearly being underreported.[59] Reports of invasion by the infidels have impact, but news of victory of the infidels must have been unwelcome to readers and authorities, and therefore to printers. It should be noted that Suleiman's siege of Vienna in 1529, which attracted so much attention in European newsbooks, was unsuccessful.

Controversy connected with matters of state, normally a magnet for newsmongers, was a warning for these printers to back off. Military defeats suffered by their motherland or fatherland must have been considered too touchy to handle; most were simply not reported. J. P. Seguin lists nearly 120 surviving reports on battles printed in France from 1498 to 1559, but his list includes no contemporary publications reporting, for example, on the decisive French defeat at Pavia in 1525 in which King Francis I was taken prisoner.[60] A fear of controversy may also explain why no printed epitaph marking the death in 1601 of the once-popular earl of Essex was registered in England until after the death in 1603 of the woman who had him executed—his former benefactor, Queen Elizabeth.[61]

News from abroad was generally less controversial than news from home—one reason English readers seemed better supplied with printed news on French politics than on their own politics. Matthias Shaaber, who in 1929 produced the most thorough study of printed news in England before the newspaper, found evidence of 38 English publications reporting on French affairs in 1590, the year of King Henry IV's greatest successes against the Catholic League. Not all foreign news was safe to handle, however. English printers apparently chose to ignore Henry's conversion to Catholicism in 1593,[62] and Turkish victories on the Continent, though they did not represent direct defeats for English armies, were certainly underplayed.

Comments on the workings of government made by those *outside* the government are also conspicuous in their absence from these early publications. We can occasionally read Queen Elizabeth's thoughts on her actions or policies: *A Declaration of the Causes mooving the Queenes Maiestie . . . to . . . send a Navy to the Seas, for the defence of her Realmes against the King of Spaines forces,* for example.[63] We cannot read the thoughts on those actions or policies of others not involved in their formulation.[64] In fact, two fully articulated positions almost never confront each other in these pamphlets and broadsides; instead, the government position wrestles with the "slaunderous" arguments of "evill and seditious" phantoms.

Dissent was not completely silenced in the 16th century—it survived in unchecked rumors, uncensored personal letters and the occasional smuggled pamphlet. Nonetheless, the control of lawfully printed news reports does appear to have been remarkably successful. With few exceptions (most the work of dedicated and print-savvy proponents of the Protestant "heresies" or, where the "heresies" had become orthodoxies, of "Papists"), the press was not available to those who challenged authority. Shaaber suggests that "practically without exception [the] tenor and the purport" of these publications "were such as the authorities themselves would have contrived had they been the authors and publishers."[65]

Chauvinism—The News Ballad

On Aug. 10, 1588, a ballad, signed T. D., about a skirmish with the Spanish armada 12 days earlier, was registered with the Stationers Company. It focused on the capture of a Spanish warship:

> . . . The chiefest Captaine,
>   of this Gallion so hie:
> Don *Hugo de Moncaldo* he,
>   within this fight did die.
> Who was the Generall,
>   of all the Gallions great:
> But through his braines w' pouders force,
>   a Bullet strong did beat.
> And manie more,
>   by sword did loose their breath:
> And maine more within the sea,
>   did swimme and tooke their death,
> There might you see
>   the salt and foming flood:
> Died and stained like scarlet red,
>   with store of Spanish blood. . . .[66]

Poetry, especially poetry worthy enough to mount a printing press, has climbed to such rarefied heights in our culture that it infrequently traffics in issues as blunt and as public as news.[67] However, a species of poet in earlier centuries was employed recording news of warring states and earthquakes, instead of mental states and landscapes. In fact, these topical ballads formed a considerable part of the output of the early presses.[68]

Three months after it was written, Columbus' letter was printed for the first time in the Tuscan language—transformed into 68 stanzas of verse by the Florentine theologian and poet Giuliano Dati.[69] In France, printed news ballads appeared alongside newsbooks from the reign of Charles VIII to the end of the 19th century.[70] In England, printers and poets frequently teamed up to disseminate information.

Of course, current events were far from the only concerns of the ballads that appeared in print. Their authors might wax poetic on the legendary adventures of Robin Hood as well as on a naval battle. Folk tales, moral instruction, romances, comic portraits, bawdy stories—all found their way into printed verses. Nonetheless, a large portion of these rhythmic, rhyming lines of print—perhaps the largest portion—was devoted to news.[71]

The debt these printed ballads owed to spoken news is clear. They were written to be performed aloud. Most included the name of a popular tune to which they could be sung and were printed on a single side of a large sheet—a broadside—so that they were easy to hold while reciting or singing. Literary exercises they were not. News was worked into verse for one reason: to make it more entertaining—especially for the large majority of the population whose tastes had been shaped by exposure to oral rather than written forms of communication. Ballad singers—part newsboy, part street musician—would sell the ballads in the streets or from stalls for a penny a copy. "Ballads! My masters, ballads! Will ye ha' any ballads o' the newest and truest matter in all London?"—is the way one 17th-century satirist rendered their cry.[72] A couple of verses might then be warbled as a sampler.

The author of one of these ballads could expect to be rewarded with 40 shillings, plus a bottle of wine.[73] Many of these rhyming journalists remained anonymous, but a few achieved a degree of fame, or infamy.[74] Among the best known was the man who signed his compositions T. D. "Thomas Deloney, the Ballatting Silke-Weaver [his previous career], of Norwich hath rime inough for all myracles," wrote Thomas Nash in 1596.[75] Another contemporary referred to Deloney more pointedly as "T. D. whose braines beaten to the yarking up of Ballades."[76]

Deloney wrote poems for print on subjects of "mere amusement," on historical events, on social issues and on contemporary events such as the confrontation with the armada. He tackled enough of the latter, with enough skill, to be considered, according to the editor of his collected works, the most popular "ballad journalist" of his day.[77]

Of 23 English printed ballads on the Spanish armada that have left evidence of their existence, three are by Thomas Deloney. In a second news ballad registered in London on Aug. 10, 1588, the poet descants upon some unusually timely news: Queen Elizabeth's visit to the troops gathered at Tilbury to defend the country against the possible Spanish invasion. The queen had left the camp at Tilbury only one day earlier, on Aug. 9.[78] In her attempt to inspire her soldiers there, Elizabeth was said to have delivered one of her more memorable lines: "I know I have the body but of a weak and feeble woman, but I have the heart and stomach of a king."[79] Deloney, perhaps operating under unusual deadline pressure, either missed that quote completely (assuming it was not simply apocryphal) or mangled the stomach metaphor:

And then bespake our noble Queene,
    my loving friends and contriemen:
I hope this day the worst is seen,
    that in our wars ye shall sustain,

Before the first European printed newspapers, major news events were discussed in printed pamphlets or broadsides, often written in verse. This "news ballad" by Thomas Deloney, printed in London in 1588, reports on a skirmish between the English navy and the Spanish armada.

> But if our enimies do assaile you,
>   never let your stomackes faile you.
> For in the midst of all your troupe,
>   we our selves will be in place:
> To be your joy, your guide and comfort,
>   even before your enimies face.[80]

Some accuracy in such news ballads must inevitably have been sacrificed to the exigencies of form. Elizabeth might, at the very least, have been surprised to find herself in Deloney's verses singing to her troops to the tune of something called "Wilsons Wilde."

These news ballads also listed heavily in the direction of chauvinism. Indeed, the tendency of news to reflect the prejudices of a society seems particularly apparent when it is arrayed in verse. Deloney's report on the queen's progress to and through the camp at Tilbury, for example, includes no mention of the difficulties her officers met with in gathering sufficient troops and supplies.[81] More significantly, although Deloney's account of the bullet the English put through the head of Don Hugo de Monçada, captain of that Spanish galleass run aground near Calais, appears to be correct, his claim earlier in that poem that the Spanish sailors had deceived the English with a false white flag does not jibe with historical accounts of the incident. Moreover, while historians report that British sailors appeared ready to plunder French civilians in the area of that battle, Deloney, if he knew about this "rude" behavior[82] by the queen's Navy, ignored it.

These apparent distortions or omissions in Deloney's reports must have owed something to the fact that his ballads were subject to government regulations (beginning with the need to register them with the Stationers Company). Europe's newswriters and printers were well aware of the aversion of Europe's rulers to seeing their slipups and setbacks published. (Had the armada fared better against the British fleet, far fewer English printers would have dared set ballads in type.) Eight years later, in a lapse of judgment, or perhaps even a display of honest concern, Deloney composed a ballad on a famine, *Complaint of great Want and Scarcity of Corn* (it has not survived). And England's best-known ballad maker apparently was forced into hiding to escape the wrath of authorities.[83] But fear alone does not explain the chauvinism that colors so many early printed news reports.

Deloney's final ballad on the confrontation with the armada, registered on Aug. 31, appears to contain little more than propaganda. It is titled: *A new Ballet of the straunge and most cruell Whippes which the Spanyards had prepared to whippe and torment English men and women: which were found and taken at the overthrow of certaine of the Spanish Shippes, in July last past, 1588.* (The lengthy titles that sat atop such publications told much of the story themselves.)

> . . . One sort of whips they had for men,
>   so smarting fierce and fell:
>
> As like could never be devisde
>   by any devill in hell . . .[84]

Given the waves of panic and pride that were breaking on the island's shores that summer, as the British Navy at once saved the motherland and made itself master of the seas, Deloney's equation of Spaniards and devils hardly seems surprising. Those who spread news—in verse or in prose—are immersed, by the nature of their profession, in the day-to-day thoughts of a society. It would take more detachment than humans can generally muster to avoid being swayed by those thoughts—especially when they reach wartime intensity (and especially in the days before the mustering of detachment was in vogue.)

Deloney certainly has had company in his patriotism and xenophobia. A random selection from the work of journalists living in virtually any country at war, no matter how free its press, could fill an anthology on jingoism. When a society falls into step, most journalists are too responsive to the stirrings of the crowd and too susceptible to martial music to do anything but grab a drum and join the parade. At these times government controls seem almost superfluous.

The inspirational efforts that pour from the pens of such loyal and committed journalists (and the stanzas and choruses of the news ballad provided a particularly suitable

Public Journalism

Public—or civic—journalism was an influential and controversial movement in late 20th century American newsrooms. The idea, originally put forward by Jay Rosen of New York University, is that journalists have a responsibility that extends beyond simply serving as "watchdogs" on the government—always cynical, constantly alert for evidence of malfeasance. The journalist's responsibility, public journalism's advocates argued, is instead to improve the dialog on civic issues, to help create a public capable of serving as a positive force in the process of governing.

Critics of public journalism feared that it would lead to a situation in which journalists spend more time organizing town meetings and reading public opinion polls than they do uncovering facts. They feared that it would make it easier for journalists to succumb to the ever-present temptation to go easy on those they cover and to become cheerleaders for their communities.

In some ways the role of facilitator of public dialog is an earlier role for journalists than that of watchdog. The first print journalists were not allowed to discuss the mistakes of their country's rulers. But they did manage—subtly and over time—to create a situation in which sections of the public felt informed on political issues and therefore in a position to take a stand on those issues. Historically, in other words, journalists have contributed to radical political change in both roles.

receptacle for their outpourings) also have a commercial advantage: An inspired audience is an enthusiastic audience. Chauvinism, in a word, sells.

In spreading news of provocative events such as Columbus' voyage with unprecedented reliability to unprecedented crowds, those who used the printing press for journalistic purposes in the first centuries after Gutenberg invented it may have helped overturn some prejudices and truly "undeceive" some minds. But more commonly newsbook writers and ballad makers exhibited a failing common to most newsmongers: Acceding to pressure from authorities and to their own rooting and commercial interests, they tended to provide their audiences with a version of what their audiences wanted to hear.

In time, the political landscape would change radically in lands irrigated by the printed word. Does this early printed news, most of it so politically timid and nonabrasive, deserve some credit for the erosion over the centuries of the authority of the old regimes of Europe and the spread of new political ideas? Probably. The printing press began amplifying the flow of news to the point where the members of these societies would gain more than a sense of participation in their societies, to the point where they would gain a sense of power. Printed news ballads on the successes of a navy increase the number of elements within a society able to share in those successes, but do they not also increase the number prepared to debate decisions affecting that navy?

As King James I and his fellow autocrats descended to place their views in print, their readers gradually began to ascend. These readers would gain a title—the public—and gain, en masse, a role in determining the legitimacy of those who attempted to gov-

ern them. Heresies and rebellions could be excised from early newsbooks and news ballads, but the development of a widening group of readers with an acknowledged interest in politics would contribute to greater heresies and more successful rebellions.

Questions

1. How might the world have been different if there had been a printing press in Greenland waiting for Leif Eriksson when he returned
   from "Vinland"?

2. Give examples from the past 10 years of news management and
   manipulation like that undertaken by Europe's rulers in the first
   centuries of printing.

3. News media today are often accused of emphasizing bad news, and
   in many ways this is true. Are there any types of stories today,
   however, where good news receives more attention than bad?
   Why?

4. To what extent can a bias similar to the chauvinism discussed in
   this chapter be found in news reports today?

Human Interests *(Faits Divers)*— Such a Deal of Wonder   7

According to Marshall McLuhan and other communication theorists, the printed page—with its thin, straight, carefully ordered lines—has had a sobering effect upon humankind. The agonistic, impassioned involvement of the "tribal age" has given way to the studied detachment of the "print age." Under the light supplied by books and journals science has flourished, and the mystical power of monarchs has succumbed to the mechanics of democracy.[2]

The printing press did eventually add a touch of sobriety to the presentation of news, but not until it began producing newspapers. For, despite government controls, in the years between the invention of the letter press in the 15th century and the development of the printed newspaper in the 17th century, printing seemed, if anything, to have made the news even more boisterous.

The reticence and timidity printers demonstrated on political news did not extend to less controversial subjects. Indeed, printers took tales of earthquakes, prodigies, fires and crimes and amplified them; they gave them the loudness of a thousand voices and the reach of a thousand handwritten letters. Outside the minefield of politics, print was bold.[3]

Newsbook and ballad writers were particularly vulnerable to what Conor Cruise O'Brien has called "the Scheherazade Syndrome." "The reader—the ultimate boss," O'Brien suggests, "is heard to say, like the Sultan, 'If you bore me, you die.'"[4] Busybodies, letter writers, or newspapers editors establish a continuing relationship with their audiences, so they can afford the occasional dull story. But each of these sporadic pamphlets and broadsides had to sell itself anew. Each arrived as a stranger, so each had instantly to establish an identity and call attention to itself.[5] Printed news had to be bold.

In addition, in transforming news into a mass-produced product, the printing press made newsmongering more than just a specialized function—it established it as a business. And as the news industry expanded, the competition in this business grew more intense. Information was no longer so scarce; each news-teller was no longer automatically in demand. The pamphlets or broadsides that came flying off the presses by the thousands were already beginning to crowd each other. To earn a profit, each had to strive not only to be bold, but to be bolder.

The result was a particularly spirited form of news—news that catered to the most obvious and reliable human interests. The techniques of "popular" journalism were not invented by the printing press, and they would certainly outlive the newsbook and the news ballad, but these techniques seem particularly naked in the news forms that were born on the early presses, news forms that were aggressive, even rude, in their attempts to attract readers.

It was not that the authors and printers of these pamphlets and broadsides were unaware of the news value of "serious" subjects. According to one 16th-century ballad, they were besieged with the query:

> What newes? or here ye any tidinges
> Of the pope, of the Emperour, or of kynges
> Of Martyn Luther, or of the great Turke,
> Of this and that, and how the world doth worke?[6]

However, encouraged by authorities who found sensationalism less offensive than political commentary,[7] newswriters devoted much of their energy not to reports on the great political, military and religious issues, but to news of "this and that," to exploring the commercial possibilities of what the French call *faits divers*.[8] Matthias Shaaber, in his study of printed news in England before the newspaper, found newsbooks and news ballads on "doings of the court; murders and other crimes; miracles, prodigies and wonders; monstrous births and strange beasts; witchcraft; the plague; acts of god such as flood and fire, and the weather; and sporting events." Shaaber speculates that in the 16th century there may have been more of this "popular news" than news of politics, government, and war.[9]

So, while a number of English ballads in the 16th and early 17th centuries were devoted to such crucial events overseas as the struggles between the Huguenots and Catholics in France, or the Spaniards and the Dutch in the Low Countries, foreign news also appeared in ballads with titles like *Tydinges of a Huge and Ougly childe borne at Arneheim in Gelderland* or *A true relacon of the birth of Three Monsters in the Citty of Namen in Flaunders*.[10] And while it was possible to read James I's explanation for his decision to dissolve Parliament in a pamphlet entitled *His majesties declaration, Touching his proceedings in the late Assemblie . . . of Parliament*,[11] readers could also brief themselves on a less politically significant piece of home news: "the Strange and Miraculous Revelation of a Murder by a Ghost, a Calf, a Pigeon, etc." in Lancashire.[12]

The English were not alone in their taste for such stories. French publications reveled in a wide variety of *faits divers,* and in discussing printed news in Germany in these years, the historian Victor von Klarwill observes, "there was hardly anything between heaven and earth, or in heaven and beneath the earth, which the *Neue Zeitung* (literally, "latest news") did not manage to talk about."[13]

Exchanging news is a way of marveling at the world. And when reporting on events like the birth of "a Huge and Ougly childe" or accusations of murder against a ghost and animals, 16th- and early 17th-century European newswriters, with all their limitations,

did demonstrate a ready eye for the world's most intense, spectacular, or amazing occurrences—its marvels.

In Shakespeare's *The Winter's Tale,* after the king has been reconciled with his lost
daughter, a gentleman asked for "the news" exclaims: "Such a deal of wonder is broken
out within this hour, that ballad makers cannot be able to express it."[14] But, as Shakespeare well knew, unless intimidated by government controls, the print journalists of his
day would at least have given such a sensational development their best effort.

Published Gossip

In 1508 Mary, daughter of Henry VII of England, was "married" to Prince Charles of
Austria, heir to the throne of the Holy Roman Empire. She was 12; he was eight. The
wedding, celebrated by proxy, was the subject of a newsbook written by Henry's Latin
secretary and printed the following year.[15] One of its purposes clearly was to marshal
public support for the alliance between England and the Holy Roman Empire. It was a
form of news manipulation:

> And it is of trouth and undoubted that there was never amytie or aliaunce hereto-
> fore made and concluded betwixt any Prynces with better wyll and mynde . . .
> than this that nowe is taken betwixt the sayde Emperour and the kynges highnes.

In approving or encouraging the printing of this pamphlet, Henry, whether consciously or not, was also accomplishing a more subtle political purpose. He was
strengthening the tenuous legitimacy of his rule by encouraging his subjects to acknowledge his performance as king:

> And . . . the kings highness beyng under his Clothe of estate the ambassadoure
> of Aragon and the lord spirituell syttynge on his right hande downeward. And
> my lorde the Prynce with other Lords temporall syttynge in the lyke wyse on the
> leftehande. . . .[16]

But this does not explain why *readers* would be interested in minute details of the seating arrangement at this celebration of a prospective marriage between two children.
Why did they care who was sitting on Henry's "right hande downeward" and who "on
the leftehande"?

One answer is that in those days royal weddings were of more than mere personal
significance. Because the sovereign embodied the state, the sovereign's or potential sovereign's birth, death or marriage could easily transform the nature of the state. The cha-
rade performed in the name of Mary and Charles was newsworthy in part because it was
the embodiment of the treaty between England and Germany.[17] And such matters as the
seating arrangements at the ceremonies, as the alignment of officials on a Soviet re-
viewing stand once did, provided clues to the disposition of power around the throne.
(While this proxy wedding may have succeeded temporarily in warming the relationship
between the two countries, it did nothing for the relationship between these two children. Charles escaped his marriage contract with Mary of England, as well as a later

agreement to wed Renée of France, before finally marrying Isabella of Portugal in 1526.)

Charades or not, such weddings also commanded readers' attention as spectacles in an age when spectacles had not yet been cheapened by overexposure. News reports on royal pomp and circumstance dwelt on the details because the events depicted were more extravagant and magnificent than anything else in their readers' experience. The newsbook *The noble tryumphaunt coronacyon of quene Anne Wyfe unto the moost noble kynge Henry the viii,* printed in 1533, lingers over such a scene:

> . . . all the worthyfull craftes and occupacyons in theyr best araye goodly besene toke theyr bargs which were splayed with goodly baners fresshe and newe. . . . And so the quenes grace in her ryche barge amonge her nobles, the cytesyns accompanyed her to London unto the toure wharfe. Also or she came nere the toure there was shot innumerable peces of ordynaunces. . . . Also to beholde the wonderfull nombre of people that ever was sene that stode on the shore on bothe sydes of the ryver. . . .[18]

(There is no evidence that any newsbooks were printed on the more newsworthy, but considerably more controversial, execution of "quene Anne" Boleyn in 1536.)

Entries of sovereigns into major cities were a particular preoccupation of these early publications because of the political statement the march through the gates represented, and also because of the majesty—and therefore the entertainment value—of the procession and reception. A 1531 French newsbook describes the entry into Paris of "the most high, most powerful, most noble and illustrious" Queen Eleanor and her two infants not only as "triumphant" but as "sumptuous."[19]

Such news stories also interest readers for another, perhaps more basic reason: all humans are curious about major events in the lives of people they know, and celebrities—the king and his family, for example—are people most of the audience, in some sense, know.

The most newsworthy event in many lives is, alas, their end. Before the advent of the formal newspaper obituary,[20] epitaphs in prose or verse were the most common form of printed personal news. Henry, the well-liked Prince of Wales, was the subject of a warm newsbook when he entered London in 1610: *Londons love, to the royal Prince Henrie, meeting him on the river of Thames . . . the last of May, 1610. With a breife reporte of the water Fight, and Fireworks.* Henry's death two years later, however, was more thoroughly covered—in at least 26 different printed epitaphs.[21] (These early forms of printed news were so accomplished at lamenting that a disconsolate character in a 1605 play cries, "O Lord, then let mee turne my selfe into a Ballad and mourne.")[22]

Beyond the royal family and occasionally their top advisers, the individuals whose exploits were celebrated in early forms of printed news were, Shaaber reports, "almost invariably soldiers, sailors, and adventurers." When Sir Francis Drake departed on a voyage, the event would be marked by a ballad of adieu, his return greeted by a ballad of welcome.[23] Sir Philip Sidney—soldier, adventurer, and poet—was another of the favorites of the early printing presses.[24] Shaaber has located 11 pamphlets and broadsides from 1586 noting Sidney's premature death and, simultaneously, recounting his suitably

More Valuable Lives?

One of the disturbing aspects of all this journalistic attention to celebrity is the nondemocratic assumption that some people are more important than others. Kings and queens have been, of course, treated that way. Others have been too—throughout the history of journalism, even in democracies.

One of the more conspicuous examples of this bias is the large, front-page *New York Times* headline following the sinking of the *Titanic* in 1912: "TITANIC SINKS FOUR HOURS AFTER HITTING ICEBERG; 866 RESCUED BY CARPATHIA, PROBABLY 1250 PERISH; /ISMAY SAFE, MRS. ASTOR MAYBE, NOTED NAMES MISSING." G. Bruce Ismay, we are told, was "head of the line" that owned the ship. Mrs. John Jacob Astor was a leading socialite. Was her possible survival really that newsworthy compared to all those deaths?

This out-of-proportion attention to the famous was mocked some years ago in a satire of the *New York Post*. The spoof reported on a nuclear war with the following headline: "KA-BOOM! IT'S WORLD WAR III/Michael Jackson, 80 Million Others Dead."

action-packed life. The demise of no other nonroyal appears to have so interested English printers in the 16th century as that of this prototypical Renaissance man.[25]

The entertainment value of reports on such dynamic figures lay not only in their personal notoriety and glamor but in the excitement of their adventures, which in Sidney's case included battles in the Netherlands and wanderings across the Continent. (Today, as military defenses increasingly are manned by silicon chips, and humans and chimpanzees seem interchangeable on voyages of discovery, the magic dust of celebrity more often settles on entertainers and athletes who, through a convenient blurring of life and performance, have inherited this ability to enthrall us with their exploits and bravado.)

An audience hangs with such interest on details of the life and death of someone like Sidney for an additional reason: The behavior of such celebrities provides guidance on how our own lives might be lived. Those who read about a royal wedding may use elements of the ceremony as a model for the proper conduct of their own infinitely more humble affairs. To be gossiped about is to be honored with the role of example.

All this fawning over the famous would prove dispiriting, however, if they did not stumble before us with some frequency. Pride, aided by aesthetic imperatives, is at work here. To protect some notion of the rightness of our own lives, it is necessary for us to believe that our heroes have received at least the hint of a frown from the fates, that they are, like the rest of us, fallible. And the fates have usually come through. There is no more conclusive proof of human limitations than death—another reason why the epitaph or obituary is such a satisfying form for celebrity news.

Effective gossip, like effective tragedy, delights in raising its subjects on a pedestal and then delights in their fall back to the ground. In the days before antibiotics and orderly succession, those falls were frequently fatal—Sir Philip Sidney died of a bullet wound received in battle at the age of 31; Prince Henry died suddenly at the age of 18 (there were rumors that he was poisoned[26]); Anne Boleyn, "Wyfe unto the moost noble kynge Henry the viii," was executed by her husband before she turned 30. (Celebrities today offer us their drug and alcohol "dependencies" or their divorces in lieu of their heads.) Blessed and cursed, exalted and debased, marvelously situated but with all too human limitations—these are the roles the celebrity, like the tragic hero, is asked to play.

Gossip on the street or over coffee has earned its negative reputation not only because it is intrusive but because it is so often exchanged with a touch of cattiness. We make comments about individuals behind their backs that we would never make to their faces, and in these comments we reveal one of our less appealing qualities: what Samuel Warren and Louis Brandeis called, in a widely cited law review article on privacy, "that weak side of human nature which is never wholly cast down by the misfortunes and frailties of our neighbors."[27] Published gossip too speaks to that unattractive side of our natures.

Backbiting was undoubtedly the furthest thing from the mind of the aide to Henry VII who wrote that printed account of the "wedding" of 12-year-old Princess Mary and eight-year-old Prince Charles in 1508. But are we to believe that his readers did not supplement the political interest, entertainment value and instruction they might have found in this pamphlet with a chance to smile, if not smirk, at such an odd occasion?

Even if celebrity news is published with impeccable decorum, it still carries personal information about its subjects well beyond the point where they can deter discussion of it by their presence. We all surrender some control of our images every time we venture into society. The subjects of celebrity news—including young Princess Mary and Prince Charles—must watch as their images are scattered all over the land. The area behind their backs is expanded enormously.

"Being a celebrity like I am is like being raped," former tennis star John McEnroe has been quoted as saying (in a *New York Times* column called "Sports People").[28] The treatment of powerful celebrities was certainly less intrusive and more discreet in the early days of printed news. It is doubtful that Princess Mary felt "raped" by the pamphlet prepared by her father's Latin secretary. But the wages of fame were known even in those years before the development of the newspaper. In *Anthony and Cleopatra,* written at the beginning of the 17th century, Shakespeare has Cleopatra express the fear that if brought to Rome, "Scald rhymers [will] ballad us out o'tune. . . ." As the historian Hyder E. Rollins, perhaps oversimplifying a bit, suggests, rather than face the gossiping media, Cleopatra applies the asp to her breast.[29] It is possible to sympathize with a McEnroe or a Cleopatra, but what tennis star, what monarch, could in fact survive complete privacy? Much of their power and glory is won in the minds of their publics, and they conquer those minds as full-bodied human beings, not as tennis-playing machines or abstract political instruments.

Warren and Brandeis worried about the effect printed gossip has not only on its subjects but on its readers: ". . . it usurps the place of interest in brains capable of other things."[30] This is undeniable. However, places in our brains that might be occupied by more robust thoughts or more delicate feelings, to use their terms, face assaults by other usurpers besides gossip, unleashed by other entertainments besides news. And these invaders have been warmly welcomed. Calls for an end to concentration upon such trivialities seem noble and decent, and perhaps futile.

Discussions of such private matters as McEnroe's relationship with the actress Tatum O'Neal, Cleopatra's relationship with Antony, or Mary's potential relationship with Charles—however upsetting to their subjects and distracting to their audiences—have always held interest. Our eyes turn to the powerful, the adventurous, the beautiful, the talented. Those of us who maintain a less dutiful watch at the gates of our minds than Samuel Warren and Louis Brandeis are not always successful in limiting our inquisitiveness to public issues and performances. The state of the projects and romances of celebrities can fire our curiosity at least as surely as the state of some proposition in some parliament. The line between news and published gossip may seem clear in sermons and civic lessons, but where exactly is that line to be drawn among the varied wanderings of the human mind?

It can be even argued that gossip, along with other *faits divers,* has an invigorating effect upon the news. Were the personal lives of the famous placed off-limits, would the news not tell a duller, less human story?

News of Crime

Early in the 17th century, the Countess of Essex became determined to divorce the Earl of Essex and marry her paramour, Sir Robert Carr, a rising star in the court of King James I. Only one man stood in the way. That man, Sir Thomas Overbury, a close adviser to Carr, campaigned against Carr's blossoming affair with the countess—whom he called a whore—and in the process infuriated the countess, her influential relatives, Carr, and apparently even the king himself.

Overbury played his cards poorly and, with these powerful forces aligned against him, soon found himself imprisoned in the Tower of London. Five months later, in Sept. 1613, Overbury was dead, poisoned in his cell. The countess had divorced Essex and married Carr by December.

The crimes that have most intrigued the readers of modern American newspapers appear to have had four qualities in common beyond mere heinousness: a woman or child as victim or suspect; a highborn or well-known victim or suspect; some doubt about the guilt of the suspect; and intimations of promiscuous behavior by the victim or suspect.* The Lindbergh kidnapping in 1932, the Manson murders in 1969, the Patty Hearst kidnapping in 1974, and the murder of O. J. Simpson's former wife in 1994—certainly among the most widely reported crimes of the 20th century—each shared at least three of those four qualities. The Overbury case had all four. No crime in England before the development of the newspaper appears to have received more attention from the printing press.

Four persons were executed in 1615 for poisoning Overbury: the lieutenant of the Tower, Overbury's servant in the Tower, an apothecary, and a widowed friend of the

---

* There is a second category of crime story, which gets its power primarily from the fear a criminal—Jack the Ripper, the Boston Strangler, Son of Sam, the Hillside Strangler, the Atlanta child murderer—spreads in a community.

countess (referred to as "Mrs. Turner").[31] One of those convicted of the murder was said to have expressed the hope before his execution that "they would not make a net to catch the little fishes and let the great go."[32] The countess, who by all accounts had contracted for the murder, and her new husband were in fact convicted of complicity in 1616, but their lives were spared by the king.

The dissemination of information about a crime such as Overbury's murder serves important purposes within a society. In raising a hue and cry it can, when necessary, assist in the apprehension of the criminal. In publicizing the punishment that is meted out, it can help deter other potential criminals. And in making the public aware of both crime and punishment, it can help clarify and reinforce the lines of acceptable behavior within a society.[33] Political bonds are also strengthened when a particularly despicable act unites a people in a great chorus of moral outrage.

These tasks appear to have been left to word of mouth and government proclamations through the earliest days of print. J. P. Seguin turned up no French newsbooks on crime in the first half of the 16th century.[34] The first English publication about a murder found by Matthias Shaaber is dated 1557. But as the century progressed, French printers began energetically exploring the journalistic possibilities of wife murders, husband murders, mass murders, and chopped-up bodies. And in England, after 1575 most interesting homicides appear to have been recorded in print.[35] Of course, these stories were not being published merely as a service to society. The journalists who were feeding the early printing presses learned what all journalists have learned: that crime news is prime news. Shaaber has located 15 different publications reporting on the murder of Sir Thomas Overbury and the executions that followed.[36]

Overbury's poisoning—like most crimes—had little direct impact on the lives of the people who read about it; crimes rarely do. But as is the case with all the most newsworthy crimes, the events surrounding Overbury's murder were filled with human drama. Readers were intrigued by the presence of female suspects (Mrs. Turner and the countess). They could contemplate the undoing of a member of the upper reaches of society (Overbury) along with the eventual tumble of two even more exalted personages (the countess and Carr). They could enjoy glimpses of society at court. They could speculate on the degree of culpability of the various suspects. (The cases against two of the four persons who were hanged were questionable, and the fact that the countess and Carr escaped execution "gave many satirical wits occasion to vent themselves"—though not, of course, in print.[37]) And readers could gossip about the sexual behavior of the suspects. (The extramarital affair of the countess and Carr, and the supposedly wanton behavior of the widow, Mrs. Turner, both became public knowledge.) Behind it all, of course, was the usual tale of cruelty, of good and evil, with Overbury cast as the innocent, and his murderers exhibiting varying degrees of depravity.

Those who attempt to pinpoint the psychological attraction of crime stories often disagree about whether the reader is identifying with the innocence and pain of the victim or with the power, freedom and eventual fall of the criminal.[38] The authors of the newsbooks and news ballads on Overbury's murder seemed prepared to exploit either possibility. Some of their accounts were related in the supposed words of the suspects: *Mistres Turners Repentance, Who, about the poysoning of . . . Sir Thomas Overbury, Was executed the fourteenth day of November last;* some in the supposed words of the victim: *Sir Thomas Overbury, or the poysoned knights complaint.*

In one news ballad, *Sir Thomas Overbury's Vision: With the Ghoasts of Weston, Mistriss Turner, the late Lieftenant of the Tower, and Franklin,* the author arranges a meeting between the ghost of Overbury and the ghosts of those executed for his murder—a conceit that enables all their tales to be told in the first person. First, we have a chance to feel Overbury's suffering, as his ghost recounts his drawn-out poisoning:

> It was not one day's space, nor two, nor three,
> In which those cruel men tormented me:
> Month after month, they often did instill
> The divers natures of that baneful ill
> Throughout these limbs; inducing me to think,
> That what I took in physick, meat, or drink,
> Was to restore me to my health; when all
> Was but with ling'ring death to work my fall. . . .

At which point the four other ghosts are allowed to put their appeals for sympathy in rhyme. For example, Mrs. Turner takes us along on her "rise from great to greater" in the world of fashion and then her inevitable (according to the logic subscribed to by such news ballads) fall into lust and crime. The author of this ballad actually devotes more space to Turner's sins of vanity and lust than to her sin of murder. It is as if the murder was being used as an excuse to delve into this even more compelling subject: "I was given up to loose desire. . . . foul lust did make me fall."[39]

Reports on crime often stand out for the intimacy of the glimpses they provide of lives like that of Mrs. Turner. Much news is taken up with public behavior, but crime news allows journalists not only to consider the lives of individual people—as published gossip does—but to penetrate beyond their public performances, to discuss such matters as "loose desire" and "foul lust." Murderers and their victims surrender all rights to privacy.

Certainly, this is among the enticements crime has for journalists. In fact, the authors of printed ballads in 16th- and 17th-century England discovered, according to the historian Charles Firth, "that a recent domestic tragedy was of all topics the most attractive and the most moving."[40] Thomas Deloney was not insensitive to the interest inherent in such a tale. One of his news ballads tells the story, in the first person, of a woman hanged for murdering the wealthy older man her parents had arranged for her to marry:

> . . . My chosen eies could not his sight abide;
> My tender youth did lothe his aged side:
> Scant could I taste the meate whereon he fed;
> My legges did lothe to lodge within his bed. . . .[41]

The historian J. A. Sharpe has collected 13 such ballads or pamphlets reporting the murder of husbands in early modern England and 12 on the murder of wives. In detailing these domestic tragedies, the news becomes highly personal. A French immigrant kills her husband and dismembers his body after he gave her a venereal disease and forced her into "a compliance with him in Villanies contrary to nature." A woman aged "near threescore" stabs her husband, who was about 30, in part because "she was not a little tainted with the passion of jealousie." An innkeeper's wife gets to know "a Person of ill fame and very desolute liver . . . in a more familiar manner, than was convenient," and together they murder her husband.[42]

Sometimes the irritants, though not the consequences, appear rather ordinary. In a 1625 French newsbook, a woman is reported to have killed her husband because he spent too much time in the tavern,[43] and a 1607 English newsbook reports on the murder of a woman who was

> not unfurnished of that fault which is too common to many women, that is, shee was milde and gentle in all her speeches and gestures to her neighbors and strangers, but to her husband she was as other manner of woman, for all, or the mooste parte of her wordes to him were sharpe, bitter, and biting, especially when they were alone.

The last straw for her husband (and apparently for our misogynous writer) came one evening when he returned home drunk and she "thought it a fitte time to ease her minde by telling him sharpely of his great and grosse faultes, which were so much the greater and grosser, by how much he made an ordinary use and custom of them."[44]

It is in accounts of such murders, paradoxically, that the news seems most alive, most human. Obviously, these marriages, all of which ended in murder, do not provide a representative sample of family relations in early modern England, just as the licentious behavior of Mrs. Turner cannot be used as an example of standard behavior at the court of James I. However, the stories that develop around these aberrations do offer glimpses of the most emotional aspects of ordinary life, aspects that would not otherwise have been made public, that would not otherwise have demonstrated the requisite uniqueness and prominence to be considered news.

An unusually long and successful French newsbook printed in 1560[45] provides another example of the intimacy of crime news. The newsbook reports on the trial and eventual execution of Arnauld du Thil for the audacious crime of impersonating the long-missing Martin Guerre in front of Guerre's friends, family and even Guerre's wife, Bertrande:

> He was led by Bertrande to her house, and received and treated like her welcome husband. And lived for a space of four years with her so peaceably, and conducted himself so well in all affaires, that no one had any suspicion of evil. . . .[46]

The commission of a crime justifies fascinating violations of privacy. "Crimes lead to all sorts of other interesting stories," Bob Woodward of the *Washington Post* has said, and he used as an example a politically motivated burglary he covered more than 400 years after Arnauld du Thil's impersonation.[47] The Watergate break-in, among its other lessons, does indeed demonstrate how much we can learn about people when they are caught violating the law. Former attorney general John Mitchell and former White House aides H. R. Haldeman, John Ehrlichman, and John Dean were all more human as criminals than they were in their roles as government officials. We were allowed to peek behind the public facades they had constructed as we were invited to peer into the lives of a Mrs. Turner or a Bertrande Guerre. In fact, criminals and their victims, even given the heavy-handedness of most crime coverage, may be the most fully drawn characters in the news.

Sensationalism

Anyone who clings to the notion that today's sensationalism, as practiced by a super-market tabloid, cable news show or even the most shameless journalist, is unprecedented could be set straight by viewing any of a number of 16th- or 17th-century newsbooks. *The crying Murther: Contayning the cruell and most horrible Butcher of Mr. Trat,* printed in 1624, would certainly do.

The victim was probably Mr. Trat, the curate of a Somerset church; however, it was not possible to firmly establish the victim's identity. Three men and a woman were convicted of the crime, which—according to what the author of this pamphlet calls "intelligence which I have received from credible persons, engaged in their trial"—went beyond murder:

> . . . these butchers, with their hands already smoking in his blood, did cut up his carcass, unbowel and quarter it; then did they burn his head and privy members, parboil his flesh and salt it up, that so the sudden stink and putrefaction being hindered, the murderers might the longer be free from [discovery].

The body of Mr. Trat, or whomever it was, was found

> all saving the head and members, disposed in this manner and form following. His arms, legs, thighs, and bowels were powdered up into two earthen steens or pots in a lower room of the house . . . , the bulk of his carcass was placed in a vat or tub. . . .

Et cetera. The murderers eventually "died [on the gallows] obstinate and unrepenting sinners"[48] (limiting the poetic uses that might have been made of their ghosts).

Here we have reached what many would consider to be the absolute nadir of journalistic endeavor: sensationalism, yellow journalism, tabloid journalism. Some would not even glorify it with the appellation "journalism." To be called "the greatest tabloid journalist of all time" is "tantamount of calling a man . . . the greatest salesman of sticky sweets in the history of dentistry," the British writer Clive James has remarked.[49]

Those who are doing the abhorring here, however, are often somewhat fuzzy on exactly what they hold in abhorrence. Is the problem the sensational *subjects* of these accounts? There is no doubt that every once in a while someone, somewhere, gets dismembered. Are writers and printers earning their contempt by being so lowminded as to trouble us with such ugly and unimportant occurrences, when they could be outlining a parliamentary debate? Or is the problem the *treatment* of such subjects? Perhaps we should be told that someone who probably was Mr. Trat has been dismembered but should be spared the exact disposition of the pieces of his corpse.[50]

If the complaint is based on an inappropriate choice of subject matter, the irritants usually turn out to be references to violence or sex. One 1598 English publication had, in an awful sense, both. The newsbook was entitled *The Examination, confessions and condemnation of Henry Robson, fisherman of Rye, who poysoned his wife in the strangest manner that ever hitherto hath bin heard of.* The strange and terrible manner of poisoning employed by Robson involved filling his slumbering wife's genitals with a mixture of ratsbane and ground glass.[51]

Sensationalism was common in 16th- and 17th-century news ballads and newsbooks. This is the cover of a newsbook, printed in London in 1624, reporting on a gruesome murder.

Over the centuries many serious journalists and a few blue-nosed censors have struggled to excise bloody and obscene stories like this from the news. If their efforts seem to come to naught, the problem may be that the news is exchanged in part because it provides the stimulation of the occasional sensation and that nothing seems to do that job quite so effectively as reports of depraved or titillating behavior. In spreading news of Columbus' voyage, "the one touch of nature that made all newsmongers kin," writes Samuel Eliot Morison, "was the naked natives, especially the women who wore nothing but a leaf."[52]

Perhaps news of violence and sex owes its attraction to its intensity, to its connection with matters of death and life. Perhaps this interest can be traced to an instinctual need to remain alert to the whereabouts of potential threats and potential mates. Whatever the explanation, most of us—with our roving eyes and rubber necks—have found these topics hard to ignore. Is it surprising, therefore, that journalists have found them so hard to ignore?

Early forms of printed news certainly did not deprive readers of an opportunity to gape at life's outsized outrages, and sensational journalists today might have envied the stories available to 16th- and 17th-century journalists. Consider, for example, "the cruel devil" Cristeman who, according to a French newsbook in 1582, was executed in Germany for having "killed and assassinated 964 people."[53]

Those who object not to the subjects being reported but to the treatment they are accorded often complain of the sensationalist's eagerness to exploit those occurrences, to squeeze every last drop of melodrama from some unfortunate circumstance. That would seem to characterize the approach taken by the news ballad *Murder upon Murder,* which tells the story of a woman and a man who were hanged in 1635 for having committed three murders together. It is not sufficient in these verses that the female half of this team be described as a "quean" (a prostitute); she must be denounced as a "filthy whore." Her partner, on the other hand, is presented as "a man of honest parentage." What went wrong? "She sotted . . . his minde." Together they live a "vile loose life," "their hearts . . . bent to cruelty." And to put things in even starker relief, one of their victims is introduced as a "goodman," another as "a gentleman of good descent/And well beloved truly."[54]

All journalists are in the business of exclaiming, "Aha!" Sensationalists add a few exclamation points.

Critics of the sensational treatment of news also take offense at the exuberance with which sex and violence (those two subjects again) are described. To our hardened eyes the sexual references in early forms of printed news appear rather tame. There was frequent condemnation in the sixteenth and seventeenth centuries of "filthy" or "undecent" ballads, but this seemed aimed more at ribald fictional tales—*Ballad of a Young Man that went a-Wooing,* for example—than at news ballads.[55] One of the more explicit newsbooks notes only that, before murdering his children, a former fishmonger had taken into his house "a Wench, whose name was Jane Blundell, who in a short time was better acquainted with her Master's bed than honesty required."[56] (In 18th-century France, underground pamphlets, or *libelles,* would go much further. One opens with a description of Queen Marie Antoinette masturbating and proceeds to accuse King Louis XVI of impotence.)[57]

Excessive concentration on blood and gore is easier to spot in the 16th and early 17th centuries. In *Murder upon Murder* we are presented with this summary of the mental state of the two perpetrators, with two murders done and one to go: "For being flushed with human blood,/They thirsteth still for more."[58]

J. P. Seguin writes that systematic research into "les 'horribles détails'" was characteristic of newsbooks on *faits divers* in France. Even the titles of many French newsbooks, like tabloid headlines, seem designed to shock: *Marvelous and frightful discourse . . . , Horrible and frightening cruelty . . . , Terrible, pitiable and frightening accident. . . .*[59] And note the title of this English newsbook about two women who were executed in 1637 for murdering their stepchildren: *Natures Cruell StepDames: or, Matchlesse Monsters of the Female Sex. . . .*[60]

All journalists are comrades in the battle against dullness; they are straining not to bore the sultan. But where the most respectable and skilled journalists might season the news they gather with some delicately applied cerebration or wit, sensationalists pour

Sensationalism: A Product of "Powerful Interests"?

Many media corporations today exploit the public's interest in sensationalism. They broadcast television talk shows that seem designed mostly to titillate: Truck-stop prostitutes were featured on one of these programs. Media corporations sell newspapers, magazines and on-line news services that include accounts of lurid crimes. When a major British actor was caught patronizing a prostitute, it was difficult to find any newspaper or newscast in Britain or the United States that did not find some way to refer to the story.

Large media corporations, no doubt, are making money off such sensationalism, but should they be blamed for the prevalence of sensationalism? Media theorist Mark Crispin Miller believes they should. "The violent, grotesque, superstitious stuff that fills certain dailies, the supermarket weeklies and—lately—much syndicated television does not come bubbling up from among the masses . . . ," he writes, "but is carefully devised and sold by powerful interests."

This is an attractive argument. We would like to have someone to blame, and who better than what Miller calls the "media monopolies." If the news they put out looks tawdry, these corporations are certainly not blameless. They could pander less. But the problem with Miller's argument is that this indulgence in sensationalism predates

"media monopolies"; it predates the late 20th century's collection of "powerful interests."

The *New York Post*—owned by one of the world's largest media companies, Rupert Murdoch's News Corporation—once ran a huge front-page headline that screamed: "LET ME DIE!" But a similar headline, amplified, could be found in crusading publisher Joseph Pulitzer's *New York World* more than a 100 years earlier: "LET ME DIE! LET ME DIE!" In fact, an emphasis on crime news was characteristic of the "penny papers" that sprang up in the United States in the 1830s—most of which began as products of one enterprising journalist, not large corporations. The first newspaper printed in America, *Publick Occurrences* in 1690, includes the tale of a man who wanted to die: a "Water-town" man who hanged himself in the "Cow-house" (see Chapters 11 and 12).

As this chapter demonstrates, similarly sensational tales were common in the earliest printed news publications. They can be found in the Roman *acta;* they were spread with enthusiasm by preliterate societies. It is difficult, therefore, to resist the conclusion—however unpleasant and unfashionable—that the bulk of the blame for the amount of sensationalism that continues to appear in the news rests not with media corporations, no matter how greedy, but with our natures.

on the catsup—not an insignificant difference in preparation for readers interested in the flavor of events.

Moreover, sensationalists, their critics complain, seem almost to delight in the depravity they have uncovered and seem unwilling to look beyond it. Notice, for example, what the ballad *Murder upon Murder* discovers when, in something of a preamble, it takes the temperature of the times:

There scarce a moneth within the yeare,
No murders vile are done,
The Son, the Father murdereth,
The Father kills the Son,
Twixt man and man there's such debate,
Which in the end brings mortall hate,
O murder, lust and murder,
Is the foule sinke of sin.

The mother loseth her owne life,
Because she her child doth kill,
And some men in their drunkenness,
Their deare friends blood doth spill,
And many more, through greedy gaine,
The brother hath the brother slaine.
O murder, lust and murder,
Is the foule sinke of sin.[61]

Might this harsh view of the world have been more justified in the 17th century? Might these publications—"mere shreds and tatters of sensation," one scholar labeled them[62]—have been accurately reflecting some truly debased times?

Early modern Europe clearly did have its share of murder, lust, and sin. However, if one murder per month is seen as creating a "foule sinke of sin," major cities in the United States today, by comparison, must be awash in mammoth cesspools of sin.

Attempts to evaluate such matters as the crime rate hundreds of years ago, let alone its causes and public attitudes toward it, are notoriously difficult.[63] A case can be made that Europe in the Elizabethan age was experiencing unusual social strains and a concomitant increase in antisocial behavior.[64] However, that case can be made for many eras—social strains, crime and violence have rarely been in short supply.[65]

Certainly, there was no cataclysmic crumbling of the social order that might explain the appearance of these sensational newsbooks and news ballads in the second half of the 16th century. The cataclysm that created them was the arrival of the printing press, with its ability to spread accounts of more or less typical outbreaks of murder, lust and sin to an audience whose size was unprecedented but whose appetite for sensation was, more or less, normal.

Moralizing

The Bloudy booke, or the Tragicall and desperate end of Sir John Fites (alias) Fitz—a no-holds-barred account, printed in 1605, of the atrocities committed by one Sir John Fites—has spared us none of the savagery, none of the perverse sexuality and none of the blood advertised in its title:

> The good wife of the house (alas poore soule) hearing the pitteous outcrie and grievous grone that her dyeing husband made, suddenly all amazed, leapes out of her bed in her smocke . . . [and] meetes Sir John with his naked rapier in his

hand, al on gore with the bloud of her husband, wherefore in hope of pitty, from his pittilesse hands, she fell down uppon her knees in her smock, and with hands erected, prayed, sweet sir, spare my life, and shew mercie; but hee, as eager and thirstie of bloud, without all compassion, twice thrust at her naked [?] body, twice he missed her, but stil reenforcing his stroke, thrust again the third time, and then wounded her greevousle in the arme (yet not mortally). . . .

So how does the author of this newsbook conclude his tale of near-pornographic violence?

Many and divers things are in this precedent lamentable discourse worthie most deepe consideration, and may serve (the true use of all such stories) to put us in mind of our duties toward God . . . the Prince, and country, and ourselves. . . .[66]

"Most deepe consideration"? "God . . . the Prince, and country"? In *The Bloudy booke?*

What we have here is the hardly uncommon but still disconcerting spectacle of the "gutter" journalist who reverses his collar, pulls a black coat on over his blood-stained shirt, grabs a mud-splattered Bible, clears his hoarse throat, and begins to harangue us with calls to avoid the path of sin. "Sitting in a bawdyhouse, he writes God's judgments," John Earle, a clergyman and essayist, quipped in 1628.[67]

Sensationalism, in fact, seemed incapable of appearing in these newsbooks and news ballads without a stern moral message as an escort. Take, for example, the story of the woman in Naples who found a lover, killed her husband, poisoned her father for refusing to let her marry her lover and then killed her sister and her two small nephews when they became nuisances. The 1577 French newsbook that presents this sordid tale concludes with advice to the young. And who of all people is dispensing the advice? The murderess, who has confessed all, herself: ". . . they should always have the fear of God in front of their eyes, render obedience to their parents & friends: & . . . they should often remind themselves of this pitiful spectacle."[68]

The moralizing often was left to the perpetrator, and it usually arrived in the form of a scaffold confession—"an essential, almost obligatory, element of pamphlets about crime in all eras and in all countries," writes J. P. Seguin.[69] One of the earliest of the "last dying speeches" to be recorded in an English publication, in 1576, began with a line that would set the tone for all that followed: "I waile in wo, I plunge in pain."[70]

Given the religious climate at the time, many 16th and 17th-century villains undoubtedly did confess their crimes—if not in verse, at least with fervor—upon beholding the noose. Here is a selection from the account reportedly provided by one such criminal, poor Anne Wallens, before she was burnt to death in 1616:

My dearest husband did I wound to death,
And was the cause he lost his sweetest breath.
. . . What hast thou don, I prethee looke quoth he,
Thou hast thy wish; for thou hast killed me.

And Wallens, according to this ballad, also managed, dutifully, to underline the moral of the story for readers: "Wives be warnd, example take by me."[71]

The dying criminal as confessional poet—this conceit had a number of advantages for a printer of sensational news: First, it invested the dastardly acts the publication recounted with the immediacy of the first person. Second, it evaded the risk that the story's protagonist might contradict or challenge the printed account by choosing a protagonist who was, conveniently, dead. And third, it provided a handy formula for the protestations of remorse and repentance, and warnings to the young, that were the responsibility of a publication on crime in those days.

The *Lamentation* of Luke Hutton, a highwayman executed at York in 1595, is a classic of the genre because of the way it alternates accounts of his dashing crimes with abject moralizing:

. . . There was no squire nor barron bold
ah woe is me, woe is me, for my great folly:
That rode the way with silver or gold,
be warned, young wantons, hemp passeth green holly
But I and my twelve Apostles gaie,
Would lighten their load ere they went away. . . .[72]

The authors of these publications must have had an additional reason for speaking, or making sure their characters spoke, from the righteous side of their mouths. The spiritual and temporal powers that were would certainly have been discomfited if the brazen outlaws in these stories had not eventually been converted into shamed penitents. Readers can enjoy vicariously the thrill of transgression for only so long before authority must reassert itself, before boundaries must triumph. Societies appear to demand that swift and excessive moralizing attend any dramatic account of affronts to their rules.

This jejune moralizing may also have satisfied a psychological need. The full horror of the behavior of someone like Sir John Fites is almost too terrible to confront straight on. We require some form of mediation, something to help us tame this horror and force it into an understandable view of life. The enunciation of the appropriate exhortations and admonitions serves to invoke the gods of normality and conformity, under whose aegis deviance retreats into a familiar moral context. Psychic order is restored. (Our hunger for meaning may be no less intense in the 21st century, but the meaning of choice increasingly is psychological rather than moral.)

Daniel Defoe was to satirize writers' slavish efforts to satisfy this need in his preface to *Moll Flanders*, written in 1722:

. . . there is not a wicked action in any part of it, but is first and last rendered unhappy and unfortunate; there is not a superlative villain brought upon the stage, but either he is brought to an unhappy end, or brought to be a penitent; there is not an ill thing mentioned but it is condemned, even in the relation. . . .[73]

What about the advice that so frequently accompanied moral messages? How, for example, might readers have responded to the tips for improving a marriage offered in a pamphlet entitled *Two horrible and inhumane Murders done in Lincolnshire, by two Husbands upon their Wives: the one strangled his wife in her sicknesse. . . . The other having killed his Wife, made a great fire, and burnt her?*

. . . husbands shall do well to have a special care, that they give not any just cause of offence to their honest wives. . . . And for wives, they shall doe as well, if in modest and milde manner, they observe the humours of their husbandes . . . not reproving them boldly or bitterly . . . lest they drive them to unmanly cruelty. . . .[74]

Sensationalists imparted like advice with such frequency that we can assume readers desired it. Humans seem, in fact, to have a weakness for worst-case examples. We ask that murdered wives and murdering husbands teach us about marriage; that homicidal knights expound on God's laws; or, to switch to a late 20th-century example, that a middle-aged headmistress who shoots her two-timing lover, a renowned Scarsdale doctor, teach us about the lot of the unmarried woman.[75] Their comments, to be sure, do have the virtue of being underlined in blood.

Many individuals in the 16th and 17th centuries were just as eager to search for meaning in the birth of a deformed child, the behavior of some witches or the appearance of a comet. Our minds, dulled to the invariant but ever alert to the unexpected, tend to make rules out of these exceptions. And journalists, who earn a living retailing such anomalies, are glad to encourage this tendency.

The Supernatural

The author of a newsbook printed in 1614 felt called upon to begin with a special note "To the Reader":

> The just rewarde of him that is accustomed to lie, is, not to be believed when he speaketh the truth. So just an occasion may sometime bee imposed upon the pamphleting pressers; and therefore, if we receive the same rewarde, we cannot much blame our accusers. . . . But, passing by what's past, let not our present truth blush for any former falshood-sake. . . .[76]

Despite the added reliability imparted by the printing press, journalists in the early 17th century clearly had something of a credibility problem. That was not unusual; the news has always had a complicated relationship with the truth.

To be considered news, information must be presented as factual, but history is full of examples of that appearance proving deceiving. In the United States in the 20th century, for example, United Press reported news of the end of World War I four days before the actual surrender,[77] the *New York Times* reported one Bolshevik defeat after another in Russia in 1919, only to have to concede, eventually, that those reported defeats had added up to a Bolshevik victory;[78] and the *Washington Post* in 1980 caused police to search frantically for an eight-year-old heroin addict who turned out to have been the product of a reporter's imagination.[79] A series of other examples of reporters fabricating news shook American newsrooms, including that of the *New York Times,* in the early years of the 21st century.

Anyone who follows the news today has seen the occasional quotation mangled, misused or possibly manufactured; the occasional occurrence distorted or possibly invented; and more than a few meanings blurred. "Truth," as one 17th-century journalist noted, "is the daughter of time."[80] And time is one luxury those who deal in news have never possessed. Sometimes in the heat of the moment, the truth falls victim to sloppiness, gullibility, ignorance or convenience; sometimes it is sacrificed to partisanship; sometimes the culprit is simple mendacity. In the late 19th century, when Charles Dana, editor of the *Sun* in New York, proclaimed, "I have never published a falsehood," his rival, Joseph Pulitzer of the *World,* responded, "That's another lie."[81]

One of the causes of the credibility problem 16th and 17th-century newswriters experienced is easy to trace. Their desire to, as one 20th-century code of ethics would put it, "inform the public of events of importance and appropriate interest in a manner that is accurate and comprehensive"[82] appears upon occasion to have been outweighed by more practical concerns.

J. P. Seguin has found proof that French printers, caught short of spectacular occurrences, were wont to reprint versions of earlier spectacular occurrences—with the dates freshened. Consider, for example, a newsbook published in Paris in 1623 reporting on the "pitiable" execution of a 17- or 18-year-old girl, Marguerite de la Rivière, in Metz in November 1623. The story may have appeared credible, but there was cause for suspicion in the fact that the exact same story had been printed six years earlier. In that version, however, the girl's execution took place in Padua in December 1616. Indeed, the identical tale had also been printed in 1607, though the girl's name was then given as Catherine de la Critonnière, her age as 15 or 16, and her "pitiable" execution dated September 1607. The first version of this story that has survived actually was printed in 1597—with Marguerite de la Rivière, 17 or 18, restored as victim, and her execution placed in Padua in December 1596.[83]

Readers with long memories or extensive libraries might have had good cause to begin to doubt that "pamphleting pressers" "speaketh the truth." And what might readers have made of some of the more unlikely occurrences reported in these newsbooks and news ballads, such as the discovery of a "marveilous straunge fishe" in 1569 or of the "hainous and horrible actes committed by . . . Fower notorious Witches" executed in 1579?[84]

The author of that 1614 newsbook, so committed to the unblushing portrayal of the truth, identified himself as "A. R./He that would send better newes, if he had it." The news he was compelled to report was indeed bad. It concerned "a strange and monstrous Serpent (or Dragon)," found living in a forest in Sussex, only "thirtie Miles from London":

> This serpent (or dragon, as some call it) is reputed to be nine feete, or rather more, in length, and shaped almost in the forme of an axeltree of a cart; a quantitie of thickness in the middest, and somewhat smaller at both endes. . . . It is likewise discovered to have large feete, but the eye may be there deceived. . . . There are likewise on either side of him discovered, two great bunches so big as a large foote-ball, and (as some thinke) will in time grow to wings: But God, I hope, will (to defend the poor people in the neighbourhood) that he shall be destroyed before he grow so fledge.

The serpent "cast his venome about four rodde from him," killing anyone who breathed it in. Its victims to this point, A. R. reports, included a man, a woman, two mastiff dogs, and some cattle.[85]

Now, to be fair, some of the news discussed in these pamphlets and broadsides was not as unlikely as it appears to 20th-century eyes. The monsters and witches, for example, were often real. "Monster" was a name for a seriously deformed animal or person. A broadside titled *The true reporte of the forme and shape of a monstrous Childe borne at Muche Horkesley* . . . , for example, described a baby born in 1562 with "neyther hande, foote, legge nor arme, but on the left syde it hath a stumpe growynge out of the shoulder."[86] We may squirm at the use of the term "monstrous" to describe so unfortunate an infant, but there is no reason to doubt the veracity of this report on his birth. Similarly, that "marveilous straunge fishe" found in 1569 may have seemed odd, but it was not fanciful; the fish appears to have been a shark.[87]

And a witch can be defined simply as a woman who worships the devil. There certainly were devil worshipers in 16th- and 17th-century Europe. ("For an Elizabethan, not believing in witches would have been like not believing in Puritans," write Joseph Marshburn and Alan Velie in their collection of Renaissance publications on crime and sin.)[88] A 168-page pamphlet printed in 1613 includes detailed testimony from the trial of some witches discovered in Lancashire. The defendants confessed to devil worship. We even learn one of their charms:

Three Bitters has thou bitten
The Hart, ill Eye, ill Tonge:
Three bitter shall be thy boote,
Father, Sonne, and Holy Ghoste . . .[89]

But what about the powers such witches were said to wield? This is from a pamphlet on the trial of three witches printed in 1589:

. . . she saith and affirmeth, that at what time so ever she would have her ferret do anything for her, she used these words, "Bidd, Bidd, Bidd, come Bidd, come Bidd, come Bidd, come Bidd, come suck, come suck, come suck," and that presently he would appear as if aforesaid: and suck blood out of her left cheek, and then performed any mischief she willed or wished him to do for her unto or against any of her neighbors.[90]

Unless Elizabethan ferrets were considerably more accomplished than those of our era, this would seem an excursion into the supernatural.

And what are we to make of a German broadside reporting the discovery of a monster in Catalonia in 1654 with "goat's legs, a human body, seven arms, and seven heads"?[91] Or of a 1635 newsbook printed in Paris discussing the three suns that had appeared over Marseille?[92] What are we to make of the demon reported by a French newsbook in 1620 to have been spotted in the middle of a fire in a church?[93] Or of the time, according to an English publication, "it rained Wheat" in Suffolk and Essex?[94] Or of Eve Fliegen of Holland who, according to more than one English newsbook in 1611, lived for 14 years without eating or drinking, simply by inhaling the perfume of roses?[95] And just how seriously are we to take A. R.'s report on that serpent (or dragon) living in Sussex?

Again, we must be careful. There is a danger in judging the credibility achieved by these reports by modern standards of credulity. As the 20th-century historian Lucien Febvre has written, "revolutions must have taken place" in mentalities in the years since these publications were written.[96] In the 16th and 17th centuries, dragons and spellbound ferrets were alive in the minds of many of those who read or heard these newsbooks and news ballads. "Pre-industrial man lived in a world of magic, wonders and marvels," explains Victor Neuburg in his book on the history of popular literature.[97]

The forces these people saw as animating their world were different from those we acknowledge, and reports of a marvel or a wonder were pounced on as signs of those forces, just as a scientific discovery might impress us today as a clue in our own schemes of causality. Sometimes the phenomena in which their forces manifested themselves were the same as those in which we find meaning—a comet, for example. (The comet of 1577 was discussed in at least 111 European books or pamphlets.)[98] But at times these people found meaning in phenomena we tend to ignore. The birth of a monstrous pig with "a head much like to a dolphin's head" near Charing Cross in 1562, for instance, was treated not just as a sensation but as a lesson:

> What might these monsters to us teache
>   Which now are sent so rife,
> But that we have Goddes word well preacht
>   And will not mend our life?[99]

It is a mistake to underestimate the sway of such logic; one French newsbook, written in 1618, dismisses attempts to find natural explanations for such wonders as evidence of "ignorance and weakness."[100]

Sometimes the message in a sign or prodigy was particularly easy to read, as was the case with the "strang monster borne of Late in Germany" to a "proude marchant's wife" who had devoted her life to vanity and fashion. The birth was recounted, and the infant described, first in a newsbook in 1608, then again in this ballad, called *Pride's fall: or a warning to all English women. . . .* , printed in 1609:

> . . . From the head unto the foote
>   monster-like was it borne.
> Every part had the shape
>   of fashions daylye worne. . . .[101]

Many of these more miraculous news stories may in fact have been invented in cynical attempts to exploit readers' superstitions and fantasies. That was the theory propounded by the author of a satire on the "Ballad-Monger" published in 1631:

> Hee ha's a singular gift of imagination, for hee can descant on a mans execution long before his confession. Nor comes his invention farre short of his imagination; for want of truer relations, for a neede he can finde you out a Sussex dragon [or] some sea or inland monster. . . .[102]

But at least a few of these reports on supernatural subjects do actually seem to have been based on what might, even in our day, pass for sound reporting.

Journalists today, often forced to read unfamiliar situations under intense time pressures, content themselves with reporting what sound like believable statements about those situations made by what appear to be believable people—a level of proof lodging somewhere between mere speculation and independently verifiable evidence. Many 16th and 17th-century newswriters professed a similar fidelity to attributable facts. A report on the behavior and trial of Sir Walter Raleigh printed in 1618, for example, proclaims that

Elvis Sightings

The most discussed supposed supernatural occurrence in the United States in the 1980s and 1990s was not a dragon, monster, or even an unidentified flying object, but the intermittent return to the corporeal world of a deceased rock music giant: Elvis Presley.

Claims of Elvis sightings quickly began to lag behind jokes about Elvis sightings. Still, the supernatural has hardly been excluded from American media. Many newspapers publish daily astrology forecasts (as has the toney magazine *Vanity Fair*), and self-proclaimed psychics are interviewed on cable talk shows.

it is "not founded upon conjectures or likelyhood, but either upon confession of the party himselfe, or upon the examination of divers unsuspected witnesses. . . ."[103]

Testaments to this respect for the importance of attribution can be found in some French newsbooks on miraculous occurrences. These publications might emphasize that they include "attestations" of their veracity, perhaps based on the "assured written testimony" of "persons deserving of credit." Sometimes such publications do seem to be protesting too much. These particular quotations are taken from two reports, printed in 1609 and 1617, on recent sightings of a "wandering Jew" who, according to one of the pamphlets, had witnessed the crucifixion of Christ.[104] But sometimes such efforts at attribution seem to indicate that the journalists had in fact talked to people who believed they had, or at least said they had, witnessed these supernatural events.

A. R. not only qualified his account of that Sussex dragon with forms of attribution familiar to modern journalists—"as some call it," "is reputed to be," "as some thinke"— but concludes with a statement that includes the names of some of his sources:

> These persons, whose names are hereunder printed, have scene this serpent, besides divers others, as the carrier of Horsam, who lieth at the White Horse in Southwarke, and who can certifie the truth of all that has been here related.
> John Steele
> Christopher Holder
> And a Widow Woman dwelling nere Faygate[105]

Would it be difficult or necessarily unreasonable today to find a few responsible-looking people who say they have seen the Loch Ness monster and to build a newspaper story or television report around their testimony?

The difference between the reports mainstream journalists produce today and A. R.'s story is more one of mind-set than of journalistic technique. We have grown more skeptical. Dragons have been chased from Sussex, "thirtie Miles from London," to the bottom of a dark lake in Scotland by the spread of what Febvre[106] calls the "awareness of the impossible."* Not that the 16th and 17th centuries were devoid of readers skeptical enough to doubt some of these wonders: despite all A. R.'s efforts, his report on that Sussex serpent was widely disbelieved.[107]

In *The Winter's Tale,* Shakespeare satirizes the gullibility of some of his contemporaries. He has a ballad maker attempt to sell to a shepherdess verses composed by "a fish, that appeared upon the coast, on Wednesday the fourscore of April, forty thousand fathom above water, and sung this ballad against the hard hearts of maids: it was thought she was a woman, and was turned into a cold fish, for she would not exchange flesh with one that loved her. . . ."

The shepherdess's response: "Is it true too, think you?"[108]

"Popular" Journalism

What audience was attracted to this news of bloody murders, monsters, witches and dragons? We have very little data on the size of the circulation of 16th- and 17th-century newsbooks and ballads, let alone about the demographics of that circulation. Can we say anything about the readership of the more sensational of these publications?

"Attempts to draw a line between the classes who take their news in earnest and those who instinctively prefer the sensational are both difficult and invidious," writes Matthias Shaaber, "but it is impossible to overlook the fact that such a difference in taste does exist."[109] Most of us would probably agree, however reluctantly, that there is an inverse relationship between level of education—and therefore to some extent social class—and susceptibility to the more emotive and fanciful forms of journalism. Most of us, in other words, probably are not surprised that Shakespeare chose a shepherdess as the gullible potential customer for a wildly unbelievable news ballad.

Among the most sensational publications printed in English today are weekly tabloids such as the *National Enquirer,* the best-selling newspaper, if it can be called a newspaper, in the United States (EXPERT CLAIMS CABBAGE PATCH DOLLS CAN BE POSSESSED BY THE DEVIL),[110] or daily tabloids such as Rupert Murdoch's *Sun,* the best-selling daily in Britain (I WANT YOU IN MY SEX SANDWICH! . . . . THREE IN A BED AT HOUSE OF TERROR or 16 NUDE WITCHES SEIZED).[111] Given the lack of advertisements for Tiffany & Co. and the presence of ads for loans to "Pay off all your debts—now!" it does seem safe to assume that the *Enquirer,* the *Sun,* and their American and British cousins attract an audience drawn from the poorer sections of the population. Why?

One obvious explanation is that the news these papers carry is more accessible.[112] The arguments in a parliamentary debate presumably require a greater degree of sophistication to decipher than do melodramatic accounts of houses of terror and nude witches. A preference for more sensational news can also be explained in political terms: The poorer classes own less of the nation and therefore have an excuse for choosing more entertaining fare over detailed reports on the nation's political and economic situation.[113]

---

* Of course, both the arrival of the printing press and the development of journalism have played a role, sometimes consciously, in this process of "exorcising consciousness" (see Chapter 13).

The wealthy and the cultured, for their part, are often anxious to display refined tastes—which usually implies paying more attention to reports on politics, economics and art, and less to nude witches—especially if by so doing they can further distinguish themselves from the masses.[114]

In the 15th and 16th centuries, the printing press began eroding one such distinction between the classes: In helping transfer responsibility for disseminating knowledge from scribes in the monasteries to printers in the cities, it furthered the shift in written communication from a language available only to the elite (Latin) to more common tongues (the vernaculars). But as the 16th century progressed, the press began creating the bases for new class distinctions: The plethora of books it churned out, while helping enlighten many of the previously unenlightened, also expanded exponentially the information available for the learned to learn and the ignorant to remain ignorant about. And the pool of printed works produced by the press was growing deep enough to accept stratification.[115]

By the second half of the 17th century, the upper classes were disdaining the old romances and heroic tales some of their servants read in favor of presumably more demanding reading matter.[116] And although the first news publications apparently were novel enough to intrigue the "educated and uneducated alike,"[117] the sophisticated soon began to proclaim their superiority to the more sensational newsbooks and news ballads, too.[118]

The more literate members of late 16th- and early 17th-century society, like so many guardians of high culture in other eras who have been forced to confront the taste of the masses, established distinctions between these popular early forms of printed news and more serious works: "The slightest pamphlet is nowadays more vendable than the works of learnedest men," complained one writer in 17th-century England.[119] They teased and disparaged the "drunken sockets and bawdye parasits" who sang the news ballads, as well as those who wrote them—Ben Jonson explained that "a poet should detest a Balletmaker."[120] They mocked the composition of their audience by noting that such ballads soon grow so familiar that "every poore milkmade can chant and chirpe it under her cow. . . ."[121] Even the melodies to which the ballads were to be sung came in for abuse: "a scurvy tune," one was called.[122]

Among the terms one civilized early 17th-century chronicler in France, Pierre de l'Estoile, used to describe the publications on *faits divers* that came his way were: "trifles, pieces of nonsense, fables, frivolities, drolleries, charlatanries and pranks."[123] (Such newsbooks were often referred to as *canards*.) A line was being drawn, and, from the point of view of the educated elite, the more sensational pamphlets and broadsides belonged on the other side. However, the distinctions drawn by serious-minded critics of journalism in any age are rarely as clear as they would have us believe.

Certainly the inanities and outrages of "popular" journalism take their toll on the content of public discourse as well as on its tone. When journalists confine themselves to the search for the violent or the miraculous, not only do they paint a grotesque face on the world, but they deprive their audiences of the opportunity to examine subtler occurrences with larger consequences. Nonetheless, as has been argued elsewhere in this chapter, without gossip, without crime—without the humanizing and stimulating touch of occasional inanities and outrages—the news would lose much of its vitality.

In succeeding centuries, publications that catered specifically to the wealthier and more cultured would seek to elevate the tone and the content of the news. As a rule, they did provide less gore and more politics, more news of economics and science. Still, in their way, most "serious" news organs have also recognized the importance of the sensational. The *New York Times* too will indulge in a murder story, particularly if the victim is someone with whom its readers can identify—a musician with the Metropolitan Opera, a Radcliffe graduate, a Scarsdale doctor, a member of the upper-middle class.[124] In the *Times* the descriptions are less graphic, the melodramatics less obvious, the cries of woe more muted, but the same human emotions and concerns are reflected in such stories in the *Times* as were reflected in news ballads on the poisoning of Thomas Overbury.

The more sophisticated forms of news may be unavailable to the less educated—due either to lack of preparation or lack of interest—but the upper classes and the cultured have not achieved full immunity to the attractions of the human interest story.[125] Cicero made a point in 51 B.C. of his distaste for "tittle-tattle," but his friend and correspondent Caelius knew better than to take him too seriously: "absolutely nothing new has occurred, unless you want such tittle-tattle as what follows— and I am sure you do— to be put in a letter to you." What follows in Caelius' letter is a collection of gossip on marriage, divorce and adultery among prominent Romans.[126] The Fugger newsletters—aimed at an audience of a few wealthy financiers—were not above catering to a taste for the sensational. Even a newssheet prepared expressly for the czar in Russia in the 17th century found room for "*curiosa*—the strange and unusual."[127]

Attempts to draw neat lines between "popular" and "serious" journalism are frustrated in the end by the nature of news itself. News is a coarse, unrefined substance, made up of events selected for their strangeness as much as their significance, their emotional appeal as much as their import. Even on the economics beat—in stories of takeovers or layoffs—the news can seem brutal. Even on the science beat—where equations can lead to bombs and humans function with mechanical hearts—the news can shock.

Scrubbed, shorn and shaved so that it can move in polite society, the news is enfeebled. In his autobiography, Lincoln Steffens recalls covering the Wall Street panic of 1893 for a newspaper—New York's *Evening Post*—that "avoided crime, scandal and the sensational generally." The fact that Steffens had seen a financier weep had, of course, to be left out of the story he wrote for the paper—it was too sensational. Serious news is about stock prices, not about people crying. But a more honest form of news judgment was applied during that economic panic not only in the unabashedly sensationalistic newspapers but in the *Evening Post*'s newsroom itself—where "the human side of Wall Street," which these journalists found it necessary to expunge from their stories, filled their conversations.[128]

Even the most high-minded cannot completely repress an interest in the more extraordinary activities of their more extraordinary contemporaries; even they will find time for some accounts of violations of society's rules, for some odd occurrences or strange tales. It would take a truly noble mind indeed to deny any interest in the fact that the financier had wept.

There is evidence that cultured individuals in the 16th and 17th centuries paid more attention to newsbooks and news ballads than their attacks on them would lead us believe. Playwrights such as Christopher Marlowe (and possibly Shakespeare) borrowed some of their plots and subplots from these publications.[129] In their letters, foreign ambassadors reveal that they kept up with printed news and reported on it to their governments.[130] Chroniclers recopied news ballads: "I hate these following railing rimes," one wrote, "Yet keepe them for president of the times."[131] And even the more outspoken critics of these publications—Pierre de l'Estoile, for instance—can be accused of demonstrating more familiarity with them than might be justified by mere sociological research.

In fact, these pamphlets and broadsides were exceedingly hard to ignore. Newsbook covers were tacked up on posts throughout the cities to interest potential buyers; news ballads could be heard in the streets; and it was common for inns, taverns and even some private homes to be wallpapered with broadsides. At the age of nine, John Aubrey, the son of a country gentleman, saw an old printed report on Sir Philip Sidney's funeral pasted over the fireplace in an alderman's parlor.[132]

If the upper classes and the educated of the 16th and 17th centuries did not purchase many of the pamphlets and broadsides on *faits divers* discussed in this chapter, they must at least, like a *New York Times* reader sitting next to a *New York Post* reader on the bus, have stolen some interested peeks.

Questions

1. What news media today display a "boldness" similar to that attributed in this chapter to early forms of printed news?

2. Why is death, as this chapter suggests, the most newsworthy event in many lives?

3. Why is a crime story, such as the murder of Sir Thomas Overbury, made more newsworthy by the presence of a highborn victim and a female suspect?

4. This chapter suggests that the prevalence of sensationalism in the news might stem in part from an instinctual human need to remain aware of sex and violence. Evaluate this argument.

5. Is there moralizing in reports of crime today?

6. What supernatural stories—besides astrology charts—appear in the news today?

7. If the more educated public disdained sensational newsbooks and news ballads in the early years of the 17th century, where else could these people turn for news? What were the advantages and disadvantages of the alternatives?

The Logic of News *(Faits Isolés)*—
People Biting Dogs

8

When the red light goes on in front of a television news camera, some of the members of a crowd will often begin jumping and waving. The statement they are making through such energetic, if indecorous, behavior is, in part, "Notice me!" Of course, according to the standards of television journalists in most of our cities, these people, as individuals, are not worthy of notice; they are not news and are not likely to become news unless they are fortunate enough to be interviewed for some "person in the street" feature or unfortunate enough to get involved in some sensational tragedy. The news is about the celebrities, politicians, or murderers who gather the crowds, not about the particular faces that happen to be bobbing up and down behind them.

The use of the printing press to publish news was a crucial step in this division of the population into two groups: the few whose lives are newsworthy and the multitude who are born, live out their lives and die without the news media paying them any mind. These early publications attracted the largest audiences news had yet known. They could not hold the interest of thousands by reporting the birth of a healthy baby somewhere in Sussex; they needed the birth of a monster or the birth of a prince. And the level of newsworthiness necessary to earn a place in these pamphlets and broadsides was raised even higher by the fact that each publication usually was devoted to a single news story. That meant each story had to be sufficiently engaging to sell on its own. This was a news medium that covered only "front-page lead stories," and journalists lead with news of marriages between royalty or marriages that end in murder, not ordinary marriages between ordinary individuals.

The year 1616, when William Shakespeare died, seems a reasonably representative year to choose for an examination of the view of the world presented in these early forms of printed news. (The oldest surviving newspaper in English would not be printed for another four years.) Fourteen publications that appear to have contained news (many of which have not survived) are listed in the Stationers Register for 1616, and Matthias Shaaber, in his comprehensive survey of printed news in England, mentions 11 additional newsbooks or news ballads printed that year. (A large portion of the publications that have survived were not registered; many evaded the licensing system, and therefore the Stationers Register, not for political reasons but because their publishers wanted to avoid paying the fee.)[2]

Among this sample of 25 English news publications, there are seven reports on murders (including four on the unfolding tale of the poisoning of Sir Thomas Overbury), three pamphlets containing highly partisan religious news[3] (primarily about prominent converts), and seven covering personal news (Prince Charles' assumption of the title Prince of Wales and "portratures" of King James, his son, daughter and grandson, and of the man who would become the King's most prominent adviser, Sir George Villiers). Newsbooks or news ballads were also printed that year containing a transcript of a speech given by the king; a political report out of France, in French; a "description of New England," written by John Smith (better known for his earlier adventures in Virginia); a report on a naval victory; the scenario for the lord mayor's annual show in London; an account of the confession and execution of a witch; news of three bodies that arose from their graves in Germany; and verses on the drowning of five drunks in the Thames.[4]

Perhaps this list is of most interest for what it does not include. There is no evidence that printed news appeared in England in 1616 on any subject that reflected the day-to-day behavior of the people of that time. Indeed the picture we get on life in the early 17th century through these news publications is notably selective and incomplete. Short of getting murdered, leading an expedition to the New World, being executed as a witch, rising from the dead, becoming an adviser to the king or, better, Prince of Wales—the English, like television news audiences today, had little chance to see their reflections in this particular mirror of their world.[5]

William Shakespeare was among those permitted no more than a brief wave of the hand in the newsbooks and news ballads of his time. Although his contemporaries left little evidence that they shared our appreciation of Shakespeare's genius, he was known during his lifetime as a gifted playwright with some following. Yet Shakespeare appears to have made only one appearance in a publication designed primarily to spread news—in the following lines from a ballad lamenting the death of Queen Elizabeth in 1603:

> You Poets all brave *Shakspeare, Johnson, Greene,*
> Bestow your time to write for Englands Queene.[6]

There is no evidence that Shakespeare's own death in 1616 was marked by any printed epitaph.[7]

Dramatic presentations were not completely ignored by these news publications. Plays might be described with some thoroughness—if the queen was in the audience. (*Certaine Devises and shewes presented to her Majestie by the gentlemen of Grayes-Inne at her Highnesse Court in Greenwich* was printed in 1587.)[8] And the Globe Theater, where many of Shakespeare's plays were presented, was itself the subject of a news ballad in 1613—but only because it burned down (*A Sonnet on the Pitiful Burning of the Globe Playhouse in London*).[9] Had Shakespeare himself wanted to command at least a printed lament upon his death, he would have done well to take some time off from writing and acting to poison his "dark lady," drown in the Thames or fight in a battle (Falstaff in *Henry IV, Part II,* labels his taking of a prisoner worthy of a ballad.)[10]

Other news media were available in England in 1616. Europeans still spread news by word of mouth. (The heyday of the coffeehouse and the *nouvelliste* was still a century away.) Those who were literate still exchanged letters filled with news. And in such conversations and correspondence—able to consider more than one story, aimed at much smaller audiences—standards of newsworthiness were undoubtedly not as high as they were in these one-shot, all-or-nothing pamphlets or broadsides. In some circles news of the death of a popular playwright would undoubtedly have been exchanged, just as the births, marriages, and deaths of less radiant personages were surely discussed when friends met or corresponded. They would appear in type with some frequency when printed newspapers—with a variety of stories in each issue—turned their attention to local news.

Nevertheless, the limitations in the perspective on humanity presented in these early forms of printed news, while not typical, are indicative of those imposed even by news media with smaller audiences or room for more stories. (The Fugger newsletters, for example, though they demonstrated a concern with English affairs, do not mention Shakespeare either—nor Marlowe, Jonson, or Cervantes.[11]) It might not always be necessary to advise a king, become a witch or commit a murder to make news, but it is necessary to do something out of the ordinary—even today, even by the standards of our most responsible news organs. And we will be repeatedly frustrated, or led into error, if we look to the often-freakish world of news for a reflection of the world most humans experience.[12] Robert Darnton, who reported for the *New York Times* off and on in the early 1960s, was one journalist who was sensitive to the limitations of news coverage. "Eight million people live out their lives every day in New York City," Darnton writes, "and I felt overwhelmed by the disparity between their experience, whatever it was, and the tales they read in the *Times.*"[13]

News tells us a great deal about what is on the mind of a society as a whole; it tells us little about how the individuals in that society are living their lives. And the danger of confusing human interests with human realities seems particularly apparent in these early newsbooks and news ballads, which had no use for any but the most compelling news items. "It is as if the quality of being extraordinary, sensational, prodigious, was regarded as essential to news," writes Matthias Shaaber.[14]

The Extraordinary

Was there room in these newsbooks and news ballads for such an important, if commonplace, phenomenon as the love between two ordinary individuals? Emotion certainly was not slighted; in one news publication from the year 1616, the author describes being "so ravished with the fullnesse of joy, which I saw in the hearts of the people, as I wished my selfe then to bee transformed into the shape of the sweete Nightingale." The emotion flowing here, however, is "the love of Wales to their soveraigne Prince" Charles.[15]

In other years there are references to more private loves. A newsbook printed in 1584 in Paris includes reports of two people kissing, fondling and caressing. The affair it describes, however, was between a man and his daughter.[16] Another French newsbook, printed in 1618, quotes some of the words a woman used to seduce a man—but he was her brother.[17] And, as noted in the previous chapter, the intimate details of relationships between husbands and wives did sometimes find their way into print in England—if one killed the other.

Whether the subject is love, birth, weather or crime, journalists' tastes inevitably run toward the unnatural, the extraordinary. The sociologist Herbert Gans, discussing modern news magazines and television newscasts, observes that most stories about ordinary people "are actually what journalists call man-bites-dog stories . . . often . . . about people who depart from expected roles."[18] In 16th- and 17th-century printed news publications, it sometimes seemed as if a person not only had to bite a dog but cook and serve it as well to be considered worthy of a newsbook or a ballad.

Notice the lengths to which "Mary, a seaman's Mistress . . . at Deptford" in England, had gone when she attracted the attention of a pamphlet. First, she had an affair with that seaman. Then, after Mary found herself pregnant by her lover following his departure on a voyage to "the Indies," she falsely told his mother that they were married in an effort to convince the seaman's mother to provide for her. And finally, when the seaman's mother demanded proof, Mary concocted a scheme to obtain a marriage certificate—a scheme that involved her friend Margaret dressing as a man and pretending to be that seaman at a wedding ceremony in another town. Mary and Margaret ended up in jail, and their story was judged extraordinary enough to fill a newsbook entitled *The She-Wedding; Or, a Mad Marriage, between Mary, a Seaman's Mistress, and Margaret, a Carpenter's Wife, at Deptford. . . .*[19]

Even a flood might not be remarkable enough to pass muster for these publications; it had, as J. P. Seguin explains, to be an unnatural flood, the heavy rains out of season.[20] These early forms of printed news were particularly susceptible to the call of the bizarre, but then no journalist is deaf to it. "Whereas sociologists summarize from recurring patterns or random samples," Gans notes, "journalists gravitate toward what sociologists term deviant cases."[21]

The vast blind spot that results from this preference for deviant cases—the unusual—not only obscures much of what passes for normal behavior in the world, it even distorts the view journalists present of subjects that are out of the ordinary to begin with—such as crime. A murder may be the most interesting of crimes—for those within range of its effects it may be the most important of crimes—but murder is also among the rarest of crimes. Its impact is felt by far fewer people than experience, for example, burglaries. Still, with the exception of the work of a colorful highwayman, like Luke Hutton with his "twelve Apostles gaie," few crimes other than the extraordinary crime of murder were mentioned in early forms of printed news.[22]

And these publications even presented a distorted perspective on murders. The historian J. A. Sharpe has found evidence in court records suggesting that the most common type of homicide committed within households in early modern England was the killing of servants and apprentices; however, these crimes are barely noticed by English newsbooks and news ballads, which are consumed with the more emotionally charged, more unnatural, subject of the murder of spouses.[23]

Man Bites

The maxim "When a dog bites a man, that is not news; but when a man bites a dog, that is news" is said to have originated at the *Sun* in New York late in the 19th century (Mott, *American Journalism;* Manoff).

Our modern news-gathering system occasionally uncovers actual examples of men biting dogs. (Stories of women biting dogs seem rarer.) Such an incident was, for example, reported in the *Los Angeles Times* in November 1987, although its news value was lessened by the fact that the dog had bitten first.

News, of course, is not the public's primary source of information on love. (Although, as noted in the previous chapter, readers are eager to solicit advice on the subject from celebrities or killers.) Most of us are not limited for examples of emotional and sexual behavior to accounts of incestuous siblings or couples whose relationships end in murder. However, because news generally is the public's primary source of information on such societal issues as the incidence of crime,[24] the members of a society, when evaluating the social climate, too often mistake the unnatural for the natural, the extraordinary for the ordinary. Married people have less to fear from their spouses—and dogs have less to fear from the teeth of humans—than it would appear from following the news.

The Conventional

The title page of a 1576 French report on a "monstrous and frightful serpent" found on the island of Cuba features a woodcut of a two-headed, winged serpent. Three years later, a French newsbook that described a "serpent or flying dragon, grand and marvelous" over the city of Paris, was also illustrated by a sketch of a two-headed, winged serpent—the exact same woodcut used to portray that serpent in Cuba.[25]

This was hardly uncommon; new woodcuts were costly. When the Seine overflowed in Paris in 1579, a newsbook printed in Lyon reporting on the flood was illustrated by a woodcut that showed water where streets should be—the same picture that had been used back in 1480 to represent a view of the city of Venice.[26] In England, a woodcut that had originally appeared in Fox's *Book of Martyrs* was then used in a series of publications on death by fire—regardless of whether the death was by execution or by accident.[27]

Woodcuts were not the only elements of these publications that might live beyond the event for which they were originally intended; a pleasing wording might also gain a certain currency. In French newsbooks earthquakes were "frightful, horrible and marvelous" (1570) or "marvelous and frightful" (1578) or "frightful" and "horrible" (1579).

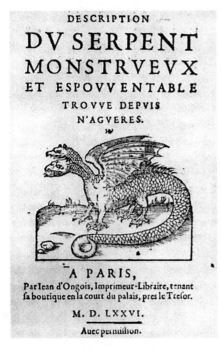

Journalists are sometimes tempted to reuse on effective wording, characterization, theme or illustration. The covers of these two French newsbooks feature the same woodcut: One, printed in 1576, reports on a "monstrous and frightful serpent" found on the island of Cuba [left]. The other, printed in 1579, on a "serpent or flying dragon, grand and marvelous" seen over the city of Paris [right].

A "monster" rarely appeared in the title of such a publication without the adjective "marvelous" or "prodigious" preceding it as a sort of fanfare.[28] Similarly, in Thomas Deloney's news ballads celebrating resistance to the Spanish armada, the English ride "gallant horses," gather in a "gallant campe" and are helped by a "gallant winde." Their ignominious but formidable foes are a "mightie power," with "mightie power," sailing in a "mightie Gallion," or "mightie vessell," which was "mightily provided."[29]

Certain themes also tended to be revisited. The French appeared particularly fond of stories recounting the arrest of innocents who, like 22-year-old Hélène Gillet, could not be executed and were therefore rescued by God, not justice.[30] And, of course, newsbooks and news ballads throughout Europe were filled with the inevitable, and inevitably repentant, "last dying speech."

Both "stereotype" and "cliché" are printing terms—referring to the metal sheets, developed in the late 18th century, on which whole pages of type could be cast. The too obvious, too familiar formulations or observations that these terms now are used to describe—observations as invariant as the words molded on those metal stereotypes or clichés—predate the printing press. Indeed such preset, formulaic wordings are crucial aids to memory in oral cultures. Still, is it surprising that the printing press— disseminator of so many popular romances, so many tales of adventure, and so many reams and reams of news—should have supplied names for the trite, the overused, the conventional?

The resort to stereotypes and clichés exacts a cost on the news, as it does on any form of communication. The idiosyncrasies of individual events are lost when they are illustrated by familiar pictures, described in familiar words and shaped into familiar themes. All serpents or all deaths by fire begin to resemble each other, the actual features of deformed creatures are obscured behind hyperbolic adjectives such as "marvelous" and "prodigious"; complex confrontations between vulnerable human beings are reduced to triumphs of the "gallant" over the "mightie"; and the last moments of criminals are bludgeoned into conformity with our expectations—categories determined, implications drawn, before the particulars have been presented.

In 16th- and 17th-century newsbooks and news ballads, criminals are "cruel" and "vicious" but revealed as "penitent" in the shadow of the noose; monarchs are "noble"; battles are "worthy"; and women usually "innocent" or vain. Theory precedes reality: Murder follows from lust, which follows from vanity, which follows from pride, which, belatedly, brings us to the sad story at hand.

A world seen through formulas is a world obscured. And even today's journalists—our eyes on the contemporary political and social world—seem to have difficulty examining the overheated events upon which their gaze falls without a set of stereotypes and clichés to reduce the glare.

Clichés are, to be sure, convenient. "Marvelous monster," alliterative in both French and English, flows from the pen. "Noble King Henry VIII," "likable President Reagan," the "mightie" Spanish, the "threat of illegal drugs"—the words spill onto the page without need for deep thought. And journalists, hustling to capture news before it decays into history, rarely have time for deep thought. Stereotypes are similarly efficient: if the exact degree of piety exhibited by each criminal on the gallows, or the exact degree to which drugs—illegal or legal—can be held responsible for particular outrages had to be calculated, the news might never get written. It would be as inefficient as carving a new woodcut every time a new dragon was spotted.

And most of these formulas became formulas because they were so effective. Readers obviously have a weakness for tales of "worthy" battles between the "gallant" and the "mightie," for "penitent" criminals and "noble" kings. Where art might challenge such stereotypes, journalism usually embraces them. News is designed to resonate through a society, and societies resonate when familiar chords are struck.

Robert Darnton received a quick lesson in the power of preconceptions and stereotypes while spending a summer as a police reporter for the *Newark Star Ledger* in 1959. On a slow news day Darnton had decided to check out a police "squeal sheet" on a boy who had been robbed of his bicycle in a park. Just for practice, Darnton wrote up this minor incident and showed it to one of the regular reporters. "You can't write that kind of a story straight," that veteran explained. Then he sat down at a typewriter to demonstrate to Darnton, the rookie, how it should be done, making up details where necessary:

> Every week Billy put his twenty-five-cent allowance in his piggy bank. He wanted to buy a bike. Finally, the big day came. He chose a shiny red Schwinn, and took it out for a spin in the park. Every day for a week he rode proudly

around the same route. But yesterday three toughs jumped him in the middle of the park. They knocked him from the bike and ran off with it. Battered and bleeding, Billy trudged home to his father, George F. Wagner of 43 Elm Street. "Never mind, son," his dad said. "I'll buy you a new bike, and you can use it on a paper route to earn money to pay me back."

Darnton got back on the telephone to find facts to fit that formula, and the story he produced appeared on the front page of the *Star Ledger,* with his first byline. Soon neighbors were taking up a collection to buy Billy a new bike, and the commissioner of parks was announcing that security would be increased in that park. "I had struck several chords by manipulating stock sentiments and figures: the boy and his bike, piggy-bank savings, heartless bullies, the comforting father," Darnton explains.[31]

After working at the *New York Times,* Darnton changed careers and went on to become a professor of history at Princeton, so he had an opportunity to learn the age of some of the stock sentiments he had manipulated. "When I did some research on popular culture in early modern France and England," Darnton recalls, "I came across tales that bore a striking resemblance to the stories that we had written from the pressroom of police headquarters in Newark."[32]

A newsbook published in Paris in 1618 provides an example of how actual stories, not just the stock sentiments of which they are composed, can live on. It tells the "admirable and prodigious" tale of a boy with a taste for adventure who had left his family to fight in Sweden. After at least a dozen years away from home, he had become a man of means and was ready to seek out his family again. Upon arriving in his hometown, the young man visited his sister, and the two of them decided to surprise their parents by hiding his identity (as sure a route to disaster in these newsbooks as it is in television soap operas). So, the young man introduced himself to his mother and father only as a man seeking lodging. Unfortunately, his parents were so dazzled by the wealth of their lodger, whom they failed to recognize, that they surrendered to an "evil and unhappy appetite for gold." By the time the man's sister arrived in the morning to reveal his identity to her parents, he had been strangled and his body burned. Criminal prosecution followed, along with "extraordinary lamentations" in response to this "secret justice of God."[33]

This story, through the hoary dramatic device of mistaken identity, plays so well to our emotions (our pity for the son, and outrage at the behavior of the parents—combined, perhaps, with some sympathy for their awful realization) and to our preconceptions (our belief in the evil inherent in greed, our expectation that it eventually will be punished) that it shows up again and again. J. P. Seguin has located reports of parents killing their sons, thinking they were rich strangers, in Toulouse in 1848, in Angoulême in 1881, and in an Algerian newspaper in this century—where Albert Camus found it and cited it in his novel *L'Etranger.* (In the version picked up by Camus, the mother and sister commit the murder.)[34]

The point here is not whether, or to what extent, these stories may have been fabricated; rather it is the fidelity to an identical news pattern, an identical story line, that all these versions, separated by hundred of years, demonstrate—almost as if, as Darnton puts it, "they were metamorphoses of *Ur*-stories [elemental story types] that have been lost in the depths of time."[35]

Camus' brief treatment of that story is different from that found in the 17th-century newsbook. His emotionless protagonist tells the tale quickly, without any hint of sentiment. Camus forces readers to confront the awful, even absurd turns life can take. Journalists, however, generally seek to move readers, not challenge them. They mention the "evil and unhappy appetite for gold," and watch us frown; they conclude that we have witnessed a "secret justice of God," and watch us smile. *Ur*-stories, stock sentiments, stereotypes, clichés are all plugged in directly to our emotions. The artist experiments with our wiring; the journalist often just pushes the buttons.

Art may dare to draw the unconventional out of the conventional; news does the opposite. Journalists start with a man biting a dog and then struggle to find a meaning in that unnatural event that their audience can share. To that end, they might emphasize the pride and lust (or recent release from a mental hospital) that had reduced this man to nipping at his fellow creatures, or they might focus on the pain and shock the dog's seven-year-old owner experienced on learning that her pet poodle had lost a piece of its hide. The journalist's work, in this sense, is to squeeze raw reality into familiar, easy to comprehend themes.

The robbery of a bike from a young boy is an unsettling occurrence, but—with the piggy bank, the bullies, the comforting father—Darnton succeeded in caging that potentially disruptive occurrence in conventionality. The stereotypes and the accompanying moralizing (and there is no more effective condemnation of a criminal than dressing the victim in stereotypes of innocence and vulnerability) provide the shield necessary to protect us from the truly new, from events—such as parents mistakenly killing their son—that are too terrible to look straight in the face.

Breaking news is extraordinary, but its fate is to be pinned down by the conventional at every turn. It is presented in routinized formats, illustrated with familiar sketches, told in clichéd wordings, and forced into stereotypical motifs. The extraordinary is made ordinary. Thus do journalists meet their deadlines; thus does their product elicit our smiles and tears; thus do we control the awful power inherent in these events.

The Unexpected

According to one of the English news ballads printed in 1616, late on the night of Oct. 15 of that year five men tried to cross the Thames in a boat:

> But, being all with drinke growne madd,
> they were in wofull manner drownd.

This is the quintessential news events—extraordinary and shockingly abrupt:

> Some riseth with the morninge Sun,
> all healthfull, lustye, stronge, and bolde;
> And yet, before the day be done,
> are changed to claye and earthy moulde.[36]

Journalists are often attacked for, as Walter Lippmann put it in 1931, seeing "life dramatically, episodically" instead of seeing it "steadily and whole." Herbert Gans complains that "journalists see external reality as a set of disparate and independent events."[37] However, if many journalists have failed to supply their audiences with perspective, connections and meaning, it is not from lack of trying. Out of the bits of shattered lives that confront them, journalists do struggle to piece together something whole, something profound.

The author of the ballad that described those deaths by drowning in 1616 devotes more verses to the significance of the accident than to the accident itself. The drowning has meaning, we are told, as evidence that "the Lord's most heavy wrath" will fall on those who not only drink to excess but who do so on a Sunday: "God's blessed Sabaoth to prophane. . . ." The drowning is placed in a larger context by approaching it from what was considered in that spiritual age to be the widest perspective available—religion:

> Therefore, let all good people then
>   take heede how they the Lord offend,
> Lest, like to these unhappy men,
>   they come to have such suddaine end.[38]

Sixteenth- and 17th-century journalists were as sensitive to such signs of the hand of God as modern-day journalists are to intimations of shifts in the Democrats' prospects in the next election, and they were just as eager to share these larger meanings.

Another strategy for placing an event in context, trying to see it whole, is to chart its emotional reverberations. The author of this news ballad sketched in reactions to the death of these five men the easy way: by trotting out the standard characterizations:

> By whose untimely losse of lives
>   their friends, bewayling, sorrowe makes:
> Their parents, kindred, and their wives,
>   now sit lamentinge for their sakes.
>
> Their children, that be fatherlesse,
>   might longe have had these loving friends,
> If that this desperate wilfulnesse
>   had not thus brought[t] them to their ends.[39]

The invocation of causes and consequences can actually ease the burden carried by hard-pressed journalists. In an analysis of press coverage of the death in 1953 of Joseph Stalin—who "had the bad taste to die in installments"—the press critic A. J. Liebling demonstrated the inverse relationship that exists between the amount of hard information actually available to journalists (only six reporters from the United States were in Moscow) and the volume of ratiocination—"on the one hand this and on the other hand that"—in which they will engage. (Pundits back home explained how Stalin's death surely would or would not lead to "WORLD CRISIS.")[40] The hidden meaning, the big picture, often helps make up for the lack of crucial details on a story.[41] In searching for significance in that 17th-century drowning, the ballad maker succeeds in fleshing out with interpretation a story that is woefully short on facts—the actual circumstances of the drowning, among other details, are missing, as hard information on the implications of Stalin's death was missing in 1953.

Finding Significance in a Bombing

The "bloodiest domestic terrorist case in the nation's history"—that is what the bombing of an office building in Oklahoma City in 1995, in which 167 people were killed, was called. Huge news. Journalists, naturally, began to search for its larger significance.

They uncovered right-wing militia groups, antigovernment crusaders, citizens furious with taxes, gun control and recent federal police actions. This, they reported, was the milieu from which came the two men accused of planting the bomb. Which was fine. News audiences learned of points of view and organizations that might not have been discussed if not for the bombing.

But that is not enough for some significance-hungry journalists. If they have just discovered something, it must be treated as if it were new (though there is a long history of such right-wing dissent in the United States). It must be described (with little evidence) as growing. The Oklahoma City bombing must be read (with no evidence) as a portent of right-wing terrorist acts to come.

An event that is awful, absurd and isolated is thus transformed by this special alchemy of journalism into a trend.

Intimations of greater significance can also increase the news value of a story. This is another old ruse: With enough huffing and puffing an accident can be inflated into a religious lesson—as Stalin's demise was expanded into a political lesson and as the behavior of one severly disturbed criminal might today be transformed into evidence of the breakdown of society.

The seer, the analyst—these are among the favorite roles of the journalist, "serious" or sensational. Journalists do not want to feed their audiences disparate, episodic news of the sort that Lippmann and Gans decry. If anything, they are *too* concerned with finding connections, with insisting that unruly events display intelligibility and coherence.

If these efforts to find meaning in the drowning of five men fail, if somehow the death of these particular men among all the Sabbath breakers, all the drunks who have to take a boat to get home, still seems sudden and meaningless, the problem is not that journalists are unwilling to see the world whole and steadily; it is that the world of breaking news is inherently disjointed and unsteady.

In observing that "any life will seem dramatic if you omit mention of most of it," the contemporary short-story writer Ann Beattie is concerned with the distortions of memory and literature, but this principle also applies to journalism; indeed, it pinpoints the source of journalism's power. The news is not about life but about a peculiar subset of life—those dramatic moments when the spell of daily reality is broken by the death of a dictator, a despicable crime, or a drowning.

The world appears through the news as it might if illuminated by strobe light—we see exaggerated poses, awkward postures, frightening faces, but the steady motions that might give meaning to those apparitions often take place in the dark. In examining reports on battles in 16th-century French publications, J. P. Seguin notes that the engagements that receive the most attention often are of little historical significance. These newsbooks, Seguin observes, tend to lose themselves in individual exploits of little impact on the military situation, in *"faits isolés"*—isolated acts—rather than the "general march of events."[42]

Journalists who attempt to keep up with fast-breaking events are not only at the whim of what one 17th-century French newsbook calls "the impetuosity of the elements,"[43] they depend on that impetuosity to power their stories. Where A inevitably leads to B, B loses news value. If we in fact had the religious, scientific, political or economic knowledge to understand and predict drownings, natural disasters, government scandals or stock market crashes, they would be diminished as news. If taking a bite out of a dog were a more reasonable act, it would not interest us so.

The great news stories are audacious: A countess and a favorite of the king plot to poison the man who stands in the way of their love affair; the Lindbergh baby is kidnapped; a popular former football star is accused of murdering his ex-wife. These stories have no real antecedents, no clear descendants. They appear suddenly out of the mist, perhaps the offspring of A, perhaps portending some ominous C, but in essence orphans, loners, fascinating anomalies.

The structure of the *fait divers,* writes Roland Barthes, the French semiologist, is based upon "disturbances of causality": the indeterminate causality of the prodigy or the mysterious crime, the "frustrated causality" of the woman who stabs her lover not for passion but in a political argument, the "'deranged' causality" of the man who "enlists in the Foreign Legion to avoid spending Christmas with his mother-in-law," the paradoxical causality of the old man who is "strangled by the cord of his hearing aid," and the reversed causality of the chief of police who kills his wife. "There is no *fait divers* without astonishment," Barthes notes.[44] He might have said, there is no news without astonishment. (*Faits divers* rarely have much practical impact, are particularly dependent on emotional impact and the element of surprise, but few stories of any sort—from a scientific discovery to a political agreement— capture wide attention without eliciting some degree of astonishment.)

It is this inevitable concentration on the unexpected, as much as the deficiencies or mercenary inclinations of individual journalists, that makes breaking news a relatively poor teacher of what to expect. The news is not political reality, social reality or daily reality. This social sense is, alas, a coarse, inexact sense—too busy trying to surprise us with the world each day to dwell on its constancies.

Journalists with the time and the talent have demonstrated that other, more thoughtful approaches might be taken to current events, approaches that lie somewhere between the reporting of breaking news and the writing of history. Publications and newscasts today do in fact attempt less hurried analyses of contemporary society; in stories labeled "news features" they do undertake examinations of more typical, more understandable circumstances—trends patterns, lifestyles. But news inevitably resists confinement in such analyses. The wild side of the news, the part that drew 17th-century crowds to ballad singers and draws millions to television newscasts, exists by definition just beyond the reach of our expectations and analyses. These more leisurely perspectives can supplement but not replace our tireless search for the odd, the shocking.

When we choose to enter the world of breaking news, we enter a fun house. Abnormities loom large in journalism's bent mirrors; perspectives are distorted; horrors materialize out of nowhere; everywhere we turn there is blood and danger. If there is a logic to the collection of intense moments that journalists package, it is a logic of discontinuity—a carnival logic of freaks and catastrophes, a logic beyond the reach of the conventional sentiments with which most daily journalists must make do. Much of the time journalists, like circus announcers, are reduced to barking and adding admonitions: "Marvelous!" "Prodigious!" "Frightful!" "Lamentable!" "Horrible!"

In succeeding centuries the news would settle within the columns of the newspaper, but the news can never be fully housebroken.

Questions

1. This chapter focuses on that which printed news in England in 1616 did *not* discuss. Analyze, based on the list of publications from that year provided in the opening section of the chapter, what it *did* discuss. Based on this sample, how does the view of the world that newsbooks and news ballads presented differ from the view of the world we get from our news media?

2. Give other examples of the journalistic tendency to "gravitate toward . . . deviant cases," from newsbooks and news ballads discussed elsewhere in this book and from contemporary news media.

3. Note some formulas, stereotypes, clichés, or story themes relied on by these newsbooks or news ballads that continue to appear in news stories today.

4. What sorts of information would have to be added to that story of the five drunk men drowned in the Thames to make it a better guide to social reality in 17th-century England?

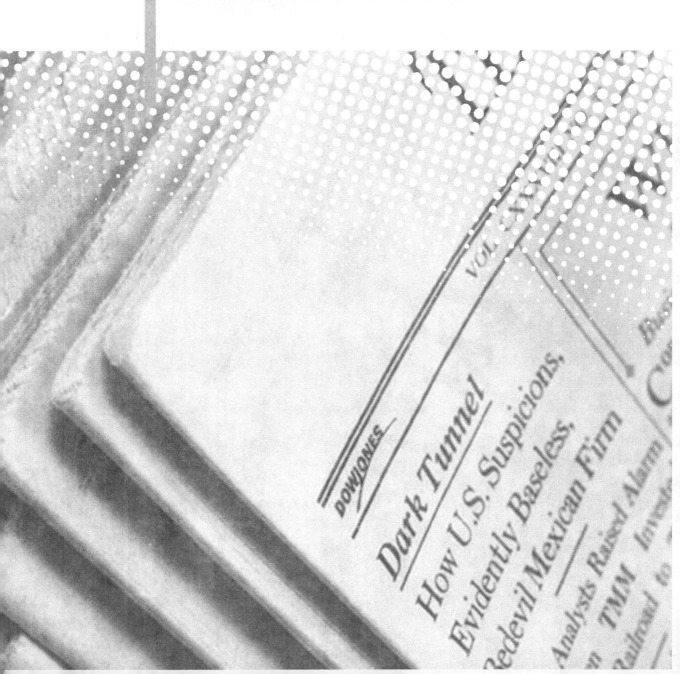

PART FOUR

NEWSPAPERS

9

The First Newspapers—
Expecting the News

The printed newspaper from which the world's dailies and weeklies would descend arrived in the early years of the 17th century. It arrived in Europe,[2] apparently without fanfare; no contemporary reference to a Gutenberg of the newspaper has been found.

Historians did not discover what may have been the first printed newspaper until 1876, when a German scholar located a collection of newsbooks that had been published in Strasbourg in 1609. A similar set of German newsbooks—also printed in 1609, probably in Wolfenbüttel—was unearthed in 1903.[3] More recent research has found reference to, though not copies of, the Strasbourg publication dating from 1605.

To qualify as a newspaper, most journalism historians would agree, a publication must be available to a significant portion of the public, as were the newsbooks or news ballads with which Europe was already familiar. But a newspaper, as it would be defined by most of these historians, has three additional attributes that distinguish it from the one-shot news publications that preceded it:[4]

- First and foremost, a newspaper is published regularly and frequently (at least weekly). Those German-language newsbooks from 1609 appeared in numbered, dated series—52 were printed in Strasbourg that year.
- Second, a newspaper, with so many issues to fill, includes a variety of different stories in each issue: The first issue of the Strasbourg weekly, printed by Johann Carolus, featured items from Cologne, Antwerp, Rome, Venice, Vienna and Prague.
- Third, a newspaper displays a consistent and recognizable title or format; in other words, it gains an identity independent of whatever particular news items it happens to be carrying. Although the long titles of these German newsbooks varied from issue to issue with the news, each issue employed a similar format;

. . . both the Reader and the Printer of these Pamphlets, agree in their expectation of weekely Newes. . . .

—Newes from Europe . . . , 1624[1]

131

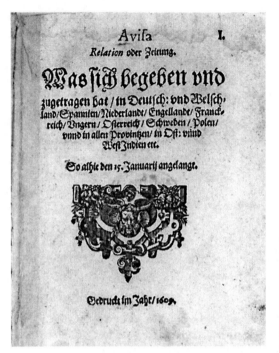

One of two publications that have claimed the title of oldest surviving European newspaper. This is the cover of the earliest known issue of the Avis[o] Relation ober Zeitung, *printed, probably in Wolfenbüttel, in January 1609. Another German-language weekly also appeared that month but probably dates from 1605.*

the earliest issues of the second paper to be discovered, printed by Lucas Schulte, would begin with the words "*Aviso Relation ober Zeitung,*" followed by a listing of the countries from which the news they contained originated, an elaborate design and the date.[5]

The word *newspaper* would not be used in English for perhaps another 60 years,[6] yet by 1609, and probably 1605, newspapers were being printed in Europe.

The debut of these first European printed newspapers, if these were the very first, may not have occasioned much comment, but the idea spread with remarkable speed. By 1610 there appears to have been a printed weekly in Basel, by 1615 in Frankfurt and Vienna, by 1616 in Hamburg, by 1617 in Berlin, by 1618 in Amsterdam, and by 1620 in Antwerp.[7] An English official at the time complained that his country was being "reproved in foreign parts" because it lacked a publication to report "the occurrents every week."[8] The first weekly newspaper printed in England appeared in 1621. France did not produce a newspaper of its own until 1631, but printers in Amsterdam were exporting weeklies in French—and English—as early as 1620. Italy's first printed weekly appeared by 1639 at the latest, Spain's by 1641.[9]

The rapidity with which the printed newspaper caught on and the anonymity of its originator are indications that the weekly printing of news was not seen as a particularly risky or revolutionary step forward in early 17th-century Europe. Europe had long been acquainted with the journalistic and commercial possibilities of printed news. And the major factor needed to transform a newsbook into a newspaper—periodicity—was very much in the air by the start of the century. Some of the same printers who had been publishing newsbooks and news ballads were also turning out periodic calendars and almanacs. By the end of the 16th century a few were even printing periodic accounts of current events, albeit with long periods between installments.

Beginning in 1588 Michael von Aitzing in Cologne published a summary of political and military events every spring and fall—timed to be available for sale at the twice-yearly Frankfurt book fair. After 1594 a second biannual account of current events, the *Mercurius Gallo Belgicus,* was also being printed in Cologne; it was written in Latin and read widely as far away as England. In 1597 the German Emperor Rudolf II apparently made an effort to quicken the pace of periodic printed news in his realm by encouraging the publication of monthly summaries of events.[10] It is not clear whether Rudolf succeeded, but against this background, the weekly printing of news hardly seems a radical idea.[11] Johann Carolus, Lucas Schulte or some unknown predecessor may deserve credit more for first acting on that idea than for conceiving it.

The newspaper, after all, required no technological innovations. The same presses that churned out individual newsbooks could print a series of weekly newsbooks. A certain amount of journalistic innovation, or at least journalistic industry, was required to fill a newssheet every week. But a stream of pamphlets, broadsides, newsletters, personal letters—and now printed weeklies—circulated from country to country in these years, and if the mails were running, an adept translator could furnish enough news for an issue.[12]

There was another important current in the air at the beginning of the 17th century. Europe had in fact already been introduced to the potential of weekly news publications. When 18th-century historians would search for the origins of the newspaper they would set off not in the direction of Strasbourg or Wolfenbüttel but toward the birthplace of these publications—toward Venice. This trail, ignored by more recent newspaper historians,[13] is worth following, but the weekly publications it leads to differ in one significant respect from those that spread across Europe in the early 17th century: They were not printed.

News in Venice—The Gazette

Cities that are centers of power and trade are also centers of news. That was true of Athens and of Rome. It would be true of Amsterdam in the 17th century and of London in the 18th and 19th centuries. It is true of New York today.

In the 16th century, as they had for hundreds of years, the goods and money of the Mediterranean world met the goods and money of Europe in the lagoons and canals of Venice. Although Venetian military power was in decline, the city remained a major political force in the Mediterranean and in Europe, and the chief point of contact with the Ottoman colossus[14]—so much on the mind of 16th-century Europe.

"Thanks to its extraordinary administrative and commercial development," writes the French historian Pierre Sardella, "Venice constituted the most important center of information at the beginning of the sixteenth century; a center of direct liaison between the most active parties of the nascent modern world."[15] Merchants and diplomats brought news into Venice, and they made it their business to collect news while they were there.

Gazettes

Pittsburgh has the *Post-Gazette*, Phoenix the *Gazette*. The dominant newspaper in France for a century and a half before the Revolution was the *Gazette de France*. Perhaps the most influential newspaper in 17th-century England was the *Oxford Gazette*, later renamed the *London Gazette*. New York's first newspaper was called the *Gazette*. The first newspaper Ben Franklin edited was the *Pennsylvania Gazette*. The Boston *Gazette* helped spur the American Revolution.

What is the origin of this word?

Gazetta was probably the name of a Venetian coin. It may have been the price charged for a copy of the weekly handwritten newssheets that circulated in Venice in the 16th century, or the price of having one read out loud. It became a name for the newssheets themselves. The fact that this word was then used in the name of so many early newspapers in so many places is one sign of how influential the Venetian gazettes were.

Here is another sign. The Russian word for newspaper is *gazeta*.

Venice appears to have functioned, for example, as a sort of news bureau for the information system maintained by the Fuggers in Augsburg.[16]

At some point in the 16th century a selection of the news that was flowing through Venice apparently began being recorded and distributed to some of the city's residents. Historians have presented sketchy and often conflicting reports about the nature of the news organs that appeared in Venice,[17] but most who have investigated the subject agree that the Venetians innovated some form of periodic news publications, which was referred to as a *gazzette*—a word which would then appear and reappear over the centuries in large type atop the front pages of many different newspapers printed in many different languages.[18] In a contribution to that pioneering French compendium of wisdom the *Encyclopédie*, Voltaire explained that the "gazette" was "invented" in Venice as a weekly newssheet.[19] "We are indebted to Italians for the idea of newspapers," Isaac D'Israeli, the English literary historian, wrote in 1791. "The first paper was a Venetian one."[20]

The most complete discussion of what the Venetians actually invented appeared in an Italian article written in 1869: "The first Italian gazettes," Salvatore Bongi explained, "were written without any special instrument. They consisted of a sheet of paper written by hand with a simple style of handwriting and the use of some abbreviations. . . . The papers were distributed every week, almost all on Saturday." Bongi suggests that these newssheets were originally produced in Venice after 1550 and that they blossomed into a public news service by 1554, with weekly publication beginning sometime thereafter. Why is so little known about these gazettes? "It is said that no respectable writer of the time even mentioned their authors," Bongi notes.[21]

A collection of these mysterious Venetian gazettes—perhaps the oldest direct ancestors of the modern newspaper—has settled in an unlikely spot. Among the letters from 16th-century British agents and diplomats abroad that have been collected in the Public Record Office in London are a number of sheets written in Italian that are clearly not letters. They contain no personal references and are unsigned. These handwritten sheets— each actually a large piece of paper folded in half to form four pages[22]—feature short news items from various locales around Europe, excepting Venice. Many were forwarded to London with diplomatic letters from Venice, where they undoubtedly were produced. They have not before been analyzed by a journalism historian.

One of the Italian newssheets in London's Public Record Office—written in 1547— predates the earliest mentioned by Bongi by a few years,[23] and the Venetian newssheets that found their way to London in 1551 are more plentiful and more advanced than his description would suggest: at least 11 such newssheets in Italian—similar in form to those of later years—accompanied letters from Venice in 1551, and two were apparently forwarded via Augsburg.[24] But otherwise the Italian sheets collected in London appear consistent with Bongi's account of these first gazettes. They also appear sophisticated and precocious enough to have impressed themselves and their nickname upon the minds of those who would circulate news in Europe in succeeding decades. (The other name by which these sheets were known, *avisi* or *avvisi*,[25] would also be widely used in the titles of printed newspapers beginning with the first issue of Lucas Schulte's printed weekly in 1609.)

The Venetian newssheets preserved in London are each divided into sets of news items forwarded from a particular city on a particular date, with the names of the cities and the dates serving as headings. The *Calendar of State Papers, Foreign Series,* which indexes and summarizes letters received from English diplomats, includes a short outline in English of the contents of a representative newssheet from September 1566:

> Intelligence from Messina, 16 Sept. 1566; from Vienna, 26 Sept., relating to the proceedings of the Turks by sea and in Hungary; from Rome, 28 Sept., concerning the Pope and Cardinals.[26]

The news in these publications was primarily political or military, but the following items, which appeared under the heading "From Constantinople 13 April," in a newssheet from May 1566, indicate that those categories might be interpreted somewhat broadly:

> The Armada, after having sailed rather speedily, has left for Gallipoli, toward the straits, and they say it goes towards [word unclear]. One hears that Selim [soon to become Sultan Selim II] is indisposed and that his father [Suleiman I] has sent for the doctor to cure him and to explain his illness, whether it is real or pretended. . . . They write from Corfu that at that place there are come 50 boats . . . loaded with different sorts of birds who, torn from the wind, had fallen into the sea.[27]

These Venetian newssheets were written decades before the first surviving printed newspapers. Do they qualify as the first post-Renaissance newspaper or, depending how the Roman *acta* or Chinese publications are classified, the world's first newspaper? Based on the evidence available in London's Public Record Office, these newssheets do appear to have possessed all the attributes that distinguish a newspaper from a one-shot news publication: Each newssheet contains a variety of different news items, and although the sheets do not display a title, they all employ a similar, presumably recognizable, format. Most significantly, enough Venetian newssheets from the year 1566 have been preserved in London to demonstrate that they were being distributed weekly by 1566.

The newssheets are not dated, but a reasonable idea of when they each appeared can be garnered from the date of the news they contain from Rome. (Each includes some news from Rome—news that probably took a day or two to reach Venice.) Here are those dates for 10 newssheets from the spring of 1566: March 9, March 16, March 23, March 30, April 6, April 13, April 20, April 27, May 4, and May 11.[28] By the spring of 1566, someone in Venice clearly was producing newssheets weekly.[29] There is no evidence of an earlier weekly news publication in Renaissance Europe.

However, one additional qualification would have to be met for these 16th-century *handwritten* weeklies to qualify as a newspaper: They must be shown to have been available, as newsbooks and news ballads were, to a substantial portion of the public. Obviously this is a difficult qualification for a handwritten publication to meet.[30] Indeed, some journalism historians have included "reduplication" by "mechanical" means in their definitions of the newspaper[31]—a requirement that forms a neat circle with the oft-repeated claim that the newspaper "is the child of printing."[32]

The issue here boils down to circulation. It is a fact that handwritten newssheets cannot achieve the distributions of printed newspapers. The *acta* in Rome were posted (and often copied), not distributed. China's *tipao* were originally circulated only among a limited audience of officials. Nevertheless, handwritten publications have on occasion been distributed to large audiences. Louis Petit de Bachaumont apparently employed 10 to 15 copyists to handle the circulation of the handwritten *Mémories Secret* he produced from the news brought to Madame Doublet's salon in 18th-century France. Such *nouvelles à la main* seem to have performed functions normally associated with printed newspapers from 1632 to 1789 in France, when the press was strictly controlled,[33] as did similar handwritten newsletters during periods of stringent press controls in England in the 17th century.[34] (Unlike the Venetian newssheets, these English and French handwritten periodicals, it must be emphasized, all appeared well *after* the first printed newspapers.)

The evidence available in London on the circulation of Venice's handwritten newssheets is far from conclusive. In a few instances two copies of individual Venetian newssheets survive in the Public Record Office[35]—an indication that they were not scarce in Venice. The fact that some copies apparently also made their way to London via Augsburg is another such indication. Had these newssheets been simply the product of a private news service, contracted for by British agents, would more than one copy have reached London? Would copies have reached Augsburg? Would they have been unsigned? Bongi notes that these sheets do not have the appearance of diplomatic or private information.[36] (There is also evidence that their audience was expanded by individuals who read them aloud, perhaps in return for a coin).[37] More research needs to be done on the distribution of Venice's gazettes, but it seems likely that Voltaire and D'Israeli were correct in looking to Venice for the origin of the newspaper.

Even if the handwritten weekly newssheets produced in Venice in the 16th century are not, in the end, deemed worthy of the title "newspaper," their important, perhaps semi-

The handwritten newssheets produced weekly in Venice as early as 1566 may qualify as the world's first newspaper. This is the front page of one of those "gazettes" written in May 1566.

nal, role in the development of the newspaper cannot be denied. We do not know who was writing the news in Venice. Some historians say the newssheets were produced by the government; some talk of a class of *avvisatori,* or professional newswriters.[38] The efforts of whoever procured and copied this news appear to have flagged by the beginning of the 17th century, if not earlier, and Venice does not appear to have been particularly quick to adopt the printed newspaper. Nevertheless, those who were responsible for the city's handwritten news publications in the 16th century contributed more than a name to printed newspapers.

Similiar handwritten newssheets soon began to appear in Rome, Bongi reports, where their circulations were higher and their news coverage less restrained. In 1574 Pope Pius V cracked down on newswriters in Rome ("They wrote things that did not sit

War and the News Business

War, perhaps the most compelling of news stories, has usually boosted circulations and therefore improved the financial prospects of those journalists who can stay out of the way of the bullets. War has also provided new news media with a chance to demonstrate their power.

The Iraq War gave the Internet a chance to show off some of its journalistic potential: Citizens, crucially, no longer had to depend only on news reports from within their own country. Americans, for example, could also get instant, and often critical, perspectives on the war their nation was fighting from the websites of newspapers such as *The Guardian* in England or *Le Monde* in France. Meanwhile, blogs and other websites began adding to the available information everything from eyewitness accounts from Baghdad, to analyses of possible American exit strategies, to calculations of civilian casualties.

The all-news cable network CNN seemed to come of age with its intensive coverage of the Persian Gulf War in 1991, which was much watched around the world—including in the capitals of the warring parties. Television flexed its impressive muscles during the Vietnam War in the 1960s, bringing burning huts and bloody soldiers into American living rooms. World War II in the 1940s gave radio a chance to show off its capacity to transmit words and sounds from afar (see Chapter 15). Newspaper reporting grew and developed rapidly during the American Civil War in the 1860s.

In 1618, less than a decade after the appearance of Europe's first printed newspapers, a war between Catholic and Protestant states began: the Thirty Years War. Many fledgling newspapers benefitted during those 30 years from public interest in battle outcomes. Newspapers had numerous opportunities to exhibit the advantages of regular publication in speed and reliability.

---

well with him," a contemporary explained),[39] with what success is unclear. News from Italy circulated widely in Germany,[40] and by 1586 a weekly handwritten newssheet appeared there—a collection survives in a library in Leipzig. The news copying service run by Jeremias Crasser and then Jeremias Schiffle (and patronized by Count Philip Eduard Fugger) in Augsburg also produced weekly collections of written news as early as 1587.[41]

In the next decade, the weekly handwritten newsletter spread to Holland with the assistance of a Dutch merchant and newswriter stationed in Cologne, Hendrik van Bilderbeek. The handwritten sheets—filled with news from Italy—Bilderbeek circulated to subscribers in Holland bear a striking resemblance to the Venetian newssheets: They include a few paragraphs of news items collected in each city, headed by the name of the city and the date on which the news was sent.[42]

The weekly Johann Carolus printed in Strasbourg in 1609 may have grown out of a handwritten weekly. (He writes in his introduction to the first issue of having previously produced "*Ordinarij avisa*.")[43] And although the earliest German printed newspapers begin with a cover page similar to that used by 16th-century printed newsbooks, the news they contain is written in the same format that had been employed in Venice. Here is one item from the first issue of Lucas Schulte's *Aviso Relation ober Zeitung* . . . from 1609:

> From Cologne 4. January
> From Amsterdam they tell/ of a great Storm with Thunder and Lightning/ and a Ship containing several 100. of Boxes of Sugar and many 1000. of Portuguese Reales was wrecked.[44]

Unlike their cousins the newsbook and the news ballad, these first European printed newspapers did not tell long stories in prose or verse; they collected short, diverse news items from different locales and organized them, as news items had been organized in Venice half a century earlier, under the place and date from which they were sent. Newspapers produced in Amsterdam in the 1620s dispensed with the title page featured by the German weeklies. They are essentially two-column, printed versions of the Venetian newssheets, with the addition only of a title in larger type atop the first page.

Perhaps this style of weekly journalism is so logical as to be inevitable; perhaps the authors of the Venetian newssheets themselves borrowed a format from the private, irregular newsletters that had circulated in Venice and elsewhere in Europe as early as the 15th century. But the journalism that was either stumbled upon or invented in these weekly Venetian gazettes—which apparently were known all across Europe—was the journalism into which the printed newspaper was born.[45]

News from Amsterdam—The Coranto

"The new tydings out of Italie are not yet com." These are the first words of the oldest surviving newspaper printed in English—in 1620.[46] English newspaper journalism begins, then, with an apology and with a hint that satisfying the "expectation of weekely newes" of "both the Reader and the Printer" would prove a formidable task. (English newspaper journalism also enters the world with a glaring typographical error: the date of this publication is given on its second page as "The 2. of Decemember.")[47]

The oldest surviving newspaper in English was printed in Amsterdam. It is an example of a printed *coranto*[48]—the brusque, businesslike news periodical in which the Dutch were beginning to specialize. Two and a half years earlier, what is now the oldest surviving printed Dutch coranto had been published in Amsterdam under the title *Courante uyt Italien, Duytslandt, &c.* (This coranto, undated but likely published on June 14, 1618, included a report from Prague on the Protestant revolt one month earlier that began the Thirty Years War and a report from Vienna on the Hapsburgs' response to it.)[49]

Amsterdam in the 17th century was transforming itself into one of the most cosmopolitan cities in Europe. Its merchants traveled widely. The man thought to have published the *Courante uyt Italien, Duytslandt, &c,* Casper van Hilten, had lived for a period of time in Germany, where he undoubtedly had encountered printed weeklies.[50] Refugees of many faiths were tolerated, often welcomed to Amsterdam; "you may be what Devil you will there, so you be but peaceable," a contemporary wrote. The city was also rapidly developing into the shipping and trading capital of Europe: the Chamber of

The oldest surviving newspaper in English was printed in Amsterdam on Dec. 2, 1620. It did not have a title; instead its first page begins with an apology.

Assurance was established in 1598, four years later the East India Company was chartered, then a new bourse in 1608, the exchange bank in 1609, a lending bank in 1614, a bourse for transactions in grain in 1616, and the West India Company in 1621.[51]

Amsterdam's merchants required news of their expanding community—a community that now extended as far as the East and West Indies. By 1619 the city would have a second weekly printed coranto. Additional corantos soon filed off the presses, and by 1645 at least eight different weeklies or biweeklies were for sale in Amsterdam.[52] These publications supplied merchants and other readers not only with news of Italy and Germany and the battles of the Thirty Years War but with news from America, Africa and Asia, including information on piracy and shipwreck—news of special interest to traders.[53]

Seventeenth-century Amsterdam, like Holland in general, tolerated ideas, including the printing of ideas, as well as it tolerated different religions. It was, in the words of one historian, "the book mart of the world." Printing was not entirely free of regulations, but the regulations—often imposed at the behest of the federal government or of a foreign government printers might have offended—were rarely enforced. Some of the work of the French philosopher René Descartes was published in Amsterdam.[54] And journalism historians in both France and England have been forced to acknowledge that their country's first printed newspapers were published in Amsterdam—"that Mart of newes," as a contemporary English news publication would call it.[55]

By September of 1620 Caspar van Hilten appears to have begun translating issues of his Dutch coranto and reprinting them the next day in French under the title *Courant d'Italie & d'Almaigne, &c.* Only four issues of this first French newspaper have survived;[56] there is no evidence that it succeeded. Early 17th-century France, with its stringent press controls, does not appear to have provided fertile ground for the printed coranto, at least not for one published in Protestant Amsterdam. It would be a decade before a printed weekly would take root in France.[57]

The first newspaper journalist to work in English appears to have been Pieter van de Keere, a Dutch map and print engraver in Amsterdam, who had lived in London for a few years. In December 1620 Van de Keere, presumably employing his ties with printers in Amsterdam and booksellers in London, printed that untitled coranto in English, which began with the apology "The new tydings out of Italie are not yet com." The bibliographer Folke Dahl has demonstrated that issues of Pieter van de Keere's newssheet were almost literal translations of Dutch corantos—with news of England (which might have offended English authorities) deleted and a few dates advanced to make the news appear fresher. Beginning with its second surviving issue, this coranto gained a name: *Corrant out of Italy, Germany, &c.*[58]

The English had to wait for the news in their first corantos to arrive, be translated, and be printed in Amsterdam. (The roundabout paths news might follow are well illustrated by this item from that first issue: *"Out of Ceulen [Cologne], the 24 of November.* Letters out of Neurenburghe of the 20 of this present, make mention, that they had advise from the Borders of Bohemia, that there had beene a very great Battel by Prage. . . .")[59] Then the English had to wait for the corantos to arrive in London. Still, this was the most timely form in which they had ever been offered news in print.

The publishers of newsbooks and news ballads of the 16th and early 17th centuries might occasionally have succeeded in rushing a story onto the press, but they were also capable of presenting months-old stories to their news-hungry readers. Coranto publishers,[60] on the other hand, not only had in their next issue a vehicle ready to deliver the latest accounts, but they had to deal with the pressure of their readers' "expectation of weekely Newes"—that vehicle was waiting impatiently to be loaded. No newsbook or news ballad publisher had to admit in print that "the new tydings out of" anywhere had "not yet com"; their publications could wait. Newspapers could not.[61] ("When a man has engaged to keep a stage coach," Richard Steele would write in his *Tatler* in 1709, "he is obliged, whether he has passengers or not, to set out; thus it fares with us weekly historians. . . .")[62]

With the introduction of a periodic news medium, a new frame of reference for judging the freshness of an item of news was introduced. Each installment of a newspaper is designed to make the previous installment obsolete, so a periodic publication in effect establishes a standard of timeliness corresponding to its period. For a weekly, news available last week will seem stale.

To underline the timeliness of the news they are able to present, radio and television reports today are often cast in the present tense: "The president *says* . . ."; "The fire *is* burning." With perhaps the same purpose, the oldest surviving issue of Pieter van de Keere's English coranto often employed the present tense: "The Hungarians continue . . ."; "the Emperour sends . . ."; "the Earle . . . doth Cause . . ."; "it is feared . . ."; "it is thought . . ."; "there is mustered. . . ."

The introduction of the newspaper might be said to have carried printed news into the present tense. Certainly it quickened the pace of the news business: Publishers in Amsterdam began to squeeze in late-breaking developments at the end of their corantos (sometimes resorting to smaller typefaces).[63] There was, after all, no such thing as "stop-the-presses news" until there was a fairly regular printing schedule to stop.

Periodicity would also cause a shift in the standards by which circumstances were evaluated as news. Newsbooks or news ballads had been concerned almost exclusively with moments of triumph or catastrophe; their subjects did not often "continue" or "send" or "muster" in any tense. Wars, with few exceptions (Charles VIII's invasion of Italy possibly among them), were reduced in these one-shot publications to a series of major battles followed by a treaty—effects stripped of causes, causes stripped of effects.

News in the newspaper would retain its fascination with outsized and anomalous events such as murders or battles.[64] However, by checking *periodically* on criminal cases or military campaigns, newspapers would be able to track their progress. Van de Keere's English coranto of Dec. 2, 1620, informed readers interested in the war in Germany and Eastern Europe that "it is thought that the Emperour will leave Austria to the Hungorians . . ."; that "the Earle . . . doth Cause the foresaid Cittie to be strongly fortified . . ."; that "it is feared that those Countrie-men are starred up. . . ." News standards were changed sufficiently by the newspaper so that the picture presented in print of the Thirty Years War now included plans and preparations. With the "expectation of . . . Newes" in these first newspapers came an increased ability to expect events.

The writing in the Dutch corantos distributed in Amsterdam and its journalistic dependencies was dense with facts. For readers familiar with the melodramatics of the newsbook or news ballad, these periodicals must have seemed rather dry, rather curt. Here is the first item, after the apology, from Pieter van de Keere's oldest surviving English coranto; it details some of the early maneuvering in the Thirty Years War:

> *Out of Weenen,* [Vienna] *the 6 November*
> The French ambassador hath caused the Earle of Dampier to be buried stately at Presburg. In the meane while hath Bethlem Gabor [prince of Transylvania] cited all the Hungerish States, to com together at Presburg the 5. of this present, to discourse aboute the Crowning [Bethlem was elected king of Hungary] & other causes concerning the same Kingdom.

A ballad maker could have found great drama in such a funeral; a newsbook writer would have delighted in Bethlem's election as king.

The lack of embellishment in these corantos owes something to the city whence they came. From the perspective of 17th-century Londoners, at least, Amsterdam was a remarkably efficient city. By 1624 the *Courante uyt Italien, Duytslandt, &c.* could be ex-

Weeklies, Dailies and Hourlies

The first newspapers in Europe appeared with a frequency—once a week—now more common to newsmagazines, yet still they helped pick up the pace of the news business. That pace would increase further with the appearance of the first printed daily newspaper in 1650 (see Chapter 10). Radio and then cable television news, with newscasts hourly or even more frequently, have provided a further acceleration. And, of course, there is the continually updated Internet.

These speedups do not only affect journalists' work lives; they make the whole world seem to move faster. Life seems more hectic. And for those who need to respond to the world's movements—government officials, business people, concerned citizens—life actually becomes more hectic as they struggle to keep up with or stay ahead of the news.

Complaints about the pace of modern life have become common. Here is one of the causes.

pected on Saturday; English publishers would not even establish a specific day of publication as a goal until 1641.[65] From Londoners' perspective Amsterdam also appeared a remarkably tidy city: One English diplomat grew perturbed during a state dinner party there because a maid was constantly wiping up his spit from the floor.[66] With similar fastidiousness, the corantos produced in Amsterdam and circulated in England seem to have been wiped clean of personal touches.

In its first years the newspaper would sell more for its relative timeliness and comprehensiveness than for its style or personality. But in what would be the first of their many contributions to newspaper journalism, the English were responsible for allowing the humanizing presence of an editor to enter the columns of the coranto to grapple with the tidy stacks of facts and rumors from around the Continent and globe that the Dutch were so adept at assembling.

An Editor in London

Newspapers are doubly disjointed publications. They reappear each day, or each week, with a different set of stories, and each issue is itself composed of diverse, often unrelated items. The earliest purveyors of periodic news inevitably faced the problem of how to organize the week's disparate set of items—items from Italy, Germany, et cetera, items that often had nothing more in common than the fact they had all arrived that same week. Like the publishers of the first German printed newspapers, Dutch written corantos and the Venetian weekly newssheets of the previous century, the publishers of printed corantos out of Amsterdam solved this problem in a fashion convenient for them but inconvenient for their readers: They simply grouped their reports under headings indicating the name of the city from which they had been sent and the date on which they had been sent.

News of Bethlem Gabor in Hungary might have been discovered under a Vienna heading, or under a Prague heading, or under the name of any of the handful of other cities in which it might have found its way into a letter or a newsbook that in turn found its way to Amsterdam. In fact, a few different references to the activities of major figures in the Thirty Years War—like Bethlem Gabor or Count Tilly, leader of the army of the Catholic League—might have been scattered in one issue among the items sent from different cities on various dates, with no regard for the actual location or chronology of the events.[67]

This journalism had taken root in England by Sept. 24, 1621—the date of the oldest surviving issue of an English coranto actually printed in England: *Corante, or weekely newes from Italy, Germany, Hungary, Poland, Bohemia, France and the Low Countreys.*[68] Its publisher—probably the first newspaper journalist in England—used only his initials, N.B., and unfortunately for the history of English journalism, there were two active printers in London with those initials—Nathaniel Butter and Nicholas Bourne.[69]

At first these more or less regular products of London print shops were faithful to the format of the Dutch corantos. By 1622, however, English publishers (mostly notably Bourne and Thomas Archer in partnership, and Butter both on his own and with others) began printing the news in the form of pamphlets, generally consisting of from eight to 24 pages, with increasingly long titles on the front page.[70] These publishers had adopted a format for their periodic newssheets that was more familiar to English readers—the format of the newsbook. (They had switched, in other words, from the Dutch to the German model for the newspaper.) And by September 1622 these English newspaper publishers—for the moment all working together on a single weekly—hired an editor.[71]

The old rubrics—"From Rome the 31. of August"—soon disappeared. Instead, this editor began to weave the various reports he had received into a coherent narrative: "May it please you next then to turne backe an eye unto *Bethlem Gabor,* of whom much hath beene expected, and little performed. . . ."[72] The editor's announced goal: putting "newes of the same nature all together."[73] At one point he explained his new method in a discussion of some reports from Venice:

> I have brought them as it were into a continued relation, which as I take it will be the pleasanter, because you need not trouble your remembrance with looking backe after former matters.[74]

This first English editor did not append his name to his work, but evidence indicates he was Thomas Gainsford, a widely traveled man who had served as a captain in the Irish wars. A letter written in 1624 refers to Captain Gainsford as "our news-monger or maker of gazets."[75] Gainsford did not always succeed in bringing all his news into a "continued relation"; occasionally he apologizes for some disjointed paragraphs on this and that—"broken stuffe . . . which will not come within the compasse of our continued discourse."[76] Nevertheless, he contributed to early newspaper journalism a sense of organization and of perspective. Though most of the news still arrived via Dutch corantos, the editor appears to have made an effort to gather news from letters and publications originating elsewhere on the Continent.[77] Gainsford also contributed an audible and appealing "voice":

> In this manner stand the affaires of *Europe,* which I cannot compare better, then to a wounded man, newly drest, and in great danger of life, so that untill his second opening, and taking the aire, the Surgion himselfe cannot tell what will become of him. . . .[78]

The techniques Gainsford employed were not new. The newsbooks and news ballads of the time were routinely organized into coherent narratives, and their authors, especially the ballad makers, frequently impressed a style upon their material. Gainsford does, however, appear to be the first journalist in England—and perhaps in the world—to apply these techniques to the newspaper.[79] "Relation" was a common term for a newsbook, and Gainsford correctly described his contribution as the "continued relation."

The application of an editorial intelligence is one means of transforming a newspaper from a hodgepodge into an attractive and reasonably coherent publication. Rather than attempting to knit stories into one "continued relation," editors in later centuries would fit individual stories, each telling a coherent tale of its own, into familiar compartments in a standardized format. Nevertheless, their goal remained the same—creating a pleasant and familiar product to which readers would regularly turn for news of the often unpleasant and unfamiliar. Their success depended in large part on creating a publication readers would come to "expect"—creating, in other words, a habit.[80]

The publishers of London's periodic newsbooks (soon exclusively in the hands of Butter and Bourne) eventually discovered that a consistent name might help make their product habit-forming. Beginning in September 1624 their lengthy titles all commenced with the phrase: *The continuation of the weekly newes.* . . .[81] (This name would be used, with minor variations, through 1632.) These early newspaper publishers were never quite able to reap the benefits of a regular day and time of publication.[82] Yet, they did succeed—as a contemporary satire notes—in making "the appetite of the reader more eager in his next week's pursuit" by closing with such suggestive phrases as, "heerafter you shall heare more."[83] These publishers or their editor also helped develop faithful readers by scripting in regular appearances by a cast of appealing characters.

The first English newspapers found their protagonists in the ongoing war on the Continent. Some of these military leaders they transformed into heroes. Perhaps the greatest of these early English newspaper celebrities was Count Ernst Mansfeld—a German mercenary fighting for the Protestants, whose troops had a disconcerting tendency to ravage the territory of friend as well as foe. Of the English periodic newsbooks that have survived from the beginning of 1622 to Mansfeld's visit to England in April 1624, nearly two-thirds mention his name somewhere in their long titles.[84]

Newsbooks and news ballads had created their own celebrities, but these stars had been allowed to fade between their heroic exploits and their epitaphs. The continual coverage the newspaper was able to grant kept Mansfeld fixed in the public mind even when he was not doing battle. Readers were told of Mansfeld's "preparations," of "the state of" his army, of "the great jollitie lately" in his camp. The effects of this coverage could be seen during Mansfeld's visit to London: cheering crowds followed him in the streets.[85]

These early newspapers were well enough established as a habit that, according to that contemporary satire, should the "Corranto-coiner" fail to "weekly performe his taske . . . he disappoints a number of no small fooles. . . . These you shall know by their Mondai's morning question, a little before exchange time; *Stationer, have you any newes.*"[86] However, after Mansfeld died in 1626 and the Protestant cause took a turn for the worse, the English newspaper fell upon hard times:[87] "It is well knowne these Novels are well esteemed in all parts of the World (but heere) by the more Judicious," Nathaniel Butter complained in a notice to his readers printed in 1641.[88] English periodic newsbooks, filled with foreign news, ceased publication sometime in 1642, as readers began demanding of their stationers copies of the newspapers specializing in home news that suddenly appeared with the approach of the English Civil War.[89]

England's first newspaper editor, Captain Gainsford, had died of the plague in 1624. After his death, the English periodic newsbooks had returned for a time to what they themselves described as "word for word" translations of corantos from Amsterdam.[90] At least one additional editor signed on with Bourne and Butter during the years they published these periodical newsbooks,[91] but it is not clear that he was able to reshape the copy in the manner of Captain Gainsford. Indeed most 17th-century and many 18th-century newspaper readers—including readers of America's first successful newspaper—would continue to have their "remembrance" troubled "with looking backe after former matters."[92] Despite Gainsford's accomplishments, the old Venetian format and rubrics would remain in wide use.

Journalism would blossom in Civil War England, but it was still not unusual to find, for example, a newspaper with a story on page four under a "Rome, January 16," heading suggesting that Cardinal Carassa is one of six men with a chance to become the next pope, and then a story on page nine of the same paper, headed "Rome, February 12," saying Carassa "is newly dead."[93]

Questions

1. What disadvantages did printed newsbooks and news ballads have compared to the printed newspapers that began appearing in Europe in 1609? What advantages did they have over those early newspapers?

2. Give the arguments for and against classifying the handwritten newssheets that appeared in Venice in the 16th century as newspapers.

3. The oldest surviving English-language newspaper was written in the present tense. What tenses do the various news media today employ?

4. England's first newspaper editor announced that his goal was putting "newes of the same nature all together." To what extent is this done in newspapers and broadcast newscasts today?

10

The Power of the Periodical—Domesticating News

Much of the history of journalism can be understood as a long struggle by written and printed forms of news to compete with that first news medium—word of mouth. Handwritten letters made some inroads but almost exclusively with the well-off and almost exclusively on news from afar. If Philip Eduard Fugger wanted news of his hometown, Augsburg, his best bet still would have been to pay some calls and ask. Early forms of printed news attracted the attention of larger audiences but only, as a rule, for the most dramatic or the most sensational stories. Fuller, if somewhat less reliable, accounts of events were still available on the street corners and in the taverns.

No previous news medium had been as successful in weaning humankind from its busybodies as the newspaper would be, but the process would take hundreds of years. In 1708, when a Dutch publisher proclaimed "this century of newspapers,"[2] he might just as well have been announcing a century of coffeehouses, of *nouvellistes,* or of salons. Each of these mechanisms through which spoken news was exchanged would continue to flourish alongside the newspaper well into the 18th century. (Handwritten periodic newsletters, *nouvelles à la main,* also continued to circulate in the 18th century, and printed news ballads remained a popular news medium through the 19th century.)

The earliest newspapers had severe limitations: They were restricted almost exclusively to foreign news. When Count Mansfeld visited England in 1624, English periodic newsbooks covered his trip over and his trip back but virtually ignored his stay in England.[3] They were often unreliable. A prayer said to have been delivered in 1632, when the king of Sweden was the latest Protestant hope in the Thirty Years War, asked for divine assistance in inspiring "the Curranto-makers with the Spirit of truth, that one may know when to praise thy blessed and glorious name and when to pray unto thee; for we often praise and Laude thy holy name for the King of Swedens victories and afterwards we hear that there is noo such

A News-Paper . . . ought to be the Register of the times, and faithful recorder of every species of intelligence; it ought not to be engrossed by any particular object; but, like a well-covered table, it should contain something suited to every palate . . . and by steering clear of extremes, hit the happy medium. . . .

—**John Walter, founder of the *Times* of London, 1785.[1]**

147

thing."[4] And these first newspapers at best appeared only weekly; news that arrived after they went to press still found its way around town by other means.

However, as the 17th century progressed and the 18th century began, the newspaper would begin to realize its potential in England and, to an extent, in France. It would cover a broader range of news, cover that news with more authority, and distribute it more frequently. The outlines were beginning to take shape of the medium that would have the strength not only to displace many of the world's busybodies but to come as close as any medium would to domesticating news, to enabling it to settle in the columns of a regular, well-ordered space.

Home News—The Breadth of the Newspaper

The following item appeared on page three of *A Perfect Diurnall of Some Passages in Parliament,* an English newspaper published in 1649 and edited by Samuel Pecke:

> Tuesday, January 30.
> This day the King was beheaded, over against the Banquetting house by White-Hall. . . .[5]

Fewer than eight years had passed since the days when English periodic newsbooks dared not mention the name of their own king, and here was a paper reporting on the loss of Charles I's head. Not only had the monarch's status changed radically in England over those years, but newspaper journalism had broken free.

The escape had been led in November 1641 by a sedate little weekly entitled *The Heads of Severall Proceedings In This Present Parliament.* This paper, apparently also edited by Samuel Pecke, was not only filled with news of English politics but with news of that particularly sacrosanct and secretive political organization—Parliament.[6] And although this weekly limited itself to the driest, most matter-of-fact of styles, it was reporting the most controversial of issues: Parliament's passage of the Grand Remonstrance, which laid out its grievances against the king. Yet the paper survived; the king's authority had ebbed to the point where he could no longer control the presses. By mid-December this weekly faced a competitor—*The Diurnall, or The Heads of all the Proceedings in Parliament.*[7] Then, at the end of December, a third weekly materialized.

Seven weeks after that first newspaper reporting on Parliament had appeared, five such weeklies were on sale in London. The publishing partnerships behind these papers might form or dissolve between issues. Titles were copied, news copied, too. Some of these newspapers lasted months; some expired after their first issue.[8] In other words, the free practice of newspaper journalism was straining fitfully to invent itself in England, in a hurry.

The experiment with a relatively free press in Amsterdam was already decades old in 1642, but that was a restrained press, which had matured gradually in a relatively restrained, business-oriented city. English journalism had been released all of a sudden into a politically polarized country whose king and Parliament would soon be facing each other across a battlefield. For the next eight years neither king nor Parliament would obtain sufficient power to force the press back into its cage.

This book has argued that no journalist, group of journalists, or society can claim credit for inventing or discovering news. The concerns of the news appear rooted in human nature. However, when a new news medium arrives, journalists do have to develop applications and techniques appropriate to that medium. Here it is possible to speak in terms of firsts, and in the history of the newspaper few publications have as strong a claim to as many such firsts as these weeklies printed during the English Civil War.[9]

In at least one of the English newspapers from this period, headlines of a sort were stacked on the front page: QUEEN'S LANDED, CESSATION INTERRUPTED. Woodcuts illustrated stories. A woman, dubbed a "sheintelligencer," was employed in the collection of news. Newsboys or, more commonly, newsgirls hawked papers in the street.[10] In other words, many of the journalistic techniques that American newspaper historians have credited to the decades surrounding the American Civil War actually date from the English Civil War two centuries earlier.

The most significant of the contributions these weeklies made to the development of the newspaper was their introduction to print of spirited coverage of national news. Word of mouth and handwritten letters had long indulged the interest of citizens in their own government. Some newsbooks and news ballads had approached national issues, but almost always from the government's side and then only with the utmost discretion. Newspapers, for the most part, had avoided these issues.[11] They were tolerated so long as their weekly searchlights were not turned on those magnanimous enough to suffer their existence.

However, the English newspapers of the 1640s found themselves with the freedom to discuss a wide range of domestic news, and, of course, they lived with a domestic story more newsworthy than any possible development abroad—a civil war. Here is more from *A Perfect Diurnall* on a particularly compelling installment of that story—the execution of Charles I:

> . . . Then the King, speaking to the Executioner said: I shall say but very short prayer and then thrust out my hands. . . .
>
> The King then said to the executioner, Is my hair well. Then the King took off his cloak . . . then looking upon the block, said to the Executioner:
>
> You must set it fast.
>
> Executioner: It is fast, Sir.
>
> King: It might have been a little higher.
>
> Executioner: It can be no higher, Sir . . .
>
> After that, having said two or three words (as he stood) to himself, with hands and eyes lift up; Immediately stooping down, laid his neck upon the block. . . .
>
> And after a very little pause, the King stretched forth his hands. The executioner at one blow severed his head from his body.
>
> That when the King's head was cut off, the Executioner held it up and showed it to the spectators. . . .[12]

What news from abroad could compete with such stories? "And now by a strange alteration and vicissitude of times," one contemporary journalist explained, "wee talke of nothing else but what is done in England, and perhaps once in a fortnight we hearken after newes sent out of Scotland." The editor who made this statement attempted to buck the trend and attract "Marchants" to a paper that emphasized foreign news, the *Exchange Intelligencer.* It lasted two months.[13]

There was occasionally some news of London in these London newspapers, but local news was for the most part still left to word of mouth. Their staple was news of the fate of the Kingdom-become-Commonwealth—what is called in England today "home news." (Like modern London newspapers, these publications attracted a national audience. Most were sold on Monday, so they could be read in the city and then sent to the provinces with the Tuesday post.)[14]

These English weeklies also began to compete with newsbooks and news ballads for *faits divers.*[15] This story about a "Yeoman not farre from Warwick, who for want of discretion or other discourse" sold his wife to a friend for 5 pounds, appeared in the *Kingdomes Weekly Intelligencer* in 1647:

> Not a quarter of an hour after, the Yeoman repented of his bargaine, and offered to restore the money, and desired to have his wife returned. His companion left it to her choyce, not without some intimation that he was loath to leave her. The good woman assured him that she was well content to live with him and had rather goe with the buyer than the seller, and accordingly expressing a courteous farewell to her Husband, she went along with his Companion. The poore Yeoman who (on better consideration) had rather lose his life than lose his wife, hath since made his complaint to all the Justices in that County. . . .[16]

Freaks and horrors were not slighted in these periodicals: Thirty-seven years after that newsbook on a dragon in Sussex, a newspaper called the *Faithfull Scout* presented a story about the body of a giant found in Sussex. Crime was covered: Readers were offered eyewitness accounts of the execution of criminals as well as of their king. In fact, the *Weekly Intelligencer of the Commonwealth* in 1655 included a story that certainly qualifies as one of the more sensational to appear in any medium, that of a woman in Kent who cooked and served to her husband the vulva of his lover.[17]

And these periodical publications were able to extend their search for the unlikely and unfortunate beyond the major catastrophes or grand oddities that could by themselves justify publication of a pamphlet or broadside. The minor human interest story, the tidbit, was for the first time finding its way into print. There was room in the pages of these weeklies for a report on a "surly" driver who ran away after his cart "bruised a child in Woodstreet," room to note that the king played golf, room for news that plays were being produced in Knightsbridge, room for the story of some troops in Bristol who fired their cannons at glowworms,[18] room to report on a man sent to prison for eloping with the Earl of Newport's daughter.[19]

Joseph Frank, a historian who had produced the most thorough account of the newspapers of this period, describes some of them as "crowded."[20] The news still concerned itself with the atypical, but the degree of extraordinariness required to catch the attention of the news was reduced in these "crowded" weeklies: the earl's daughter had not been maimed; the troops were not firing at a dragon.

The freedom the English press achieved in the 1640s can be exaggerated. These newspapers did have, for the first time, the opportunity to discuss not only the king's golf game but the major issues facing their divided government. They did not have immunity

Calls for Press Freedom

"Let [Truth] and Falsehood grapple," the English poet John Milton proposed in his *Areopagitica;* "who ever knew Truth put to the worse in a free and open encounter. . . ." This was a controversial suggestion in 1644; it would also upset some today who still struggle to "protect" people from information they consider false.

The *Areopagitica* is certainly among the most eloquent arguments for press freedom: "Who kills a Man kills a reasonable creature . . .," Milton wrote, "but hee who destroyes a good Booke, kills reason it selfe. . . . Truth and understanding are not such wares as to be monopoliz'd. . . ."

John Stuart Mill, the English philosopher, argued for this freedom perhaps less poetically but equally powerfully in his book *On Liberty* 200 years later: "If all mankind minus one, were of one opinion, and only one person were of the contrary opinion, mankind would be no more justified in silencing that one person, than he, if he had the power, would be justified in silencing mankind" (Siebert, *Four Theories* . . .).

against prosecution for offending whichever faction in that government had jurisdiction over them. Editors could still be jailed for too enthusiastic coverage of a controversial issue, as Samuel Pecke learned when one of his newspapers apparently devoted too much space to a petition calling for peace with the king.[21] The old shackles had been lifted, but they still dangled above the English presses, ensnaring editors who reached too high.

The lifting of the shackles had represented no great triumph of libertarianism to begin with. The papers stumbled upon this freedom three years before the ideal of freedom of the press would be articulated so eloquently by John Milton in his *Areopagitica*.[22] Nor was this freedom the result of a calculated experiment. It was an unforeseen consequence of the breakdown of the power of King Charles I under the assault of the Long Parliament and the Puritan revolution.

For a time, there were two separate centers of power in the country, each offering shelter to its supporters. The young journalist Marchamont Nedham, for example, had described King Charles in his paper, among the boldest of the anti-Royalist organs, as having "a guilty Conscience" and "bloody Hands." Then, two years later, Nedham was kissing one of those hands, asking forgiveness, launching a new royalist weekly, and referring to Oliver Cromwell, the leader of Parliament's forces, as "Crum-Hell."[23] Nedham had simply switched protectors.

Most editors, however, were not only more loyal but more cautious than Marchamont Nedham. Most seem to have recognized the basic conservatism of the medium in which they were working. A newspaper is to a pamphlet or a broadside as a store is to a peddler; it is an established business with a reputation to uphold and an investment to protect.

As would most of their successors, the newspapers in England during the Civil War struggled to establish a recognizable name and format. (These papers were, however, more likely than their successors to borrow, word for word, another paper's recognizable name and its format.) And these newspapers, with a few notable exceptions, remained remarkably temperate in intemperate times, as their successors, with a few notable exceptions, would remain. When presented with particularly controversial, and therefore dangerous, discussions in Parliament, Samuel Pecke, one of the most successful of those journalists, might tell readers only that "divers particulars . . . not convenient to be published at this time" had been discussed.[24]

Newspaper editors, unlike ballad makers or newsletter writers, could rarely hide—as Pecke, after his stay in jail, well knew. They had to return to the same shop next week. "Whosoever undertakes to write weekly in this nature," noted one anonymous editor in 1647, "undertakes to sayle down a narrow Channell, where all along the shore on each side are Rocks and Cliffs that threaten him. . . . He onely is the happy steersman that can keep his course in the middle of the channell."[25]

By 1649, with the parliamentary side triumphant, the king decapitated, and authority reestablished in the form of the Commonwealth, the relative freedom the English press had experienced began to evaporate. Marchamont Nedham was apprehended and sent to Newgate prison; the royalist point of view began to disappear from print. Oliver Cromwell, Lord Protector of England, great believer in freedom of conscience, great admirer of John Milton, gradually reimposed most of the press controls the Tudor monarchs had perfected—from licensing requirements to jail terms for insufficiently loyal editors.[26]

By 1655 only two English newspapers were being printed, both by the same publisher—the irrepressible Marchamont Nedham, reeducated, rehabilitated and now the only journalist Cromwell would trust.[27] Milton, for a final irony, aided Cromwell in his attempts to silence the opposition and was the official responsible for licensing one of his friend Nedham's newspapers.[28]

When Charles II was restored to his dead father's throne in 1660, he cleared the field for his own authorized newspapers—Roger L'Estrange's *Intelligencer*, then Henry Muddiman's *Oxford*, soon *London Gazette*. In 1663 L'Estrange, who doubled as censor, caught a printer in the act of printing sheets that supported, among other heresies, the doctrine that "the execution of judgment and justice is as well the people's as the magistrate's duty." The printer was sentenced to be hanged by the neck, cut down before he was dead, mutilated, disemboweled, and decapitated.[29] The shackles had returned, but the world, at least the English-speaking world, would retain a vision of the potential of the unfettered newspaper.

News of Science—The Authority of the Newspaper

French journalism historians tried for a time to promote Théophraste Renaudot for the still-vacant position "father of the newspaper."[30] There have been few more distinguished candidates. Renaudot was educated as a doctor, and he completed his education by introducing himself to most of the capitals of Renaissance Europe. Upon his return to France, Renaudot, a protégé of Cardinal Richelieu, was selected by the king to tackle the problem of poverty in the realm. Unfortunately, as even French historians have grudgingly conceded, the case for Renaudot's paternity was weakened considerably by the realization that when he began his weekly, the *Gazette de France,* in May 1631 he was not only 22 years too late to have published the first printed weekly and 11 years too late for the first printed weekly in French, but even a few months too late to have produced the first weekly printed in France. (*Nouvelles Ordinaires de Divers Endroits* had appeared on Jan. 1, 1631.)[31]

Still, Renaudot deserves credit for having published one of the most influential newspapers of the 17th century. News in the *Gazette* was organized under the same sort of rubrics used in the Venetian newssheets Renaudot is said to have seen during his travels. However, he was apparently able to select that news, discreetly of course, directly from government dispatches, and under those rubrics, Renaudot presented his information in a fluid, almost literary style. Few contemporary newspapers were as authoritative or as sophisticated. The king himself not only read the *Gazette,* Renaudot once explained, but supplied Renaudot with memoranda for his paper. The king also supplied Renaudot with an exclusive privilege to print weekly news and with a salary.[32]

No early newspaper better represents the conservative nature of the medium than Théophraste Renaudot's *Gazette de France.* It survived in essentially the same form until the Revolution in 1789, providing a reliable, regular and readable forum for the news of the world, and it covered that news intelligently but, first and foremost, inoffensively. "Was it for me to examine the acts of the government?" Renaudot once asked.[33] This was the newspaper as civilizing force, as a corral into which breaking events could be driven.

Among the more significant of the events Renaudot allowed into his *Gazette* in 1634 was the trial and condemnation of Galileo Galilei. The science practiced by individuals like Galileo is a particularly difficult subject to reduce to news. Their work not only resists popularization but challenges that which journalists—as transmitters of society's common thoughts—often seem to hold most dear: conventional wisdom. Renaudot supplied a lengthy account of the proceedings against Galileo, whose crime, the *Gazette* explained, was holding that "the sun is the center of the universe." But the publisher's sympathies lay with the Inquisition, not with Galileo's "absurd and false" ideas.[34]

Scientists, wary of this sort of response, long resisted placing their work before untutored eyes. Leonardo da Vinci disdained the printing press; Nicholas Copernicus shunned publicity; Isaac Newton once explained that he wrote in "a cryptic and complicated manner to discourage ignorant quibblers."[35] Nevertheless, the scientific revolution of the 17th century might not have been possible without the efforts of journalists to spread news about science both within the profession and, as Renaudot did in his clumsy way, to lay people.

Scientists, if they are to build on each other's advances and mistakes, require information on each other's work. "A scientific laboratory without a library is like a decorticated cat," writes the physicist John Ziman. "The motor activities continue to function, but lack coordination of memory and purpose."[36] Galileo's work on the telescope began in 1609 with a piece of news: "In Venice, where I happened to be at the time," he recalled years later, "news arrived that a Fleming had presented to Count Maurice a glass by means of which distant objects could be seen as distinctly as if they were nearby." (A description of this invention had been included in a widely circulated printed newsbook.)[37] Galileo also benefited from the chance to read the book Copernicus finally consented to publish; Newton benefited from the chance to read Galileo. Many of Leonardo's scientific ideas, however, remained undeveloped, locked in his notebooks.[38]

The public too must be kept informed of what is being discovered in laboratories and recorded in notebooks. The spread of news about science is part of the educational process that activates the interest of new scientists and prepares nonscientists to accept innovations such as the telescope and innovative ideas such as Galileo's. Indeed the hostility Galileo encountered might be seen, in part, as evidence of the failings of the system for spreading news of science that was available early in the 17th century.

Scientists traditionally communicated with each other by meeting each other, and as the scientific community expanded in the 17th century, attempts were made to regularize and formalize such contacts. Scientists in the major cities began to organize themselves into groups, such as England's Royal Society, founded in 1660.[39] Nevertheless, such organizations did little for the spread of information across borders or even into the provinces. In 1641 a physician who had studied in Paris but had left the city to practice complained, "I have no one here to confer with; it is as if I have been relegated to an island. . . ."[40]

To communicate from one city to another, or one "island" to another, 17th-century scientists resorted to the mails. Perhaps the most important scientific correspondence of Galileo's age flowed out of and into the quarters of Friar Marin Mersenne in a Paris convent. Mersenne was a perceptive, knowledgeable and incredibly energetic letter writer, who, in the words of one of the scientists to whom he wrote, "filled the air of the universe with his correspondence."[41] Mersenne exchanged letters with many of the top scientists of the day, including Descartes and Galileo, going out of his way to inform them of each other's work and to keep ideas, particularly Galileo's ideas, circulating. Less renowned scientific thinkers were also favored by the good Friar. That lonely doctor on his "island" in the provinces, for example, had the honor of having some of his thoughts and letters forwarded to Descartes, via Mersenne.[42]

The shortcomings of even such an extensive epistolary network[43] are apparent, however. A correspondent such as Friar Mersenne, for all his industriousness and dedication, could keep current only a limited number of scientists. And although Descartes may have learned of Galileo through such written correspondence, who outside of Mersenne and his circle was able to learn what Descartes thought of Galileo? The handwritten word was simply not up to the task of keeping the expanding "Republic of Letters" informed. Indeed, by 1661 the unofficial secretaries of Europe's various convocations of scientists were complaining that their time was being eaten up by the task of copying and recopying news for their correspondents.[44]

The printing press certainly had the potential to ease the strain on the hands of Friar Mersenne and other faithful letter writers. Multiple copies of major scientific works, including Copernicus's *De Revolutionibus,* were now available. Still, without any regular system of communication, such books were difficult to direct to the appropriate audience. And much interesting research was ignored by publishers because it was not sufficiently extensive, definitive and earth-shaking to command an entire volume.[45] The newsbook and news ballad, for their part, had little interest in any but the most newsworthy occurrences, and they were much more likely to see news value in a miracle than an experiment.[46] Communication within the "Republic of Letters" would require a news medium with a broader scope and greater seriousness.

Periodicity provided the answer. Even general interest weeklies, because they had more room for more events, carried occasional items on science. For example, an issue in 1609 of one of the two oldest surviving printed newspapers, Johann Carolus' Strasbourg weekly, includes an interesting tidbit—a brief report on the invention of the telescope by "Signor Galileo."[47] And Renaudot, though he approached Galileo's work with none of the understanding of a Friar Mersenne, was still able to focus the attention of thousands of readers on the dispute about the structure of the heavens.[48]

Newspapers like Renaudot's *Gazette de France* not only had more space for these matters, they could approach them with an authority that was new to printed journalism. This is an easy point to miss. The newspapers of the 17th century appear anything but authoritative at first glance. An English weekly from 1648, for example, included a report from Arabia via Warsaw on "the invention of a Machine, being Airie & of a construction so light, nevertheless so sound and firm, that the same is able to bear two men, and hold them up in the Air . . . after the same manner as you see represented in the old Tapistry hangings [of] the Dragons flying."[49] According to Joseph Frank, nearly one-tenth of the earliest English newspapers contained news of either an apparition, a vision, or a monstrous birth.[50] Renaudot's unenlightened view of Galileo was among the least of the errors of these early newspaper journalists.

Nonetheless, unlike the newsbooks and news ballads of the time, periodical publications had reputations to protect; they planned to face the public again. Although this did not eradicate mistakes or reports on the supernatural (news gatherers remained fallible and readers credulous), it certainly increased the price that might be paid for a report readers did not believe or learned that they should not have believed. English newspapers were pouncing on the errors of their competitors as early as 1622, printing critical letters from readers as early as 1624 (debunking, for example, a report on "the strange birth of Antichrist" in Babylon) and perhaps most significantly, newspapers in England were correcting their own errors as early as 1626: "In our laste newes where is spoken of the ship of Schoonhouen, which is cast away upon the Coast of Portugall reade that it was bound for the East, and not the West Indies. . . ."[51]

A publication that lived on to be corrected, and to correct itself, could aspire to and be held to a higher standard of truth.[52] The newspaper—like writing, like the printing press itself—moved the news a bit further along in the direction of credibility. Periodicals tended to be not only cautious politically but cautious in their assertions of fact. Those interested in science soon recognized their potential.

As early as 1633, in addition to his *Gazette* Théophraste Renaudot appears to have begun publishing *Feuilles du bureau d'adresses,* a weekly account of the public debates he was holding at his Bureau d'Adresses et de Rencontre (a center Renaudot organized, as part of his assignment to alleviate poverty, to bring together rich and poor—prospective employers, for example, with prospective employees). Many of those debates concerned science. The *Feuilles* has been called the first learned periodical; however, it was more record than newssheet, more dogmatic than inquisitive. "Journalism enters the world of learning," in the view of the historian Harcourt Brown, not with Renaudot's *Feuilles* but "with the *Journal des savants* in 1665."[53]

The French did not award the title *journal* lightly. According to a French history of journalism written in 1734:

> A *journal* is a periodic work that, appearing regularly at indicated intervals, announces new or newly reprinted books, provides an idea of their contents and serves to conserve the discoveries that are made in the sciences; in brief, a work in which one records everything that occurs daily in the Republic of Letters.[54]

The weekly *Journal des savants*[55] was the prototypical *journal.* Its pages were filled with scientific observations—that the shadows of four moons could be seen on Jupiter, for example. The major books of the time were reviewed ("For the comfort of those who are too busy or too lazy to read entire books," Diderot's *Encyclopédie* sneered).[56] And, of course, the more intriguing "monsters" of the time were discussed—a "human born near Chartres," for example, "who had a head with two faces, one in front the other behind."[57]

England's first scientific journal—the Royal Society's *Philosophical Transactions*—began monthly publication later in 1665 under the supervision of the Society's secretary, Henry Oldenburg.[58] The first issue included a report on the observation of a spot on Jupiter by "the ingenious Mr *Hook*" and "An Account of a very odd Monstrous Calf."[59] (That misshapen calf is analyzed in this and succeeding issues with a thoroughness that would soon make the pages of these journals inhospitable to the more fabulous of these monsters.) Of the 10 items in the first issue of *Philosophical Transactions*, three were borrowed from the *Journal des savants.*[60]

New journals soon debuted in other major European cities. Their effect upon the scientific community was dramatic. When Isaac Newton's *Principia mathematica* appeared in 1687, it had already been the subject of a long prepublication notice in *Philosophical Transactions.* It was then reviewed in the *Journal des savants.* (The reviewer found its mechanics "the most perfect one could imagine" but expressed disappointment at the limitations of the physics "Mr. Newton has given us.") More thorough accounts of the book appeared in a French journal published in Holland, *Bibliothèque universelle* (perhaps written by John Locke), and in a Latin journal published in Leipzig, *Acta eruditorum.*[61]

Newton revised his text after reading the review in the *Acta eruditorum,* and the German philosopher and mathematician Leibniz is said to have been inspired by that review to write three papers.[62] But such direct contributions to scientific discourse are overshadowed by the more generalized blessing of awareness these publications bestowed upon Europeans interested in science: Now for the first time they could be sure of being informed about *any* new work by a scientist of stature.

This information was available to anyone capable of passing the literacy test for citizenship in the "Republic of Letters"—scientist and nonscientist alike. "There is scarcely any literature better received by the public, nor read with more eagerness . . . ," an observer noted in 1721.[63] News of science was spreading faster, farther and with more accuracy than ever before. Unlike Galileo, Newton faced no Inquisition; instead he was sent to Parliament, elected president of the Royal Society and knighted. The gap between scientists and the public had narrowed.

The Long March to Credibility

Yes, we continue to have our complaints about journalists. They get this or that fact wrong. They ignore something they should cover; they cover something we wish they would ignore. Nevertheless, we have come to more or less trust the information we receive in newspapers and newscasts and increasingly online.

This book discusses a number of factors that have contributed to the growing credibility of news. The first was writing, which enabled stories to be preserved over distances. The next was the printing press, with its ability to make exact copies. This chapter discusses the contributions the newspaper made to the credibility of the news. Two developments in later centuries would also play key roles: the telegraph and the development of reporting (see Chapters 13 and 14).

Radio and cable television, then, made sure this information would be available to us 24 hours a day; satellites spread it around the world (see Chapters 15 and 16).

It took a few thousand years, but human beings have finally succeeded in constructing a news system upon which they can—more or less, most of the time—rely.

That gap would widen again, however, with increased specialization. Between 1665 and 1730 Europe witnessed the birth of 30 publications devoted to natural science.* The competition would force these publications to seek out narrower, more specialized audiences—11 of these journals, for example, concentrated on medicine.[64] At the same time, the line between newspaper and scholarly journal, blurred in some of these early weeklies, would grow firmer with the arrival of dailies. Science would continue to be popularized for the readers of the newspaper,[65] but scientists increasingly would communicate with each other in more esoteric publications.

News of Business—The Speed of the Newspaper

In 1663 Samuel Pepys, an English official and businessman, was attempting to buy insurance on an overdue ship when, according to his diary, he had the good fortune to call "at the Coffee-house, and there by great accident hear that a letter is come that our ship is safe come to Newcastle."[66] In Pepys' London news was as likely to save money—the cost of additional insurance in this case—or to make money as it was in Fugger's Augsburg. Letters and word of mouth, like that exchanged at London's coffeehouses, were

---

* There are signs even at this early date of the traditional problem of too little information giving way to the modern problem of too much information. At least six of the publications founded during these years were digests, which offered to sift through this growing mass of printed material for readers.

still disseminating much of that news. However, the newspaper was becoming an economic force in the second half of the 17th century. Indeed, the symbiotic relationship between news and business—established in bustling marketplaces and strengthened by the handwritten newsletter—would be formalized in the newspaper.

Early printed weeklies began to attract merchants, traders and financiers both with reports on Continental events and with more customized services. Dutch corantos included specific reports on the fate of investment-laden ships,[67] and although Pepys did not obtain initial word on *his* ship from a newspaper, such information was becoming available in English periodicals. By 1655 in England, Marchamont Nedham's *Mercurius Politicus* featured long lists of vessels, their port of origin and cargo—"Oyls, Sugar[,] Cinamon and Fruit," for example—under the heading: "Ships this week arrived in the Port of London."[68]

These lists of ships, ports, and cargos do not exactly represent breaking news. They fit instead in the category of "service feature," and are indeed among the first of the wide variety of listings and practical data—weather forecasts, recipes, movie timetables, television schedules—that newspapers would eventually offer their readers. Newspaper publishers were discovering that a periodic publication could have other selling points besides its accounts of breaking news. And it is fitting that they began to make this discovery while catering to those most loyal and valued of their customers—the commercial classes.

The cooperation between newspaper publishers and merchants was also manifest in the advertising the early weeklies began to carry. Advertisements, as McLuhan has noted, can be considered a form of news;[69] however, they represent not only an unusually purposive, self-interested variety of news, but a quiet news, usually with minimal news value. As cities grew larger, this information on products and services was beginning to have difficulty being heard. Renaudot's center to facilitate economic transactions of benefit to the poor, his Bureau d'Adresses et de Rencontre, was in part a response to the challenge of spreading news of available jobs throughout a city the size of Paris.[70] Newsbooks and news ballads occasionally were placed at the service of what we would call advertisements. In 1612, for example, the Virginia Company printed a ballad to publicize a lottery held to support its settlements:

> . . . Let no man thinke that he shall loose,
>   though he no Prize poscesse:
> His substance to Virginia goes,
>   which God, no doubt will blesse. . . .[71]

Newspapers, however, provided a much more attractive setting for advertisements. For a price, this quiet news of goods and services (itself something of a "service feature") was allowed to share the newspaper's crowded pages with the more compelling news journalists collected. Battles and crimes gathered a group of readers; advertised products took their money. This gentle grab-and-fleece trick paid some of the bills of 17th- and 18th-century English newspapers; it would finance most of the grandest 19th- and 20th-century news organizations.

Publishers placed the first advertisements in their newspapers themselves. In *The continuation of the weekly newes* . . . for September 16, 1624, Nathaniel Butter and Nicholas Bourne note that they will be printing and selling a map of one of the battles

Types of Advertising

A line—a thin, wavy line, to be sure—might be drawn between two types of advertising. The first, and the closest to news, simply announces that a product or service is available. This is the kind of advertising that began to appear in these early newspapers.

The second type goes further: It attempts to imbue its audience with a need for the products and services it mentions. It is a form of psychological manipulation, not news.

There is considerable overlap, certainly, between these two types of advertising. An attractive picture of a product, for example, can be both informative and manipulative. Nonetheless, the advertising that has fired the economy of the United States and other modern capitalist countries—and filled so many homes with unneeded products—seems primarily of the second type.

mentioned in that issue; they are, in effect, advertising the map.[72] Publishers in England began more fully exploiting the potential of this form of income in the 1640s and 1650s, when advertisements appeared for the return of stolen horses, lost articles, and lost children and for medical remedies such as apples and frankincense. Nedham's newspapers included ads for tea, beer and fire extinguishers.[73]

Still, for all their hospitality to advertising and their willingness to monitor the ports, these newspapers had a major limitation as a business-news medium: They were published only once or twice a week, which made it difficult for them to keep up with the daily fluctuations of the markets and exchanges where the most news-sensitive forms of capitalism were being practiced. Some attempts were made to monitor the markets. In 1667, for example, the *City and Country Mercury* (a semiweekly) published such information in dialogue form:

> *Countryman.* But pray, how goes the Grocer's Trade . . . we are concern'd for the Belly?
> *Citizen.* It is a hard matter to deal with a Grocer, but I will the best I can inform you. Coarse Barbado's Sugars, formerly sold for thirty five shillings, are now worth forty five shillings the Hundred. Malaga Raisons rarely to be had. . . . Currans, formerly sold at about three pound, are now £3 10s. Brandy at about forty five pound the Tun. . . .
> *Countryman.* But I pray, how goes fish?
> *Citizen.* Fish of all sorts are very dear. . . .[74]

But if newspapers were to provide those who played the markets and exchanges with more timely data for use in their speculations, newspapers would have to gain speed. The world's oldest surviving *printed* daily, *Einkommende Zeitung* (Incoming News) was published in Leipzig in 1650.[75] (Of course, the handwritten *acta* had been posted daily in Rome before the birth of Christ.)

After the weakening of the king's authority that led to the second English revolution, in 1688, and the lapsing of the Licensing Act (temporarily in 1679, permanently in 1695), London witnessed a journalistic explosion that would produce a wide variety of vigorous and more frequent periodicals. In 1709, when the *General Postscript* published a list of the newspapers available in London, it included more than a dozen thrice-weeklies. (Their titles—*Post-Boy, Post-Man, Flying Post,* and *Evening Post,* for example—demonstrate not only that these papers relied heavily on the post for news, but that newspaper journalists generally are no more adventurous in their choice of titles than they are in their choice of format.) The *General Postscript*'s list also included one daily: England's first successful daily, the *Daily Courant,* which had first appeared in 1702 and would survive for 12 years.[76]

Dailies require (and favor) news that changes daily. (Their hunger for news would help invigorate the art of news gathering.) The *Daily Courant* succeeded in filling its two pages a day with the latest news of the ongoing war on the Continent—the War of the Spanish Succession (referred to by one contemporary as "the great Fountain of News").[77] But thicker dailies in later years began to turn to the flow of business data for much of their quotidian quota of news. The *Daily Advertiser,* which began publication in London in 1730, included the following notice about its contents:

> This paper will consist wholly of Advertisements, together with the Prices of Stocks, Course of Exchange, and Names and Descriptions of Persons becoming Bankrupts; as also in Alphabetical Manner a Daily Account of the Several Species and Quantities of Goods Imported into the Port of London. . . .[78]

The journalism historian Stanley Morison, who labels the *Daily Advertiser* the "first modern newspaper," says it soon gained "a hold on the commercial classes which it never lost." Its success inspired all of London's growing number of morning dailies in the 1740s to feature such "commercial intelligence."[79] The word *Advertiser* began to supplant the word *Post* in the titles of England's newspapers.

In accounts of the behavior of the markets and exchanges, daily newspapers found a subject matter that justified daily publication and that attracted a well-heeled, influential readership. In these daily papers, merchants, traders and financiers, for their part, found the first news medium quick enough to compete with word of mouth for news of their affairs and speculations. (Some 18th-century newspapers and journals were even sufficiently thoughtful and authoritative to attempt discussions of economic theory.[80]) It was a successful partnership. Their reports on business helped gain Grub Street* journalists a measure of respectability, while newspapers, by organizing prices in precise, formal columns, helped transform haggling into business transactions. London merchants might still visit coffeehouses as the 18th century progressed, but they would spend much of their time there reading newspapers.

Nevertheless, the commercial classes did not view the publication of commercial intelligence as an unmitigated blessing. Many a government official had already discovered how unpleasant it can be to see one's affairs published in a newspaper. Now

---

* Grub Street—the name of a street in London inhabited by many impecunious scribblers—was used as early as the 17th century to refer to writers driven by want and ill-fortune to hackwork.

merchants and traders had that opportunity. In business, as in government (or subatomic particle physics), the presence of an observer can distort the process being observed. In this case regular publication of prices tended to reduce disparities in prices, disparities upon which many traders based their incomes.[81]

America's fledgling newspapers in the early 18th century took a special interest in the trade upon which the colonies were so dependent. However, when the second newspaper to establish itself in America, the *Boston Gazette,* proposed carrying a "Price Currant" in 1719, the paper reported with some annoyance that local merchants "made their Objections."[82] Of course, like most such publicity-shy newsmakers, those Boston merchants were fighting a losing battle. Lists of prices would join maritime news as a staple of the newspaper in America.

Indeed, once the political ferment that resulted in the American Revolution quieted, Americans began to take the lead in the development of the daily newspaper. They would create a press uniquely situated for domesticating political as well as economic news.

Questions

1. This chapter notes ways in which the 18th century was and was not a "century of newspapers." What news media dominated the 20th century? What seem likely to dominate the 21st century?

2. How might the story, quoted in this chapter, of the yeoman who sold his wife to a friend for five pounds be told differently in newspapers or newscasts today?

3. How might the scientific revolution have been delayed without the printing press and periodic publication?

4. How did daily publication change the nature of the news that appeared in newspapers?

News and Revolution—
A Junction of All the People

11

There is nothing so fretting and vexatious, nothing so justly TERRIBLE to tyrants, and their tools and abettors, as a FREE PRESS.

—Samuel Adams, 1768[1]

The first story in the first newspaper printed in America seems remarkably well chosen:

> The Christianized *Indians* in some parts of *Plimouth,* have newly appointed a day of Thanksgiving to God for his Mercy in supplying their extream and pinching Necessities under their late want of Corn & for His giving them now a prospect of a very *Comfortable Harvest.* Their Example might be worth mentioning.

However, if survival was its goal, other items in this issue of *Public Occurrences Both FORREIGN and DOMESTICK,* printed in Boston on Sept. 25, 1690, appear to have been selected rather cavalierly. The paper's publisher, Benjamin Harris, included an attack on some Indians who had fought with the English against the French—"miserable Salvages," he called them—and an allusion to a rumor that the king of France had cuckolded his son.[2]

The instructions given the governor of Massachusetts by the British government had included a warning about the "great inconvenience [that] may arise by the liberty of printing."[3] When *Publick Occurrences* appeared, the governor and council of the colony expressed their "high Resentment and Disallowance of said Pamphlet," which, they said, "contained Reflections of a very high nature: As also sundry doubtful and uncertain Reports."[4] The first issue of America's first newspaper was also its last.

Benjamin Harris does not seem the sort of publisher capable of convincing a governor to endure the "inconvenience" of a newspaper. Harris was a rabid anti-Catholic with an eye for the sensational. The first issue of a newspaper he had published in London in 1679, *Domestick Intelligence,* not only began with a report on a man found hanging "by the Arms in a Wood . . . with his Head and Hands cut off, and his Bowels pulled out" but included a tidbit about "a Popish Priest . . .

The first American newspaper, Publick Occurrences Both FORREIGN and DOMESTICK, *was published in Boston on Sept. 25, 1690. The paper's third page reports that the king of France had cuckolded his son; this reference may have helped ensure that its publisher, Benjamin Harris, would not be permitted to print a second issue.*

who . . . had occasion to make use of his Ladies Chamber maid."[5] Before fleeing to Boston in 1686, Harris had been imprisoned for printing a pamphlet containing a particularly incendiary exposé of the supposed "Popish plot" against England. *Publick Occurrences* appears to have been edited with Harris' usual disregard for official sensibilities.[6]

When 14 years later someone again ventured to publish a newspaper in America, it also appeared in Boston, the largest town in the colonies. But this time the paper was designed more to survive than to excite. The *Boston News-Letter* grew out of a handwritten newsletter that had been distributed by its editor and publisher—the town's post-master, John Campbell. Campbell filled his printed weekly primarily with news of English and European politics taken from London papers—usually in the form of procla-mations, formal letters or official statements, such as the pair of speeches introduced by these deferential phrases in the fourth issue of the *News-Letter:* "The Humble Address of the House of Commons, Presented to Her Majesty . . . To which Her Majesty re-turn'd Her most Gracious Answer, in the following words. . . ." Campbell's paper also included news of the arrival of ships and even reports on fires, accidents, court cases and acts of piracy. (Blackbeard's death in a hand-to-hand battle was reported in 1719.) The failings of England's allies, the sexual activities of monarchs, and other potentially "in-convenient" stories, however, appear to have been ignored. The *Boston News-Letter* survived for 72 years.[7]

Along with its argument that the news in general tends to bind societies, this book has maintained that the newspaper in particular tends of necessity to be a temperate, if not a conservative medium. The failure of Harris' incautious paper would seem to sup-port this theory, as does the survival of Campbell's tame *Boston News-Letter.* However, Harris' and Campbell's successors in colonial print shops in the years leading up to the American Revolution, along with the editors involved in the struggles that grew out of the French Revolution later in the century, would help create quite a different perception of this medium. "Four hostile newspapers are more to be dreaded than a hundred thou-sand bayonets," Napoleon would declare.[8]

The politics of journalism appeared to change in the 18th century. Why were news-papers, with investments and reputations to protect, leading revolutions? And how were rebels such as Samuel Adams able to forge news, that great unifier of societies, into a weapon in their struggles to topple "tyrants"?

The American Revolution

"The Revolution was effected before the war commenced," John Adams concluded. "The Revolution was in the minds and hearts of the people. . . . This radical change in the principles, opinions, sentiments, and affections of the people, was the real Amer-ican Revolution."[9]

The struggle for "minds and hearts" in the years leading up to the Declaration of In-dependence was fought with word of mouth in the streets. It was fought with handwrit-ten letters, often sent by formalized "committees of correspondence." It was fought with pamphlets, such as those written by Thomas Paine. But the most powerful weapons in this struggle to persuade, in what Adams calls the "real American Revolution," were the colonial newspapers.

Britain's American colonies learned their journalism from the Mother country. En-glish newspapers were widely circulated after they arrived in American harbors, and ar-ticles reprinted from their pages dominated early colonial newspapers. However, the ex-ample set by London's journalists in the 18th century was not necessarily one British monarchs and the governors they appointed wanted Americans to follow.

The burst of freedom England's press had experienced with the expiration of the Licensing Act in 1695 had made possible the development (alongside fact-laden publications such as the various *Posts* and the *Daily Courant*) of a group of remarkably literate journals of opinion edited by writers the likes of Joseph Addison, Richard Steele, Jonathan Swift, and Daniel Defoe. At a time when public opinion seemed to have gained an increased hold on the political fortunes of the nation, the British public had access to a variety of unusually well-argued points of view for use in formulating its opinions. "What I approve I defend; what I dislike I censure," Defoe proclaimed in 1712 in the preface to a collection of articles from his *Review*.[10]

American journalists borrowed a style from these publications; the young apprentice printer Benjamin Franklin, for one, consciously set out to imitate Addison's writings from the *Spectator*.[11] They also borrowed a political aggressiveness. As early as 1721, Benjamin's older brother, James, editor of Boston's fourth newspaper, the *New-England Courant*, took the liberty of censuring a policy he disliked; he began printing essays and letters assailing efforts to inoculate people against the smallpox then raging through Boston. (This, alas, was the first American newspaper crusade.)[12]

However, the freedom to write their minds that colonial newspaper editors appropriated from their models in Britain had its limits. Daniel Defoe had served time in jail before he founded his *Review*. (Defoe's professed likes and dislikes may also have been influenced by subsidies from patrons in the government.)[13] James Franklin served time in jail when a satire in his *Courant*, implying that the governor was slow to pursue pirates, hit too close to home for the governor of Massachusetts to tolerate.[14] Prior restraint of the press had indeed become more difficult to establish in England or its colonies now that publications no longer had to be approved in advance by licensers, but editors were still subject to postpublication penalties, particularly under the common-law prohibition on the printing of derogatory, potentially inflammatory remarks about the government or its members—known as "seditious libel." That had been Defoe's crime.[15]

Here America was to make a contribution of its own. In 1735 John Peter Zenger was tried for seditious libel following a series of attacks in Zenger's newspaper, the *New-York Weekly Journal*, on the colony's particularly arbitrary and self-interested governor, William Cosby. There was no doubt that Zenger had printed the criticism, and the judge accurately instructed the jury that under the common-law definition of seditious libel the criticism was no less libelous if true. But Zenger's lawyer, Andrew Hamilton, delivered an impassioned call to defend the "cause of liberty . . . the liberty both of exposing and opposing arbitrary power . . . by speaking and writing truth." The jury ignored the judge's instructions and found the German-born printer innocent.[16]

So American newspapers inherited a style with which to criticize; they inherited and, through the Zenger case, even expanded the freedom to criticize. And when the British attempted to impose taxes upon colonies already suffering from the depression that followed the French and Indian War, American newspapers were presented with perceived injustices at which they could aim their criticisms. The cycle of tax and protest began in 1765 with the Stamp Act, which required, among other things, that printers pay for a stamp on each sheet of paper they used.

English newspapers had been subject to a stamp tax since 1712, but American journalists saw in the Stamp Act—the "fatal *Black-Act*," one termed it[17]—not only an ex-

Women in Journalism

No woman could simply choose to get a job working at a colonial newspaper. That is made clear by the stories of a few of the women who managed to succeed in finding such work.

- Anna Catharine Zenger edited the *New-York Weekly Journal* for eight months, but this was only because her husband, John Peter Zenger, was in jail awaiting his momentous trial in 1735. Anna Catharine Zenger also ran the newspaper for more than two years after her husband's death in 1746.
- Elizabeth Timothy published the *South Carolina Gazette* after her husband Lewis died in 1738. According to Benjamin Franklin, who was a business partner in the paper, Elizabeth made a success out of what had been a floundering, poorly run operation.

A number of other women also found their way into American print shops in these years by inheriting them. For men, the normal first step to newspaper work was an apprenticeship, but apprenticeships in print shops were not given to young women. And women faced an even earlier obstacle: getting an education.

- The first woman to apply for a license to print in the English colonies, Diana Nuthead, in 1693, widow of the printer William Nuthead, signed with a mark instead of signature. Apparently, like many women (and a significant but much smaller percentage of men), no one had bothered to teach her to write. If Diana Nuthead printed anything it has not survived.

The level of the talent denied American journalism by such discrimination is made clear by two others of the exceptions, a mother and daughter.

- William Goddard founded the *Providence Gazette* in 1762 and then the *Pennsylvania Chronicle* in 1767. Each time William, who was an argumentative and inconstant fellow, ran into trouble and each time his mother, Sarah, and his sister, Mary Katherine, took over and improved the business. In 1773, William started yet another newspaper, the *Maryland Journal.* Sarah had died in 1770, but Mary Katherine Goddard ended up publishing that paper for 10 years. She earned a reputation as one of the best printers in the colonies.

ample of taxation by a body, the English Parliament, in which they were not represented, but a severe threat to the survival of their businesses. In the weeks before the act was to take effect, the *Maryland Gazette,* to choose one example, expressed its anger and fear by affixing to its title the line *"Expiring: In uncertain Hopes of a Resurrection to Life again."* In its last issue before that dreaded day, Nov. 1, 1765, the *Gazette* dressed itself in black borders and bid farewell to its readers.[18]

These suddenly aroused publications would not succumb without a struggle, however. New York's lieutenant governor, Cadwallader Colden, complained that they employed "every falsehood that malice could invent to serve their purpose of exciting the People to disobedience of the Laws & to Sedition."[19] They succeeded. The virulence and the scope of the protest made the Stamp Act impossible to enforce. An issue of an unstamped paper appeared in Maryland on Dec. 10 tiled *An Apparition of the late Mary-*

During the protest over the Stamp Act, many colonial newspapers proclaimed themselves ready to cease publication rather than pay for the hated stamp. These paper tentatively began to reappear, without the stamp, in the months after the act was supposed to take effect (on Nov. 1, 1765). Here are issues of the Maryland Gazette *for Oct. 10, 1765; Jan. 30, 1766; and Feb. 20, 1766.*

land Gazette which is not Dead but only Sleepth. On Jan. 30, 1766, *The Maryland Gazette, Reviving* was published, also on unstamped paper; on Feb. 20 *The Maryland Gazette, Revived* appeared.[20] The Stamp Act was repealed on March 18.

Colonial newspapers were roused to a new wave of protests the next year when Parliament approved the Townshend Acts, which imposed duties on American imports of glass, lead, paint, tea and, significantly, paper. "Nonimportation agreements," policed in large part through the press, led the colonies to another victory: the removal in 1770 of all the duties except that on tea.

The period of quiet and renewed prosperity that followed was not shattered until 1773, when Parliament decided to allow the East India Company to market its tea directly in America, with a price advantage over local merchants. The press worked to awaken the colonies to this new, if more subtle, threat, and from that point events proceeded rapidly. The Boston Tea Party, planned in the house of an editor of the *Boston Gazette,* Benjamin Edes, was staged in 1773. Parliament retaliated against Boston in 1774 with the Intolerable Acts. (The name by which these laws became known is itself evidence of the hold revolutionaries had gained on the levers of opinion.) The First Continental Congress met in 1774. The first shot was fired in 1775.

There may be no better historical example of a press *engagé* than the American newspapers that led this decade-long struggle. They festooned themselves with polemical woodcuts: divided snakes, death's-heads as mocking substitutes for tax stamps, or coffins (designed by Paul Revere) to represent the victims of the Boston Massacre. They displayed the names of those "Enemies to their Country" who persisted in importing proscribed British goods. Their rhetoric was heated (and occasionally almost prescient): "Shall the island BRITAIN enslave this great continent of AMERICA which is more than ninety nine times bigger, and is capable of supporting hundreds of millions of millions of people?" demanded the *Massachusetts Spy* in 1773. "Be astonished all mankind, at her superlative folly!"[21]

These newspapers spared no pejoratives. British officials and their supporters were, variously, "serpents," "guileful betrayers," "diabolical Tools of Tyrants," or "*Men totally abandoned to Wickedness.*"[22] When the goal was a boycott of tea, the newspapers directed their scorn at tea, which one writer called "a slow poison," which causes "spasms, vapors, hypochondrias, apoplexies of the serous kind, palsies, dropsies, rheumatisms, consumptions. . . ."[23] Even advertising columns were turned over to the cause, as in this takeoff on the ads run by unhappy spouses, signed "American Liberty": "My reason for leaving him was because he behaved in an arbitrary and cruel manner. . . ."[24]

News coverage too was bent to political purposes. During the extended campaign against the Townshend Acts, for example, papers throughout the colonies began printing a regular series called the "Journal of Occurrences," which detailed outrages alleged to have been committed by British troops in Boston:

> *Dec.* 12, 1768. A Married Lady of this Town was the other Evening, when passing from one House to another, taken hold of by a Soldier, who otherways behaved to her with great rudeness. . . . Another Woman was pursued by a Soldier into a House near the North End, who dared to enter the same, and behave with great Insolence. . . .[25]

Clues to the reliability of these reports can be found in the facts that victims went unnamed and that the Boston papers themselves waited months to reprint them. This installment—from John Holt's *New-York Journal,* Dec. 29, 1768—did not appear in the *Boston Evening-Post* until Feb. 6, 1769.[26]

After American protests succeeded in forcing the British to retreat, the papers were effusive with pride in their accomplishments:

> 'Tis truth (with deference to the college)
>> Newspapers are the spring of knowledge,
> The general source throughout the nation,
>> Of every modern conversation.
> What would this mighty people do,
>> If there, alas! were nothing new.

This poem, from the *New-York Journal* in 1770, concluded with even less humility:

> Our service you can't express,
>> The good we do you hardly guess;
> There's not a want of human kind,
>> But we a remedy can find.[27]

A Son of Liberty, writing in the *Providence Gazette,* was similarly enthusiastic: "The press hath never done greater service since its first invention."[28] Tory commentators agreed on the scope, though not the merit, of the press's accomplishment. "Every suggestion that could tend to lessen the attachment to the mother Country, and to raise an Odium against her," wrote Lieutenant Governor Colden in a letter to England, "have been repeatedly published."[29] Whatever potential the news and the newspaper have as weapons against authority appears to have been exploited in Britain's American colonies during the years 1765 to 1775. What powers were these Patriot editors tapping?

News organs—from busybodies to television networks—fret and vex "tyrants" simply by casting a harsh light on machinations intended to be viewed through a romantic haze or accomplished in the dark. The more thoughtful or aggressive journalists peek behind carefully constructed facades and deconstruct carefully constructed policies. No "civilized Government upon Earth," Massachusetts Governor Francis Bernard complained in 1768, could function effectively with its private deliberations "canvassed by Tavern Politicians, and censured by News Paper Libellers."[30] It is at least true that no government on earth, civilized or uncivilized, has relished such intrusions.[31]

Those who govern societies are also discomfited by the newsmonger's interest—driven by an attraction to controversy and the unusual—in imbalances within a society (a price advantage for the East India Company) or injustices within a society ("taxation without representation"). Authorities thrive on good news, while news organs, though they may prefer victory to defeat for the society as a whole, thrive on disputes, errors and scandals among those who lead the society. "The printers," Thomas Jefferson would complain years later, "can never leave us in a state of perfect rest and union of opinion."[32] Of course, "a state of perfect rest and union of opinion," were it possible to achieve, would be disastrous for newspaper sales.[33]

In the decade leading up to the American Revolution, a hostile press certainly created unrest and helped dissolve whatever union of opinion had existed between British officials and their American subjects. But was this primarily an expression of the anti-authoritarian power of the press? British authorities, from Governor Bernard to King George himself, may have felt the sting of American newspapers. Nonetheless, the pain of having private deliberations made public, the pain of having injustices and imbalances publicized, would hardly have proved fatal to British rule by themselves. Because it wields neither stick nor stone, the press's own direct power to hurt boils down to a power to embarrass. And embarrassment alone does not topple systems of governments.

The true power of the prerevolutionary press is not to be found in its ability to wound the British. The true power of this press was its ability to enfranchise and unify the Americans. "Had it not been for the continual informations from the Press," wrote "A Countryman" in the *Providence Gazette* during the battle against the Stamp Act, "a junction of all the people on this northern continent . . . would have been scarcely conceivable."[34] The role of the news in the American Revolution is best understood not as an uncharacteristic anti-authoritarian outburst but as an entirely characteristic exercise in animating and binding a new society, in producing "a junction" of a majority of the American people.

"The basic problem facing the propagandists in nearly every period," writes Philip Davidson in his study of the use of propaganda in the American Revolution, "was the unification of their own group. . . ."[35] In attempting to quantify the growing sense of unity and community expressed in American newspapers in the years leading up to the Revolution, the political scientist Richard Merritt found that from 1762 to 1775 these papers referred to the American colonies as a single unit almost four times as frequently as they had from 1735 to 1761. Merritt discovered a similarly dramatic increase in the newspapers' use of terms such as "Americans" to describe the colonists, terms that imply the existence of an American political community.[36]

Early African Newspapers

Colonialism ended in parts of Africa after Africans began to gain control of their countries' newspapers.

Africa's first newspaper, the *Cape Town Gazette and African Advertiser* of 1800, and most of those that followed, were settlers' newspapers—published by and in support of whites. Newspapers published by Africans—where they were possible, where the journalists behind them eventually got out of prison—helped power the continent's independence movements. They spoke up for Africans. They unified Africans.

The individuals who led the movements were often the individuals who had edited the newspapers. In 1928, Johnstone Kamau became the founding editor of a seminal, native-language newspaper in Kenya, *Mwigwithania;* thirty-five years later, under the name Jomo Kenyatta, he became independent Kenya's first prime minister. Nnamdi Azikiwe founded the influential *West African Pilot* in Nigeria in 1937; he became the first president of the Republic of Nigeria in 1963 (Hachten).

These newspapers undoubtedly were both reflecting and effecting a change in the attitudes of their readers. Residents of Britain's American colonies were beginning to see themselves as Americans, and the news they exchanged—of resistance to the Stamp Act in Virginia or harassment by Redcoats in Boston—helped direct their gaze toward fellow inhabitants of the continent, as written news media had helped direct the gaze of Romans toward Rome.

But did American newspapers not also assault the British with another set of journalistic weapons—well-reasoned, forceful arguments? Opinions are not news, though they can make news and contain news. They tend, obviously, to be more politically charged than news. The opinions newspapers were promulgating in America then had an impact and, consequently, a news value difficult for Americans now to imagine. For example, in late 1767 the *Pennsylvania Chronicle* began running a series of what might today be termed "opinion pieces," called "Letters from a Farmer in Pennsylvania to the Inhabitants of the British Colonies." The "Pennsylvania Farmer"—actually a Philadelphia lawyer and politician, John Dickinson—supplied the previously missing constitutional argument against the new Townshend Acts (that because their purpose was primarily to raise revenue, not regulate imperial trade, Parliament had no right to impose them on the colonies). The "Letters" were received with so much enthusiasm that almost every newspaper in America chose to reprint them.[37]

The thoughts of this "Farmer" gave evidence of a political power that famous columnists such as Walter Lippmann or George Will could only dream about. Thomas Paine's ringing call for independence, "Common Sense," had a similar effect in 1776. But still that power had little to do with any direct effects these arguments may have had on the British. Opinions hurled against an oppressor are as pebbles against a fortress; enemy minds are not that easily turned. The "Farmer's Letters" circulated in Britain, but King George and his ministers did not don sack cloth or decide to rescind the Townshend

Thomas Paine

On Jan. 9, 1776, one of the great "opinion pieces" of all time, Thomas Paine's "Common Sense" was published as a pamphlet. "The sun never shone on a cause of greater worth . . . ," Paine wrote. "The blood of the slain, the weeping voice of nature cries, 'TIS TIME TO PART." "Common Sense" sold, Paine estimated, 120,000 copies in three months. It includes this example of persuasive writing at its most poetic:

Every spot of the old world is overrun with oppression. Freedom hath been hunted round the Globe. Asia and Africa have long expelled her. Europe regards her like a stranger, and England hath given her warning to depart. O! receive the fugitive, and prepare in time an asylum for mankind.

Paine stepped to the fore once again in Dec. 1776 when the first of his "Crisis" papers, published in the *Pennsylvania Journal,* helped to rally Washington's dejected troops: "These are the times that try men's souls," Paine wrote. "The summer soldier and the sunshine patriot will, in this crisis, shrink from the service of his country; but he that stands it NOW deserves the love and thanks of man and woman. Tyranny, like hell, is not easily conquered. . . ."

After later taking on "tyranny" in England and France and almost getting himself executed in the process, Paine, the classic international revolutionary, died in poverty in the United States.

Acts upon reading them. Instead, such arguments operate behind the lines as morale boosters, means of rallying and even recruiting troops. The "Letters" wielded power insofar as they agitated and further unified the colonists. Town meetings and grand juries voted thanks to the "Farmer," and the boycott of British goods—an act that did directly influence the British—intensified.[38]

The political role of such arguments was, therefore, similar in effect to the political role played by the news. Arguments supply rationales and common purpose; the exchange of news solidifies a common identity. Together in the pages of the colonial newspapers they strengthened a developing society—a subsociety within the British Empire.

"Men are governed by the weaknesses of their imaginations," Walter Bagehot, the 19th-century English social scientist, suggested.[39] But the argument here is that they are governed *by* their imaginations, by their ability to conjure up an image of a societal organism deserving of significant sacrifice. American newspapers helped the inhabitants of the colonies imagine themselves Americans.

In his diary, John Adams describes spending a Sunday evening in 1769 with his second cousin Samuel Adams, the Patriot editor John Gill and others, "preparing for the next day's newspaper,—a curious employment, cooking up paragraphs, articles, occurrences, &c., working the political engine!"[40] When they are in a position to hazard the role, newspapers do make remarkably effective "political engines." A pamphlet or broadside can bang the drum; a newspaper, reappearing weekly or biweekly, can roll the drum.

Gandhi: Journalist

Mohandas Gandhi, the apostle of nonviolence who led India's struggle against British rule in the first half of the 20th century, worked for much of his life as a journalist. "I have taken up journalism," he explained, "not for its sake but merely as an aid to what I have conceived to be my mission in life."

He began in 1903, while living in South Africa, by founding a weekly, aimed at improving treatment of Indians there. It was called *Indian Opinion*. In 1919, back in India, Gandhi took over direction of two weeklies, *Young India* and *Navjivan*. In 1933, he founded the weekly *Harijan*. Gandhi's editorship of these publications was interrupted at times by the jail terms he received for his writings and political activities.

The newspapers Gandhi published had a few things in common: He tended to write the bulk of the articles—all of which were connected to his causes; he accepted no advertising; and he tried to give away copies to those who could not afford them.

"It is wrong to use a newspaper as a means of earning a living," Gandhi wrote. "Newspapers are meant primarily to educate the people. They make the latter familiar with contemporary history. This is a work of no mean responsibility."

Benjamin Franklin made the point with a different metaphor; The press not only can "strike while the iron is hot," he noted, but it can "heat it by continually striking."[41]

Nevertheless, that "the next day's newspaper" in those years should have been full of revolution was something of a fluke. It resulted from a lapse in authoritarian controls in a situation that may have been inherently unstable without them. It resulted from Parliament's unwise insistence on aiming its taxes directly at printers. It resulted, too, from a historical moment in which the newspaper business was unprofitable enough to deny most of its proprietors an investment in the status quo yet respected enough to attract such men of ideas and intelligence as the Adamses.

Still, newspapers did not entirely surrender their traditional wariness and conservatism in the years before the American Revolution. They remained aware enough of their vulnerability to tone down or silence their attacks when British authorities seemed ready to hazard a crackdown. (The campaign in New York quieted for a few weeks in 1765, for example, when word leaked out that New York's lieutenant governor and its council had debated suing some newspapers for seditious libel.) Colonial printers also chose to save some of the more incendiary attacks on the British for broadsides and mock journals such as the "*Constitutional Courant* . . . Printed by ANDREW MARVEL, at the Sign of *the Bribe refused*, on *Constitutional Hill, North-America*." Paul Revere's angriest woodcuts appeared in broadsides with such titles as *Bloody Massacre* or *A Warm Place—Hell*.[42] And Thomas Paine initially had his radical views on independence published in a pamphlet "on account of the impossibility of getting them generally inserted" in newspapers.[43]

Furthermore, the more aggressive actions American newspapers did take, although they may have outraged British authorities, were condoned and even encouraged by the new authorities on the continent—the Patriots, the "Sons of Liberty." As the campaign against the British intensified, these leaders of the new society newspapers were helping create gained substantial power. There was considerable Tory sentiment in America, but newspapers plumping for the Tory side experienced increasing difficulty surviving without the protection of a British garrison. The editor of a paper that dared to print Tory viewpoints in Boston in 1769 had his windows broken and his business signs daubed with filth, and eventually was forced to flee to England. A mob smashed the press of the editor of a Tory paper in New York in 1775.[44] In short, journalistic behavior that appears free and revolutionary when considered in the context of British society may have been restricted, even conservative, in the context of the newly developing American society.

"It was by means of News papers," John Holt, the leading anti-British editor in New York, wrote to Samuel Adams, "that we receiv'd & spread the Notice of the tyrannical Designs formed against America, and kindled a Spirit that has been sufficient to repel them."[45] These newspapers operated within a society more than against a society. Their great accomplishment was kindling a spirit in the "minds and hearts" of their readers, and that is something news, especially when accompanied by inspiring arguments, has always done well.

The French Revolution

Crusading newspapers helped make the American Revolution. The role of newspapers in the French Revolution was considerably more ambiguous. French gazettes and *journals*—among the most sophisticated in the world—undoubtedly helped enlighten portions of the public to the point where the old inequities seemed less tolerable.[46] However, these periodicals were also distinguished by the extent to which they were controlled by the government, and they responded to the first stages of the French Revolution by discreetly averting their gaze. Indeed, the absence of an aggressive, aboveground press to cover events and channel dissent itself contributed to the Revolution.

The virtues of freedom of expression were acknowledged by the most enlightened citizens of Enlightenment France: "It is as much a natural right to use one's pen," wrote Voltaire, "as it is to use one's tongue. . . ."[47] Nevertheless, France's kings, spared the tribulations of their counterparts in England, had not felt called upon to loosen their hold on the means of expression until they finally began losing their hold on the country.

French *journals* and gazettes could not be published without a privilege from the king; they were prohibited on threat of death from attacking religion, stirring up passions, infringing on the authority of the government, disturbing order and tranquility and discussing the administration of finances. (A French publisher did not find a sufficient amount of sanctioned news to fill a successful daily until 1777).[48] The system of regulations was filled with contradictions and was notoriously corrupt. However, if the authorities decided to crack down, the penalties could be severe: one publisher, for example, was locked in a cage at Mont Saint-Michel until he died.[49]

Among the consequences of these strict press controls upon a country awash with self-proclaimed critics and *philosophes* was the growth of an overpopulated and underfed literary underground. The borders were too porous, the garrets too difficult to police, the police too corrupt for it to be possible to snuff out all unauthorized publications. So the inhabitants of this underground, denied privileges and state pensions, denied even the right to publish, expressed themselves and supported themselves, after a fashion, by writing for a variety of illegal publications, including handwritten newsletters—*nouvelles à la main*—and, their staple, scandalous newsbooks—*libelles.*

These underground writers, "a sort of literary proletariat" the historian Robert Darnton calls them, represented something more extreme than a subsociety; they were an antisociety—"not merely unintegrated but beyond the pale." Their journalism outraged even Voltaire: "There has just appeared one of those satanic works where everyone from the monarch to the last citizen is insulted with furor," he fumed, "where the most atrocious and most absurd calumny spreads a horrible poison on everything one respects and loves."[50]

The authors of such *libelles* directed their furious insults at the academies, the aristocracy, the church, the court and the monarch, all portrayed as irredeemably debased and corrupt. Louis XV was reported in such publications to have consumed two girls a week; the woman reputed to be his mistress, Mme. Dubarry, to have passed "directly from the brothel to the throne"; his grandson, Louis XVI, to have been unable to consummate his marriage; Louis XVI's queen, Marie Antoinette, to have been impregnated by a cardinal. Born beyond the law, these publications knew no restraints on their sensationalism, their irreverence and their licentiousness.[51]

Though these were not generally political tracts, the *libelles* may have had profound political effects: Their acidic mix of scathing truth and wild exaggeration ate away at the spiritual, moral and even genetic legitimacy of the Old Regime. As the Revolution approached, even the offer of money could not convince crowds to applaud the queen.[52]

There is a lesson in press relations here for would-be rulers: Make your journalists postmasters or professionals, get them started on investments and a fashionable wardrobe, loosen your controls sufficiently to allow them the satisfaction of an occasional exposé. Journalists who are part of society will eventually strengthen a society. The pens most likely to challenge your swords are those wielded by journalists left to smolder—alienated and oblivious to fashion—on Grub Street.

Louis XVI did keep a corps of fat and loyal journalists. His mistake was in leaving too many others hungry and angry, and denying those journalists to whom he did grant privileges the right to cover the news their readers required. The July 17, 1789, issue of the venerable *Gazette de France,* for example, contained reports from various European capitals as well as coverage of a fire in Paris; it even found room to note that the king had been presented with a book at Versailles on July 15. However, a significant event that had transpired since the last issue of the *Gazette*—the storming of the Bastille—went unmentioned.[53] The *Gazette* also ignored the crucial meetings of the Assembly during this period.[54]

"The Parisians had more of a propensity to believe the malicious rumors and *libelles* that circulated clandestinely," the king's chief of police complained, "than the facts printed and published by order or with the permission of the government."[55] The Parisians had good reason. The gaping omissions in the sanctioned newspapers added to the credibility of those who were steadily eroding the regime's credibility in unsanctioned publications. And significant portions of the population outside Paris were left in the dark.

When a Press Goes Underground—1765 to 1968

Legal, respected newspapers have certainly created their share of difficulties for authorities. However, rarely have they proved as troublesome as a press that sees itself as operating beyond the law or at least beyond the bounds of respectable society.

Many of the newspapers in Britain's American colonies crossed that line during the uproar over the Stamp Act in 1765. It was a liberating experience. Once they took the step of publishing without the stamp—without paying the new tax, in other words—these papers began to realize that they could get away with additional disobediences and impassioned attacks. After another decade or so of those attacks, they had helped unite the colonies in their desire for independence.

Because of the tight and corrupt system of regulation in France before the Revolution, a generation of French publications was born beyond the law. Their publishers had no debt to those in power and little fear of them. If they were vulnerable to arrest just by publishing, what did they have to lose by gossiping about the king's mistress?

A similar underground press—the "pauper press"—would appear in England in the first half of the 19th century. They were illegal, as were those colonial newspapers in 1765, because they refused to pay for a stamp. They were also revolutionary, calling for an end of the domination of the poor by the rich (see Chapter 12).

The term "underground press" is most commonly used in the United States today to describe the often outrageous, multicolored periodicals that appeared in the late 1960s and early 1970s. The *Berkeley Barb,* the *San Francisco Oracle,* the *East Village Other,* the *Boston Phoenix,* and the *Los Angeles Free Press* were some of the better known.

Were they in fact underground? Certainly they challenged the views of mainstream news organs and mainstream society in general on such subjects as drug use, the Vietnam War and popular culture. And in 1968 members of the underground press alleged that no less than 28 such papers had been subject to official harassment, on charges ranging from obscenity to libel to resisting the military draft.

Were they revolutionary? Well, the Underground Press Syndicate, meeting outside San Francisco in 1967, saw itself, in its statement of purpose as warning "the 'civilized world' of its impending collapse."

In the provinces during the crucial summer of 1789, the *Gazette* was often the only paper available,[56] if it was available. A Moulins resident remarked, "It would have been easier to get an elephant than a newspaper."[57] The *libelles,* although they certainly had broadened the French view of the monarchy, hardly provided an effective substitute for a regular and reliable news medium. So most of the citizens of France had not only a propensity but a need to rely on rumor—on word of mouth—for information on what may have been the most important political events of their lives.[58] The town of Machecoul selected two reliable citizens to go to Nantes to gather some news. The wealthy sent their servants on similar expeditions. When at a town meeting in Charlieu the innkeeper announced that a merchant staying with him seemed to possess news, that merchant, a traveling jeweler, was immediately summoned and asked for a report.[59]

Spoken news, however, did not have the reach, the capacity and, most significantly, the reliability necessary to sustain a large nation in crisis. So the Revolution, which toppled the Old Regime, began in something of a news vacuum. A hint of the effect the *absence* of adequate and reliable news might have on that society had been available as early as 1750, when a riot was sparked by a rumor that the police were kidnapping working-class children to provide a prince with blood in which to bathe.[60] The crucible of the Revolution produced more conclusive evidence of this effect: The crowd that marched on the Bastille on July 14, 1789 (and freed a total of seven prisoners), was inspired, in part, by an *erroneous* report that 30,000 Royalist troops had begun to slaughter citizens in a section of Paris.[61]

In the provinces—farther removed from these profound and terrifying events—the effects of the absence of hard news were perhaps even more dramatic. That traveling jeweler called on to report to the people of Charlieu told them a brigand had been arrested in one of the towns the jeweler had visited—which was true; then he passed on a report that 80 brigands had extorted money from the people of another town—which was false. "Everywhere people talk of nothing but brigands," the jeweler added. And immediately the people of Charlieu—in their anxiety about the overthrow of the only system of authority they had ever known—were talking of nothing but brigands. A local merchant recalled that "when he was in Digoin a week ago he noticed the bourgèoisie mounting guard to defend themselves." Others contributed similar scare stories.[62]

Rumors such as these, burning through the news-dry countryside, contributed to a remarkable phenomenon: the "Great Fear" of the summer of 1789. Beginning, according to the historian Georges Lefebvre, on July 20 in the west and ending on Aug. 6 in the south, a panic swept across the country. The inhabitants of one town after another became convinced that armies of brigands sent by the aristocracy were about to storm down upon them. In Charlieu, for instance, a day or two after that town meeting, the threat had been inflated to 1,300 brigands camped "on the heights of the Beaujolais." In their fear and their fury, many of these towns organized themselves and moved against the local aristocracy. The most tangible result of the "Great Fear" was this spread of the Revolution to the countryside.[63]

The people of rural France in 1789, deprived of reliable sources of news, were left to wonder, hope, panic and eventually revolt.[64] The crowds in Paris, too, grew restive when rumor filled the vacuum left by the lack of accurate information. The French Revolution, then, provides evidence not only of the anti-authoritarian power of news in the hands of a subculture of disfranchised journalists but of the anti-authoritarian power of the *absence* of reliable vehicles for news. No news may actually be more destabilizing than bad news. Might a couple of accurate, widely distributed newspapers have saved Louis XVI's head?

The incidents discussed here represent, of course, only a small part of the drama that was unfolding in France. Journalists would play a different role in the Revolution's later acts.

Article 11 in the Declaration of the Rights of Man, adopted by the Constituent Assembly in France in 1789, labeled "the freedom to communicate thoughts and opinions . . . one of the most precious" of those rights. Newspapers were able to partici-

Jean-Paul Marat's *L'Ami du peuple was one of the most aggressive of the horde of partisan newspapers that circulated in Paris during the French Revolution. Marat was assassinated in 1793, and this copy of an issue of his paper is said to be stained with his blood.*

pate fully in the political turmoil that followed the upheavals of the summer of 1789. There had been four newspapers in Paris in 1788; in 1790, 335 appeared.[65] A wide range of views was represented, as even a small sample of their titles indicates: *L'Ami du citoyen* (The Friend of the Citizen), *L'Ami du roi* (The Friend of the King), *L'Ami de la révolution, L'Ami des Jacobins, L'Ami de la constitution,* and so on. The incorrigibly out-spoken and iconoclastic Jean-Paul Marat's *L'Ami du peuple* provides a dramatic, if extreme, example of the tenor of these papers, and of the times: "In fighting against the enemies of the state," Marat wrote, "I attack the cheats without fear, I unmask the hypocrites, I denounce the traitors." A few of those whom *L'Ami du peuple* attacked, unmasked and denounced were eventually killed by elements of the people.[66]

In a country divided into bitterly antagonistic factions, the major achievement of many of these newspapers seemed their ability to strengthen and rally particular factions. Their loud partisanship obscured whatever lessons the fate of the Old Regime might have provided on the importance of a reliable, above-ground press in stabilizing a modern state. (Of course, at times after the breakdown of the old authority there was no coherent state to stabilize.)

Efforts were soon under way to force this perhaps misunderstood genie—a free press—back into its bottle. In 1792, under the orders of the Paris Commune, the editors of the royalist journals, including *L'Ami du roi,* were arrested. In 1793 Marat was assassinated, a copy of *L'Ami du peuple* stained with his blood.[67]

A few years later, Napoleon would deal with the inconveniences caused by France's brief experiment with a free press the same way he dealt with those caused by its experiment with representative government: He would end what was left of the experiment. There would be no declaration of rights in the constitution Napoleon promulgated in 1799. Paris would again have only four newspapers—all strictly monitored—and the emperor would help edit and censor his official newspaper, the *Moniteur,* himself.[68] "If I loosened the reins on the press, I would not stay in power three months," Napoleon declared.[69] The struggle to reconcile modern news forms with the modern state would be continued elsewhere.

A Free Press

"I have lent myself willingly as the subject of a great experiment," Thomas Jefferson wrote in 1807, "to demonstrate the falsehood of the pretext that freedom of the press is incompatible with orderly government."[70] It may be difficult today to understand how compelling that "pretext" seemed when Jefferson wrote, but in 1807 a truly free press was a rare and suspect phenomenon.[71] Certainly revolutionary France had done nothing to disabuse the world of the notion that a society without controls on the press, like a society without a king, was inherently unstable. And the results of the American experiment were still very much in doubt.

An injunction stating that "Congress shall make no law . . . abridging the freedom of speech, or of the press" was added, belatedly many thought, to the Constitution in the Bill of Rights, which was adopted by the first Congress in 1789. However, many politicians continued to wonder whether the often nasty newspapers they were reading deserved that protection.

In the decades following the War for Independence, America discovered that a revolutionary press, like a revolution, is difficult to turn off. Editors will not simply return to reprinting speeches from abroad; the political engine continues to churn. After the departure of the British, ideological differences that were submerged during the struggle with the British surfaced, and Americans, already in the habit of filling newspapers with vituperation, directed that vituperation against each other.

One of the most outspoken of this generation of journalists was Benjamin Franklin Bache, called "Lightning Rod Junior" in honor of his illustrious grandfather. Bache's paper, the *Aurora,* greeted the end of the first president's second term in 1797 by printing this comment:.

> . . . the man, who is the source of all the misfortunes of our country, is this day reduced to a level with his fellow-citizens, and is no longer possessed of power

to multiply evils upon the United States—If ever there was a period of rejoicing, this is the moment—every heart in unison with the freedom and happiness of the people ought to beat high with exultation, that the name of Washington from this day ceases to give a currency to political iniquity and to legalized corruption.[72]

Journalists of this, the "partisan period" in the history of the press in America were equally unsparing in their attacks upon each other. An editor whose allegiance lay with the other party might be labeled in print an "impious, disorganizing wretch," "a scoundrel and a liar," "the equal of the most atrocious felon ever executed at Tyburn," or, in Bache's case, an "atrocious wretch . . . abandoned liar . . . [and] an ill-looking devil." Such disputes occasionally grew violent: A gang of former Revolutionary War soldiers rewarded Bache for that attack on George Washington by sacking his print shop.[73]

The second president of the United States, the Federalist John Adams, flirted with Napoleon's solution for the problem of an obnoxious, destabilizing press. (Adams would later refer to the work of some anti-Federalist editors of this period as "terrorism.")[74] In 1798, when war with France appeared imminent, the Federalist-controlled Congress passed, and Adams signed, the Alien and Sedition Acts. The Alien Acts were aimed at immigrants—particularly French immigrants—some of whom were active in anti-Federalist politics. The Sedition Act, aimed at the press, declared:

> That if any person shall write, print, utter or publish . . . any false,* scandalous and malicious writing . . . against the Government of the United States, or either house of the Congress . . . or the President . . . with intent to defame . . . or to bring them . . . into contempt or disrepute; or to excite against them . . . the hatred of the good people of the United States . . . , [that person] shall be punished by a fine not exceeding two thousand dollars, and by imprisonment not exceeding two years.

During the debate over the Alien and Sedition Acts, Bache's *Aurora* had reprinted, without comment, an early draft of the acts under the text of the First Amendment.[75] The contradiction may have been apparent, but the Supreme Court would not take upon itself the power of judicial review until 1803, so there was no authority capable of acting upon it.

Adams' secretary of state, Timothy Pickering, spent much of his time reading anti-Federalist papers in search of violators. Under his direction, the leading Republican (anti-Federalist) editors in New York and New England, and the leading Republican editor in Philadelphia (Benjamin Franklin Bache) were all indicted for violating the Sedition Act or its cousin—resuscitated for the occasion by the Federalists—the hoary old British common-law prohibition against seditious libel (which had been used against Zenger). There were at least 15 convictions. (Bache, however, died before he could be tried.) The nature of the charges is well illustrated by the case of Matthew Lyon, a congressman known as "the roaring Lyon of Vermont," who was convicted of violating the Sedition Act for having written a letter to an editor accusing Adams of "unbounded thirst for ridiculous pomp, foolish adulation, or selfish avarice." After an unsuccessful attempt

---

* The Sedition Act did establish truth as a defense, but the truth of partisan charges made by anti-Federalist editors often was impossible to prove to the satisfaction of Federalist judges.

America's Not-Always-Free Press

The "experiment" with a free press in the United States has continued to suffer significant setbacks even after the Sedition Act lapsed. Before the Civil War, some Southern states simply outlawed abolitionist newspapers. Wartime brought numerous crackdowns and prohibitions, ranging from the temporary shutdown of a few pro-South Northern newspapers during the Civil War to the successful effort to prevent any independent reporting of the U.S. military invasion of the Caribbean island of Grenada in 1983.

Among the most upsetting of these setbacks for partisans of a free press was the treatment of socialist newspapers under the Espionage Act of 1917. (In 1913 socialist newspapers had a total U.S. circulation of 2 million.)

Again the country was involved in a war—World War I. The Espionage Act, supplemented by the Sedition Act of 1918, made it a crime to write or publish disloyal or profane language that was intended to cause contempt for, or scorn for, the federal government, the Constitution, the flag, or the uniform of the armed forces. As with the Sedition Act of 1798, this seems a clear violation of the First Amendment. Judges debated. These laws stood.

Many nonmainstream publications lost their mailing privileges under the Espionage Act, including *The Masses,* a widely read socialist magazine. The "treasonable" material in *The Masses* included a cartoon showing a crumbling Liberty Bell. *The Masses,* like many of these publications, was forced to close.

---

to prove the president's taste for pomp by cross-examining the judge, who had been a dinner guest of Adams, Lyon was fined $1,000 and sentenced to four months in jail.[76]

Unlike France under Napoleon, however, the United States turned back from this road—perhaps because the social and political distance between its factions was not as great as in France, perhaps because the rhetoric of press freedom had been too central to the American Revolution for it to be so quickly forgotten. While in jail, Matthew Lyon was reelected to Congress by almost a 2-1 vote, and crowds hailed him as a hero as he traveled from his jail cell in Vermont to the capital. The nation's third president, Thomas Jefferson—the hero of this tale—was elected in part because of resentment over the Alien and Sedition Acts, which he allowed to lapse.[77]

Even after the Sedition Act, the United States government has not always been scrupulous in its fidelity to the principles of a free press, nor were Jefferson's Republicans, for that matter.[78] Nevertheless, the "great experiment" to which Jefferson lent himself can be said to have resumed with his administration, to have continued and to have proved a success. Once partisan fires cooled, the press demonstrated not only a compatibility with the maintenance of "orderly government," under what is now one of the oldest continuing governments on earth, but a talent for it.

The United States government has survived the challenge of an unfettered press in part because of its underlying flexibility. "A public Mercury [a newspaper]," the English editor and censor Roger L'Estrange had cautioned in 1663, "makes the multitude too familiar with the actions and counsels of their superiors, too pragmatical and censorious, and gives them, not only an inch, but a kind of colourable right and licence to be meddling with the government."[79] Republican government is designed to channel the meddling of the multitude into elections and other forums for political debate. It can, therefore, face the intrusions, exposés and criticisms of a free press without fear that the system itself will be washed away (though not necessarily without resentments), and it is, therefore, in a position to take advantage of the feeling of participation and belonging that a free press also cultivates in the "multitude" by making them "familiar with the actions and counsels of their superiors."

The role of the *public,* in other words, was formalized and institutionalized in the United States, with journalists functioning as the public's ministers—bringing issues before it, interpreting its wishes, and promulgating its edicts. Indeed, republican government may require a free and energetic press. That was James Madison's conclusion: "A popular government without popular information, or the means of acquiring it," he said, "is but a prologue to a farce or a tragedy."[80]

American newspapers set themselves to the task of providing the American people with a wide variety of information. In 1800 the editor of the *Bee* in New London, Conn., summed up the content of these papers with some candor:

> Here various news we tell, of love and strife,
>   Of peace and war, health sickness, death and life,
> Of loss and gain, of famine and of store,
>   Of storms at sea, and travels on the shore,
> Of prodigies, and portents seen in air,
>   Of fires, and plagues, and stars with blazing hair,
> Of turns of fortune, changes in the state,
>   The fall of fav'rites, projects of the great,
> Of old mismanagements, taxations new,
>   *All neither wholly false, nor wholly true.*[81]

By 1825, the United States was said to have more newspapers circulating to more people than any nation on earth. "The influence and circulation of newspapers is great beyond any thing ever known in Europe," an English visitor wrote: "Newspapers penetrate to every crevice of the Union."[82] And these newspapers were carrying to "every crevice of the Union" not only news about America but crucial information about the government of America.

"The supreme merit of monarchy," wrote the historian and communication theorist Harold Innis, "is its intelligibility."[83] Representative governments, insofar as they obtain their right from something more subtle than inheritance or might, can be more difficult to comprehend. In discussing "changes in the state, the fall of fav'rites, projects of the great," even in assaulting George Washington, American newspapers helped make intelligible a system in which leaders were held fallible and truth subject to dispute; they were at once establishing the parameters of that system, animating it with their energies and impressing its issues upon the minds of the populace—ensuring that the government's issues became the people's issues.

"The newspaper brought them together," Alexis de Tocqueville concluded after his visit to America in 1831 and 1832, "and the newspaper is still necessary to keep them united."[84] And American newspapers would have additional contributions to make to the stability of American society, particularly as those newspapers grew to the point where the interests of their proprietors became more tightly entwined with the interests of that society.

Questions

1. Discuss which is more typical of modern newspapers: Benjamin Harris's *Publick Occurrences* or John Campbell's *Boston News-Letter*.

2. What opinions expressed in print or in the broadcast media in recent decades have changed people's minds in the way that John Dickenson's "Letters from a Farmer in Pennsylvania" apparently did?

3. Is "the newspaper . . . still necessary," in Alexis de Tocqueville's words, "to keep" Americans "united"?

12 Mass Circulation—For All

Two truths have governed the economics of the newspaper business: One is that well-to-do readers are more attractive to advertisers; the second is that poorer readers, because they are much more numerous, build higher circulations. The history of journalism has been punctuated by periods when publishers have honored one of these truths at the expense of the other.

In the United States, as the partisan disputes of the post–Revolutionary War period began losing some of their urgency, newspapers increasingly turned their attention to business—their own and their readers'. In 1820 more than half of all the newspapers in seven of the country's largest cities featured the words *advertiser,* *commercial,* or *mercantile* in their titles.[2] These papers were often printed on extra-large sheets—"blanket sheets," they were called—and much of their space was devoted to a patchwork of advertisements and information of interest to the commercial or mercantile class (shipping reports and tables of prices, for example).[3]

Publishers, in other words, had begun catering to a readership capable of paying a substantial fee for advertised goods and services and, not incidentally, capable of paying a substantial fee for the newspapers themselves—6 cents a copy, or $8 to $10 a year for a subscription to a daily. With nonfarm workers in the United States earning only about 75 cents a day, circulations remained low: By 1833 the highest circulation claimed by an American newspaper (the *Courier and Enquirer* in New York, a city with a population of more than 218,000) was 4,500 copies a day. Were statistics on newspaper readership in the United States charted on a graph, the "mercantile period" would stand out: Between 1790 and 1820, the number of newspaper copies distributed per capita in the United States had grown at a rate of 14 percent annually; from 1820 to 1835, it grew by only 1 percent annually.[4]

Per capita circulation growth had also leveled off in England in these years. The *Times* of London, which was beginning to dominate the field, sold more than 10,000 copies daily in 1830,[5] but this was in a city of 2 million. English newspa-

"The popular commercial press, because it is popular and profitable, has finally broken the ancient monopoly of intelligence."

—Walter Lippmann[1]

per circulations were held down not only by the search for a monied readership but by the stamp tax, which, in a deliberate effort to keep news and opinion from the lower orders, sharply increased the price of newspapers. In 1815 the stamp tax had been increased to fourpence on each copy sold.[6]

The second economic truth of the newspaper business was rediscovered in both the United States and England in the 1830s. Newspapers reached out to poorer readers—of which there were, in the cities, masses. In the process, the owners of these newspapers would eventually become much richer.

The Penny Press and Newspaper Ownership

On Sept. 3, 1833, in New York City, Benjamin Day, a printer in his early 20s, began publishing a small unimpressive paper sold on the streets for 1 penny. Within four months, Day was selling 5,000 copies daily of the *Sun,* whose motto became "It Shines for All." Within two years the paper was bragging in its pages of a circulation of 15,000, "far surpassing that of any other daily paper in the Union, and with one, perhaps two, exceptions in London, in the whole world."[7]

Day attached his audience with a breezy mix of crime and human interest stories. In other words, he practiced a form of "popular" journalism similar to that featured in many 16th- and 17th-century newsbooks and news ballads, similar to that employed during some of the more exuberant periods of British newspaper history from the 1640s on. Indeed, Day had stumbled upon a form of journalism not unlike that Benjamin Harris had attempted to transplant to America in 1690 with *Publick Occurrences.*

Day's ability to bring his potpourri of odd occurrences and police news to a mass audience at such a low price was facilitated by a series of technological developments. The old Gutenberg-type printing presses had been able to produce perhaps 125 papers per hour. But in the early decades of the 19th century the process was made considerably speedier and more efficient by machines that manufactured type and paper, and by the use of cast iron, toggle joints, springs, levers and then cylinders to improve and eventually replace the old screw presses. The most powerful of these technological advances was the steam engine, which was first put to work driving presses at the *Times* of London in 1814. In 1835 Day purchased a steam press for the *Sun.* By 1840 4,000 copies of the *Sun* could be printed per hour; by 1851 the *Sun*'s steam-powered presses were turning out 18,000 copies per hour.[8]

Day's model of the cheap, popular newspaper was adopted by enterprising publishers in New York and other major cities. Among those who scored the largest successes with it were two acquaintances of Day who had initially ridiculed his plan to sell a newspaper for 1 cent, William M. Swain and Arunah S. Abell. Together with Azariah H. Simmons, they started two penny papers, the Philadelphia *Public Ledger* in 1836 and, a year later, the *Baltimore Sun* (which still exists today but costs considerably more).[9]

From 1835 to 1840, per capita newspaper circulation in the United States increased at an annual rate of more than 8 percent.[10] The most notable of the new penny papers, the *Herald,* which Bennett founded in New York in 1835, was, he bragged, selling 20,000 copies daily by its second year (despite a price increase to 2 cents a copy).[11]

The Frontier Press

In the 19th century, the lead in the development of the American press, and to some extent the world's press, was being taken by newspapers in the large Eastern cities, particularly New York. Nonetheless, some of the most intrepid journalists of the period were trying to establish old-fashioned one-person, newspapers out on the American frontier.

They lugged presses across the mountains, endured floods and printed in tents, sod houses, and log huts. When newsprint did not make it up river, they printed on everything from cartridge paper to wallpaper. Yet somehow they managed to endow towns sometimes too small and new to have a schoolhouse with a sense of identity. The United States government encouraged their spread by requiring that federal laws be printed in three papers in each state or territory.

The first new newspaper published in what was then viewed as the "west" was the *Pittsburgh Gazette* in 1786. Wisconsin Territory got its first newspaper, the *Green Bay Intelligencer,* in 1833; the *Telegraph and Texas Register* appeared in the Republic of Texas in 1835.

The first newspaper on the Pacific Coast was the *Oregon Spectator* in 1846. California's first newspaper, the *Californian,* appeared later that year in Monterey. One side of its single large sheet was printed in Spanish, the other in English, but only Spanish type was available. So the printers explained that instead of a W "vve must use tvvo V's" (Mott, *American Journalism*).

Legh Freeman, perhaps the classic frontier journalist, simply moved his newspaper as construction on the Union Pacific Railway moved west. Beginning in 1865, the *Frontier Index,* was printed, sometimes under different names, in 13 places from Nebraska to Washington state.

In England in the 1830s, a group of publishers also began selling newspapers for a penny or two.[12] These papers—the "pauper press," they were called—also trafficked in human interest and crime stories in an effort to attract a mass audience. For instance, Henry Hetherington, publisher of the *Twopenny Dispatch,* promised readers in 1834 that his paper would:

> be a repository of all the gems and treasures, and fun and frolic and "news and occurrences" of the week. It shall abound in Police Intelligence, in Murders, Rapes, Suicides, Burnings, Maimings, Theatricals, Races, Pugilism, and all manner of moving "accidents by floor and field." In short, it will be stuffed with every sort of devilment that will make it sell.

Hetherington bought a steam press, and by 1836 the *Twopenny Dispatch* was reported to have a circulation of 27,000.[13]

Unlike their American cousins, however, the English penny papers could not manage daily publication, and unlike the American penny papers, these weeklies were illegal. The pauper press could not have kept its prices low enough to reach a mass audience had it paid the stamp tax. Some publishers tried to evade the tax by pretending their publications were not actually newspapers. (One printed his "paper" on calico and called it the *Political Handkerchief.*) Most simply ignored the stamp. More than 560 different unstamped newspapers appeared between 1830 and 1836 to pursue this mass readership.[14]

The "license to be meddling" that newspapers might offer "the multitude" had thrilled democrats and terrified autocrats even in the days when newspaper circulations were measured in the hundreds. Now the United States and England had newspapers selling tens of thousands of copies and, because copies were still widely shared, being read by hundreds of thousands of people. (The "cheap" newspaper took root in Paris in 1836 with Émile de Girardin's *La Presse.*)[15] What were the political implications of laying this news before the masses?

Politics was an afterthought for Benjamin Day, a hobby for James Gordon Bennett. Still, the American penny press did play a significant role in informing the poorer classes—particularly the artisans and mechanics in the cities, in other words, the workers—and therefore in helping involve them in the political process.[16] The rise of the penny papers in the United States has been connected with the spread of Jacksonian democracy—Bennett's *Herald* and many of the other cheap papers were indeed staunch supporters of Jackson and his Democratic party. Some who have analyzed this period, Walter Lippmann among them, also see significance in the independence from party "tutelage" (that is, party subsidies) these newspapers achieved through the profits made possible by their huge circulations; editors no longer were financially dependent on politicians—a point Bennett, for one, made much of.[17] And some have even discerned echoes of a radical working-class rhetoric in the pages of these papers—the *Sun* shone "for *all.*"[18] Nevertheless, the political comments the penny papers did insert between their police stories eventually drifted safely into the mainstream.

Horace Greeley, who began the 1 cent *New York Tribune* in 1841, was the most politically active of these editors. Greeley was an abolitionist and something of a socialist, but for most of his career he found a home in one of the two major political parties. In fact, Greeley (though he had been a Whig and then a founding member of the Republican party) was the Democratic candidate for president in 1872. The American penny papers posed no threat to the American government. "They are not given to harsh language with regard to public men," Greeley himself noted in 1851; "they are very moderate."[19]

The situation in England was different. On one side of the chasm that separated the classes in Britain a subsociety had developed—denied the right to vote, denied representation in Parliament, even denied the right to affordable legal newspapers. The July Revolution in France in 1830 gave the more radical members of the British working class a sense of their potential power; the illegal pauper papers gave them a voice and a sense of identity.

Many editors of unstamped papers were crusaders first, journalists second. After detailing the "fun and frolic . . . and every sort of devilment that will make it sell" with which he would fill his *Twopenny Dispatch,* Henry Hetherington explained that "our object is not to make money, but to beat the Government." This statement is consistent with the way Hetherington approached his newspapers and his life: His projects for the working class took precedence over his business.[20]

The depth of the critique of society published in the more political of these unstamped papers can be seen in this passage from another of Hetherington's papers, the *Poor Man's Guardian:*

Horace Greeley of the New York Tribune.

Politics is the noble art of dividing society into two classes—*Slaves* and *Robbers;* the former including the *poor* and *ignorant,* the latter all the *rich* and *crafty.* . . . [This robbery] has been done by politics and can only be prevented by having done with politics. . . . By politics, then, we mean all the operations of Government, in which the people have no share. Under the existing system, all Government operations are of this kind.[21]

In the 1830s Britain's leaders had to face the fact that newspapers published outside the law were encouraging "the multitude" to do considerably more than "meddle" in the affairs of the government. The Torys' nightmare—a press written by revolutionaries and read by the masses—was coming true. (England's best-selling stamped newspaper, the *Times,* was also frequently at odds with the government in the early decades of the 19th century, but its cry—like the cry of most established news organs—was for nothing more radical than "reform.")

For 140 years British authorities had struggled to control a press that no longer required their approval before publication. Friendly newspapers had been subsidized and rewarded with official advertising; recalcitrant editors had been prosecuted (John Walter, founder of the *Times,* had spent more than 15 months in jail for libeling the Prince of Wales and the Duke of York).[22] And the stamp tax had been used to hike the price of newspapers. The weaknesses of this policy had been noted as early as 1733:

Can statutes keep the British press in awe,
When that sells best, that's most against the Law?[23]

Now it was apparent that that policy had failed.

Between 1830 and 1836 almost 800 publishers and venders of unstamped publications were thrown in jail. Hetherington's presses were impounded once, and he was imprisoned three times. But prosecution failed to silence the pauper papers; in fact the publicity surrounding arrests boosted sales.[24]

Finally, in 1836, Parliament, listening to the advice of the liberals, arrived upon a strategy for legislating the unstamped press out of existence: It reduced the stamp tax on newspapers to 1 penny. With the tax so low, avoiding it was no longer worth the bother. Not only were the publishers of the pauper papers—exhausted by six years of struggle—drawn back into the fold, but the legal, stamped papers were now in a position to compete with them for a mass audience. By 1855 the *Times* had a circulation of almost 60,000.[25]

The reformers, who had pressed for the reduction of the stamp tax, had seen the political situation of the press with unusual clarity: "Is it not time to consider whether the printer and his types may not provide better for the peace and honour of a free state, than the gaoler and the hangman?" Edward Bulwer-Lytton had asked in 1832. "Whether . . . cheap knowledge may not be a better political agent than costly punishment?"[26]

A few radical newspapers would flicker to life in Britain in subsequent years. Some—wearing the stamp—participated in the Chartists' struggle for universal suffrage that followed the depression of 1837 and 1838. And the Sunday papers that built mass circulations in England in the 1840s and succeeding decades borrowed some working-class rhetoric, along with an emphasis on crime news, from the unstamped papers of the 1830s. But most of their proprietors saw these Sunday papers primarily as business investments.[27] The rhetoric had simply become part of the formula; soon it would be dropped.

The British stamp tax was abolished entirely in 1855. The previous year the president of the Association for the Repeal of the Taxes on Knowledge had predicted that removing the stamp tax entirely would create "a cheap press in the hands of men of good moral character, of respectability, and capital."[28] That argument had been strengthened by the testimony before a committee of the House of Commons of the American publisher and editor Horace Greeley, who had as good a view as anyone of the hands that controlled the cheap press in the United States.

James Gordon Bennett had founded the *Herald* in 1835 with $500 to his name. When Greeley started his *Tribune* six years later, he had about $2,000 in cash in hand (at least half of which he had borrowed) and another $1,000 in printing equipment.[29] But mass circulation was turning newspapers into big businesses, with growing staffs and increasingly expensive presses. In 1849 the *Sun* was sold for $250,000 and Greeley called the price "very cheap." In 1851 Greeley's former assistant Henry J. Raymond and two partners needed about $70,000 to found a new penny paper, the *New York Times*.[30]

Greeley and Bennett had begun their careers without money—now Bennett was rich and Greeley had avoided that state only by distributing stock in the *Tribune* to some of its employees and "loans" to all comers. Raymond's two partners in the *Times* were both bankers.[31] The press in New York was indeed passing into the hands of "men of capital." And the sums were at least as large in London. In 1846, 100,000 British pounds were reportedly required to launch Charles Dickens' *Daily News;* another 100,000

British pounds had to be invested in the paper before it became profitable (long after Dickens had escaped the editorship).[32]

The penny newspapers attracted large working-class audiences. However, the size of those audiences inevitably lifted the ownership of those newspapers into the upper classes. Despite the egalitarian rhetoric of the early penny papers, significant conservative, even reactionary, political forces were unleashed by mass circulation.

Other Voices

In 1846, the editor of the New York *Sun* informed Willis A. Hodges, an African-American who was protesting the newspaper's policy on voting rights, that "the *Sun* shines for all white men, and not for colored men."[33] Clearly, the masses to whom 19th-century newspapers were beginning to circulate excluded significant segments of the population. The *Sun*, as this statement indicates, was relegating women, too, to the shade.

The *Sun*'s editor suggested that if Hodges wanted his people's views aired he could start his own newspaper. Hodges did—the *Ram's Horn*. Frederick Douglass, the former slave who had become an eloquent spokesman for the African-American cause, became the paper's nominal editor. The circulation of the *Ram's Horn*—which peaked at about 2,500 in the year and a half it survived—was, of course, miniscule compared to that of newspapers such as the *Sun*, but in its pages the perspectives of African-Americans could, at least, be expressed.[34] This is the route that many who felt themselves ignored or mistreated by the mainstream press followed.

The first newspapers in America designed to speak for particular ethnic groups were intended for immigrants who wanted to read the news in their native languages. Benjamin Franklin helped start the first foreign-language newspaper in Britain's American colonies, the *Philadelphia Zeitung*, printed in German, in 1732. It lasted only a few issues. The *Germantown Zeitung*, founded in 1739, was much more successful. The first Spanish-language newspaper in what became the United States, *El Misisipi*, appeared in New Orleans in 1808. (*El Misisipi* kindly provided English translations of all its Spanish news.) A Native American newspaper, the *Cherokee Phoenix*, written, in part, in a newly devised Cherokee writing system, appeared in 1828.

African-Americans got their first newspaper, *Freedom's Journal*, in 1827, 19 years before the *Ram's Horn*. Its publishers were Samuel Cornish and John B. Russwurm, the first African-American to graduate from college in the United States. *Freedom's Journal* began with a sentence that summed up the purpose of many such alternative newspapers: "We wish to plead our own cause." After the failure of the *Ram's Horn*, Frederick Douglass started his own, much more successful, newspaper, the *North Star*, in 1848. "The object of the *North Star* will be to Attack Slavery in all its forms and aspects," he wrote.[35]

Women formed one marginalized group that could not be completely ignored by mainstream publishers; there were too many of them. *Godey's Lady's Book*, an early women's magazine, debuted in Philadelphia in 1830. The Godey behind this publication was a man, Louis A. Godey, but Mr. Godey did employ a woman—Josepha Hale, the author of "Mary Had a Little Lamb"—as an editor. In the 1850s, *Godey's* achieved a circulation of 150,000.

Cherokee Writing

A member of the Cherokee tribe, Sequoyah, or George Gist, was convinced that his people should be able to communicate with "talking leaves" as the white settlers did. He neglected his farm while working on the problem, but, by 1819, despite opposition from his family and a trial for witchcraft, Sequoyah devised an 86-character phonetic system for writing the Cherokee language. Each symbol represented a sound.

His daughter was the first to learn how to write Cherokee. Tribal elders were impressed. Within a few years, thousands of Cherokee were writing in their own language. The *Cherokee Phoenix* newspaper was printed, in part, using Sequoyah's writing system.

A couple of newspapers intended for women flickered in and out of existence in New York in the early years of the penny press: *Woman* in 1834 and the *Ladies Morning Star* in 1836. This was a time when many who wrote for women felt called upon to adopt a moralistic or sentimental style. "The *Ladies' Morning Star*," the paper announced in its first issue, "will sustain the character of a Literary Moral Newspaper, which it shall be the endeavor of the proprietor to enrich with every variety that may improve and adorn the female mind, enlarge and strengthen the understanding, purify the soul, and refine the senses. . . ." This did not prove a particularly successful formula. Soon, with its circulation stalled at about 2,000, the paper's editor—a man, William Newell—changed its name to the *Morning Star*.[36]

Women's career possibilities in journalism were, of course, severely limited throughout the 19th-century (as they would remain for much of the 20th century). As late as the 1880s, biographer Brooke Kroeger reports, "The newsroom was a crude, tobacco-stained, white-male environment." Margaret Fuller was one of the first females to attempt to surmount the barriers. Fuller's father had helped her secure the sort of rigorous, classical education then almost exclusively reserved for boys. In 1844, after her success as editor of the transcendalist publication the *Dial* in Boston, Fuller was hired by Horace Greeley, perhaps the most open-minded of the major 19th-century editors, to write for his *Tribune*.[37]

In her *Tribune* articles—Greeley asked that she write three a week—Fuller pondered literature, attacked slavery, criticized capital punishment, defended the Irish, welcomed immigrant Jews and called for better educational and employment opportunities for the poor and for women. In 1846, Fuller left for Europe to become one of America's first foreign correspondents. She was killed, along with the man she had met and married in Italy and their infant son, in a shipwreck off Fire Island on the return passage in 1850. "Margaret was always a most earnest, devoted champion on the Emancipation of Women, from their past and present condition of inferiority . . . ," Greeley wrote, after Fuller's death.[38]

For many liberal-minded American women in the first half of the 19th century, emancipation of the slaves must have seemed a more pressing issue than the emancipa-

The first issue of the first African-American newspaper published in the United States: Freedom's Journal, *March 16, 1827.*

tion of women. At the World Anti-Slavery Convention in London in 1840, however, some of them received a blunt lesson on the importance of fighting for their own cause: The conference voted not to seat female delegates, many of whom had made major contributions to the abolitionist movement. The first women's rights convention was held in Seneca Falls, New York, in 1848.[39]

In the United States at that time, the contribution a newspaper could make to unifying and strengthening a political movement was already clear. The *Lily,* edited by Amelia Bloomer with the help of women's rights leader Elizabeth Cady Stanton, first appeared in 1849. Stanton's own newspaper, the *Revolution,* followed in 1868, with another famous crusader for women's rights, Susan B. Anthony, as its business manager. The *Revolution*'s motto: "Men, Their Rights and Nothing More; Women, Their Rights and Nothing Less."[40]

Margaret Fuller, one of the first women to obtain a job as a reporter, in 1849.

Publishing a newspaper that tries to express a point of view that others are not expressing is never an easy task. It certainly wasn't in 19th-century America. Here, for example, is 19th-century press historian Frederic Hudson on William Lloyd Garrison's abolitionist newspaper, the *Liberator:*

> For 35 years it fulminated against the institution of slavery in spite of persecution, tar and feathers, denunciation, rewards for its editor's head, threatened assassination, hanging in effigy, assaults, and mobs, from which the bold editor barely escaped with his life.[41]

Frederick Douglass had his house destroyed and his papers burned by proponents of slavery. Jane Grey Swisshelm, a feminist journalist who covered Washington for Greeley's *Tribune* and then started her own newspaper in Minnesota, had her presses destroyed and her type thrown in the river by a mob. Another abolitionist editor, Elijah Lovejoy, was killed by a mob in Alton, Ill., outside of St. Louis, on Nov. 7, 1837. Even as late as 1892, the African-American journalist Ida B. Wells was rewarded for her investigation into the lynching of three black businessmen by having a mob wreck her press and threaten to lynch her. Her newspaper, which Wells was forced to abandon, was called the *Memphis Free Speech.*

Frederick Douglass

Frederick Douglass, who became one of the most influential journalists in American history, guessed he was born in February 1817; no birth records were kept for slaves. When a white woman tried to teach him to read, she was scolded by his master: "A nigger should know nothing but to obey his master—to do as he is told to do."

Douglass escaped in 1838. Four years later he was writing for William Lloyd Garrison's fiery *Liberator*. By 1845 friends in England raised enough money to officially buy Douglass' freedom. That year he wrote his autobiography. "For genuine eloquence," editor Horace Greeley noted, Douglass' work "would do honor to any writer of the English language."

Frederick Douglass' newspaper, first called the *North Star,* would be published, weekly and then monthly, from 1847 to 1863 and have a circulation that extended to the West Indies and Europe. Douglass died while fighting for another kind of human rights, at a women's suffrage convention in 1895.

Frederick Douglass, the former slave who became an eloquent crusader against slavery.

Mobs can impinge upon free speech, as governments can. And mass circulations—as they fund larger, better capitalized, more complacent news organizations—can limit the range of speech heard in a society. The best ideas are often presented to the smallest circulations. Journalists with the courage to stand up to the mobs, to stand apart from the masses, are a rare and valuable commodity.

The New Journalism and Consolidation

The profit for American mass-circulation newspapers, Horace Greeley had explained to the British in 1851, was in the advertising their huge circulations attracted, not in the circulations themselves.[42] But when attracting advertisers is the goal, attention inevitably returns to the spending power of the readership. As the decades passed, there came times when it seemed too many publishers had again become captivated by the charms of a "respectable," monied readership, when newspaper prices crept higher and their pages grew more "serious." But then the journalism world again would be refreshed by a new wave of "popular" journalism, bringing new readers and even larger circulations.[43]

Among the most powerful of these waves of journalistic renewal in the United States was that led by Joseph Pulitzer—a German immigrant who had arrived penniless in St. Louis in 1865 and had left in 1883 owner of a thriving newspaper, the *Post-Dispatch.* Pulitzer purchased the moribund *New York World*—circulation under 20,000—in 1883 and filled it with a unique journalistic mix: one part sensationalism (CORNETTI'S LAST NIGHT/SHAKING HIS CELL-DOOR AND DEMANDING RELEASE, read a front-page headline in the first issue of Pulitzer's *World*); one part crusading, progressive politics (Pulitzer's 10-line editorial program, announced in 1883, included: "1. Tax Luxuries. 2. Tax Inheritances. 3. Tax Large Incomes. 4. Tax Monopolies. 5. Tax the Privileged Corporations. . . ."); one part attention-getting campaigns (The *World* took the lead in 1885 in the drive to erect the Statue of Liberty, then waiting in storage in France); and one part aggressive, intelligent news coverage—specifically including coverage of the concerns of the city's huge population of impoverished immigrants. Readers were offered eight pages of this a day, as the paper bragged in its "ears," for only 2 cents. By 1887 the *World* had a circulation of 190,000 during the week and a quarter of a million on Sunday.[44] Pulitzer's mix, soon widely imitated, became known as the "new journalism."

The most successful of the imitators was the son of a wealthy California miner turned United States senator. William Randolph Hearst's expulsion from Harvard (for sending instructors chamber pots with their names engraved on the bottom) had barely fazed his father, but his obsession with taking over management of a failing, seemingly hopeless business—the *San Francisco Examiner*—upset his father deeply. Hearst trained himself with a job as a reporter on Pulitzer's *World,* then in 1887 he returned to San Francisco to transform the *Examiner* into a sensationalistic, crusading, self-promoting, progressive newspaper, and, by 1890, a financial success. (In his version of the new journalism, however, Hearst neglected to include Pulitzer's respect for accuracy and truth: The *Examiner*'s exaggerations of minor accidents on the hated Southern Pacific Railroad foreshadowed exaggerations in later Hearst newspapers of the offenses

Ida B. Wells, who used newspapers in a courageous crusade against lynching.

committed by the Spanish in Cuba or of the talents of Hearst's paramour, the actress Marion Davies.)[45]

Hearst landed in New York City in 1895, purchased the New York *Morning Journal* and cut its price to a penny. Pulitzer would eventually be forced to follow suit. Hearst also hired away many of the *World's* top journalists, including the artist behind a popular cartoon, "The Yellow Kid," engaged Pulitzer in a battle over whose paper could most overdramatize Spanish injustices in Cuba and initially lost millions. Pulitzer soon had another artist drawing yellow kids for the *World*. Out of the battle between Pulitzer and Hearst in New York—fought with what became known as "yellow journalism"—came war with Spain in 1898,[46] circulations that occasionally surpassed 1 million, and a new burst of growth for the newspaper business. Pulitzer had purchased the *World* for

New York World *Publisher Joseph Pulitzer. This portrait is by John S. Sargent.*

$346,000; by 1898 the various editions of the paper were turning a profit of about $500,000 dollars a year.[47]

Magazines were becoming a major journalistic force in these years, led by *McClure's,* which used tough investigations into government and business corruption to win a circulation of a half million. Henry R. Luce and Briton Hadden launched *Time,* the first weekly "newsmagazine" in 1923. The *New Yorker*—which would be distinguished by the quality and depth of its reporting, analysis, criticism and fiction—was founded by Harold Ross in 1925.

Newspapers, too, were booming. The population of the United States doubled between 1870 and 1900; the number of daily newspapers quadrupled. By 1915, more than 2,200 U.S. English-language daily newspapers were publishing, plus an additional 160 foreign-language dailies. (One, the *Vorwarts,* a Yiddish newspaper started in 1897 and known in English as the *Jewish Daily Forward,* was eventually published daily in 11 cities.) In 1913 there were 323 socialist newspapers in the United States, including two large metropolitan dailies, with a total circulation of 2 million.[48]

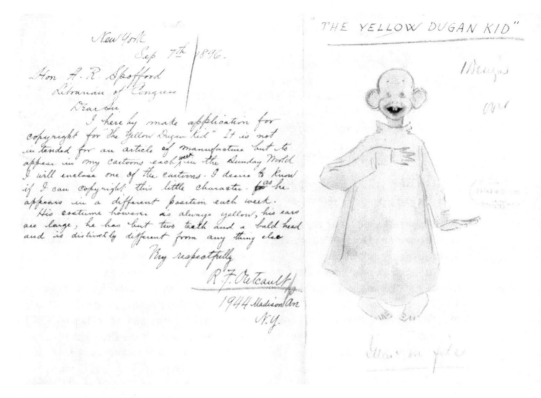

"The Yellow Kid"—a popular cartoon character that ran first in the New York World *and then, as the papers battled, in both the* World *and the* New York Journal, *giving rise to the phrase "yellow journalism" in the 1890s.*

But a shakedown began. First ownership began to narrow. The pattern became clear in London. In 1896, Alfred Harmsworth invested about a half million British pounds in an effort to start a new popular daily, the *Daily Mail.*[49] By 1908 Harmsworth, now Lord Northcliffe, also owned the *Evening News,* the *Daily Mirror,* the *Observer,* and the *Times.*

In the United States, E. W. Scripps put together a "chain" of 33 newspapers by 1914. William Randolph Hearst owned 20 daily papers and 11 Sunday papers by 1922, plus two wire services, the largest newspaper feature syndicate, a newsreel company, and a motion picture production company.[50] Henry Luce followed *Time* with *Fortune, Life* and *Sports Illustrated.* The business grew bigger still, and ownership of it became concentrated in fewer hands.

In 1903 Frank A. Munsey, a not particularly successful newspaper publisher who had accumulated a fortune in other businesses, made a prediction: "In my judgment it will not be many years—five or ten perhaps—before the publishing business of this country will be done by a few concerns—three or four at most." It took much longer, of course, but Munsey himself played a major role in getting the process going. In New York City he merged or contributed to the merger of the *Press* into the morning *Sun,* the morning *Sun* into the *Herald,* the *Herald* (Bennett's old paper) into the *Tribune* (Greeley's old paper), and, finally, the *Globe* into the *Evening Sun,* and the *Mail* into the *Evening Telegram.*[51]

"Consolidation" this process was called. The number of daily newspapers in the United States would begin to decline after 1915. And when there are fewer of any kind of news organ, those that survive inevitably aim to attract more general audiences. American newspapers began migrating away from where many of their wildest but most creative ancestors had lived—the fringes.

Tabloids and Corporations

The 20th century saw one more great reaching-out for new masses of newspaper readers. The newspapers that attracted them used a design introduced by the British publisher Alfred Harmsworth.

At the end of the year 1900, Joseph Pulitzer and Harmsworth found themselves on the same transatlantic ship, and Pulitzer invited Harmsworth to experiment with the Jan. 1, 1901, edition of the *World.* The paper the English publisher produced—"the first twentieth-century newspaper"—was only nine inches wide and 18 inches high.[52] The size was hardly new—Day's *Sun,* for example, had been even smaller—but in the years since the first penny papers, most newspapers had grown large enough to accommodate six to eight columns across and a fold halfway down the page. The *World* returned to its normal size the next day, but in London a few years later Harmsworth would introduce his own small newspaper, the *Daily Mirror*—a "tabloid." (The term had been coined in the pharmaceutical industry in the 1880s as the trade name for compressed, easy-to-digest medicine.)[53] The *Daily Mirror* was selling 1.2 million copies a day by 1914.[54]

The first modern tabloid in the United States, the *Daily News* in New York, was founded in 1919 by Robert McCormick and Joseph Patterson—two cousins who had inherited control of the *Chicago Tribune* and who had been inspired by the success of Harmsworth's *Mirror.* The tabloids were easy to hold on a train or trolley and easy to read, with their black headlines and plethora of photographs. Soon the United States was undergoing another wave of "popular" journalism ("gutter journalism" was then the current pejorative) and another wave of circulation growth. By 1925 the *Daily News* was selling almost 1 million copies a day; by 1940 close to 2 million.[55]

The tabloids, for the most part, disdained the progressive crusades that had been an integral part of the "new journalism" of the 1880s and 1890s. In the 1920s Hearst himself, having difficulty making do on an income of perhaps $15 million a year, became increasingly devoted to the decidedly nonprogressive cause of tax cutting.[56] Progressive crusades were seldom found in the newspapers run by Hearst's heirs, either.

As the 20th century progressed, new mass audiences would be introduced to the news by radio and then television newscasts, without any discernible radicalizing of the masses. In the United States, the stations that broadcast these newscasts were at least as well capitalized as the local newspaper; in many cases they were owned by the local newspaper. In Britain, the major broadcast network began as a government-regulated monopoly.

Ruth Snyder is executed in the electric chair in 1928 for the murder of her husband. New York's Daily News *obtained this dramatic picture, which the paper touched up, through a camera hidden on the ankle of a photographer. The paper printed 1 million extra copies.*

Harold Innis has suggested that "the tendency of each medium of communication [is] to create monopolies of knowledge to the point that the human spirit breaks through at new levels of society and on the outer fringes."[57] The newspaper, in the hands of Patriot editors in colonial America, or perhaps pauper-press editors in England, can be said to have served as a tool of this renegade, radical "human spirit." An "ancient monopoly of intelligence," as Walter Lippmann put it, was broken. However, the newspaper itself began to contribute to the formation of a new "monopoly of knowledge" (or "information") as the dissemination of news came more and more under the control of "men of . . . capital."[58]

"Freedom of the press," A. J. Liebling noted in an oft-quoted remark, "is for those who own one." Perhaps new multichannel, computer-aided forms of communication will once again lower the price of reaching the masses. But as things currently stand, without the aid of rich patrons, radicals on the order of a Henry Hetherington, or enter-

Karl Marx: Journalist

A newspaper could still be a powerful tool in the hands of a radical in the 19th century. That is demonstrated by the journalistic career of perhaps the most influential political radical of all time: Karl Marx.

Between 1852 and 1862, Marx wrote, or cowrote with Friedrich Engels, a total of 362 articles as a European correspondent for Horace Greeley's *New York Tribune,* a newspaper with undisguised socialist leanings. These articles, according to Greeley's top assistant Charles Dana, were "widely reproduced" and "most highly esteemed" (Christman).

However, Marx's most revolutionary journalism came earlier, when he edited his own newspaper in Germany. In 1848, as a wave of unrest and revolution swept across Europe, Marx moved to Cologne, Germany, where he obtained control of the *Neue Rheinische Zeitung,* and used it to fight for the cause of democracy. (The "bourgeois revolution," Marx believed, had to be won before the working-class could strike for its demands.)

Marx sank what was left of his patrimony and his wife's money into the newspaper. But while struggling to obtain additional funds to keep the paper afloat, Marx was finally banished from the city. He printed the last issue of his *Neue Rheinische Zeitung* entirely in red ink (Edmund Wilson).

prising but poor journalists such as Bennett and Greeley, can no longer afford a press (or television transmitter or cable system) technologically sophisticated enough to compete for a mass audience.

This change in the status of the owners of the news media would prove to be among the major political effects of mass circulation. The case can be made that it has led to a subtle or not-so-subtle conservative bias in news coverage: "When the shares of a newspaper lie in the safe-deposit box cheek by jowl with gas, telephone, and pipe-line stock," Edward Alsworth Ross suggested in 1910, "a tenderness for these collateral interests is likely to affect the news columns."[59] If news columns are not often directly tampered with today, the corporate structure implanted by publishers with "gas, telephone, and pipe-line stocks" does effectively ensure that these columns will not be written by aggressive proponents of anti-establishment ideas. Frederick Douglass, William Lloyd Garrison, Elizabeth Cady Stanton and Ida B. Wells were not corporate types.

Certainly the aging news behemoths that preside over our political and social affairs pose no threat to the basic assumptions of society. And certainly the increased capital needed to run a newspaper (or broadcast station) has decreased the chances that a group of rebels might marshal the attention of a subsociety large enough to challenge the existing order.[60]

Many may see this as a sign of progress; yet the absence of this ability to unite a substantial community of rebels may be felt should new ideas again overtake an old regime.

Questions

1. What news organs today try to reach a well-to-do audience? What news organs attempt to reach large masses of poorer people?

2. Discuss the intended and the unintended effects of the British stamp tax on newspapers.

3. Are there news media today that struggle to express minority points of view? How are they treated by more mainstream media?

4. What are the negative effects of "consolidation" in the newspaper business? Are there any positive effects?

5. How might a radical on the order of a Henry Hetherington or an Ida B. Wells communicate today?

PART FIVE

REPORTING

13 Before Reporting—No Data by Which We Can Correctly Reason

Upon occasion we receive a small hint of what it must have been like: On Sept. 11, 2001, two planes smash into the twin towers of the World Trade Center, and for a couple of hours exaggerated accounts of the number of hijacked planes still in the air spread on the streets and on the airwaves. A nuclear reactor explodes and burns near Kiev in the Soviet Union in 1986, and our newspapers and newscasts, denied hard facts for a few days, must content themselves with speculation ("It could burn for months") and rumors ("two thousand dead").[2] The United States invades the small Caribbean island of Grenada in 1983 without bringing along any representatives of the press, and for two days we hear little but what the military itself chooses to tell us about the fighting.

But in general those of us with access to the Western news system possess a confidence that most of our ancestors would have found remarkable: We are confident that the world, at least on its more superficial levels, is knowable. We put down a newspaper or turn off a newscast confident that we have learned of, if not understood, the more dramatic recent events in the world. We take for granted a feeling of awareness that extends not only through our town or nation but around our planet.

To appreciate how unprecedented this confidence is it is necessary to double back and examine more closely the information available in previous centuries. Consider, for example, the problems Americans in 1814 experienced in trying to follow events in Europe. Allied troops, led by the English, were pushing French armies back through Germany, and Napoleon's great adventure appeared to be approaching its climax. Americans, though sharply divided in their feelings toward the French emperor, shared a fascination with his fate. Moreover, a defeat for the French would free England to concentrate its energies on its war with the United States, begun in 1812 and still sputtering along in 1814 (making communication with Europe even more difficult than usual). "Public attention, naturally enough,

I doubt not, but it is without doubt that it hath beene newes to most men, that they have beene so long without newes. . . .

—**Untitled English "newspaper," 1625[1]**

205

appears so rivetted on the present momentous act of the great European drama," the *Baltimore Patriot* observed on May 23, 1814, "that it would be vain to attempt to attract it to any other object."[3]

Yet the news that trickled into the United States of this "momentous act" of this "great drama" was late, incomplete and sometimes inaccurate. On March 22 a ship carrying French papers published as late as Feb. 8 reached Boston with the shocking news that the allies had entered France. But the United States had to wait three weeks to learn more. When additional information arrived, it arrived via some circuitous routes: On April 11 a newssheet appeared in Boston that had been printed in Halifax on March 20, bearing news taken from London papers published as late as Feb. 12. The story was advanced another couple of days on April 13 by a merchant who had traveled by ship to New York from Venezuela, where he had somehow obtained a copy of the *Morning Chronicle,* printed in Portsmouth, England, on Feb. 14.

News of what happened next—the emperor's fall—arrived with maddening difficulty. By May 16 three different ships had reached the United States carrying reports that the allies had entered Paris, but two false reports that Napoleon had retaken his capital also received wide currency in the American press. Then, with some sort of resolution clearly in sight, the news stopped. On June 1 the New York *Evening Post* moaned:

> The latest news, reader, arrived a little more than a fortnight ago. . . . As at the closing scenes of the drama the curtain fell just at the most interesting moment of the tragedy, as if for the purpose of leaving us for a while in a state of breathless anxiety.[4]

For two weeks Americans were left to try to reconcile the conflicting reports and guess the outcome of the drama. "It was evident that Napoleon's star was set and his power and resources decaying like a rope of sand; and that nothing short of a miracle could save him," wrote the *Columbian Centinel* on May 21. Other papers, swayed by other wishes, reached different conclusions: "Is it to be supposed for a moment that a nation like France, with thirty millions of people, can be subdued by 200,000 savages?" thundered the Boston *Yankee* on May 20. "Away with such folly!"[5]

When news finally arrived of Napoleon's abdication on April 11, of his exile, of the restoration of the Bourbon monarchy and of the end of the Continental war, it arrived in the form of oral reports spread on the night of May 31 by the crew of a privateer, which had captured an English ship more than two weeks before anchoring at Portsmouth, N.H. The *Democratic Press* of Philadelphia labeled this news "incredible and absurd." "What a whale!" exclaimed Boston's *Independent Chronicle.*[6] "The story of a continental peace we entirely discredit . . . ," wrote the Baltimore *American.* However, the "MOMENTOUS AND HIGHLY IMPORTANT NEWS!" was confirmed on June 3 when a gentleman riding the Eastern Stage brought some Halifax papers, filled with London news, to Boston. By then, of course, the news was more than a month and a half old.

From the American perspective, it was as if a haze had covered Europe in the winter and early spring of 1814. There were moments when the haze dissipated, and it was possible to see events across the ocean with some clarity. But most of the time Americans were unable to discern what was transpiring. "The details are so broken, the times when, or places where, or the manner how . . . are entirely unsatisfactory," wrote the

Democratic Press. The Boston *Yankee* summed up the plight of the Continent when it complained, "There is really no data by which we can correctly reason. . . ."[7]

The specific difficulties Americans experienced in obtaining "data" on events in France in 1814 were intensified by the war with Britain and by weather conditions on the Atlantic. News traveled somewhat more easily in peacetime and in summertime. Nevertheless, a similar haze obscured distant events from the view of most of humanity for most of human history.

The Haze

The methods our more distant ancestors employed to exchange news tended to be near-sighted. Word of mouth—bolstered by busybodies, messengers and criers—might offer peeks into even the most intimate affairs of the inhabitants of a village; it presented a reasonably clear view of major events within a day's walk, perhaps a day's run. But events beyond the range of a busybody or a messenger grew blurry, and beyond the reach of caravans or travelers they were almost entirely obscured.

This nearsightedness presented few problems when life was centered on villages or tribes, but people dependent on spoken news were often lost when their villages or tribes were subsumed by countries. In Thailand in 1953, for example, only 38 percent of the residents of one such village were aware that their country was not currently at war.[3]

Even in 15th-century England, where letters were beginning to supplement spoken news, it was difficult to keep track of who was king during periods of crisis, let alone who had won the latest battles. A letter written to John Paston on April 4, 1461, explained that it had not been possible to send news earlier of the battle of Towton, fought on March 29, "be cause we had non certynges tyl now; for un to this day London was as sory cite as myght."[9]

Any European city in the 15th century whose fate rested on complex events taking place out of town might be classified as "sorry"; mechanisms for gathering and disseminating news of such events were just beginning to develop. At one point during the War of the Roses, the City of London had to resort to dispatching men "to make reaporte unto us of the disposicioun" of each of the warring parties after a battle.[10]

The increased use of writing and then print helped news items maintain their integrity over distance. But distance, even with improved roads and postal services, still reduced the number of written or printed reports likely to arrive and, consequently, reduced the likelihood that an accurate or comprehensive report would find its way through. According to reports collected by Philip Eduard Fugger, for example, news that the formidable Spanish armada had been decisively defeated by the English on Aug. 8, 1588, was available in relatively nearby Middelburg, near the coast in Holland, four days later. However, on Aug. 27, many in Rome were of the belief—thanks to a printed newssheet, a messenger and a letter from France—that the Spanish armada had triumphed. And as late as Sept. 8, Prague was still celebrating news, brought by messengers, of a Spanish victory.[11]

The fact that faraway events, even when communicated by letter or set in type, tended to be seen in soft focus, their images occasionally inverted, helps explain why

The Speed of News

Some comparisons:

1481. A handwritten letter reporting on the death of a Turkish sultan took two years to make its way to England.

1644. News on the Manchus' conquest of China appeared in a Dutch newspaper six years later.

1702. Unofficial news of King William's death in England first reached his subjects in North America after two months and nine days.

1775. News of the battles of Lexington and Concord in Massachusetts appeared in the *Georgia Gazette* after one month and 12 days (Mott, "The Newspaper Converage . . .")

1790. Average time lag between foreign events and their publication in Philadelphia newspapers: London, 67.5 days; Paris, 80.8 days; Constantinople, 147.0 days (Pred).

1800. News of George Washington's death in Virginia appeared three weeks later in the *Western Spy* in Cincinnati (Mott, *American Journalism*).

1815. New England learned of the American victory in the Battle of New Orleans 20 days later. The Northeast learned of the treaty that ended the war (signed two weeks before the battle was fought) six weeks after it was signed.

1841. News of President William Henry Harrison's death in the East reached Los Angeles after three months and 20 days.

1844. A telegraph operator sent news of the Whig presidential ticket from Annapolis Junction to Washington on the world's first telegraph line almost instantly.

1963. Sixty-eight percent of Americans learned that President John F. Kennedy had been shot within $1/2$ hour of the attack (Pred).

relatively distant lands seem to appear in these early forms of news predominantly as the sites of bizarre occurrences. In his discussion of early English newsbooks and news ballads before the arrival of the newspaper, Matthias Shaaber notes that the view to the east was often distorted: "Germany, for instance, was a prolific source of miraculous wonders but of little else."[12] The view to the west from Germany was no more reliable: A newsbook printed in Augsburg in the middle of the 17th century on a monster born with goat's legs, a human body, seven arms, and seven heads placed that birth in Spain.[13]

Along with misunderstandings and mysticism, the haze that hung over the outer boroughs of the news world supported the growth of xenophobia. The more obscure the view of distant peoples, the less comprehensible their behavior seemed. The residents of Barbary (Morocco), for instance, were described in one 1579 English newsbook as "a barbarous people observinge the lawes of Mahomet, geven (for the most part) to idlenes and sundry supersticions."[14] As late as the 19th century, the inhabitants of the less-developed portions of the world were routinely dismissed in French newsbooks as "savages."[15]

Insofar as they regularized and institutionalized the distribution of news, newspapers boosted the reliability of the reports that were available. But the newspapers of the

17th, 18th and early 19th centuries could not gather or distribute news over a distance any faster than a horse or a ship could travel. The format used by the early newspapers, in which news was listed under its date and place of origin, makes apparent the delays enforced by travel. An issue of the *Gazette de France,* printed in Paris on Jan. 2, 1632, for example, contains day-old news from Paris, three-day-old news from Metz in Lorraine, six-day-old news from London, week-old news from Brussels, more than two-week-old news from Madrid and two-and-one-half-month-old news from Constantinople. This spread was typical.[16]

Because the oldest news was usually placed first, any news that had completed the journey from Constantinople usually sat atop 17th-century European corantos or newspapers. On rare occasions news arrived from even farther afield: One of Nathaniel Butter's periodic newsbooks published in London in the middle of January 1642 featured a report on a battle fought in "Brazeil" on Aug. 26 of the previous year.[17] And the Manchu conquest of China in 1644 was mentioned in a Dutch paper in 1650 and then again in 1653—among the first times "the calamities of the ingenious China" were discussed in print anywhere in Europe.[18]

North America, although more accessible than Brazil or China, was perhaps as remote from Paris or London as was Constantinople. Details of battles in and around Quebec between French troops and "savages"—the Iroquois—in October and November 1666, for example, did not appear in the *Gazette de France* until March 11 of the next year.[19]

The nearsightedness of European news systems was felt perhaps most profoundly by those Europeans who chose to settle in America. The haze began obscuring the homelands of these emigrants even as their boats left shore. And difficulties in transmitting news to and from North America would have definite political consequences, because, unlike the "infidels" in Turkey, the settlers implanted in America had a political allegiance to Western European governments, an allegiance they were asked to maintain.

The *minimum* time it would have taken for news from England to cross the ocean to Massachusetts at the beginning of the 18th-century has been estimated at 48 days. Delays in getting on board a ship, delays at sea, and delays once the news reached America all helped make the *average* time lag much greater.[20] King William III died on March 8, 1702, but unofficial news of the king's death did not reach his subjects on the North American continent until May 17; official word, in the form of a copy of the *London Gazette,* did not arrive in Boston until May 28.[21]

Americans today may expect to learn of a leader's death within minutes or, at most, hours.[22] Americans in 1702, however, grew accustomed to a delay of months while news from their homelands made its way across that seemingly irreducible impediment—the Atlantic Ocean.[23] Indeed, on June 4, 1702, the colony of Massachusetts officially and un-self-consciously grieved for a king who had been dead for nearly three months.[24]

Such delays, though expected, cannot simply be factored out. The pace of events itself necessarily slows with a large time lag in the transmission of news. For instance, the resolutions attacking the Stamp Act passed or considered by the Virginia House of Burgesses at the end of May 1765 were widely discussed in English publications—but not until August. And news that the stamp tax had finally been repealed took 65 days to reach America in 1766.[25] Such delays in the spread of news substantially prolong reaction time and consequently reduce a society's ability to respond to developments in an efficient and coordinated fashion. In fact, the time lag imposed on the transmission of news by the Atlantic may be another possible explanation for the fact that the British Empire broke apart along the Atlantic in the 1770s.

Similar time lags in the transmission of news persisted into the 19th century. Perhaps the most dramatic example of the temporal dislocations they caused in America is the Battle of New Orleans (in which about 2,000 soldiers were killed). The battle was fought on Jan. 8, 1815—two weeks *after* a peace treaty ending the war with Britain had been signed in Belgium. (The Northeast did not receive news of the battle until Jan. 28 or news of the treaty until Feb. 11.)[26]

News today is certainly not immune to confusion. The first reports on heated events are still occasionally inaccurate. When President Ronald Reagan and some members of his party were shot in 1981, Americans were told by television reporters that the president's press secretary, James Brady, had died. Brady was, in fact, seriously wounded but alive. The error, however, was corrected within about half an hour as additional reports arrived. In the days when news arrived slowly and sporadically, such errors might remain uncorrected for weeks; the confusion might persist for months. The result—probably the most palpable consequence of the weakness of the news systems used by our ancestors—was a universal sense of uncertainty.

Testaments to that uncertainty can be found throughout the letters Fugger received on the fate of the Spanish armada: "As the news reached here so quickly and unexpectedly, little credence was placed in it . . . ," a correspondent writes; "it is rumoured here . . . but where this news comes from I cannot find out," admits another; "whether it is correct we shall not know for certain till the regular mail comes," explains a third Fugger agent.[27] A similar uncertainty runs through the reports on the Thirty Years War carried by the oldest surviving coranto printed in English ("The new tydings out of Italie are not yet com"), which is spotted with phrases like "here comes no certainty thereof"; "it is to[o] wondered at"; and "there is different writing & speaking there uppon." The uncertainty was so pervasive that, according to this coranto, merchants in Nuremberg were betting "many 100 Florins" on whether enemy troops had in fact entered Prague.[28]

The development of the printed newspaper may have begun to ease this uncertainty somewhat, but it surely did not put an end to it. Early in the 18th century Daniel Defoe complained that his fellow journalists

> daily and monthly arouse mankind with stories of great victories when we are beaten, miracles when we conquer, and a multitude of unaccountable and inconsistent stories which have at least this effect, that people are possessed with wrong notions of things, and wheedled to believe nonsense and contradictions.[29]

For while news systems were gaining strength over these centuries, the world about which Europeans wanted to be informed was expanding; the distances were growing. And, of course, few were as susceptible to "wrong notions of things" as those Europeans who had moved 3,000 miles from the sources of much of the news that was of interest to them, to a place where the data necessary to "correctly reason" seemed perpetually in short supply.

The problem was not just communicating with those they had left behind; Americans also faced substantial obstacles in communicating with each other, in spreading the news necessary to maintain a society across this large continent dotted with European settlements. A report on the first battles of the American Revolution, fought in Lexington and Concord, Mass., on April 19, 1775, for example, did not make its way into the pages of the *Georgia Gazette*, in Savannah, until May 31.[30]

After the success of the Revolution, the European inhabitants of America's coastal settlements and its growing number of inland outposts found themselves sharing a government. Human experience had shown, to paraphrase Henry Adams, that even the minimal internal communication necessary to sustain a nation of this size would require a system of rivers and roads much more efficient than any available or contemplated in America (a system European nations had had centuries to develop), and Americans did not yet dream that the experience of humankind was useless to them.[31]

In the 19th and 20th centuries, the "distance decay"[32] to which news had been subject would be eliminated in large part by technological developments—many emanating from news-hungry America—that would eventually enable news to cross forests and oceans at the speed of light. Newspaper journalists themselves, particularly in America and Britain, would also play an important part in clearing the haze, though that would require a change in the methods by which they operated: They would have to leave their print shops.

The Print Shop

"No mail yesterday," complained the *Orleans Gazette* in 1805. "We hardly know what we shall fill our paper with that will have the appearance of news."[33]

Early American newspaper editors/publishers/printers[34]—the titles were interchangeable because the positions were often filled by the same person—fretted, paced and held their presses, waiting for the mail. The post might bring a letter with a few facts from afar or some printable opinion; it might bring out-of-town papers and a chance to borrow enough news to fill a couple of issues. If there was no news in the mail, there would be a spate of hastily composed essays in the paper that week. The promises the early newspapers made to their readers often were qualified with such caveats as "if the Post faile us not"; their apologies, too, often allude to problems with the post: "The failure of all the mails must plead our excuse for the barrenness of our columns to-day," the *Mobile Advertiser* explained in 1833.[35]

"Reporter" was not among the titles used by these ink-stained editors. What little local news there was in their papers, what little they attempted to compete with word of mouth for, could usually be obtained in the course of conversations with visitors to the shop or acquaintances at the tavern: National and foreign news was taken from letters or, more commonly, from other papers. When Lewis and Clark returned from their expedition to the West on Sept. 23, 1806, for example, Boston newspapers obtained the news from the *National Intelligencer* in Washington, which itself was reprinting a letter from President Thomas Jefferson based on a letter he had received from William Clark in St. Louis. The news was not published in Boston until Nov. 6, 1806.[36]

Early newspapers were not ashamed about having "stolen" another's news; instead the scope of their borrowings was a point of pride: the first issue of the *Evening Post* in

London in 1709, for example, boasted that it would contain "an extract of all the foreign as well as domestic prints."[37] It was not uncommon to read attributions like the following from the *Boston Evening Transcript* in 1841: "We learn from the *Albany Daily Advertiser* of yesterday from the *Buffalo Commercial Advertiser* of Saturday. . . ."[38]

As a consequence, news often reached readers only after some lengthy wanderings. Before settling into the pages of a newspaper, it might have traveled through the mails, through conversations and through other papers. Note, for example, how this significant piece of news dribbled into the New York *Gazette and Mercury* of Feb. 2, 1778:

> The Hartford Post, tell us, That he saw a Gentleman in Springfield, who informed him that he (the Gentleman) saw a Letter from an Officer in Gen. Howe's Army to another in Gen. Burgoyne's, giving him to understand, WAR was declared on the sides of France and Spain, against the MIGHTY Kingdom of Britain.

This item, which the *Gazette and Mercury* had actually lifted from a month-old Boston paper,[39] had an additional weakness: It was untrue. Neither France nor Spain had yet declared war on Britain.

To the extent that they merely collected, passively, whatever information happened to drift through the door, early newspaper editors left themselves vulnerable to the errors of other newspapers, of the Hartford postmaster, and of gentlemen in Springfield. These editors also surrendered the ability to pursue the subjects about which they wanted to know more. The limitations of the print-shop way of knowledge deepened the frightening opacity of this expanding world.

The printing press and the newspaper are marvelous devices for disseminating news, but in these years they may actually have represented a setback for news gathering. Some earlier newsmongers had collected news more aggressively. Busybodies did not simply wait at home, they strolled from courtyard to courtyard. Messengers might travel for days in an effort to secure some piece of information. Medieval heralds might accompany their masters into battle in order to regale those who missed the carnage with first-hand accounts of their lord's valiant deeds.[40]

Newspaper journalists seemed not to have inherited this skill. Perhaps they were made complacent by their ability to enthrall the community simply by printing a couple of essays, a letter someone in town had received from London, and a few stories taken from a reasonably fresh copy of the *London Gazette* by a recent edition of the *Boston News-Letter.*[41] Perhaps they were deterred by their inability to compete with word of mouth for the stories they might have most easily covered—local events. Perhaps they were simply too busy with the chores and responsibilities of their print shops to chase fires or observe battles. In London, a newsman might find time to visit nearby Saint Paul's Cathedral in search of information. "But long he must not walke," a critic observed in 1631, "lest he make his newes presse stand."[42]

Despite the depth of American interest in the fall of Napoleon in 1814, there is no evidence of an American journalist actually having hazarded a journey to Europe to gather and send back information; there is no evidence that anyone was hired to forward European newspapers from a neutral port (admittedly not a simple task given the vagaries of shipping, particularly during wartime). In Boston in 1814, a few journalists were beginning to gather at the Exchange Coffee-House where the stage coach lines ended and news reports were transcribed for patrons; one or two newsmen were beginning to row out to the harbor to meet ships from Europe. But as late as 1814 most American journalists were still waiting—for the mails, for an American paper that might have stumbled upon some news from Europe or even for that rare commodity, a European newspaper. "The editor of this paper," read a plaintive notice in the *Democratic Press* of Philadelphia in May 1814, "will sincerely thank any of his friends, who will favor him with loan of foreign papers, particularly French or English."[43]

The news flow was further obstructed by the musings, conjectures and diatribes with which many of these journalists filled the spaces between and around the details that did become available. "I gave myself over to some meditations . . ." is how the editor of a French-language weekly in New York in 1814 explained one such departure from the tight confines of established fact.[44] These journalists were interested in information, even anxious for information, but they were not yet worshipful of information. Occasionally they would ignore news that challenged their preconceptions: Federalist newspapers in America underplayed the more optimistic reports on Napoleon's fate; Republican newspapers were far more likely to swallow the false reports that French forces had regained the offensive.[45]

News was being covered in early 19th-century America, but it was being covered in fits and starts, often hazily, often laggardly, usually in third- or fourthhand reports, often obscured by the prejudices of partisans. And with few exceptions, news was not being *uncovered.* American newspapers had yet to discover the power of reporting.

Questions

1. Are there any parts of the world—or areas of society—that a "haze," as described in this chapter, still appears to cover?

2. How might uncertainty caused by the unreliability of news have affected the worldviews of our ancestors?

3. It seems strange to us that early newspaper editors did not take more aggressive steps to improve the flow of news. What factors held them back?

The Development of Reporting— The Journalistic Method 14

"What has become of space?" the *New York Herald* asked in 1844. In the first half of the 19th century, distance—space—seemed to have been, to use the *Herald*'s term, "annihilated."[2] The time it took to traverse distances within the United States had been cut first by the use of Pony Express systems, then by steam-powered ships on coastal and inland waterways, then by railroads. Charleston newspapers, for example, which had been reprinting 20-day-old New York news in 1794, were able to report on New York events an average of only five and a half days after they occurred by 1839. In similar fashion, the frequency, reliability and speed of the intercontinental exchange of news had been improved by the institution of regular packet-ship service between New York and Liverpool in 1818, which would reduce the time needed to cross the ocean to as few as 22 days. In 1838 steamships had begun making the trip, and the next year one arrived after only 13 days.[3]

But the space between news event and audience truly began to disappear on May 1, 1844. With the Whig convention meeting in Baltimore, a crowd had gathered at a railroad station in Washington that afternoon to await reports on the convention's decisions. (Railroad stations had become news organs for those too impatient to wait for the next day's newspaper.) Shortly after the convention had settled on its presidential and vice presidential nominees, a train left Baltimore. It stopped briefly at Annapolis Junction, then arrived in Washington, buzzing with the news. However, by the time that train pulled in, the inventor Samuel Morse had already announced the composition of the ticket to the skeptical crowd at the station. Morse had stationed a telegraph operator at Annapolis Junction to transmit the news to Washington on the completed section of the first extended telegraph line. It had taken the train an hour to cover the distance from Annapolis Junction to Washington. The world's first telegraphed news message—reporting, as Morse announced, that "the ticket is Clay and Frelinghuysen"—had arrived almost instantaneously.[4]

FIRST TELEGRAPH LINE
CONSTRUCTED.

The first telegraph line—constructed for Samuel Morse between Baltimore and Washington. A portion of this line was used to send the first news report by telegraph.

Within a month newspapers began taking advantage of Morse's telegraph—which would allow them to publish *today* news of the major events *yesterday* in any city to which they were connected by a reliable wire. Newspapers would soon become the primary customers of the telegraph companies. Within four years James Gordon Bennett's *New York Herald* was boasting of having printed "ten columns of highly important news received by electric telegraph" in a single issue.[5]

Bennett was among those who recognized the political significance this rapid flow of news held for this rapidly growing country:

This means of communication will have a prodigious, cohesive, and conservative influence on the republic. No better bond of union for a great confederacy of
states could have been devised. . . . The whole nation is impressed with the
same idea at the same moment. One feeling and one impulse are thus created and
maintained from the centre of the land to its uttermost extremities.[6]

But from an American perspective, perhaps the most dramatic result of the invention of
the telegraph was the "annihilation" of the Atlantic Ocean: America and England were
connected by a cable laid under the Atlantic for a few weeks in 1858, permanently in
1866.

The extent to which the business of gathering news had been transformed was apparent in 1870 when Americans turned their attention to a story similar to the one that
had proved so elusive in 1814: the fall of a second French emperor, Napoleon III. On the
evening of Sept. 4, 1870, two days after the Prussians defeated Napoleon III's army, the
Republic was proclaimed in Paris. The *New York Tribune* carried the news on the morning of Sept. 6. In fact, the issues of the *Tribune* that discuss this act in this European
drama are filled with similarly prompt reports on the military and political situation, and
on the emperor's exact whereabouts and activities.[7] There appeared, in other words,
columns and columns of timely data by which readers could "correctly reason."

The *Tribune*'s reports on Napoleon III's fall arrived by telegraph via the transatlantic cable. Without the cable, the facts might have straggled in weeks later; had packet
ships, railroads, and steamships also been unavailable, months later. However, these
technological changes, these methods of accelerating news, are not sufficient in themselves to explain the sharp contrast between the accounts Americans were given of the
fall of the first Napoleon and of the fall, 56 years later, of his nephew.

The *Tribune*'s editors in 1870 did not simply wait to see what information on the situation in France had managed to find its way across the cable. They were not dependent
on the flow of private reports or accounts from other papers. Instead, the *Tribune* was able
to make use of "special correspondents" stationed with the Prussian and French armies
and "at the leading capitals." These "specials" forwarded the key documents and letters;
they contributed firsthand battle reports ("I was with the King throughout the day on
the hill above the Meuse, commanding a splendid view of the valley, of the river and the
field. . . ."); they struggled to uncover information and even interviewed the principals
("I broke ground by asking Count Bismarck what were likely to be the conditions of peace
demanded by the King of Prussia's Government").[8] By 1870 reporters had arrived on the
scene.

Reporting—embarking into the field in search of news—is an act of deference toward
facts, an acknowledgment of the limitations of one's own deductive or creative powers.
Many other systems of knowledge have relied on similar information-gathering expeditions: Herodotus traveled for his histories. At the end of the 15th century, a number of
Italians were stationed in France to gather diplomatic intelligence for their governments.
In the 16th century, naturalists set out on "field trips," while astronomers sailed across
the Equator in order to map the southern sky. In the 17th century, industrial spies were
sent from England to Italy to learn how to build a machine to throw silk.[9]

Indeed, the strategy for gathering information now employed by most journalists—
what might be called the "journalistic method"—is a product of the same spirit that

spawned the techniques of historical research and intelligence gathering, the same spirit that gave birth to the scientific method. All such activities are motivated by a belief that the world has something to teach the mind, that rumination will be unproductive without the opportunity to graze on fresh information. "Sit down before a fact as a little child," commanded the 19th-century English biologist Thomas Henry Huxley, "be prepared to give up every preconceived notion, follow humbly wherever and to whatever abyss nature leads, or you shall learn nothing."[10]

Not all journalists have possessed sufficient humility to stand, notebook open, before an event; not all have had the know-how, the opportunity or the time. But when journalists do commit themselves to looking, asking and listening, events—even highly charged events as far away as France or Prussia—can be seen with a remarkable degree of clarity.

The journalistic method is the pursuit of independently verifiable facts about current events through enterprise, observation and investigation. This method does have important limitations; nevertheless, along with the telegraph and other technological wonders, it deserves credit for clearing the haze.

Enterprise

Most of the news included in early newspapers occurred out of town. The first sign that editors were prepared to devote energy to hastening and deepening the flow of news was their effort to seek out informed individuals in the provinces or abroad who might be counted upon to forward a regular supply of letters containing such news. In the first issue of his newspaper, the *Intelligencer,* in 1663, Roger L'Estrange discusses "the planting and securing of my correspondents."[11] Henry Muddiman—England's leading newsletter writer at that time, soon to become England's leading newspaper editor—was kept informed by postmasters and other correspondents, often in return for a discount on his publications. In 1663, for example, a postmaster from Newcastle wrote:

> Mr. Muddyman. I received your last paper and give you many thanks, and I hope it will continue and that I shall have a further correspondence. As for the Scotts affairs . . .[12]

Such correspondents could be counted upon to forward reports of newsworthy occurrences in their bailiwick directly to the newspaper—a considerably more efficient system than waiting for the haphazard arrival of private letters. By 1792 the use of correspondents by London newspapers had increased to the point where a commercial daily, *Lloyd's List,* could name 32 individuals who supplied information to the paper from 28 ports.[13]

Eighteenth-century American newspapers had made attempts of their own to obtain news from correspondents, often without great success. "Our Country Correspondents are desired to acquaint us, as soon as they can conveniently, with every remarkable Accident, Occurrence, &c fit for public Notice," Benjamin Franklin requested—or pleaded—in his *Pennsylvania Gazette* in 1729.[14] As the century progressed, however, most American newspapers settled into the habit of relying on each other, on foreign papers and on private letters for word of newsworthy occurrences.

Correspondents exported news, and given the perishability of the merchandise, their business was dependent on a reliable means of transportation. Consequently, correspondents did not arrive in force in American journalism until packet ships, railroads and steamships began to make travel, particularly transatlantic travel, more dependable. By 1837 Bennett's *New York Herald* claimed to have "occasional correspondents all over the country, in France, England, and other foreign nations." A year later Bennett traveled to Europe (on the return trip of the first steamship to cross the Atlantic) to arrange for additional correspondents.[15]

Along with securing correspondents, there was another relatively simple step impatient newspaper journalists could take to improve their coverage of news from afar: They could reach out for it at earlier points in its long journeys. Some American editors, with their omnipresent hunger for news from Europe, began by walking down to the docks to obtain news from the most recently arrived ships. Among the first to demonstrate such enterprise was Benjamin Russell of the *Massachusetts Centinel and Republican Journal,* who was gathering news on the docks of Boston by 1790. The next frontier was the harbor itself. In the early years of the 19th century, Henry Ingraham Blake, of the *Mercury and New England Palladium* in Boston, boarded a boat and began meeting the ships.[16]

In New York City, in the middle of the 1820s, the use of such "news boats" resulted in one of the world's first ventures in cooperative news gathering: Most of the major New York newspapers joined together to send a boat into the harbor in search of European newspapers and European news. When that cooperative venture split apart in 1828, it led to some intensely competitive races through New York harbor. Rowboats were soon replaced by schooners, and the schooners began venturing farther and farther out in the sea lanes to intercept ships.[17]

Bennett had observed the utility of news boats on his first job in journalism—with the *Courier* in Charleston in 1823. (The *Courier*'s editor, Aaron Smith Willington, was an early devotee of the news boat, which he had used to obtain one of the first reports on the treaty ending the War of 1812.)[18] By 1840 Bennett, now established in New York, owned his own newspaper and, he claimed, the fastest sailboat. An issue of the *Herald* exults in a description of its boat "skimming o'er the bright blue waters" and passing the competition's boat "almost without an effort, and with a sort of gentle smile on the figurehead which adorns her prow." "In every species of news the Herald will be one of the earliest of the early," Bennett had proclaimed in one of the first issues of his paper.[19]

The competition to be "one of the earliest of the early" would also be conducted in those years with horse relays, trains and pigeons—and journalists were not above hijacking each other's trains or shooting down a rival's pigeons. In England in 1835, Charles Dickens, then reporting for the *Morning Chronicle,* raced a *Times* reporter to London with some news from Exeter. "The *Times* and I changed horses together," Dickens wrote a colleague. "They had the start two or three minutes, I bribed the post-boys tremendously and we came in literally neck and neck—the most beautiful sight I ever saw."[20]

The reporter's obsession with such competitions has been dismissed as a professional "fetishism" by one journalism critic.[21] That is unfair. This concern with speed stems, as did the news boats and to some extent the correspondents, from an effort to satisfy the most basic desire of the news audience: the desire to be aware of what is occurring, if not *now,* then as close to *now* as possible. It is unlikely that readers of the *Morning Chronicle* would have experienced any material loss had an edition of the paper been printed without Dickens' report from Exeter. However, they may have had to suffer the comment "Oh, you haven't heard?"; they may have felt the echo of some ancient fear upon learning that they had, for a time, been left in the dark. And, worse, when the *Morning Chronicle* finally arrived with that report, readers might have found it familiar, dull. "We would not nauseate the Reader," promised an English newspaper, the *True Protestant Mercury,* in 1680, "with cold Pye."[22]

The public may not follow the results of these races as closely as do journalists themselves, but the public certainly does want its news kept up to date or even, given the increased speed enterprising journalists and their machines have achieved in the 20th and 21st centuries, up to the minute. The competition to be "one of the earliest of the early" grows out of one of the most basic exigencies of journalism: timeliness.

Observation

On Aug. 16, 1819, perhaps 50,000 English men and women gathered on Saint Peter's Field in Manchester in support of parliamentary reform. The field and the events that transpired there would both become known—in a sarcastic reference to the Torys' great triumph at Waterloo—as "Peterloo." This massive crowd of protesters, probably the largest yet gathered in England, had been urged by the radical leader Henry Hunt to "come . . . armed with no other Weapon but that of a self-approving conscience."[23] However, a brigade of soldiers, including volunteer yeomanry cavalry, was stationed in and around the field, and they bore more conventional weapons.

Two wagons lashed together formed the hustings, and Hunt was addressing the huge assemblage from this makeshift platform when the yeomanry began pressing their way through the crowd to arrest him. The wagons were soon surrounded. Hunt, still urging nonviolence, surrendered. But then in a flash Saint Peter's Field erupted in violence and terror as the yeomanry bared their sabres and began hacking at the crowd. Approximately 420 people would be wounded; perhaps a dozen would die. And on the wagons with the speakers at that moment, staring down upon the very center of the horror that was Peterloo, was John Tyas—a reporter for the *Times* of London.[24]

The writers whose letters had been reprinted in early newspapers or in still earlier forms of printed news occasionally had witnessed an event themselves. One newsbook in 1538, for example, is filled with the result of an intrepid effort to report on an eruption on Mount Vesuvius, with "fire still burning and smoking under the layer of ashes." "When I came to the top of the mountain," the author explains, "I saw that it was not full inside, but empty. . . ."[25] More frequently, however, printed reports were based on second- or thirdhand information. Even the correspondents secured by enterprising early editors like L'Estrange or Muddiman were relied upon more to forward whatever information had come into their hands about events than actually to observe those events themselves. Many of these correspondents, after all, were postmasters—with access to a variety of letters and newspapers but little time to go prowling about. They were not likely to be found at the center of news events, staring down at horrors.

Charles Dickens, Reporter

Before and even after he turned to fiction, Charles Dickens reported for newspapers. His subject matter often was, as in his fiction, the lives of poor or working-class people. His writing often was, as in his fiction, impassioned and captivating.

This description of a London slum was published in *Household Words,* a publication Dickens founded in 1850 with the announced purpose—one that journalists of many eras would share—of "the raising up of those that are down."

How many people may there be in London, who, if we had brought them deviously and blindfold, to this street . . . would know it for a not remote part of the city . . . ? How many, who amidst this compound of sickening smells, these heaps of filth, these tumbling houses, with all their vile contents, animate and inanimate, slimely overflowing into the black road, would believe that they breathe this air? How much Red Tape may there be, that could look round on the faces which now hem us in . . . the infected, vermin-haunted heaps of rags . . . and say I have thought of this. I have not dismissed the thing. I have neither blustered it away, nor frozen it away, nor tied it up and put it away, nor smoothly said pooh, pooh! to it, when it has been shown to me?

Without a new emphasis on firsthand observation, the race to implant correspondents and intercept news from afar in the 19th century would have been a race to obtain distanced and diluted accounts of that news. The development of our modern reporting systems, of the journalistic method, required more than schooners and friendly postmasters, more than telegraphs or telephones; it required newspaper journalists who, like John Tyas of the *Times,* had rediscovered a skill many busybodies, messengers and heralds had possessed: the ability to gather news through direct observation.

Newspaper journalists would not learn to behave like aggressive newsmongers until they could compete with aggressive newsmongers for the news that was breaking around them—for local news. While the cities in which newspaper journalists operated remained small and their publications appeared infrequently, the gains an energetic editor might have made by leaving the print shop were small; whatever news might have been uncovered at the scene of an event would have been old news to most of the town well before a weekly might reach the streets. Perhaps the first signs of change appeared in London. Greater London, with a population of about 670,000 by 1700, had grown too large for spoken news to easily traverse, and its newspapers were beginning to be published more frequently.

Local news had begun making sporadic appearances in the newly liberated London newspapers of the 1640s. Those appearances became common in the twice-weeklies that appeared following the failure to renew the Licensing Act in 1679, beginning with a paper published by Benjamin Harris (11 years before he would print the first newspaper in America) and titled, significantly, *Domestick Intelligence Or News both from CITY and Country*.[26]

The newspapers published in London by Harris and his growing number of competitors detailed numerous crimes, executions, accidents, and fires—in London. According to the newspapers historian James Sutherland, the first 36 issues of the twice-weekly published by Thomas Benskin in 1681, also under the name *Domestick Intelligence,* included accounts of 12 drownings in the Thames (it was an unusually hot summer), "seven suicides, four attempted suicides, four murders, four fatal quarrels, one rape (followed by the suicide of the victim), one attempted abduction . . . several muggings, burglaries and highway robberies," and the death of a man hit by a falling tile in Covent Garden.[27]

Some of this information newspaper proprietors must have gathered firsthand; some they may have sent an employee after; much must have been based on hearsay picked up in a coffeehouse.[28] The specialized reporter probably had not arrived in 17th-century London—but the development of newspaper reporting had begun.

The thrice-weeklies and then the dailies of the first decades of the 18th century accelerated the chase after local news. London's second successful daily newspaper—Joseph Addison and Richard Steel's *Spectator,* which debuted in 1711—was a vehicle for essays rather than breaking news, yet the *Spectator* contributed to the development of reporting simply by living up to its name. Addison frequently filled its columns with his observations on the scene at the various coffeehouses, and in 1712 his partner, Steele, anticipated the sports reporter with a detailed account of a boxing match:

> It is not easy to describe the many Escapes and imperceptible Defences between two Men of quick Eyes and ready Limbs; but *Miller*'s Heat laid him open to the Rebuke of the calm *Buck,* by a large Cut on the Forehead. Much Effusion of Blood covered his Eyes in a Moment, and the Huzzas of the Crowd undoubtedly quickened the anguish. . . .[29]

"This article call'd Home News is a new Common Hunt . . . ," wrote Daniel Defoe in 1725.[30] Reporters—spectators for hire—were well enough established by then in London that they became an issue in a battle, fought by pamphlet, between newspaper publishers and coffeehouse owners. The "Proprietors of the Papers" admitted to giving "a *Salary* for *better Advices*" to "*Collectors of Home News*."[31] The "coffee-men," writing in 1729, treated this organized snooping, eavesdropping and loitering with contempt:

> Persons are employed (One or Two for each Paper) at so much a Week, to haunt Coffee-Houses, and thrust themselves into Companies where they are not known; or plant themselves at a convenient Distance, to overhear what is said, in order to pick up Matter for the Papers. . . .
>
> The same Persons are employed to scrape Acquaintance with the Footmen and other Servants of the Nobility and Gentry; and to learn from those Knowing and ingenious Persons the Motions and Designs of the Lords and Masters, with such Occurrences as come to the Knowledge of those curious and inquisitive Gentlemen. . . .

> The same Persons hang and loiter about the Publick Offices, like House-
> breakers, waiting for an Interview with some little Clerk, or a Conference with a
> Door-Keeper, in order to come at a little News, or an Account of Transactions;
> for which the Fee is a Shilling, or a Pint of Wine. . . . [32]

These persons who "thrust themselves into Companies where they are not known"
would seem to qualify as paid reporters.[33] However, judging from the fees they commanded, it appears unlikely that they were full-timers. Most such *Collectors of Home
News*" probably were "stringers," like the correspondents then collecting news in the
provinces. But 18th-century London newspapers—circulating in a metropolitan area
that held roughly one-tenth the population of the nation and a considerably higher proportion of its wealth—were growing prosperous enough to support full-time news gatherers. They arrived in force in the 1770s when journalists finally gained access to the
most newsworthy ongoing event in London—the debates of Parliament.

With the exception of the burst of journalistic freedom during the Civil War in the
1640s and a period in 1680 and 1681 when the House of Commons sought publicity for
its argument against the king, Parliament had generally been successful in preventing
printed newspapers from revealing its proceedings to nonmembers (including that most
powerful of nonmembers, the monarch). Some handwritten newsletters, some printed
pamphlets and a few monthly magazines had gotten away with publishing outlines of
parliamentary debates.[34] But London's newspapers did not succeed in evading and then
overturning Parliament's prohibition against publication of its proceedings until the second half of the 18th century.[35]

No note taking was permitted in the gallery, where the public was seated, and at first
the reports that appeared in the newspapers about parliamentary debates (usually under
purposely ambiguous headings, such as a A GREAT ASSEMBLY) were short and incomplete. But in 1770, with interest in parliamentary affairs running particularly high, newspapers began to compete with each other in providing fuller reports. They were further
encouraged in 1771 by the failure of an effort by the House of Commons to crack down
on these violations of its privacy.[36]

By 1774 at least seven London newspapers were covering Parliament.[37] Each of
these newspapers was required to have a representative in attendance at the often
lengthy debates. The editor of the *Morning Chronicle,* William "Memory" Woodfall, un-
dertook the task himself and achieved considerable renown for his ability to paraphrase
or even re-create the debates. Other editors hired reporters to do the work for them—a
few depending on freelancers, but most employing full-time reporters.[38]

Parliamentary reporters might sit for 12 hours and then be asked to excerpt or summarize from memory 12 hours of debates in time for their papers to go to press. These
early, perhaps earliest, full-time newspaper reporters complained, as their successors
would, of the hours and the deadline pressure: "The poor weary reporter was always im-
portuned for the utmost possible dispatch," one moans in his memoirs.[39] Their job was
more to record than to interpret, but under the circumstances this required considerable
political acumen and forensic skill. One member of Parliament upon being asked if a
newspaper had correctly reported a speech of his is reputed to have replied, "Why, to be
sure, there are in that report a few things which I did say, but many things which I am
glad I did not say, and some things which I wish I could have said."[40] (Even Woodfall's

texts in the *Morning Chronicle,* despite his apparently formidable memory, did not generally retain the actual phrases used by the speakers.)[41]

Whatever their fidelity to the speeches, these reports from the gallery had become crucial features in London's newspapers. After one of England's most enterprising journalists, James Perry, began outdoing "Memory" Woodfall's coverage of Parliament by deploying a team of young barristers to cover the debates in relays for his *Gazetteer,* Woodfall's *Morning Chronicle* began to decline.[42]

Reporters in the gallery were finally permitted to take notes in 1783, and a knowledge of shorthand replaced an exceptional memory as a qualification for a job as a full-time reporter. (John Dickens and, later, his son Charles were among those who would use shorthand to report on parliamentary debates.)[43] With their technique honed and their power made manifest in the gallery of Parliament, London reporters also began training their gaze, and their stenographic abilities, upon other aspects of public life in London. The courts provided an obvious target.

In 1789 one of the best-known actresses in England, Mary Wells, devoted herself to covering a trial for her paramour's newspaper, the *World.* (Clerks were stationed outside the courtroom to transcribe her recollections of the testimony.) Indeed, when Wells sat on and broke a bottle she had with her while sitting in court, she herself became an example of the extent to which prominent Londoners were now under observation. The broken bottle was noted in the *Times,* which questioned Wells' assurance that it was filled only with lavender.[44]

The effort required to record all these observations at the dawn of the modern age of reporting in London occasionally took its toll: At one point the *Times* was forced to explain that its coverage of a major trial would be delayed "in consequence of the excessive fatigue, which the gentleman who is the principal reporter of this Paper has daily undergone."[45]

By the last decade of the 18th century, reporters were also being sent where only correspondents previously had tread—out of town. Following a riot in Birmingham in 1791, the *Times* announced to its readers:

> . . . we have thought proper, in order to meet the wishes and expectation of the public, to send down to Warwick the Gentleman who takes the Law Reports for this paper, to write down the [Birmingham] trials in short hand.[46]

That same year James Perry—now co-owner of Woodfall's old paper, the *Morning Chronicle*—dispatched himself to Paris to observe the unfolding French Revolution firsthand: Perry's reports helped the *Chronicle* achieve what a contemporary labeled an "amazing circulation."[47]

Nothing concentrates the attention of publishers as effectively as a sharp jump in circulation. In the spring of 1794 John Bell, proprietor of the *Oracle and Public Advertiser,* set out on a similar mission to Flanders—where the English and their allies were battling French troops. Bell's ostensible purpose was to secure correspondents on the Continent, but soon after he arrived he announced: "I shall be my own Journalist." The *Oracle* devoted many columns to Bell's reports from "close to the Field of Battle." How close he occasionally came to the fighting was apparent in sentences like this: "There has been an incessant cannonading, of which I have been a spectator a great part of the time from a tower."[48] From 1807 to 1809, the *Times* of London assigned a talented man of letters and of society, Henry Crabb Robinson, to attain a similar proximity to the field of battle in the ongoing Napoleonic Wars, first in Altona, Germany, then to Corunna, Spain.[49]

The dashing war correspondent—distinguishable from the most gallant soldier only by facility with a pen, critical spirit and the technicality of full-time journalistic employment—had not yet charged onto the battlefield. William Howard Russell of the *Times* is given credit—in his epitaph in Saint Paul's Cathedral as well as in many journalism histories—for introducing that role during the Crimean War in 1854.[50] Unlike Russell and his successors, early war reporters such as Bell and Robinson never saw fit actually to ride and camp with the troops; nonetheless, they covered the fighting and upon occasion even observed the fighting—Bell from his tower, Robinson from a ship in the harbor.[51]

Firsthand news gathering had become sufficiently important in London by 1808 that the *Times* employed, in addition to Henry Crabb Robinson, at least five full-time reporters (some, though, were on salary only when Parliament was in session).[52] Reporting developed considerably more slowly in the United States.

The first American daily, the *Pennsylvania Evening Post,* did not appear in Philadelphia until 1783.[53] Newspaper staffs remained small, and there was insufficient emphasis on local news in most American newspapers to justify diverting a staff member to a courthouse or city hall. Philadelphia had a population of about 69,000 in 1800—less than 7 percent of the population of Greater London at the time; New York had about 60,000 inhabitants that year. These cities were small enough—Broadway was still "a country drive"[54]—that their residents had little difficulty obtaining local news by word of mouth. ("There were too many spectators there," the *New-England Courant* had explained about Boston's reaction to an eclipse, "to make it now a piece of public news.")[55]

Certainly there were some American journalists too peripatetic to resist the occasional foray outside their print shops, as well as some local stories too newsworthy for the papers to ignore. In fact, the first successful newspaper in America, the *Boston News-Letter,* had included a description of the execution of six pirates on the Charles River in 1704.[56] But such efforts were relatively rare in these early American newspapers. Firsthand news coverage in America did not begin to come into its own until the 1820s and 1830s.

At the turn of the century, the federal government had relocated to a city —Washington, D.C.—so obscure that Abigail Adams, the wife of the first president to live there, had gotten lost in the woods trying to find it.[57] Early coverage of the activities of this government had been left primarily to a newspaper or two in Washington, whose articles would then be reprinted in papers throughout the country and supplemented by a few private letters, often from members of Congress.[58] The first clear evidence that a full-time reporter from one of the nation's large cities had been sent to Washington appeared in 1822, when the New York *Statesman and Evening Advertiser* announced that its senior editor, Nathaniel Carter, "departed this morning for Washington, where he will remain the greater part of the winter,"[59] At least three reporters were in town for the session of Congress in the winter of 1827—James Gordon Bennett, then working for the *New York Enquirer,* prominent among them. At least one out-of-town reporter would attend every session thereafter.[60]

Unidentified Sources

Nathaniel Carter's first report in 1822 as probably the first correspondent sent to cover Washington included an unidentified source: "I have to-day learned from a source, which may be depended on, that a resolution will soon be offered. . . ."

This was fitting. Unidentified sources of information or quotations are now quite common in Washington stories—so common that they have become the subject of much hand-wringing in Washington bureaus.

Sources who are permitted to withhold their names can gripe and snipe with impunity. Some, clearly, are using reporters to grind axes, settle scores or float trial balloons. And readers have no way of judging whether a source whose name is not given is, in fact, someone who "may be depended on."

Nevertheless, there is some information—often crucial information—that sources will not give journalists if their names are to be used, for a very good reason: It might cost them their jobs. Much wrongdoing has been uncovered with their aid. For that reason Nathaniel Carter's successors likely will never entirely wean themselves of unidentified sources.

In the summer of 1830, with Congress in recess, Bennett—covering Washington for the paper that had incorporated the *Enquirer,* James Watson Webb's *Courier and Enquirer*—was sent to report on a news story of a different kind:

> Mr. Bennett, our associate editor, left here Saturday last, the 17th, for Salem. . . . Knowing the interest which is felt by all classes of the community in the pending trial of the murderers of Capt. WHITE, he will from day to day furnish us with the proceedings of the Court, which will be laid before our subscribers at the earliest moment.[61]

In furnishing reports on this trial of three men accused of arranging for the murder of Joseph H. White, a wealthy retired sea captain, Bennett had to contend with the judge's attempt to prevent reporters from printing their accounts of the trial, or at least prevent them from taking notes. Indeed, in the United States the struggle for freedom to cover the courts began to resemble the struggle for the right to cover Parliament in England. "The Press is the *living* Jury of the Nation," Bennett, a partisan in this dispute, exclaimed during the White trial.[62] The point was being won: Pennsylvania had passed a statute limiting the power of judges to hold reporters in contempt of court in 1809, New York in 1829; the federal government passed a similar law in 1831.[63]

Protected by these new statutes, American reporters began peeking more regularly into courtrooms in their own cities, too—cities that were growing too large to know themselves by word of mouth. New York City's population had soared to about 218,000 by 1830, and in 1827 the country's first scheduled urban transit system arrived in the form of a 12-passenger coach on Broadway—a sign of the difficulty people, and therefore spoken news, were now experiencing traveling from one end of town to the other.[64]

New York newspapers began to find a regular source of local news in the city's police courts, where a parade of petty but apparently diverting crimes (usually involving alcohol) were adjudicated. Police court coverage was institutionalized in the earliest penny papers.[65] One week after the initial issue of the *Sun* appeared in 1833, Benjamin Day agreed to pay an out-of-work printer, George Wisner, $4 a week to visit the police court at 4 a.m. daily. (In 1834, in lieu of a raise, Day presented Wisner with half ownership in the paper.)[66] Here are two items from one of the Wisner's reports:

> William Briggs, labored under the physical infirmity of *deafness,* and not satisfied with this, superadded the moral infirmity of drunkenness, and remaining *deaf* to all entreaties, was committed.

> John McMann, at the corner of King and Varick, who had been up before for the same sin against matrimonial felicity, and against the peace and dignity of his *rib,* was brought up again at midnight, for beating his wife Jane. As she did not appear, he was discharged.[67]

In early editions of his *New York Herald,* Bennett supplemented these sardonic encapsulations of minor crimes with lengthy transcripts of major trials.[68] He would soon lead his paper and American reporting in general beyond the limits of stenographic observation. But the more aggressive reporting that would follow should not obscure the very real accomplishments of these observers—stationed in the gallery of Parliament, on the battlefield, at police court; stationed, increasingly, wherever news might be expected to break.

No newspaper in the early decades of the 19th century observed more of the political world, and observed it more intently, than the *Times* of London. To complement its foreign correspondents and its firsthand coverage of Parliament, wars and crimes, the *Times,* under its editor, Thomas Barnes, was now dispatching reporters to public assemblies, to country demonstrations, and to "radical meetings," such as Peterloo.[69]

"Just as our paper was going to press," the *Times* announced on Aug. 19, 1819—three days after the bloodshed on Saint Peter's Field—"we received from the gentleman deputed by us to report the proceedings at Manchester, the following account." John Tyas, the reporter Barnes had sent to cover that rally, had been taken into custody after the violence started (probably for his own protection), delaying his report. But when it appeared, Tyas' detailed, dispassionate description of how, in the words of the *Times* editorial that day, "nearly a hundred of the King's unarmed subjects have been sabred by a body of cavalry in the streets of a town of which most of them were inhabitants," sent a chill through many of the paper's influential readers. The key sentences were those that described the events immediately following Henry Hunt's arrest by the yeomanry cavalry who had surrounded the wagons from which he was speaking:

> . . . a cry was made by the cavalry, "Have at their flags." In consequence, they immediately dashed not only at the flags which were in the waggon, but those which were posted among the crowd, cutting most indiscriminately to the right and to the left in order to get at them. This set the people running in all directions, and it was not till this act had been committed that any brick-bats were hurled at

Press Power

The ability of the news media to influence elections or humble government leaders has often been marveled at in the United States in recent decades. Editors such as Benjamin Bradlee of the *Washington Post* and A. M. Rosenthal of the *New York Times*, television journalists such as Walter Cronkite of CBS and Tom Brokaw of NBC and, most recently, talk-show hosts such as Rush Limbaugh and Bill O'Reilly seem to have accumulated unprecedented power. "Who elected them?" has been a much-repeated moan. Journalists have appeared to wield power, rather than simply report on those who wield power.

That is true, but it is hardly new. Journalists, after all, helped lead the revolution that resulted in the formation of the United States. In the 19th century, the opinions of newspaper editors reverberated through the political parties and the government. *New York Tribune* editor Horace Greeley, for example, helped form the Republican Party, haggled over Whig and then Republican presidential candidates and was himself the Democratic candidate for president in 1872. The world's most powerful news organ in the 19th century, however, was in London.

The *Times* of London, under the leadership of editor Thomas Barnes, reported on the Peterloo massacre and then took the lead in the struggle for reform in British politics. The newspaper's power may have reached its height in 1834, when a new British government, desperate for the newspaper's support, actually negotiated with Barnes until it could win his approval for its policies. "Barnes is the most powerful man in the country," a member of that government commented.

The *Times* continued to dominate public opinion in Britain under Barnes's successor John Delane, who sent William Howard Russell to cover the Crimean War in 1854. Russell's critiques of British planning and the conditions of British soldiers eventually brought down the government. "If England is ever to be England again, this vile tyranny of the *Times* must be cut off," a former British prime minister, Lord John Russell, argued.

When William Howard Russell arrived in the United States to cover the Civil War, he was taken to meet President Abraham Lincoln, who remarked: "The London *Times* is one of the greatest powers in the world. In fact, I don't know anything which has much more power—except perhaps the Mississippi" (Woods).

the military. From that moment the Manchester Yeomanry Cavalry lost all command of temper. . . . [70]

One of the major points of controversy on Peterloo remains whether the yeomanry did indeed provoke the violence themselves. Tyas' report was and is the firmest piece of evidence against them.

The *Times* stayed with the story of Peterloo. A *Times* reporter walked the streets of Manchester, looking for signs of further trouble and covering the initial proceedings against Henry Hunt:

". . . The magistrates, whose organ I am, have therefore unanimously deemed it their duty to remand you upon a charge of high treason."

Hunt.—I presume I am not allowed to say any thing.

The Bench.—No.

He then was going down, but returned and said, "I beg to state one word: I am perfectly innocent of the charge, and ready to meet it." Having done so he bowed and retired.[71]

The *Times* devoted pages and pages to detailed coverage of Hunt's trial in 1820. (The charge of high treason had been withdrawn, but Hunt was sentenced to two and a half years in prison for organizing, or conspiring to organize, the allegedly seditious meeting at Saint Peter's Field.) And the paper covered the various inquests, all held outside of Manchester, on the deaths at Paterloo.[72]

The deployment of reporters to events such as this portentous rally, and the trials and inquests that followed, represented more than an effort to *find* news; it represented a commitment on the part of editors such as Thomas Barnes not to *miss* news. Such a commitment is inherent too in the "beat" system that arrived in these decades: Reporters assigned to Parliament or police court offered readers the assurance that they would learn of *any* important bills, of *any* intriguing crimes.

The reporter's regular observations, combined with the newspaper's regular distribution, enabled journalists to keep a systematic watch on the world. Floodlights were being lit. There were fewer dark corners in which outrages, such as the Peterloo massacre, could be hidden.

It is fitting that reform was adopted by the *Times* as its cause in the years following Peterloo. Reform would become the dominant political current during the change-over from the old journalistic order to this new world in which the behavior of those in positions of public trust—from members of Parliament to the yeomanry of Manchester—was vigilantly observed and, soon, investigated by reporters.

Investigation—The World Asked to Explain Itself

"The sun broke out for a moment in splendor" on April 10, 1836, as James Gordon Bennett set out from his office at the corner of Nassau and Beekman streets in Manhattan and walked across Chapel Street to "a large, four story elegant" yellow house on Thomas Street.[73]

As pundit or political thinker, Bennett did not rank with Greeley, Barnes or the other great 19th-century editors (though he proclaimed himself worthy of comparison to Napoleon or even Moses).[74] Bennett was a misanthropic, hyperbolic, self-promoting, apparently shameless newspaperman—capable of announcing his own marriage under a boldface headline: TO THE READERS OF THE HERALD—DECLARATION OF LOVE—CAUGHT AT LAST—GOING TO BE MARRIED—NEW MOVEMENT IN CIVILIZATION.[75] His destination on this spring afternoon in 1836 was "one of the most splendid establishments devoted to infamous intercourse that the city can shew." Bennett was on the trail not of some gov-

"Newspapers Have Made Them Know"

Robin Jeffrey was at work on a book (published in 2000) about the growth of newspapers written in India's various languages when he met a police official from the southern part of the Indian state Andhra Pradesh. "Newspapers have made the police's job more difficult," that official told Jeffrey.

Newspapers reporting on local events—and written in a language villagers could easily understand—had come to this dry, poor part of India only relatively recently. A popular, Telugu-language, socially minded daily, *Eenadu*—with a large network of local correspondents—was being published in two towns near that official's territory by the early 1990s.

Why was that a problem for the police? "Once," the official explained to Jeffrey, "if one policeman went to a village, the people were afraid. Now, six police may go to a village and people are not afraid. Newspapers have made them know that the police are not supposed to beat them" (Jeffrey).

ernment scandal but of the ax murder of a young prostitute.[76] Yet, in walking from his office to that yellow house, Bennett helped introduce the world to the power of journalistic investigation.

Seventeen years earlier, John Tyas of the *Times* of London had made a revealing comment in his report on Peterloo. Tyas had gone out of his way to assure his readers that "the individual who furnishes this report . . . had never previously spoken to" Henry Hunt, who had acceded to Tyas' request that he be allowed to stand on the wagons with the speakers, "nor would he have thought of addressing him upon this occasion."[77] Tyas wanted to make clear that he was no cohort of or sympathizer with the radical Hunt. Still, it is shocking to hear an experienced reporter—the only London reporter covering this unprecedented rally—announce that he would not normally have thought of speaking to its organizer, leader and main orator! But such was the state of newspaper journalism in the years before James Gordon Bennett walked to the house on Thomas Street.

Reporters were beginning to fan out across the globe; they were observing, even exposing. However, most reporters accomplished all this as mere members of the crowd. Their great achievement was simply to earn the right to sit with the other interested citizens in the gallery overlooking the House of Commons, with the spectators at trials, and to write a faithful account of what they had witnessed. Reporters might go so far as to request, as Tyas did at Peterloo, a spot from which they might better be able to hear, but they did not yet claim for themselves the right to behave differently from the other spectators. And the behaviors we associate with the most searching modern-day reporting—the interrogations, the rummagings—would have been considered extraordinary, even impolite behaviors.

A few reporters, to be sure, had been prepared to supplement the testimony of their eyes and ears by asking what others had seen and heard. Ten days after Peterloo, the *Times* published a story by a reporter in Manchester who acknowledged having made

James Gordon Bennett Sr. of the New York Herald.

some "inquiries on the spot" and who wrote of having "procured the testimony of individuals from every part of the area" of the massacre.[78] But more commonly the procurement of testimony was left to the magistrates, and reporters confined themselves to recording their own observations and what evidence official bodies presented. They did not print quotes, unless the statements were made in public; they may have made inquiries, but they did not interview; they refrained from addressing the principals; they did not intrude; they did not investigate.

On Monday, April 11, 1836, New York's best-selling newspaper, the *Sun,* printed a long account of the crime that drew Bennett to that house on Thomas Street. Relying on testimony before the coroner's jury, the *Sun* reported that the body of the 23-year-old prostitute Ellen Jewett had been found on her bed early Sunday morning with a deep gash in her skull, that her bed had been set afire and that she had spent the evening with a young clerk named Richard P. Robinson, who had been arrested for the murder.[79] The *Herald* included a similarly detailed report on the information heard by the coroner's jury, but the *Herald*'s editor was not content to simply pass on that information. Bennett's great strength as a journalist was his alertness to news and the energy and ingenuity he brought to the pursuit of news. In this he has had few equals. And Bennett's talents shone through this account of Ellen Jewett's murder, one section of which was headed: VISIT TO THE SCENE.

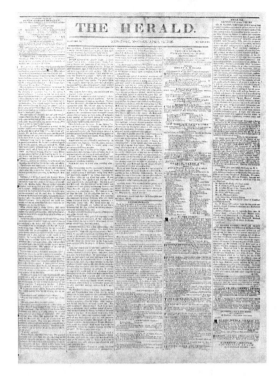

Remarkably industrious reporting by James Gordon Bennett on the ax murder of a young prostitute helped introduce the world to the power of journalistic investigation. This is a portion of the front page of the New York Herald *that followed this "Most Atrocious Murder" in 1836. It includes Bennett's path-breaking "Visit to the Scene."*

In the *Herald* that morning, Bennett described how he had walked through the crowd gathered on Thomas Street, entered the house where Jewett had been killed and commenced what would amount, over the next few days, to his own investigation of the crime. ("Why do you let that man in?" he quoted a member of the crowd as having asked the police officer guarding the door. "He is an editor—he is on the public duty" was the reply.) In this first report, Bennett presented his readers with the information he had uncovered on the circumstances of the arrest and the crime, including the moment of death itself:

> . . . he then drew from beneath his cloak the hatchet, and inflicted upon her head three blows, either of which must have proved fatal, as the bone was cleft to the extent of three inches in each place.

And Bennett also went so far as to lead his readers inside the prostitute's bedroom, where her corpse still lay:

> The countenance was calm and passionless. Not the slightest appearance of emotion was there. One arm lay over her bosom. . . . For a few moments I was lost in admiration at this extraordinary sight—a beautiful female corpse—that surpassed the finest statue of antiquity. I was recalled to her horrid destiny by seeing the dreadful bloody gashes on the right temple, which must have caused instantaneous dissolution.[80]

"Great excitement prevailed throughout the city yesterday," Tuesday's *Sun* announced, "occasioned by the disclosure of the details of the horrible murder of Miss Jewett." However, the *Sun* that day was able to produce only two long paragraphs to feed that excitement.[81] The *Herald,* on the other hand, again rose to the occasion. For this second-day story Bennett discovered the real name, family history and original *nom de guerre* (used in her years in Boston) of the victim. He outlined the series of wrong turns that had led her to that yellow house, described the dress she was known to wear while parading on Broadway and revealed this young prostitute's "great intellectual passion"—the poems of Byron.[82]

When he made that initial "VISIT TO THE SCENE," Bennett had been convinced that Robinson had wielded the ax. He had reported all the evidence against the suspect: the presence of Robinson's cloak in Jewett's room, reports that she had threatened to expose him. "His intentions can scarcely be doubted," the *Herald* concluded, "when it is known that he carried the hatchet with him."[83] But Bennett did not remain convinced.

On April 13, 1836, the *Herald* reported on "ANOTHER VISIT TO THE SCENE" undertaken by its editor. With the unerring instinct of a master sensationalist, Bennett returned to Ellen Jewett's disheveled bedroom, where he discovered under the linen sheets of this unfortunate prostitute something sure to mist the eyes of his more sentimental readers: "It was a recent splendid work of Lady Blessington's entitled the 'Flowers of Loveliness,' and treating on the resemblances of females and flowers to each other." Then, after pawing through her desk—her "*écritoire*"—and playing to a different set of human feelings by reprinting a love letter she had saved (" 'Oh! lovely creature, what a form! what a figure! what a fine bust!' "), Bennett turned to a reevaluation of the circumstances that implicated Robinson in the murder:

> Can they not be shown to be naturally growing out of other persons' guilt—of a deep laid conspiracy of female rivals—of the vengeance of female wickedness—of the burnings of female revenge?[84]

The press was no longer merely the "Jury of the Nation" for Bennett. In one of the stories he wrote about Ellen Jewett's murder, he concluded that editors are "just as useful" as police justices in "ferreting out crime, and aiding to bring criminals to justice."[85] Newspaper readers were now the jury; Bennett was ready to claim a more active role for journalists. And in his new role of proto-investigative reporter, Bennett did in fact do his best to bring to justice the person responsible for Jewett's death.

In the next day's paper, cheered on by the sudden "RAPID INCREASE" in circulation the *Herald* was experiencing, Bennett responded to his enthusiastic public by announcing that he had "made another visit to . . . Thomas Street." This time he included a paraphrase of comments by Rosina Townsend, "the keeper of the house," and by now Bennett's choice for the role of "wicked female" and chief conspirator. In his wanderings about Townsend's establishment—with which he should by then have been quite familiar (there were whispers, but no evidence, that he had been familiar with the house before the murder)[86]—Bennett seized upon one piece of evidence: a painting showing a woman about to be struck by an Indian's tomahawk. "Would not that picture perpetually hanging there—visible at all hours," Bennett asked, "suggest to female vengeance or female design—the very act that was perpetrated?"[87]

On April 16 Bennett printed what he said was a transcript of a conversation he had had with Rosina Townsend. Here is a sample of the dialogue (similar in format and content to the transcripts of courtroom cross-examinations in earlier editions of the *Herald*):

> *A* [Townsend]: . . . The house was locked up for the night at twelve o'clock P.M.—I returned to rest.—about three o'clock A.M. . . . I smelt smoke, and on going into the parlor I found the back door open, and Helen's [Ellen's] lamp standing on the marble side table, by the door—I went directly to Helen's room, and found the door shut—I opened it, and on so doing, the smoke rushed out and nearly suffocated me. . . .
>
> *Q* [Bennett]: How did you know that the lamp on the table belonged to Helen's room?
>
> *A:* There are but two lamps alike in the house, the one used by Helen and the other by myself.
>
> *Q:* Did you hear no other noise previous to the knocking of the young man you let in?
>
> *A:* I think I heard a noise and said who's there, but received no answer.
>
> *Q:* How did you know that the person you let in was Frank [the name Robinson was said to have been using]?
>
> *A:* He gave his name.
>
> *Q:* Did you see his face?
>
> *A:* No—his cloak was held up over his face, I saw nothing but his eyes as he passed me—he had on a hat and cloak. . . .[88]

One of Bennett's biographers, Oliver Carlson, credits him, probably overgenerously, with having invented the "formal interview" by reprinting this conversation. (Bennett's competitors at the *Sun* accused him of having invented the conversation.)[89] Assuming Bennett can be trusted—and he was never proved a fake—this was something more than a *tour de force* of observation. This was the journalist as opener of closed doors, as inquisitor, as detective.

In a packed courtroom in June 1836, Richard Robinson was found innocent of the murder of Ellen Jewett. (Police would make no additional arrests in the case.) "The publication and perusal of the evidence in this trial will kindle up fires that nothing can quench," Bennett had written the day before the verdict.[90] He had in mind moral fires (like most sensationalists, Bennett often surrendered to the urge to moralize), but the most profound result of the Ellen Jewett murder case was the kindling of journalistic fires.

New York journalists had seen a tragedy without political content, a local tragedy at that, exploited on a scale that may have been without precedent west of the Atlantic. ("We have no news from Europe," Bennett wrote during his coverage of the Jewett case. "Who cares? We have enough of interest on this dear delightful continent to occupy all our feelings—all our soul—and all our sensibilities. . . .")[91] New York journalists had watched a newspaperman go beyond the official sources and public records, and search for information on his own through a house of prostitution, under the sheets, in an *écritoire* and through a private interview with one of the principals. They had observed a journalist struggling—with whatever lack of taste, restraint and even good sense—not just to arrive at the truth, or to be there when the truth arrived, but to uncover the truth. Lest they ignore those lessons, New York journalists had also seen the circulation of the *Herald* triple.[92]

Bennett may not have been the first journalist to commit himself to such an effort. Many others preceded him to "THE SCENE"; a few others must have nosed about a bit on their own once there. Still, Bennett's investigations in the yellow house on Thomas Street stand out for their visibility, their manifest commercial success and their timing.

Facts—brought forth by schooners in the harbor and notepads in the courtroom—were beginning to tumble into journalists' laps. The time had come to determine how reporters might impress their talents upon this world of information. In the early decades of the 19th century, the choice had seemed between the work of what Henry Crabb Robinson called "matters of fact men" and journalists disposed to adding "*intelligence raisonée*"[93] or between shorthand transcriptions of political debates and the partisan romps that committed journalists still turned out on demand—between, in other words, "mere reportage" and some form of comment or interpretation. In entering that yellow house on Thomas Street, in searching for the facts behind the facts authorities had made public—at a time when newspaper journalists were in the process of evolving into reporters— Bennett had helped present a third alternative.

Bennett himself did not make an attractive role model. Indeed, in 1840 many other dailies joined in a "moral war" against the saucy *Herald* and its rude editor.[94] Nevertheless, the path Bennett blazed clearly led to news and, therefore, to circulation.

His footsteps would soon feel the tread of a parade of newly commissioned reporters—not all working for his *Herald*. The *Herald* sent a reporter to cover the Mexican War in the 1840s. Under Bennett's direction, it dispatched no less than 63 reporters to cover the Civil War. The *New York Tribune* and the *New York Times* each fielded at least 20 reporters of their own.[95] Wars, even more than murders, spur the development of reporting, and the Civil War furnished numerous examples of zealousness in the pursuit of information. Among the adventures of one of the *Tribune*'s Civil War reporters, Albert D. Richardson, was a trip incognito through the South (he could have been hanged if discovered). Richardson also perched atop a tall tree between Fort Henry and the gunboats that were bombarding it, and attempted to run the blockade at Vicksburg, which led to his arrest by Confederate troops (he eventually escaped).[96] Bennett's view of the importance of aggressively uncovering news would also be adopted by his equally flamboyant, if somewhat less talented, son and successor—James Gordon Bennett Jr.— who instructed Henry Morton Stanley to find Dr. David Livingstone in Africa for the *Herald* in 1869.

Among the first to receive the full political force of these new journalistic weapons was William Marcy Tweed, the leader of New York City's Democratic party during and after the Civil War. Tweed and his associates had slipped perhaps $30 million into their pockets through such scams as the submission of fictitious or widely inflated bills on city projects, particularly the construction of the new county courthouse. Their activities were hardly secret, but hard evidence of the Tweed Ring's thievery was not available to ordinary reporting. The city controller firmly refused to make public the city's books, and no investigative agency dared take on the Democratic party organization—Tammany Hall.

The "Moral War"

The people who have done the most to advance the news business are not always the most respected figures in the news business. Rupert Murdoch is a contemporary example.

Murdoch is now publisher both of the conservative *Times* and the sensationalistic *Sun* in London. When he first purchased the *New York Post*, he filled the paper's news columns with crime, sex and his own political views. Yet, Murdoch has managed to create a fourth television network in the United States, the Fox network, plus the successful Fox News Channel, and he has pioneered satellite television-delivery systems around the world. He has been both reviled and celebrated by media critics.

James Gordon Bennett was a similarly complex character. Journalism historians credit him with as many advances in newspaper journalism as anyone, including the development of reporting. Yet many of his contemporaries were disgusted by his behavior.

Perhaps it was the sensationalism of reports such as that on the murder of the prostitute Ellen Jewett. Perhaps it was his impudence in using the word "legs" instead of the more proper "limbs," of writing "shirt" instead of "linen," or "trousers" instead of "unmentionables." Perhaps it was the gossipy society items he printed. Perhaps it was his not-always-sympathetic reports on goings-on in the churches. The last straw, Bennett's critics said, was when he called the disability of a rival editor, Park Benjamin of the *Evening Standard* a "curse by the Almighty."

In 1840, a "moral war" was launched against Bennett's *New York Herald* by newspapers in New York and as far away as England. Bennett was scorned as an "obscene vagabond," a "polluted wretch," a "venomous reptile," a "common bandit," a "turkey buzzard" and a "ribald vehicle" of "moral leprosy." All "respectable people" were called upon to boycott the *Herald*. Many did. Its circulation fell for a time by about one-third. But it recovered. And by 1850 Bennett's *Herald* was selling 30,000 copies daily—more than any other newspaper in the United States (Mott, *American Journalism*).

The *New York Times* in 1870 was between masters. The newspaper's founder, Henry Raymond, one of the top journalists of his day, had died in 1869. The *Times* would not be purchased by Adolph Ochs—and set on the path that would lead to its current respectability and authoritativeness—until 1896. The interregnum between these two eras was marked by financial difficulties, declining circulation and by one of the first of the great political investigations—The *New York Times*'s exposé of the Tweed Ring.[97]

Almost alone among the New York dailies—most of which were cowed by, if not beholden to, Tweed—The *Times* had begun questioning Tammany Hall's management of the city's government, and the paper soon was uncovering facts to support its charges. In the months before the election of 1870, the reporter John Foord revealed that Tweed had added 1,300 new names to the city payroll in six weeks, that park lamps were being painted only on rainy days—to ensure that they would have to be painted again at lucrative rates—and that in some of the city's election districts there were as many as 70 percent more registered voters than male citizens over the age of 21 (as counted by the recent census).[98]

Nelly Bly and Stunt Journalism

Elizabeth Cochrane (1864–1922)—who used the pen name Nellie Bly—was one of the most enterprising reporters in American history. "In the 1880s, she pioneered the development of 'detective' or 'stunt' journalism, the acknowledged forerunner of full-scale investigative reporting," states her biographer, Brooke Kroeger.

Cochrane got her first job in journalism at the *Pittsburgh Dispatch* when she wrote a letter in response to a column making fun of young unmarried women. Cochrane's letter, signed "Lonely Orphan girl," was not printed, but was noticed by the paper's editor. He reached the author through a notice in the paper and began giving her writing assignments.

After moving to New York and Joseph Pulitzer's *New York World,* "Nelly Bly" feigned insanity to expose conditions at the asylum on Blackwell's Island in the fall of 1887, and also took on prison conditions and Albany lobbyists.

In 1889 the *World* sent Bly around the world in one of the greatest "stunts" in this era of journalistic stunts. Her goal was to complete the journey faster than Phileas Fogg, the hero of Jules Verne's novel, *Around the World in Eighty Days.* "If I fail," she said at one point in her around-the-world race, "I will never return to New York. I would rather go in dead and successful than alive and behind time." Bly returned to New York alive and successful in 72 days (Kroeger).

Elizabeth Cochrane, better known as Nellie Bly, whose investigations and stunts, including a dash around the world begun in 1889, made her one of the most famous journalists of her era.

The summer after the election—which Tweed and his candidates had still won easily—a Tammany insurgent walked into the offices of the *Times* editor Louis Jennings carrying an envelope stuffed with copies of pages from the city controller's closely guarded books. While fending off Tweed's bribes and attempts to wrest away control of the paper, the *Times* published lists of supposed expenditures from the books—$1,231,817.76 for plumbing and gas fittings in the new courthouse, for instance—in a series of installments in July 1871.[99] And the paper followed up on these astounding figures with further investigations:

> Throughout yesterday morning one of the reporters attached to the *Times* was busy searching through the City in the hope of finding a large carpet dealer by the name of J. A. SMITH, who during the years of '68, '69 and '70 had furnished the City Government with $779,117 worth of "carpet, shades &c. . . ."

(Checks made out to J. A. Smith had been cashed by a Tweed crony, James Ingersoll.)[100]

William Marcy Tweed was tried and sentenced in his expensive new courthouse in 1873—his fall a direct result of the revelations published in the *New York Times*. The Progressive Era, which arrived in the last years of the century, would reverberate with the explosion of similar journalistic bombshells—fashioned by such crusading reporters as Ida Tarbell, Jacob Riis, and Lincoln Steffens, and by such crusading editors as Joseph Pulitzer—who while sharing the elder Bennett's enthusiasm for news and sensation possessed a considerably more vigorous social conscience. Pulitzer's *New York World* featured, for one example, an exposé of conditions in the Blackwell's Island Women's Lunatic Asylum by a reporter, Nellie Bly, who had feigned insanity to get inside. In the late 19th century and the 20th century, the way of investigation would also lead into meatpacking plants, migrant labor camps, and the Nixon White House. In the 21st century, it would expose abuse of prisoners by members of the American military. Another journalistic weapon had been presented to the forces of reform.

Journalistic investigation is not an entirely benevolent force. It is responsible—as Rosina Townsend, Boss Tweed, and the managers of the Blackwell's Island Asylum learned—for exaggerating the inherent intrusiveness of journalism and therefore for intensifying the animosity inevitably directed at journalists by those whose lives, careers or scams have been intruded upon. The men who commanded troops in the Civil War were not particularly pleased to find reporters staring down at them from trees. Upon being informed of the death of three "specials" who had been reporting on his army during the Civil War, General William T. Sherman is said to have replied, "Good! Now we shall have news from hell before breakfast!"[101] Oscar Wilde viewed journalists from a similar perspective in 1892: "In the old days men had the rack. Now they have the press. That is an improvement, certainly. But still it is very bad, and wrong, and demoralizing."[102]

There is a threat not only to privacy but to a type of personal liberty inherent in an active, investigative press—though Bennett's analogy to police justices is perhaps more appropriate than Wilde's comparison to the rack. Reporters inspired to uncover scandal do begin to exhibit an uncomfortable resemblance to law enforcement officers. A history of journalism written in 1859 called the press "a police of public safety, and a sentinel of public morals."[103] The payment exacted from societies for knowledge of some of what happened in their prostitutes' bedrooms or city controller's offices is the burden of having to put up with these unlicensed sentinels of public morals sneaking into position to monitor behavior in bedrooms and offices.

It is possible in some Orwellian nightmare to imagine investigative reporters surpassing even repressive authorities as persecutors of what the majority judges immoral. Historically, however, investigative reporting has seemed one of our best defenses against Orwellian nightmares. To preserve their liberties, modern democratic societies seem to require that their muck periodically be raked; that inequities and injustices be revealed; that public figures be held to standards of public morality; that buried facts—from the circumstances of the death of a prostitute to allegations of corruption in city government—be brought to the surface. This is the service performed by reporters who uncover. Journalistic investigation is not without its hazards and costs, yet it gives the journalistic method much of its power as a tool for understanding and as a force for justice and progress.

Reporters with an inclination to investigate have also demonstrated an additional, more subtle, though equally profound power. In aiming their searchlights into the nooks and crannies of society, they have altered more than perceptions; they have altered behaviors. Modern reporters did not simply arrive in a world of unheralded police detectives, of public relations specialists writing unread press releases, of stadiums lacking only press boxes. The modern world was not waiting to be discovered by newspaper reporters; their investigations helped shape the modern world.

These prying, fact-hungry reporters asked questions that penetrated more deeply, forcing newsmakers to explain themselves more thoroughly. The reporter for the *New York Tribune* who asked Count Bismarck to outline likely conditions for peace, on the day Napoleon III was defeated in 1870, was putting the Prussian leader on the spot—Bismarck had to supply a list of carefully formulated conditions capable of withstanding scrutiny by an international public. That spot would grow crowded in succeeding decades. Reporters in the field, like sergeants in the barracks, can be placated only by order and tidiness. They force those they scrutinize to prepare, to organize themselves. Adjustments must be made not only in explanations but in actions. The consequences include significant changes in the way a society's institutions are managed and structured.

Obviously, other forces were also at work in remaking these institutions. Indeed, aggressive, intrusive reporting was in part a response to the growing size and density of 19th-century institutions. Police forces were expanding; governments and businesses were thickening with bureaucracies; ad hoc teams of sportsmen were arranging themselves in professional leagues. Journalists had to leave their print shops if they were to follow the police, account for the bureaucracies and report on the new leagues. But the growing sophistication of these institutions was itself partly a response to reporters' inquiries.

In peering over the shoulders of police as they attempted to solve crimes, journalists such as James Gordon Bennett increased the pressure on police officials to commission crime-solving specialists—detectives. (Some of them—along with the increasingly professional rogues who served as their foils—were then elevated to celebrity status through exposure in the press.)[104] Governments and businesses hired public relations experts to hand out measured portions of news to hungry reporters and then were forced to

Or he may be this

Art Young drew this cartoon for Collier's *in 1911.*

hire additional functionaries to prepare and refine the positions their public relations specialists were to distribute. Sports teams found themselves performing to crowds much larger than those drawn to a field on any given day—the audience of potential paying customers that might read of their exploits in the newspaper. And the promoters of these teams were motivated to offer the reporters who represented that audience the clarity and dramatic structure of leagues and championships and to appease them by removing the more obvious irritants—such as open gambling in the ball parks.[105]

There is something of a paradox here. Reporters of the James Gordon Bennett type open doors in hope of catching a glimpse of naked reality. Yet the more aggressive reporters become, the more self-conscious their subjects become. The deeper reporters peer, the more layers of polish, even pretense will be applied to the truth. Through their investigations, newspaper reporters exposed new areas of the world to public view, but in so doing they fostered an obsessive concern with appearances and encouraged new efforts to manipulate appearances. The age of reform would be succeeded by the age of public relations.

Veneration of the Fact

In 1835 the New York *Sun* had printed a series of exclusive reports on an examination of the moon with a new telescope "of vast dimensions" located at the Cape of Good

Improving Baseball

Some journalists play an even more direct role in organizing the events they are writing about.

Henry Chadwick, who began covering baseball regularly for the *New York Herald* in 1862, wrote the first baseball rule book, popularized the box score and supervised an annual preseason game in which the season's new rules were demonstrated.

Chadwick is now in the baseball Hall of Fame.

Hope. Among the more startling of the discoveries recorded in these articles, which sent the paper's circulation soaring, was a new life form:

> They averaged four feet in height, were covered, except on the face, with short and glossy copper-colored hair, and had wings composed of thin membrane . . . whenever we afterwards saw them, these creatures were evidently engaged in conversation. . . .[106]

The *Sun's* hoax eventually was discovered, but with little resentment and some admiration. "From the epoch of the hoax," wrote Edgar Allan Poe, who had followed the affair closely, "the *Sun* shone with unmitigated splendor."[107] Its circulation growth continued unabated.

"The epoch of the hoax" passed, however.[108] As the century progressed, violations of the truth, while they were certainly not eliminated from journalism, began to be looked upon more seriously. By the end of the century, the newsroom of Joseph Pulitzer's *New York World* was decorated with a printed card demanding ACCURACY, ACCURACY, ACCURACY![109] Accuracy had become a sacred duty because facts increasingly were held sacred.

The enterprise reporters were beginning to demonstrate, the observations they made, the investigations they conducted were all efforts to gain facts: facts from Parliament, facts from Europe, facts from Rosina Townsend's house of prostitution; data, not speculation; information, not comment; fact *uber Alles*. "The world has grown tired of preachers and sermons," wrote Clarence Darrow in 1893; "to-day it asks for facts."[110] Journalists were not only affected by the 19th-century movement toward realism in literature and art, they took the lead in that movement. The historian Richard Hofstadter has noted how large a percentage of "the makers of American Realism . . . were men who had training in journalistic observation."[111]

A reverence for facts was difficult to express in the newswriting forms available to reporters through much of the 19th century. The essay—perfected by 18th-century journalists such as Joseph Addison, Richard Steele and Daniel Defoe—placed too much emphasis on point of view; there was to be no point of view in the new world of unambiguous fact. The narrative style—relied on throughout history by those newsmongers who had the time or space (James Gordon Bennett, reporting on Ellen Jewett's murder:

A depiction of life on the Moon as it was described in the New York Sun's *famous "Moon hoax" in 1835.*

"I returned to take a last look at the corpse")[112]—began to seem too subjective and leisurely a vehicle to be trusted with cold, crisp facts. The experiences of the narrator, like the views of the essayist, were simply distractions. And the stenographic reports early reporters had produced on debates in Parliament or testimony in court failed for another reason: They profaned hallowed facts by ignoring essential distinctions between them—between mere procedural questions and smoking guns, for example. The great facts were buried in such transcripts under columns of dull detail.

Facts found their true voice only with the arrival of the "inverted pyramid" composition style in the second half of the 19th century. After the American Civil War, journalists rushing to transmit their most newsworthy information over often unreliable telegraph lines developed the habit of compressing the most crucial facts into short, paragraph-long dispatches, often destined for the top of a column of news, as in this dispatch printed in the *New York Tribune:*

> *To the Associated Press*
>
> WASHINGTON, Friday, April 14, 1865
> The President was shot in a theater to-night and perhaps mortally wounded.[113]

From here it was not a long distance to reserving the first paragraph of their stories, the "lead," for the most newsworthy facts and then organizing supporting material in descending order of newsworthiness. (The news value of the facts stacked in these stories, like the width of an inverted pyramid, grows smaller as you read down.) Theodore Dreiser recalled being introduced to this style, including the "who, what, how, when and where" lead,* with his first job in journalism at the *Chicago Globe* in 1892. "News is information," his copy editor would proclaim. "People want it quick, sharp, clear—do you hear?"[114]

This example of the inverted pyramid appeared in the *New York Times,* Aug. 23, 1927:

> CHARLESTOWN STATE PRISON, Mass., Tuesday, Aug. 23—Nicola Sacco and Bartolomeo Vanzetti died in the electric chair early this morning, carrying out the sentence imposed on them for the South Braintree murders of April 15, 1920.
>
> Sacco marched to the death chair at 12:11 and was pronounced lifeless at 12:19.
>
> Vanzetti entered the execution room at 12:20 and was declared dead at 12:26.
>
> To the last they protested their innocence, and the efforts of many who believed them guiltless proved futile, although they fought a legal and extra legal battle unprecedented in the history of American jurisprudence. . . .[115]

The inverted pyramid organizes stories not around ideas or chronologies but around facts. It weights and shuffles the various pieces of information, focusing with remarkable single-mindedness on their relative news value.

This style of newswriting had taken decades to establish its dominance. Newspapers continued to dawdle over an engaging tale, as did the *New York Herald* in this famous narrative by Henry Morton Stanley in 1872:

> There is a group of the most respectable Arabs, and as I come nearer I see the white face of an old man among them. He has a cap with a gold band around it, his dress is a short jacket of red blanket cloth, and his pants—well, I didn't observe. I am shaking hands with him. We raise our hats, and I say:
> "Dr. Livingstone, I presume?"
> And he says, "Yes."[116]

In addition, much information continued to be placed in newspapers first come, first served—the dispatches arrayed, as they were in the *New York Tribune*'s initial coverage of Lincoln's assassination, in the order in which they arrived. However, more and more reports of breaking news began to assume the form not of the narrative or the transcript but of this upside-down pyramid of facts.

When words are herded into any rigid format—from news ballad to two-minute videotape report—their ability to recreate events in their fullness may suffer. The demands of format, especially when enforced under deadline pressure, undoubtedly contribute to the journalist's habit of, in Norman Mailer's words, "munching nuances like peanuts." In the 16th and 17th centuries, newsmakers found their sentences transformed into verse; in the 20th century they found their statements chopped into 15-second "sound bites." The inverted pyramid is no more accommodating a host to nuances than other news forms. Facts—a quotation here, a number there—shine through these hier-

---

* There is something beyond a desire for a more perfect alliteration behind the recent tendency to substitute "why" for "how" in these lists; it is indicative of the increased emphasis on analysis and interpretation to which newspapers have been forced to retreat by the arrival of swift broadcast newscasts.

Mark Twain, Irreverent Journalist

"I was a reporter on the *Morning Call* of San Francisco," the novelist Mark Twain once recalled in an autobiographical dictation. "I was more than that—I was the reporter. There was no other. There was enough work for one and a little over, but not enough for two—according to Mr. Barnes's idea, and he was the proprietor and therefore better situated to know about it than other people."

Twain was also the reporter or an editor for the *Examiner* in Montana, and the *Territorial Enterprise* and the *Placer Weekly Courier* in Nevada. He covered, in his characteristically sardonic style, a "Grand Bull Drivers' Convention" for the *Weekly Courier:* "I journeyed to the place yesterday to see that the ovation was properly conducted. I traveled per stage. The Unreli-

able of the *Union* went also—for the purpose of distorting the facts. The weather was delightful. It snowed the entire day . . ." (Snyder).

Twain clearly was no romanticizer of the journalist's calling:

Our duty is to keep the universe thoroughly posted concerning murders and street fights, and balls, and theaters, and pack-trains, and churches, and lectures, and school-houses, and city military affairs, and highway robberies, and Bible societies, and hay-wagons, and a thousand other things which it is in the province of local reporters to keep track of and magnify into undue importance for the instruction of the readers of this great daily newspaper. (Mott, *American Journalism*)

archical columns of information, but the temporal, historical, atmospheric or ideological connections between these facts are often weakened, occasionally severed.

That *New York Times* account of the execution of Sacco and Vanzetti, written by Louis Stark, is an example of this form of newswriting at its most powerful:

. . . Then [Vanzetti] spoke his last words:

"I wish to forgive some people for what they are now doing to me."

Vanzetti stepped into the chamber at 12:20:30. At 12:26:55 he was declared dead.

Before midnight Warden Hendry told reporters how he broke the news to Sacco and Vanzetti.

"I simply told them that it was my painful duty to convey to them the information that they were to die shortly after midnight," he said. . . .

One dramatic fact after another: Details asked to speak for themselves—without political context, acknowledged point of view, sense of outrage, or even chronological telling. Despite the lack of explicit prompting by the writer, a conception of the nature of these executions does begin to take shape as the roll of facts is called: The event, we come to believe, consisted of a series of distinct and emotional moments. The protagonists spoke clearly and profoundly. Elsewhere in the story we learn that at the appropriate moments relatives cried, protestors marched, police drove crowds back, defense lawyers rushed about "breathlessly" and the warden himself was "almost overcome."[117]

It is a powerful tableau and a familiar one. This view of events as composed of discernible and dramatic instants, acted by coherent and recognizable characters, is the view that most newspaper readers have come to accept as valid. But this was not the only possible representation of the electrocution of Sacco and Vanzetti. Had it been considered from a political perspective, the behavior of victims, protestors, police, lawyers and warden might have taken on different meanings. Or had the *Times* reporter, alternatively, approached events from his own point of view, the scene would have reflected what he described years later as a situation of "the utmost confusion" with his and his fellow reporters' nerves "stretched to the breaking point."[118] Such partisan or personal perspectives, however, cannot be compressed into the sort of facts that echo through the inverted pyramid.

The concern with facts that led to this change in the style of newswriting was also causing a shift in the ethics of newswriting: a renewed belief in the importance of impartiality. Protestations of impartiality have been a part of the rhetoric of journalism at least since the development of the newspaper. Some English newspapers in the 1640s wore their claim to impartiality atop their front pages: *Mercurius Civicus,* for example, was subtitled *London Intelligencer or, Truth impartially related from thence to the whole Kingdome, to prevent mis-information.*[119] Editors often pledged impartiality in the notes they wrote to their readers: "The Author . . . promises to keep strictly to truth, and avoid partiality and imposition," announces the first issue of the *London Mercury* in 1719.[120] A similar promise can even be found in an English newsbook printed in 1548: "I shal never admit for any affection towards countree or Kyn, to be so partial, as wil wittingly either bolster the falsehood or bery the truthe. . . ."[121]

Did these early journalists match word with deed? Some did. In many cases partisan comment simply did not fit in crowded news columns (like those of the early corantos) or was suppressed for fear of offending the authorities. In his diary, Samuel Pepys judged the first issue of Henry Muddiman's cautious *Oxford Gazette* in 1655 "very pretty, full of news, and no folly in it."[122] Some publishers went further, however, and seem actually to have made a positive effort to balance their coverage.

Few publications proclaimed commitment to impartiality as insistently as the first English-language daily, London's *Daily Courant,* which was pledged to "delivering Facts as they come related, and without inclining to one Side or the other."[123] And if balance is accepted as a measure of impartiality, this first successful English daily appears to have lived up to its promises. As evidence we have the testimony of a cynical contemporary on the *Courant's* coverage in 1709 of the "Whig War" with France over the Spanish succession. In a satire on partisanship and exaggeration in war coverage, Joseph Addison was forced to concede that the *Courant's* editor, Sam Buckley, though a Whig, "generally kills as many of his own side as the enemy's."[124]

Mercurius Civicus in the 1640s, which billed itself as presenting the *Truth impartially related,"* is another example of a paper that might be said to have lived up to its rhetoric by including relatively balanced reports on the various anti-Royalist factions.[125] But there are many more publications, with and without the rhetoric, that seem to 21st-century eyes to have been severely out of balance. The 1548 newsbook that promised "never . . . to be so partial, as wil wittingly either bolster the falsehood or bery the

. . . And the Archduke Perished

Here is a classic example of a story that does *not* begin with the most important facts. It appeared in the Berlin newspaper *Vossische Zeitung* in 1914 under the following dateline: SARAJEVO, June 28.

This afternoon, as the Archduke and heir to the throne, Franz Ferdinand, and his spouse, Duchess von Hohenburg, were on the way to a reception at the local city hall, a bomb was thrown at the archduke's automobile, and an explosion took place right after his automobile passed the place where the bomb landed. Count Boos-Waldeck, a major in the royal military office, and Lieutenant Colonel Merizzi, a personal adjutant of the governor of Bosnia, who were riding in the following car, suffered multiple wounds. Six members of the public were heavily injured. The bomb was thrown by a typography worker by the name of Cabrinowitch. The criminal was immediately put under arrest.

After a festive reception at the city hall, the royal couple went on a ride through the city streets. Not far from the government building a gymnasium student in the eighth class named Princip, a native of Grabow, fired a series of shots from his Browning into the royals. The duke was shot in the face, and the duchess in the lower abdomen. Both perished from the injuries shortly after they were transported into the governmental building. . . . (La Roche)

The assassination of Archduke Ferdinand of Austria in Sarajevo, which this story finally gets around to reporting, was the spark that soon ignited World War I.

truthe . . . ," for example, goes on to describe the pope as "that hydeous monster, that venemous . . . Antichriste."[126]

The appeal of impartiality to early journalists—and there is no doubt that it had an appeal—was often insufficient to outweigh that of partisan causes. The partisanship exhibited might be subtle: Samuel Johnson was proud of the "impartiality" of his parliamentary reports for the *Gentleman's Magazine* in the 1740s, yet he admitted that he "took care that the Whig dogs shall not have the best of it."[127] Or that partisanship might be bold: A weekly supporting the king during the English Civil War in the 1640s twitted the enemy, the Puritans on Parliament's side, even in its day of publication—Sunday, the Sabbath.[128] And in 1793, to choose a particularly exuberant example, a French newspaper printed an account of the execution of the queen under the subheadline "The head of Female Veto separated from her fucking neck."[129] Political struggles would lose their ability to commandeer the minds of such journalists only when those minds were turned to a new adventure, offering a new perspective on their work—the quest for facts.

The journalist's hunt for facts reduced the time available for opinion: "I shall frequently write in the field, or under the first hedge that can afford me a safe retreat," John Bell of the *Oracle* explained to his readers while covering the battles with the French in 1794; "and therefore you must be satisfied with facts, without ornament or exaggerated colouring. . . ."[130] The accumulation of facts in newspapers also reduced the space available for opinion—especially when those facts had to be sent over unreliable telegraph wires at so much per word: In 1894 a correspondent for the *Times* of London was instructed that "telegrams are for facts; appreciation and political comment can come by post."[131] And the outpouring of fact from newspapers inevitably began diverting attention from opinion: "The people of England at large have not so much taste for discussion as for information," a British commentator noted in 1851. "They care more for the facts, or what they suppose to be the facts, than for the most luminous reasoning in the world upon those facts."[132]

Many newspapers retained political allegiances through the 19th and into the 20th century. Nevertheless, news increasingly was seen as an independent substance, composed of facts; opinion as something else entirely, something slightly disreputable—safe only when segregated in editorials or caged in quotation marks. Attribution, heretofore simply a method of winning additional credibility (according to the "assured written testimony" of "persons deserving of credit") now became a requirement for maintaining impartiality ("According to the mayor, the plan has no chance for success"); reporters might handle without contamination only the *independently verifiable* fact that someone held an opinion. Narrators were no longer omniscient, but the facts reporters gathered were treated as omnipotent.

For these new defenders of the fact, partisanship was merely an impediment to the free and clear movement of information; rooting, wishing, decrying were all synonymous with failing to see. "When a man acquires the scientific spirit . . . ," Walter Lippmann had Socrates explain in a dialogue written in 1928, "it means that he is ready to let things be what they may be, whether or not he wants them to be that way. It means that he has conquered his desire to have the world justify his prejudices."[133] Partisans made the mistake of equating "validity . . . with utility."[134] They were insufficiently respectful of facts.

Among the factors that led journalists to, in Honoré de Balzac's words, "venerate the fact" was the growth of news agencies in the 19th century. The first of these large-scale wholesalers of news may have been the British post office, which for a fee was supplying English summaries of articles in the foreign press to the London papers twice a week in the first years of the century.[135] The first major private news agency was established by Charles Havas in France.[136] Havas set up an office in Paris in 1832 and soon began distributing translations of foreign news to the newspapers. In 1840 Balzac expressed concern that the Agence Havas has become the only source of foreign news in France.[137]

News wholesaling was a logical outgrowth of the increased costs inherent in competing in the intensifying race to obtain news. Speed and enterprise were the *raison d'être* of any news agency. Initially Havas relied on carrier pigeons and the semaphore telegraph. The first effort at cooperative news gathering by New York's newspapers had been their decision to split the cost of news boats to the harbor in the 1820s; in 1848 the city's major newspapers, at times using the name "Associated Press," agreed to share both the expense of chartering a steamer from Boston to meet ships from Europe at Halifax, Nova Scotia, and the expense of telegraphing the news that that steamer obtained from Boston to New York.[138] Bernard Wolff began distributing telegraphic news to newspapers in Berlin by 1855; Paul Julius Reuter began a similar service in London by 1858 (both men had worked for Agence Havas).[139]

When no photos of an event were available, the wildly sensational New York Daily Graphic *(known as the "pornographic") in the mid-1920s simply posed and cut up photos until they had re-created the event. In this, their first "composograph," the* Graphic *re-creates the scene at a steamy trial where a witness was required to partially undress in the judge's chambers. She is trying to demonstrate—in this unenlightened age—that her husband must have known she was part African-American (not the term used at the time). A "show girl" plays the witness. Most of the other faces are real—taken from other photographs.*

The business in which these news agencies were engaged disposed them to treat news as a commodity—rather than as a political weapon. Indeed, partisanship had to be excised from the stories Havas, Wolff, Reuter and the Associated Press distributed if they were to be suitable for use by newspapers of all stripes.[140]

The growth in the size of newspaper staffs in these years was an additional force working against partisanship. By the middle of the 19th century, to be competitive a newspaper in England had to field a dozen parliamentary reporters, six court reporters, correspondents in the provinces and the major European capitals and a team of editorial or "leader" writers. By 1854 the *New York Tribune* employed 14 reporters and 10 editors.[141] With newspapers now produced not by one or two journalists but by dozens, enforcing a standard political line became a more difficult proposition. Moreover, with the journalists on these larger staffs increasingly segregated into separate teams of reporters and editorial writers, the distinction between gathering news and formulating opinions was re-enforced. "An editorial is a man speaking to men," exclaimed the 19th-century writer James Parton, "but the news is Providence speaking to men."[142]

And while reporters were differentiating themselves from fellow inhabitants of the newsroom, journalists as a group were differentiating themselves from the newsmakers

Dividing Up the World

As telegraph cables, and the news agencies that controlled them, began to circle the planet, information began to flow as never before. At the same time, however, information began to be centralized as never before.

In 1870, the three most powerful news agencies in the world, Britain's Reuters, France's Havas, and Germany's Wolff agreed to divide up the world. Reuters, for example, got the British empire, including China and India; Havas took the French empire, including much of Africa plus all of South America. These three companies would no longer compete for news; indeed they would share all the news they received. The Associated Press in the United States eventually became part of this "ring combination," which survived until 1934.

Thanks to the domination of news by these few Western organizations, a country in Africa might learn of events in South America only through Paris. This form of "news imperialism"—though hardly as overtly monopolistic—continues today. The major news agencies in the world remain Reuters, the Associated Press, and Havas, now known as Agence France Press. The major international broadcast news organizations, CNN and the British Broadcasting Company (BBC) are also in Western hands.

A growing reluctance for governments to continue funding news organizations has also weakened some national news agencies. In the 1990s national news agencies in Tanzania and several other African states ceased operations (De Beer and Merrill). However, the growth, beginning in the late 1990s, of Al-Jazeera, an influential Arabic-language satellite channel out of Qatar, has shown that in the world of satellites and cables it might be possible to challenge this Western domination of the news.

with whom their interests and activities had traditionally been entangled. Early newsbooks about trials had been written, on judges' instructions, by court clerks. Soldiers, even kings, had supplied news reports on battles. The Federalist leader Alexander Hamilton had helped found and edit the New York *Evening Post,* and journalists such as Thurlow Weed, who in 1830 founded the *Evening Journal* in Albany, N.Y., doubled as party leaders and political bosses.

However, as mass circulations endowed newspapers with the financial strength to survive on their own, their newsrooms were increasingly populated by individuals for whom journalism was vocation, politics at best avocation.[143] A line was being drawn: Reporters reported on positions; politicians and editorial writers held positions. Standards of acceptable behavior gradually changed to reflect this new situation: Reporters began to appear somewhat awkward sporting a second hat, or tossing one into the ring.

Of course, the journalist's new political independence posed a threat to the politician's traditional hold on the levers of public opinion. When William of Orange landed in England to lead the "Glorious Revolution" in 1688, he brought with him his own printing press. Thomas Jefferson helped persuade a reliable newspaper editor, Samuel Harrison Smith, to move to the new capital, Washington, shortly before Jefferson assumed the presidency there in 1801, and then rewarded Smith with government printing contracts.[144] However, 60 years later President Abraham Lincoln had to contend with a largely autonomous, often hostile press. The leading Republican newspaper in the country, for instance—Horace Greeley's *New York Tribune*—was frequently critical of this Republican president's performance, particularly his hesitation to free the slaves. ("Well, I do not suppose I have any right to complain," Lincoln once remarked to a *Tribune* correspondent. "Uncle Horace . . . is with us at least four days out of seven.")[145]

Nevertheless, the individuals who presumed to lead societies did not so easily surrender their influence over the news. Those most blatant of press controls—censorship, threats and punishments—were, and still are, widely employed in many parts of the world. At one point during the Civil War, Lincoln moved to deny postal privileges to the leading pro-Southern newspaper in New York, the *Daily News* (a paper unrelated to the tabloid begun in 1919). Nineteenth-century officials also refined and expanded upon their predecessors' less heavy-handed methods for managing and manipulating the news. Lincoln devoted hours to conversations with reporters. He sent letters and emissaries to their editors, he made offerings of exclusive information or patronage, he presented Bennett with the opportunity to become ambassador to France (which the editor declined).[146] And Lincoln was a comparative amateur.

In Germany in the second half of the 19th century, imprisonment was so constant a threat for journalists that some newspapers hired "sitting editors"—specialists in sitting out jail terms. Nevertheless, Count Bismarck, as his willingness to be interviewed by a reporter from New York indicates, also employed a repertoire of more sophisticated techniques for managing public opinion, not only in Germany but throughout the Western world. The German chancellor and his staff wrote paragraphs, editorials and articles that were funneled to newspapers in England and Belgium as well as Germany. (Where necessary, acceptance of these submissions was encouraged by subsidies.) Bismarck himself helped write a letter sent to a paper as if it were from a Frenchman in Paris; similar letters were sent as if from an Italian in Rome. When he perceived Empress Augusta as a threat, Bismarck was not above commissioning an article attacking her loyalty, then leaking to a journalist word that he was "indignant at" that "notorious article."[147]

Specialization would soon overtake the craft of news manipulation too. Future presidents, chancellors and businesses would delegate responsibility for influencing a press they could no longer simply own—and for protecting their institutions against the intrusions of independent and increasingly inquisitive journalists—to experts in "public relations." The Democratic National Committee and President Grover Cleveland himself used a former newsman, George F. Parker, as a "press agent" in the 1880s. (Parker would join Ivy L. Lee in one of the nation's first independent public relations firms in 1905.) In 1889 the Westinghouse Electric Company, with its new system of alternating electrical current under attack as hazardous, employed a former journalist as a full-time press agent. And one week after President Woodrow Wilson led the United States into World War I, he hired a press agent to organize support for the war effort.[148]

These specialists can also be seen as filling a vacuum left by increasingly nonpartisan reporters. "Since in the daily routine reporters cannot give a shape to facts," wrote Walter Lippmann in 1922, "and since there is little disinterested organization of intelligence, the need for some formulation is being met by the interested parties."[149] Through the use of public relations, those interested parties were able to maintain control over

"Yes, Virginia" . . .

Reporting was not the only beneficiary of the increasing separation between fact and opinion in 19th century American newspapers. Editorial writing, viewed now as a specialty in its own right, also flourished.

Perhaps the best known editorial of this period appeared in the *New York Sun* in 1897. Editorial writer Francis P. Church had received a letter from a girl named Virginia: "Dear editors: I am 8 years old. Some of my little friends say there is no Santa Claus. Papa says 'If you see it in THE SUN it's so.' Please tell me the truth; is there a Santa Claus? . . .

Here is a selection from Church's response:

VIRGINIA, your little friends are wrong. They have been affected by the skepticism of a skeptical age. They do not believe except what they see. They think that nothing can be which is not comprehensible by their little minds. All minds, Virginia, whether they be men's or children's, are little. In this great universe of ours man is a mere insect, an ant, in his intellect, as compared with the boundless world about him, as measured by the intelligence capable of grasping the whole of truth and knowledge.

"Yes, VIRGINIA, there is a Santa Claus. He exists as certainly as love and generosity and devotion exist, and you know that they abound and give to your life its best beauty and joy. Alas! how dreary would be the world if there were not Santa Claus. . . ."

many of the opinions that appeared in the news. Yet reporters could still point to their success in placing a distance between themselves and those opinions.

Economic imperatives would strengthen the need to maintain that distance, as so many newspapers fell victim to competition with radio and television in the 20th and 21st centuries. It would no longer make sense to tailor a newspaper for Republicans or Democrats or Progressives. Those newspapers that would survive—often the only papers in their towns—would seek to maintain a broadly based readership, which meant they could not afford to offend large groups of potential customers with overtly partisan coverage. Corporate advertisers—concerned about the effect controversy might have on sales—would also prove more comfortable associating themselves with newspapers that maintained what the journalism critic Ben Bagdikian terms an "appearance of neutrality."[150]

The pages of newspapers throughout the past 120 years have offered numerous examples of partisanship overwhelming facts. The front-page news headlines in William Randolph Hearst's *New York Journal* before the start of the Spanish-American War, for example, would have made the most enthusiastic polemicist proud: Feb. 16,1898—CRUISER MAINE BLOWN UP IN HAVANA HARBOR; Feb. 17—DESTRUCTION OF THE WAR SHIP MAINE THE WORK OF AN ENEMY; Feb. 18—THE WHOLE COUNTRY THRILLS WITH THE WAR FEVER . . . ; Feb. 20—JOURNAL HERE PRESENTS, FORMALLY, PROOF OF A SUBMARINE MINE.[151] But the outrage with which other journalists began to greet the more blatant examples of partiality in news coverage was itself a sign that a new ethic

After playing a major role in building "war fever" through his newspapers, William Randolph Hearst himself went to Cuba to help report on the Spanish-American War. Here he takes a photograph during the war from his yacht.

was in place, if not always honored. On Feb. 19, 1898, an editorial in the New York *Evening Post* had this to say about coverage of the sinking of the *Maine* in Hearst's *Journal* and Pulitzer's *World:* "Nothing so disgraceful as the behavior . . . of these newspapers this week has ever been known in the history of American journalism."[152]

By the end of the 19th century and the early decades of the 20th, journalists were beginning to think of themselves as professionals. Like other upstanding professions, journalism was gaining a place in the universities, and professional organizations of publishers and editors were formed. Journalists had formulated a "service ideal": "the people's right to know" (essentially the right of access to facts). They were perfecting a set of specialized techniques: methods of observation and investigation, the inverted-pyramid writing style (procedures for obtaining and communicating facts). And they had developed a set of professional norms, headed by the need for impartiality (untainted facts).[153] When the American Society of Newspaper Editors drafted the "Canons of Journalism" in 1923, it included the pronouncement: "News reports should be free from opinion or bias of any kind."[154]

Objectivity

In the last years of the 19th century, while covering the police beat for the New York *Evening Post,* Lincoln Steffens created a crime wave.

The explosion of the Maine *in the* New York Journal, *Feb. 17, 1898. The cause of the explosion is still not known, but William Randolph Hearst's* Journal *showed no reluctance in blaming it on the Spanish.*

According to Steffens' autobiography, his crime wave began in the cool basement of New York's police headquarters, where detectives, prisoners and reporters would gather on hot days to "gossip or doze or play cards."[155] Steffens had been among the dozers one day when he heard the conversation turn to the burglary of the house of a well-known Wall Street broker—a burglary that did not happen to be among the daily allotment of crimes the police chose to share with the press. In a display of roguish enterprise uncharacteristic of his fellow police reporters, Steffens stretched, rose, walked back to his office and wrote a story about the burglary.

That afternoon the respectable *Evening Post* found itself with an exclusive—a "beat"—while the police reporters for the other evening papers suffered the embarrassment of having been beaten. Under pressure from their editors, they joined this new competition. An assistant to Jacob Riis, then covering crime for the *Evening Sun,* had discovered the pigeonhole where the list of all the major thefts in the city was kept. By making daily raids on that pigeonhole, Riis was able to score two or three such beats a day. And the other police reporters, by pooling their resources, also succeeded in ferret-

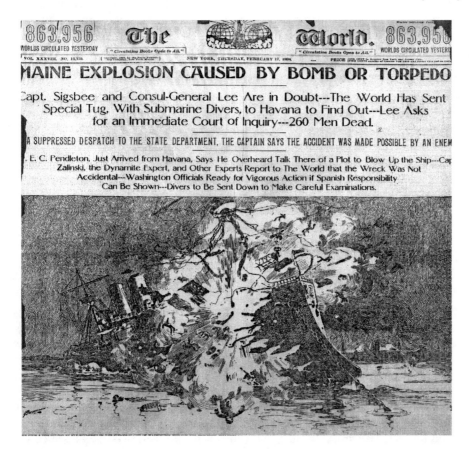

863,956
WORLDS CIRCULATED YESTERDAY

The **World.** **863,956**
WORLDS CIRCULATED YESTERDAY

" Circulation Books Open to All." " Circulation Books Open to All."

VOL. XXXVIII., NO. 13,339.   NEW YORK, THURSDAY, FEBRUARY 17, 1898.   PRICE

MAINE EXPLOSION CAUSED BY BOMB OR TORPEDO

Capt. Sigsbee and Consul-General Lee Are in Doubt---The World Has Sent Special Tug, With Submarine Divers, to Havana to Find Out---Lee Asks for an Immediate Court of Inquiry---260 Men Dead.

A SUPPRESSED DESPATCH TO THE STATE DEPARTMENT, THE CAPTAIN SAYS THE ACCIDENT WAS MADE POSSIBLE BY AN ENEM

. E. C. Pendleton, Just Arrived from Havana, Says He Overheard Talk There of a Plot to Blow Up the Ship---Cap
Zalinski, the Dynamite Expert, and Other Experts Report to The World that the Wreck Was Not
Accidental---Washington Officials Ready for Vigorous Action if Spanish Responsibility.
Can Be Shown---Divers to Be Sent Down to Make Careful Examinations.

The front page of the New York World, *Feb. 17, 1898, reporting on the explosion of the* Maine—*an event Joseph Pulitzer's* World *and William Randolph Hearst's* Journal *used to intensify anti-Spanish feeling and push the country toward war.*

ing out their share of those burglaries the police were not announcing. To keep pace, Steffens was reduced to additional eavesdropping in the basement of police headquarters.

Suddenly the newspapers were filled with news of burglaries supplied by their newly bestirred police reporters. It was "one of the worst crime waves I ever witnessed," Steffens writes in his autobiography. Editorial writers began pointing fingers; sociologists set to work; those with possessions to protect presumably took steps to protect them; and the city's reformers, who had recently gained control of the police department, came under attack. Lost in the rush to purchase additional locks and assign blame was the fact that the rate of crime in the city had not budged.

Objectivity is a term journalists began using in the 20th century to express their commitment not only to impartiality but to reflecting the world as it is, without bias or distortion of any sort. European journalists have been slower to raise the banner of objectivity,[156] but in the United States this commitment is central to the modern reporter's self-image. Nevertheless, Steffens' crime wave demonstrates that it is impossible to fulfill.

Public Relations

Journalists—however clumsily, however imperfectly—pursue truth. Good public relations people also deal in truths, but it is their business to give the truth a "spin"—an interpretation that favors their client. Occasionally they accomplish that by creating truths that might not otherwise have existed: pseudo-events.

Ivy Lee, one of the fathers of public relations, advised the Pennsylvania Railroad early in the 20th century that instead of trying to cover up a train wreck it should assist reporters in their efforts to cover it. That, for journalists, is the good side of public relations.

However, Lee also advised a client, John D. Rockefeller, who was widely disliked for his monopolistic and anti-union practices, to improve his image not by ending those practices but by publicly handing out dimes to school children. Staged events like that have grown increasingly common. Some fear that they may overwhelm public life.

No one who proposes to communicate facts about an event will be able to treat those facts entirely dispassionately and evenhandedly—to treat them as if they were *objects*. A bias of sorts appears the moment the flow of life is broken down into discrete "events," those events are in turn broken down into discrete "facts" and a few of the infinite number of possible facts are singled out as sufficiently compelling to be newsworthy. Additional subjective distinctions inevitably are injected with each new attempt to narrow the focus or impose organization. Journalists, in other words, do not simply "mirror" the world for their audiences.[157] The view with which their audiences are presented will vary depending on where in this large world journalists direct their small allotment of attention.

Steffens decided to cover a burglary, and a crime wave appeared. Once the origin of this apparent burst of burglaries was explained to the president of New York City's police board, Theodore Roosevelt, he decided to put a stop to it. Roosevelt called in Steffens and Riis and convinced them to return to their gossip, dozing and card games before they damaged the reform movement. Riis surrendered to Roosevelt the secret of the pigeonhole; Steffens promised not to mix reporting and napping. The crime wave disappeared. What was the objective reality? The burglaries had been real enough, but public perception of their significance depended almost entirely on how eager the press was to report them.

Journalists' supposed objectivity is further compromised by the narrative frameworks they impose on their stories—their decision, for example, on which combination of formulas a particular crime might be made to fit: woeful victim ("his life savings"), noble victim ("a former Boy Scout"), tearful relatives ("their only child"), twist of fate ("had his car not been in the shop"), awful irony ("scoffed at fear of crime"), despicable criminal ("despite the victim's pleas"), psychologically scarred criminal ("abandoned by his parents"), shocked acquaintances ("seemed such a quiet boy"), the wages of poverty ("unemployed for seven months"), the scourge of drugs ("to support his habit"),

William Allen White, Small-Town Editor

Most of the big news in American journalism was being made in the big cities. But some of the best work was being done in small towns.

William Allen White bought the *Emporia Gazette* for $5,000 in 1895. The next year he wrote a folksy, conservative editorial—"What's the Matter with Kansas?"—which defended development and attacked populism and "shabby, wild-eyed, rattle-brained fanatics." It was reprinted by most of the country's Republican newspapers.

White never took the opportunity to move to a larger paper. His politics, however, did move—toward the left. By 1912, the former conservative was a national committeeman of the Progressive party. In 1922, he challenged Kansas Governor Henry Allen's use of a new compulsory arbitration law to ban the display in store windows of signs that read: "We are for the striking railroad men 100 percent." White put one of the banned signs in his office window, altered it to read "49 percent," and declared that he would boost that number 1 percent every day the railroad strikers remained nonviolent. White also distinguished himself with his battles against the Ku Klux Klan (Mott, *American Journalism*).

or the breakdown of societal values ("the fourth such crime this month"). Most events provide sufficient facts to support a multiplicity of possible formulas; journalists choose among them.

Reporters may initially be in the position of the messenger in Euripides' *The Suppliant Women,* who returns from a battle and exclaims, "I know the many horrors there, but not where to begin."[158] But, like that messenger, reporters do begin, and where they begin and where they end, and how they travel from beginning to end, helps condition their audience's response to the news. "No story is the inevitable product of the event it reports," writes the media critic Robert Karl Manoff; "no event dictates its own narrative form. News occurs at the conjunction of events and texts, and while events create the story, the story also creates the event."[159]

As they tell their stories, journalists are encumbered with belief systems, social positions, workaday routines and professional obligations—all of which affect their selection and presentation of facts. Before the apparent crime wave, Steffens and his fellow police reporters allowed the unwritten rules of society in the basement of police headquarters to limit their reporting on burglaries. During the crime wave, competition and pressure from editors had them scurrying after burglaries. The crime wave ended because Steffens and Riis respected Roosevelt and the reformers. So much for dispassion and evenhandedness.

The Federalist editor William Cobbett called claims of impartiality "perfect nonsense" in 1797.[160] Since then the biases journalists impose on the news have grown subtler and, given the forest of facts in which modern reporters operate, more difficult to discern; but despite reporters' great show of reverence for those facts, these biases have not been eliminated. "To hear people talk about the facts you would think that they lay about like pieces of gold ore in the Yukon days waiting to be picked up," the British journalist Claud Cockburn wrote in 1967; "all stories are written backwards—they are supposed to begin with the facts and develop from there, but in reality they begin with a journalist's point of view, a conception. . . ."[161]

The impossibility of journalistic objectivity has not prevented it from being elevated to the status of commandment: Thou shalt tell the news "straight"! Thou shalt not taint thy news columns with biases of any kind![162] In truth, however, the actions of the more dutiful modern reporters indicate that they have chosen to obey a considerably less rigorous, less philosophically demanding injunction. Journalists have settled upon a working definition of objectivity that allows them to reach the end of their stories each day without the feeling of having sinned. It is this "objectivity for realists" that guides the behavior of practitioners of the journalistic method.[163]

The first rule these reporters follow is to make sure their personal preferences are not readily apparent in their stories. Democrats may strain to give a fair shake to Republicans, conservatives to be fair to liberals. The better journalists may achieve considerable success in suppressing their more visible rooting interests; however, more widely held political beliefs—beliefs that are nearly invisible because they are disguised as accepted wisdom—can never be entirely eradicated.

"The men and women who control the technological giants of the mass media [in the United States] are not neutral, unbiased computers," the *Village Voice* writer Jack Newfield noted in 1970. "They have a mind-set. They have definite life styles and political values, which are concealed under a rhetoric of objectivity. . . . Among these unspoken, but organic, values are belief in welfare capitalism, God, the West, Puritanism, the Law, the family, property, the two-party system, and perhaps most crucially, in the notion that violence is only defensible when employed by the State."[164] Today we might remove the words "welfare" and "Puritanism" from this list. But, in either version, these are, of course, the values of the society in which publishers, editors and reporters operate. The news—unlike the most challenging forms of art, literature or history—speaks with the voice of a society, and in so doing commonly takes for granted the predominant values of that society.

Much has traditionally been made of the difference in class, politics and even ethics between newspaper proprietor and newspaper reporter: "The reporter comes, unless he be a supple knave, and brings his true report," wrote a more radical William Cobbett in 1823. "The vile hunks of the proprietor, then garbles, guts, swells out, cuts short, or otherwise manages the report according to his interest."[165] Reporters as a rule remain more liberal than their publishers; there would be a measurable shift in the editorial positions of major American news organizations were they controlled by their news staffs. Smaller news organizations, run by less business-oriented people, would likely hire and promote some more rebellious spirits. However, as reporters have gained in salary and status and learned to survive in our large corporate news organizations, and as newspaper managements have grown more bureaucratic, the image of the conservative owner censoring and coercing a radical staff has lost much of its validity. Though there have been some notable exceptions,[166] early 21st-century American publishers infrequently resort, or have to resort, to anything as heavy-handed as managing news reports according to their interest. Most of the values and interests that do find their way into news stories today arrive more quietly and are commonly shared by reporter and publisher.

Another step journalists today take to satisfy themselves that they are being objective is to avoid the use of obviously value-laden terms—such as "foolish" or "reactionary." However, the work of these journalists is still filled with loaded, if less obviously offensive, characterizations such as "terrorist" (to be distinguished from "freedom fighter"), "sect" (to be distinguished from "denomination"), or "fanatic" (to be distinguished from "partisan").

Modern journalists also use balance (or "fairness," as the Federal Communications Commission in the United States labeled it) as a measure of their objectivity. They attempt to chain opinions to their opposites, hoping, it seems, that these beasts will annihilate each other, leaving what passes in journalistic thinking for the truth. This technique conveniently frees journalists from responsibility for looking beyond competing arguments to find the truth. Some events and issues, after all, are unbalanced, and the effort to balance them in itself adds a kind of bias. Moreover, there rarely is sufficient room on this seesaw to seat the whole range of arguments issues inspire. As a result, usually no more than two or three widely held—mainstream—points of view per issue are deemed worthy of balanced consideration. The choice of where to place the fulcrum in this balance is necessarily a subjective decision.

In addition, the working definition of objectivity subscribed to by modern journalists demands that they rely on "responsible" sources for their information and attribute any potentially controversial statements to those sources. But in selecting the persons whose views they will publicize, journalists invariably demonstrate a bias—usually toward those invested by society with some credentials or authority. "The economically and politically powerful can obtain easy access to, and are sought out by, journalists," Herbert Gans argues; "those who lack power . . . are generally not sought out until their activities produce social or moral disorder news."[167]

And even if journalists were able to be more scrupulous in ignoring their own beliefs and values in their reporting, they would still be influenced by the pressures and requirements of the news organization for which they work. Some stories are cheaper or easier to report than others—the logistics of satellites, telephone company land-lines, or freeways at deadline time have all entered into news judgments. In his study of television coverage of the Vietnam War, Edward Jay Epstein noted how the amount of blood in television news reports varied depending on how those reports were transmitted to New York. When the film was flown by plane to New York, a number of news executives would have a chance to preview it and, frequently, sanitize it; news films that were transmitted back in a rush by satellite—as they often were during the Tet offensive in 1968—tended to be rawer.[168]

Some stories also are more likely to please management or colleagues than others. Most journalists in the United States are now members of the middle or upper-middle classes;[169] they may be more interested in, for example, the problems of commuter lines to the suburbs than the problems of mass transit in the ghettos. Many of their ideas for features or investigations grow out of conversations on the patio, over white wine, after tennis. Were facts indeed lying about "like pieces of gold ore in the Yukon days," journalists still would be likely to grab those positioned on certain well-trodden paths.

The effort modern reporters make to reach, somewhat clumsily, for the unreachable ideal of objectivity not only involves them in something of a sham but forces them to surrender what can be a powerful weapon in the search for understanding—an above-board point of view. It is difficult to examine the work of those late 19th, 20th and 21st-century journalists who have dedicated themselves to the goal of impartiality without wishing at some point that they would acknowledge their inherent biases, that they would break free of the straitjacket of the inverted pyramid and the rules of attribution, that they would unsheathe their points of view and more vigorously prod and puncture. For along with their ability to shout out opinions, have journalists not sacrificed much of their ability to effect substantial change? "Minds and hearts" were not turned to revolution in America by newspapers that struggled to find a balancing quote from King George III. In learning to fetch and dig, have journalists not lost much of their ability to bite?

The apparent defanging of these journalists would seem to leave them even more vulnerable to the wily and professional news manipulators who occupy the news arena in ever-increasing numbers. As was demonstrated when Senator Joseph McCarthy waved his pseudo-lists of pseudo-Communists in front of the notepads of dutiful reporters in the early 1950s, quotation marks do not protect journalists from complicity in the misrepresentations of their sources. And reporters reduced to the phrasings "he said," "she said" are often in no position to cut through the smoke and the fluff to what *is*.

But this line of argument can be carried too far. A mass retreat back to the staunchly partisan journalism of the days of the lone editor ensconced in a print shop—were it somehow possible—does not seem a particularly appealing alternative. Conservative opponents of a return to a crusading, overtly opinioned journalism would note that not all authorities are King George III or Joseph McCarthy; the more radical proponents of such a move must remember that most present-day journalists are not Samuel Adams or even Joseph Pulitzer. Given the declining number of news organs in recent decades and the nature of their ownership—in the United States predominantly large corporations or gray-suited grandsons of great editors—a marketplace in which modern newspaper and broadcast journalists were freer to peddle their political ideas would not necessarily be any better stocked than our current supermarket of quasi-objective news. And if the editors and publishers of our most powerful news organs did not at least nod in the direction of objectivity, to what standard would victims of their lapses and distortions appeal?

The facts brought to us through the application of the journalistic method are less "objective" than their champions would have us believe. Yet these facts, coddled and cared for by journalists who are attempting at least to restrain their personal prejudices, can lend some clarity to our view of the political world—a clarity that was not available in the unabashedly partisan papers (in which everything from smallpox inoculation to tea was fair game for attack in service of a cause) that helped make the American Revolution.

Perhaps the most effective response to the thinness and arbitrariness of journalistic facts is to buttress them with even more facts. The journalistic presentation that is credited with having done the most to expose Joseph McCarthy was a compilation, on the CBS television program *See It Now* on March 9, 1954, of the senator's own statements, with some brief comments by Edward R. Murrow. This was advocacy journalism. Murrow hazarded a few conclusions; he quoted from Shakespeare ("The fault, dear Brutus,

The Postmodern Journalist

American journalism seemed, in the last third of the 20th century, to be the last redoubt of a hard-headed, just-the-facts realism that had long ago faded in art, literature and much of the academic world.

However, by the turn of the millennium it became rather difficult to ignore the extent to which information of all kinds is "spun"—turned or even twisted to make some sort of point, put to political or business uses, packaged. It became increasingly difficult to conceive of news that did not consist of facts plus "spin." In one sign of the growing awareness of spin, the area outside the halls where American presidential candidates hold their quadrennial debates became known as "spin alley." The vast mound of interpretation upon interpretation that blogs began producing contributed to this increasing sensitivity to the primacy of interpretation.

A change in mind-set seemed underway. Journalists seemed to be moving from realism to a postmodern acceptance of the idea that facts cannot be separated from point of view. The spinning began to be seen as part of the story.

Such postmodern journalists were left with a new task: reporting not only on what happened but on the role and veracity of various competing interpretations of what happened. The trick is to report the spinning with as much enterprise as any other part of the story. But there is another trick: not becoming so obsessed with that spinning that whatever truths might be discerned beyond it are ignored (Stephens, "We're All Postmodern Now.").

is not in our stars, but in ourselves"); but his guns were loaded primarily with facts. (McCarthy on film, interrogating a witness: "You know the Civil Liberties Union has been listed as a front for . . . the Communist Party?" Murrow: "The attorney general's list does not and never has listed the A.C.L.U. as subversive. Nor does the F.B.I. or any other federal agency.")[170] The rules of balance were honored to the extent that McCarthy was allowed to produce his own response, paid for by CBS and broadcast in the *See It Now* time slot four weeks later.[171] Still, this and other *See It Now* documentaries on McCarthyism were able to help turn the tide against Senator McCarthy.

Controlling the News—Still

In the 20th century ideals of free expression—first formulated in classical Greece, developed in the Netherlands, England, France and the United States—seemed to spread around much of the world. But the 20th century also saw some of the most organized, effective and brutal controls on expression.

Newspapers appeared, for example, in dictator Francisco Franco's Spain with white spaces in place of stories removed by government censors. In Communist countries, out-of-favor individuals had their faces deleted from photographs and their biographies subtracted from encyclopedias; those who tested the narrow boundaries of acceptable discourse often found themselves tossed into labor camps or executed. And in the 1930s and 1940s, of course, Nazi leaders practiced the strictest and most brutal forms of censorship.

African journalists, most of whom had shed colonial controls in the second half of the 20th century, often then found themselves stifled by government controls. The government owned or controlled newspapers in all but five countries in sub-Saharan Africa by 1978. Among the results: Ethopia's drought and famine in the 1980s was not reported in that country until at least two years after it began. For his BBC reports on the famine in the Sudan in 1986 journalist Mike Kilongson was rewarded in that country by imprisonment and torture.[172]

Perhaps the most draconian attempt to stop the spread of information in the 20th century came in the last decade of the century, in Afghanistan. Under the Islamic fundamentalist regime of the Taliban, not only were newspapers shut down and only one radio station—the Taliban's own—allowed to broadcast, but citizens were ordered to throw out their television sets. Internet access was also banned, as were photographs of any living people or animals.[173]

As a result, a significant portion of the world's population woke up most mornings in the 20th century unable to trust much of what it read in its newspapers or heard on its newscasts—if it had access to newspapers or newscasts. A significant portion of the world's population woke up, in other words, with the basic human need for awareness unsatisfied.

The situation has improved with the fall, in the second half of the 20th century, of right-wing dictatorships in Spain, Portugal, Greece, Chile, Argentina and elsewhere. It improved rapidly and dramatically with the collapse of the Soviet Union and the end of European Communism. The press is now free in some African countries—South Africa and Ghana among them. And the Taliban were overthrown in most parts of Afghanistan in response to the Sept. 11, 2001, attacks on the United States. In much—but still far from all—of the world, democracy seems now to be in fashion, a free press to be a prerequisite for participation in the global economic system.

Nevertheless, the Western democracies themselves have not always been scrupulous in protecting free expression. The United States, for example, cracked down on those who expressed socialist or Communist ideas during World War I, in the McCarthy era during the 1950s and in various lesser ways at various times since.

As the 21st century began, authoritarian governments still strictly limited the information available to their citizens in China as well as in much of the Middle East and Africa. And there were significant signs of backsliding elsewhere in the world —in Russia, for example.

"Russia's poor press climate is declining at an alarming rate," Ann Cooper, executive director of the Committee to Protect Journalists, wrote in 2005. Economic, legal and extra-legal threats—against journalists and media owners — have repeatedly been used to discourage reporting critical of government officials. Cooper noted that, since 2000, "a dozen journalists have been murdered in Russia in contract-style killings" and that only one of those murder cases has been solved (and that one unpersuasively).[174] There has not been a wholesale return to the Soviet days when criticism of the government was impossible. However, in President Vladimir Putin's Russia, as well as in some other former Soviet states, criticism of the government in the media is often difficult and sometimes dangerous. And in Russia the situation has been getting worse, not better.

The greatest current threat to press freedom in the Western democracies may come from concentration of ownership of news outlets. One of the most frightening examples of that concentration is in a Western democracy in the East: Australia. Early in the 21st century, 70 percent of the copies of newspapers people bought in that country were published by one company: Rupert Murdoch's News Corporation, and Murdoch has never been shy about using his news organs to push his political causes.

In Italy, former Prime Minister Silvio Berlusconi, a political cause himself, owns the company, Mediaset, that has had a near monopoly on private television in the country, while as prime minister he had also been in a position to influence public television. Berlusconi's brother has owned one of Italy's top newspapers, and Berlusconi himself, the country's richest man, controls one of its two current affairs magazines, along with its largest publishing house and its major advertising agency.

It is difficult to imagine critical information on politics flowing freely and easily in such circumstances. With sufficient concentration, it is possible to imagine such circumstances occurring in other democracies. Perhaps our notion of what is required for a free press will have to be revised in the 21st century to fend off such politically potent concentrations of ownership.

The press, Samuel Johnson observed, "affords sufficient information to elate vanity, and stiffen obstinacy, but too little to enlarge the mind. . . ."[175] This failing can be explained both by the resistance human vanity and obstinacy tend to demonstrate when confronted with wisdom and by the limitations of news—unrepresentative, written in haste—as a source of wisdom, but it must also have been exaggerated by the specific limitations of the press with which Dr. Johnson was familiar.

In the 200 years since Johnson's death, the arrival of several vigorous new information technologies and the growth of a system of reporting based on the journalistic method have enabled the news media to offer their audiences not only considerably more information, but considerably more reliable information. This journalism—in whose development England and the United States have often taken the lead—has adapted successfully to many different cultures, although its acceptance has been far from universal. (The fear that accepting Western-style journalism would mean submitting to a sort of cultural imperialism may have contributed to the restrictions so many countries have placed on the pursuit of facts, but a more pressing concern is the perceived need to protect officials, ideologies, or the goal of development from the contention and disruption inevitably generated by free-floating reporters.)[176]

Still, where journalists today can practice the journalistic method in relative freedom, their audiences are the recipients of masses of data on politics, war, crime and the benefits of smallpox inoculation—data that is recorded, even uncovered, by reporters who are on the scene and who often have been instructed, however naively, however imperfectly, not to defer to their biases. The news audience remains adept at resisting information that challenges its preconceptions, and journalists remain preoccupied with the extraordinary and the unexpected. Nonetheless, the chances that the press might succeed in enlarging a mind would seem to have grown.

Questions

1. Can "one feeling and one impulse," as James Gordon Bennett predicted, now be "created and maintained from the center" of this country "to its uttermost extremities"? Did the telegraph accomplish that? What might be its consequences?

2. How is the competition to be "one of the earliest of the early" waged in journalism today?

3. Why does the growth of reporting tend to make journalists into apostles of "reform"?

4. Explore the connection between the development of what this chapter calls "the journalistic method" and the development of public relations.

5. Discuss the pluses and minuses of the inverted-pyramid writing style.

6. Discuss the pluses and minuses of the effort modern reporters make to "reach, somewhat clumsily, for the unreachable ideal of objectivity."

PART SIX

ELECTRONIC NEWS

15

New Technologies—Improved Means to an Unimproved End

In 1854 one of the telegraph's many boosters raved about its ability "to whisper to the four corners of the earth the lordly behests of lordly man!"[2] Henry David Thoreau—whose book *Walden* was published that year—viewed such electronic devices with a colder eye:

> We are in great haste to construct a magnetic telegraph from Maine to Texas; but Maine and Texas, it may be, have nothing important to communicate. . . . We are eager to tunnel under the Atlantic and bring the Old World some weeks nearer to the New; but perchance the first news that will leak through into the broad, flapping American ear will be that Princess Adelaide has the whooping cough.[3]

The argument for the profundity of the various changes society is undergoing—so galling to Thoreau—has had no greater champions than journalists themselves. Journalists peddle reports on change. Consciously or not, they devote themselves to promoting their product—trumpeting the importance of the latest election, the latest crime wave, the latest invention; impressing upon their audiences the notion that yesterday's election, crime and invention gave history a direction and that today society approaches another turn. The belief that society is making triumphant progress or suffering catastrophic decline—or, somehow, both—is a powerful inducement to read newspapers and heed newscasts.

"No other public teacher lives so wholly in the present as the Editor," bragged Horace Greeley.[4] No other is as enchanted by the present, either. Indeed, the currently common view of the present as uniquely exciting and frightening may owe as much to the spell woven by journalists as it does to the reality of technological development. And journalists see change nowhere as evident as in journalism itself.

"This sheet presents such a specimen of journalism," exclaimed an issue of James Gordon Bennett's *Herald* in the early days of the telegraph, "as has never

Our inventions are wont to be pretty toys, which distract our attention from serious things. They are but improved means to an unimproved end.

—Henry David Thoreau, *Walden*[1]

New Technologies, Their Fans and Foes

The debate over the telegraph echoed earlier debates over other new inventions Enthusiasts gushed over each of them; critics moaned. Writing, it was recognized, provided a great intellectual tool, but Socrates, according to Plato, complained that the ability to write things down would weaken our memories.

And such debates flared anew with the introduction of the telephone, radio, television, cable television and calculators. The arguments are particularly heated now on the subject of computers. Enthusiasts such as Nicholas Negroponte of MIT's Media Lab have seen digital communication leading to a world "free of old prejudices" and "released from the limitation of geographic proximity." Others—in the Thoreau role—fear that it will lead to laziness and physical isolation.

Who is correct? Neither side, of course, to the extent that they predict utopia or apocalypse. Human nature—both pleasant and unpleasant, both perky and perverse—has yet to find a technology that can hold it down. Yet these new technologies all do have lesser effects—positive and negative. Writing *has* to some extent weakened our memories.

before been equalled, from the creation of the world up to this morning, in the history of mankind. It . . . is enough to . . . bring us actually to believe that either the end of the world or the beginning of the millennium is at hand."[5] Journalists from many different periods, if not quite as excitable as Bennett, have shared this belief that the contours of their field were shifting even as they worked it. And journalism has indeed changed. Newspaper journalists were subject to a revolution of sorts in technique with the arrival of the journalistic method; and few endeavors have benefited as directly as the exchange of news from such new technologies as the telegraph, radio, television, satellites and computers. In Thoreau's day, Maine and Texas, the Old World and the New, found they had pages and pages of news to exchange with each other over telegraph wires.

Still, Thoreau had a point. Bennett, far from alone in his enthusiasm, prophesied that with the arrival of the telegraph "mere newspapers—the circulators of intelligence merely—must submit to destiny, and go out of existence . . . [while] the intellectual, philosophic, and original journalist will have a greater, a more excited, and more thoughtful audience than ever."[6] But such a miracle, as Thoreau suggested, seems beyond the power of electrons. The telegraph and the Atlantic cable do not appear to have aided the "the intellectual" journalist at the expense of "mere newspapers."

Thoreau did not live long enough to see electrons trained to carry the human voice, to see radio waves transformed into flying messengers, to see images themselves transported from news event to living room. Yet do his hesitations not also apply to these even prettier toys? The capabilities of each of these new news media—their speed, their breadth—amazed those who witnessed their births, but the categories of information with which they each would occupy themselves might not have surprised a resident of the island of Tikopia. News would grow substantially more plentiful, timely and reliable, but would the nature of news be significantly "improved" (or corrupted, for that

Photography

Our 21st-century media world was not built by electronic technologies alone. Indeed, when the only messages that could be sent electronically still had to be transformed into the dots and dashes of Morse code, optical and chemical processes were already allowing whole images to be preserved and displayed.

In 1829, Louis Jacques Mande Daguerre, a French painter, succeeded in capturing images on metal plates by using light-sensitive salts. "Daguerreotypes," those early photographs were called.

Photography developed to the point where, during the Civil War, photos taken on the battle-field, showing some of the blood and death glossed over by romantic illustrators, were displayed in galleries. By the 1880s, the first photographs began appearing in newspapers.

Then in 1877, Edward Muybridge and John D. Isaacs used a series of successive photographs to analyze the footwork of a galloping horse, and the age of moving images began—not electronically, but on film.

matter) by the telegraph, radio or television? The public's "broad, flapping . . . ear" would still listen for a similar mix of information on wars, accidents, crimes and the lives of princesses—from Adelaide to Diana.

Thoreau, it should be noted, took a rather extreme position on journalism, viewing a preoccupation with news with the same scorn he directed at most of the preoccupations of his contemporaries: "I am sure I never read any memorable news in a newspaper," he announced in *Walden:*

> If we read of one man robbed, or murdered, or killed by accident, or one house burned, or one vessel wrecked, or one steamboat blown up, or one cow run over on the Western Railroad, or one mad dog killed, . . . we never need read of another. . . . To a philosopher all *news,* as it is called, is gossip, and they who edit and read it are old women over their tea.[7]

Thoreau omits mention of news of politics, economics, art or science from this list. He did not have an opportunity to see the news fortified with investigations of governmental corruption. Nevertheless, if the charge is that news can seem repetitious, ephemeral and frivolous, again he has a point. And although a mastery of electromagnetic waves would enable news to be moved anywhere instantly, although it would make possible further increases in the quantity and credibility of the data available to the news audience, it would not prove capable of making news significantly more "memorable" to a philosopher with Thoreau's standards.

This is not to say that the nature of news has been entirely unaffected by its voyage through the atmosphere. Vacuum tubes, transistors and silicon chips have not remade human interests, but they have amplified some and resisted others. The peccadilloes of electronic news organs, like those of their predecessors, have been reflected in the information their audiences have obtained. And this information, however repetitious, ephemeral and frivolous it occasionally appears, continues to affect the political and social behavior of those of us it preoccupies—all of us old men and women gossiping over our tea.

Radio—An Electronic Meeting Place

Radio was the product of a series of breakthroughs: the discovery of electromagnetic waves in "the ether" by James Clerk Maxwell of Scotland and Heinrich Hertz of Germany in the second half of the 19th century; the innovation of methods for freighting those waves with coded messages—"wireless telegraphy"—by Guglielmo Marconi of Italy at the end of the century; the development of techniques for transforming human speech into and out of such codes—"wireless telephony"—by Lee De Forest and Reginald Fessenden of the United States early in the 20th century. These inventions had a number of intended results: Ships could communicate with the shore, war planes and soldiers with their bases, amateur radio operators with each other. But the most significant use to which radio would be put was apparently unforeseen by its inventors.

In 1920 the Westinghouse executive Harry P. Davis experienced an epiphany. The attention attracted by an amateur radio transmission, broadcast from a garage, "caused the thought to come to me," Davis later wrote, "that the efforts that were then being made to develop radio telephony as a confidential means of communication were wrong, and that instead its field was really one of wide publicity. . . ."[8] Davis realized, in other words, that radio could gather a crowd.

On Nov. 2, 1920, at Davis's urging, Westinghouse launched the first commercial radio station—KDKA in Pittsburgh. Westinghouse hoped to make its profit by selling the radios needed to listen to such stations. By the end of 1922, 576 radio stations were in operation in the United States;[9] about 100,000 radios were purchased that year. And the American Telephone and Telegraph Company was already introducing an alternative method for financing broadcasting in 1922: charging a "toll" for access to the mass of listeners radio could attract. The United States system of advertiser-supported radio and television networks would evolve from AT&T's fledgling network of "toll" stations. (AT&T's broadcast operation was purchased in 1926 by the newly formed National Broadcasting Company.) By 1925, $5\frac{1}{2}$ million radio sets were in use in the United States—nearly half the number in use in the world.[10]

Whether gathered in a sun shelter, a marketplace or within earshot of one of hundreds of thousands of radio receivers, crowds hunger for news. KDKA had first gone on the air with the results of the Harding-Cox presidential election (news not only gathered but, for the first time, distributed at something approaching the speed of light). In 1923 the first French radio station, Radiola, arranged for the Havas news agency to furnish dispatches for its *"bulletins d'information."*[11] Radio was far from exclusively a news medium (nor is print or the newspaper itself, for that matter), but news gained, and would maintain, a position second only to music as a staple of radio programming.

Following the apprenticeship system all new news media follow, radio journalism established itself by borrowing the product and imitating the techniques of newspaper journalism. In France, Radiola's newscasts were initially conceived as a *"gazette parlée."*[12] Early broadcast journalists appropriated much of their copy, often with permis-

The first commercial radio broadcast: the Harding-Cox presidential election returns on KDKA in Pittsburgh, Nov. 2, 1920.

sion, from newspaper journalists. Westinghouse's KDKA had obtained results of the Harding-Cox election by telephone from the wire service room of the Pittsburgh *Post.* Results of the Coolidge-Davis-LaFollette presidential election in 1924, broadcast on AT&T's network to an audience of perhaps 20 million, were supplied by United Press.[13]

Radio journalists frequently were drawn from newspaper staffs: One of the first to develop a following, H. V. Kaltenborn, maintained his regular job as an editor of the *Brooklyn Eagle* until 1930. When William Paley decided that the presentation of news was one of the few areas in which his fledgling Columbia Broadcasting System could surpass NBC, he put together a staff composed primarily of newspaper journalists under the leadership of Ed Klauber, former night city editor of the *New York Times,* and Paul White, a former United Press editor.[14]

Radio journalists adopted, by and large, the dispassionate voice of the newspapers at which they had trained. But speaking to an audience of news hearers, rather than news readers, required modification of the vocabulary and sentence structure newspapers had employed. When radio arrived, newspaper writers (along with novelists such as Ernest Hemingway) were already beginning to grow impatient with the dense wordings and long-winded constructions of formal written language—a style perhaps better appreciated in contemplative quiet than in the din of the 20th century. Radio newswriters had an even more compelling reason for abandoning those elevated and circumlocutory sentences: Newscasters lacked the wind to deliver them, and their listeners, denied the ability to reread, lacked the concentration to comprehend them.

The modern newswriting style—short sentences, simple, clear, concise wordings—was honed on the radio. Here is a selection from one of the reports of Edward R. Mur-

First Lady Eleanor Roosevelt attempted to encourage the careers of women reporters by refusing to allow men to cover her press conferences. This picture was taken in 1933.

row (that rare American radio journalist who had never reported for a newspaper) on the German bombing of London:

> Suddenly all the lights dashed off and a blackness fell right to the ground. It grew cold. We covered ourselves with hay. The shrapnel clicked as it hit the concrete road nearby. And still the German bombers came.[15]

In the United States, radio news began to prove that it had arrived as a significant journalistic force when the Japanese attacked Pearl Harbor on Dec. 7, 1941—a Sunday. There were no evening papers on Sunday. From the first bulletin—interrupting a football game on the small Mutual radio network, right after the wires flashed the news at 2:22 p.m. EST[16]—until Monday morning, the news was a radio exclusive.

World War II gave radio news what the Civil War had given newspapers: a taste of the medium's power to bring news home. Murrow had communicated the feel of the Battle of Britain to Americans—at one point aiming his microphone at the sidewalk to pick up the sound of feet walking calmly to the bomb shelters.[17] Other radio journalists were taking their microphones onto battlefields or into landing craft.

Most radio news was still being reported live. (Murrow from London: "I think probably in a minute we shall have the sound of the guns in the immediate vicinity. . . . You'll hear two explosions. There they are!") Americans did not discover what would become the mainstay of radio journalism—the tape recorder—until the Allies entered

Reporting World War II

All of America's major wars—not just Vietnam—have inspired opposition. Perhaps a third of the population of the colonies was Tory before the Revolution. Every Federalist member of Congress voted against the War of 1812. Abraham Lincoln was one of many Whig members of Congress who believed the Mexican War to be "unnecesary and unconsitutional." "Copperheads"—Southern supporters in the North during the Civil War—staged some of the largest riots in U.S. history. In 1898, the declaration of war against Spain passed the Senate by only seven votes. Opponents of the decision to involve the United States in World War I filled Madison Square Garden. By January of 1951, according to one poll, 49 percent of Americans believed that sending troops to Korea had been a mistake. Only 44 percent of Americans, a *New York Times* poll reported, said "the United States made the right decision in taking military action against Iraq" in Sept. 2005, a year and a half after that war began. In all cases opposition to these wars was aired in, if not led by, sections of the press.

Some Americans opposed entry into World War II also, but very few. Perhaps because the United States had clearly been attacked first at Pearl Harbor, or perhaps because the cause—opposing Nazism and Japanese expansionism—seemed so just, this was the least controversial war in American history.

The great journalistic tales of World War II, therefore, do not feature obstinacy or investigation but foresight (as in Dorothy Thompson's early warnings of Hitler's malevolence), human drama (as in Edward R. Murrow's reports on the bombing of London), or an ability to capture the little torments and large tragedies of the sol-

diers. It was in the latter that Scripps-Howard correspondent Ernie Pyle, known as "the friend of the G.I.," excelled.

Pyle's "The Death of Captain Waskow" is a classic example of the power of those two staples of journalism —-simple language and quiet observation:

. . . One soldier came and looked down, and he said out loud, "God damn it." That's all he said, and then he walked away. Another one came. He said, "God damn it to hell anyway." He looked down for a few last moments, and then he turned and left.

Another man came; I think he was an officer. It was hard to tell officers from men in the half light, for all were bearded and grimy dirty. The man looked down into the dead captain's face, and then he spoke directly to him, as though he were alive. He said: "I'm sorry, old man."

. . . Then, the first man squatted down, and he reached down and took the dead hand, and he sat there for a full five minutes, holding the dead hand in his own and looking intently into the dead face, and he never uttered a sound all the time he sat there.

And finally he put the hand down, and then reached up and gently straightened the points of the captain's shirt collar, and then he sort of rearranged the tattered edges of his uniform around the wound. And then he got up and walked away down the road in the moonlight, all alone. . . .

In 1944, Pyle won the Pulitzer Prize for his war reporting in Europe. He was killed while covering the war in the Pacific in 1945.

Edward R. Murrow of CBS in London during World War II.

Berlin and learned that the Germans had developed a device that could preserve electronic codes for voices on a coated paper tape. Before then sound could be recorded only on primitive wire recorders (the wire was coated with a magnetic substance) or on records. (An announcer for WLS in Chicago had been recording in the field for his station's record library when the *Hindenburg* dirigible exploded in flames in 1937; his emotional narration, played on NBC hours later, was the first recorded material broadcast on a radio network.)[18]

In the United States, millions attended radio news reports, as they did such entertainment programs as *Amos 'n' Andy*. This was a national audience. America's citizenry could now be gathered around their radios, and America's chief executive regained a privilege most tribal chiefs had taken for granted: His voice could reach a significant portion of those he governed. War news, the country's news, his news, could be spread among them almost instantaneously. Another significant step had been taken toward unifying this widely scattered nation. Citizens crowded around President Franklin Roosevelt's fireside to hear him talk, as they crowded around Murrow—their messenger from the battlefield.

The presence of national networks—radio stations across the country all fed the same program over telephone company long-lines—undoubtedly played a role in the growth of federal political power in the 1930s and 1940s. The president's fireside had become more accessible than the mayor's.

All methods for moving information over distances more effectively—from the use of writing and the printing press to the telegraph and the railroad—have contributed to the expansion of human societies, to the extension of bonds of identity and interests. Radio accelerated that process and its corollary: the weakening of smaller communities.

Not only did allegiance to neighborhood or town begin to slacken as attention turned from ward leader or mayor to the president, but the likelihood that individuals would remain residents of their neighborhoods or towns lessened as trains and automobiles made it possible to move across the country more easily and as radio (and movies) made it possible to do so without losing contact with accustomed leaders, accustomed subjects of gossip, accustomed newsmongers. Radio listeners were residents of an ethereal community, populated by familiar, if unreachable, presences whose voices were accessible anywhere in the nation.

In the 1950s, radio's stars, including many of its star newscasters, left for television, and radio surrendered its position as the nation's central gathering place. However, although the activation of a great national community had been invaluable for national leaders, its value for those who had been funding commercial radio in the United States was not as obvious as it initially had appeared. Advertisers, particularly local advertisers searching for more efficient uses of their monies, began to develop a taste for media that might gather more defined and homogeneous crowds—teenagers, eager for acne remedies; African-Americans, looking for stores near their neighborhoods and store owners without prejudice; farmers, shopping for fertilizer and tractors. Radio managed to survive and thrive in the television era through its ability to target specific demographic groups for advertisers, through "*narrow*casting."[19]

Non-network stations began broadcasting rock and roll records for teenagers, rhythm and blues for African-Americans, country music for farmers. Those audiences were soon further segmented: the realm of rock and roll, for example, divided into hard rock, soft rock, oldies, and Top Forty. And, gradually, broadcasters began to offer the specialized groups gathering around these stations news suited to their special interests: news-casts on rock stations discussed concerts, rock stars, demonstrations; African-American stations emphasized civil rights issues; farm stations discussed soybean prices, foreign wheat purchases and, as thoroughly as possible, the weather.[20]

Radio and radio news were now binding new communities within cities and towns—communities bound by age, ethnicity or profession, not neighborhood. (Another news medium—the magazine—has also specialized of late in providing advertisers with such segmented audiences.) The result is that American teenagers, for example, may now be more likely to share an interest in personalities, issues and events with their fellows on the other side of town, or even on the other side of the country, than they are with a middle-aged neighbor. In the electronic age, community increasingly is based on commonality of wave length, not locale.

Television—The Distant Newsmonger

Radio gave newsmongers back their voices; television restored their faces. Indeed, the television newscast seems to resemble that most ancient of methods for communicating news: A person telling other people what has happened. But this resemblance, as with much of what we see when we first examine this most powerful of news media, can be misleading.

Newsreels

Those who contend that forms of communication today, ranging from videotape recorders to newspapers, will survive growing competition from new interactive, multichannel, digital technologies like to point to other unexpected survivors: radio and film, for example, neither of which succumbed, as many predicted, to television.

Unfortunately, however, there are counter-examples: not just the criers, newsletters, news ballads, and newsbooks discussed in the early sections of this book—all of which are now mostly extinct—but more recent inventions such as telegrams and, perhaps most conspicuously, newsreels.

Newsreels began in the days of nickelodeons as short, nonfiction features. At first their producers were content merely to show a baby being fed or Annie Oakley posing in a studio, but soon they began to record significant news events: the coronation of a Russian czar, an America's Cup Race. Some events were faked: The San Francisco earthquake and fire was filmed on a miniature created in New York, and a boxing match was filmed in Thomas Edison's studio.

Movie theaters began to appear in the United States in the early years of the 20th century, and newsreels—each one reel of film long—began to play as shorts before main features. They would open with major news events and then conclude with news of fashion or sports. An announcer's deep voice would squeeze all the drama out of the events being shown.

Newsreels had one feature no other news medium of the time could match: moving images. But they also had one distinct, usually fatal disadvantage as a news medium: They were slow. It look time to shoot the stories, develop and edit the film, and then get the reels to theaters.

The earliest television newscasts in the United States contracted with newsreel companies for their visuals. But television news, which could distribute moving images much faster, quickly finished the newsreel.

A method for transforming moving pictures into and out of electronic signals, using a rotating disk with spiral perforations, had been devised as early as 1884 by Paul Nipkow of Germany. By the 1920s experimenters in Britain and the United States had succeeded in sending such signals through the air to receivers, and the rotating disk was soon replaced by an electronic scanning system. The technology of television was perfected by radio networks. And by 1941 CBS was broadcasting to a tiny audience two 15-minute newscasts daily on its New York television station.[21]

The problem facing the producers of early television news broadcasts, most of whom were veterans of radio, was how to fill the screen. Those first newscasts on CBS were "chalk talks," with a newsman named Richard Hubbell standing, pointer in hand, in front of a map of Europe. Picture quality was so poor that it was difficult to make out Hubbell, let alone the map. When Pearl Harbor was attacked, CBS did not ignore its handful of television viewers, but for visuals they had to make do with a shot of an undulating American flag, blown by a fan in the studio.[22]

One of the first television newscasters, John Cameron Swayze, preparing to take viewers "hopscotching the globe" on NBC's Camel News Caravan *in 1953.*

World War II placed television's development on hold, but by 1949 Americans who lived within range of a couple of the approximately 100 television stations that now dotted the country could *watch* the *Kraft Television Theater* or *Howdy Doody,* and choose between two 15-minute newscasts—*CBS TV News,* with Douglas Edwards, and NBC's *Camel News Caravan,* with John Cameron Swayze. The visuals on these newscasts consisted mostly of what would become known as "talking heads": shots of the somber Edwards or the boutonniered Swayze reading to the camera. Don Hewitt, the director of the CBS newscast, was constantly searching for a way to increase the newscaster's eye contact with the camera, but Edwards drew the line at Hewitt's suggestion that he learn to read his script in Braille.[23]

What film there was of news events was supplied by newsreel companies. Television journalism was seen initially as an amalgam of radio news and movie newsreels. Coverage of events was severely limited by the scarcity of film crews, by the bulkiness of their 16mm or 35mm cameras, by the time-consuming process of developing the film and transporting it to New York, and by the limitations of the genre—the newsreel emphasized on-scene photography, not on-scene reporting. Filmed reports might not be aired for days after they were shot, therefore, film tended to be reserved for planned events and timeless features. Nonetheless, viewers were captivated simply by the op-

The Italian liner Andrea Doria *sinks off the coast of Nantucket in 1956—an event covered by Don Hewitt and Douglas Edwards of CBS Television.*

portunity to witness, from their living rooms, a ribbon cutting, a submarine christening, the dedication of a dam, a beauty contest or, on the first installment of Edward R. Murrow and Fred Friendly's hallowed *See It Now* in 1951, live shots of the Brooklyn Bridge and the Golden Gate Bridge side by side.[24]

Even with this primitive equipment, television journalists obviously possessed a power to re-create the sights and sounds of events that went well beyond anything even the most verbally skilled of their predecessors might have achieved, and it was not long before they were more fully exploiting that power. In 1949 a former radio journalist and former movie cameraman set out to cover a balloon race for France's first television news program. They were reporting on the race from the vantage point of their own balloon when storm winds swept it onto a high-tension wire. The two newsmen escaped with camera rolling, and film of their balloon exploding and burning provided the first great example of the potential of this new news medium in France. *"Le journal télévisé"* originally was broadcast three times a week; by the end of the year, it was aired twice a day.[25]

In the United States CBS and NBC began producing their own film reports in the 1950s. Camera crews were stationed in the largest cities, and their film flown to New York by plane.[26] Correspondents in Washington and a few other cities might also appear live via a cable hookup. The quadrennial political conventions were covered; the earliest stirrings of the space program were covered, as were the initial struggles of the civil rights movement.[27] Occasionally, the "anchorman" (a term apparently first used to describe Walter Cronkite's central role in CBS's convention coverage in 1952) himself ventured out of the studio on a story. In 1956 Hewitt's aggressiveness, Edwards' fame, and some fortuitous timing secured a place for Edwards and a film crew in a Navy plane circling the Italian liner *Andrea Doria* as it sank off the coast of Nantucket. The film,

Morley Safer of CBS in Vietnam in 1965.

combined with Edwards eyewitness narration, which led off CBS's newscast that evening, provided further evidence of the potential power of this medium.[28]

That power was realized in the 1960s. John Kennedy defeated Richard Nixon on television; Lee Harvey Oswald was shot on television; presidents dissembled and protesters protested in front of the cameras, indeed with their eyes fixed upon the cameras. In August 1965 a CBS reporter, Morley Safer, accompanied a group of United States Marines in Vietnam on a "search and destroy" mission to a complex of hamlets called Cam Ne. The Marines, who faced no resistance, held cigarette lighters to the thatched roofs and proceeded to "waste" Cam Ne. And this, too, appeared on television.[29]

Television news was no tool of radicals. Safer's report, the exception rather than the rule in television coverage of Vietnam, caused considerable consternation among the management at CBS; the network made an effort in the following days to air more positive stories about the war.[30] Television journalists in the United States were subject not only to the moderating influence of their own allegiance to a working definition of the ethic of objectivity, but to the moderating influence of their corporate owners, their government regulators (the Federal Communications Commission), and their corporate sponsors. (The film cameras that fed the *Camel News Caravan* had dared not happen upon any NO SMOKING signs.[31])

In England, the nonprofit British Broadcasting Corporation—controlled by a board of governors appointed by the government and financed by an annual license fee on radio and television sets—maintained a similarly moderate tone. In France, where television for many decades was entirely under government control, television journalists placed a stricter interpretation upon their obligations to their superiors and became more open partisans of government policies. French President Charles De Gaulle once explained that "my enemies have the press, so I keep television."[32]

Nevertheless, television news, where it was free from direct censorship, was too sensitive an instrument to ignore the tremors radiating through the United States and Western Europe in the 1960s and early 1970s. And the workings of television news were not yet transparent enough to public relations experts employed by the established institutions that its reports might have been prevented from amplifying some of those tremors. Perhaps on television in these years the "human spirit," to use Harold Innis terms, was breaking through before a new "monopoly of knowledge" had a chance to consolidate itself. Society, in the United States at least, has not since appeared on the television screen in such a state of disarray.

The morning after CBS aired Morley Safer's filmed report on Cam Ne, the network's president, Frank Stanton, was awakened by a telephone call. "Frank, are you trying to fuck me?" a voice said. "Frank, this is your president, and yesterday your boys shat on the American flag." This brief, unsolicited piece of journalism criticism, contributed by the president of the United States, Lyndon Johnson, is an indication of the political pressure under which television news operates. That Stanton, a good friend of the president, is reported to have "had it in for Safer" for a time after the call is an indication that journalistic principles may occasionally have sagged under the pressure.[33] Johnson's deep concern with one piece of news film on one network newscast also helps demonstrate another point: the extent to which television news had come to fascinate, if not obsess, the nation. President Johnson stationed three television sets in his office, so he could monitor coverage on all three networks. Many an evening, after Walter Cronkite would finish anchoring the *CBS Evening News,* Cronkite would find his secretary waiting to hand him the telephone: "White House on the line."[34]

And now, though it has been around for decades, television news continues to fascinate leaders and citizenry alike; it continues—like those French newsmen in a balloon—to make news as it covers news. Our interest in this "pretty toy" has, if anything, increased as it has brought us images of inner-city riots and of men hopping on the moon. We've seen images, in color and via increasingly portable videotape equipment, from the scene of famines and earthquakes and murders; images, via satellite, from Iran; images, live and then replayed endlessly on videotape, of space shuttles disintegrating, of Los Angeles police beatings, of Persian Gulf War bombings; images, via embedded journalists, of American tanks racing to Baghdad and then of insurgents' "explosive devices" maiming those tanks. We remain fascinated, too, by the irreverence with which television seems to treat the news—by its mix of bantering sportscasters, cavorting weathercasters, overexposed celebrities, shootings, stabbings, crashes and sobbing mothers invited to explain to a microphone how it feels to have lost all.

The perfect expression of this fascination may have been a scene during the intensely covered New Hampshire presidential primary in 1984 when television news cameras reported on the phenomenon of television news cameras reporting on the presence of so many television news cameras. And enthralled as we are with this seemingly omnipotent product of our seemingly omnipotent technology, we tend to overstate some of its accomplishments— pretty and ugly.

To begin with, despite the presence of satellites and 24-hour cable news services, the television audience is hardly unique in its interest in news in general, or in events over the oceans in particular. Nor is this audience, to recap another point made earlier in this book, uniquely well informed about all aspects of the world. A television camera is trained on the president of the United States every moment that he spends in public, but in the larger television "markets," at least, such cameras are rarely in a position to supply news of neighborhood occurrences to the residents of what is left of such neighborhoods.

Some of the criticism television journalism inspires is equally shortsighted. Journalists did not become encumbered by celebrity for the first time when Barbara Walters was offered $1 million to work for ABC television news; Horace Greeley was well enough known to obtain the Democratic nomination for president, and James Gordon Bennett, Henry Morton Stanley, Nellie Bly, Joseph Pulitzer and William Randolph Hearst are all examples of journalists who achieved considerable renown without appearing on television. Nor did news and entertainment meet and mate for the first time on often giggly, often frivolous, local television newscasts in the United States; their affair dates back at least as far as criers and minstrels. Television news, in other words, did not inject a foreign substance—playfulness—into the news; news has been enjoyed for as long as it has been exchanged.

Like the penny papers of the 1830s, the yellow journals of the 1880s and 1890s, and the tabloids of the 1920s, television has succeeded in attracting a new audience to the news. Once television sets became affordable, news became available to audiences of many millions, including even those lacking the energy, skill or maturity to read a newspaper or concentrate on a radio narrative. Television newscasts are, if anything, easier to watch than news events themselves, in the sense that it is easier to turn the set on than to walk outside and into the street.

From this perspective, it is remarkable that television journalists took so long to adopt sensationalistic techniques to cater to this largest of mass audiences. For many decades, local and particularly network television newscasts were relatively decorous affairs. Their blood, sex and depravity content was surprisingly low compared, say, to Joseph Pulitzer's *New York World* in 1883,[35] compared even to television entertainment programs.

Competition for larger circulations traditionally has spawned increases in sensationalism. But such competition was often absent on television. Large audiences enabled the handful of local stations in each market and the few networks to divide large profits. Genteel news directors were able to steer their productions onto the high road. They took their directions more from their prissy triumvirate of governors —corporate owners, corporate sponsors, and government regulators—than from popular preferences.

Yes, crime was reported, sometimes with great industriousness, but those stories tended to be told in the friendly but earnest equitone that had, give or take the occasional quip, become the voice of the medium worldwide. The overheated prose—teeming with adjectives, admonitions and sobriquets—of the tabloid journalist was rarely heard on television.

The first edition of this book suggested that this might change, and to some extent it has. Cable then satellite television arrived, bringing dozens then hundreds of new

News and Hollywood

The long and complicated relationship between news and entertainment took an interesting turn with the growing power of the Hollywood film studios in the 1920s and 1930s. (The first film was produced in Hollywood in 1911.)

Journalists had long had famous artists and entertainers to fawn over. When the novelist—and journalist—Charles Dickens visited the United States in 1842 his travels were well covered by American journalists. (Dickens was not thrilled by the experience, grumbling that the "Press has its evil eye in every house. . . .") Eight years later, Jenny Lind, a soprano known as "the Swedish Nightingale," created a similar fuss in the press when she toured the United States under the management of that master fussmaker P. T. Barnum.

But Hollywood presented the American press with a whole, homegrown industry devoted to the creation of celebrity. Louella Parsons, whose column was "syndicated" (sold to newspapers across the country) by Hearst, was among the first to exploit it. Parsons became a power in Hollywood and journalism in the 1920s with her movie-industry gossip. In 1938 Parsons got serious competition from Hedda "the Hat" Hopper of the *Los Angeles Times,* who became know for the "juicy" scoop. The two matched each other gossip item for gossip item until Hopper's death in 1972, their columns at times reaching—via syndication—a combined circulation of 75 million.

Hollywood was also being covered in these years by an increasingly aggressive group of newspaper photographers. George Watson was the first full-time photographer hired by the *Los Angeles Times.* Some of his famous shots: 18 "starlets" high-kicking on an airplane's wing and silent-movie king Charlie Chaplin arm in arm with the physicist Albert Einstein.

Hollywood and journalism have also crossed paths in another significant way. News organizations increasingly have found themselves tied to entertainment organizations. This trend began, perhaps, when newspaper publisher William Randolph Hearst made himself a power in the early decades of Hollywood and even set up his own film studio, Cosmopolitan Pictures (mostly to make a star of his mistress, Marion Davies).

The trend continued when many newspapers—the *Chicago Tribune* and *Washington Post* among them—became owners of radio and television stations. The television networks themselves were part of the trend: CBS produces, for example, both 60 *Minutes* and *The Late Show with David Letterman.* And that trend seems to have intensified recently with the development of large multimedia corporations such as Time Warner, which owns a film studio, cable television systems and many top magazines. Disney owns a movie studio, theme parks, the ABC television network and, therefore, *ABC News.*

News is and always has been entertainment. But it also has been something more: a source of sometimes critically important information. Some fear that new, Hollywood-oriented proprietors will forget that.

channels and, consequently, a more aggressive form of competition. Local television newscasts in many cities in the United States—trying to compete with movies and music videos and other channels of news—now often confine national and international politics to short "briefs," as they luxuriate in crime and celebrity gossip. Talk shows dwell on misfits and misfortunes. "Reality shows" often home in on the embarrassing, the cut-

John Walsh—host of the television program America's Most Wanted, *in which viewers are asked to help locate crime suspects—is interviewed on NBC's Sunday morning news show* Meet the Press.

throat or the titillating. And leering "magazine" programs have now earned themselves the label "tabloid television." Even all-news networks seem eager to lose themselves in racy crimes.

The use of the term "tabloid" could be useful in reminding critics that these forms of sensationalism are not new and, therefore, are not likely to lead to the end of journalism as we know it or the fall of the republic. But the use of this term can also be misleading. The analogy between these programs and tabloid newspapers is far from perfect.

There is a sense in which sensationalism on television is more intense than it is in print. Seeing the blood, watching a mother sob is in some ways more disturbing than reading about it. But the fact is that television cameras, even as they become much smaller and much more widely available, are still not sufficiently swift and dexterous to capture most of life's rawest moments. It is only the rare stabbing or beating that is available on videotape. Tabloid and crime reality shows will attempt to re-create some crimes or accidents. But more earnest television newscasts are reduced to showing mostly scenes of crimes, not crimes. Newspaper writers, on the other hand, can always recall what they did not witness. No act of violence is beyond the reach of the still formidable magic of words.

With the exception of a city such as New York, which still has three English-language dailies, competition is almost gone in the U.S. newspaper business. Sensationalism has, therefore, quieted. Television appears even wilder by comparison. Still, it is foolish to argue that this relatively new medium has achieved new levels of sensationalism. Those levels, after all, reached some daunting heights in the past.

The charge that television news treats events with particular superficiality is more difficult to refute. Television newswriters have room for fewer words than their newspaper counterparts. Their stories are measured in seconds, not column inches. Moving pictures (particularly now-omnipresent moving graphics) certainly contribute informa-

Journalism Criticism

Journalism criticism goes back at least as far as Cicero, with his complaints about being sent "tittle tattle" and other impertinences. In the United States, the governor and council of the colony of Massachusetts played the role of press critics where they complained that America's first newspaper, *Publick Occurrences,* "contained . . . sundry doubtful and uncertain Reports" in their statement shutting it down.

American newspapers have had no fiercer critic than the novelist James Fenimore Cooper, who sued for libel at every opportunity and inserted digs at the press into a couple of his novels. This from *Home as Found,* 1838:

> The press, throughout the country, seized with avidity on anything that helped fill its columns. No one appeared disposed to inquire into the truth of the account. It was in print, and that struck the great majority of the editors and their readers, as a sufficient sanction.

However, regular press criticism in the United States is mostly a post–World War II phenomenon. A. J. Liebling began writing his pointed, informed and witty column, "The Wayward Press," in the *New Yorker* magazine in 1946. This is Liebling in 1961 on the decline of the newspaper:

The corrective for the deterioration of a newspaper is provided, in nineteenth-century theory, by competition. . . . Theoretically, a newspaper that does not give news, or is corrupt, or fails to stand up for the underdog, attracts the attention of a virtuous newspaper looking for a home, just as the tarantula, in the Caribbees, attracts the blue hornet. Good and bad paper will wrestle, to continue our insect parallel. Virtue will triumph, and the good paper will place its sting in the bad paper's belly and yell, "Sic sember Newhouse management!" or someting of the sort. Then it will eat the advertising content of the bad paper's bread basket.

This no longer occurs. Money is not made by competition among newspapers, but by avoiding it. . . .

In 1961, the first regularly published magazine critiquing the media—the *Columbia Journalism Review*—was founded at Columbia University. *CJR* would have a few imitators, Liebling dozens. Indeed, by the 1990s it seemed as if no major story could be covered—the Persian Gulf War, the O. J. Simpson trial, presidential elections—without newspapers, magazines and newscasts going on at great length about how it

tion of their own, but to the extent that depth of coverage correlates with volume of words, television stories are undeniably shallower than most newspaper stories. And because their words are intended for a less acute, less painstaking sense—hearing—television newswriters must forswear the more complex formulations a newspaper reporter might hazard. But these are differences of degree.

Journalists, whatever their medium, tend to swim close to the surface—concerned with the splashes and waves more than the underlying currents. Whether communicating by print, newsletter or cry, journalists are not often endowed with the time or the endurance to delve deeper. More thorough discussions may accompany breaking news coverage in extended newspaper series or columns, in television documentaries or in-was being covered. And with the 21st century came a multiplicity of blogs eager to note the biases, errors and omissions of the "mainstream media." Some proved quite adept at it.

This new era of sometimes obsessive self-consciousness is certainly healthy for journalism. At its best, it awakens news audiences to some of the limitations of the news they receive. This book argues, however, that journalism criticism suffers, as does much journalism, from a lack of historical perspective.

152

A. J. Liebling, the press critic of the New Yorker, *photographed in 1963.*

terview programs, in magazine articles. But here, too, the hurry and fascination with the moment that permeates most newsrooms, and is indeed inherent in the journalistic enterprise, appears to discourage longer perspectives and more searching analyses.

Some years ago, a writer visiting an Eskimo village in Canada's Northwest Territories was asked by one of the residents how long he planned to stay. Before the writer could answer, the Eskimo suggested, in English: "One day—newspaper story. Two days—magazine story. Five days—book."[36] It is not clear whether that Eskimo was familiar yet with the three-hour, hit-and-run operations mounted by television news crews, with their complex equipment and harried schedules, but he hardly required acquaintance with a television reporter to grasp the journalist's tendency toward superficiality.

Television is also routinely accused of having debased contemporary politics. But newspapers had faced similar accusations before television cameras began to steal the attention and abuse. When reporters were first beginning to cover Parliament in England in the late 18th century, one of its members, William Windham, fumed that politicians were being treated like "actors." "What was to become of the dignity of the House," Windham demanded, "if the manners and gestures, and tone and action of each member were to be subject to the license, the abuse, the ribaldry of newspapers?"[37]

Television favors candidates who are attractive, skilled at producing a newsworthy eight-second statement, and able to afford airtime for political commercials. Modern newspapers have favored candidates whose views are easily capsulized in headlines, and, in the days before circulation measured in the hundreds of thousands, publishers demonstrated a less subtle bias—toward parties and candidates willing to help subsidize their operations.

Our impatience with television's view of politics represents, in part, a longing for an era when the news regularly achieved the depth, impartiality and seriousness of the civics lesson—an era that never was.[38] Journalists throughout history have been as prone to oversimplification as the politicians about whom they write. Certainly, there is substantial room for improvement in television's coverage of politics, but such efforts should not be based on a false nostalgia.

Of course, television has had some profound effects on journalism. Particularly noticeable are the changes it has imposed upon newspapers. With broadcast newscasts now routinely beating them to breaking news, newspapers increasingly are emphasizing news features and more analytical approaches to events. They are moving away from pure news reporting toward some hybrid of news, opinion, history and pop sociology. (Network television newscasts have begun moving in the same direction in the face of competition from lengthier, more frequent local and cable television newscasts.)[39] Television, along with radio, also deserves some credit for the modern American newspaper's return to less constricted writing styles—at the expense of the five W's lead, the inverted pyramid and even the sobriquet. The anecdotes or turned phrases that now lead off so many front-page stories are there to compensate for the breaking news lost to broadcast journalists, but they are also there in imitation of broadcast journalists, who have long recognized that their wordings, written to be read aloud, had to sound conversational.[40] Television's influence on newspapers is nowhere more apparent than in the national daily *USA Today*—a colorful confection of graphics and short, breezy stories when it debuted in 1982.

But perhaps the most significant effect the television newscast has had on journalism has been the added distance it has placed between news purveyor and audience (in this it has continued the work of the newspaper). Television news is deceptive; it looks so friendly. The vast pool of live, videotaped and computer-generated images available to television newscasts have never succeeded in forcing the "talking head" of the newscaster from the screen. Audiences apparently prefer having their news delivered by a familiar, affable, *human* presence—these apparent throwbacks to criers or busybodies. Yet, the television screen is too flat and impenetrable for this to be much more than mimicry. No news medium offers less of the *actual* interaction and neighborly contact characteristic of spoken news than does television.

Newspapers, in the Age of Television

Even before the Internet the news had been mostly bad. Yes, there were some great journalistic triumphs, most prominent among them the Watergate investigation by *Washington Post* reporters Bob Woodward and Carl Bernstein in the early 1970s—an investigation that helped lead to the resignation of President Richard Nixon. But newspaper readership has been declining at a frightening rate.

Changes in newspaper penetration into American households and per capita American newspaper readership over the second half of the 20th century both form graphs you could ski down. According to time use studies compiled at the University of Maryland, the share of the adult population that "read a newspaper yesterday" declined from 85 percent in 1946 to 73 percent in 1965, and to 55 percent in 1985. According to one survey, that number had dropped to 39 percent by 2002.

The cause of newspapers' problems can be summed up in one word: television. Television newscasts get the news much faster than newspapers, and they deliver them not in gray words but in colorful moving images. Then there are all those networks upon networks full of entertainment programming. The average American spends many hours a day in front of a television set. That time had to be taken away from something.

The Persian Gulf War in 1991 provides further evidence of how far the newspaper has fallen. A survey by Birch/Scarborough reported that a grand total of 8.9 percent of Americans kept up with war news primarily through newspapers.

The result of this declining readership is not surprising: Newspapers are dying. Only a handful of American cities now have competing daily newspapers—a sad development for those who believe in the value of competition and a variety of points of views.

In their attempts to survive, newspapers have tried everything from changing their beat system—sending reporters, say, to shopping malls, not city halls—to promoting "news" readers can "use"—health or shopping tips, for example. They emphasize analysis as much as breaking news. Following *USA Today,* they have brightened up their graphics, employing color, and have shortened their stories. But it often seems a losing battle.

The arrival of the World Wide Web in the 1990s provided some reason to be cheerful about the future of newspapers. It gave them a new quicker, cheaper way to distribute the unmatched collection of information on current events their teams of reporters gathered each day. However, the Web has also brought waves of new competitors: news sites and, with the new century, blogs.

If newspapers continue to decline, it is not at all clear what might replace them as industrious gatherers of comprehensive accounts of daily occurrences, particularly local occurrences. It is clear that the public now has many other potential sources of accounts and entertainment.

It is possible that the increasing number of channels made possible by cables and satellite dishes will drive television newscasts toward the smaller, demographically segmented audiences now sought by many radio stations. But for now, television speaks predominantly to the large communities of nation or metropolitan area. The chances of a member of those communities being heard—still a vague possibility for newspaper readers through a letter or a canceled subscription—have almost entirely disappeared with television. This is one-way news.

Television viewers live in a world of mediated reality. Increasingly they talk and think about people they have not met, places they have not been. Television has, in McLuhan's terminology, "extended" dramatically our access to news but, as cars weaken the legs they have "extended," reliance on television news may have weakened our ability to hear and tell our *own* news. We borrow facts, perceptions, even opinions from newscasters, and we borrow the newscasters themselves—with whom we fancy ourselves on a first-name basis—as surrogate busybodies, surrogate friends. It is important to remember, as we allow one of these well-known, well-dressed personalities to present our news, that the exchange of news has not always been a spectator sport, that the pursuit of news once encouraged even nonjournalists to move, observe, investigate, remember and talk, that for an individual to be fully informed, it was once necessary to leave the house.

One accomplishment of television seems impossible to overstate: It brings a wealth of news into our homes with astounding speed and immediacy. The development of television news has capped centuries of improvements in the means of news dissemination and news gathering, centuries in which the perennial shortage of reliable information about current events has been transformed into a surplus. We can learn more and see more of a President Bush or Prince Charles than most of Thoreau's contemporaries could have dreamed of learning and seeing of President Pierce or Princess Adelaide. But we pay a price.

Questions

1. Consider the merits of Thoreau's argument that "to a philosopher all *news,* as it is called, is gossip, and they who edit and read it are old women over their tea."

2. What are the consequences of a society divided into communities based, as this chapter puts it, on "wave length, not locale"?

3. What are the similarities and dissimilarities between television news and spoken news?

16

The Information Explosion—
A Surfeit of Data

Whereas our ancestors had too little, middle-class residents of the most developed countries of the world today have too much. That may be the most profound difference between us. They struggled to feed themselves; our struggle is to resist the temptation of rich foods and excess calories. They might expect one new set of clothes in a lifetime; our drawers are filled with barely worn shirts or blouses. And whereas previous generations suffered from a constant shortage of news, "a starvation of print," and were often left "in a state of breathless anxiety," reduced to speculation and wonder, we complain that it is difficult to "keep up" with the voluminous amounts of news presented to us each day in print, on the air and on the Web.

The amount of available news from afar had swelled with the arrival of dailies, with the use of the steam press and the telegraph, with the development of radio and then of television and, of course, with the Internet. But if it were necessary to select one occurrence to represent this transformation from shortage to excess, a strong candidate would be an event that occurred on May 6, 1961: the radio innovator Gordon McLendon's conversion of a rock and roll station, XEAK, into XETRA—a station that broadcast news 24 hours a day. The law required that the station, which was aimed at Los Angeles listeners, identify its location once an hour, but McLendon instructed that this obligation be fulfilled only in Spanish—in such a fashion that its English-speaking audience would think it was hearing an advertisement for tourism in Mexico. XETRA—the first successful all-news radio station in North America, and probably the first in the world—was broadcasting with 50,000 watts of power from Tijuana, Mexico.[2]

Much of the news offered by modern news organizations is repetitious: Reporters tend to follow the same trails, stop at the same events, and partake of similar sets of facts. Newspaper stories repeat background information; newscasts repeat each other. At first XETRA began telling the top stories over again every

Now let's go hopscotching the world for headlines

—John Cameron Swayze, on NBC's *Camel News Caravan*[1]

seven and a half minutes, though the cycle was eventually extended to a half hour. (All-news stations are designed to serve as frequencies upon which itinerant listeners might pause to be briefed on the latest happenings, as men paused to hear the news at Siwan sun shelters.) McLendon's team of 12 newscasters did no original reporting; they simply rewrote news taken from the wire services—the same news available to newspapers and other radio stations. Future all-news stations (New York City had two by 1967) would mix liberal doses of features, reviews, and commentary into their programming in an effort to fill those endless hours.[3] Twenty-four hours of news has never meant 24 hours' worth of information.

Nonetheless, those who tuned in to these stations—while making coffee in the kitchen, driving in a car, sitting at a desk—had gained the ability to obtain an update on the world's news just about whenever they wanted it. And when Ted Turner introduced the first all-news television network, the Cable News Network, in 1980, the sights as well as the sounds of the news became available 24 hours a day. Then, beginning in the 1990s, the Web gave us easy, anytime access to words, sights and sounds.

Even subtracting the redundancies, even taking into account those forced to wait minutes, perhaps even hours, for their next newscast in towns without all-news radio or homes without cable or computer, most of the members of the news audience in the United States now have ready access to more stories than they can remember, more details than they can grasp, more news of the world beyond their communities in a half-hour than many of their ancestors could have expected in a year.

The most obvious and perhaps the most important comment that can be made about the onset of this surfeit of data is that it is welcome. Modern journalists have a right to be satisfied with their accomplishments. Whatever the limitations of the view they present of events across the country or the oceans, it is a blessing to be able to see so far, so frequently, and with such clarity. Plumpness is preferable to malnutrition; too much news of the world is preferable to too little.

That said, progress having received its due, a harder look can be taken at our flabby midsections—at some of the more ambiguous consequences of the heaping portions journalists are so busy loading onto our plates.

Many years ago, the entertainer Eddie Fisher divorced Debbie Reynolds and married Elizabeth Taylor, revealing himself as someone likely to test the attentiveness of the public with a string of wives. Former *New York Times* columnist Russell Baker says that was when he realized, for the first time, that "there might be a lot of things that were not worth keeping up with. This," Baker explains, "was a moment of liberation."

Once food became inexpensive and plentiful in many parts of the world, thinness became fashionable. With the masses now able to gorge themselves at our fast-news outlets, will "not keeping up," though it comes no more naturally to human beings than passing up desserts, attain a similar status? Will ignorance of the exact cause of death, of the subcommittee's vote, or of the names of Eddie Fisher's wives (or the paramours of today's tabloid idols) come to be seen as a sign of a disciplined resistance to the blandishments of the current noise?

"To this day I do not know how many times Eddie has married," Baker admits. "I do know, however, that Eddie Fisher gave me my first glimpse of what freedom could

Radio News: Still Around

Radio sometimes seems like the medium that will not die. Television can do everything radio can do plus show moving images. Why hasn't television killed radio? Because of something television audiences can't do: drive a car while watching. Radio has added to its essentially captive audience of automobile commuters enough people who are waking, working, walking, or washing the dishes to enable its stations to survive.

As radio channels continue to hone themselves in the search for narrow, specialized audiences, the news has taken a beating. Music stations pay less and less attention to news, and much of what news they do carry now comes in short, upbeat bursts from satellite-delivered national networks. At one time stations were pressured by the Federal Communications Commission to fulfill their "public service obligations" with news programs, but such pressures eased and then disappeared with the deregulation frenzy of the 1980s and 1990s.

Current events continue to be discussed on the air in talk shows hosted by budding Daniel Defoes. Web broadcasts, podcasts and news channels on satellite-radio systems promise to provide additional room for news. But perhaps the most encouraging development in radio news in the United States in recent decades has been National Public Radio. Established in 1967 under the Public Broadcasting Act, NPR came of age in the 1980s with such programs as *Morning Edition* and *All Things Considered.* Borrowing a style from the British Broadcasting Company's distinguished World Service, these programs feature longer, more serious reports on major national and international issues, as well as some not so major but still intriguing issues. Many news-hungry listeners now set a button on their car radios to the often weak-signaled, sometimes university-owned stations that carry NPR programs.

Radio has taken yet another blow from two relative new technologies—CD and digital music players, both of which work in cars. But these media seem too slow for news. It is also hard to access news through a computer while driving. So radio looks good into the next century, too.

be. . . . Soon thereafter, I was not keeping up with so many things that I had time to read Henry James."[4] Given our new situation of abundance, the argument that we ought to show more restraint in "keeping up" has considerable power. Instincts—a taste for sweets, for instance—that developed in a world of scarcity can run amok in a world of plenty. The desire for news, which kept our ancestors awake and aware, often leaves us prone on a couch—a remote control in hand, some faraway oddity on the screen.

Moreover, with the vast pool of occurrences available to modern news organs, our ancestors' need to be alert to potential threats is now satisfied by daily, hourly immersions in a selection of tragedies so unrelievedly black that the world itself, always grim when viewed through the news, may appear actually to have darkened. And the glimpses of lives and events newsmongers once struggled to present to their audiences have been replaced, thanks to the swiftness and power of our journalists, by a dizzying merry-go-round of personalities and situations—displacing each other with remarkable speed but not fast enough for us to realize that we often travel in circles.

The huge surplus of news we live with may be unique in human history. This final chapter is an attempt to explore a few of the more subtle, perhaps more ominous, effects an excess of such information—or from the newsmakers' point of view, an excess of publicity—is likely to have on humankind.

Publicity

Providing newsmakers with publicity is not normally a goal of the exchange of news, but it is and always has been a by-product of that exchange. When word of the man who fell into a rain barrel while exiting from a woman friend's window spread among the Nootka of Vancouver Island, it bestowed a degree of renown upon that ill-starred suitor. Sixteenth- and 17th-century newsbooks and news ballads helped focus public attention on criminals such as the murderer Sir John Fites, while the earliest English newspapers, to recall another example, helped transform the German mercenary Count Ernst Mansfeld into a celebrity.

Publicity, as newsmakers from William of Orange to P. T. Barnum have recognized, can be turned to political or financial gain. Public relations professionals are desperate to consecrate their clients with but a few drops of attention from a popular news organization. Still, many who have been touched by publicity remain uneasy about it.

When writers gather at conferences, explains the writer and critic Susan Sontag, the occasion should provide an opportunity "precisely to talk among ourselves," not "to attract the attention of the press or television." Yet one of the more important purposes of the press and broadcast news is precisely to intrude upon such potentially newsworthy conversations and share their more interesting or entertaining moments with the public.

Sontag laments the "abridged and simplified version . . . of what is being said" that escapes to the public through news coverage, and she protests the loss of the ability "to have a context for one's remarks," to be able to address them "to some and not others."[5] Her concerns are justified, of course. In becoming news, statements and events must necessarily undergo some degree of abridgment, simplification and isolation from their contexts. They always have. As an unintended by-product of what can itself be a rather clumsy force, publicity's glare rarely does justice to its subjects.

Publicity is also widely criticized for the manner in which it is distributed. Many look askance upon the tendency of news organs to huff and puff and blow out of proportion, particularly their readiness to grant attention to the determined, demented or diabolical. But this too is not new. Was Sir John Fites more deserving of a chance to be heard than Charles Manson or an airplane hijacker?

The world has long accommodated this tendency of publicity to distort or to fall on the undeserving; publicity has grown no coarser, no less discriminating. But with the mammoth publics modern news media now address, publicity has become an even stronger force. An international audience now hears the remarks of participants in the most interesting writers' conferences; the image of a teenager with a grenade bounces off satellites to mesmerize tens of millions of people across the globe. The real danger inherent in this intensified publicity may lie not in its distortions or in its tendency to shine on the diabolical, but in the intensity of the light it shines on the merely different.

John Cameron Swayze invited his audience to "go hopscotching the world for head-lines" in the earliest days of television. And we have been hopscotching with Swayze and his successors ever since—hopscotching ever more animatedly, the far corners of the world ever more brightly illuminated. Those who have access to this news of the globe may indeed be beginning to coalesce into a sort of global society. We share news across continents and cultures, and the sharing of news, first, tends to undercut xeno-phobia and, second, tends to encourage the spread of common values—the importance of famine relief, perhaps—and even a sense of common identity.

This slow drift in the direction of a more unified species, should it continue, would obviously have important implications for the possibility of understanding and peace— among the most noble of goals. But is there not also a dark side to a vision of humankind joined together over news of famine, earthquakes, hijackings and the latest pop super-star? Might not such a global society begin to overrun the wide variety of smaller soci-eties the globe has till now supported?

When prices are reported in the papers, the disparities between them begin to shrink. As the behavior of disparate cultures increasingly finds its way into the news, might the result not be the same? For a time the ways of some unfamiliar society satisfy the jaded audience's hunger for the exotic, but with exposure this culture becomes less exotic. We watch them; eventually they obtain their own television sets and watch us. Fashion designers are inspired by their costumes; a member of their society considers purchasing a tie. Along with travel, trade and other forms of communication, news has allowed us to feast on the world's diversity, but we risk exhausting the supply.

Each culture, like each species, represents a separate experiment in adaptation and development. But as a culture is exposed to international publicity, its customs may begin to fade, to lose their unique colorations, and when cultural diversity is endangered, as the physicist Freeman Dyson argues, the number of alternatives available to hu-mankind as it selects possible futures could begin to shrink; human progress may be en-dangered.[6] Is the potential depletion of a human culture not as serious a concern as the potential extinction of an animal species?

Our high-tech news organs take us hopscotching not only to the more exotic corners of the world but to the more exotic corners of our own societies—including the downtown clubs, the laboratories, and the writers' conferences where innovations first surface. Should an odd or otherwise diverting art form, or a likely looking scientific discovery, peck its way out of an egg, a notepad, microphone, and camera are sure to be present to record its first peep. Previous generations of innovators might be ignored for decades, if not lifetimes, in their garrets and laboratories. The members of our avant-garde, on the other hand, seem to face an inquisition before juries of hundreds of thousands the mo-ment they take a step in a newsworthy direction. Publicity surrounds them, seduces them, seems to overwhelm them.[7]

And our news hounds, with their swiftness and ubiquity, are able to trap innovations in earlier and earlier stages of their development. The new management style developed by the computer companies in California's Silicon Valley in the late 1970s and early

1980s, for example, received so much exposure so quickly that it seemed exhausted before it was even mature. The work of our experimenters is now frequently clipped and displayed before it flowers.

"The prophets of the presses," notes the architecture critic Ada Louise Huxtable, may now spring into action to discuss architects based only on their drawings—before they have built any major buildings.[8] The same premature publicity now shines on all aspects of public life. The news increasingly is filled with reports on deliberations rather than decisions, on plans rather than actions, on predictions rather than votes, on potentiality rather than actuality. Publicity arrives so quickly that its subjects often appear half-formed and seem likely to remain that way.

Early 21st-century journalists are able to intrude with ever-increasing efficacy. The public dialogue, to be sure, is invigorated by exposure to the odd and innovative scenes they penetrate, but the air too quickly turns stale again. For although the world these journalists re-create each day, each hour, appears relentlessly new and different, it is a world that may contain fewer and fewer dark corners in which the truly new or different might be sheltered long enough to fully develop. When news of occurrences moves this far, this fast, does less of consequence actually occur?

The Weight of the Present—
News, Rumors and Ideas

The world has always been complex. It is arguable whether the arrival of microprocessors and current account deficits, which most of us do not understand, has made life any more perplexing than it was under the sway of the biological and physical principles most of our ancestors did not understand. There has always been more taking place around us than we can comprehend or even notice. But there is a difference between the world that exists for us to stumble upon and the world that is announced to us by our journalists. What has changed with our superabundance of news is that the obtrusive world *as announced* now competes in its complexity with the unobtrusive world *as is*. With their speed and reach increased by the teaming of electronics and the journalistic method, journalists—despite their inclination to simplify—are now acquainting us with, haranguing us with, complexity after complexity.

The massive pile of information deposited in front of us by hyperactive news organs and energetic reporters has, of course, had significant positive effects: Dragons and miracles are expiring as we become less likely, with another fact always available, to paper over gaps in the known with recourse to the unknown. Furthermore, as newspapers, radio and television spray the planet with facts, rumor—the least responsible variety of news—is gradually being eradicated; the haze that shelters rumor dissipating; the periods of uncertainty in which rumor breeds shrinking.[9]

This effort to inoculate societies against the more virulent forms of superstition, misinformation, misunderstanding and panic is commendable, of course. It would be absurd to contemplate rereleasing the contagion of error into the environment. Still, it is worth considering the effect this noble effort may have upon the ecology of the psyche.

The news exchanged by the inhabitants of the island of Tikopia, according to the anthropologist Raymond Firth, often drifted into rumor. If a ship bringing food to the island was due to arrive, a rumor would start that it had arrived. If no ship was due, word would spread that one was on its way. These rumors, Firth surmises, accomplished a number of psychological purposes: They were a form of wish-fulfillment, no doubt, but they may also have given the Tikopia the ability to release tensions, to cushion blows, to manage the unknown.[10] Phantom ships, in other words, may be of some use in filling the gaps between real ships. Moreover, by adding an element of doubt to all reports, periodic injections of rumor may help dilute some of the awful finality of the news. Under the aegis of our ever-vigilant news organs, defeats are defeats; deaths, deaths; ship arrivals and destinations incontrovertible. The Tikopia lacked this reassuring confidence in the intelligibility of the world, but they did have one consolation: room for hope.

When news is built around hard information, it loses some of its flexibility, even some of its ability to cohere. With so few facts on patrol our ancestor's minds were able to wander with impunity. Rumor benefited from this freedom, but another more reputable form of thought also gained room to play in the open spaces that stretched between facts: ideas.

After detailing all the problems Americans faced in obtaining news of the fall of Napoleon in 1814, the French historian Guillaume de Bertier de Sauvigny concedes that the analyses of these events produced in faraway, news-poor America sometimes proved more perceptive than those composed in Europe—within full range of the barrage of facts. American journalists, from their vantage point deep within the haze, were among the first to suggest, for example, that Napoleon's fall would bring the restoration of the Bourbons.[11] This may have been luck. Europeans, consumed by an even more rabid partisanship, may have been too blind to see the obvious; press controls in some countries curtailed speculations. Certainly Bertier de Sauvigny's regard for their perspicacity would have surprised those American editors who were complaining at the time of the lack of sufficient data by which to reason. However, there is a sense in which pauses in the flow of data can stimulate deeper reflection. Access to a superabundance of news limits rumormongers, but can it not also confound those engaged in the formulation of ideas?

"When ideology is in the saddle," writes former *New York Times* columnist Anthony Lewis, "inconvenient facts are pushed aside. . . ."[12] But the converse is also true. When facts are in the saddle, conceptions, beliefs and opinions (all, like rumor, dependent on some degree of speculation) risk getting trampled underfoot.

As they accumulate over time, facts eventually overflow most theories designed to contain them. News brings forth these inconvenient facts, and improvements in the gathering and dissemination of news speed up their accumulation. We learn, with leering journalists as our guides, of socialists profiting, democrats dictating, capitalists colluding, revolutionaries repressing. A Marxist would need a shut-tight mind to escape news of communism's inefficiencies and brutalities; a free-market capitalist would have to quickly turn the channel to miss news of the boats that sink as the economic waters rise and fall. Sufficient contradictions are eventually presented for exception to be taken to most ambitious formulations about societal behavior.

In the past century the flow of news has grown into a torrent. Facts now storm through the air, rain down from satellites, pour out of computers or even cell phones. The 18th- and 19th-century ideas so many have lived by for so long have eroded under this deluge. That these aged philosophies have failed to account for the 20th and 21st centuries is not surprising. What is interesting is our failure to replace them.

"Though those with what they take to be one big idea are still among us, calls for 'a general theory' of just about anything social sound increasingly hollow," notes the anthropologist Clifford Geertz, "and claims to have one, megalomaniac."[13] As they march into battle, lined up in their dress uniforms, such theories prove easy targets for snipers firing facts from behind the trees. In the more esoteric disciplines, a new piece of research always seems poised to refute. And in politics or economics, even the pluckiest theories seem no match for the maneuverability and tactical command of the fact-wielding modern journalist.

Yes, we still have opinions, but many of us now wear our louder opinions somewhat self-consciously. And the formulations that might knit these opinions into ideologies are in short supply. We seem to have difficulty creating syntheses that can stand up to our analyses. The full weight of the present, with which a vigorous and uninterrupted supply of news has burdened us, may be too much for our conceptual abilities to support.

Neither the size nor the amount of ideas lends itself to quantification, making this a difficult point to prove. In scholarship the predominant trend seems to have been away from the grand theory toward the solution of smaller problems. In politics, on the one hand, doctrines supporting the rights of blacks and other minorities, women, and gays became increasing mainstream in the mid- to late 20th century in the United States. On the other hand, ambitious attempts to account for more general political behaviors seem in short supply. Has levelheadedness—the ability to balance bunches of information—not become, by default, the dominant political philosophy of the age? And what economist of the left or right is capable of constructing a theory strong and supple enough to withstand the daily releases of economic statistics?

Access to this surfeit of data has saved us from many flawed theories and oversimplified beliefs. The chief beneficiary of any ideological impotence it has produced may be clear thinking. Nevertheless, where governments themselves are not based on demanding ideologies, a climate inhospitable to their growth also benefits the status quo. Revolutionaries must talk in the subjunctive, but the news overwhelms their *would be*'s and *could be*'s with its incessant reminders of what *is*. Where on the streets of this crowded city of facts is it possible to gain a long and unobstructed view?

The news maintains a constant sense of political frustration, portraying the moment, any moment, as "a time of so much violence and injustice," as Anthony Lewis characterized late 1986 in a column in the *Times*.[14] Yet the news so entrances its audience with the quotidian mechanics of the extant institutions and social realities that presumably less violent, less unjust, more radical alternatives may seem inconceivable. The news is society's deeply dissatisfied spouse: always complaining, never leaving.

"When no opinions are looked upon as certain," wrote Alexis de Tocqueville, a century and a half ago, "men cling to the mere instincts and material interests of their position, which are naturally more tangible, definite, and permanent than any opinions in the world."[15] Is this not our situation?

Many political opinions have lost currency in recent decades. Communism has crumbled. Socialists (or at least parties with that name) trade places with conservatives in Western democracies and the ground does not shake. The left sometimes seems almost as eager to hack away at the "welfare state" as the right. Radical protests (except in France) often fizzle. The only political philosophy that has seemed able to increase its grip on power has been neo-conservatism, and the contradictions inherent in this movement have grown increasingly apparent as it has attempted to wield that power. We have seen new wars. We have seen new atrocities. We have not seen that many new ideas.

Yes, the proliferation of television channels and blogs has given voice to the intensely partisan, the often shrill. But beyond the name-calling, and beyond efforts to start or end those wars, the issues often seem circumscribed: reduced to the question of how the economic fires might most effectively be stoked. The personal accumulation of money—the essence of practicality—threatens to become the only goal.

Is this just a stagnant moment—a pause after centuries of revolution and decades of liberation? Or are we in the West beginning to see the outlines of a new order: a world without dragons, rumors and ideologies—the age of information? Has news—the thought stream of the group mind—been amplified to the point where individuals are beginning to have difficulty concentrating on anything else?

The Future of News

The toys grow prettier and prettier. Each wondrous invention spawns new wondrous inventions. Each—the alphabet, paper, the printing press, electronic and broadcast communication, satellites, computers—has worked for us and on us, and each continues to practice its magic. None of these revolutionary technologies has yet exhausted itself. The alphabet perfected by the Greeks has served fewer than 95 generations; its latest challenge is on the keyboard of computers. The printing press is still expanding bookshelves, newsstands, and consciousnesses. The electronic media are just reaching adulthood. And the computer—mere child—is just beginning to escape those gray metal cases and integrate itself into our lives. Revolution upon revolution upon revolution. Early 21st-century living provides the opportunity to watch these technologies compete to eradicate the tiniest imperfections in our access to data.

Much of the globe has already been wired. Although the electronic conduits promise to become still more numerous and efficient, we already possess the technological capability to collect news instantly from almost anywhere in the world, where government controls do not interfere, and then transmit it instantly to almost anywhere in the world where government controls do not interfere. And the number of governments brazen enough to impose such controls declined sharply after 1989. It is difficult to imagine the news becoming much faster or more far-reaching. But technology has outstripped our imagination before. This book suggested in its first edition in 1988 that "there remains room for improvement, if not in the methods by which news is gathered and transmitted, then in the methods by which that news is sorted and distributed." The Internet has further improved the way news is collected and sent, but its main effect

Television News in the Age of Cable

This book has been filled with the stories of sometimes eccentric characters who were able to peek a little further into the future than their contemporaries: James Gordon Bennett Sr. was one; so was Joseph Pulitzer. Ted Turner may also qualify.

The principle upon which Turner based his analysis of the future is an old one: narrowcasting. Cable systems would allow television sets to receive more channels, so those channels could grow—as London coffeehouses once did—more specialized. The three traditional broadcast networks mixed news and various sorts of entertainment programming in their search for broad audiences. On cable there would be room for a news-only network. In 1980, Turner started the Cable News Network, CNN, with news or news-related programs 24 hours a day

Turner was prescient, too, in his view of global broadcasting. He was quick to see the international market for his all-news channel. After a number of money-losing years, CNN established itself during the Persian Gulf War as the place where much of the United States and, increas-

ingly, much of the world, turns for information on breaking news events.

With an explosion in the number of channels—arriving on cable, via satellite and, eventually, on the Internet—came room for more specialized news channels: one, for example, emphasizing a more opinionated, more conservative point of view. Soon Rupert Murdoch's Fox News Channel, launched under the guidance of Roger Ailes in 1996, was garnering higher ratings in the United States than CNN.

Of course, those extra channels are not only available to American news organizations or those of the West. The first real threat to Western domination of international television news came from Al-Jazeera, which was founded in Qatar in 1996. This Arab-language satellite news channel began broadcasting 24 hours a day in 1999 and was soon capturing large numbers of viewers in the Arab world. The station garnered considerable attention, and inspired considerable controversy, by reporting on the Iraq War in 2003 from a perspective sometimes quite different from that of American news organs.

Satellite news channels allow television viewers—such as this man in Baghdad who is setting up a dish—access to a wider range of perspectives.

has indeed been on the sorting and distribution of news—the way it is made available to us.

When they met on the beach, residents of the island of Tikopia each maintained some control over the news they received: They could attempt to satisfy individual interests by expressing them in questions and reactions. We could, back in 1988, choose to receive our news from one newscaster or another, in one newspaper or another, but after this initial decision we sat still for bulky, heterogeneous collections of information—much of which might have been of little interest to us. Reading a newspaper we could at least pick and choose; watching television our only recourse was to modulate our attention—to drift off. "The next challenge for journalists," that first edition said, "may be allowing the members of their audiences as flexible an access to the oceans of news at their disposal as the Tikopia had to their trickles of news."

And that challenge is indeed being met. On the Internet we can obtain news from many thousands of valuable news sites whenever we want, just by fingering a keyboard or the buttons on our cell phones. We can get that news in print on our screens but also, more and more, in the form of audio podcasts or video. In fact, video news reports—which for many decades were distributed only on hugely inflexible, you-watch-when-we-want, *mass*-audience newscasts—can now often be played at any moment on well connected screens of all sizes.

Our maps are already growing inadequate as representations of electronic societies—where airwaves serve as paths and websites as meeting places, where we are much more likely to know friends' e-mail addresses than their physical addresses and where we can satisfy our need for awareness without ever having to step out into the street. A teenager in Prague with a taste for hip-hop may now have more in common with a teenager in Houston than with a Chopin-loving neighbor. And as traditional "vertical" communities of neighborhood or nation—communities based on geographic proximity—decline, the news will likely speak more regularly to these new, ethereal, "horizontal" communities of interest: boroughs, perhaps, of a more homogeneous, perhaps more homogenized, global society.

Computers face an additional challenge: We undoubtedly will look to them not only to route news more efficiently to us but to help us digest the huge volume of information they are directing our way. A small first step toward the use of computers to analyze the news has already been taken with the now common use of computer-generated charts and graphs in newspapers, magazines and television newscasts. More substantial progress will depend on more sophisticated modeling and artificial intelligence programs. In other words, our minds—hard-pressed to circumnavigate the masses of facts brought forth by electronically amplified news organs—may themselves turn to electronics for assistance. And the solution to the apparent shortage of large-scale political and economic ideas may be found in computer-aided conceptualization.

Might these improved means of handling and even digesting news ever succeed in improving news? Perhaps access to so much information will make us more selective in our consumption of this information. Perhaps with the help of computers we will become more adept at picking our way through news of tragedies, outrages, politics and Eddie Fisher's wives. Should idea processors join word processors in our newsrooms, perhaps this first gloss on the world will even gain in wisdom some percentage of what it has gained in speed.

The Changing Style of Television News

Television news has been growing much faster and more visually alive.

The fact that "sound bites"—on-air quotations from news makers-have grown shorter has been much lamented. During recent presidential elections they were down to about eight seconds each. But it is not just the sound-bites. Each shot in a videotape report—the candidate waving, the balloons going up—is on the air for much less time, too.

Meanwhile, more and more is going on behind the "talking heads" of the newscasters who read the introductions to stories. Graphics and words move around to the left or right of their heads.

Computerized graphics, first introduced in weather maps, have establish themselves in videotape reports. Television reporters and producers are not just limited to telling their stories with videotaped scenes, now they can mix in moving arrows, maps, and graphs.

Many critics still look at television with eyes accustomed to print. All this looks hyperactive and distracting to them. They much prefer seeing Jim Lehrer of PBS simply sitting and talking with someone. But if television is ever to really compete with print as a means of storing and transmitting intelligence, it is going to have to carry more interesting pictures than the back of Jim Lehrer's head. These recent changes in style, by this way of thinking, may be a step in the right direction.

We can hope. We can hope too that journalists will look more regularly beyond the concerns of their own social class or their employer's social class and that they will wander more frequently beyond the boundaries of news itself and occasionally adopt less hurried, more searching perspectives. And there is always the hope that further improvements in the flow of the news, and in the efforts of journalists, will further increase the chances that the news will, in Dr. Johnson's words, enlarge a mind. After all, the exchange of news, with all its limitations, remains an expression of our desire for awareness, and that impulse is always at least a start.

If the past is any guide, however, many future databanks will be stocked with gruesome murder stories, and more online news services will concentrate on Hollywood and baseball than on African politics. For no matter how sophisticated news organs become, unless human beings are also rewired, they are likely to continue to satisfy their desire to remain aware with a spicy, hastily prepared mix of the portentous and the anomalous similar to that with which they have satisfied that desire for the past few thousand years.

The more profound, more sober side of our nature may never succeed in transforming news into an ideal vehicle for its concerns. Still, is there not something wonderfully human in this image of a future in which layer upon layer of finely worked circuitry is placed at the service of subject matter as unrefined, unruly and irrepressible as news?

Questions

1. Is there any sign that, as this chapter suggests might happen, "not keeping up" with the news is becoming fashionable? The upper classes used to be better informed than the lower classes. Is this still true?

2. Give examples of recent avant-garde artistic, social or political movements. Have they been hurt by premature publicity?

3. Give arguments for or against this chapter's suggestion that the masses of news we receive have made it more difficult to construct new ideas.

4. Give examples of what this chapter calls "ethereal, 'horizontal' communities of interest." What might the consequences be of their growing importance?

Endnotes

See the Bibliography for complete citations of the books and journal articles referred to here. Supplementary material in the timeline is taken from such histories as Mott, *American Journalism,* Edwin Emery, Folkerts, Woods, Bellanger, Lee, Kroeger, Hudson, and Bleyer.

Introduction

1. II, 484–486; translated, Lippmann, "A Test of the News." The term given here as "news" is often translated as "tales" or "rumor."

2. C. S. Lewis, 1.

3. Peters.

4. Thomas Deloney, *A Proper Newe Sonet Declaring the Lamentation of Beckles Suffolke* . . . ; cited, Neuburg, 33–37.

5. *Boston Evening-Post,* Nov. 4, 1765.

6. "Leading Article," *Times Literary Supplement,* Nov. 18, 1955, 689.

7. Other, more complex definitions of news have been formulated, but this seems the heart of the matter. News is usually a report on an *event*—a fire, a murder, a vote—although word on the president's *position* on Mideast peace would also be news. News is usually about *recent* occurrences, although fresh information on whether Napoleon was or was not poisoned on the island of Saint Helena in 1821 would be news. News is usually gathered for the purpose of dissemination, although we can obtain news simply by stumbling upon the fact that there was a burglary last night at a house down the street. News is always introduced to us as *true,* but—as anyone who has spent some time following or making news knows—that characterization occasionally proves misleading.

Chapter 1. Why News?—The Thursty Desyer That All Our Kynde Hath to Know

1. *Spectator,* 452, Aug. 8, 1712; reprinted, Donald F. Bond, IV, 90–94.

2. Cited, Thomas Whiteside, "Standups," *New Yorker,* Dec. 2, 1985, 92.

3. *British Mercury,* July 30–Aug. 2, 1712; cited, Nichols IV, 86–87.

4. Sir Roger North; cited, Edward Forbes Robinson, 82.

5. William Patten, *The Expedicion into ScotLande* . . . (London: 1548).

6. *First Philippic;* Demosthenes, 17.

7. Shooter, 232. The previous year, for another example, Richard Burton had noted that the Somali Bedouins "have a passion for knowing how the world wags"; Burton, 188.

8. Maiskii, 91. In the American South at the beginning of the 19th century, the first question settlers put to travelers was, "Where might you be coming from?" The second question was whether they might be "acquainted with any news"; Henry Adams, 41.

9. This discussion is based on Raymond Firth, "Rumor in a Primitive Society."

10. The information on the Tikopia in this section is from Raymond Firth, "Rumor in a Primitive Society."

11. Gairdner, *Paston Letters,* III, 267; New York *Evening Post,* June 1, 1814.

12. "Latest Intelligence," *Times,* London, April 26, 1871; John McPhee, "Annals of the Former World: Rising from the Plains-II," *New Yorker,* March 3, 1986, 42.

13. *The Newspaper;* reprinted, *Life and Poems of the Rev. George Crabbe,* II (London: 1834), 129.

14. The information on this study of the effects of the strike is from Berelson.

15. *The Newspaper;* reprinted, *Life and Poems of the Rev. George Crabbe,* II (London: 1834), 129.

16. Berelson, 125–126.

17. Sardella, 9.

18. Molotch.

19. Granqvist, 84.

20. See Gans, 122.

21. Paine, 102.

22. Coulet, 18.

23. McIlwraith, 184.

24. Silva, 204–205 (144).

Chapter 2. News in Preliterate Societies—In the Ordinary Way

1. Ferrars, 124.

2. Shooter, 232–233.

3. The term *Zulu* is used broadly in this chapter to refer to the various tribes that have been dominated by the Zulu kings.

4. Bryant, *The Zulu People,* 1.

5. Samuelson, 47–48.

6. Titiev, 330.

7. Havelock, 6.

8. The background of these observers raises the question whether they might not have imposed inappropriate modern categories upon indigenous behaviors. To the extent that the exchange of news was limited by social or religious taboos, or entwined with religious behaviors, it must have taken on some meanings in preliterate societies that Western observers and modern readers might find unfamiliar. Nevertheless, the evidence collected in this chapter indicates that these societies did acknowledge an interest in a set of subjects that bears a remarkably close resemblance to what we call news. It would be useful to have an anthropological analysis of the precise meaning news held for one such preliterate culture; it would be surprising, however, if such an analysis uncovered a radically different conception of news or of its importance.

9. Lebzelter, 4(2); Barnett, 18; Belgrave, 145; Haas, 105.

10. Raum, 333.

11. Vilakazi, 90–91, discusses Zulu mourning rituals.

12. Umeasiegbu, 27; Adriani, II, 373 (256).

13. Cline, 50a.

14. Belgrave, 145.

15. Samuelson, 47–48.

16. For the Ute in Utah the gambling ground was "the major clearinghouse for all reservation news"; Collins, 149. Among the more exotic examples of such gathering places are the palm trees at the bottom and tops of which people would gather to smoke and talk on hot days on Negros Island in the Philippines or the date grove where the Hasawis of Saudi Arabia congregated to exchange gossip, transact business, discuss family affairs and "listen to news"; Donn Vorhis Hart, 383; Vidal, 150–151.

17. Leith-Ross, 87–88.

18. For the Khasis in India the market was where they exchanged "information of all kinds"; McCormack, 108B. The crowds drawn to the bazaar in Iran in the 1930s, for an additional example, made it the place where "news arrives first from everywhere"; Haas, 105.

19. Raum, 403, 411.

20. The Navaho, for example, announced press conferences through smoke signals; Willard Williams Hill, 19(2). Some of the Zapotecs of Mexico used seashells to spread warnings and calls to assemble; Steininger, 9. Adriani, I, 246 (165).

21. Drucker, 331–332. The Thonga, on the eastern coast of South Africa, built the exchange of news with travelers into a ritual—the ceremony of *djungulisana;* see Junod, 354.

22. For an analysis of the synergistic relationship between trade and "information flows" in early American history, see Pred, 19, 208.

23. Katzin, ix, 37. In Korea, "package carriers" played a similar role—they were also expected to carry information; Keir, 821. In Poland, beggars, because they moved from village to village, were once "greatly valued . . . as carriers of news and gossip"; Benet, 233.

24. Iliff, 126.

25. The role of busybodies has also been noted in a study of an Indian village, where elderly women who roved about "visiting" were relied on to carry news; Cornell University, 552. In Uttar Pradesh, a state in northern India, this role was filled by washermen's wives and any other women who frequently "circulate through courtyards other than their own"; Wiser, 108–109.

26. Gluckman, 38–39.

27. Michelson, 9–47.

28. Crawfurd, 336.

29. A group of Tewa Indians in New Mexico, for another example, had a crier who would call out word of events ranging from the loss of an animal, to a race, to the arrival of Mexicans for trade; Parsons, 102–103.

30. Radin, 210.

31. Belgrave, 221–222.

32. Voth, following 6-B.

33. Gurdon, 91.

34. Mijatovich, 99–101.

35. David Montgomery Hart, 82.

36. Cornell University, 549.

37. ". . . for it is part of their duty to go daily to the marketplace and collect and bring back all the latest news"; Gorer, 55–56; Bebey; see also Le Coeur, 53. For a discussion of the use of songs, *"corridos,"* to spread news in the 20th century in Hispanic south Texas, see Peter Applebome, "Outrages and Brave Deeds Live on in South Texas Ballads," *New York Times,* Dec. 12, 1986.

38. Bebey.

39. McIlwraith, 160, 218.

40. McIlwraith, 247.

41. Reader, 231.

42. For an example of the use of a large tom-tom to call villagers together in an emergency in Den Pasar on the island of Bali, see Covarrubias, xxix, 65, 406.

43. The Zapotec's bells have a language of sorts: For a major threat "the three bells are run slowly in succession, one clap from each, beginning with the highest pitched one"; Robert Bartley Taylor Jr., 317–318.

44. See Nelson, 6–7, for the use of a riddle song to warn the inhabitants of a squatter village in Nairobi, Kenya, of surprise police raids.

45. Cited, Anthony Smith, *The Newspaper: An International History,* 81.

46. Dobritzhofer, 424–425.

47. Raymond Firth, "Rumor in a Primitive Society"; Raswan, 104.

48. Parsons, 103.

49. Drucker, 331–332; the talk of plans for war is attributed to "ancient times."

50. Adriani, II, 373 (256), 376 (258).

51. Nambiar, 2-A.

52. The uses of news, or even attitudes toward news, do not appear to have undergone a radical restructuring similar to that Michel Foucault, for example, writes of having found in his study of mental illness. The influence of various cultural and political systems upon the news is of interest but appears to have been relatively small.

53. Bryant, *Olden Times in Zululand and Natal,* 172.

54. Gusinde, 931–932 (1020).

55. Bohannan, 226–227.

56. Raymond Firth, "Rumor in a Primitive Society."

57. See Ong, 38–39, 58–59, 70–71.

58. Stock, 16.

59. Cornell University, 517.

Chapter 3. The Survival of Spoken News— Publishing the Whisper of the Day

1. *The Spleen;* reprinted, Chalmers, XV, 164.

2. Samuelson, 47; Maiskii, 91–92; Redfield, 186; Schram, 115a.

3. Bryant, *Olden Times in Zululand and Natal,* 172; Bryant, to be fair, does include a reference to the spread of news in English villages.

4. W. Warde Fowler, 272. Romans also shared information in the popular public baths.

5. Guillaume de la Villeneuve; cited, Alf Franklin, *La Vie Privée d'Autrefois,* 14–19. Records also survive of major events in the 16th century—the taking of Milan, the treaty with Pope Clement VII, and the birth of a crown prince, for instance—being "cried at the sounding of a horn at the crossroads of Paris"; Bourrilly, 177, 180; Bellanger, I, 33–34. Crying, of course, is also one of the oldest forms of advertising; see Alf Franklin, *La Vie Privée d'Autrefois,* and Galliot.

6. Armstrong, 444. Few European nations were as dependent on travel as Russia. The struggle to overcome the isolation imposed by its geography caused travelers to retain their importance as sources of news in Russia well into the 17th century. Merchants, diplomats, clergy,

captives and others who arrived from abroad were interrogated in search of news; Waugh, "The Publication of Muscovite *Kuranty,*" 112.

7. Cited, Armstrong, 433–434.

8. In summer, the city's newsmongers moved outside to Moorfields; Trevelyan, 175–176. In a periodic newsbook published in 1630 "Pauls walkers" are singled out as among "the greatest talkers of Newes"; *The Continuation of the Most Remarkable Occurrences of Newses,* July 16 [?], 1630; cited, Dahl, *A Bibliography of English Corantos and Periodical Newsbooks,* 167–168. See also Stanley Morison, *Ichabod Dawks and His Newsletter,* 16.

9. Cited, Armstrong, 433. For a discussion of the importance of communication in the development of cities, see Meier, 13.

10. Sydney, 17; Pearson, 473. Watchmen served as "news-bearers" more recently in India, where they were expected to keep the locals up to date on births, deaths, and crimes, as well as on threats to the village's security; Thorner, 577–578. In Detroit in 1798, a priest appointed a town crier, who would stand on the church steps each Sunday and tell the news; Lee, 179.

11. Ducey, 301.

12. Arensberg, 177. This method is not, of course, limited to the West: In China early in this century, "drinking tea with friends . . . [was]the farmer's chief means of obtaining news"; Buck, 405–406.

13. Edward Forbes Robinson, 72.

14. Cited, Edward Forbes Robinson, 80.

15. Cited, Ellis, 189.

16. *News from the Coffe-House. In which is shewn their several sorts of Passions, Containing Newes from all our Neighbor Nations. A Poem* (London: 1667).

17. *Spectator,* 403, June 12, 1712.

18. Ellis, 119.

19. Wright, 111.

20. Lillywhite, 366, 656–658.

21. Lillywhite, 328, 409, 551, 571, 573, 577–578; Wright, 9. Britain's outposts in America were not populous enough to support more than a few coffeehouses. Benjamin Harris, who would play an important role in the history of American journalism, opened the London Coffee House, probably Boston's first, in 1686. As late as 1734, New York appears to have had only a single coffeehouse—upon occasion forcing members of the city's bitterly antagonistic political factions to share the same table; Kobre, *Development of American Journalism,* 3–4; "Old New York Coffee Houses," *Harper's Monthly,* March 1882, 481–499.

22. *Spectator,* 457, Aug. 14, 1712; reprinted, Donald F. Bond, IV, 111–114.

23. Ellis, 223–229, 238–239.

24. Guérard, 243; Funck-Brentano, 219–241.

25. See Weil, 76.

26. Livois, 50–53.

27. Desmond, 20–22; Funck-Brentano, 81.

28. Cited, Hatin, *Histoire Politique et Littéraire de la Presse*, I, 40–41. Another comment of Montesquieu's on the *nouvellistes*: *"Leurs discours de cinquante ans n'ont pas d'effet différent de celui qu'aurait pu produire un silence aussi prolongé";* cited, Livois, 50.

29. Tate, 120, 135.

30. R. de Livois writes, *"Au XVIIIème siècle, le goût pour l'information est presque devenu un vice ayant intoxiqué les Parisiens";* Livois, 53.

31. Havelock, 167.

32. Cited, William Harlan Hale, 65.

33. For example, Matthias Shaaber, in his extensive study of early forms of printed news in England, says local news was "utterly neglected" in these publications; Shaaber, *Some Forerunners of the Newspaper in England*, 9; see also Steward, 21.

34. Modern editors and producers are aware, as Horace Greeley was, of the news value of proximity, but their audiences are drawn from too many different neighborhoods for them to consistently focus on any particular neighborhood.

35. Michelson, 13.

Chapter 4. News and Literacy—The First Story That Comes to Hand

1. Thucydides, I, 21.

2. Gurdon, 80.

3. Cicero, *Epistulae ad Familiares,* VIII, vii, 2.

4. Goody, 105.

5. See Goody, Ong, Havelock, and Stock.

6. McLuhan traces a related turn of mind—"detachment"—to literacy; McLuhan, 20.

7. Petronius refers to a crier of lost children; Brewster, 45.

8. See Havelock, 40, 185–187, 328–339; Innis, *Empire and Communications*, 81.

9. Havelock, 50. "Of the some three thousand languages . . . that exist today only some seventy-eight have a literature," notes Walter Ong; Ong. 7.

10. Jack Goody, "Alphabets and Writing," in Raymond Williams, 106–113.

11. Jack Goody, "Alphabets and Writing," in Raymond Williams, 106–126; Gordon, 153–156.

12. Gordon, 191–195.

13. Might parts of the Bible have originally served to spread news? One of the stronger possibilities is the Song of Deborah, an account of a victory over the Canaanites about the 12th or 13th century B.C. It appears to have been based on a contemporary composition. If the Hebrews had mastered writing by then (an open question), and if this account was written down at the time, it may have played some role in disseminating news of the battle; see Grant, 57.

14. Jack Goody, "Alphabets and Writing," in Raymond Williams, 117–118, 124.

15. Innis, *Empire and Communications*, 67–68.

16. Havelock, 185.

17. See Lanson, " 'Trust me' Journalism."

18. Herodotus, I, 1.

19. Thucydides, I, 22.

20. Plato, *Charmides,* translated by Rosamond Kent Sprague (Indianapolis: 1973), 57–58.

Chapter 5. News and Empire—The Thought Stream of the Group Mind

1. Cicero, *Epistulae ad Familiares,* XII, ix, I.

2. See Richard Taylor.

3. "Face to face interaction" is particularly effective in "creating and maintaining groups," notes Richard L. Meier in his study of communication and urban growth; Meier, 42.

4. Herbert Gans makes a similar point when he says, "The judgment that the president and leading public officials represent the nation . . . carries with it an acceptance of, if not a preference for, this state of affairs; otherwise, stories which investigate whether the president does, in fact, represent the nation would be more numerous"; Gans, 39.

5. Sapir.

6. See Rossi.

7. Borza.

8. Rossi, 15, 17.

9. Rossi, 43–45.

10. McLuhan credits the creation of a "social consciousness" variously to the press or to electronic communication; see McLuhan, 56, 64–65, 190–193, 218. But it must be much older. How can people be expected to share even the most primitive economies or politics without sharing an outlook, a set of interests, an awareness?

11. Cicero, *Epistulae ad Familiares,* II, ix, 1.

12. Cicero, *Epistulae ad Familiares,* II, viii, 1.

13. Cicero, *Epistulae ad Familiares,* II, iv, 1.

14. Cicero, *Epistulae ad Familiares,* VIII, i, 1.

15. Cicero, *Epistulae ad Familiares,* VIII, ii, 2.

16. Cicero, *Epistulae ad Familiares,* VIII, xi, 4.

17. Cicero, *Epistulae ad Familiares,* VIII, i, 1.

18. According to Evan T. Sage, these men, mostly Greeks, were called *"operarii"*; Sage, 203. The *Oxford Latin Dictionary* defines *compilationem* as "burglary";

the *Thesaurus Linguae Latinae,* as "compilation." See also Giffard, 107.

19. Giffard, 107–108.

20. Giffard, 107.

21. Suetonius, I, xx. J. V. Le Clerc, in his thorough though aged, study of the *acta,* reads this quote from Suetonius as suggesting that the *acta populi* were already being published; Le Clerc, *Des Journaux chez les Romains,* 197.

22. Giffard, 106.

23. Cicero, *Letters to Atticus,* VI, 2.

24. Giffard, 106.

25. Le Clerc includes the most complete collection of such references; *Des Journaux chez les Romains,* 375–421.

26. Cicero, *Epistulae ad Familiares,* XII, xxiii, 2.

27. Cicero, *Epistulae ad Familiares,* XII, viii, 1.

28. See Giffard, 109.

29. Jebb, 159–160.

30. Tacitus, XIII, xxxi.

31. Pliny, VIII, lxi, 145; X, ii, 5.

32. Cited, Giffard, 108.

33. Le Clerc, *Des Journaux chez les Romains,* 407–419.

34. Giffard, 132.

35. Starr, 117.

36. Giffard, 132.

37. Cicero, *Epistulae ad Familiares,* VIII, vii, 1.

38. Pliny, *Letters,* IX, 15, 3; cited, Giffard, 109.

39. Tacitus, XVI, xxii.

40. Giffard, 107–108. Dion-XLIV, ii; cited, Le Clerc, *Des Journaux chez les Romains,* 383.

41. See, for example, Schramm, 26–31.

42. The "Spring and Autumn Annals"—written compilations of information in China that date back even further, as early as the eighth century B.C.—appear to have had the recording of history rather than the dissemination of news as their purpose; see Ko. 22.

43. Lin, 14.

44. Ko, 23.

45. Lin, 15.

46. Ko, 23. Ko states that the *tipao* began during the Han; 24.

47. Lin, 14–16.

48. Ko, 24, 30, 63.

49. Lin, 11–16; see also Carter, 26–32.

50. Lin, 3.

51. Cited, Lin, 17–18.

52. Lin, 18–19, 77.

53. Warton, I, 44–46, 58, 331–335. See Hall, and Halliwell, *A Selection from the Minor Poems of Lydgate.*

54. Havelock, 339.

55. Carolingian script, for example, was originally developed late in the eighth century; it began establishing itself in the 11th and 12th centuries.

56. See Armstrong, 439–440; Weill, 15–16.

57. C. A. J. Armstrong, "A Present for a Prince: The Survival of a Newsletter," *Times,* London, May 23, 1936, 15–16. See Ünver.

58. Armstrong, 430–437.

59. Armstrong, 432; Kingsford, 174–176.

60. Reprinted, Bruce, 29–30.

61. "The courtiers also have so great a knowledge of our affairs, so that I could fancy myself at Rome"—the Milanese ambassador to England writing to the Duke of Milan, Sept. 8, 1497; Great Britain, Public Record Office, *Calendar of State Papers, Milan,* 323.

62. Bücher, 221.

63. Norman Davis, II, 189.

64. Norman Davis, II, 273.

65. Stapleton, 48.

66. Corti, 158–159.

67. *Diarri* of Marino Sanudo; cited, Sardella, 23.

68. Innis, *Empire and Communications,* 147.

69. Sardella, 29, 34.

70. A similar dependence by merchants on written news can be seen as late as the 19th century in the United States; see Pred, 81.

71. Klarwill, *The Fugger News-Letters,* xiii–xxviii; Matthews, 13–18.

72. Klarwill, *The Fugger News-Letters,* xx; and Klarwill, *The Fugger News-Letters, Second Series,* xii.

73. Klarwill, *The Fugger News-Letters,* 175. These selections are English translations of the German texts of Victor von Klarwill, who himself attempted to make the "mode of speech" in the letters less baffling to 20th-century readers. (Most of the original copies are in German or Italian.) These wordings, then, are two or more steps removed from the originals.

74. Klarwill, *The Fugger News-Letters,* 242–243.

75. See Klarwill, *The Fugger News-Letters,* 121–130; and Klarwill, *The Fugger News-Letters, Second Series,* 154–183.

76. The claim has been made that the letters were copied and sold; although this view has gained some currency (see Desmond, 24, or Kortepeter, 118), both Klarwill, *The Fugger News-Letters,* xvii, and Matthews, 16–18, following Kleinpaul, *Die Fuggerzeitungen, 1568–1605,* 6–8, dismiss it as unfounded.

77. Cited, Ravry, 32.

78. Schottenloher, 172–174.

79. Bücher, 229; see Klarwill, *The Fugger News-Letters,* xviii, and Kleinpaul, *Die Fuggerzeitungen,*

1568–1605, 107, for further discussion of the "ordinary" and the "extraordinary."

80. Klarwill, *The Fugger News-Letters,* xviii; and Kleinpaul, *Die Fuggerzeitungen, 1568–1605.* The Nuremberg merchants were Reiner Volckhardt and Florian von der Bruck, but the exact relationship between Crasser, Schiffle, these merchants and Fugger requires more investigation. Crasser and Schiffle are intriguing characters in the history of journalism. It is not clear whether they were relatively passive copyists with some correspondents who simply had the good fortune to become involved with the Fuggers or whether they were creative forces in the developments that would lead to the printed newspaper. Their enterprise provides a connection between the massive Fugger collection and one of the first weekly written-news services in Germany, and a potential connection to the introduction of the printed weeklies in German at the beginning of the next century. (Some of the newsletters collected by Reiner Volckhardt and Florian von der Bruck in Nuremberg—presumably from Crasser and Schiffle—have survived, and they appear to have circulated weekly; see chapter 9. Kleinpaul speculates that Schiffle may have turned to printing; Kleinpaul, *Die Fuggerzeitungen, 1568–1605,* 126.).

81. Armstrong, 441.

82. See Sardella, 16.

83. Sardella, 16.

84. Sardella, 53–54.

85. Klarwill, *The Fugger News-Letters,* xx–xxi.

Chapter 6. Controlling the News—The Undeceiving of the People

1. *The Anatomy of Melancholy* . . . ; cited, Nichols, IV, 37.

2. Jones, 295–303; and Foote, xx, 17; Wahlgren, 74.

3. Samuel Eliot Morison, 353–354, 357–358.

4. Samuel Eliot Morison, 375–376.

5. Samuel Eliot Morison, 340, 376–378.

6. Schulte, 67.

7. Columbus, "The Spanish Folio Letter."

8. Samuel Eliot Morison, 379.

9. Eames.

10. Cited, Eisenstein, 3.

11. Innis, *Empire and Communications,* 139; Henri-Jean Martin, "Printing," in Raymond Williams, 131; Warren Chappell, 8–16; see also Carter.

12. See Desmond, 21; Desmond is wrong, however, in suggesting that the Columbus letters were printed by this method.

13. Lent, 66–68.

14. Carter, 166.

15. Weill, 16–17; for dates on the progress of the printing press, see Henri-Jean Martin, "Printing," in Raymond Williams, 128–150.

16. McLuhan, 158.

17. Eisenstein, 46.

18. Armstrong, 430, 437; Bellanger, I, 34.

19. Stock, 13; Schwoerer, 857; see also Natalie Zemon Davis.

20. Samuel Eliot Morison, 379.

21. In a statement of purpose in the first issue of his newspaper, *Observator,* April 13, 1681; reprinted, Anthony Smith, *The Newspaper: An International History,* 43.

22. Great Britain, Public Record Office, *Calendar of State Papers, Foreign Series,* 1578–1579, July 19, 1578.

23. Columbus, "The Spanish Folio Letter."

24. Aston, 76.

25. See John R. Hale.

26. Shaaber, *Some Forerunners of the Newspaper in England,* 39.

27. Knightley, for example, begins his history of war correspondents with the Crimean War.

28. Seguin, "L'Information à la Fin du XVe Siècle en France," I, 319. That was the fate of many similarly ephemeral publications. According to the "law of bibliography," as outlined by Marshall McLuhan, "the more there were, the fewer there are"; McLuhan, 146–147.

29. Seguin "L'Information à la Fin du XVe Siècle en France," I, 310–311; see also Renata V. Shaw, 4.

30. Seguin, "L'Information à la Fin du XVe Siècle en France," I, 319–320; II, 53.

31. Seguin, "L'Information à la Fin du XVe Siècle en France," I, 320–327.

32. The citations are from Seguin, "L'Information à la Fin du XVe Siècle en France," I, 322–323.

33. Seguin, *L'Information en France, de Louis XII à Henri II,* 46.

34. Shaaber, *Some Forerunners of the Newspaper in England,* 41–42.

35. Shaaber, *Some Forerunners of the Newspaper in England,* 41–42.

36. Shaaber, "Forerunners of the Newspaper in America," 340.

37. Hester, 74; Gutiérrez.

38. Shaaber, *Some Forerunners of the Newspaper in England,* 56–57; for an example of the French King Charles IX's secret distribution of propaganda pamphlets in England, see Bakeless, 20.

39. Shaaber, *Some Forerunners of the Newspaper in England,* 35–64.

40. The early printing press, which would change little from the 15th through the 18th centuries, was sup-

ported by two thick upright pieces of wood (often braced to the ceiling). A sheet of paper was placed on top of the *bed*—a form containing the type. The bed moved along a horizontal platform, about desk high, until it was under a heavy platen. A large screw then lowered the platen, pressing the paper against the inked type; Henri-Jean Martin, "Printing," in Raymond Williams, 132–133; Warren Chappell, 53–57.

41. Siebert, *Freedom of the Press in England,* 98–100.

42. Chief Justice Holt of the Court of King's Bench, 1704; cited, Siebert, *Four Theories of the Press,* 24.

43. Siebert, *Freedom of the Press in England,* 34–39.

44. Shaaber, *Some Forerunners of the Newspaper in England,* 45–48; Du Maurier, 16–17.

45. Schulte, 68–69.

46. Siebert, *Freedom of the Press in England,* 49, 56–63, 67, 71–74.

47. The Edict of Worms is reprinted in De Lamar Jensen, 75–111.

48. Kortepeter, 115–116, 122.

49. Bellanger, I, 65.

50. Bellanger, I, 64–65; Siebert, *Freedom of the Press in England,* 58, 88–89.

51. Shaaber, *Some Forerunners of the Newspaper in England,* 66.

52. Pottinger, 79.

53. Shaaber, *Some Forerunners of the Newspaper in England,* 76–77.

54. Cited, Göllner, I, 175.

55. Cited, Göllner, I, 338.

56. See Göllner, II, 303–305.

57. *The true Report of all the successe of Famagosta* . . . , translated by William Malin (1572).

58. Göllner, I, 241–242; II, 121–122, 154, 269–270, 273–274, 382, 482.

59. Matthias Shaaber suggests that military defeats might only be covered in print if, as was the case with Famagusta, they demonstrated the cruelty of the enemy; Shaaber, *Some Forerunners of the Newspaper in England,* 184. "Bad news" appears to have fared somewhat better in histories, as in this English publication from 1600: *The historie of the troubles of Hungarie: containing the pitifull losse and ruine of that Kingdome and the Warres happened there, in that time, between the Christians and Turkes;* cited, Göllner, II, 719.

60. Seguin, *L'Information en France, de Louis XII à Henri II,* 30, 83–84.

61. Charles Firth, "Ballads and Broadsides," 522. Shaaber notes that there is some reason to believe that epitaphs for Essex were printed but immediately sup-

pressed; none survive; Shaaber, *Some Forerunners of the Newspaper in England,* 33, 123.

62. Shaaber, *Some Forerunners of the Newspaper in England,* 168–172, 184.

63. This pamphlet was printed in six languages in 1596; Shaaber, *Some Forerunners of the Newspaper in England,* 44.

64. Shaaber, *Some Forerunners of the Newspaper in England,* 107–108.

65. Shaaber, *Some Forerunners of the Newspaper in England,* 35.

66. Thomas Deloney, *A joyful new Ballad, declaring the happie obtaining of the great Galleazzo* . . . (London: 1588).

67. In fairness, poetry has lost most of its ability to compete for the news in the more developed societies now that newspapers and broadcast newscasts transmit prose accounts with such speed. Those few topical songs or poems composed today are vehicles more for agitation or celebration than for news. (The commentaries in verse written by the CBS Radio newscaster Charles Osgood are an exception to this rule: Osgood frequently succeeds in forming the news of the day into lively rhymes.).

68. Neuburg, 24; Rollins, "The Black-Letter Broadside Ballad," 258. They are called *black-letter* ballads because of the dense Gothic type the printers used.

69. Samuel Eliot Morison, 379.

70. *"Qui ne rimait pas à cette époque?"*—Seguin *L'Information en France, de Louis XII à Henri II,* 24–25.

71. Rollins, "The Black-Letter Broadside Ballad," 333, 338.

72. Cited, Rollins, "The Black-Letter Broadside Ballad," 308.

73. Sheavyn, 72–73; ballad makers are accused with such frequency of showing an untoward affection for ale and wine that it may have been true; Rollins, "The Black-Letter Broadside Ballad," 299.

74. There is one piece of evidence that William Shakespeare tried his hand at the composition of news ballads and produced a "song" or two on the Spanish armada; see Halliwell, *A Discovery that Shakespeare Wrote One or More Ballads or Poems on the Spanish Armada,* 22–23. No news ballads attributed to Shakespeare have survived.

75. Cited, Mann, xii. Lawlis, xxiii, maintains that the mention of "Norwich" here is based on a misquoting of Nash.

76. Robert Greene in 1592; cited, Mann, viii.

77. Mann, viii, xxxvii. Deloney also wrote fiction, in prose, and these long, relatively well-constructed tales

earn him a place, alongside so many later journalists, in the history of the novel; see Mann, xiv–xxxi.

78. The poet and the printer might not have worked quite that quickly; however, it is possible that the printer registered the ballad before it was actually complete.

79. Neale, 103–106; Michael Lewis, 195; Mattingly, 349–350.

80. Reprinted, Mann, 474–478.

81. See Mattingly, 343–344.

82. See Michael Lewis, 173–175; and Mattingly, 328–329.

83. Mann, ix; Lawlis, xxviii–xxix.

84. Reprinted, Mann, 479–482.

Chapter 7. Human Interests *(Faits Divers)*—Such a Deal of Wonder

1. Phillip Massinger, *The Bondman,* edited by Benjamin Townley Spencer (Princeton: 1932), 159.

2. See McLuhan, 157, for example.

3. McLuhan was not unaware of this characteristic of typography; see McLuhan, 147.

4. Cited, *Observer,* London, Aug. 5, 1984.

5. It is not clear to what extent the reputation—if known—of an individual printer, bookseller, or author might have contributed to the sales of a pamphlet or broadside.

6. Cited, Bennett, 135.

7. Seguin, *L'Information en France Avant le Périodique,* 15.

8. The term *faits divers*—literally, "diverse acts" or "diverse facts"—is used broadly here, as it is used by the bibliographer J. P. Seguin, as a name for news that appeals to readers not because the events it describes are of any obvious historical consequence, but because they are particularly unusual or have a particular emotional appeal; see Seguin, *L'Information en France Avant le Périodique,* 65–66. In French journalism today the term is sometimes used more narrowly to refer to a series of brief reports on relatively trivial events.

9. Shaaber, *Some Forerunners of the Newspaper in England,* 138.

10. Mann, xxxvi–xxxvii.

11. Shaaber, *Some Forerunners of the Newspaper in England,* 40.

12. Rollins, "The Black-Letter Broadside Ballad," 295.

13. Klarwill, *The Fugger News-Letters, Second Series,* xv.

14. *The Winter's Tale,* V, ii, 25–27.

15. Alexander, 159, 210; Shaaber, *Some Forerunners of the Newspaper in England,* 23.

16. The *solemynities and triumphes doon and made at the spousell and mariage of the kyng daughter* . . . (London: 1590).

17. The diplomatic discussions that took place upon the occasion of the wedding were described by this newsbook in terms whose vagueness should be familiar to followers of reports on 20th century diplomacy: ". . . they had longe contynued and talked of and upon many great and weyghty matiers. . . ."

18. *The noble tryumphaunt coronacyon of quene Anne Wyfe unto the moost noble kyng Henry the viii* (London: 1533).

19. Seguin, *L'Information en France, de Louis XII à Henri II,* 98.

20. The word *obituary* was used to refer to death notices in English newspapers as early as the 18th century; *Oxford English Dictionary.*

21. Shaaber, *Some Forerunners of the Newspaper in England,* 24. Prince Henry appears to have been a partisan of the anti-Catholic, pro-war forces in the country, and that may have affected coverage of these events; see Christopher Hill, "The Man Who Should Be King," *New York Review of Books,* Oct. 23, 1986.

22. *The History of the Tryall of Chevalry;* reprinted, Arthur H. Bullen, ed., *A Collection of Old English Plays,* III, (New York: 1964) 312.

23. Shaaber, *Some Forerunners of the Newspaper in England,* 28–29.

24. There may also have been a political element in the attention devoted to Sidney, who was, like Prince Henry, associated with efforts to involve Britain in the religious wars on the Continent; see Christopher Hill, "The Man Who Should Be King," *New York Review of Books,* Oct. 23, 1986.

25. Shaaber, *Some Forerunners of the Newspaper in England,* 32.

26. Marshburn, *Murder and Witchcraft in England,* 156.

27. Samuel D. Warren, 196.

28. *New York Times,* Nov. 27, 1985.

29. *Antony and Cleopatra,* V. 2, 214–215; Rollins, "The Black-Letter Broadside Ballad," 278.

30. Samuel D. Warren, 196.

31. Marshburn, *Murder and Witchcraft in England,* 154–168. *The five Years of King James* . . . (1643); reprinted, *Harleian Miscellany,* VII, 407–449.

32. Marshburn, *Murder and Witchcraft in England,* 158.

33. See Erikson, 14.

34. Seguin, *L'Information en France, de Louis XII à Henri II,* 31; and see Seguin, *L'Information en France Avant le Périodique.*

35. Shaaber, *Some Forerunners of the Newspaper in England,* 141.

36. Shaaber, *Some Forerunners of the Newspaper in England,* 142–143.

37. Gardiner, II, 338–344. Charles Firth, "The Ballad History of the Reign of James I," 43.

38. See Stephens, "Crime Doesn't Pay, Except on the Newsstands."

39. Richard Niccols, *Sir Thomas Overbury's Vision . . .* (1616); reprinted, *Harleian Miscellany,* VII, 178–188.

40. Charles Firth, "Ballads and Broadsides," 530–531.

41. Thomas Deloney, *The Lamentation of Mr. Pages Wife . . .* (1591); reprinted, Mann, 482–485.

42. J. A. Sharpe, 42–43.

43. Seguin, *L'Information en France Avant le Périodique,* 31.

44. J. A. Sharpe, 43.

45. Seguin, *L'Information en France Avant le Périodique,* 66n.

46. *Histoire admirable d'un faux et supposé mari, advenue en Languedoc l'an 1560;* reprinted, Fournier, VIII, 99–118. The dramatic possibilities of this story were explored again in 1983 in a French film, *The Return of Martin Guerre.*

47. Stephens, "Crime Doesn't Pay, Except on the Newsstands."

48. *The crying Murther: Contayning the cruell and most horrible Butcher of Mr. Trat;* reprinted, Marshburn, *Blood and Knavery,* 40–57.

49. Cited, Philip Elliott, "Professional Ideology and Organizational Change: The Journalist Since 1800," in Boyce, 180; John Pauly has noted how the pejorative term *sensationalism* is used by journalists to "fix the boundaries of normal journalism" and "affirm the high moral standing" of their own profession; Pauly.

50. The confusion between attacks on subject matter and treatment is noted in Stevens, 53.

51. J. A. Sharpe, 41.

52. Samuel Eliot Morison, 380.

53. Seguin, *L'Information en France Avant le Périodique,* 30.

54. *Murder upon Murder;* reprinted, Marshburn, *Blood and Knavery,* 65–73; see also Marshburn, *Murder and Witchcraft in England,* after page 164.

55. Rollins, "The Black-Letter Broadside Ballad," 285–286.

56. J. A. Sharpe, 42.

57. Darnton, *The Literary Underground of the Old Regime,* 200–201.

58. *Murder upon Murder;* reprinted, Marshburn, *Blood and Knavery,* 65–73; see also Marshburn, *Murder and Witchcraft in England,* after page 164.

59. Seguin, *L'Information en France Avant le Périodique,* 28, 30n.

60. Reprinted, Marshburn, *Murder and Witchcraft in England,* after page 164.

61. *Murder upon Murder,* reprinted, Marshburn, *Blood and Knavery,* 65–73, see also Marshburn, *Murder and Witchcraft in England,* after page 164.

62. Gummere, xxiv.

63. See J. A. Sharpe, "Enforcing the Law in the Seventeenth-Century English Village," in Gatrell, 99–100.

64. See Salgādo, 11.

65. For a discussion of the extent of social and economic changes and the attendant threat to public order in the 14th and 15th centuries, see Bellamy, 1.

66. *The Bloudy booke, or the Tragicall and desperate end of Sir John Fites (alias) Fitz;* reprinted, Halliwell, *Murder Narratives,* 25–26, 32.

67. The quote begins: "The death of a great man or the burning of a house furnish him with an argument, and the nine muses are out strait in mourning gowns, and Melpomene cries fire! fire!" John Earle, *Microcosmographie* (1628); cited, Charles Firth, "Ballads and Broadsides," 519n.

68. *Le Vray Discours d'une des plus Grandes Cruaultez qui ait esté veuë de nostre temps, avenue àu Royaulme de Naples* (Paris: 1577).

69. Seguin, *L'Information en France Avant le Périodique,* 56.

70. George Mannington, *Sorrowfull Sonet made at Cambridge Castle* (1576); cited, Charles Firth, "Ballads and Broadsides," 531–532.

71. Cited, Waage, 735–736.

72. *Luke Huttons lamentation: which he wrote the day before his death* (London: 1598).

73. Daniel Defoe, *Moll Flanders* (New York: 1978), 30.

74. *Two horrible and inhumane Murders done in Lincolnshire,* reprinted, Halliwell, *Murder Narratives,* 54–55.

75. Jean Harris, a headmistress, shot Dr. Herman Tarnower in March 1980.

76. *True and Wonderfull. A Discourse relating a strange and monstrous Serpent . . . ;* reprinted, *Harleian Miscellany,* III, 109–112.

77. Stephens, *Broadcast News,* 161.

78. *Times* headlines included such phrases as: . . . BROKEN RED ARMY and RED RULE TOTTERS . . . ; Lippmann, "A Test of the News."

79. The article, written by Janet Cooke, appeared in 1980 and was exposed shortly after it was awarded a Pulitzer Prize in 1981; see Goldstein, 28–29.

80. Sir Henry Waller; cited, Anthony Smith, *The Newspaper: An International History,* 34–36.

81. Cited, Tebbel, *The Compact History of the American Newspaper,* 199.

82. "Code of Broadcast News Ethics: Radio-Television News Directors Association"; as of 1981.

83. Seguin, *L'Information en France Avant le Périodique,* 20, 71.

84. Shaaber, *Some Forerunners of the Newspaper in England,* 152, 156.

85. The complete title: *True and Wonderfull. A Discourse relating a strange and monstrous Serpent (or Dragon) lately discovered, and yet living, to the great Annoyance and divers Slaughters both of men and Cattell, by his strong and violent Poyson: In Sussex, two Miles from Horsam, in a Woode called St. Leonard's Forrest, and thirtie Miles from London, this present Month of August, 1614. With the true Generation of Serpents.* (London: 1614); reprinted, *Harleian Miscellany,* III, 109–112.

86. Reprinted, Lilly, 27–30.

87. Shaaber, *Some Forerunners of the Newspaper in England,* 152.

88. Marshburn, *Blood and Knavery,* 74–75.

89. Thomas Potts, *The Wonderfull Discoverie of Witches in the Countie of Lancaster* (London: 1613).

90. *The Apprehension and Confession of Three Notorious Witches* (1589); reprinted, Marshburn, *Blood and Knavery,* 87.

91. Paisey, 62.

92. *Discours et Interprétation sur L'Apparition Merveilleuse de Trois Soleils sur la Ville de Marseille* (Paris: 1635); reprinted, Claudin.

93. Seguin, *L'Information en France Avant le Périodique,* 41.

94. Rollins, "The Black-Letter Broadside Ballad," 267.

95. Shaaber, *Some Forerunners of the Newspaper in England,* 147.

96. Febvre, *A New Kind of History,* 191.

97. Neuburg, 78. King James I himself wrote a treatise on witches; Christopher Hill, 3.

98. Hellman.

99. Charles Firth, "Ballads and Broadsides," 534.

100. Seguin, *L'Information en France Avant le Périodique,* 48–53.

101. *Pride's fall: or a warning to all English women . . .* (1609); reprinted, Clark, 133–139.

102. Clitus-Alexandrinus, 17.

103. *A Declaration of the Demeanor and Cariage of Sir Walter Raleigh . . .* (London: 1618).

104. Seguin, *L'Information en France Avant le Périodique,* 21, 22n, 124; *Discours merveilleux d'un juif, lequel va errant . . .* (1617).

105. *True and Wonderfull. A Discourse relating a strange and monstrous Serpent . . .* ; reprinted, *Harleian Miscellany,* III, 109–112.

106. Febvre, *A New Kind of History,* 192; James, 15.

107. Shaaber, *Some Forerunners of the Newspaper in England,* 152–154.

108. *The Winter's Tale,* IV, iv, 276–284.

109. Shaaber, *Some Forerunners of the Newspaper in England,* 137.

110. Cited, Waters. The *Enquirer* is apparently oblivious to our presumed increased "awareness of the impossible."

111. *Sun,* June 30, 1984; June 22, 1984.

112. See Hughes, "The Social Interpretation of News," 14.

113. Gans, 308, makes a related argument.

114. A subscription card enclosed in the *New Yorker* magazine, Jan. 6, 1986, reads: "Separate yourself from the crowd. Subscribe to *The New Yorker.*"

115. There is also evidence that the economic gap between the classes, at least in rural England, was widening in those years; see J. A. Sharpe, "Enforcing the Law in the Seventeenth- Century English Village," in Gatrell, 99–100.

116. Crane, 165–167.

117. Renata V. Shaw, 3.

118. This tendency would be exaggerated when a variety of alternative *periodical* publications—including newspapers and even the first scientific journals— began appearing in the 17th century.

119. Cited, Innis, *Empire and Communications,* 150.

120. Phillip Stubbs, *Anatomy of Abuses* (1583), edited by Frederick J. Furnivall (London: 1879), 171; Jonson, 406.

121. Clitus-Alexandrinus, 19.

122. Cited, Rollins, "The Black-Letter Broadside Ballad," 314n.

123. Cited, Seguin, *L'Information en France Avant le Périodique,* 23.

124. The Metropolitan Opera musician Helen Hagnes was killed in July 1980; the Radcliffe graduate Caroline Isenberg in December 1984; and Dr. Herman Tarnower in March 1980.

125. Peter Burke makes this point in his discussion of early modern Europe: "The elite participated in the little tradition, but the common people did not participate in the great tradition." Burke, 28.

126. Cicero, *Epistulae ad Familiares,* VIII, vii, 2.

127. Waugh, "News of the False Messiah," 308.

128. Steffens, 179–186; and Hughes, "The Social Interpretation of News," 11.

129. See Bakeless. Printed news reports on the shipwreck of Sir Thomas Gates and his expedition to Virginia may have helped inspire *The Tempest; see Newes from Virginia. The lost Flocke Triumphant;* reprinted, Alexander Brown, I, 420–426.

130. Rollins, "The Black-Letter Broadside Ballad," 335.

131. John Rous; cited, Rollins, "The Black-Letter Broadside Ballad," 336.

132. Rollins, "The Black-Letter Broadside Ballad," 336–337.

Chapter 8. The Logic of News *(Faits Isolés)*—People Biting Dogs

1. "Snow," *Vanity Fair,* September 1983.

2. See Rollins, "The Black-Letter Broadside Ballad," 283; Neuburg, 24n.

3. One of which was also printed in Latin, and one of which was printed abroad.

4. See Arber, III, 580–599. (In determining which titles to label news publications for this list, I have, where possible, used Shaaber as a guide; some of the decisions on which publications to include or exclude in this list—often based only on titles—are arguable; however the addition, or subtraction, of a few publications would not affect my point here.). See also Shaaber, *Some Forerunners of the Newspaper in England,* 23, 26, 45, 90, 134, 142–143, 150, 243, 251, 272. In 1606, for another example, 27 news publications were registered with the Stationers—six of which were on the arrest of some traitors, five on the pomp surrounding the visit of the king of Denmark to England—but in general their subject matter appears similar to that of this selection of newsbooks and news ballads from 1616.

5. A number of sermons were registered in 1616, including some occasioned by funerals. If these contained any news of the life or death of the deceased, then "Master Thomas Dutton" and "Ladie Anne Glover wife to Sir Thomas Glover Ambassador to Constantinople"—two subjects of printed funeral sermons that year—might qualify as exceptions to this rule.

6. *A mourneful Dittie, entituled Elizabeth's losse, together with a welcome for King James;* cited, Ingleby, I, 124; there are a few other references to the playwright or his plays in contemporary poems or prose, but their content or their method of publication indicate that they did not serve to spread news; see, for example, Ingleby, I, 24, 46, 50.

7. Ingleby, I, xxvi–xxvii.

8. Shaaber, *Some Forerunners of the Newspaper in England,* 22.

9. Charles Firth, "Ballads and Broadsides," 519–520; Shaaber reports that this and a second news ballad on the fire were registered the very next day; *Some Forerunners of the Newspaper in England,* 163.

10. *Henry IV, Part II,* IV, iii, 45–50.

11. Matthews, 19, see also Klarwill, *The Fugger News-Letters,* xxxi.

12. Such a tendency to confuse news with reality is common, especially among journalists themselves. Note, for example, the assumption behind this statement from a Sept. 26, 1984, *New York Times* editorial celebrating the success of the Chicago Cubs: "New Yorkers . . . can applaud the fact that something is going right in Chicago. Its citizens, troubled by corruption probes and rancorous political rivalries, deserve some good news." Is it not possible that things unnoticed by the *New York Times* had previously been going right in Chicago? One hesitates to underestimate the importance of baseball, but is the mood of the citizenry in fact inexorably tied to the local political scandals that preoccupy journalists?.

13. Darnton, "Writing News and Telling Stories," 192.

14. Shaaber, *Some Forerunners of the Newspaper in England,* 9; see also Gans, 15.

15. Cited, Shaaber, *Some Forerunners of the Newspaper in England,* 243.

16. *Discours emerveillable contenant la vie d'une Jeune Damoiselle Flamande, native de Mons en Hainaut, quie fuiant le mauvais voulloir de son Pere . . . ;* cited, Seguin, *L'Information en France Avant le Périodique,* 32, 70.

17. *La grande cruaute et Tyrannie. Exercee en la ville d'Arras . . . Par un jeune Gantil-homme et une Damoiselle Frere et Soeur on commis inseste . . . ;* cited, Seguin, *L'Information en France Avant le Périodique,* 32–33, 77.

18. Gans, 156.

19. (London: 1684); reprinted, *Harleian Miscellany,* VI, 402–404.

20. Seguin, *L'Information en France Avant le Périodique,* 48.

21. Gans, 92.

22. In this bias journalists have been remarkably consistent: In one typical month in Houston in 1973, for example, the most common crime, according to police reports, was larceny, but larceny received no coverage in Houston's two daily newspapers that month. Instead, almost all the crime stories in those two papers that month

involved a murder or a justifiable homicide. Police reports, however, showed murder to be the least common crime in Houston: only 0.24 percent of all reported crimes that month were murders; Antunes.

23. J. A. Sharpe, 33–41. There is also evidence of a class bias in this lack of attention to murders of servants and apprentices (though the conviction rates were extremely low), a bias perhaps similar to that expressed in the disproportionately small amount of attention given in the United States in the 20th century to the murders of blacks; see Stephens, "Crime Doesn't Pay, Except on the Newsstands."

24. See Antunes.

25. *Description du Serpent Monstrueux et Espouventable* . . . (Paris: 1576); *Du Serpent ou Dragon Volant* . . . (Paris: 1579).

26. Seguin, *L'Information en France Avant le Périodique*, 13, 85.

27. Rollins, "The Black-Letter Broadside Ballad," 263. Twentieth-century newspapers have been known to make use of a similar convenience—stock photographs.

28. For example, *Briefz discours d'un merveilleus monstre né a Esrigo* . . . (1578) or *Discours prodigieux et veritable, D'un monstre né pres de Franc-Fort* . . . (1606); cited, Seguin, *L'Information en France Avant le Périodique*, 91–92, 121–123.

29. Reprinted, Mann, 468–478.

30. *Histoire lamentable, d'une jeune damoiselle fille du Chastellain de Bourg en Bresse, condamnée à mort au Parlement de Dijon, menée au supplice, et miraculeusement sauvée* . . . (Paris: 1625); reprinted, Seguin, *L'Information en France Avant le Périodique*, 33–34, 78.

31. Darnton, "Writing News and Telling Stories," 190–191; he has apparently re-created this draft of the bike story from memory.

32. Darnton, "Writing News and Telling Stories," 191.

33. *Histoire Admirable et prodigieuse d'un Pere & d'une Mere qui ont assassiné leur propre fils sans congnoistre. Arrivée en la ville de Nismes en Languedoc, au mois d'Octobre dernier,* 1618 (Paris: 1618).

34. Darnton, "Writing News and Telling Stories," 189; see also Camus' Play *Malentendu*.

35. Darnton, "Writing News and Telling Stories," 189. For another illustration of Darnton's point, see Neuburg, 69–73.

36. *A dolefull ditty of five unfortunat persons that were drowned in their drunknes in crossing over the Thames neare Ivy Bridge* . . . ; reprinted, Clark, 67–71.

37. Lippmann, "Two Revolutions in the American Press," 438; Gans, 167–168. Lippmann is criticizing the

authors of "Human interest stories," Gans journalists in general.

38. *A dolefull ditty of five unfortunat persons that were downed in their drunknes in crossing over the Thames neare Ivy Bridge* . . . ; reprinted, Clark, 67–71.

39. *A dolefull ditty of five unfortunat persons that were drowned in their drunknes in crossing over the Thames neare Ivy Bridge* . . . ; reprinted, Clark, 67–71.

40. Liebling, 226–250.

41. "The order of explanation runs as follows," explains James Carey in a study of contemporary journalism: "If you can find a motive, state it; if you can't find a motive, search for a cause; if you can't find a motive or a cause, look for consequences; if you can find none of the above, read the tea leaves of the event for its significance"; James Carey, "Why and How? The Dark Continent of American Journalism," in Manoff, 172.

42. Seguin, *L'Information en France, de Louis XII à Henri II,* 30.

43. Cited, Seguin, *L'Information en France Avant le Périodique,* 53.

44. Barthes, 185–195.

Chapter 9. The First Newspapers—Expecting the News

1. One of the early English newspapers, published by Nathaniel Butter, March 19, 1624; cited, Shaaber, "The History of the First English Newspaper," 581–582.

2. The newspapers eventually adopted by the rest of the world would be modeled on or at least strongly influenced by the European newspaper. Missionaries' journals and foreign-language publications in Shanghai and Hong Kong in the 19th century helped introduce modern journalism to China. What may qualify as the first Japanese-language newspaper—*Batavia Shimbum*, begun in 1861—was modeled on a Dutch newspaper; Lent, 34–36, 65–66; Lin, 78–80. See also Anthony Smith, *The Newspaper: An International History,* 14–15.

3. Weill, 20–21. The earliest newspapers often withheld mention of the city in which they were printed in an effort to forestall complaints to their local governments from other governments; see Baschwitz, 102. It had been believed that this second set of newsbooks from 1609 had been printed in Augsburg, but more recent research has pointed to Wolfenbüttel; see Lindemann, 92–93. The first surviving issue of the Strasbourg paper includes an introduction; the first surviving issue of the Wolfenbüttel paper does not—an indication that issues of that

paper may have been printed before 1609; see Heide, 15, 24.

4. One widely used definition adds some additional qualifications to the list presented here; see Edwin Emery, 6, who cites Allen, who in turn cites Groth. These qualifications seem unhelpful.

5. Weill, 21–22; Allen, 313–315; copies of the early weekly printed by Lucas Schulte are reproduced in Heide.

6. The term "newes paper" appears in a letter dated Sept. 10, 1670; Alfred F. Robbins, "The Earliest Newspaper of English News," *Times Literary Supplement,* April 23, 1925, 284.

7. Weill, 21–22; Allen, 315–316, features a slightly different list of dates. Some still maintain that Abraham Verhoeven's *Nieuwe Tydinghen* was published periodically in Antwerp as early as 1605; however, the introduction to a collection of the newssheets printed in Ghent in 1899 makes a strong case for this later date; see Verhoeven.

8. In a draft memorandum, probably written in 1621; cited, Herd, 12n.

9. Bellanger, I, 80; Castronovo, 20; Schulte, 74.

10. Weill, 19–20; Muddiman, *A History of English Journalism,* 11–12.

11. Half-yearly publications were timed to coincide with the fairs, weekly publications with the weekly posts. Monthly publication, lacking fairs or posts to establish a rhythm, may have been skipped; Bücher, 238.

12. Fledgling weeklies that managed to stay out of the path of the armies were also helped by the outbreak of the Thirty Years War in 1618. That struggle, centered in Germany between Protestant and Catholic forces, provided, as all wars do, the double blessing of ready news and eager readers.

13. In *The Newspaper: An International History,* Anthony Smith gives these Venetian publications less than a sentence, 26; Desmond devotes about the same amount of space to them, 25; the authors of the standard American journalism history textbook, Edwin and Michael Emery, do not mention them, nor do Folkerts and Teeter.

14. McNeill, 123–146.

15. Sardella, 14.

16. Ancel, 119, 159–160.

17. Some historians have implied that they were printed; see "Origin of Newspapers," *Notes and Queries,* 4th ser., IV (Sept. 4, 1869), 191; but more commonly they are conceded to have been handwritten. Some report that they appeared monthly; "Gazette," *Notes and Queries,* 8th ser., IX (May 2, 1896), 347–348. Some that they were distributed *daily* and as early as 1536; Kortepeter, 117; see also *Encyclopedia Italiana* XVII (1933), 184.

18. The etymology of the word *gazette* is hashed over in Hatin, *Bibliographie Historique et Critique de la Presse Périodique Française,* xlvii–xlix; and in *Notes and Queries,* 3rd ser., I, 365; 4th ser., IV, 191–192, 256–257, 468, 569, V, 263; 8th ser., IX, 347–348, 492–493. Whatever its derivation, by 1596 this Italian word was being used as far away as England as a name for collections of current information; see "Origin of Newspapers," *Notes and Queries,* 4th ser., IV (Sept. 4, 1869), 191.

19. Cited, Ravry, 26. However, Voltaire appears to have gotten the dates wrong: He places the invention of the gazette in Venice at the beginning of the 17th century.

20. D'Israeli, I, 224. D'Israeli believed the *gazetta* to have been monthlies, published by the government.

21. Bongi, 315–326.

22. Often pages or half pages at the end are left blank; a typical page is about 19 $\frac{1}{2}$ centimeters wide and 28 $\frac{1}{2}$ centimeters long.

23. A letter dated March 7, 1547, from Edmond Harvel, apparently an English agent in Venice, to the Earl of Hertford, the lord protector, in London included an enclosure in Italian, headed "di Roma nel 26 di Febraro" and reporting on the Council of Trent and on hopes, following the death of Henry VIII, "that the Kingdom of England may return to the ancient obedience of this Holy See." This enclosure is the earliest of the Venetian newssheets in the Public Record Office. It differs from the others only in that it includes news originating in only one city—Rome; see Great Britain, Public Record Office, *Calendar of State Papers, Foreign Series,* 1547–1553, under March 7, 1547.

24. In letters sent "to the council" in England by another English agent in Venice, Peter Vannes, between May 23 and Dec. 5, 1551; see Great Britain, Public Record Office, *Calendar of State Papers, Foreign Series,* 1547–1553, under the following dates in 1551: May 23, June 11, June 21, July 9, July 18, July 24, Aug. 28, Sept. 12, Oct. 10, Nov. 13, Dec. 5; and for the letters from Augsburg: August 4 and Oct. 20. The Oct. 20 letter from Augsburg features news from Rome dated Sept. 26.

25. The newssheet accompanying Vannes's letter of July 18, 1551, was unusual in that it displayed a title of sorts, written at the top of the first page in the same hand as the rest of the sheet: "*Diversi avisi da piu bande.*" "*Avisi,*" it should be noted, appears also to have been used as a term for the *private* diplomatic and business intelligence that was flowing out of Venice in these years; see Ancel and Houtte.

26. Great Britain, Public, Record Office, *Calendar of State Papers, Foreign Series,* 1566–1568, under Sept. 28, 1566.

27. Great Britain, Public Record Office, *Calendar of State Papers, Foreign Series,* 1566–1568, under: May 4, 1566; this translation is by Donna J. Klick.

28. These newssheets from 1566 are not filed with diplomatic letters; they can be found listed separately in Great Britain, Public Record Office, *Calendar of State Papers, Foreign Series,* 1566–1568, under the dates March 9, March 16, March 23, "[April]," April 9, April 16, April 20, April 30, May 4 and May 13. Evidence that these sheets originated in Venice includes the fact that the sheets were always written in Italian, that they contained news from everywhere but Venice and that they so closely resemble the newssheets forwarded from Venice by Vannes in 1551. A look through the *Calendar of State Papers, Foreign Series* for this period has turned up no evidence of similar unsigned newssheets in other languages or with other apparent origins.

29. Sufficient evidence to make the case has not been preserved in London, but these newssheets may even have been distributed regularly as early as 1551.

30. There is some evidence that some such Italian newssheets may have found their way to a printing press; an Italian publication at the British Library, *Diversi Avisi de le cose Piu notabili seguite nouamente in Transilvania & Ongaria circa li grã combattiment che a fatte il s. Lazaro Suendi con la prefa de dua fortezze . . .,* printed at Padua in 1567, looks intriguing, for example. However, there is no evidence that they were regularly printed.

31. Allen, 311; Edwin Emery, 6.

32. Hatin, *Histoire Politique et Littéraire de la Presse,* I, 4; see also Weill, viii, 16.

33. Interview conducted by the author with the French journalism historian François Moureau, June 5, 1984.

34. Stanley Morison, *The English Newspaper,* 47–48. The importance of handwritten newsletters in the early history of the newspaper can be seen in the career of Henry Muddiman, writer of a handwritten newsletter in England "sent to subscribers all over the country." In 1665 Muddiman was selected to found a printed newspaper, the *Oxford Gazette,* which became the *London Gazette*—the dominant English newspaper of the second half of the 17th century; Anthony Smith, *The Newspaper: An International History,* 42–44; Muddiman, *A History of English Journalism,* 176–193. The first successful American newspaper, the *Boston News-Letter,* grew out of a handwritten newsletter, and it is worth noting that at least one printed London newspaper, *Dawk's*

News-Letter, was consciously designed to imitate the look of handwritten newsletters; see Anthony Smith, *The Newspaper: An International History,* 54.

35. April 20, May 4, and May 11 (under May 13 in the *Calendar*), 1566, for example; see Great Britain, Public Record Office, *Calendar of State Papers, Foreign Series,* 1566–1568, under these dates.

36. Hatin, in his *Bibliographie Historique et Critique de la Presse Périodique Française,* xlvii–xlviii, passes on the argument that the Venetian government was too suspicious to allow public distribution of news and that the handwritten sheets never circulated beyond the patricians, but Bongi, who seems to believe in a wider circulation, explains that the Venetian newssheets were cautious and that the Republic was able to keep them under control; Bongi, 315.

37. Castronovo, 10.

38. Bongi, 314–321.

39. Cited, Bongi, 315–317.

40. See Werner, 21, 26–27.

41. Opel, 9–19; Kleinpaul has established that the news Opel says was written for the Nuremberg merchants Reiner Volckhardt and Florian von der Bruck originated with Crasser and Schiffle; Klarwill, *The Fugger News-Letters,* xxi.

42. See Stolp, 3, 35–36, 49–51, and especially the facsimiles on 34 and 50.

43. Heide, 15.

44. *Avisa Relation ober Zeitung . . . ,* Jan. 15, 1609; reprinted, Heide, after page 36.

45. There are tempting social and political explanations for the rapid development of the printed newspaper in the 17th century. (Anthony Smith, for example, notes that religious wars stimulated the demand for news in the early 17th century and that the growth of cities stimulated interest in public affairs; Anthony Smith, *The Newspaper: An International History,* 17–18.) Without discounting such factors entirely, however, it seems more accurate to view the printed weekly as having grown organically out of 16th century *journalistic* developments: printed newsbooks and news ballads, printed monthlies and, perhaps of most importance, handwritten weeklies.

46. Here and elsewhere in this chapter it is important to remember that "oldest surviving" does not necessarily equal "first." The bibliographer Folke Dahl estimates that only .013 percent of the copies of these periodic news publications have survived and been located, and he explains that we have at least one copy of only 349 of the perhaps 1,000–1,200 issues of English newspapers that were printed between 1620 and 1642; Dahl, *A Bibliography of English Corantos and Periodical News-*

books, 22–23. Earlier issues may have been printed without copies having survived. On the other hand, it seems unlikely that a printed newspaper could have been published in England with any regularity for any period of time before 1620 without having left any evidence of its existence.

47. A facsimile of the back page of this publication appears in Frank, *The Beginnings of the English Newspaper,* after page 194.

48. *Coranto* and its cognates have been used to refer to newssheets and newspapers in many different countries. The term, like the related English word *current,* may have originated in Italy (it appears originally to have referred to a type of running, perhaps a messenger); *Oxford English Dictionary.*

49. Dahl has dated the *Courante uyt Italien, Duytslandt, &c.* based on the date of the news it contains from The Hague. The Dutch are sometimes given credit for inventing the printed newspaper. The case for them is based on a reference to Dutch "corantos" in 1607, but the word *coranto* seems also to have been used to refer to handwritten newssheets; Dahl, *Amsterdam—Earliest Newspaper Centre of Western Europe,* 167–168, 171–176.

50. Dahl, *Dutch Corantos,* 33–34.

51. Murray, 10, 25, 53; Barbour, 17–18.

52. Dahl suspects that two additional corantos, of which no copies have survived, may also have been in circulation in the city in 1645; Dahl, *Amsterdam— Earliest Newspaper Centre of Western Europe,* 186.

53. Dahl, *Dutch Corantos,* 25.

54. Murray, 91–92, 109, 111–112; Baschwitz, 99–103.

55. *The continuation of our former newes,* April 24, 1623; cited, Frank, *The Beginnings of the English Newspaper,* 300. The realization that the first English and French newspaper journalists were Dutch arrived early in the 20th century when collections of these corantos surfaced. This realization, along with the discovery in the previous century that the Germans had been printing weeklies as early as 1609, may have been responsible for cooling interest in the early history of the newspaper in both England and France.

56. Dahl has compared one of these French papers with the Dutch paper printed the previous day and found it to be a "nearly verbatim translation;" Dahl, *Amsterdam—Earliest Newspaper Centre of Western Europe,* 195–197.

57. Support for the Protestant cause tended to be understated in Dutch corantos; nonetheless, they frequently were caught having exaggerated Protestant victories. For example, the number of Poles reported by one Dutch publication to have been killed in a battle with the Swedes—9,000—had to be revised downward in the following issue of that coranto—to 250; Dahl, *Amsterdam—Earliest Newspaper Centre of Western Europe,* 185. Publications imported from the Netherlands would enjoy considerably greater success in France later in the 17th century and in the 18th century; see Bellanger, I, 285–298; Baschwitz, 98–99.

58. Later, *Courant newes out of Italy, Germany, Bohemia, Poland, &c.;* Dahl, "Amsterdam—Cradle of English Newspapers," 166–170; Dahl, *A Bibliography of English Corantos and Periodical Newsbooks,* 31–41.

59. "The new tydings out of Italie are not yet com," Dec. 2, 1620.

60. The word *publisher* is used as early as 1630 in an English newspaper; the publishers of the Dutch corantos usually called themselves "corrantiers"; see Dahl, *A Bibliography of English Corantos and Periodical Newsbooks,* 167–168; Dahl, *Dutch Corantos,* 33–35.

61. Actually, this oldest surviving English newspaper barely qualifies as a periodical. Copies of sixteen different issues of Van de Keere's English coranto have survived. A few of the surviving copies are dated only six days apart, a few as much as two months apart; see Frank, *The Beginnings of the English Newspaper,* 3.

62. *Tatler,* 12, May 7, 1709; reprinted Richard Steele.

63. Dahl, *Dutch Corantos,* 23–26.

64. "As for ordinary people," writes Matthias Shaaber about these earliest English newspapers, "the scarcely ever cut a figure in this news except *en masse . . .*"; Shaaber, "The History of the First English Newspaper," 569.

65. See Dahl, *Dutch Corantos,* 33–40; Shaaber, "The History of the First English Newspaper," 560.

66. Murray, 15–16.

67. See Shaaber, "The History of the First English Newspaper," 573–574.

68. The title of these English corantos varied somewhat; this is from the Sept. 30 issue; see Dahl, *A Bibliography of English Corantos and Periodical Newsbooks,* 51–54. The last of the group of English corantos printed in Amsterdam was dated Sept. 18, 1621. It seems reasonable to assume that the commencement of one publication was related to the demise of the other.

69. Butter seems the current favorite; see Dahl, *A Bibliography of English Corantos and Periodical Newsbooks,* 51. For the argument in favor of Bourne, see Shaaber, *Some Forerunners of the Newspaper in England,* 316.

70. These long summaries of the news within functioned as combination titles, headlines and tables of contents. Here is the full title of the periodic newsbook pub-

lished by Nicholas Bourne and Thomas Archer on Aug. 19, 1622:

> The entertainment of Count Mansfield, and the Duke of Brunswick, into the service and pay of the Duke of Bulloygne, being both dismissed by the King of Bohemia. As also the invasion made upon the countrey of Ser Bruggen by Count Mansfield, with his arrivall in the province of Namure, so that some part of his armie lyeth not about sixe leagues from Bruxelles. With strange tidings from Bergen up Zome of a battaile very lately fought about the enemies surprising of a sconce belonging to the out-workes of the towne, with more especiall passages before the same. Likewise the wonderfull proceedings of Monsieur Tilly and Don Cordua in the Palatinate. Moreover the late commotion which happened in Turkie, wherein about 60000. Turkes were slayne: with the warlike actions of Bethlem Gabor, and the Switzers and Grisons great victories obtained against the usurpers of their state, besides the recovery of their countrey.

Cited, Dahl, *A Bibliography of English Corantos and Periodical Newsbooks,* 77.

71. There are hints of an editorial presence in slightly earlier periodicals; see Dahl, *A Bibliography of English Corantos and Periodical Newsbooks,* 72–73, 78.

72. Nov. 16, 1622; cited, Shaaber, "The History of the First English Newspaper," 578.

73. Sept. 12, 1623; cited Shaaber, "The History of the First English Newspaper," 575.

74. Aug. 29, 1623; cited Shaaber, "The History of the First English Newspaper," 575.

75. John Chamberlain, Sept. 4, 1624; cited, Shaaber, "The History of the First English Newspaper," 578–579; see also Frank, *The Beginnings of the English Newspaper,* 9.

76. April 21, 1623; cited Shaaber, "The History of the First English Newspaper," 576.

77. Shaaber, "The History of the First English Newspaper," 576–577. Still, the bibliographer Folke Dahl estimates that for the next decade "between sixty and seventy percent of the news material in the English periodical press originated from the Netherlands and particularly from Amsterdam"; Dahl, "Amsterdam—Cradle of English Newspapers," 173.

78. Aug. 29, 1623; cited, Shaaber, "The History of the First English Newspaper," 574.

79. Dahl explains that personal notes from the editor were "almost unknown in the German, Dutch, Belgian or Italian papers at this time," though there would be a few such notes in Théophraste Renaudot's *Gazette de France,* which began publication in Paris in 1631; Dahl, *A Bibliography of English Corantos and Periodical Newsbooks,* 20.

80. When readers are invited to return each week for a continual update on events, bad news becomes more difficult to ignore. The Turks, whose victories rarely earned a mention in 16th-century English newsbooks, would fare much better in these early periodicals. (See the newspapers dated Sep. 5, 1623, and Sept. 17, 1623, for example; Dahl, *A Bibliography of English Corantos and Periodical Newsbooks,* 111–112.) By the end of the decade, English newspaper publishers were left with but one response to their readers' continued resistance to bad news: They simply published less frequently when the Catholic side took the initiative in the Thirty Years War; see Frank, *The Beginnings of the English Newspaper,* 13.

81. Their sluggishness in adopting such a title may have stemmed from a fear that readers—used to newsbooks and news ballads—might suspect that a familiar title meant a familiar—that is, stale—collection of news; see Dukes, 198.

82. Frank, *The Beginnings of the English Newspaper,* 15.

83. Clitus-Alexandrinus, 21.

84. This count is based on the titles of surviving publications or publications registered with the Stationers listed in Dahl, *A Bibliography of English Corantos and Periodical Newsbooks..*

85. Gardiner, V, 222.

86. Clitus-Alexandrinus, 22.

87. In 1632, soon after a new Protestant hero, King Gustavus Adolphus of Sweden, took the field and reader interest in foreign news revived, the government banned the periodic newsbooks. (To fill the void, a publisher in Amsterdam began printing in English again.) Butter and Bourne were able to wrangle an exclusive license to resume printing foreign news in 1638, but they had the new annoyance of having to submit their newsbooks to an apparently quite censorious censor.

88. Jan. 11, 1641; cited, Dahl, *A Bibliography of English Corantos and Periodical Newsbooks,* 250–251.

89. Frank, *The Beginnings of the English Newspaper,* 13–16.

90. Sept. 11, 1624; cited, Shaaber, "The History of the First English Newspaper," 579.

91. Frank, *The Beginnings of the English Newspaper,* 14.

92. See Henry Crabb Robinson's suggestion in 1807 that the *Times* of London place its foreign intelligence in the hands of a "*rédacteur . . .* and not merely a *traducteur*"; *Times* of London, I, 138–139.

93. Marchamont Nedham's *Mercurius Politicus,* March 1–8, 1655.

Chapter 10. The Power of the Periodical—Domesticating News

1. First issue of the *Universal Daily Register*, forerunner of the *Times*, Jan. 1, 1785; reprinted, *Times* of London, I, after page 26.

2. Cited, Anthony Smith, *The Newspaper: An International History*, 13.

3. Shaaber, "The History of the First English Newspaper," 571.

4. Cited, *Notes and Queries*, 7th ser., XI (Jan. 17, 1891), 45.

5. Jan. 29–Feb. 5, 1649; reprinted, Frank, *The Beginnings of the English Newspaper*, after page 194; and Bilainkin, 12–13.

6. This was not the first effort at reporting on the House of Commons. During the intensifying struggle with the king, texts of speeches in the House of Commons, though secret by law, had appeared in handwritten newsletters an the occasional printed pamphlet; Frank, *The Beginnings of the English Newspaper*, 19–21, 25.

7. A "diurnall" represented a variation on the old Venetian format: The past week's news was presented day by day, usually beginning with Monday. The beheading of the king was relegated to Page 3 of *A Perfect Diurnall of Some Passages in Parliament* in 1649 because it took place on a Tuesday. The international news the early corantos had gathered from distant and diverse locales would have been much more difficult to organize into a diurnall.

8. Frank, *The Beginnings of the English Newspaper*, 21–25, 279.

9. For an example of the extent to which these early newspapers are overlooked in the history of journalism, see Richard Kluger's statement that before the 1830s, or at least the American Revolution, "*news*papers, as such, remained unconceived, if not inconceivable, and totally impractical"; Kluger, 22–24.

10. Frank, *The Beginnings of the English Newspaper*, 36–37, 39, 41, 146.

11. In freer countries, such as the Netherlands, some domestic news might have found its way into print—a coranto printed in Delft in the Netherlands in 1623 was titled, significantly: *Courante uyt Italien, Duytslandt ende Nederland*. Nevertheless, even in the Netherlands foreign news predominated.

12. Reprinted, Frank, *The Beginnings of the English Newspaper*, after page 194; and Bilainkin, 12–13.

13. Frank, *The Beginnings of the English Newspaper*, 95–96. The English Civil War was sufficiently newsworthy that it also became the dominant story in Dutch corantos at this time; Dahl, *Amsterdam—Earliest Newspaper Centre of Western Europe*, 176.

14. Frank, *The Beginnings of the English Newspaper*, 29, 41, 124, 227.

15. Such news was also appearing in Dutch corantos. For a sea monster with a human face and a calf with eight legs and two heads, see Dahl, *Amsterdam—Earliest Newspaper Centre of Western Europe*, 177.

16. Oct. 12–19, 1647; cited, Frank, *The Beginnings of the English Newspaper*, 123. Frank notes the similarity between this story and the first chapter of Thomas Hardy's *The Mayor of Casterbridge*. Perhaps this is another *Ur*-story.

17. Frank, *The Beginnings of the English Newspaper*, 227, 239.

18. The examples are from Frank, *The Beginnings of the English Newspaper*, 129.

19. Nedham's *Mercurius Politicus*, Feb. 22–March 1, 1655.

20. See Frank, *The Beginnings of the English Newspaper*, 129, 227.

21. Muddiman, *A History of English Journalism*, 42–43; Frank, *The Beginnings of the English Newspaper*, 36–42.

22. The *Areopagitica*, published in 1644, had almost nothing to say about these weekly newsbooks and was not much noticed by them; Frank, *The Beginnings of the English Newspaper*, 94.

23. Herd, 19–21; Frank, *Cromwell's Press Agent*, 26, 45, 55.

24. Frank, *The Beginnings of the English Newspaper*, 79.

25. *London Post*, Jan. 14–21, 1647; cited, Frank, *The Beginnings of the English Newspaper*, 131–132.

26. Noah.

27. A rather innocuous French-language newspaper intended for foreign eyes also survived, *Nouvelles Ordinaires de Londres*; Frank, *The Beginnings of the English Newspaper*, 210. A few additional newspapers sprang briefly to life following Cromwell's death and the fall of his son in 1659—demonstrating once again, as Frank has noted, "that the greater the chaos, the freer the press."

28. Saillens, 155–156; Frank, *The Beginnings of the English Newspaper*, 210, 253–255. One possible explanation for Nedham's shifts—"a Jack of all sides," a contemporary called him—is money: he was well paid by all his protectors. The readiness of former targets to rehabilitate Nedham can probably be explained by his substantial talents as a journalist and "press agent"; see Frank, *Cromwell's Press Agent*, 45, 74, 89, 107, 170–174, 179–181.

29. Fox Bourne, I, 37–39.

30. For an example of the argument that had been made in favor of Renaudot, see Hatin, *Bibliographie*

Historique et Critique de la Presse Périodique Française, lx-lxi; and Hatin, *Histoire Politique et Littéraire de la Presse,* I, x.

31. Bellanger, I, 80, 86.

32. Bellanger, I, 83–95.

33. Bellanger, I, 94.

34. *Gazette de France,* Jan. 5, 1634; see also Bellanger, I, 91.

35. Eisenstein, 564–565, 575–577, 679.

36. Ziman, 102.

37. Drake, *Galileo at Work,* 137–138; Drake, *The Unsung Journalist.*

38. Koyré, 66, 209–213; Drake, *Galileo at Work,* 27; Eisenstein, 565.

39. The history of these organizations is discussed in Harcourt Brown.

40. Cited, Rochet, 20.

41. Huygens; cited, Rochet, 9.

42. Rochet, 20, 25.

43. Kearney, 108.

44. See Harcourt Brown, 185–186.

45. Ziman, 104–105.

46. One exception was a German pamphlet published in 1632, reporting on an observation of the transit of Mercury across the sun, which confirmed Kepler's theory; Eisenstein, 631. That early report on the telescope, another exception, found its way into a newsbook almost by accident: A telescope had been displayed during a visit to the Hague by an embassy from the King of Siam and a Spanish general, and their visit were newsworthy enough to interest a printer; Drake, *Galileo at Work,* 138; Drake, *The Unsung Journalist.*

47. Cited, Allen, 314.

48. That Galileo's work in particular should have been the subject of reports in these newborn newspapers may have been due in part to his own precocious awareness of the value of publicity; see Eisenstein, 525–527.

49. Cited, Frank, *The Beginnings of the English Newspaper,* 158.

50. Frank, *The Beginnings of the English Newspaper,* 302; see also Dahl, *A Bibliography of English Corantos and Periodical Newsbooks,* 94–96.

51. *A relation of many memorable passages . . . ,* Sept. 14, 1622; cited, Dahl, *A Bibliography of English Corantos and Periodical Newsbooks,* 82–83. *Our last news . . . ,* Oct. 2, 1623; cited, Shaaber, "The History of the First English Newspaper," 582. *The Continuation of our weekly newes . . . ,* May 23, 1626; cited, Dahl, *A Bibliography of English Corantos and Periodical Newsbooks,* 147.

52. There was evidence of this as early as the 16th century: The handwritten Venetian periodic newssheets were commended for their readiness to confirm or deny previous reports in subsequent issues; Bongi, 324.

53. Harcourt Brown, 21–25.

54. Camusat, I, 5–6. It should be noted that the French government prohibited most published discussions of politics.

55. Originally spelled *"scavants."* It would have considerable trouble achieving its goal of weekly publication; Harcourt Brown, 199.

56. Cited, Kronick, *A History of Scientific and Technical Periodicals,* 20.

57. For the shadows of the moons of Jupiter, see *Journal des savants,* Feb. 22, 1666; the baby with two faces is mentioned in the index for the *Journal des savants,* under the year 1677.

58. What may have been the first *weekly* English journal of science, *Weekly Memorials for the Ingenious . . . ,* appeared in 1682; *Notes and Queries,* 3rd ser., IV (Dec. 2, 1893), 444–445.

59. *Philosophical Transactions,* March 6, 1665.

60. Harcourt Brown, 200.

61. Axtell.

62. Eisenstein, 638n.

63. Cited, Barnes, 257.

64. Barnes.

65. For a survey of science coverage in the American newspaper, see Krieghbaum.

66. Pepys, I, 344–345.

67. Dahl, *Amsterdam—Earliest Newspaper Centre of Western Europe,* 163.

68. Mercurius Politicus, March 8–15, 1655.

69. McLuhan, 187–188.

70. A British editor, Oliver Williams, operated a similar "Office of Intelligence" for profit in London in the 1650s; Frank, *The Beginnings of the English Newspaper,* 263.

71. Charles Firth, "The Ballad History of the Reign of James I," 57–61. The Virginia Company had also published a broadside in 1610 in an effort to recruit settlers—"honest sufficient Artificers"; Alexander Brown, I, 439.

72. Dahl, *A Bibliography of English Corantos and Periodical Newsbooks,* 125; an advertisement for a book had appeared in two Dutch corantos one month earlier. For the development of advertising in the Dutch corantos, see Dahl, *Amsterdam—Earliest Newspaper Centre of Western Europe,* 179–183.

73. Frank, *The Beginnings of the English Newspaper,* 124, 172, 219, 256–257.

74. Cited, Sutherland, 82; Sutherland includes some additional examples of early efforts to cover this news, 82–83.

75. Lindemann, 94–95. A newspaper (published by Lucas Schulte) had begun appearing two times weekly

in Germany in 1625. Amsterdam had gained a twice-weekly by 1645; Dahl, *Amsterdam—Earliest Newspaper Centre of Western Europe,* 186.

76. *General Postscript,* Oct. 24, 1709; cited, Nichols, IV, 84. The paper that was apparently England's first daily, *A Perfect Diurnal or the Dayly Proceedings in Parliament,* had survived for only four weeks in 1660; C. Edward Wilson.

77. Rosenberg, *Spectator,* 452, Aug. 8, 1712; reprinted, Donald F. Bond, IV, 90–94.

78. *Daily Advertiser,* Feb. 26, 1730; cited, Stanley Morison, *The English Newspaper,* 123–151.

79. Stanley Morison, *The English Newspaper,* 123–151. The business and advertising newspaper—*Intelligenzblatt*—had begun appearing in German with the *Wienerisches Diarium* in 1703; Lindemann, 250.

80. See *Mémoires de Trévoux* for January 1714 for one example; according to an analysis of this publication, one percent of its articles during the years 1705 to 1720 concerned economics, eight percent from 1755 to 1762; Retat, 44–51. By 1768 France had a publication called the *Journal oeconomique;* and Defoe's *Review* earlier in the century had included essays on economic affairs.

81. For a discussion of the role of improved communication in producing a drop in the disparity in prices in different cities in 19th-century America, see Pred, 57.

82. *Boston Gazette,* Dec. 28, 1719–Jan. 4, 1720.

Chapter 11. News and Revolution—A Junction of All the People

1. Writing as "Populus," *Boston Gazette,* March 14, 1768.

2. *Publick Occurrences,* Sept. 25, 1690.

3. Cited, Kobre, "The First American Newspaper."

4. Cited, Paltsits, "New Light on *Publick Occurrences.*" For a new theory on the "Disallowance" of Harris' paper, see Sloan.

5. *Domestick Intelligence,* July 7, 1679.

6. Harris' imprisonment became an issue in the struggle between Parliament and the king. Oddly, Harris was appointed printer to the governor of Massachusetts after *Publick Occurrences* was suppressed. Muddiman suggests that this may have been an attempt to console Harris; Muddiman, *The King's Journalist,* 214–219, 227, 231, 245–247.

7. *Boston News-Letter,* May 8–15, 1704; reprinted, Oswald, 9. Mott, *American Journalism,* 11–14. Hudson, 52–58.

8. Cited, Hudson, xvi.

9. Letter to Hezekiah Niles, Feb. 13, 1818; in John Adams, X, 282–283.

10. Reprinted, Defoe, 50.

11. Benjamin Franklin, *The Autobiography,* 22–26.

12. Mott, *American Journalism,* 15–21.

13. Siebert, *Freedom of the Press in England,* 330–331, 336–337.

14. Mott, *American Journalism,* 19–20.

15. Downie, 61.

16. *A Brief Narrative of the Case and Tryal of John Peter Zenger* (New York: 1736); reprinted, Snyder, 21–25.

17. James Parker in a letter to Benjamin Franklin, June 14, 1765; in *Proceedings of the Massachusetts Historical Society,* 2d ser., XVI (1902): 198.

18. *Maryland Gazette,* Oct. 10, 1765; Schlesinger, 76.

19. Letter to Henry Seymour Conway, Sept. 23, 1765; in "Colden Papers," *New-York Historical Society Collections* X (1877): 33.

20. *Maryland Gazette,* Dec. 10, 1765; Jan. 30, 1766; Feb. 20, 1766.

21. "Sydney, *Massachusetts Spy,* Nov. 11, 1773.

22. The citations are from Schlesinger, 96–97, 109, 171.

23. "T. Young," *Boston Evening-Post,* Oct. 25, 1773.

24. *Pennsylvania Packet,* Nov. 22, 1773.

25. "Journal of Occurrences," *New-York Journal,* Dec. 29, 1768.

26. Schlesinger, 101–102.

27. "The Newspaper," *New-York Journal,* April 19, 1770.

28. *Providence Gazette Extraordinary,* March 12, 1766.

29. Letter to the Earl of Shelburne, Nov. 23, 1767; in "Colden Papers," *New-York Historical Society Collections* X (1877): 135.

30. Cited, Schlesinger, 99.

31. In this sense, the complaints of authorities at having their deliberations exposed echo the complaints of merchants in having their prices published: An informed public limits their prerogatives.

32. Cited, Innis, *Empire and Communications,* 158.

33. "Happy times are barren; calamitous periods only are fruitful of interesting materials for historians and gazettes," concluded "Speculator" in the *Independent Ledger and American Advertiser* in Boston on Jan. 26, 1784.

34. *Providence Gazette Extraordinary,* March 12, 1766.

35. Davidson, 43.

36. Merritt, 1, 56, 144–145.

37. Schlesinger, 87–90.

38. The value of colonial imports fell from £2,157,000 in 1768 to £1,336,000 in 1769. English merchants began to protest; *Encyclopaedia Britannica* (1964), XXII, 747.

39. Cited, Innis, *Empire and Communications,* 29.

40. John Adams, II, 219.

41. Letter to Richard Price, June 13, 1782; in Benjamin Franklin, *The Writings,* VIII, 457.

42. Schlesinger, 43, 73, 114–117.

43. Hawke, 41.

44. Schlesinger, 107–108, 240.

45. Jan. 29, 1776; in Paltsits, "John Holt—Printer and Postmaster," 494.

46. In addition, by providing readers with a feeling of involvement in some of the issues facing society, French gazettes and *journals,* like newspapers in England and America, must have accelerated the transformation of elements of the populace into a political force—a public. In a country that provided as few opportunities for meaningful political participation as did France under the Old Regime, the elevation of a public was inevitably a destabilizing development; see Keith Michael Baker, "Politics and Public Opinion Under the Old Regime: Some Reflections," in Censer, 204–246.

47. Cited, Ballangere, I, 166.

48. The *Journal de Paris;* Bellanger, I, 240–241.

49. Bellanger, I, 161–162; Funck-Brentano, 11; for contradictions, see Varloot, 71.

50. Darnton, *The Literary Underground of the Old Regime,* 16, 25, 36.

51. Darnton, *The Literary Underground of the Old Regime,* 35, 145–147, 203.

52. Darnton, *The Literary Underground of the Old Regime,* 205.

53. *Gazette de France,* July 17, 1789.

54. Lefebvre, 68–69.

55. Darnton, *The Literary Underground of the Old Regime,* 201.

56. Unauthorized newspapers were just beginning to appear in Paris by July 1789, as the king's power faded; Bellanger, I, 428.

57. Lefebvre, 68–69.

58. Private letters also circulated in France during the Revolution, but those letters in turn were usually based on hearsay; Lefebvre, 72.

59. Lefebvre, 69–73.

60. Darnton, *The Literary Underground of the Old Regime,* 202.

61. Rudé, 53–54.

62. Lefebvre, 73.

63. Lefebvre, x–xiii, 181.

64. There have been numerous examples of this phenomenon: Rumors that King James II's son was illegitimate, fanned in print by William of Orange, for example, played a role in the English Revolution of 1688–1689; Schwoerer, 852–854. A rumor that Abraham Lincoln's running mate, Hannibal Hamlin, was a mulatto helped spread resentment in the South in the days before printed photographs; Tebbel, *The Press and the Presidency,* 177.

65. For additional statistics on the explosive growth of the French press during the Revolution, see Edelstein, 17–18.

66. Bellanger, I, 431, 436–437, 455–456.

67. Bellanger, I, 501–502.

68. Bellanger, I, 550.

69. Cited, Salmon, *The Newspaper and Authority,* 31.

70. Letter to Thomas Seymour, Feb. 11, 1807; in Levy, 369–370.

71. The Dutch press, even before Napoleon, had still, for the most part, been limited to discussion of foreign news, and in England the stamp tax tended to restrict newspaper circulation to the well-to-do; see Baschwitz, 106–107; Olson, 155; Anthony Smith, *The Newspaper: An International History,* 79.

72. *Aurora,* March 6, 1797.

73. Mott, *American Journalism,* 146; Pickett, 68–69; Hudson, 211.

74. Letter to Thomas Jefferson, June 30, 1813; in John Adams, X, 48.

75. *Aurora,* June 6, 1798. James Morton Smith reprints the text of the acts, 435–442.

76. James Morton Smith, 182–204; Mott, *American Journalism,* 147–152; Austin, 108–118.

77. Austin, 124–127; Stewart, 486.

78. For some of the 20th-century setbacks to the right to free expression in the United States, see Davidowitz. Some Federalist editors were prosecuted for seditious libel in state courts during the Jefferson administration, but there is no evidence that the president himself "supported a systematic prosecution" or federal prosecutions; Richard Buel, Jr., "Freedom of the Press in Revolutionary America," in Bailyn, 93.

79. In the first issue of his own "public Mercury," *Intelligencer,* Aug. 31, 1663; cited, Nichols, IV, 56.

80. Cited, Desmond, x.

81. *Bee,* March 26, 1800.

82. Hamilton, II, 73–74.

83. Innis, *Empire and Communications,* 29.

84. Tocqueville, II, 120

Chapter 12. Mass Circulation—For All

1. Lippmann, "Two Revolutions in the American Press," 437.

2. New York, Boston, Baltimore, Philadelphia, Washington, Charleston, and New Orleans; Schudson, 17.

3. See George Rogers Taylor, 150–151.

4. Pred 144, 256; see chart, Pred, 21. For a debate on the significance of the penny press, see Nerone.

5. Ivon Asquith, "The Structure, Ownership and Control of the Press, 1780–1855," in Boyce, 100; Wadsworth, 9.

6. Fox Bourne, I, 291.

7. Cited, Mott, *American Journalism,* 224–225.

8. Kobre, *Development of American Journalism,* 156–159, 216–217; Hudson, 418.

9. Mott, *American Journalism,* 239–241.

10. See chart, Pred, 21.

11. Mott, *American Journalism,* 234.

12. A decade and a half earlier a few radical political weeklies had also achieved large circulations in England; Raymond Williams, "The Press and Popular Culture," in Boyce, 46–47.

13. Hollis, 121–123, 126; James Curran, "The Press as an Agency of Social Control," in Boyce, 63.

14. Hollis, 160; James 13.

15. Bellanger, II, 114–115.

16. Herbert Gans calls this process "cultural democratization"; Gans, 304. These newspapers were particularly useful, as radio and television would be in the 20th century, in teaching English to the many immigrants in their audiences. The newspaper, Horace Greeley maintained, "is worth all the schools in the country. I think it creates a taste for reading in every child's mind. . . ."; cited, Hudson, 547.

17. Lippmann, "Two Revolutions in the American Press," 437.

18. This argument is made by Dan Schiller. It rests, in part, on what appears to be a tenuous reading of coverage in Bennett's *Herald* of the Robinson-Jewett murder case; Schiller, 57–67. (Coverage of this case is considered, from a different perspective, in Chapter 14.) Bennett and Day can be squeezed under the heading "radical" only with great difficulty.

19. Cited, Hudson, 546.

20. See Hollis, 122, 135.

21. March 22, 1834; cited, Hollis, 248.

22. *Times* of London, I, 53–60.

23. James Branston, *The Man of Taste* (Los Angeles: 1975), 8.

24. Ivon Asquith, "The Structure, Ownership and Control of the Press, 1780–1855," in Boyce, 112; Hollis, 311.

25. See Koss, 57–58; Woods, 55–56.

26. Cited, James Curran, "The Press as an Agency of Social Control," in Boyce, 55.

27. James Curran, "The Press as an Agency of Social Control," in Boyce, 62; Virginia Berridge, "Popular Sunday Papers and Mid-Victorian Society," in Boyce, 251–254.

28. Cited, James Curran, "The Press as an Agency of Social Control," in Boyce, 60.

29. Kluger, 46.

30. Mott, *American Journalism,* 230, 268; Schiller, 12–13; Berger, 15.

31. William Harian Hale, 185–188. Mott, *American Journalism,* 278–279.

32. Fox Bourne, II, 140–149.

33. Bryan, 18–19.

34. Bryan, 19.

35. Bryan, 19.

36. Bleyer, 169–171.

37. Kroeger, 192. Chevigny, 21, 290.

38. Chevigny, 235–236, 290–292, 305.

39. Folkerts, 184–185.

40. Edwin Emery, 304–305. Folkert, 289.

41. Hudson, 387.

42. Hudson, 542–543.

43. The role sensationalism could play in attracting new publics was demonstrated time and time again over the decades. The *Norfolk News* in England, for example, was founded by Dissenters in 1845, but it became successful after it published two exclusives: an account of a bridge that collapsed under the weight of the crowd watching a clown float down a river in a tub towed by geese, and a shorthand account of a murder trial; Eric Fowler, 183.

44. *New York World,* May 11, 1883; Swanberg, *Pulitzer,* 6, 86, 88, 91–92, 121–122, 150.

45. Swamberg, *Citizen Hearst,* 39–41, 47–68, 385–387.

46. Hearst probably came as close as has any private citizen in the United States to single-handedly starting a war (see Chapter 14), and Pulitzer, whose love of circulation proved stronger than his commitment to fairness, followed along; Swanberg, *Citizen Hearst,* 89–97, 137, 163–164.

47. The *World* declined rapidly after Pulizer's death in 1911, but still brought $5 million when his sons sold it to Scripps-Howard in 1931; Swanberg, *Pulitzer,* 80, 258, 479.

48. Edwin Emery, 231, 305–306.

49. Alan Lee, "The Structure, Ownership and Control of the Press, 1855–1914," in Boyce, 124.

50. Mott, *American Journalism,* 551, 646–647.

51. Mott, *American Journalism,* 637–640.

52. Swanberg, *Pulitzer,* 316–317.

53. See A. W. Haggis, "The Life and Work of Sir Henry Wellcome," unpublished manuscript, the Wellcome Foundation, London, 115–118.

54. Graham Murdock and Peter Golding, "The Structure, Ownership and Control of the Press, 1914–1976," in Boyce, 130.

55. Mott, *American Journalism,* 666–673.

56. Swamberg, *Citizen Hearst,* 464, 479.

57. Innis, *Empire and Communications,* 117; see also Bagdikian, *The Information Machines,* 1–27.

58. See Raymond Williams, "The Press and Popular Culture," in Boyce, 47–48.

59. Ross, 305.

60. The youth movement in the United States and Western Europe during the 1960s may have represented a flickering attempt to pose such a challenge. These movements were briefly unified by "alternative" newspapers and rock and roll music. (The role television may have played is discussed in Chapter 15). But most of the participants in the protests and counterculture gatherings never entirely surrendered an attachment to the larger society, and their newspapers and music both quickly succumbed to the commercial imperatives of that larger society.

Chapter 13. Before Reporting—No Data by Which We Can Correctly Reason

1. Cited, Dahl, *A Bibliography of English Corantos and Periodical Newsbooks,* 275.

2. The "two thousand dead" figure appeared in a United Press International dispatch, later retracted.

3. Unless otherwise indicated, the citations of newspaper coverage in this section are from Bertier de Sauvigny.

4. New York *Evening Post,* June 1, 1814.

5. Boston *Yankee,* May 20, 1814.

6. *Independent Chronicle,* June 2, 1814.

7. Boston *Yankee,* May 13, 1814.

8. Kingshill, 226.

9. Gairdner, *Paston Letters,* III, 267.

10. Letter of May 9, 1471, from the City of London to Thomas Faucomberge, Captain of Kent; in Reginald R. Sharpe, III, 390.

11. See Klarwill, *The Fugger News-Letters, Second Series,* 170–176.

12. Shaaber, *Some Forerunners of the Newspaper in England,* 180.

13. *Ein warhafftiges Monstrum,* Augsburg, 1655[?]; cited, Paisey, 62. For those who lived in Russia, foreign events must have seemed hazier still. News reports compiled in Moscow on the Shabbetaian Jewish movement in 1665 and 1666, to choose a somewhat exotic example, announced erroneously that Shabbetai Zevi, who had proclaimed himself the messiah, had been killed by the Turks. And the stories through which the more informed citizens of Moscow learned of this movement are replete with news of omens and miracles—including comets, fire from heaven, shriveling hands, and Muhammad's coffin crashing to the ground. These reports are from the *kuranty*—based primarily on European newsbooks, newspapers and letters, and intended, at first, exclusively for the czar and his advisers; Waugh, "News of the False Messiah."

14. *A Dolorous discourse, of a most terrible and bloudy Battel, fought in Barbarie, the fourth Day of August last past 1578* (London: 1579).

15. Seguin, "Les 'Canards' de Faits Divers de Petit Format en France," 41.

16. *Gazette de France,* Jan. 2, 1632. For additional examples, see Bellanger, I, 87–91, 105.

17. *A little true forraine newes . . . ;* cited, Dahl, *A Bibliography of English Corantos and Periodical Newsbooks,* 262.

18. *Hollandtsche Mercurius,* July 22, 1650; November 1653; cited, Van Kley, 562.

19. Rossel, *Historie de France à travers les Journaux du Temps Passé: Le Faux Grand Siècle,* 290–291.

20. The news was occasionally slowed further by a lack of space to print it; John Campbell, editor of the *Boston News-Letter,* at one time fell more than a year behind in printing foreign news; Mott, *American Journalism,* 13.

21. I. K. Steele, 6–9, 19.

22. See Pred, 12.

23. It was not the water but the vast distance it spanned that caused the problem; although the Atlantic was often treacherous, travel by sea was still considerably faster than long-distance travel by land; I. K. Steele, 1n.

24. I. K. Steele, 10–11, 20–21.

25. Hinkhouse, 56; Pred, 13.

26. Mott, *American Journalism,* 196–197; Edwin Emery, 122.

27. Klarwill, *The Fugger News-Letters, Second Series,* 165–175.

28. "The new tydings out of Italie are not yet com," Dec. 2, 1620.

29. Cited, Charlton, 224.

30. Mott, "The Newspaper Coverage of Lexington and Concord," 504.

31. See Henry Adams, 9.

32. This term is used in Pred, 240.

33. *Orleans Gazette* (New Orleans), May 28, 1805.

34. These terms were still in the process of acquiring their modern meanings. For notes on the arrival of the "editor" in English journalism, see Anthony Smith, "The

Long Road to Objectivity and Back Again," in Boyce, 165.

35. *The continuation of the forraine occurrents . . . ,* Jan. 11, 1641; cited, Dahl, *A Bibliography of English Corantos and Periodical Newsbooks,* 250–251; *Mobile Advertiser,* April 17, 1833; cited, *Niles' Weekly Register* (Baltimore), May 18, 1833.

36. Marbut, 1–3.

37. Sept. 6, 1709; cited, Nichols, IV, 83. This practice would be curtailed by the development of wire services in the 19th century.

38. *Boston Evening Transcript,* Dec. 2, 1841.

39. "Extract from Rebel Papers," New York *Gazette and Mercury,* Feb. 2, 1778.

40. Warton, I, 332.

41. Much foreign and national news arrived via Boston and later New York City. News of southern cities was often available in New York newspapers well before it appeared in papers elsewhere in the South; Pred, 49–50, 203. Newspapers in these cities exercised a dominance over the nation's news system in the first half of the 19th century similar to that attributed to American wire services by Third-World countries today.

42. Clitus-Alexandrinus, 21.

43. *Democratic Press,* May 18, 1814.

44. *Le Médiateur,* May 14, 1814; cited, Bertier de Sauvigny, 352.

45. Bertier de Sauvigny, 344–345, 348–350.

Chapter 14. The Development of Reporting—The Journalistic Method

1. *New York Herald,* May 6, 1835.

2. *New York Herald,* June 4, 1844.

3. Pred, 29, 32, 55.

4. Kirk.

5. *New York Herald,* Jan. 5, 1848; see Czitrom, 15–16.

6. Cited, Pray, 364.

7. *New York Tribune,* Sept. 5–7, 1870.

8. *New York Tribune,* Sept. 5–6, 1870.

9. Pélissier; Eisenstein, 110–111, 600; Cipolla, 47–48.

10. Cited, Stephen Jay Gould, "Between You and Your Genes," *New York Review of Books,* Aug. 16, 1984, 30.

11. Aug. 31, 1663; cited, Nichols, IV, 57.

12. Muddiman, *The King's Journalist,* 146. Muddiman, and probably L'Estrange, also took advantage of a close relationship with what was still the largest information-gathering organization in Britain, the government; Muddiman, *The King's Journalist,* 146; as did the *Gazette de France* in France; see Anthony Smith, *The Newspaper: An International History,* 48–50; Bellanger, I, 197.

13. Wright, 72–75.

14. *Pennsylvania Gazette,* Oct. 9–16, 1729.

15. *New York Herald,* Dec. 8, 1837; Hudson, 450–451.

16. Samuel Topliff Jr. of the Exchange Coffee-House also spent time in a rowboat in Boston Harbor in these years, gathering news which was then made available—for a fee—to readers in the coffeehouse. Journalism historians have yet to sort out the accomplishments of these various explorers; see Rosewater, 5–10; Lee, 154–155; Hudson, 189–190; Buckingham, II, 104; Mott, *American Journalism,* 194–195.

17. Rosewater, 14–19; Bleyer, 144–145; Mott, *American Journalism,* 195.

18. Mott, *American Journalism,* 195; Rosewater, 10–11; Pray, 46.

19. *New York Herald,* May 18, 1840; Aug. 31, 1835.

20. Cited, Woods, 60.

21. Michael Schudson, "What Time Means in a News Story," Gannett Center for Media Studies, Occasional Paper No. 4, Aug. 1986; a version of this paper appears in Manoff.

22. Jan. 1, 1681; cited, Sutherland, 54. A satire on the "Ballad-Monger" in 1631 made a similar point: "stale ballad-news, like stale fish, . . . are not for quesie stomacks;" Clitus-Alexandrinus, 19.

23. Read, vii, 123.

24. *Times,* Aug. 19, 1819; Woods, 40–45.

25. Cited, Seguin, *L'Information en France, de Louix XII à Henri II,* 40.

26. One early issue of Harris' paper featured, for example, a detailed report on a local fire; *Domestick Intelligence Or News both from CITY and Country,* Aug. 14, 1679.

27. Sutherland, 76–77.

28. Sutherland, 44–47.

29. *Spectator,* 436, July 21, 1712.

30. ". . . the Miseries of Mankind are the chief Materials," *Applebee's Original Weekly Journal,* Aug. 21, 1725; cited, Bleyer, 24.

31. *The Case Between the Proprietors of the News-Papers, and the Subscribing Coffee-Men, Fairly Stated* (London: 1729), 6.

32. "Coffee-Man," *The Case of the Coffee-Men of London and Westminster. Or, an Account of the Imposition and Abuses put upon them and the whole Town, by the present Set of News-Writers* (London: 1728), 5–7.

33. For evidence the paid reporters could also be found in the provinces as early as 1758, see Wiles, 253.

34. Samuel Johnson wrote such outlines, based on others' recollections of the debates, for the *Gentleman's Magazine* from 1740 to 1743. Indeed, Dr. Johnson claimed credit for the widely praised wording, as reported in the magazine, of a speech by William Pitt; Fox Bourne, I, 129–130.

35. Sutherland, 21; Peter David Gannen Thomas, 623.

36. The gallery could still be closed and "strangers" excluded from some of the more controversial debates; Peter David Gannen Thomas, 626–631.

37. Here are three paragraphs from the "*Summary of Yesterday's* Proceedings in the House *of* Commons" in the *London Chronicle,* March 3–5, 1774, 223:

Lord North acquainted the House, that his Majesty has signified a desire for the papers respecting the late unhappy disturbances at Boston, and other parts of America, to be laid before them on Monday next, and at the same time move an address to his Majesty. . . .

Mr. Dempster desired to know what address the noble Lord meant.

Lord North said, it was only a usual complimentary address to his Majesty, for his great goodness and condescension in desiring those papers to be laid before the House.

38. Peter David Gannen Thomas, 632–633.

39. James Stephen, 291.

40. Alexander Wedderburn; cited, Peter David Gannen Thomas, 634.

41. Peter David Gannen Thomas, 635–636. See MacDonagh, 275–279, for a comparison of Woodfall's account of a famous five-and-one-half-hour speech by Richard Brinsley Sheridan in 1787 with the accounts of another paper and of historical sources.

42. Christie, 338–339; Anthony Smith, "The Long Road to Objectivity and Back Again," in Boyce, 166.

43. Anthony Smith, "The Long Road to Objectivity and Back Again," in Boyce, 160–162; Peter David Gannen Thomas, 632.

44. Stanley Morison, *Edward Topham,* 13–19.

45. Cited, *Times* of London, I, 41.

46. *Times,* Aug. 20, 1791.

47. Christie, 344–345. The hordes of newspapers that appeared on the streets of revolutionary Paris had not yet begun to deploy specialized reporters of their own, but their editors were beginning to visit the assemblies and cafés in search of news; Bellanger, I, 440.

48. *Oracle and Public Advertiser,* May 5, 22, 30, 1794.

49. Morley, 41–54.

50. See Knightley, 4–5. Knightley writes that "before the Crimea, British editors either stole war news from foreign newspapers or employed junior officers to send letters from the battlefront." He does not mention Perry, Bell or Robinson.

51. Henry Crabb Robinson, 185–186.

52. William Collier, John Payne Collier, James Murray, John Ross and Charles Ross; *Times* of London, I, 136.

53. Its publisher, Benjamin Towne, was indicted as a traitor a few months later; he had supported the Tories during the British occupation of Philadelphia; Mott, *American Journalism,* 115.

54. Henry Adams, 22.

55. Cited, Mott, *American Journalism,* 51.

56. Hudson, 57.

57. Alfred Kazin, "In Washington," *New York Review of Books,* May 29, 1986, 11–18.

58. A start had been made on coverage of Congress while the government of the United States was ensconced in Philadelphia from 1790 to 1800; see Hudson, 228; Mott, *American Journalism,* 155n.

59. Dec. 11, 1822; reprinted, *Statesman and Advertiser for the Country,* Dec. 12, 1822.

60. Marbut, 30–32.

61. *Morning Courier and New York Enquirer,* July 24, 1830.

62. *Morning Courier and New York Enquirer,* Aug. 6, 1830.

63. Eberhard, 461–462. See Sutherland, 49, for a discussion of limitations on courtroom coverage in 17th century England.

64. Pred, 242. The sense of companionship and identity readers obtain from regular perusal of a newspaper must also have taken on new significance in these larger, lonelier cities, see Kluger, 39.

65. Driven by their desire for a mass audience, and fortified by the resources a mass audience brought, the penny papers in the United States made a substantial contribution to the development of reporting; however, the extent of that contribution is frequently exaggerated; see Schudson, 22; Robert E. Park in Hughes, *News and the Human Interest Story,* xiii; and Desmond, 77.

66. O'Brien, 17, 23.

67. *Sun,* Jan. 12, 1835.

68. See, for example, *New York Herald,* Jan. 13, 1836, or Jan. 15, 1836.

69. *Times* of London, I, 253.

70. *Times,* Aug. 19, 1819.

71. *Times,* Aug. 23, 1819.

72. See *Times,* Aug. 30, 1819; *Times,* March 18–22, 1820, Walmsley, 345–357; *Times* of London, I, 238. This

remarkably thorough reportage dovetailed nicely with the *Times's* editorial "thundering"—its professions of outrage at what it labeled "the dreadful fact" of this attack upon unarmed civilians; *Times,* Aug. 19, 1819. The columns the newspaper devoted to Peterloo sufficiently discomfited the government to help inspire a libel prosecution, a tightening of the laws on seditious libel, an effort to bar a *Times* reporter from an inquest on a death at Peterloo, and the publication of a sheet called the *Anti-Times.* But, in the end, the effect of these reports and opinions was to strengthen rather than weaken the paper and its editor. By 1834, when the Tories were asked to form a new government, their program was submitted to Barnes in advance for approval; Walmsley, 319; *Times* of London, I, 236–240; Woods, 57–59.

73. *New York Herald,* April 11, 1836.

74. Mott, *American Journalism,* 235. Bennett on poverty: "The philosophers of the *Tribune* are eternally harping on the misery, destitution and terrible sufferings of the poor of this city and throughout the country. There is nothing more ridiculous than all of these tirades about this fancied distress. . . . [Poverty arises] out of indolence, licentiousness or drunkenness"; cited, Kluger, 53.

75. *New York Herald,* June 1, 1840.

76. *New York Herald,* April 11, 1836.

77. *Times,* Aug. 19, 1819.

78. This reporter also writes that he walked over to the police depot to examine sticks some members of the audience had carried to make sure none of the points had been sharpened; *Times,* Aug. 26, 1819.

79. *Sun,* April 11, 1836.

80. *New York Herald,* April 11, 1836.

81. *Sun,* April 12, 1836.

82. *New York Herald,* April 12, 1836.

83. *New York Herald,* April 12, 1836.

84. *New York Herald,* April 13, 1836.

85. *New York Herald,* April 15, 1836.

86. Bennett responded, in print, that he had visited such an establishment only once in his life and had been turned away as "too ugly"; cited, Carlson, 164.

87. *New York Herald,* April 14, 1836.

88. *New York Herald,* April 16, 1836.

89. Carlson, 161. The historical significance of this article can be overstated. Carlson's claim is based on a rather outdated definition of the interview as a transcription of questions and answers. The products of less formal interviews, while remarkably rare in early newspapers, have made occasional appearances in print since the earliest days of print. And, as Nils Gunnar Nilsson has noted, one or two earlier editions of the *Herald* had included what appear to be similar transcriptions of conversations with newsmakers, though none seems as

clearly the product of industrious news gathering as the interview with Rosina Townsend; see Nilsson.

90. *New York Herald,* June 8, 1836.

91. *New York Herald,* April 15, 1836.

92. Mott, *American Journalism,* 233.

93. Cited, *Times* of London; I, 139.

94. Carlson, 168–190.

95. Seitz, 123; Hudson, 495 (Frederic Hudson served as managing editor of the *Herald* in the mid-19th century); Knightley, 20.

96. Mott, *American Journalism,* 334–335. There is no doubt that reporting techniques matured rapidly to meet the challenge presented by the Civil War, however, some exaggerated claims have been made for the contributions of Civil War reporters; see, for example, Knightley, 20–21.

97. Talese, 195.

98. Berger, 35–38; *New York Times,* Nov. 7, 1870.

99. Berger, 41–50.

100. *New York Times,* July 29, 1871; July 22, 1871.

101. Mott, *American Journalism,* 337. There is evidence that Confederate General Robert E. Lee obtained information on Union troop movements from Northern newspapers, Mindich.

102. Wilde, "The Soul of Man Under Socialism," 40–41. Wilde's view of journalism were shaped by his aestheticism before they were hardened by his persecution. "One has merely to read the ordinary English newspapers and the ordinary English novels of our day," he wrote in 1891, "to become conscious of the fact that it is only the obvious that occurs. . . ." Wilde, *The Letters of Oscar Wilde,* 295–296.

103. Andrews, II, 347.

104. See Lane, 65–67.

105. See Vincent, 87, 132; Cozens, 113–114; Noverr, 21.

106. *Sun,* Aug. 28, 1835; the series ran from Aug. 25 to Aug. 31, 1835.

107. Cited, O'Brien, 37–57. For Bennett's reaction, see *New York Herald,* Aug. 31, 1835.

108. It did not pass all at once. Poe essayed a hoax of his own—he wrote in the *Sun* in 1844 of a balloon that had crossed the Atlantic in three days; Mott, *American Journalism,* 227. On Nov. 9, 1874, the *New York Herald* panicked many of its readers with a page full of news of an "AWFUL CALAMITY"—THE WILD ANIMALS BROKEN LOOSE FROM CENTRAL PARK./TERRIBLE SCENES OF MUTILATION/A SHOCKING SABBATH CARNIVAL OF DEATH. At the bottom of this nightmarish story, however, diligent readers did discover a paragraph explaining that "Not one word of it is true"; *New York Herald,* Nov. 9, 1874. The *Sun* had made no such concession to veracity in 1835 and

had in fact continued its hoax for days. (Orson Welles's version of *War of the Worlds* on radio in 1938, despite its success at imitating actual news programming, was presented on a drama program. It was not a journalistic hoax.) Evidence on the extent of which attitudes have changed can be seen in the outrage that greeted a more recent journalistic hoax; Janet Cooke's fabricated story about an 8-year-old heroin addict in the *Washington Post,* Sept. 28, 1980.

109. Dreiser, 467.

110. Darrow, 109.

111. Hofstadter, 198; he gives as examples Mark Twain, William Dean Howells, Stephen Crane, and Theodore Dreiser, among others.

112. *New York Herald,* April 12, 1836.

113. *New York Tribune,* April 15, 1865. Mindich makes a convincing case for Secretary of War Edwin M. Stanton's role in the early use of the inverted pyramid, Mindich.

114. Dreiser, 52.

115. *New York Times,* Aug. 23, 1927.

116. *New York Herald,* Aug. 10, 1872.

117. *New York Times,* Aug. 23, 1927.

118. Snyder, 455.

119. Cited, Stanley Morison, *The English Newspaper,* 25.

120. March 14, 1719; cited, Nichols, IV, 91.

121. William Patten, *The Expedicion into Scot-Lande.* . . . (London: 1548).

122. Pepys, II, 279.

123. *Daily Courant,* Oct. 22, 1702.

124. *Tatler,* 18, May 21, 1709, reprinted, Richard Steele, 48.

125. This balance apparently did not extend to Royalists; Frank, *The Beginnings of the English Newspaper,* 84–85.

126. Patten, William, *The Expedicion into Scot-Lande.* . . . (London: 1548). In his discussion of English newsbooks and news ballads before the publication of the first newspapers, Matthias Shaaber explains that "at that time news was almost invariably partial, without scruple or apology. Comment never lagged far behind it . . ."; Shaaber, *Some Forerunners of the Newspaper in England,* 5.

127. Cited, Koss, 30.

128. *Mercurius Aulicus;* Frank, *The Beginnings of the English Newspaper,* 33.

129. *Père Duchesne,* Oct. 1793; cited, Darnton, *The Literary Underground of the Old Regime,* 205.

130. *Oracle and Public Advertiser,* May 5, 1794.

131. Cited, Michael Palmer, "The British Press and International News, 1851–1899," in Boyce, 208.

132. William Johnson; cited, Philip Elliott, "Professional Ideology and Organizational Change," in Boyce, 184.

133. Lippmann, *American Inquisitors,* 46. Some minimal ability to conquer emotional involvement in the news seems almost prerequisite to its flow. "Men who frequent Coffee-houses and delight in News," remarked a correspondent to the *Spectator* (probably Alexander Pope) in 1712, "are pleased with every thing that is Matter of Fact, so it be what they have not heard before. A Victory, or a Defeat are equally agreeable to them." *Spectator,* 452, Aug. 8, 1712; reprinted, Donald F. Bond, 90–94. This writer seems discomfited by such detachment, but without it would the news not be transformed from "delight" to horror? The leader of the Mossi in West Africa apparently had been permitted to indulge in a more emotional involvement in the news. According to an anthropologist, he "had the right to execute anyone who brought him unwelcome news, and often did so"; Skinner, 68.

134. This wording is used by Molotch and Lester to refer to a formally controlled press; it is, however, equally relevant to an ideological press; see Molotch, 105.

135. *Times,* of London, I, 96–98.

136. The activities of Samuel Topliff Jr. at the Exchange Coffee-House in Boston, might also qualify as a wholesale news operation, though on a somewhat smaller scale; see Rosewater, 4–8.

137. *Revue Parisienne,* Aug. 25, 1840; reprinted, Balzac, 671–675. Bellanger, II, 124–125.

138. Rosewater, 64–66.

139. UNESCO, 11–12.

140. The old system in which newspapers were forced to rely on papers closer to events for their coverage had, however, occasionally enforced a balance of its own. In 1775, for example, the *Salisbury Journal* in England reprinted a report on the first battles of the American Revolution from the *Essex Gazette* in New England, which accused British troops of "cruelty not less brutal than what our venerable ancestors received from the vilest Savages of the wilderness . . ."; June 5, 1775; cited, Keith Williams, 35.

141. Anthony Smith, *The Newspaper: An International History,* 144; Edwin Emery, 263.

142. Cited, Hudson, 548.

143. The *Times* was one of the first newspapers formidable enough to demonstrate independence from political parties in England; the penny papers—beginning with the *Sun* and the *Herald*—began to flex similar muscles in the United States. The withdrawal of reporters from active political involvement did not come all at

once: Horace Greeley, Joseph Pulitzer and William Randolph Hearst, for example, all harbored political ambitions. And there remain occasional examples of journalists who find a place in politics and politicans who pursue careers in journalism.

144. Schwoerer, 856; Ames, 15.

145. Cited, Pollard, 353.

146. Tebbel, *The Press and the Presidency,* 167–201; Seitz, 191–195.

147. Salmon, *The Newspaper and Authority,* 94 –97, 325–329; Busch, III, 183–189.

148. Tebbel, *The Press and the Presidency,* 270–271; Pollard, 502; Mott, *American Journalism,* 597; Kelley, 13–44; Raucher, 2, 8–9, 71–73. In the early decades of the 20th century considerable thought was devoted to drawing lines between the uses of press agentry that were legitimate—promotion of civic improvements or universities, perhaps—and those that seemed illegitimate—promotion of political candidates or products; see Salmon, *The Newspaper and Authority,* 311–315. Such lines, earnestly drawn, have, however, been washed away like beaver dams before a flood as public relations and advertising have come into their own.

149. Lippmann, *Public Opinion,* 345.

150. Ben Bagdikian, "The Five Ws," *Progressive,* March 1987.

151. *New York Journal,* Feb. 16–20, 1898. Rupert Murdoch's newspapers have provided more current examples of obviously biased news coverage; see Stephens, "Clout: Murdoch's Political *Post*,"; and Mills.

152. New York *Evening Post,* Feb. 19, 1898.

153. These standards for definition as a profession are from Wilensky.

154. Reprinted, Mott, *American Journalism,* 726–727.

155. This account is based on that in Steffens, 285–291.

156. Perhaps journalistic objectivity has won fewer converts in Europe because the number of newspapers concentrated in European capital cities encourages more diverse political stances, because Europeans' attachments to explicit ideologies runs deeper or because advertising revenues have not been sufficient to allow European newspapers to sustain a similar independence from party ties. There is evidence, however, that the importance of party affiliations for European newspapers has been declining; see Hoyer, 29–30.

157. An example of the importance this mirror analogy continues to hold for journalists appeared in a *New York Times* editorial on Feb. 10, 1985: "All storytelling involves some distortion. But the difference between news and fiction is the difference between a mirror and a painting"; cited, Carlin Romano, "What? The Grisly Truth About Bare Facts," in Manoff, 39.

158. Euripides, *The Suppliant Women,* 686–687, translated by Frank William Jones, in *Euripides, The Complete Greek Tragedies,* edited by David Grene and Richmond Lattimore (Chicago: 1960), 163.

159. "Writing the News (by Telling the 'Story')," Robert Karl Manoff, in Manoff, 228.

160. *Porcupine's Gazette,* March 4, 1797.

161. Cockburn, 147.

162. "In the twentieth century," explains Carlin Romano, literary editor of the *Philadelphia Inquirer,* "doubt about 'naive realism' seems to have gained the upper hand in every field except American journalism"; Carlin Romano, "What? The Grisly Truth About Bare Facts," in Manoff, 76.

163. Journalists often underestimate the distance between ideal and reality. Here is A. M. Rosenthal, for many years executive editor of the *New York Times,* on modern reporters and objectivity: "They accept it as given that while nobody can achieve pristine objectivity every journalist can strive incessantly toward fairness. And they are sophisticated enough to know the test. Substitute your own name in a story for the person you are writing about and if you can say, Well I am going to get hurt but the facts are right and there is no innuendo or anonymous attack, your story is fair. If not, do it over"; A. M. Rosenthal, "Minding Our Own Business, " *New York Times,* April 12, 1987. Were it only so simple.

164. Newfield, 56.

165. *Political Register,* Feb. 8, 1823; cited, *Times* of London, 1, 251.

166. See Alexander Cockburn, "Beat the Devil," *Nation,* March 7, 1987, 279, for a dramatic instance of an investor throwing his weight around at a news magazine in 1943; two examples of publishers controlling news to protect advertisers are discussed in Stephens, *Writing and Reporting the News,* 476–477.

167. Gans, 81.

168. Epstein, 220–225.

169. H. L. Mencken noted the beginnings of this change in the social position of journalists in 1942: "They undoubtedly get a great deal more money than we did in 1900 . . . ," he wrote. "I well recall my horror when I heard, for the first time, of a journalist who had laid in a pair of what were then called bicycle pants and taken to golf: it was as if I had encountered a studhorse with his hair done up in frizzes, and pink bowknots peeking out of them"; Mencken, 26.

170. Cited, Sperber, 437.

171. Barnouw, *Tube of Plenty,* 178–180.

172. Hachten, 35.

173. De Beer and Merrill, 50.

174. Ann Cooper, "Violent Censorship," *Moscow Times,* March 10, 2005.

175. Cited, Koss, 31.

176. Rationales for controlling the press are cited in Siebert, *Four Theories of the Press,* 32, 116; Carlin Romano, "What? The Grisly Truth About Bare Facts," in Manoff, 74; and Righter, 18.

Chapter 15. New Technologies—Improved Means to an Unimproved End

1. Thoreau, 66–67.

2. Taliaferro P. Shaffner, "The Ancient and Modern Telegraph," *Shaffner's Telegraph Companion* 1 (Feb. 1854): 85; cited, Czitrom, 9.

3. Thoreau, 67.

4. Cited, Kluger, 50.

5. *New York Herald,* Jan. 5, 1848; this is the same issue in which Bennett bragged of having 10 columns of news received by telegraph.

6. Cited, Pray, 363–364.

7. Thoreau, 110.

8. Harry P. Davis, 5.

9. Licenses were issued to anyone who applied by the Secretary of Commerce; true regulation of broadcasting in the United States arrived with the Radio Act of 1927, which established the Federal Radio Commission (replaced by the Federal Communications Commission in 1934).

10. Barnouw, *Tube of Plenty,* 43–48; Barnouw, *A Tower in Babel,* 31–32, 69–72, 96, 104, 185–186; Czitrom, 72. Advertising's central role on American radio was by no means conceded in these early years; see Briggs, 19.

11. Miguel, 32, 47.

12. Miguel, 47. One American station, WWJ in Detroit, expressed a debt to older predecessors—its news service was dubbed "the Town Crier"; Barnouw, *A Tower in Babel,* 138.

13. Carl Warren, 4; Harry P. Davis, 7. As this young "talking gazette" gained strength in the 1920s and 1930s, newspapers became somewhat more reluctant masters; for attempts by newspaper publishers to deny radio networks use of news from the wire services, see Coase, 104; and Barnouw, *The Golden Web,* 18–22.

14. Barnouw, *A Tower in Babel,* 138–142, 245; Barnouw, *the Golden Web,* 19–20; Metz, 39–45. The British Broadcasting Corporation, committed to the "avoidance of sensationalism," did not hire its first former newspaper journalist until 1932; Briggs, 117.

15. Cited, Metz, 98.

16. Edwin Emery, 475–476.

17. Sperber, 163.

18. Fornatale, 96–97.

19. Fornatale, 11–33.

20. For examples of such demographically tailored news, see Stephens, *Broadcast News,* 321–322, 328–330.

21. Barnouw, *Tube of Plenty,* 5, 48–49, 86; Gates, 55.

22. Gates, 55.

23. Barnouw, *Tube of Plenty,* 102, 112–113; Gates, 59–60, 66, 76.

24. Barnouw, *Tube of Plenty,* 102, 168–171; Gates, 59–60, 67–68.

25. Miguel, 193–194.

26. Barnouw, *The Image Empire,* 42.

27. For an account of some of these early efforts, see Reasoner.

28. Gates, 73–74, 79.

29. Halberstam, 488–490; Gates, 165–170. See also Hallin.

30. Epstein, 213–214; Halberstam, 491.

31. Barnouw, *Tube of Plenty,* 170.

32. Cited Paul Lewis, "French TV Battle Grows as Rightist Wins Contract," *New York Times,* Feb. 25, 1987.

33. Halberstam, 490–491. This story is also told in Gates, 128, although Gates does not specifically connect Johnson's call to Safer's report on Cam Ne.

34. Barnouw, *Tube of Plenty,* 388.

35. Some examples of headlines from the first week after Pulitzer took control: SCREAMING FOR MERCY, LOVE AND COLD POISON, WHILE THE HUSBANDS WERE AWAY; *New York World,* May 12, 16, 17, 1883.

36. Cited, Herbert Mitgang, "Barry Lopez, a Writer Steeped in Arctic Values," *New York Times,* March 29, 1986.

37. Cited, MacDonagh, 293–295.

38. In the first half of the 18th century, English periodicals featured the work of Addison, Steele, Swift, Defoe, and Johnson. But it was during this apparent "golden age" that Defoe complained that his fellow journalists left readers "possessed with wrong notions of things, and wheedled to believe nonsense and contradictions," and that Dr. Johnson suggested that the press "affords . . . too little" information "to enlarge the mind."

39. See Lanson, " 'Trust Me' Journalism."

40. For a critique of one aspect of this change in writing style—the use of "soft leads"—see Lanson, "Jell-O Journalism."

Chapter 16. The Information Explosion—A Surfeit of Data

1. Cited, Barnouw, *Tube of Plenty,* 102–103.

2. Station KFAX in San Francisco had instituted a similar format in 1960; however, after seven months and

$250,000 in losses, KFAX again began playing records. Fornatale, 100–102.

3. Fornatale, 101–105.

4. Russell Baker, "Keeping out of Touch, " *New York Times Magazine,* Nov. 9, 1986.

5. Susan Sontag, "When Writers Talk Among Themselves," *New York Times Book Review,* Jan. 5, 1986.

6. Dyson, 218–224.

7. Todd Gitlin's account of the effect of news coverage on Students for a Democratic Society in the 1960s includes evidence of the danger premature publicity holds for a radical movement; see Gitlin.

8. Ada Louise Huxtable, "After Modern Architecture," *New York Review of Books,* Dec. 1983.

9. One category of rumor that retains some importance is the consciously planted rumor: the trial balloon, the flown kite, the smear. "Men of rank" on the island of Tikopia demonstrated some facility with such instrumental uses of rumor (Raymond Firth, "Rumor in a Primitive Society," 132), as do many men and women of rank in more technologically sophisticated societies today. Nevertheless, the scope and power of these rumors have diminished. In 15th century Europe it was possible to convince significant portions of the populace that dead kings were alive. Today, given the ability of reporters to penetrate government, it can strain the talents of skilled news manipulators to maintain even a persuasive rumor that a bill will be vetoed.

10. Raymond Firth, "Rumor in a Primitive Society," 127–131.

11. Bertier de Sauvigny, 375.

12. "When Reason Flees," *New York Times,* March 10, 1985.

13. Geertz, 4.

14. "Beacon of Hope," *New York Times,* Dec. 25. 1986.

15. Tocqueville, I, 197.

16. Videotext has not proved particularly popular with those who do not have money wagered on the news, but that might be remedied by stronger presentations that mimic more successfully the excitement of a traditional news exchange and that are careful to satisfy the need for an overall feeling of awareness, of having been filled in.

Bibliography

This list includes most of the books and articles that were consulted and all of the books or articles that are cited, with the exception of works of fiction, reviews, short notes or comments, and the original newsletters, newsbooks, news ballads, and newspapers themselves. (Complete citations for these publications are included in the endnotes.) Most of the anthropological works listed here are collected and indexed on microfiche in the *Human Relations Area Files* (New Haven, Connecticut).

Adams, Henry. *History of the United States of America During the Administrations of Thomas Jefferson.* New York: 1986.

Adams, John. *The Works of John Adams,* edited by Charles Francis Adams. 10 vols. Boston: 1850–1856.

Adams, Randolph G. *The Case of the Columbus Letter.* New York: 1939.

Adriani, N., and Albert C. Kruyt. *De Bare'e Sprekende Toradjas van Midden-Celebes (de Oost-Toradjas).* 2d ed. I, II. Amsterdam: 1950–1951. Translated in *Human Relations Area Files.*

Alexander, Michael Van Cleve. *The First of the Tudors.* Totowa, NJ.: 1980.

Allen, Eric W. "International Origins of the Newspapers: The Establishment of Periodicity in Print." *Journalism Quarterly* 7 (1930): 307–319.

Ames, William E. *A History of the National Intelligencer.* Chapel Hill, N.C.: 1972.

Ancel, Dom René. *"Etude Critique sur Quelques Recueils d'Avvisi." Mélanges d'Archéologie et d'Histoire. Ecole Française de Rome* 28 (1908): 115–139.

Andrews, Alexander. *The History of British Journalism.* 2 vols. London: 1859.

Antunes, George E., and Patricia A. Hurley. "The Representation of Criminal Events in Houston's Two Daily Newspapers." *Journalism Quarterly* 54 (1977): 756–760.

Arber, Edward, ed. *A Transcript of the Registers of the Company of Stationers of London, 1554–1640.* 5 vols. London: 1875–1894.

Arensberg, Conrad Maynadier, and Solon Toothakev Kimball. *Family and Community in Ireland.* Cambridge, Mass.: 1940.

Armstrong, C. A. J. "Some Examples of the Distribution and Speed of News in England at the Time of the Wars of the Roses." In *Studies in Medieval History: Presented to Frederick Maurice Powicke,* edited by R. W. Hunt, W. A. Pantin and R. W. Southern. Oxford: 1948.

Aspinall, A. "Statistical Account of the London Newspapers in the Eighteenth Century." *English Historical Review* 68 (April 1948): 201–232.

Asquith, Ivon. "Advertising and the Press." *Cambridge Historical Journal* 18 (1975): 723.

Aston, Margaret. *The Fifteenth Century: The Prospect of Europe.* London: 1968.

Austin, Aleine. *Matthew Lyon.* University Park, Penn.: 1981.

Axtell, James L. "Locke's Review of the *Principia.*" *Notes and Records of the Royal Society of London* 20 (1965): 152–161.

Ayerst, D. *The Guardian: Biography of a Newspaper.* London: 1971.

Bachaumont, Louis Petit de. *Mémoires Secrets pour Servir à l'Histoire de la République des Lettres.* 36 vols. London: 1777–1787.

Bagdikian, Ben H. *The Information Machines.* New York: 1971.

———. *The Media Monopoly.* Boston: 1983.

Bailyn, Bernard, and John B. Hench, eds. *The Press and the American Revolution.* Worcester: 1980.

Bakeless, John. "Christopher Marlowe and the Newsbooks." *Journalism Quarterly* 14 (1937): 18–22.

Baldasty, Gerald J. *The Commercialization of News in the Nineteenth Century.* Madison, Wis.: 1992.

Balzac, Honoré de. *Ouevres Complètes,* edited by Calman Lévy. XXIII. Paris: 1879.

Barbour, Violet. *Capitalism in Amsterdam in the Seventeenth Century.* Ann Arbor: 1963.

Barnes, Sherman B. "The Scientific Journal, 1665–730." *The Scientific Monthly* 38 (January–June 1934): 257–260.

Barnett, Donald L., and Karari Nijama. *Mau Mau from Within: Autobiography and Analysis of Kenya's Peasant Revolt.* New York: 1970.

Barnouw, Erik. *The Golden Web: A History of Broadcasting in the United States.* II. New York: 1968.

———. *The Image Empire: A History of Broadcasting in the United States.* III. New York: 1970.

———. *A Tower in Babel: A History of Broadcasting in the United States.* I. New York: 1966.

———. *Tube of Plenty: The Evolution of American Television.* New York: 1975.

Barthes, Roland. *Critical Essays.* Translated by Richard Howard: Evanston, Ill.: 1972.

Baschwitz, K. "The History of the Daily Press in the Netherlands." *Bulletin of the International Committee of Historical Sciences* 10 (1938): 96–113.

Beasley, Maurine, ed. *The White House Press Conferences of Eleanor Roosevelt.* New York: 1983.

Bebey, Francis. "The World of the Griots." *Balafon: For a Greater Knowledge of Black Africa* (Air Afrique) 1 (1983): 30–33.

Belgrave, C. Dalrymple. *Siwa: The Oasis of Jupiter Ammon.* London: 1923.

Bellamy, John. *Crime and Public Order in England in the Later Middle Ages.* London: 1973.

Bellanger, Claude, Jacques Godechot, Pierre Guiral and Fernand Terrou, eds. *Histoire Générale de la Presse Française.* I, II. Paris: 1969.

Benet, Sula. Song. *Dance and Customs of Peasant Poland.* New York: 1951.

Bennett, H. S. *English Books and Readers, 1475–1557.* 2d ed. Cambridge: 1969.

Berelson, Bernard. "What 'Missing the Newspaper' Means." In *Communications Research, 1948–1949,* edited by Paul Lazarsfeld and Frank Stanton. New York: 1949.

Berger, Meyer. *The Story of* The New York Times 1851–1951. New York: 1951.

Bertier de Sauvigny, Guillaume de. "The American Press and the Fall of Napoleon in 1814." *American Philosophical Society Proceedings* 98 (1954): 337–375.

Bilainkin, George. *Front Page News—Once.* London: 1937.

Black, Jeremy. *The English Press in the Eighteenth Century.* London: 1987.

Blanchard, Margaret A. *Revolutionary Sparks: Freedom of Expression in Modern America.* New York: 1992.

Bleyer, Willard Grosvenor. *Main Currents in the History of American Journalism.* Boston: 1927.

Bohannan, Paul, and Laura Bohannan. "Three Source Notebooks in Tiv Ethnography." New Haven: 1958.

Unpublished, available in *Human Relations Area Files.*

Bond, Donald F., ed. *The Spectator.* 5 vols. Oxford:1965.

Bond, Donovan H., and W. Reynolds McLeod, eds. *Newsletters to Newspapers: Eighteenth-Century Journalism.* Morgantown, W.Va.: 1977.

Bongi, Salvatore. "Le Prime Gazzette in Italia." *Nuova Antologia* 11, Florence (1869): 311–346.

Boorstin, Daniel. *The Image: A Guide to Pseudo-Events in America.* New York: 1961.

Borza, Eugene N. "Alexander's Communications." *Ancient Macedonian* 2 (1977): 295–303.

Bourrilly, V.-L., ed. *Journal d'un Bourgeois de Paris* (1515–1536). Paris: 1910.

Boyce, George, James Curran and Pauline Wingate, eds. *Newspaper History: From the Seventeenth Century to the Present Day.* London: 1978.

Braestrup, Peter. *Big Story.* 2 vols. Boulder, Colo.: 1977.

Brewster, Ethel Hampson. *Roman Craftsmen and Tradesmen of the Early Empire.* Menasha: 1917.

Bridge, John S. C. *A History of France from the Death of Louis XI.* 5 vols. Oxford: 1921–1936.

Briggs, Asa. *The BBC: The First Fifty Years.* Oxford: 1985.

British Museum Catalogue of Books . . . Printed in England, Scotland and Ireland and of Books in English Printed Abroad to the Year 1640. 3 vols. London: 1884.

Brown, Alexander. *The Genesis of the United States.* 2 vols. New York: 1964.

Brown, Harcourt. *Scientific Organizations in Seventeenth Century France.* Baltimore: 1934.

Bruce, John, ed. *The Histoire of the Arrivall of Edward IV* (1471). London: 1838.

Bryan, Carter F. "Negro Journalism Before Emancipation." *Journalism Monographs,* 1969.

Bryant, Alfred T. *Olden Times in Zululand and Natal.* London: 1929.

———. *The Zulu People: As They Were Before the White Man Came.* New York: 1970.

Bücher, Carl. *Industrial Evolution.* Translated by Wickett S. Morley. New York: 1901.

Buck, John Lossing. *Chinese Farm Economy.* Chicago: 1930.

Buckingham, Joseph T. *Specimens of Newspaper Literature.* 2 vols. Boston: 1852.

Burke, Peter. *Popular Culture in Early Modern Europe.* London: 1978.

Burton, Richard. *First Footsteps in East Africa.* London: 1856.

Burton, Robert. *The Anatomy of Melancholy.* London: 1621.

Busch, Mortiz. *Bismarck: Some Secret Pages of His History.* 3 vols. London: 1898.

Camusat, Denis-François. *Histoire Critique des Journaux.* 2 vols. Amsterdam: 1734.

Carlson, Oliver. *The Man Who Made News.* New York: 1942.

Carter, T. F., and C. L. Goodrich. *The Invention of Printing in China and Its Spread Westward.* New York: 1955.

Castronovo, Valerio, and Nicola Tranfaglia, eds. *Storia della Stampa Italiana.* I. Rome: 1976.

Censer, Jack R., and Jeremy D. Popkin, eds. *Press and Politics in Pre-Revolutionary France.* Berkeley: 1987.

Chalmers, Alexander. *The Works of the English Poets.* 21 vols. London: 1810.

Chappell, Warren. *A Short History of the Printed Word.* Boston: 1980.

Chappell, William, and J. W. Ebsworth, eds. *Roxburghe Ballads.* 9 vols. London: 1869–1897.

Charlton, J. E. "De Foe—the Journalist." *Methodist Review* 91 (1909): 219–230.

Chevigny, Bell Gale. *The Woman and the Myth: Margaret Fuller's Life and Writings.* Boston: 1994.

Christie, Ian R. *Myth and Reality.* London: 1970.

Christman, Henry M., ed. *The American Journalism of Marx and Engles.* New York: 1966.

Cicero, *Epistulae ad Familiares.* Translated by W. Glynn Williams. 3 vols. London: 1927–1929.

———. *Letters to Atticus.* Translated by E. O. Winstedt, 3 vols. London: 1912–1918.

Cipolla, Carolo M. "The Diffusion of Innovations in Early Modern Europe." *Comparative Studies in Society and History* 14 (1972): 46–52.

Clark, Andrew, ed. *Shirburn Ballads, 1585–1616.* Oxford: 1907.

Claudin, Anatole. *Diverses Pièces Curieuses.* Lyon: 1875–1876.

Cline, Walter Buchanan. *Notes on the People of Siwah and El Garah in the Libyan Desert.* Menasha: 1936.

Clitus-Alexandrinus [Richard Brathwait?]. *The Whimzies or a News Cast of Characters* (1631), edited by James O. Halliwell. London: 1859.

Coase, R. H. *British Broadcasting: A Study in Monopoly.* Cambridge, Mass.: 1950.

Cockburn, Claud. *I Claud . . .* Harmondsworth: 1967.

Collins, Thomas William. *The Northern Ute Economic Development Program. Social and Cultural Dimensions* (University Microfilms). Ann Arbor: 1971.

Columbus, Christopher. *The Columbus Letter of 1493.* Translated by Frank E. Robbins. Ann Arbor: 1952.

———. *The Letter of Columbus on the Discovery of America: A Facsimile.* New York: 1892.

———. "The Spanish Folio Letter from Christopher Columbus to Luis de Santangel," a literal translation bound along with a photostate of the letter (the original is in the New York Public Library) at Bobst Library, New York University.

Cornell University, Department of Far Eastern Studies, India Program. *India: Sociological Background.* New Haven, Conn.: 1956.

Corti, Egon Caesar. *The Rise of the House of Rothschild.* Translated by Brian Lunn and Beatrix Lunn. New York: 1928.

Coulet, George. *L'Organisation Matérielle du Théâtre Populaire chez les Annamites.* Saigon: 1926. Translated in *Human Relations Area Files.*

Covarrubias, Miguel. *The Island of Bali.* New York: 1938.

Cozens, Frederick W., and Florence Scovil Stumpf. *Sports in American Life.* Chicago: 1953.

Crane, Ronald, S. "The Vogue of Guy Warwick." *Publication of the Modern Language Association* 30, 2 (1915): 125–194.

Crawfurd, John. *Journal of an Embassy from the Governor-General of India to the Courts of Siam and Cochin China.* 2d ed. I. London: 1830.

Crouse, Timothy. *The Boys on the Bus.* New York: 1974.

Czitrom, Daniel J. *Media and the American Mind: From Morse to McLuhan.* Chapel Hill, N.C.: 1982.

Dahl, Folke. "Amsterdam—Cradle of English Newspapers." *The Library,* 5th ser., 4 (December 1949): 166–178.

———. *Amsterdam—Earliest Newspaper Centre of Western Europe.* The Hague: 1939.

———. *A Bibliography of English Corantos and Periodical Newsbooks, 1620–1642.* London: 1952.

———. *Dutch Corantos, 1618–1650: A Bibliography.* The Hague: 1946.

———. *Nouvelles Contributions à l'Histoire des Premiers Journaux d'Anvers.* Brussels: 1939.

Dann, Martin E. *The Black Press, 1827–1890.* New York: 1971.

Darnton, Robert. *The Great Cat Massacre and Other Episodes in French Cultural History.* New York: 1983.

———. *The Literary Underground of the Old Regime.* Cambridge, Mass.: 1982.

———. "Writing News and Telling Stories." *Daedalus* 104, 2 (1975): 175–194.

Darrow, Clarence S. "Realism in Literature and Art." *The Arena,* 9 (December 1893): 98–113.

Davidowitz, Esther, and Mitchell Stephens. "Floyd Abrams: The Lawyer with Press Appeal." *Washington Journalism Review,* April 1985, pp. 35–41.

Davidson, Philip. *Propaganda and the American Revolution, 1763–1783.* Chapel Hill, N. C.: 1941.

Davis, Harry P. "The History of Broadcasting in the United States." Address delivered before the Harvard University Graduate School of Business Administration, April 21, 1928.

Davis, Natalie Zemon. "Printing and the People." In *Society and Culture in Early Modern France.* Stanford: 1975.

Davis, Norman, ed. *Paston Letters and Papers of the Fifteenth Century.* I, II. Oxford: 1971.

De Beer, Arnold S., and John C. Merrill, eds. *Global Journalism: Topical Issues and Media Systems.* 4th ed. Boston: 2004.

Defoe, Daniel. *The Best of Defoe's Review: An Anthology,* edited by William L. Payne. Freeport, N.Y.: 1970.

De Lange, William. *A History of Japanese Journalism.* Richmond, Surrey: 1998.

Demosthenes. *The Orations of Demosthenes.* Translated by Thomas Leland. New York: 1900.

Deschamps, Léon. "*Les Découvertes et l'Opinion en France au Seizième Siècle.*" *Revue de Géographie* 16 (1885): 370–378.

Desmond, Robert W. *The Information Process: World News Reporting to the Twentieth Century.* Iowa City: 1978.

Dicken-Garcia, Hazel. *Journalistic Standards in Nineteenth-Century America.* Madison, Wis.: 1989.

D'Israeli, Isaac. *Curiosities of Literature.* 4 vols. Boston: 1859.

Dobritzhofer, Martin. *An Account of the Abipones, an Equestrian People of Paraguay.* Translated by Sara Coleridge. II. London: 1822.

Downie, J. A. *Robert Harley and the Press.* Cambridge: 1979.

Drake, Stillman. *Galileo at Work: His Scientific Biography.* Chicago: 1978.

———. *The Unsung Journalist and the Origin of the Telescope.* Los Angeles: 1976.

Dreiser, Theodore. *Newspaper Days.* New York: 1931.

Dresler, A. *Geschichte der italienischen Presse.* I. Munich: 1931.

Drucker, Philip. *The Northern and Central Nootkan Tribes.* Washington, D.C.: 1951.

Ducey, Paul Richard. *Cultural Continuity and Population Change on the Isle of Skye* (University Microfilms). Ann Arbor: 1956.

Duff, Arnold Mackay. *Freedmen in the Early Roman Empire.* Oxford: 1928.

Dukes, Graham. "The Beginnings of the English Newspaper." *History Today* 4 (1954): 197–204.

Du Maurier, Daphne. *The Winding Stair: Francis Bacon, His Rise and Fall.* London: 1976.

Dyson, Freeman. *Disturbing the Universe.* New York: 1979.

Eames, Wilberforce. "Columbus' Letter on the Discovery of America." *Bulletin of the New York Public Library* 28, 8 (August 1924): 595–599.

Eberhard, Wallace B. "Mr. Bennett Covers a Murder Trial." *Journalism Quarterly* 47 (1970): 457–463.

Edelstein, Mel. *La Feuille Villageoise: Communication et Modernisation dans les Régions Rurales pendant la Révolution.* Commission d'Histoire Economique et Sociale de la Révolution Française. *Mémoires et Documents,* 34. Paris: 1977.

Eisenstein, Elizabeth L. *The Printing Press as an Agent of Change.* 2 vols. Cambridge: 1979.

Ellis, Aytoun. *The Penny Universities: A History of the Coffee-Houses.* London: 1956.

Emery, Edwin, and Michael Emery. *The Press and America.* 5th ed. Englewood Cliffs, N.J.: 1984.

Emery, Walter B. *National and International Systems of Broadcasting.* East Lansing, Mich.: 1969.

Epstein, Edward Jay. *Between Fact and Fiction: The Problem of Journalism.* New York: 1975.

Erikson, Kai T. "Notes on the Sociology of Deviance." In *The Other Side: Perspectives on Deviance,* edited by Howard S. Becker. London: 1964.

Escott, T. H. S. *Masters of English Journalism.* London: 1911.

Fattorello, Francesco. *Le Origini del Giornalismo in Italia.* Udine: 1929.

Febvre, Lucien. *A New Kind of History,* edited by Peter Burke. Translated by K. Folca. London: 1973.

———. *Le Problème de l'Incroyance au Seizième Siècle.* Paris: 1947.

Ferrars, Max, and Bertha Ferrars. *Burma.* 2d ed. London: 1901.

Fincham, H. W., ed. *Caoursin's Account of the Siege of Rhodes in 1480.* London: 1926.

Firth, Charles. "The Ballad History of the Reign of James I." *Transactions of the Royal Historical Society,* 3rd ser., 5 (1911).

———. "The Ballad History of the Reigns of the Later Tudors." *Transactions of the Royal Historical Society,* 3rd ser., 3 (1909).

———. "The Ballad History of the Reigns of Henry VII and Henry VIII." *Transactions of the Royal Historical Society.* 3rd ser., 2 (1908).

———. "Ballads and Broadsides." In *Shakespeare's England,* II, edited by Charles Talbut Onions. Oxford: 1916.

Firth, Raymond. *Rank and Religion in Tikopia.* Boston: 1970.

———. "Rumor in a Primitive Society." *Journal of Abnormal and Social Psychology* 53 (1956): 122–132.

———. *We the Tikopia.* New York: 1936.

Fischer, Henry W. "Newspapers 3,609 Years Old." *Inland Printer* 43 (1909): 244.

Folkerts, Jean, and Dwight L. Teeter Jr. *Voices of a Nation.* 2d ed. New York: 1994.

Foote, Peter, and David M. Wilson. *The Viking Achievement.* London: 1970.

Fornatale, Peter, and Joshua E. Mills. *Radio in the Television Age.* Woodstock, N.Y.: 1980.

Fortes, Meyer. "Communal Fishing and Fishing Magic in the Northern Territories of the Gold Coast." *Journal of the Royal Anthropological Institute of Great Britain and Ireland* 67 (1937): 131–142.

Fournier, Edouard. *Variétés Historiques et Littéraires, Recueil de Pièces Rare et Curieuses.* 10 vols. Paris: 1855–1863.

Fowler, Eric. "Norwich Newspapers and Their Editors." *East Anglican Magazine* 22 (April 1963): 182–183.

Fowler, W. Warde. *Social Life at Rome.* New York: 1927.

Fox, Robin Lane. *Alexander the Great.* New York: 1974.

Fox Bourne, H. R. *English Newspapers.* 2 vols. London: 1887.

Frank, Joseph. *The Beginnings of the English Newspaper, 1620–1660.* Cambridge, Mass.: 1961.

———. *Cromwell's Press Agent: A Critical Biography of Marchamont Nedham.* Lanham, Md.: 1980.

Franklin, Alf. *Les Rues et les Cris de Paris au Treizième Siècle.* Paris: 1874.

———. *La Vie Privée d'Autrefois.* I. *L'Annonce et la Réclame: Les Cris de Paris.* Paris: 1887.

Franklin, Benjamin. *The Autobiography of Benjamin Franklin.* New York: 1965.

———. *The Writings of Benjamin Franklin,* edited by Albert Henry Smith. 10 vols. London: 1905–1907.

Funck-Brentano, Frantz: *Les Nouvellistes.* Paris: 1923.

Gairdner, James, ed. *Paston Letters.* 6 vols. London: 1904.

———. *Three Fifteenth Century Chronicles.* Westminster: 1880.

Galliot, M. "La Publicité à travers les Âges." *Hommes et Techniques* 10 (1954): 113, 291–298; 117, 613–616; 144, 381–386.

Gans, Herbert J. *Deciding What's News.* New York: 1980.

Gardiner, Samuel R. *History of England, 1603–1642.* 10 vols. New York: 1965.

Gates, Gary Paul. *Air Time: The Inside Story of CBS News.* New York: 1979.

Gatrell, V. A. C., Bruce Lennan and Geoffrey Parka, eds. *Crime and the Law.* London: 1980.

Geertz, Clifford. *Local Knowledge: Further Essays in Interpretive Anthropology.* New York: 1983.

Gelb, I. J. *A Study of Writing.* Chicago: 1963.

Ghiglione, Loren. *The American Journalist.* Washington, D.C.: 1990.

Giffard, C. A. "Ancient Rome's Daily Gazette." *Journalism History* 2, 4 (Winter 1975–1976): 106–109, 132.

Gilbert, Allison, Phil Hirschkorn, Melinda Murphy, Robyn Walensky and Mitchell Stephens. *Covering Catastrophe: Broadcast Journalists Report September 11.* Chicago: 2002.

Gitlin, Todd. *The Whole World Is Watching: Mass Media in the Making and Unmaking of the New Left.* Berkeley: 1980.

Gluckman, Herman Max. "The Kingdom of the Zulus in South Africa." In *African Political Systems,* edited by Meyer Fortes and Edward Evans-Pritchard. London: 1955.

Goldie, Marc. "The Revolution of 1689 and the Structure of Political Argument." *Bulletin of Research in the Humanities* 83, 4 (1980): 473–564.

Goldstein, Tom. *The News at Any Cost.* New York: 1985.

Göllner, Carl. *Turcica: Die europäischen Turkendrucke des XVI. Jahrhunderts.* 2 vols. Bucharest: 1961.

Goody, Jack. *The Domestication of the Savage Mind.* Cambridge: 1977.

Gordon, Cyrus H. *Forgotten Scripts: Their Ongoing Discovery and Decipherment.* New York: 1982.

Gorer, Geoffrey. "Senegalese." In *Africa Dances: A Book about West African Negroes.* London: 1935.

Goris, J. A. *Etude sur les Colonies Marchandes Méridionales à Anvers, 1488–1567.* Louvain: 1925.

Granqvist, Hilma Natalia. *Birth and Childhood Among the Arabs: Studies in a Muhammadan Village in Palestine.* Helsinki: 1947.

Grant, Michael. *The History of Ancient Israel.* London: 1984.

Great Britain, Public Record Office. *Calendar of State Papers, Foreign Series, 1547–1553,* edited by William B. Turnbill. London: 1861.

———. *Calendar of State Papers, Foreign Series, 1566–1568,* edited by Allan James Crosby. London: 1863.

———. *Calendar of State Papers, Foreign Series, 1578–1579,* edited by Arthur John Butler. London: 1903.

———. *Calendar of State Papers, Milan.* I, edited by Allan B. Hinds. London: 1912.

Groth, Otto. *Die Zeitung ein System der Zeitungskunde.* 4 vols. Mannheim: 1928–1930.

Guérard, Albert Léon. *France in the Classical Age.* New York: 1956.

Gummere, Francis, B. *Old English Ballads.* New York: 1967.

Gurdon, Philip Richard Thornhagh. *The Khasis.* London: 1907.

Gusinde, Martin. *Die Yamana*. Mödling bei Wein: 1937. Translated in *Human Relations Area Files*.

Gutiérrez, Felix, and Ernesto Ballesteros. "The 1541 Earthquake: Dawn of Latin American Journalism." *Journalism History* 6, 3 (Autumn 1979): 79–83.

Haas, William S. *Iran*. New York: 1946.

Hachten, William A. *The Growth of Media in the Third World: African Failures, Asian Successes*. Ames, Iowa: 1993.

Halberstam, David. *The Powers That Be*. New York: 1979.

Hale, John R. "War and Public Opinion in the Fifteenth and Sixteenth Centuries." *Past and Present* 22 (July 1962): 18–36.

Hale, William Harlan. *Horace Greeley: Voice of the People*. New York: 1950.

Hall, Joseph. *The Poems of Laurence Minot*. Oxford: 1914.

Halle, J. *Newe Zeitungen, Relationen, Flugschriften Flugblätter, Einblattdrucke von 1470 bis 1820*. Munich: 1929.

Hallin, Daniel C. *The Uncensored War: Media and Vietnam*. Berkeley: 1989.

Halliwell, J. O., ed. *A Collection of Letters Illustrative of the Progress of Science in England*. London: 1841.

———. *A Discovery That Shakespeare Wrote One or More Ballads or Poems on the Spanish Armada*. London: 1866.

———. *Murder Narratives*. London: 1860.

———. *A Selection from the Minor Poems of Lydgate*. London: 1840.

Hamilton, Thomas. *Men and Manners in America*. 2 vols. London: 1833.

Harleian Miscellany, The 10 vols. New York: 1965.

Harris, Michael. "Newspaper Distribution During Queen Anne's Reign." In *Studies in the Book Trade*. Oxford: 1975.

Harrison, S. *Poor Man's Guardians*. London: 1974.

Harrisse, Henry. *Christophe Colomb*. Paris: 1884.

Hart, David Montgomery. "An Ethnographic Survey of the Riffian Tribe of Aith Wuryaghil." *Tamuda* 2, 1 (1954): 55–86.

Hart, Donn Vorhis. "Barrio Caticugan: A Visayan Filipino Community." Dissertation, Syracuse University, 1954.

Hatin, Eugene. *Bibliographie Historique et Critique de la Presse Périodique Française*. Paris: 1866.

———. *Histoire Politique et Littéraire de la Presse*, 8 vols. Paris: 1859–1861.

Havelock, Eric A. *The Literate Revolution in Greece and Its Cultural Consequences*. Princeton: 1982.

Hawke, David Freeman. *Paine*. New York: 1975.

Heide, Walther. *Die älteste gedruckte Zeitung*. Mainz: 1931.

Hellman, Clarisse Doris. *The Comet of 1577: Its Place in the History of Astronomy*. New York: 1944.

Herd, Harold. *The March of Journalism: The Story of the British Press from 1622 to the Present Day*. London: 1952.

Herodotus. *The History*. Translated by David Grene. Chicago. 1987.

Hertsgaard, Mark. *On Bended Knee: The Press and the Reagan Presidency*. New York: 1989.

Hester, Al. "Newspapers and Newspaper Prototypes in Spanish America." *Journalism History* 6, 3 (Autumn 1979): 73–77, 88.

Hill, Christopher. *The Century of Revolution, 1603–1714*. Edinburgh: 1961.

Hill, Willard Williams. *Navaho Warfare*. New Haven: 1936.

Hinkhouse, Free Junkin. *The Preliminaries of the American Revolution as Seen in the English Press*. New York: 1926.

Hofstadter, Richard. *The Age of Reform*. New York: 1985.

Hollis, P. *The Pauper Press*. Oxford: 1970.

Houtte, Hubert van. "*Un Journal Manuscrit Intéressant (1557–1648). Les Avvisi du Fonds Urbinat et d'autres Fonds de la Bibliothèque Vaticane.*" *Bulletins de la Commission Royale d'Histoire* 89 (1926): 359–440.

Hoyer, Svennik, S. Hadenius and L. Weibull. *The Politics and Economics of the Press: A Developmental Perspective*. Beverly Hills: 1975.

Hudson, Frederic. *Journalism in the United States, from 1690 to 1872*. New York: 1873.

Hughes, Helen MacGill. *News and the Human Interest Story*. Chicago: 1940.

———. "The Social Interpretation of News." *Annals of the American Academy of Political and Social Science* 219 (1942): 11–17.

Huth, Henry. *Fugitive Tracts Written in Verse*, edited by William Carew Hazlitt. 2 vols. London: 1875.

Hutt, Allen. "The Gothic Title-Piece and the English Newspaper." *Alphabet and Images* 3 (1946): 3–20.

Hyde, H. Montgomery. *Oscar Wilde: A Biography*. London: 1975.

Iliff, Flora Gregg. *People of the Blue Water: My Adventures Among the Walapai and Havasupai Indians*. New York: 1954.

Ingleby, C. M., L. Toulmin Smith, F. J. Furnivall and John Munro. *The Shakspere Allusion-Book*, edited by John Munro. 2 vols. London: 1932.

Innis, Harold A. *Empire and Communications*. Toronto: 1972.

———. "The Newspaper in Economic Development." *Journal of Economic History,* supplement, December 1942, pp. 1–33.

James, Lewis. "Economic Literature: The Emergence of Popular Journalism." *Victorian Periodicals Newsletter* 5, 14 (December 1971): 13–20.

Jebb, Richard C. "Ancient Organs of Public Opinion." In *Essays and Addresses.* Cambridge: 1907.

Jefferson, Thomas. *A Jefferson Profile as Revealed in His Letters,* edited by Saul K. Padover. New York: 1956.

Jeffrey, Robin. *India's Newspaper Revolution.* New York: 2000.

Jensen, De Lamar, *Confrontation at Worms.* Provo, Utah: 1973.

Jensen, Merrill. *The Founding of a Nation.* New York: 1968.

Johnson, Samuel. "Introduction." In *Collection of Gentleman's Magazine.* 1740.

Jones, Gwyn. *A History of the Vikings.* Oxford: 1968.

Jonson, Ben. "Conversations with William Drummond." In *The Works of Ben Johnson,* edited by W. Giffard and F. Cunningham, IX. London: 1875.

Junod, Henri Alexandre. *The Life of a South African Tribe.* 2d ed. I. London: 1927.

Katzin, Margaret Fisher. *Higglers of Jamaica* (University Microfilms). Ann Arbor: 1959.

Kearney, Hugh F. "Puritism and Science: Problem of Definition." *Past and Present* 31 (1965): 104–110.

Keir, R. Malcolm. "Modern Korea." *American Geographical Society Bulletin* 46 (1914): 756–769, 817–830.

Kelley, Stanley, Jr. *Professional Public Relations and Political Power.* Baltimore: 1956.

Kingsford, Charles L. *English Historical Literature in the Fifteenth Century.* Oxford: 1913.

Kingshill, Konrad. *Kudaeng—The Red Tomb: A Village Study in Northern Thailand.* Chiangmai, Thailand: 1960.

Kirk, John W. "The First News Message by Telegraph." *Scribner's Magazine* (May 1892): 652–656.

Klarwill, Victor von. *The Fugger News-Letters.* Translated by Pauline de Chary. London: 1924.

———. *The Fugger News-Letters, Second Series.* Translated by L. S. R. Byrne. London: 1926.

Kleinpaul, Johannes. *Die Fuggerzeitungen, 1568–1605.* Leipzig: 1921.

———. *Das Nachrichtenwesen der deutschen Fürsten im 16. und 17. Jahrhundert.* Leipzig: 1930.

Kluger, Richard. *The Paper: The Life and Death of the New York Herald Tribune,* New York: 1986.

Knightley, Phillip. *The First Casualty.* New York: 1975.

Knowlton, Steven R., and Karen L. Freeman, eds. *Fair and Balanced: A History of Journalistic Objectivity.* Northport, Ala.: 2005.

Kobre, Sidney. *Development of American Journalism.* Dubuque, Iowa: 1969.

———. "The First American Newspaper. A Product of Environment." *Journalism Quarterly* 17 (1940): 335–345.

Ko Kung-chên. *History of Chinese Journalism.* Peking: 1955.

Komroff, M. *Contemporaries of Marco Polo.* London: 1928.

Kortepeter, Max. "German Zeitung Literature in the Sixteenth Century." In *Editing Sixteenth Century Texts,* edited by R. J. Schoeck. Toronto: 1966.

Koss, Stephen. *The Rise and Fall of the Political Press in Britain: The Nineteenth Century.* Chapel Hill, N.C.: 1981.

Koyré, Alexander. *Newtonian Studies.* London: 1965.

Krieghbaum, Hillier. "American Newspaper Reporting of Science News." *Kansas State College Bulletin* 25, 5. *Industrial Journalism Series* 16 (Aug. 15, 1941).

Kroeger, Brooke. *Nellie Bly.* New York: 1994

Kronick, David A. *A History of Scientific and Technical Periodicals.* Metuchen, N.J.: 1976.

———. *The Literature of the Life Sciences.* Philadelphia: 1985.

Lane, Roger. *Policing the City: Boston, 1822–1885.* Cambridge, Mass.: 1967.

Lanson, Gerald, and Mitchell Stephens. "'Trust Me' Journalism," *Washington Journalism Review,* November 1982, pp. 43–47.

——— ———. "Jello Journalism: Reporters Are Going Soft in Their Leads." *Washington Journalism Review,* April 1982, pp. 21–23.

La Roche, Walther von. *Einführung in den praktischen Journalismus.* 10th ed. Munich: 1987.

Lawlis, Merritt E. *The Novels of Thomas Deloney.* Bloomington, Ind.: 1961.

Lebzelter, Viktor. *Eingeborenenkulturen in Südwest- und Südafrika.* II Leipzig: 1934. Translated in *Human Relations Area Files.*

Le Clerc, J.V. *"Extrait d'un Mémoire sur les Journaux chez les Anciens Romains." Institut Royal de France, Recueil de Pièces* (May 3, 1836.)

———. *Des Journaux chez les Romains.* Paris: 1838.

Le Coeur, Charles. *Dictionnaire Ethnographic Téda.* Paris: 1950. Translated in *Human Relations Area Files.*

Lee, James, Melvin. *History of American Journalism.* Boston: 1923.

Lefebvre, Georges. *The Great Fear of 1789: Rural Panic in Revolutionary France.* Translated by Joan White. Princeton: 1982.

Leith-Ross, Sylvia. *African Women: A Study of the Ibo of Nigeria.* London: 1939.

Lent, John A., ed. *The Asian Newspaper's Reluctant Revolution.* Ames, Iowa: 1971.

Leonard, Thomas C. *The Power of the Press.* New York: 1987.

Levy, Leonard W., ed. *Freedom of the Press from Zenger to Jefferson.* Indianapolis: 1966.

Lewis, C. S. *The Allegory of Love: A Study in Medieval Tradition.* Oxford. 1958.

Lewis, Michael. *The Spanish Armada.* London: 1966.

Liebling, A. J. *The Press.* New York: 1961.

Lilly, Joseph, ed. *A Collection of Seventy-Nine Black-Letter Ballads and Broadsides.* London: 1867.

Lillywhite, Bryant. *London Coffee Houses.* London: 1963.

Lindemann, M. *Die Deutsche Presse bis 1815.* Berlin: 1969.

Lindsay, James L. *Bibliotheca Lindesiana.* Aberdeen: 1910.

Linton, David, and Ray Boston, eds. *The Newspaper Press in Britain: An Annotated Bibliography.* London: 1987.

Lin Yutang. *A History of the Press and Public Opinion in China.* New York: 1968.

Lippmann, Walter. *American Inquisitors.* New York: 1928.

———. *Public Opinion.* New York: 1922.

———. "Two Revolutions in the American Press." *Yale Review* 20 (March 1931): 433–441.

———, and Charles Merz. "A Test of the News." *The New Republic* 23, supplement (August 4, 1920).

Livois, R. de. *Histoire de la Presse Française.* 2 vols. Lausanne: 1965.

McCormack, Anna P. "Khasis." In *Ethnic Groups of Mainland Southeast Asia,* edited by Frank M. LeBar, Gerald C. Hickey and John K. Musgrave. New Haven, Conn.: 1964.

MacDonagh, Michael. *The Reporter's Gallery.* London: 1913.

McElwee, W. *The Murder of Sir Thomas Overbury.* Cambridge, Mass.: 1952.

McFeely, William S. *Frederick Douglass.* New York: 1991.

McIlwraith Thomas Forsyth. *The Bella Coola Indians.* I. Toronto: 1948.

McKibben, Bill. *The Age of Missing Information.* New York: 1993.

McLuhan, Marshall. *Understanding Media: The Extensions of Man.* New York: 1964.

McNeill, William H. *Venice: The Hinge of Europe, 1081–1797.* Chicago: 1974.

McPherson, Elizabeth Gregory. "Reporting the Debates of Congress." *Quarterly Journal of Speech* 28 (1942): 141–148.

Maiskii, I. *Sovremennaia Mongoliia.* Irkutsk: 1921. Translated in *Human Relations Area Files.*

Mann, Francis Oscar, ed. *The Works of Thomas Deloney.* Oxford: 1912.

Manoff, Robert Karl, and Michael Schudson, eds. *Reading the News.* New York: 1986.

Marbut, F. B. *News from the Capital: The Story of Washington Reporting.* Carbondale, Ill.: 1971.

Marlow, Joyce. *The Peterloo Massacre.* London: 1969.

Marshburn, Joseph H. *Murder and Witchcraft in England, 1550–1640, as Recounted in Pamphlets, Ballads, Broadsides and Plays.* Norman, Okla.: 1971.

———, and Alan R. Velie. *Blood and Knavery: A Collection of English Renaissance Pamphlets and Ballads of Crime and Sin.* Rutherford, N J: 1973.

Matthews, George T., ed. *News and Rumor in Renaissance Europe.* New York: 1959.

Mattingly, Garrett. *The Armada.* Boston: 1959.

Meier, Richard L. *A Communications Theory of Urban Growth.* Cambridge, Mass.: 1962.

Mencken, H. L. *The Vintage Mencken,* edited by Alistair Cooke. New York: 1955.

Merritt, Richard L. *Symbols of American Community, 1735–1775:* New Haven: 1966.

Mersenne, Marin. *Les Nouvelles Pensées de Galilée,* edited by P. Costabel and Michel-Pierre Lerner. 2 vols. Paris: 1973.

Metz, Robert. *CBS: Reflections in a Bloodshot Eye.* New York: 1975.

Michelson, Thomas. "Notes on the Ceremonial Runners." In *Contributions to Fox Ethnology.* Washington, D.C.: 1927.

Miguel, Pierre. *Histoire de la Radio et de la Télévision.* Paris: 1984.

Mijatovich, Chedo. *Servia of the Servians.* New York: 1914.

Mills, Joshua, and Mitchell Stephens. "The Election According to Murdoch." *More,* November 1977, pp. 22–23.

Mindich, David T. Z. "Edwin M. Stanton, The Inverted Pyramid, and Information Control." *Journalism Monographs* 140 (1993).

Mindich, David T. Z. *Just the Facts: How "Objectivity" Came to Define American Journalism.* New York: 1998.

Mindich, David T. Z. *Turned Out: Why Americans Under 40 Don't Follow the News.* New York: 2005.

Mitton, Fernand. *La Presse Française: Des Origines à la Révolution.* Paris: 1943.

Molmenti, Pompeo G. *La Storia di Venezia nella Vita Privata.* III. Trieste: 1973.

Molotch, Harvey, and Marilyn Lester. "News as Purposive Behavior: On the Strategic Use of Routine Events, Accidents and Scandals." *American Sociological Review* 39 (February 1974): 101–112.

Money, John. "Taverns, Coffee Houses and Clubs." *Historical Journal* 14 (1972).

Morison, Samuel Eliot. *Admiral of the Ocean Sea: A Life of Christopher Columbus.* Boston: 1946.

Morison, Stanley. "The Bibliography of Newspapers and the Writing of History." *The Library,* 5th ser., 9, 3 (September 1954): 153–175.

———. *Edward Topham, 1751–1820.* Cambridge: 1933.

———. *The English Newspaper, 1622–1932.* Cambridge: 1932.

———. *Ichabod Dawks and His Newsletter.* Cambridge: 1931.

———. *John Bell, 1745–1831.* Cambridge: 1930.

Morley, Edith J. *The Life and Times of Henry Crabb Robinson.* London: 1935.

Morton, Frederic. *The Rothschilds.* New York: 1962.

Mott, Frank Luther. *American Journalism: A History of Newspapers in the United States Through 250 Years.* New York: 1941.

———. "The Newspaper Coverage of Lexington and Concord." *New England Quarterly* 17 (December 1944): 489–505.

Muddiman, J. G. [J. B. Williams] *A History of English Journalism to the Foundation of the Gazette.* London: 1908.

———. *The King's Journalist, 1659–1689,* London: 1923.

Murray, John J. *Amsterdam in the Age of Rembrandt.* Norman, Okla.: 1967.

Myers, Gustavus. *The History of Tammany Hall.* 2d ed. New York: 1917.

Nambiar, P.K., and T. B. Bharathi. "Kankagiri." *Village Survey Monographs* 6. Delhi: 1964.

Neale, J. E. *Essays in Elizabethan History.* London: 1958.

Negroponte, Nicholas. *Being Digital.* New York: 1995.

Nelson, Nici. "Informal Sector Economic Activity in a Squatter Neighborhood." London: 1976. Unpublished, available in *Human Relations Area Files.*

Nerone, John C. "The Mythology of the Penny Press," with response by Michael Schudson, Dan Schiller, Donald L. Shaw, and John J. Pauly. *Critical Studies in Mass Communication,* December 1987.

Neuburg, Victor E. *Popular Literature: A History and Guide.* New York: 1977.

Newfield, Jack. "Journalism: Old, New and Corporate." In *The Reporter as Artist,* edited by Ronald Weber. New York: 1974.

"The Newspapers," *The Metropolitan,* January 6, 1833.

Nichols, John. *Literary Anecdotes of the Eighteenth Century.* 9 vols. London: 1812–1816.

Nilsson, Nils Gunnar. "The Origin of the Interview." *Journalism Quarterly* 58 (1971): 707–713.

Noah, J. E. "Oliver Cromwell, Protector, and the English Press." *Journalism Quarterly* 39 (1962): 57–62.

Nordin, Kenneth D. "The Entertaining Press: Sensationalism in Eighteenth-Century Boston Newspapers." *Communication Research* 6, 3 (July 1979): 295–320.

Noverr, Douglas A., and Lawrence E. Ziewacz. *The Games They Played: Sports in American History, 1865–1980.* Chicago: 1983.

O'Brien, Frank. *The Story of The Sun.* New York: 1928.

Olson, Kenneth. *The History Makers: The Press of Europe From Its Beginnings Through 1965.* Baton Rouge, La.: 1966.

Ong, Walter J. *Orality and Literacy: The Technologizing of the Word.* New York: 1982.

Opel, Julius Otto. *Die Anfänge der deutschen Zeitungspresse, 1609–1650.* Leipzig: 1879.

Oswald, John Clyde. *Printing in the Americas.* New York: 1968.

Paine, Robert. *Coast Lapp Society.* I. Tromso, Norway: 1957.

Paisey, D. L. "Illustrated German Broadsides of the Seventeenth Century." *British Library Journal* 2, 1 (1976): 56–69.

Paltsits, Victor Hugo. "John Holt—Printer and Postmaster." *Bulletin of the New York Public Library* 24, 9 (1920): 483–499.

———. "New Light on *Publick Occurrences.*" *Proceedings of the American Antiquarian Society* 58 (April 1949): 75–88.

Parry, Edward A. *The Overbury Mystery.* New York: 1925.

Parsons, Elsie Worthington Clews. *The Social Organization of the Tewa of New Mexico.* Menasha: 1929.

Pauly, John J. "Rupert Murdoch and the Demonology of Professional Journalism." Paper presented at the conference "Sensationalism and the Media." University of Michigan, April 1986.

Pearson, Lu Emily. *Elizabethans at Home.* Stanford: 1957.

Pélissier, Léon-G. "Nouvellistes Italiens à Paris en 1498." *Bulletin de la Société d'Histoire de Paris et de l'Ile-de-France,* September–October 1892.

Pepys, Samuel. *The Diary of Samuel Pepys,* edited by Henry B. Wheatley. I, II. New York: 1942.

Perkins, H. J. "The Origins of the Popular Press." *History Today* (1957): 425–435.

Peters, John Durham. "From Hylemorphism to Hubris: A History and Analysis of Information." Paper presented to the International Communication Association, 1984.

Pickett, Calder M. *Voices of the Past: Key Documents in the History of American Journalism.* Columbus, Ohio: 1977.

Piffl, Meinhard. "Deutschlandsberg und sein Nachrichtenwesen bis zur Errichtung der Briefsammlung im Jahre 1847." *Mitteilunger des Steiermarkischen Landesarchivs* 24 (1974): 39–74.

Pilorgerie, J. de la. *Campagnes et Bulletins de la Grande Armée d'Italie.* Paris: 1866.

Pliny the Elder. *Natural History.* Translated by H. Rackham. London: 1940.

Pollard, James E. *The Presidents and the Press.* New York: 1941.

Pottinger, David T. *The French Book Trade in the Ancien Régime, 1500–1791.* Cambridge, Mass.: 1958.

Pray, Isaac Clark ["A Journalist"]. *Memoirs of James Gordon Bennett and His Times.* New York: 1855.

Pred, Allan R. *Urban Growth and the Circulation of Information.* Cambridge, Mass.: 1973.

Radin, Paul. "The Winnebago Tribe." *United States Bureau of American Ethnology Annual Report* 37 (1915–1916, 1925): 35–560.

Raswan, Carl R. *Black Tents of Arabia.* New York: 1947.

Raucher, Alan R. *Public Relations and Business, 1900–1929.* Baltimore: 1968.

Raum, Otto Friedrich. *The Social Function of Avoidance and Taboos Among the Zulus.* Berlin: 1973.

Ravry, A. "Les Origines de la Presse et de l'Imprimerie." *Union Syndicale des Maîtres Imprimeurs de France, Bulletin Officiel,* Christmas edition, 1937.

Read, Donald. *Peterloo: The 'Massacre' and Its Background.* Manchester: 1958.

———. *The Power of News: The History of Reuters.* Oxford: 1992.

Reader, D. H. *Zulu Tribe in Transition.* Manchester 1966.

Reasoner, Harry. *Before the Colors Fade.* New York 1981.

Redfield, Robert. *Tepoztlán, A Mexican Village: A Study of Folk Life.* Chicago: 1930.

Reid, John C. *Bucks and Bruisers: Pierce Egan and Regency England.* London: 1971.

Retat, Pierre, ed. *Le Journalism d'Ancien Régime.* Lyon: 1982.

Richardson, Florence Elsa. *The Old English Newspaper.* London: 1978.

Righter, Rosemary. *Whose News? Politics, the Press and the Third World.* London: 1978.

Robbins, Frank E. *The Columbus Letter of 1493.* Ann Arbor: 1952.

Robinson, Edward Forbes. *The Early History of Coffee Houses in England.* London: 1893.

Robinson, Henry Crabb. *Diary, Reminiscences and Correspondence,* edited by Thomas Sadler. I. Boston: 1869.

Rochet, Bernard. *La Correspondance Scientifique du Père Mersenne.* Paris: 1966.

Rollins, Hyder E. "The Black-Letter Broadside Ballad. " *Publication of the Modern Language Association,* 34 (1919): 258–339.

———. "Notes on Some English Accounts of Miraculous Fasts." *Journal of American Folk-Lore* 34 (1921): 357.

Rosen, Edward. "The Invention of Eyeglasses." *Journal of the History of Medicine and Allied Sciences* 11 (1956): 13–46, 183–218.

Rosenberg, Marvin. "Rise of England's First Daily Newspaper." *Journalism Quarterly* 30 (1953): 3–14.

Rosewater, Victor. *History of Cooperative News-Gathering in the United States.* New York: 1930.

Ross, Edward Alsworth. "The Suppression of Important News." *Atlantic Monthly* 105 (March 1910): 303–311.

Rossel, André. *Histoire de France à travers les Journaux du Temps Passé: Le Faux Grand Siècle, 1604–1715.* Paris: 1982.

———. *Journaux du Temps Passé.* 2 vols. Paris: 1965–1966.

Rossi, Gwen Haddad. "Methods of Communications of Alexander the Great." Unpublished thesis, Pennsylvania State University, June 1973.

Rudé, George. *The Crowd in the French Revolution.* Oxford: 1959.

Sage, Evan T. "Advertising Among the Romans. " *Classical Weekly* 9, 26 (May 6, 1916): 202–208.

Saillens, Emile. *John Milton.* Oxford: 1964.

Salgādo, Gāmini. *The Elizabethan Underworld.* London: 1977.

Salmon, Lucy Maynard. *The Newspaper and Authority.* New York: 1923.

———. *The Newspaper and the Historian.* New York: 1923.

Samuelson, L. H. *Zululand: Its Traditions, Legends, Customs and Folklore.* Natal, South Africa: 1928.

Sapir, Edward. "Communication." In *Encyclopaedia of the Social Sciences.* IV: 78. New York: 1931.

Sardella, Pierre "Nouvelles et Spéculations à Venice au Debut du XVIe Siècle." *Cahiers des Annales* 1 (1948).

Schiller, Dan. *Objectivity and the News: The Public and the Rise of Commercial Journalism.* Philadelphia: 1981.

Schlesinger, Arthur M. *Prelude to Independence: The Newspaper War on Britain, 1764–1776.* Boston: 1980.

Schottenloher, Karl. *Flugblatt und Zeitung.* Berlin: 1922.

Schram, Louis M. J. *The Mongours of the Kansu-Tibetan Frontier.* Philadelphia: 1954.

Schramm, Wilbur, and William E. Porter. *Men, Women, Messages, and Media.* 2d ed. New York: 1982.

Schudson, Michael. *Discovering the News: A Social History of American Newspapers.* New York: 1978.

Schulte, Henry F. *The Spanish Press, 1470–1966.* Urbana, Ill.: 1968.

Schwoerer, Lois G. "Propaganda in the Revolution of 1688–1689." *American Historical Review* 82, 4 (1977): 843–874.

Seguin, Jean-Pierre. "Les 'Canards' de Faits Divers de Petit Format en France, au XIXe Siècle." *Arts et Traditions Populaires* (1956) 1: 30–45; 2: 113–130.

———. "Faits Divers Sensationnels dans Seize Bulletins d'Information Imprimés en France, pendant le Règne de François Ier." In *Mélanges F. Calot.* Paris: 1960.

———. "L'Information à la Fin du XVe Siècle en France: Pièces d'Actualité Imprimées sous le Règne de Charles VIII." I, II. *Arts et Traditions Populaires* (1956) 4: 309–330; (1957) 1: 46–74.

———. *L'Information en France Avant le Périodique: 517 Canards Imprimés entre 1529 et 1631.* Paris: 1964.

———. *L'Information en France, de Louis XII à Henri II.* Geneva: 1961.

———. *Nouvelles à Sensation: Canards du XIXe Siècle.* Paris: 1959.

Seitz, Don C. *The James Gordon Bennetts, Father and Son.* Indianapolis: 1928.

Shaaber, Matthias A. "Forerunners of the Newspaper in America." *Journalism Quarterly* 11 (1934): 339–347.

———. "The History of the First English Newspaper." *Studies in Philology* 29 (1932): 551–587.

———. *Some Forerunners of the Newspaper in England, 1476–1622.* New York: 1966.

Sharpe, J. A. "Domestic Homicide in Early Modern England." *Historical Journal* 24, 1 (1981): 29–48.

Sharpe, Reginald, R. *London and the Kingdom.* 3 vols. London: 1894–1895.

Shaw, Donald Lewis. "At the Crossroads: Change and Continuity in American Press News, 1820–1860." *Journalism History* 8, 2 (Summer 1981): 38–50.

Shaw, Renata V. "Broadsides of the Thirty Years' War." *Quarterly Journal of the Library of Congress* 32, 1 (1975): 2–24.

Sheavyn, Phoebe. *The Literary Profession in the Elizabethan Age.* Manchester: 1909.

Shooter, Rev. Joseph. *The Kafirs of Natal and Zulu Country.* London: 1857.

Siebert, Fredrick Seaton. *Freedom of the Press in England, 1476–1776.* Urbana, Ill.: 1952.

———. Theodore Peterson and Wilbur Schramm. *Four Theories of the Press.* Urbana, Ill.: 1963.

Silva, Álcionilio Brüzzi Alves da. *A Civilização Indigena do Uaupés.* São Paulo: 1962. Translated in *Human Relations Area Files.*

Skinner, Elliott Percival. *The Mossi of the Upper Volta.* Stanford: 1964.

Sloan, William David. "Chaos, Polemics and America's First Newspaper." *Journalism Quarterly* 30 (1993): 666–668.

Smith, Anthony. *The Geopolitics of Information.* New York: 1980.

———. *The Newspaper: An International History.* London: 1979.

Smith, James Morton. *Freedom's Fetters: The Alien and Sedition Laws and American Civil Liberties.* Ithaca, N.Y.: 1956.

Snyder, Louis L., and Richard B. Morris, eds. *A Treasury of Great Reporting.* 2d ed. New York: 1962.

Sperber, A. M. *Murrow: His Life and Times.* New York: 1986.

Stapleton, Thomas, ed. *The Plumpton Correspondence in the Reign of Henry VII.* London: 1839.

Starr, Chester G. *The Roman Empire, 27 B.C.–A.D. 476: A Study in Survival.* New York: 1982.

Steele, I. K. "Time, Communications and Society: The English Atlantic, 1702." *Journal of American Studies* 8, 1 (1974): –21.

Steele, Janet E. *The Sun Shines or All.* Syracuse, N.Y.: 1993.

Steele, Richard. *The Tatler,* edited by J. J. Woodward. Philadelphia: 1831.

Steffens, Lincoln. *The Autobiography of Lincoln Steffens.* New York: 1931.

Steininger, George Russel, and Paul Van de Velde. *Three Dollars a Year: Being the Story of the San Pablo Cuatro Venados, A Typical Zapotecan Indian Village.* Detroit: 1971.

Stephen, James. *The Memoirs of James Stephen,* edited by Merle M. Bevington. New York: 1954.

Stephen, Leslie. "The Evolution of Editors." In *Studies of a Biographer.* London: 1898.

Stephens, Mitchell. *Broadcast News.* 2d ed. New York: 1986. 3d ed. Ft. Worth, Tx.: 1993.

———. "Clout: Murdoch's Political *Post.*" *Columbia Journalism Review.* July/August 1982, pp. 44–46.

———. "Crime Doesn't Pay, Except on the Newsstands." *Washington Journalism Review,* December 1981, pp. 39–43.

——— "We're All Postmodern Now: Even Journalists Have Realized that Facts Don't Always Add up to the Truth." *Columbia Journalism Review* July/Aug 2005.

———, and Gerald Lanson. *Writing and Reporting the News.* New York: 1986. 2nd ed. Ft. Worth, Tx.: 1994.

Stevens, John D. *Sensationalism and the New York Press.* New York: 1991.

———. "The Social Utility of Sensational News: Murder and Divorce in the 1920s." *Journalism Quarterly* 62 (1985): 53–58.

Stewart, Donald H. *The Opposition Press of the Federalist Period.* Albany, N.Y.: 1969.

Stock, Brian. *The Implications of Literacy.* Princeton: 1983.

Stolp, Annie. *De Eerste Couranten in Holland.* Haarlem: 1938.

Suetonius. *The Lives of the Caesars.* Translated by J. C. Rolfe. London: 1924.

Sutherland, James. *The Restoration Newspaper and Its Development.* Cambridge: 1986.

Swanberg, W. A. *Citizen Hearst.* New York: 1971.

———. *Pulitzer.* New York: 1967.

Sydney, William Connor. *England and the English in the Eighteenth Century.* I. London: 1891.

Tacitus. *The Annals of Tacitus.* Translated by Alfred John Church and William Jackson Brodribb. New York: 1942.

Talese, Gay. *The Kingdom and the Power.* New York: 1970.

Tarabasova, N. I., V. G. Dem'ianov and A. I. Sumkina. *Vesti-Kurant, 1600–1639.* Moscow: 1972.

Tate, Robert S., Jr. "Petit de Bachaumont: His Circle and the *Mémoire Secrets.*" In *Studies on Voltaire.* LXV. Geneva: 1968.

Taylor, George Rogers. *The Transportation Revolution, 1815–1860. Economic History of the United States,* IV. New York: 1951.

Taylor, Richard. "The Basis of Political Authority." *The Monist* 66 (October 1983): 457–471.

Taylor, Robert Bartley, Jr. *Teotitlan del Valle: A Typical Mesoamerican Community* (University Microfilms). Ann Arbor: 1960.

Tebbel, John. *The Compact History of the American Newspaper.* New York: 1963.

———, and Sarah Miles Watts. *The Press and the Presidency: From George Washington to Ronald Reagan.* New York: 1985.

Thomas, Isaiah. *The History of Printing in America.* New York: 1970.

Thomas, Peter David Gannen. "The Beginnings of Parliamentary Reporting in Newspapers, 1768–1774." *English Historical Review* 74,293 (October 1959): 623–636.

Thoreau, Henry David. *Walden.* New York: 1951.

Thorner, Daniel, and Alice Thorner. "India and Pakistan." In *Most of the World,* edited by Ralph Linton. New York: 1949.

Thucydides. *The Complete Writings of Thucydides: The Peloponnesian War.* Translated by R. Crawley. New York: 1951.

Times of [London]. *History of the Times.* 5 vols. London: 1935–1952.

Titiev, Mischa. *The Hopi Indians of Old Oraibi: Change and Continuity.* Ann Arbor: 1972.

Tocqueville, Alexis de. *Democracy in America,* edited by Francis Brown and Phillips Bradley. Translated by Henry Reeve. 2 vols. New York: 1945.

Trevelyan, George Macaulay. *England Under the Stuarts.* 16th ed. London: 1933.

Tuchman, Gaye, "Objectivity as Strategic Ritual: An Examination of Newsmen's Notions of Objectivity." *American Journal of Sociology* 77, 4 (January 1972): 660–679.

Umeasiegbu, Rems Nna. *The Way We Lived: Ibo Customs and Stories.* London: 1969.

UNESCO *News Agencies; Their Structure and Operation.* New York: 1969.

Ünver, A. Süheyl, ed. *Fâtih Sultan Mehmed' in* Ölümü. Istanbul: 1952.

Van Kley, Edwin J. "News from China: Seventeenth-Century European Notices of the Manchu Conquest." *Journal of Modern History* 45, 4 (1973): 561–582.

Van Stockurn, W. P., Jr., ed. *The First Newspapers of England Printed in Holland, 1620–1621: A Faithful Reproduction Made from the Originals.* The Hague: 1914.

Varloot, Jean and Paule Jansen, eds. *L'Année 1768: A travers la Presse Traitée par Ordinateur.* Paris: 1981.

Verhoeven, Abraham. *Nieuwe Tydinghen.* Ghent: 1899.

Vidal, Frederico S. *The Oasis of al-Hasa.* Publication of the Arabian American Oil Company, 1955.

Vilakazi, Absolom. *Zulu Transformations: A Study of the Dynamics of Social Change.* Pietermaritzburg: 1962.

Vincent, Ted. *Mudville's Revenge: The Rise and Fall of American Sport.* New York: 1981.

Voth, Henry R. *The Oráibi Oáqöl Ceremony.* Chicago: 1905.

Waage, Federick O. "Social Themes in Urban Broadsides of Renaissance England." *Journal of Popular Culture* 2, 3 (1977): 730–742.

Wadsworth, A. P. "Newspaper Circulations, 1800–1954." *Transactions of the Manchester Statistical Society, 1954 –1955.*

Wahlgren, Erik. *The Vikings and America.* London: 1986.

Walmsley, Robert. *Peterloo: The Case Reopened.* Manchester: 1969.

Warren, Carl. *Radio News Writing and Editing.* New York: 1947.

Warren, Samuel D., and Louis D. Brandeis. "The Right to Privacy." In *Harvard Law Review* 4, 5 (Dec. 15, 1890): 193–220.

Warton, Thomas. *The History of English Poetry.* 3 vols. London: 1774.

Waters, John. "Why I Love the *National Enquirer.* " *Rolling Stone* 458 (Oct. 10, 1985): 43–44, 71–72.

Watson, Francis. "Daniel Defoe, Father of Modern Journalism." *Bookman* 80 (1931): 16–18.

Waugh, Daniel Clarke. "News of the False Messiah: Reports on Shabbetai Zevi in Ukraine and Muscovy." *Jewish Social Studies* 41 (1979): 301–322.

———. "The Publication of Muscovite *Kuranty.*" *Kritika: A Review of Current Soviet Books on Russian History* 9 (1973): 104–120.

Wedgwood, C. V. *The Thirty Years War.* London: 1981.

Weed, K. K., and R. P. Bond. "Studies of British Newspapers and Periodicals from their Beginning to 1800: A Bibliography." *Studies in Philology* 2, extra series (December 1946).

Weil, Francoise. "Les Nouvellistes." In *La Régence Colloque de 1968 sur la Régence.* Paris: 1970.

Weill, George. *Le Journal: Origines, Evolution et Rôle de la Presse Périodique.* Paris: 1934.

Weiss, R. "Earliest Account of the Murder of James I." *English Historical Review* 2 (1937): 479–491.

Werner, Theodor Gustav "Das kaufmännische Nachrichtenwesen im späten Mittelalter und in der frühen Neuzeit und sein Einfluss auf die Entstehung der handschriftlichen Zeitung." *Scripta Mercaturae* 2 (1975): 3–52.

Wickwar, William H. *The Struggle for the Freedom of the Press, 1819–1832.* London: 1928.

Wight, John. *More Mornings at Bow Street.* London: 1827.

Wilde, Oscar. *The Letters of Oscar Wilde,* edited by Rupert Hart-Davis. New York: 1962.

———. "The Soul of Man Under Socialism." In *The Complete Works of Oscar Wilde,* edited by John Cowper Powys. X. Garden City, N.Y.: 1923.

Wilensky. "The Professionalization of Everyone." *American Journal of Sociology* 70, 2 (September 1964): 137–158.

Wiles, R. M. *Freshest Advices: Early Provincial Newspapers in England.* Columbus, Ohio: 1965.

Williams, Keith. *The English Newspaper: An Illustrated History to 1900.* London: 1977.

Williams, Raymond, ed. *Contact: Human Communication and Its History.* London: 1981.

Wilson, C. Edward. "The *First* First Daily Newspaper in English." *Journalism Quarterly* 58 (1981): 286–288.

Wilson, Edmund. *To the Finland Station.* Garden City, N.Y.: 1953.

Wiser, Charlotte, and William H. Wiser. *Behind Mud Walls.* New York: 1930.

Woods, Oliver, and James Bishop. *The Story of The Times.* London: 1983.

Wright, Charles, and C. Ernest Fayle. *A History of Lloyd's.* London: 1928.

Yardeni, Myriam. "Journalisme et Histoire Contemporaine a l'Epoque de Bayle." *History and Theory* 12 (1973): 208–229.

Ziman, John. *Public Knowledge: An Essay Concerning the Social Dimension of Science.* Cambridge: 1968.

Credits

Page 3:   © SOQUI TED/CORBIS SYGMA

Page 10:   Raymond Firth's Social Change in Tikopia

Page 21:   © Bettmann/CORBIS

Page 23:   © The Field Museum, #A110553_A

Page 35:   Reproduced by courtesy of the Department of Special Collections, General Library System, University of Wisconsin-Madison.

Page 54:   © Araldo de Luca/ CORBIS

Page 63:   Princeton University Library

Page 72:   Rare Books and Manuscripts Division, the New York Public Library, Astor, Lenox and Tilden Foundations

Page 75:   © Authenticated News/ Hulton Archive/ Getty Images

Page 86:   By permission of the British Library, London

Page 101:   The Crying Murther (London 1624). STC 24900. Courtesy of Houghton Library, Harvard College Library.

Page 121:   Bibliotheque Municipale D'amiens, France

Page 132:   Courtesy of the Niedersachsische Landesbibliothek, Hannover, Germany

Page 137:   The National Archives of the UK, ref. SP70/84

Page 140:   By permission of the British Library, London

Page 163:   The National Archives of the UK, ref. CO5/855

Page 167:   (left) Courtesy of Maryland State Archives, Special Collections (Maryland State Law Library Collection of the *Maryland Gazette*). Printer, Jonas Green, *The Maryland Gazette,* Thursday October 10, 1765, No. 1066. MSA SC 2311-1-9. (center) Courtesy of Maryland State Archives, Special Collections (Maryland State Law Library Collection of the *Maryland Gazette*). Printer, Jonas Green, *The Maryland Gazette,* Thursday, February 20, 1766, No. 1068 MSA SC 2311-1-11. (right) Courtesy of Maryland State Archives, Special Collections (Maryland State Law Library Collection of the *Maryland Gazette*). Printer, Jonas Green, *The Maryland Gazette,* Thursday January 30, 1766, No. 1067 MSA SC 2311-1-11.

Page 177:   Library of Congress, Microform: LC control #: 38661

Page 187:   © Bettmann/CORBIS

Page 191:   Library of Congress, MicRR 22992 E.

Page 192:   © Bettmann/CORBIS

Page 193:   The Library of Congress, LC-USZ62-24165

Page 195:   © Bettmann/CORBIS

Page 196:   © Hulton Archive/ Hulton Archive/Getty Images

Page 197:   The Library of Congress, LC-USZC4-12966

Page 199:   © New York Daily News

Page 217:   Library of Congress, LC-USZ62-17523

Page 230:   Matthew Brady/Hulton Archive/Getty Images

Page 231:   Collection of the New York Historical Society, New York City

Page 236:   © Bettmann/ CORBIS

Page 239:   Library of Congress

Page 241:   Library of Congress, LC-USZ62-2310

Page 247:   Library of Congress, general collection

Page 251:   AP/World Wide Photos

Page 252:   Historical Pictures Service/Stock Montage

Page 253:   ©UP/Bettmann

Page 269:   Courtesy of News/Talk 1020 KDKA, Pittsburgh, PA/CBS Radio

Page 270:   Stock Montage, Inc.

Page 272:   © CBS Photo Archive/ Hulton Archive/ Getty Images

Page 275:   © Hulton Archive/Getty Images

Page 276:   © Bettmann/CORBIS

Page 277:   CBS Photo Archive/ Hulton Archive/ Getty Images

Page 281:   © Alex Wong/ Getty Images

Page 283:   © Bettmann/CORBIS

Page 296:   CORBIS

Index

Bold page numbers indicate illustrations.

CPSIA information can be obtained at www.ICGtesting.com
Printed in the USA
BVOW04s0422201114

375815BV00005B/13/P